Susanne Blumesberger, Igor Eberhard, Elisabeth Hafeneder, Gertraud Novotny, Elisabet Torggler (Hg.)

Handbuch Repositorienmanagement. Grundlagen – Anwendungsfelder – Praxisbeispiele

SCHRIFTEN DER VEREINIGUNG ÖSTERREICHISCHER BIBLIOTHEKARINNEN UND BIBLIOTHEKARE

Band 17

Herausgegeben von
Christina Köstner-Pemsel, Josef Pauser, Lisa Schilhan und Markus Stumpf

Die Bände dieser Reihe sind peer reviewed.

SUSANNE BLUMESBERGER,
IGOR EBERHARD,
ELISABETH HAFENEDER,
GERTRAUD NOVOTNY,
ELISABET TORGGLER (HG.)

HANDBUCH REPOSITORIEN-MANAGEMENT

Grundlagen – Anwendungsfelder – Praxisbeispiele

Graz University Library Publishing

Zitiervorschlag:
Susanne Blumesberger, Igor Eberhard, Elisabeth Hafeneder, Gertraud Novotny, Elisabet Torggler (Hg.), Handbuch Repositorienmanagement. Grundlagen – Anwendungsfelder – Praxisbeispiele. Graz 2024.

Graz University Library Publishing
Universitätsplatz 3a
8010 Graz
https://library-publishing.uni-graz.at
Grafische Grundkonzeption: Roman Klug, Presse und Kommunikation, Universität Graz

Coverbild: © Martin Ellinger und Reinhard Öhner; CC BY-NC-SA 4.0
Lektorat: Victoria Eisenheld und Sonja Edler
Typografie: Source Serif Pro und Roboto

ISBN (Paperback) 978-3-99165-932-7
eISBN 978-3-903374-23-2
DOI 10.25364/9783903374232

Druck und Vertrieb im Auftrag der Herausgeber:innen: Buchschmiede von Dataform Media GmbH, Wien
Printed in Austria

Inhaltsverzeichnis

Anwendungsfelder

Praxisbeispiele

Eva Ramminger

Grußwort

Handbuch Repositorienmanagement, Hg. v. Blumesberger et al., 2024, S. 9–11
https://doi.org/10.25364/97839033742321

Eva Ramminger, Universität Innsbruck, Universitäts- und Landesbibliothek Tirol, eva.ramminger@uibk.ac.at |
ORCID iD: 0000-0002-8942-2247

Wissenschaftlicher Fortschritt hängt heute wesentlich von einer reibungslos funktionierenden digitalen Forschungsinfrastruktur ab. Eine Voraussetzung dafür ist die zuverlässige Dokumentation und Zugänglichmachung der in Forschung und Lehre entstehenden Daten und Dokumente. Dreh- und Angelpunkte dieser Entwicklung sind Repositorien, auf denen Daten und Dokumente in der Regel von den Forschenden selbst bereitgestellt werden, mit dem Ziel, die an der eigenen Institution entstandenen Ergebnisse für die Diskussion innerhalb der Science Community sichtbar zu machen. Durch Zitieren in weiteren Publikationen ist eine Vernetzung dieses Wissens möglich und die Grundlage dafür gelegt, dass neue Ideen und innovative Lösungen darauf aufbauen können. In Kombination mit den modernen Möglichkeiten der Forschungskommunikation und den Erfolgen der Open-Access-Bewegung können die Ergebnisse wissenschaftlicher Forschung heute mit einer bislang nie dagewesenen Reichweite zugänglich gemacht werden.

Im Rahmen des Gesamtösterreichischen Universitätsentwicklungsplans, spielen Repositorien eine maßgebliche Rolle in der Umsetzung der dort definierten Systemziele. So sollen dort u. a. Maßnahmen für eine „[l]okale, überregionale und internationale Sichtbarkeit bzw. Wirkung von Lehre, Forschung/Entwicklung und Erschließung der Künste sowie starke Kooperationen und inter-institutionelle Verbundstrukturen“[1] gesetzt werden. Für die Arbeit der wissenschaftlichen Bibliotheken bedeutet die Implementierung von Repositorien einen unverzichtbaren Entwicklungsschritt im systematischen Auf- und Ausbau digitaler Forschungsinfrastrukturen. Eine Vielzahl der dafür notwendigen Aktivitäten wurde bereits vor etwa zehn Jahren in den mit Sondermitteln des Bundes geförderten Projekten zum Thema E-infrastructures Austria[2] bearbeitet. Im Zentrum standen damals die Konzeption und Entwicklung von Lösungen für ein professionelles Datenmanagement an den nationalen Universitäten und Forschungseinrichtungen. In diesen Projekten wurden auch wichtige juristische, prozessuale und technische Grundlagen für die heutige Repositorienlandschaft gelegt.

Die heutige Struktur und Situation institutioneller Repositorien baut auf der Erfahrung von Bibliotheken auf, Wissen zu dokumentieren und zu beschreiben. Aktuellste Forschungsergebnisse werden über Metadaten erfasst, die auf der Basis internationaler Standards und technischer Austauschformate weiterverarbeitet werden können. Repositorienmanagement bedeutet jedoch nicht nur das Dokumentieren

---

1 Gesamtösterreichischer Entwicklungsplan 2022 - 2027 (GUEP) des Bundesministeriums für Bildung, Wissenschaft und Forschung, Stand: Oktober 2020, https://www.bmbwf.gv.at/Themen/HS-Uni/Hochschulgovernance/Steuerungsinstrumente/GUEP.html

2 Siehe Projekthomepage: www.e-infrastructures.at

und Beschreiben, sondern auch das Erstellen von entsprechenden Workflows, Policies und Schnittstellen, die sinnvoll in die einzelnen Phasen des Forschungszyklus eingreifen.

Die bibliothekarischen Kompetenzen fließen hier an einer Schnittstelle zwischen Forschung, Forschungsservices und IT-Infrastruktur ein. Ziel aller beteiligten Partner ist es, die jeweiligen Leistungen der Wissenschaftler:innen sowie der jeweiligen Forschungseinrichtung eindeutig zu identifizieren und die Urheberschaft transparent zu dokumentieren. In Zeiten, in denen die Themen Wissenschaftsskepsis und Fake News die öffentliche Diskussion immer mehr bestimmen, ist ein freier Zugang zu genau diesen Forschungsergebnissen nicht zu unterschätzen.

Das vorliegende Handbuch bildet nun den Status quo der Entwicklungen in Österreich und darüberhinaus ab und ermöglicht einen detaillierten Einblick in die verschiedenen Ansätze und Problemstellungen. Es zeigt auch, wie beeindruckend breit die Behandlung des Themas in der Zwischenzeit geworden ist.

Ich möchte an dieser Stelle den zahlreichen Expert:innen, die ihre Erfahrungen und ihr Fachwissen in dieses Handbuch eingebracht haben, sehr herzlich danken! Ohne ihr bereits viele Jahre währendes Engagement für das Thema Repositorienmanagement – sowohl in der Praxis als auch im Rahmen des Netzwerks Repositorienmanager:innen (RepManNet)[3] – wäre dieses Werk nicht möglich gewesen!

3 Siehe: https://ubifo.at/netzwerk-repositorienmanagerinnen-repmannet/

Susanne Blumesberger, Igor Eberhard, Elisabeth Hafeneder,
Gertraud Novotny, Elisabet Torggler

Einleitung

Handbuch Repositorienmanagement, Hg. v. Blumesberger et al., 2024, S. 13–18
https://doi.org/10.25364/97839033742322

Susanne Blumesberger, Universität Wien, Universitätsbibliothek, susanne.blumesberger@univie.ac.at |
ORCID iD: 0000-0001-9018-623X
Igor Eberhard, Universität Wien, Ethnographisches Datenarchiv, igor.eberhard@univie.ac.at |
ORCID iD: 0000-0002-5631-7109
Elisabeth Hafeneder, Anton Bruckner Privatuniversität, Bibliothek, elisabeth.hafeneder@bruckneruni.at |
ORCID iD: 0000-0002-6197-5798
Gertraud Novotny, Wirtschaftsuniversität Wien, Universitätsbibliothek, gertraud.novotny@wu.ac.at |
ORCID iD: 0000-0002-8816-4936
Elisabet Torggler, Institut für Höhere Studien, Bibliothek und Publikationsservices, elisabet.torggler@ihs.ac.at |
ORCID iD: 0000-0002-1802-1091

Die Aufgabenfelder im Repositorienmanagement sind sehr vielfältig. Der Bogen erstreckt sich über bibliothekarisches Wissen, technisches Know-how, strategisches Handeln, Weitergabe von Wissen, ethisches Denken, erfordert aber auch kommunikative Kompetenz und den Willen, in einem sehr dynamischen und heterogenen Umfeld zu arbeiten.

Der Wunsch, institutionenübergreifend gemeinsam ähnliche Fragestellungen und Herausforderungen zu diskutieren, mündete 2016 in die Gründung des Netzwerks für Repositorienmanager:innen (RepManNet)[1], das in Kooperation mit der ubifo (Forum Universitätsbibliotheken Österreichs) betrieben wird. Dort haben alle, die sich im weitesten Sinn mit Repositorien beschäftigen, die Möglichkeit, rasch und unkompliziert miteinander in Kontakt zu treten und Informationen auszutauschen.

Arbeitsgruppen zu unterschiedlichen Themen laden ein, gemeinsam an einem Thema zu arbeiten und Lösungen zu finden. Im Rahmen des RepManNet entstand die Idee zu diesem Handbuch, das den Einstieg ins Repositorienmanagement erleichtern und Know-how aus unterschiedlichen Perspektiven weitergeben soll, auch oder gerade weil die Entwicklung in diesem Bereich so rasch fortschreitet.

Mit diesem Handbuch beabsichtigen wir daher, auf möglichst breiter Ebene niederschwellig über unterschiedliche Aspekte von Repositorien zu informieren, sowie Use-Cases und Best-Practice-Modelle anzubieten. Damit soll eine praxisnahe Handreichung geschaffen werden, die als gemeinsame Wissensbasis für dieses komplexe Thema dienen und in Fortbildungen, da Open Access verfügbar, unkompliziert weitergegeben werden kann. Durch die Vielfalt im Bereich des Repositorienmanagements werden auch immer wieder Themen wichtig, denen vielleicht nicht immer die gleiche Relevanz zugesprochen wurde oder die erst ins Bewusstsein der Arbeit dringen (wie etwa Barrierefreiheit, Zertifizierungen, ethische und kollaborative Aspekte oder Schulungsmaterialien). Auch deshalb ist uns dieses Handbuch ein Anliegen.

Wir freuen uns, dass wir zahlreiche Kolleg:innen unterschiedlicher Institutionen in Österreich und darüber hinaus als Autor:innen gewinnen konnten und sind dankbar für ihre inspirierenden Beiträge. Dieses Buch soll zum Austausch und Diskurs untereinander beitragen. Das Thema wird nie abgeschlossen sein und bleibt spannend.

1 https://datamanagement.univie.ac.at/forschungsdatenmanagement/netzwerk-fuer-repositorien-managerinnen-repmannet/

Grundlagen

Die Beiträge im ersten Abschnitt thematisieren theoretische Grundlagen und strategische Gesichtspunkte im Repositorienmanagement. Das Spektrum reicht von der Entscheidung für ein Repositorium über dessen Implementierung, Fragen zu Datenmanagement bis zu Maßnahmen, die Sichtbarkeit der Repositorien und deren Inhalte zu erhöhen. Zunächst werden in den zwei Beiträgen „Research Data Repositories and What to Consider When Choosing One for Deposit" von Thomas Seyffertitz und „Open-Access-Repositorien an Hochschulen – ein Zukunftsmodell?" von Michael Katzmayr die verschiedenen Arten von Repositorien und deren Charakteristika thematisiert. Von zentraler Bedeutung ist von Anfang an die Einbindung der unterschiedlichen Akteur:innen mit Blick auf den gesamten Workflow, wie die Beiträge „Die Rolle von Repositorien im Forschungsdatenmanagement aus unterschiedlichen Perspektiven. Eine abwechslungsreiche und fordernde Tätigkeit" von Susanne Blumesberger, „Das OAIS-Referenzmodell. Grundlage für das Repositorienmanagement" von Elisabeth Steiner und „Workflow-Modell für das Datenmanagement" von Raman Ganguly zeigen. In „OAI-PMH. Grundstein und Prüfstein der Open-Access-Bewegung" stellt Herbert Hrachovec die Entwicklung des Datenaustausches und der Open-Access-Bewegung dar, die durch neue Herausforderungen, durch leistungsfähige Big-Data-Algorithmen und durch die Verbesserung der Suchmaschinen vor notwendigen Adaptionen und Herausforderungen steht.

Diese grundlegenden Beiträge werden durch praktische Anwendungsfelder im folgenden Abschnitt ergänzt.

Anwendungen

Die Beiträge im zweiten Abschnitt widmen sich konkreten Anwendungsfeldern im Bereich des Repsitorienmanagements. Hier steht die Vertiefung von grundlegenden Perspektiven und Anwendungen im Vordergrund.

Eine wesentliche Rolle im Repositorienmanagement spielt etwa die Erfassung und Verwaltung von Metadaten. Das zeigen die Beiträge „Modelling (Meta)Data in a Digital Repository. Methodological Tips in Practice" von Anna Bellotto und Kolleg:innen der Universität Padua sowie „Metadaten und kontrollierte Vokabulare" von Moritz Strickert. Sonja Fiala ergänzte diesen Bereich mit einer „Schritt-für-Schritt-Anleitung: Metadatenmapping". Ebenso essentiell für die langfristige Verfügbarkeit ist die Wahl der richtigen Dateiformate, wie Kristina Andraschko mit ihrem Beitrag „Dateiformate in der Langzeitarchivierung" zeigt, und die Wahl der Lizenzen, wie Joachim Losehand mit seinem Text „Creative Commons im Repositorien-

Management" belegt. Adelheid Mayer arbeitet in ihrem Beitrag über „Hochschulschriften-Repositorien" die Begriffsdefinitionen und rechtlichen Aspekte aus. Auf Barrierefreiheit wird leider oft nicht ausreichend geachtet. Andreas Jeitler zeigt mit seinem Beitrag „Repositorium? Ja, aber bitte barrierefrei! ", dass es auch auf scheinbar kleine Schritte ankommt. Wie die Sichtbarkeit und Nutzung von Repositorien bzw. deren Inhalten innerhalb der Institution und darüber hinaus verbessert werden können, wird im Beitrag von Daniel Beucke und Kolleg:innen „Synergien und Herausforderungen bei der Integration von Repositorien mit Forschungsinformationssystemen" deutlich. Mit einem weiteren wichtigen Aspekt, nämlich der Frage, wie interne Schulungsmaßnahmen gelingen, befassen sich Claudia Hackl und Tereza Kalová in „Kompetenzen rund um die Repositoriennutzung vermitteln. Ein Leitfaden zur Entwicklung von Schulungsmaßnahmen". Claudia Hackl und Kolleg:innen greifen in einem weiteren Beitrag das Thema Open Educational Resources auf: "An der Schnittstelle von E-Learning-Zentren, Zentralen IT-Services und Bibliotheken. Interdisziplinäre Zusammenarbeit zur Entwicklung einer nationalen Infrastruktur für Open Educational Resources (OER) aus dem österreichischen Hochschulraum". Die Brücke zu EU-Projekten schlägt Daniel Spichtinger mit "The Role of Repositories in Horizon 2020 and Horizon Europe Open Access and Data Management Requirements. A Comparative Perspective". Der zweite Abschnitt dieses Handbuchs schließt mit einem Beitrag zur Qualitätssicherung von Repositorien durch deren Zertifizierung von Elisabeth Steiner.

Die vertiefenden Beiträge dieses Abschnitts werden durch die konkreten Fallbeispiele im letzten Teil abgerundet.

Fallbeispiele

Der dritte Abschnitt bietet Einblicke in die Praxis von Wissenschaftler:innen, Repositorienmanager:innen und Mitarbeiter:innen aus Bibliotheken, zentralen IT-Services bzw. forschungsunterstützenden Services. Wie kann der Entscheidungsprozess an einer Universität für ein Produkt aussehen? Thomas Haselwanter und Heike Thöricht berichten darüber unter dem Titel „Erste Schritte zum Repositorium für Forschungsdaten an der Universität Innsbruck". Edith Leitner und Lisa Schilhan stellen „Marketingtools für Bibliotheksdienstleistungen am Beispiel von Open-Access-Zeitschriften" vor und Georg Mayr-Duffner erläutert in seinem Text „Erste Schritte in Goobi workflow mit Goobi-to-go", wie das Workflow-Management bei der Arbeit mit einer bestimmten Digitalisierungssoftware funktioniert. Einen weiteren Einblick in die Praxis liefert János Békési mit dem Thema „UNIDAM. Ein Bildrepositorium für Forschung und Lehre. Erfahrungsbericht und Schlüsse aus der Praxis". Gregor Neuböck berichtet: „Zeitgemäße visuelle Darstellung von Digitalisaten in einem Repository – am Beispiel der DLOÖ – kann nur gelingen, wenn Daten geeignet in Format gebracht werden". Harald Eberle zeigt unter dem Titel „Inhaltsbasierte Bilderschließung durch Crowd und Cloud", welche technischen Möglichkeiten es zur Datenanreicherung bzw. -visualisierung gibt. Christopher Pollin schließt mit dem Text „Datenvisualisierung" daran an. Friedrich Summann stellt in seinem Beitrag „Sichtbarkeit und Qualität von Repositorien – aus Sicht eines Service-Providers am Beispiel BASE" die Frage , welche Qualitätsmerkmale die Sichtbarkeit über das institutionelle Repositorium hinaus in globalen Suchservices verbessern. Schließlich wird am Beispiel sozialwissenschaftlicher Forschungsdaten dargestellt, dass dem Paradigma größtmöglicher Offenheit und Sichtbarkeit von Daten durchaus auch rechtliche und ethische Fragen gegenüberstehen können, etwa bei Lisa Hönegger, „Das Teilen und Archivieren von Daten in den Sozialwissenschaften" und bei Wolfgang Kraus und Anna Nindl, „Managen, Öffnen und Teilen qualitativer Forschungsdaten in den Sozialwissenschaften. Herausforderungen für Forschende und Repositorien".

In diesem Handbuch kann nur eine Auswahl an Themen behandelt werden. Dennoch haben wir uns bemüht, einen differenzierten Überblick über das Feld des Repositorienmanagents zu bieten, der hoffentlich auch Lust auf eine weitere Vertiefung des Themas macht.

Ein großer Dank ergeht an alle Peer-Reviewer:innen, die sich die Mühe gemacht haben, die Beiträge kritisch zu lesen und wertvolles Feedback zu geben sowie an Sonja Edler und Victoria Eisenheld für die tatkräftige Unterstützung.

Wir wünschen Ihnen viel Freude beim Lesen!

Die Herausgeber:innen

Susanne Blumesberger ist Leiterin der Abteilung Repositorienmanagement PHAIDRA-Services an der Universitätsbibliothek Wien. Sie veröffentlicht zu den Themen Forschungsdaten-, Repositorienmanagement, zu Open Science und Open Data.

Igor Eberhard ist wissenschaftlicher Leiter des Ethnographischen Datenarchivs an der Universität Wien. Er ist Kultur- und Sozialanthropologe. Außerdem ist Eberhard Sammlungsleiter der Ethnographischen Sammlung des Instituts für Kultur- und Sozialanthropologie der Universität Wien, wo er auch lehrt und forscht. Er veröffentlicht vor allem zu den Themenbereichen Forschungsethik und -daten, Tätowierungen und Skin Studies sowie zu sensiblen bzw. kolonialen Sammlungen.

Elisabeth Hafeneder ist seit 2016 Bibliothekarin an der Anton Bruckner Privatuniversität und dort unter anderem für das Repositorium PHAIDRA und die Verwaltung der elektronischen Ressourcen zuständig. Davor Studium der Anglistik und Amerikanistik sowie Musik- und Tanzwissenschaft mit anschließenden wissenschaftlichen und administrativen Tätigkeiten an der Paris Lodron Universität Salzburg.

Gertraud Novotny ist seit 2007 an der Universitätsbibliothek der WU Wien beschäftigt. Sie ist Fachreferentin für Wirtschaftswissenschaften (Wirtschaftsgeschichte), zuständig für Open Access und Forschungsdatenmanagement.

Elisabet Torggler studierte Geschichte und Altertumswissenschaften mit Schwerpunkt auf jüdischer Frauengeschichte. Zunächst in der Bibliothek des Jüdischen Museums Wien mit Provenienzforschung beschäftigt, leitet sie seit 2010 die Abteilung Bibliothek und Publikationsservices am Institut für Höhere Studien (IHS).

Grundlagen

Thomas Seyffertitz

Research Data Repositories and What to Consider When Choosing One for Deposit

Handbuch Repositorienmanagement, Hg. v. Blumesberger et al., 2024, S. 21–45
https://doi.org/10.25364/97839033742323

Thomas Seyffertitz, Wirtschaftsuniversität Wien, Universitätsbibliothek, thomas.seyffertitz@wu.ac.at |
ORCID iD: 0000-0002-7444-6780

Abstract

The main purpose of the present contribution is to provide practical guidance with regard to selecting a suitable data repository for research data. It might be helpful for researchers, librarians, and research support staff. Choosing a research data repository (RDR) that is appropriate for research data can be challenging and may be influenced by various factors such as the specific character of the data, requirements imposed on the researchers by third parties, e.g. a funding agency or publisher. Therefore, different types of repositories are briefly characterized in recognition of the fact that scientific disciplines or research communities have different requirements for their data management – sometimes due to the characteristics of their data, and to some extent due to the specific academic culture that has evolved. Further, directories of data repositories are presented that may be helpful in finding an appropriate place for research data storage and/or data publication. Next, data policy frameworks of some scientific journal publishers are summarized pointing to a broad spectrum of potential data sharing requirements when submitting to a journal. The final section discusses some important issues and questions to be considered in the repository selection process.

Keywords: Research data; research data repository; data archive; data policy; scholarly journal; journal publisher

Zusammenfassung

Repositorien für Forschungsdaten und was bei der Auswahl eines Repositoriums zu beachten ist

Das vorliegende Kapitel soll Forscher:innen, Bibliothekar:innen und Mitarbeitenden von Forschungseinrichtungen als praktische Orientierungshilfe zur Auswahl eines Datenrepositoriums dienen. Die Wahl oder Empfehlung eines für Forschungsdaten geeigneten Repositoriums (RDR) kann eine Herausforderung sein und von verschiedenen Faktoren beeinflusst werden, wie z. B. dem spezifischen Charakter der Daten, oder den Anforderungen, die den Forscher:innen von Dritten, z. B. einer Fördereinrichtung oder einem Verlag, auferlegt werden. Zuerst werden verschiedene Arten von Repositorien kurz charakterisiert, um der Tatsache Rechnung zu tragen, dass wissenschaftliche Disziplinen oder Forschungsgemeinschaften unterschiedliche Anforderungen an ihr Datenmanagement stellen – manchmal aufgrund der Merkmale ihrer Daten und in gewissem Maße auch aufgrund der spezifischen akademischen Kultur, die sich entwickelt hat. Außerdem werden einige Verzeichnisse von Datenrepositorien vorgestellt, die bei der Suche nach einem geeigneten Ort für die Speicherung und/oder Veröffentlichung von Forschungsdaten hilfreich sein können. Anschließend werden am Beispiel einiger großer wissenschaftlicher Zeitschriftenverlage Rahmen-Datenrichtlinien zusammenfassend vorgestellt. Die abschließende Zusammenfassung liefert Überlegungen, die zur Auswahl eines geeigneten Datenrepositoriums von Bedeutung sind, und formuliert Fragen, die von den jeweiligen Datenautor:innen zuvor beantwortet werden sollten.

Schlagwörter: Forschungsdaten; Datenrepositorium; Daten teilen; Datenpolitik; Forschungspublikation; Zeitschriftenverlag

1. Introduction

In recent years, depositing datasets associated with published research has become more common. Amongst other factors, such as proper research data management as an element of Good Scientific Practice (cf. DFG, ÖAWI and others), this is due to an increase in journals requiring data sharing[1]. It has been evidenced that journal-based data archiving policies could be very effective in ensuring that research data are available to the scientific community to enable reuse and reproducibility of results, especially when journals require a data accessibility statement to be provided in the published paper[2]. Key contributions towards the increasing availability and accessibility of research data have been the OECD Principles and Guidelines for Access to Research Data from Public Funding[3] as well as the formulation of the FAIR data principles[4]. In the case of publicly funded research projects (e.g. EU H2020 projects, FWF-funded projects), the funding bodies are increasingly demanding that the associated research data are stored in a data repository and openly accessible as far as possible (ERC, H2020, FWF, etc.).

The first objective of this contribution is to present different types of research data repositories to the reader, being one of the ways to publish and share research, and second, to provide some guidance when selecting a repository for the data deposit. The contribution primarily aims at staff generally offering research services or advising researchers on data repositories, but it may also serve as a helpful source of information for researchers themselves.

1 Resnik, D. B. et al. (2019)
2 Vines, T. H. et al. (2013 and 2020)
3 OECD (2007)
4 Wilkinson, M. et al. (2016)

In the next section (section 2), by including definitions concerning data and data repositories, the different types of RDR are described in more detail. Additionally, examples of some RDR are given. Where available, links to the relevant websites or related content are provided. However, the development of the landscape of RDR is dynamic, and finding an appropriate data repository may be a daunting task. The emerging of directories of research data repositories can be helpful for finding a suitable place to deposit research data (section 3). Data (sharing) policies and recommendations on data deposits by publishers and research funders are another important aspect in the publishing process. Hence, in section 4, some examples from important publishers of scholarly journals are presented. Finally, section 5 summarizes and considers issues of choosing a proper repository for data deposit.

2. Types and characteristics of research data repositories (RDR)

Data repositories not only serve as a storage infrastructure but can also help to make a researcher's research data more discoverable, accessible, and hence leading to potential reuse and an increased citation of scientific work. Furthermore, they can enable the reproducibility of results, making research outcomes more transparent. There is also evidence for a statistically well-supported citation benefit from open data[5]. Research tradition or discipline requirements imposed by publishers and funders, as well as institutional or national policies, may influence if, how and where researchers archive or publish the data that underlie their published research in dedicated repositories. There are different types of RDR. Looking at the scope of research areas a repository covers, two core types of data repositories can be distinguished: discipline-specific RDRs and general-purpose (or generic) RDRs. Following the US Geological Survey[6], throughout this contribution, the terms "data repository" and "data archive"[7] will be used synonymously. The same will apply to the term "research data repository" (RDR) and "research data archive".

A professionally operated data repository should always be the first choice for depositing research datasets. There, the data published in a thematically appropriate ecosystem, such repositories are recognized in their respective discipline, and the

5 Piwowar, H. A. et al. (2013)
6 U.S. Geological Survey (2022)
7 From different perspectives, the two terms may represent different concepts. Further details will not be discussed as it is beyond the scope of this contribution. The USGS approach will be followed here. For more details, see the terms archive and repository in the online dictionary of the Society of American Archivists (2022) or the German RDM information platform forschungsdaten.info. https://www.forschungsdaten.info/praxis-kompakt/glossar

visibility of the data is high. A domain- or discipline-specific repository is likely a good choice for data that can be publicly shared[8]. If there is no suitable repository available, or the requirements for the datasets cannot be met, a generalist repository such as Zenodo[9] could be an alternative[10]. If these services are not an option, e.g. because the amount of data is too large, or external storage is not possible for legal reasons, institutional research data repositories are a good place for publication. For the institution (and its researchers), providing its own repository can have several advantages. By having control over the published datasets, it is possible to specify the quality of the metadata and to ensure that the data remain in-house. Additionally, the publication process can be designed and controlled independently of third parties. It also increases the visibility of the institution and improves the overview of the published datasets of an institution. A general discussion and a good overview of these topics can be found in some recently published books[11].

There are various options available for the storage of research data. They can be stored in data archives or data repositories. An important step is to find out whether your institution operates such a platform (an institutional data archive or repository) or collaborates with a data centre where it may be compulsory to store your data. If this is not the case, it is advisable, particularly with a view to allowing other researchers to reuse your data, to find out whether any subject-specific repositories exist for your particular discipline where your data can be stored. Directories of repositories are useful tools for finding a suitable repository, an example being re3data[12], which currently lists more than 2.600 repositories (see section 3 for more details). Repositories can make data accessible in different ways: open (no access barriers), with restricted access (i.e. only metadata are accessible; or there is an embargo on a particular dataset for a certain period of time), or closed (no access rights at all)[13].

2.1. Research data

Research data are generated by various methods – depending on the research question. Data used or created within a research project may be primary data generated in the course of source research, experiments, measurements, interviews,

8 Whyte, A. (2015)
9 https://about.zenodo.org/policies/
10 See for example the data repository guidance for the Journal Scientific Data https://www.nature.com/sdata/policies/repositories
11 Cox, A. M. et al. (2018) and Corti, L. et al. (2020)
12 http://www.re3data.org/
13 re3data.org (2021)

surveys or polls. If data have been collected or produced by others than the author(s) and are already available (e.g. census data), they are termed secondary data. Depending on the research design, datasets may consist of both. These research data usually form the basis for scientific publications. Beside the different perspectives and concepts of what data generally are[14], quite a lot of different definitions of research data can be found in the relevant literature[15]. The definition by the German Research Foundation[16], and that by the Office of Management and Budget at the US Whitehouse (2020)[17] exemplify the diversity of viewpoints on research data. The OECD[18] defines research data "as factual records (numerical scores, textual records, images and sounds) used as primary sources for scientific research, and that are commonly accepted in the scientific community as necessary to validate research findings. (...)". For reasons of simplicity, the term "research data" refers to (digital) data that, depending on the subject context[19], are the subject of a research process, and are generated during a research process or are its result.

2.2. Research data repository (RDR)

In general terms, a research data repository (or data archive) can be characterized as the technical infrastructure and final destination for research data that is intended to be stored for the long term. The structure and characteristics of scientific data – the content of an RDR – differ greatly depending on the research discipline. Legal regulations may also influence the decision if, where and how to archive research data. Another reason for the different requirements of data management is the diversity of research traditions and publication cultures that have developed over time in the numerous disciplines. In simple terms, a research data repository represents an institutionalized storage location for digital research data. If you look more closely, it is not that simple, and there are definitions that are more detailed. For example, a data archive can be defined as the organizational unit that responsibly takes on the task of data management within a defined frame of reference, and a data repository as the realization of a data storage facility in that data archive[20].

14 Kitchin, R. (2021)
15 Cox, A. M. and Verbaan, E. (2018), pp. 19.
16 DFG (2009), p. 2.
17 Office of Management and Budget [=OMB] (2020); see also https://www.whitehouse.gov/wp-content/uploads/legacy_drupal_files/omb/circulars/A110/2cfr215-0.pdf and for further details on OMB's functions within the US Government, see https://www.whitehouse.gov/omb/
18 OECD (2007), p. 13.
19 Kindling, M.; Schirmbacher, P. (2013), p. 130.
20 Ludwig, J.; Enke, H. (2013), p. 47-48.

Types of research data repositories

Selecting a research data repository that is appropriate for the data in question can be quite challenging and sometimes depends on very specific requirements that may arise from the data itself, but also from requirements imposed on the researcher by third parties, such as publishers or funders (see section 4 below for data policy issues). Data repositories can be distinguished along different attributes: the disciplinary context of data, functional criteria, organizational embedding, how they are operated (commercial/non-commercial) and special purposes. Hence, a certain repository may fall into more than one of the below-mentioned categories. Nevertheless, the following types of data repositories can be distinguished[21]:

(i) Domain-specific research data repositories (dedicated to a certain discipline, or a certain research field, hence sometimes called subject-repository),
(ii) Generic data repositories usually open for all kinds of research data (for example Zenodo),
(iii) Institutional (data) repositories (e.g. operated by a university[22])
(iv) Software repositories (e.g. Github, specifically for depositing software or software projects)
(v) Commercially operated repositories, usually operated by a profit-oriented company (or part of it; e.g. Figshare)

It should be noted that repositories of the types (i), (ii), and (iv) can also be commercially oriented (i.e. they fall into category (v)). In general, the types of data repositories do not represent disjoint types or classes. In table 1, some typical characteristics of research data repositories are presented. Software repositories differ from the traditional research data archives for several reasons. They are rather generic in their nature, usually not focusing on specific scientific disciplines. Another characteristic is the availability of services for private or commercial projects as well as research projects. The initial or further development of a software is a process that may take months or years, and software may be updated over time by releasing new versions. In summary, this indicates a significant difference in use compared to traditional research data repositories, where the archived data have usually reached a final state. A recent short overview on software repositories provides some factors to be considered in the selection process[23]. It should be noted

21 See for example, Baker, K. S.; Duerr, R. E. (2017), pp. 139-144, for more details.
22 For example, GAMS, which is the Humanities' Asset Management System of the University of Graz and contains not only research data https://gams.uni-graz.at/archive/objects/context:gams/methods/sdef:Context/get?mode=about (Stigler J. H.; Steiner, E. (2018)).
23 Hong, N. (2020)

that the RDR landscape is dynamic in its nature: for example, a repository may be subject to changes in its business model or extend the scope of the data to be archived. Therefore, features listed in the table below may not exclusively apply to one type of repository. In the author's recent experience, researchers are sometimes looking for a quick fix for their data deposit, not attaching equal importance to the options listed below. Instead, they try to meet the minimum requirements set by funders or publishers.

Table 1. Data repository types[24]: characteristics, potential advantages and disadvantages. Features may not be available for all repositories listed in the example column, but rather indicate usual core features that can be expected for this class of repositories.

Repository type	**Description of features typically present/expected**		**Examples**
	Potential advantages	Potential problems or shortcomings	
Domain specific digital repositories/data archives (disciplinary repositories)	• meeting data quality standards • PID • long-term preservation • data catalogues for discovery • licensing arrangements • promotion of data • monitoring secondary use of data • management of • access to data • management of user requests on behalf of data owner • enhanced consulting services for data depositors • training offers	• may accept only specific data that are typical for the respective research domain • (possibly) costs involved in depositing data or curation services • data depositing process may be a little more complex, i.e. time and effort of the depositing process may be an entry barrier for potential submitters	UKDA (UK Data Archive)[26] AUSSDA (Austrian Social Science Data Archive)[27] DARIAH-DE (Digital Research Infrastructure for the Arts and Humanities)[28] CESSDA (Consortium of European Social Science Data Archives)[29] ICPSR (Inter-University Consortium for Political and Social Research)[30]

24 Parts of the table have been adopted from Haaker, M.; Corti, L. (2020), pp. 276-277.

26 https://www.data-archive.ac.uk/ (UK's largest digital collection of social sciences and population research data).

27 https://aussda.at/

28 https://de.dariah.eu/en/dariah-de-in-kurze or https://de.dariah.eu/en/home

29 https://datacatalogue.cessda.eu/ As a consortium CESSDA rather acts as a data-catalogue.

30 https://www.icpsr.umich.edu/web/pages/

	• data curation services • may provide self-deposit for partner institutions • additional tools and services along the research cycle[25] • usually highly acknowledged by funders' policies		
Special purpose repositories / data community driven repositories	• characteristics similar to those of domain specific repositories • homogeneous data and data ingest process[31]	• for smaller research communities, operating their own data repository may not be commensurate with the effort required	BMRB (Biological Magnetic Resonance Data Bank)[32] wwPDB[33] x-econ.org[34] (focus on experimental economics data)
Institutional digital repositories[35] (For more examples, use a query at re3data.org[36])	• Usually accepting all data collections created by their staff • Deposit usually at no cost to staff • Locality of data (may be important in case e.g. of highly sensitive data) • Visibility via institutional channels • Suitable for small datasets	• Probably lacking data management and diversity of metadata profiles for managing data from different disciplines • Limited data curation in smaller institutions due to limited staff resources or lack of expertise • Number of datasets sometimes	GAMS (Humanities Asset Management System)[37] IST Austria (Institute of Science and Technology – Austria) PHAIDRA[38] (Permanent Hosting, Archiving and Indexing of Digital Resources and Assets)

25 See for example https://de.dariah.eu/web/guest/dienste-und-werkzeuge

31 This means usually the data that are to be deposited in such repositories are homogeneous in terms of their characteristics, contents and structure, which is advantageous to the ingest process.

32 https://bmrb.io/

33 https://www.wwpdb.org/

34 A repository on experimental economics, since 2018: https://x-econ.org/xecon/#!AGB.

35 Operated by a research institution and usually only available for faculty members of the entire institution or projects where at least one project member must be affiliated with the institution.

36 Example query at re3data.org using "European Union" AND "institutional" as filter terms: https://www.re3data.org/search?query=&types%5B%5D=institutional&countries%5B%5D=EEC.

37 GAMS is the Humanities' Asset Management System of the University of Graz and contains not only research data but also other digital objects https://gams.uni-graz.at/archive/objects/context:gams/methods/sdef:Context/get?mode=about; (see also Stigler, J. H.; Steiner, E. (2018), for more details on GAMS).

38 https://phaidra.univie.ac.at/

		rather small compared to efforts required to run this service	
Generic digital repository (ranging from general purpose[39] to cross-disciplinary data repositories)	• Accepting a wide range of data types • Suitable for cross-disciplinary data • Suitable for smaller datasets • Data owner usually controls publishing of and access to dataset	• No or less editorial control over quality of data or metadata • No or limited data curation services • Limited metadata profiles • Location of physical storage of data may be legally relevant[40]	Zenodo (non-profit) Figshare (commercial) Harvard dataverse (non-profit, based on the dataverse project[41]) Dryad[42] RADAR[43] (Research Data Repository)
Software repositories[44]	Exemplary characteristics[45]: • Available for private, commercial and research projects • Usually for open-source licensed[46] projects • Some allowing for data hosting (e.g. git-annex for very large data files) • Depersonalization of services • Different version control systems • Certain services are fee-based • Developer- vs. project-focused environments		Github (a more developer focused environment) Bitbucket Sourceforge CRAN[47] (Comprehensive R Archive Network)

A further distinction can be made between special purpose repositories and disciplinary repositories. While the latter have their emphasis on research data (and the related research papers) in a certain scientific discipline or sub-discipline as a whole, the former focus on a specific topic or the type of data collected in these repositories is very narrow and homogeneous in its structure. Especially in the STEM-fields[48] the emergence of such repositories can be facilitated by the formation and longer-term

39 Generalist repositories accept data regardless of data type, format, content, or disciplinary focus.

40 For example, a research institution does not allow data deposits if the physical cloud-storage is located in the US.

41 For more details on the project, see King, G. (2007)

42 https://datadryad.org/stash/our_mission

43 https://www.radar-service.eu/en; for details, see Potthoff, J. et al. (2014) and Kraft, A. et al. (2016) and https://radar.products.fiz-karlsruhe.de/en/radarabout/ueber-radar.

44 Hong (2020)

45 (The +/- descriptions do not apply for SW-repositories.)

46 See, for example, the GNU General Public Licenses (https://www.gnu.org/licenses/gpl-3.0.html).

47 https://cran.r-project.org/

48 Abbr. for Science, Technology, Engineering and Mathematics.

existence of so-called data communities that focus on lively data exchange or sharing[49]. In a blogpost[50] at Springer Nature, Matthews (2022) states: "Each community repository is built around a specific data type, and this data-specificity yields several advantages", this term refers to the more common terms subject-specific or domain-specific repository. The following two databanks serve as examples for special purpose archives: The Biological Magnetic Resonance Databank[51] is a special purpose repository for experimental and derived data gathered from nuclear magnetic resonance spectroscopic studies of biological molecules[52]. As a second example, the Protein Data Bank[53] archive (PDB) serves as the only repository of information about the 3D structures of proteins, nucleic acids, and complex assemblies. The Worldwide PDB (wwPDB) organization manages the PDB archive and ensures that the PDB is freely and publicly available to the global community[54]. At the same time, these two repositories serve a highly specialized data community.

3. Directories of RDR – or where to search for an appropriate repository

Directories of repositories are internet portals hosted by different organizations or bodies and provide information about available repositories as well as related information. Based on the respective functionalities, this information can be discovered by browsing and search options. The scope of searchable content may vary quite a lot. In addition, repository descriptions may differ in comprehensiveness and detail among the registries. In the following, some of the most prominent directories are provided:

re3data.org[55] is by far the most comprehensive registry of RDRs. Since 2021, it has been providing information about more than 2.600 data repositories from different

49 Cooper, D.; Springer, R. (2019)
50 Matthews, T. (2022)
51 BMRB (https://bmrb.io/) is a special purpose repository for experimental and derived data gathered from nuclear magnetic resonance (NMR) spectroscopic studies of biological molecules.
52 Ulrich, E. L. et al. (2007)
53 https://www.wwpdb.org
54 wwPDB consortium (2018)
55 http://re3data.org/; online since 2012

academic disciplines all over the world[56], offering a broad set of functions and features[57]. It uses an icon system for visually indicating important features of a repository[58]. See table 2 for exemplary entries in this registry.

OpenDOAR (since 2005)[59] is a quality-assured, global directory of open-access repositories. It is not limited to data repositories. Thousands of registered repositories can be searched and browsed, based on a range of features, such as location, software or type of material held.

FAIRsharing[60] provides curated information on data repositories, data and metadata standards, as well as data policies[61].

Datacite's Repository Finder[62] can help to find an appropriate repository to deposit research data. The tool is hosted by DataCite[63] and queries the re3data registry. It further provides two predefined queries via the re3data registry resulting in a list of RDR that meet the criteria of the Enabling FAIR Data Project and the FAIRsFAIR Project[64]. Recently, DataCite has further developed its search tool: the "Repository Search" feature replaces the previous tool and merges metadata from re3data and DataCite[65].

Core Trust Seal[66] provides a (searchable) list of data repositories that are certified by at least one of the following data service providers: WDS (World Data Systems)[67], DSA (Data Seal of Approval). DSA is a certification body for repositories and was merged into CoreTrustSeal (CTS) in 2018, together with the ICSU Word Data System (WDS).

The Federal Ministry for Education, Science and Research in Austria (abbr. BMBWF) provides a search interface on its research infrastructure website, which

56 Strecker, D.; Weisweiler, N. L. (2021)

57 Vierkant, P. et al. (2018) and Pampel, H. et al. (2013)

58 Pampel, H. et al. (2015); for a more detailed description of the icons' meanings, see the FAQs at https://www.re3data.org/faq.

59 https://v2.sherpa.ac.uk/opendoar/

60 https://fairsharing.org/

61 Sansone, S.-A. et al. (2019)

62 https://repositoryfinder.datacite.org/: It is a pilot project of the Enabling FAIR Data Project led by the American Geophysical Union (AGU) in partnership with DataCite and the Earth, space and environment sciences community.

63 DataCite is a global provider of DOIs for research data.

64 https://www.fairsfair.eu/

65 Vierkant, P. (2022)

66 https://www.coretrustseal.org/

67 https://www.worlddatasystem.org

can be searched for data repositories in Austria[68], with the option to display the search results as a map.

Table 2. Selected examples of RDR (taken from the re3data.org directory of RDR)

re3data record	About	Content focus
re3data.org: **Comprehensive R Archive Network (CRAN)**; editing status 2021-09-02; re3data.org – Registry of Research Data Repositories. http://doi.org/10.17616/R3J88J	CRAN is a network of ftp and web servers around the world that store identical, up-to-date, versions of code and documentation for R.	Statistical computing
re3data.org: **AUSSDA** Dataverse; editing status 2021-11-25; re3data.org – Registry of Research Data Repositories. http://doi.org/10.17616/R39G72	Data archive for the social science community in Austria, offers a variety of research support services, primarily data archiving and help with data re-use[69].	Social sciences
re3data.org: **DARIAH-DE** Repository; editing status 2020-11-26; re3data.org – Registry of Research Data Repositories. http://doi.org/10.17616/R30G8N	Digital long-term archive for human and cultural-scientific research data.	Digital humanities
re3data.org: **RADAR**; editing status 2021-03-18; re3data.org – Registry of Research Data Repositories. http://doi.org/10.17616/R37X96	RDR for archiving and publishing research data from completed scientific studies and projects, focusing on data from subjects that do not yet have their own discipline-specific infrastructures for research data management.	Cross-disciplinary
re3data.org: **DRYAD**; editing status 2021-09-03; re3data.org – Registry of Research Data Repositories. http://doi.org/10.17616/R34S33	All material is associated with a scholarly publication.	General purpose

68 https://forschungsinfrastruktur.bmbwf.gv.at/en
69 https://aussda.at/en/

For researchers intending either to deposit data or search for reusable data, access is an important feature. Concerning the different types of access, for example, the re3data directory groups repositories according to four different levels[70]:

open: There are no access barriers. Both the data and their respective metadata are accessible.

embargoed: External users cannot overcome access barriers until the data are released and openly accessible. This refers only to the data themselves.

restricted: External users can overcome access barriers. Metadata can be accessed, but not the related data set.

closed: External users cannot overcome access barriers. Restriction refers to both metadata and the data themselves.

Restrictions may include the requirement of fees, registration or institutional membership. After the identification of one or more potential RDR for deposit, it is recommended to look at the respective homepages for specific deposit conditions (policies or the general terms and conditions) and for detailed information on the depositing process. This is important in so far as a data deposit to a data archive with a highly professional data curating process (including a moderated deposit process, such as AUSSDA or ICSPR) may take more time and cost than simply uploading data files to, for example, Zenodo. On the other hand, these larger disciplinary data archives usually comply with data policies provided by funders and publishers. Furthermore, they are often approved by relevant repository certification organizations, hence guaranteeing high quality standards.

70 How open are repositories in re3data? https://coref.project.re3data.org/blog/how-open-are-repositories-in-re3data

4. Publishers' data (sharing) recommendations and policies

In recent years, in the scholarly publication landscape, journal publishers have started developing (data) policies around the sharing or publication of research data underlying the manuscripts they publish. Some publishers or journals also refer authors to different data repositories in their policies or guidelines, or recommend searching a directory of data repositories (see section 3 in this contribution) – such as re3data – to find a suitable data archive for the relevant research data[71]. As this may be important to the authors submitting their publication, it is worth looking at some journal data policies here. For example, Springer Nature developed a framework for the research data policies of all its journals[72]. The Data Policy Standardisation and Implementation Interest Group (IG) of the Research Data Alliance further developed this framework around existing scholarly publishers' research data policies of Springer Nature, Elsevier, Wiley, and PLOS[73]. An overview of the research data policies of universities and other research institutions is omitted here, as it would go beyond the scope of this contribution. Also, research data policies provided by public funders (e.g. Austrian Science Fund, ERC[74], NSF[75] or ESRC[76]) will not be discussed in detail. For an example, the reader is referred to a comparison on requirements of the Austrian Science Fund and the European Union's Horizon 2020 Programme[77]. The summary section provides a few noteworthy tips for the repository selection decision considering funding agency guidelines. Journal publishers' data policies are probably the most relevant ones for researchers in everyday scholarly life. Therefore, some key elements and characteristics of these policies are summarized below. However, the reader should bear in mind that this represents only a small section and does not reflect the entire scientific journal publisher universe. In table 3, four prominent scholarly publishers and their research data guidelines (or policies) are exemplified in a condensed manner.

---

71 See for example https://authorservices.taylorandfrancis.com/data-sharing/share-your-data/repositories/

72 Hrynaszkiewicz, I. et al. (2017)

73 Hrynaszkiewicz, I. et al. (2020)

74 European Research Council: Data Guidelines and Open Data Policy https://open-research-europe.ec.europa.eu/for-authors/data-guidelines

75 See the National Science Foundation Proposal & Award Policies & Procedures Guide: https://new.nsf.gov/policies/pappg/23-1

76 See the Economic and Social Research Council's Research Data Policy https://www.ukri.org/publications/esrc-research-data-policy/

77 Spichtinger, D.; Blumesberger, S. (2020)

Table 3. A condensed summary of the policy framework spectrum of four large publishers

Publisher	Weakest (all features encouraged)	………	Strongest (all features required)
Wiley[78]	• DAS*	………	• DAS • Peer review of data
Taylor & Francis[79]	• DAS	………	• DAS • PID for data • Data citation
Elsevier[80]	• Data deposit in a relevant data repository • Citing this dataset in the article	……… ………	• Data deposit • Data citation and linking (or a DAS) • Peer review of data prior to publication
Springer[81]	• Data sharing • Data citation • DAS	………	• Data sharing • Evidence of data sharing • Peer review of data

Note: *DAS = Data Availability Statement/Data Access Statement; PID = Permanent Identifier (e.g. DOI)

There may be certain differences in the detailed wording and expressions, but their policy frameworks show some common core features:

They provide a general framework – with a spectrum ranging from encouraging recommendations to strictly mandatory data (sharing) policies.

They provide a set of data policies focusing on different groups of journals. The features within a certain type of policy range from a simply recommending to a highly encouraging nature to absolutely mandatory features.

It may also depend on the journal editors/editorial board what type of policy is implemented at journal level. Hence, the respective journal author guidelines should be read (see, for example Nature's editorial and publishing policies[82]).

78 John Wiley & Sons Inc. (2022); As of July 2023 the provision of a DAS has become mandatory for all original articles.
79 Taylor & Francis (2018)
80 Elsevier (2022a, 2022b)
81 Springer Nature (n.d.)
82 https://www.nature.com/palcomms/journal-policies/editorial-and-publishing-policies

The "Data Availability Statement" (DAS) is the feature most often provided as mandatory instrument. It states where data supporting the results reported in a published article can be found. It may contain links (e.g. a DOI) to publicly archived datasets.

Data journals[83] that specialize in publishing (research) datasets (so-called data papers[84]), are amongst those with the most rigid data policies. As datasets themselves are the main subject of publication, these journals require a peer review of the data. The data must be made available to editors and referees at the time of submission.

For more details on the scope and design of the policies summarized in table 3, see the respective pages at the publishers' websites. Two further examples of data sharing policies are those by SAGE[85] and PLOS[86]. Other journals, like those published by the American Economic Association (AEA), have a so-called data editor[87] who defines and monitors the journal's approach to data and reproducibility. Similarly, INFORMS's[88] Management Science Journal[89] has a data editor installed and adopted some of the data policy features from the AEA. In general, it is strongly recommended to take a close look at editorial guidelines, author guidelines and – if explicitly mentioned – a journal's data policy (sometimes termed data disclosure policy) before submitting the paper. In case of ambiguity, one should contact the journal editor or any data editor in advance.

5. Summary

Within research projects or multi-authored research articles that include or generate research data, certain questions are very important and should be addressed at the earliest possible point of time – at its best at the beginning of such a research endeavor: Which data policies may apply, whether and where which data shall be archived. As mentioned in the previous section, the publisher's or funder's guidelines may include specific requirements regarding the provision or archiving of research data (e.g. open data by default, certified repository, etc.). Even if there are no legal or contractual requirements regarding data archiving, there are a number

83 Candela, L. et al. (2015)
84 For a detailed description of this type of journal articles see for example Chavan, V.; Penev, L. (2011).
85 https://uk.sagepub.com/en-gb/eur/research-data-sharing-policies
86 https://journals.plos.org/plosone/s/data-availability
87 See https://aeadataeditor.github.io/ and American Economic Association (2019).
88 The Institute for Operations Research and the Management Sciences is an internationally recognized association for professionals in operations research, analytics, management science, economics, and many other related fields.
89 https://pubsonline.informs.org/page/mnsc/datapolicy

of issues that should always be considered when selecting a suitable data repository.

Only recently, in the United States, a set of desirable characteristics of online, public access data repositories have been formulated to help ensuring that research data are findable, accessible, interoperable, and reusable (i.e. FAIR-principles[90]) to the greatest extent possible, while integrating privacy, security, and other preventive measures.

Table 4. Desirable characteristics of repositories for managing and sharing data from federally funded or supported research[91]

Organizational infrastructure	Digital Object Management	Technological issues	Human Data related considerations[92]
• Free and easy access • Clear use guidance • Risk management • Retention policy • Long-term organizational sustainability	• Unique persistent identifiers • Metadata • Curation and Quality assurance • Broad and Measured reuse • Common formats • Provenance	• Authentication • Long-term technical sustainability • Security and Integrity	• Fidelity to consent • Security • Limited use compliant • Download control • Request review • Plan for breach • Accountability

Usually it is preferable to use a domain-specific or disciplinary repository, or alternatively an institutional data repository. If neither of these is available, a generalist repository may be an option (see section 2 above). There are some key issues to consider when depositing research data[93] and there are different options of where and how data can be archived, published and disseminated. The choice may depend on the project, the nature and characteristics of the dataset itself, the kind of access control needed for the data, the length of preservation desired, costs associated with publishing data and many other factors.

90 For details see https://www.go-fair.org/fair-principles/ or Wilkinson, M. et al. (2016).
91 For a detailed description of the features, see The National Science and Technology Council (2022), p. 4-6.
92 Very important to human data protection (see Wilkins 2021).
93 Haaker, M.; Corti, L. (2020), p. 301.

Table 5. Data-related characteristics[94]

Data format	• Hosting of common file formats (e.g. csv, xlsx, doc, pdf etc.) • Hosting of proprietary file formats (e.g. raw image files)
Data size	• Limits to size per file or to total dataset size • Small/medium datasets (e.g. spreadsheets): datasets may be uploaded by the researcher, or transferred through university network drives to a server or the cloud, and/or uploaded by a data archivist into a repository. • Medium-to-large datasets (i.e. requiring terabyte/petabyte drives): there is a larger weight toward data curation, adding robust metadata for access points and considering logical divisions of datasets/fields in consultation with researchers • Very large datasets may require consortial services or national data preservation and archiving infrastructure. At this level, the storage costs and cost for data curation may become an important issue.
Data licensing	• Types of licenses available (CC0, waiver; software license etc.) • Take care in advance whether the data are licensed (e.g. from a third-party, like a commercial data-provider)
Data attribution and citation tools	• Assignment of dataset DOIs, PIDs • References to related publications
User access controls	• Tiered access (e.g. administrator-level, collaborator-level, curator-level) • Journal-integrated, anonymous access (for peer review pre-publication) • Optional embargo to data release following publication
Data access tools	• Comprehensive data and metadata search tools • Data access via direct download • Data downloading via API • Built-in tools for reading proprietary file formats • Integrated data analysis tools

While there are many important issues to be considered when choosing a repository or archive for depositing data, some of these issues may be more relevant in the ongoing research project, whereas others may be important at the end of the project when research data are archived for the long term. Therefore, in the following table a list of some important questions is presented. These questions should be considered at the beginning of the project. However, some of them may not be answered in advance and have to be tackled again at a later stage in the project.

94 Uzwyshyn, R. (2016), p. 21.

Table 6. Important questions with regard to the choice of a research data repository

- Who operates the repository? A major publicly funded organization may be a safer choice than a commercial provider, particularly where ***long-term availability*** is concerned. Is the archive well recognized within the respective research field?
- What does the ***collection policy*** of the archive look like, i.e. what data are collected?
- What ***legal requirements*** (data protection, location of the repository, etc.) need to be taken into account? Which GDPR rules apply?
- Are the research data or parts thereof subject to ***special restrictions*** (e.g. requirement of de-identification, copyright protection)?
- What recommendations or ***data policies*** are provided by the journals where the research output is supposed to be submitted?
- What specifications regarding the provision of the research data are required by a ***funder's policy*** (e.g. is there an open data mandate; what type of repositories are recommended)?
- Is there a suitable choice of different ***licensing models*** defining how data can be reused?
- Does the repository ***enable collaborative work*** with the data? This may be of interest during the project, especially in projects with researchers from different institutions (e.g. access to data; versioning of data sets).
- Do ***charges*** apply for data storage? What does the funder's policy say about cost coverage (e.g. the SNSF does not cover costs for data deposits if the repository is commercial[95])?
- Do you need a ***trustworthy data infrastructure***; is the data archive certified (e.g. CoreTrustSeal)?
- Are the search functions useful, and is it easy to cite the data (e.g. for data reuse), for instance through the assignment of ***persistent identifiers***? What about versioning of data sets (especially during a project)?
- Does the repository provide appropriate ***metadata*** schemes for data description?

Without claiming to be exhaustive, the above questions offer some first clues for the selection of a data repository. There are quite a few tools, provided either by a special interest group in the respective research community, or by a university's research support office. For example, in 2018, the AGU Enabling FAIR Data project's Repository Guidance Targeted Adoption Group developed a detailed "decision tree" for researchers in the earth, space and environmental sciences[96], as a tool to determine an appropriate repository in which to deposit their data. The tree is applicable to most domains of research, funding scenarios and project stages (i.e., proposal vs. project completion), and considers many of the above-listed issues with which the researcher may need to comply. If neither a domain-specific repository nor an institutional repository is a solution or none of them is available, a

95 Swiss National Science Foundation (2022), p. 15.
96 Enabling FAIR Data Community et al. (2018); see also https://doi.org/10.5281/zenodo.1475430

"generalist repository comparison" chart97 may assist researchers in finding a generalist repository. Such a comparison chart can be a first starting point, as it provides some basic feature information on, for example, size limits for data, supported metadata standards, versioning support, potential costs etc.

Finally, for those not having any potential repositories in mind yet, it is recommended to visit one of the most comprehensive sources for data repositories and archives: the re3data registry[98]. It has not only search options, but also allows filtering of and browsing for data repositories along several indicators, such as content type, country, subject and many others. A further important source is FAIRsharing[99], a community-driven portal that provides repository search and additionally features a searchable database on standards and policies.

If it is still unclear what repository or data archive fits best, it is highly recommended to contact the institution's research service support or the research data management office, respectively.

Bibliography

American Economic Association (2019): Data and Code Availability Policy. July 10, 2019. https://www.aeaweb.org/journals/policies/data-code (retrieved 17.04.2023)

Baker, Karen S.; Duerr, Ruth E. (2017): Data and a Diversity of Repositories. In: Lisa R. Johnston (ed.): Curating Research Data Vol. 2: A Handbook of Current Practice. Chicago, Illinois: Association of College and Research Libraries, pp. 139-144.

Candela, Leonardo; Castelli, Donatella; Manghi Paolo; Tani, Alice (2015): Data Journals. A survey. In: Journal of the Association for Information Science & Technology 66 (9), pp. 1747-1762. https://doi.org/10.1002/asi.23358

Chavan, Vishwas; Penev, Lyubomir (2011): The Data Paper. A Mechanism to Incentivize Data Publishing in Biodiversity Science. In: BMC Bioinformatics 12 (Suppl. 15), p. 2. https://doi.org/10.1186/1471-2105-12-S15-S2

Cooper, Danielle Miriam; Springer, Rebecca (2019): Data Communities. A New Model for Supporting STEM Data Sharing. In: Ithaka S+R Issue Brief (13.05.2019). https://doi.org/10.18665/sr.311396

Corti, Louise; Van den Eynden, Veerle; Bishop, Libby; Woollard, Matthew; Haaker, Maureen; Summers, Scott (2020): Managing and Sharing Research Data. A Guide to Good Practice. 2nd edition. Los Angeles: Sage.

Cox, Andrew M.; Verbaan, Eddy (2018): Exploring Research Data Management. London: Facet Publishing.

---

97 Stall, S. et al. (2020), see also https://doi.org/10.5281/zenodo.3946719

98 re3data.org (2023); see also https://www.re3data.org

99 Sansone, S.-A. et al. (2019); see also https://fairsharing.org/

Deutsche Forschungsgesellschaft [DFG] (2009): Empfehlungen zur gesicherten Aufbewahrung und Bereitstellung digitaler Forschungsprimärdaten. https://www.dfg.de/resource/blob/169298/51f011ec1a047637243ea95a994a49e6/ua-inf-empfehlungen-200901-data.pdf (retrieved 17.04.2023)

Elsevier (2022a): Research Data Guidelines. https://www.elsevier.com/authors/tools-and-resources/research-data/data-guidelines (retrieved 17.04.2023)

Elsevier (2022b): Policies. Research Data. https://www.elsevier.com/researcher/author/tools-and-resources/research-data/data-guidelines (retrieved 17.04.2023)

Enabling FAIR Data Community; Duerr, Ruth; Kinkade, Danie; Witt, Michael; Yarmey, Lynn (2018). Data Repository Selection Decision Tree for Researchers in the Earth, Space, and Environmental Sciences. https://doi.org/10.5281/zenodo.1475430

Haaker, Maureen; Corti, Louise (2020): Publishing and Citing Research Data. In: Corti, Louise; Van den Eynden, Veerle; Bishop, Libby; Woollard, Matthew; Haaker, Maureen; Summers, Scott (eds.): Managing and Sharing Research Data. A Guide to Good Practice. 2nd edition. Los Angeles: Sage, pp. 275-307.

Hong, Neil Chue (2020): Choosing a Repository for Your Software Project. The Software Sustainability Institute. University of Edinburgh. https://www.software.ac.uk/guide/choosing-repository-your-software-project (retrieved 17.04.2023)

Hrynaszkiewicz, Iain; Simons, Natasha; Hussain, Azhar; Grant, Rebecca; Goudie, Simon (2020): Developing a Research Data Policy Framework for All Journals and Publishers. In: Data Science Journal 19 (1), p. 5. https://doi.org/10.5334/dsj-2020-005

Hrynaszkiewicz, Iain; Birukou, Aliaksandr; Astell, Mathias; Swaminathan, Sowmya; Kenall, Amye; Khodiyar, Varsha (2017): Standardising and Harmonising Research Data Policy in Scholary Publishing. In: International Journal of Digital Curation 12 (1), pp. 65-71. https://doi.org/10.2218/ijdc.v12i1.531

ICSPR [Inter-university Consortium for Political and Social Research] (2020). Guide to Social Science Data Preparation and Archiving. 6th edition. https://www.icpsr.umich.edu/files/deposit/dataprep.pdf (retrieved 17.04.2023)

John Wiley & Sons Inc. (2022). Wiley's Data Sharing Policies. https://authorservices.wiley.com/author-resources/Journal-Authors/open-access/data-sharing-citation/data-sharing-policy.html (retrieved 26.09.2022)

King, Garry (2007): An Introduction to the Dataverse Network as an Infrastructure for Data Sharing. In: Sociological Methods & Research 36 (2), pp. 173-199. https://doi.org/10.1177/0049124107306660

Kitchin, Rob (2021): The Data Revolution. A Critical Analysis of Big Data, Open Data and Data Infrastructures. 2nd revised edition. London: SAGE Publications.

Kindling, Maxi; Schirmbacher, Peter (2013): „Die digitale Forschungswelt" als Gegenstand der Forschung. In: Information – Wissenschaft & Praxis 64 (2-3), S. 127-136. https://doi.org/10.1515/iwp-2013-0017

Kraft, Angelina; Razum, Matthias; Potthoff, Janet al. (2016): Archivierung und Publikation von Forschungsdaten. Die Rolle von digitalen Repositorien am Beispiel des RADAR-Projekts. In: Bibliotheksdienst 50 (7), S. 623-635. https://doi.org/10.1515/bd-2016-0077

Ludwig, Jens; Enke, Harry (Hg.) (2013): Leitfaden zum Forschungsdaten-Management – Handreichungen aus dem WissGrid-Projekt. Glückstadt, Deutschland: Verlag Werner Hülsbusch.

Marker, Hans Jørgen; Fink, Anne Sofie (2018): CESSDA – a History of Research Data Management for Social Science Data. In: Thestup, Jesper Boserup; Kruse, Fillip (eds.): Research Data Management – a European Perspective. Berlin, Boston: De Gruyter Saur, pp. 25-42. https://doi.org/10.1515/9783110365634-003

Matthews, Tristan (2022): Community Repositories. The Best Way to Share the Data Underlying Your Research. https://authorservices.wiley.com/author-resources/Journal-Authors/open-access/data-sharing-citation/data-sharing-policy.html (retrieved 30.08.2022)

Office of Management and Budget [OMB], Executive Office of the President (2020): Guidance for Grants and Agreements. 2 CFR parts 25, 170, 183, and 200. In: Federal Register 85 (157), p. 49551. https://www.federalregister.gov/d/2020-17468 (retrieved 17.04.2023)

OECD (2007). OECD Principles and Guidelines for Access to Research Data from Public Funding. Paris: OECD Publishing. https://doi.org/10.1787/9789264034020-en-fr

Pampel, Heinz; Vierkant, Paul; Scholze, Frank et al. (2015): The re3data.org Icon System Depicting All Possible Values for Each Icon. In: PLoS ONE. Figure. https://doi.org/10.1371/journal.pone.0078080.g002

Pampel, Heinz; Vierkant, Paul; Scholze Frank et al. (2013): Making Research Data Repositories Visible. The re3data.org Registry. In: PLoS ONE 8 (11) e78080. https://doi.org/10.1371/journal.pone.0078080

Piwowar, Heather A.; Vision, Todd J. (2013): Data Reuse and the Open Data Citation Advantage. In: PeerJ 1, e175. https://doi.org/10.7717/peerj.175

Potthoff, Jan; Wezel, Jos Van; Razum, Matthias; Walk, Marius (2014): Anforderungen eines nachhaltigen, disziplinübergreifenden Forschungsdaten-Repositoriums. In: Müller, Paul; Neumair, Bernhard; Reiser, Helmut; Rodosek, Gabi D. (Hg.): 7. DFN-Forum – Kommunikationstechnologien. Bonn: Gesellschaft für Informatik e.V., S. 44136.

re3data.org (2023). re3data.org – Registry of Research Data Repositories. https://doi.org/10.17616/R3D (retrieved 28.01.2023)

re3data.org. (2021). How Open Are Repositories in re3data? (Dec. 6th, 2021). https://coref.project.re3data.org/blog/how-open-are-repositories-in-re3data (retrieved 17.04.2023)

Resnik, David B.; Morales, Melissa; Landrum, Rachel et al. (2019): Effect of Impact Factor and Discipline on Journal Data Sharing Policies. In: Accountability in Research 26 (3), pp. 139-156. https://doi.org/10.1080/08989621.2019.1591277

Ruediger, Dylan (2022): Guest Post. The Outlook for Data Sharing in Light of the Nelson Memo. https://scholarlykitchen.sspnet.org/2022/09/06/guest-post-the-outlook-for-data-sharing-in-light-of-the-nelson-memo/ (retrieved 17.04.2023)

Sansone, Susanna-Assunta; McQuilton, Peter; Rocca-Serra, Phipippe et al. (2019): FAIRsharing as a Community Approach to Standards, Repositories and Policies. In: Nature Biotechnology 37 (4), pp. 358-367. https://doi.org/10.1038/s41587-019-0080-8

Society of American Archivists [SAA] (2022): Dictionary of Archives Terminology. SAA. Society of American Archivists. https://dictionary.archivists.org/index.html (retrieved 11.08.2022)

Spichtinger, Daniel; Blumesberger, Susanne (2020): Fair Data Management Requirements in a Comparative Perspective. Horizon 2020 and FWF policies. In: Mitteilungen der Vereinigung Österreichischer Bibliothekarinnen und Bibliothekare 73 (2), S. 207-216. https://doi.org/10.31263/voebm.v73i2.3504

Springer Nature (n.d.). Research Data Policy. Legacy Data Policy Types. https://www.springernature.com/gp/authors/research-data-policy/research-data-policy-types (retrieved 06.09.23)

Stall, Shelley; Martone, Maryann E.; Chandramouliswaran, Ishwaret al. (2020): Generalist Repository Comparison Chart. https://doi.org/10.5281/zenodo.3946720

Stigler, Johannes H.; Steiner, Elisabeth (2018): GAMS – Eine Infrastruktur zur Langzeitarchivierung und Publikation geisteswissenschaftlicher Forschungsdaten. In: Mitteilungen der Vereinigung Österreichischer Bibliothekarinnen und Bibliothekare, 71 (1), S. 207-216. https://doi.org/10.31263/voebm.v71i1.1992

Strecker, Dorothea; Weisweiler, Nina Leonie (2021): Wie wird das Registry of Research Data Repositories re3data verwendet und referenziert? – Eine kurze Literaturanalyse. Blog der DINI AGs FIS & EPUB. https://doi.org/10.57689/DINI-BLOG.20210527

Swiss National Science Foundation (2022). General Implementation Regulations for the Funding Regulations, Version: 1.1.2023 (76 p.). Bern: Swiss National Science Foundation. https://www.snf.ch/media/en/B0SWnPsrDCRTaiCx/snsf-general-implementation-regulations-for-the-funding-regulations-e.pdf (retrieved 17.04.2023)

Taylor & Francis (2018): Data Sharing Policies. https://authorservices.taylorandfrancis.com/wp-content/uploads/2019/04/Author-Services-Data-sharing-policies.pdf (retrieved 17.04.2023)

The Software Sustainability Institute. (2018): Software Deposit Guidance for Researchers. The Software Sustainability Institute, University of Edinburgh. https://softwaresaved.github.io/software-deposit-guidance/ (retrieved 30.01.2022)

Ulrich, Eldon, L.; Akutsu, Hideo; Doreleijers, Jurgen F. et al. (2008): BioMagResBank. In: Nucleic Acids Research 36 (Issue suppl., 1 January 2008), pp. D402–D408. https://doi.org/10.1093/nar/gkm957

U.S. Geological Survey [USGS] (2022): Archive vs. Repository. Is There a Difference? USGS (U.S. Department of the Interior). https://www.usgs.gov/data-management/archive-vs-repository-there-difference (retrieved 11.08.2022)

Uzwyshyn, Ray (2016): Research Data Repositories. The What, When, Why, and How. In: Computers in Libraries 36 (3), pp. 18-21. https://www.proquest.com/docview/1792217242?accountid=29104&sourcetype=Trade%20Journals (retrieved 17.04.2023)

Vierkant, Paul; Pampel, Heinz; Elger, Kirsten; Kindling, Maxi; Ulrich, Robert; Witt, Michael; Fenner, Martin (2018): Status Quo and Perspective of re3data. Paper presented at the MERIL-2 Interoperability Workshop, Athens, Greece. https://doi.org/10.5281/zenodo.1297432

Vierkant, Paul (2022). How to find a repository for your research outputs. In: DataCite Blog. DataCite. https://doi.org/10.5438/mz0y-7j88

Vines, Timothy H.; Albert, Arianne (2020): The effect of a strong data archiving policy on journal submissions (Part II). In: The Scholarly Kitchen (Aug 26, 2020). https://scholarlykitchen.sspnet.org/2020/08/26/__trashed/ (retrieved 17.04.2023)

Vines, Timothy H; Andrew, Rose L. et al. (2013): Mandated data archiving greatly improves access to research data. In: The FASEB Journal 27 (4), 1304-1308. https://doi.org/10.1096/fj.12-218164

Wilkins, R. Bert (2021): Do You Know Me?: The Subtle Distinction Between "Anonymous" and "De-identified" Data in Clinical Research (White Paper, Western-Copernicus Group Institutional Review Board). https://www.wcgclinical.com/insights/do-you-know-me-the-subtle-distinction-between-anonymous-and-de-identified-data-in-clinical-research/ (retrieved 11.10.2023)

Wilkinson, Mark; Dumontier, Michel; Aalbersberg, IJsbrand et al. (2016): The FAIR Guiding Principles for scientific data management and stewardship. In: Scientific Data 3, 160018. https://doi.org/10.1038/sdata.2016.18

Whyte, Angus (2015): Where to keep research data. DCC checklist for evaluating data repositories (v.1.1). Edinburgh: Digital Curation Centre. https://www.dcc.ac.uk/guidance/how-guides/where-keep-research-data (retrieved 17.04.2023)

wwPDB consortium (2018): Protein Data Bank: the single global archive for 3D macromolecular structure data. In: Nucleic Acids Research 47 (D1), D520-D528. https://doi.org/10.1093/nar/gky949

Thomas Seyffertitz ist seit 2013 an der Universitätsbibliothek der WU Wien beschäftigt. Er ist Fachreferent für Wirtschaftswissenschaften sowie Mathematik, Statistik und Finanzierung und zuständig für Forschungsdatenmanagement. Darüber hinaus ist er Mitglied der Kommission für Forschung an der WU Wien.

Michael Katzmayr

Open-Access-Repositorien an Hochschulen – ein Zukunftsmodell?

Handbuch Repositorienmanagement, Hg. v. Blumesberger et al., 2024, S. 47–60
https://doi.org/10.25364/97839033742324

Michael Katzmayr, Wirtschaftsuniversität Wien, Universitätsbibliothek, michael.katzmayr@wu.ac.at |
ORCID iD: 0000-0003-1571-2329

Zusammenfassung

Institutionelle Repositorien, die Forschungsergebnisse einer Hochschule oder Forschungseinrichtung frei zugänglich im Internet anbieten, sind seit vielen Jahren ein wichtiger Bestandteil der Informationsinfrastruktur. Sie mussten sich jedoch seit Anbeginn gegen fachspezifische Repositorien behaupten, die für die Wissenschaftler:innen oft die nachgefragtere Alternative sind. Darüber hinaus stellen akademische soziale Netzwerke wie ResearchGate oder Academia.edu für (institutionelle) Repositorien eine weitere Herausforderung dar. Zudem führt der Trend zur Integration von Informationssystemen an Hochschulen zu Überlegungen, bisher getrennt bestehende Forschungsinformationssysteme und Repositorien zusammenzuführen. Angesichts dieser Entwicklungen stellt sich die Frage, inwieweit für die Verbreitung und langfristige Archivierung wissenschaftlicher Ergebnisse institutionelle Open-Access-Repositorien auch heute noch die Lösung der Wahl sind und wie Repositorien ausgestaltet sein sollten, um für gegenwärtige und zukünftige Anforderungen gerüstet zu sein.

Schlagwörter: Hochschule, institutionelles Repositorium, fachspezifisches Repositorium, Forschungsinformationssystem, akademisches soziales Netzwerk

Abstract

Open-Access Repositories at Universities – a Model for the Future?

Institutional repositories, which make the research results of a university or research institution freely accessible on the internet, have been an important part of the information infrastructure for many years. However, since their introduction, they have had to hold their own against subject-specific repositories, which are often the more sought-after alternative for researchers. Furthermore, academic social networks such as ResearchGate or Academia.edu pose another challenge for (institutional) repositories. Moreover, the trend towards integration of information systems at universities is leading to considerations of merging previously separate current research information systems and repositories. In view of these developments, the question arises as to what extent institutional open access repositories are still the solution of choice today for the dissemination and long-term archiving of research results, and how repositories should be designed in order to be equipped to meet current and future requirements.

Keywords: University, institutional repository, subject repository, current research information system, academic social network

1. Einleitung in die Thematik

Vor rund 20 Jahren wurden im Zuge der aufkommenden Open-Access-Bewegung die ersten institutionellen Repositorien gegründet. Sie verfolgten dabei insbesondere zwei Ziele: Open Access als neues Publikationsparadigma voranzutreiben und die wissenschaftlichen Leistungen von Institutionen wirksam nach außen darzustellen. Damals wie heute können diese Informationssysteme im Wesentlichen wie folgt beschrieben werden[1]:

- Institutioneller Fokus: Es werden die intellektuellen Leistungen der Mitglieder einer Institution unabhängig thematischer Einschränkungen zur Verfügung gestellt. Dadurch ergibt sich eine Abgrenzung zu themenspezifischen Repositorien bzw. Repositorien ohne institutionelle Einschränkung.
- Es geht um wissenschaftliche Inhalte wie Publikationen, Forschungsdaten oder auch Lehrmaterialien. Repositorien mit Dokumenten aus dem Berichtswesen oder Archivgut aus der Verwaltung sind in der folgenden Betrachtung ausgeklammert.
- Dauerhafte Archivierung und wachsender Dokumentenbestand: Die Inhalte sollen dauerhaft zur Nutzung vorgehalten werden, wobei aufgrund der wachsenden Datenmenge das Repositorium auch skalierbar sein muss.
- Offener Zugang und Interoperabilität: Open Access steht im Vordergrund, geeignete Schnittstellen und Protokolle erlauben den freien Zugriff auf die Metadaten durch andere Systeme.

Seither haben sich allerdings nicht nur die informationstechnologischen Rahmenbedingungen und die damit verbundenen Praktiken der Wissenschaftskommunikation verändert, sondern auch die Geschäftsmodelle im Bereich des Open-Access Publizierens. Es stellt sich also die Frage, ob institutionelle Repositorien nach wie vor die geeigneten Instrumente sind, um die freie Versorgung mit wissenschaftlichen Ergebnissen und die Außendarstellung der wissenschaftlichen Leistungen einer Institution zu gewährleisten[2]. Die neuen und zum Teil auch altbekannten Herausforderungen für institutionelle Repositorien sollen im Folgenden dargelegt werden.

1 Vgl. dazu und zum Folgenden Crow, R. (2002).
2 Siehe dazu auch Novotny, G.; Seyffertitz, T. (2018).

2. Herausforderungen für institutionelle Repositorien

2.1. Repositorien ohne institutionelle Einschränkung

Themenspezifische Repositorien, die nicht an Forschungsergebnissen bestimmter Institutionen, sondern an Fachgebieten ausgerichtet sind, gibt es schon wesentlich länger als deren institutionelle Pendants. Insbesondere in Disziplinen, deren Publikations- und Forschungskulturen stark durch die Zirkulation von Arbeitspapieren geprägt sind, finden sich schon früh Beispiele des erfolgreichen Betriebs themenspezifischer Repositorien. Hier sind vor allem die Physik (arXiv[3], gegründet 1991), Wirtschaftswissenschaften (RepEc[4], gegründet 1997), Psychologie (Cogprints[5], gegründet 1997) und andere, insbesondere naturwissenschaftliche, Fächer zu nennen. Für viele Forschende jedoch waren – und sind – bestehende themenspezifische Repositorien für ihren Fachbereich nicht vorhanden oder nicht geeignet. Wenig überraschend wurden daher nach deren Vorbild die ersten institutionellen Repositorien gegründet. Dies bedeutet im Umkehrschluss aber auch, dass es hinsichtlich der Open-Access-Verbreitung von Inhalten Disziplinen gibt, die auf eine institutionelle Lösung schlicht nicht angewiesen sind und wenig Anreiz sehen, ihre Forschungsergebnisse dort zusätzlich abzulegen, zumal Probleme mit unterschiedlichen Versionen eines Objekts bzw. unterschiedlichen Richtlinien der Repositorien häufig vorkommen[6].

Ähnlich verhält es sich mit Repositorien, die sich inhaltlich weder an einer bestimmten Institution ausrichten noch an eine Disziplin gekoppelt sind. Ein bekanntes Beispiel ist das von der Kernforschungseinrichtung CERN betriebene Repositorium Zenodo[7], das für eine Vielzahl von Dokumenttypen – von Forschungsdaten über Publikationen bis hin zu Videos, Software etc. – offen ist und eine besonders niederschwellige Möglichkeit zur Selbstarchivierung durch Forschende darstellt, dabei aber eine hohe funktionale Qualität aufweist[8].

Angesichts der Leistungsfähigkeit dieser Art von Repositorien stellt sich die Frage, ob institutionelle Repositorien überhaupt eine Rolle spielen sollen und ob sie den Aufwand, den sie in Erstellung und Betrieb verursachen, rechtfertigen. Hierzu ist anzumerken, dass sie auch Vorteile bieten, die gerade in ihrem institutionellen Fokus begründet liegen:

---

3 https://arxiv.org
4 http://repec.org
5 http://cogprints.org
6 Vgl. Jones, R. et al. (2006), S. 6f.
7 https://zenodo.org
8 Vgl. Pujol Priego, L.; Wareham. J. (2019).

- Außendarstellung: institutionelle Repositorien sind geeignet, die Leistungen ihrer Institutionen gleichsam wie in einem Schaufenster zu präsentieren. Das kann zwar auch durch andere Lösungen bewerkstelligt werden (z. B. durch Content-Management-Systeme oder Forschungsdokumentationen), diese weisen aber nicht immer die erforderlichen Schnittstellen zur optimalen Verbreitung der Inhalte auf.
- Governance: institutionelle Repositorien sind zumeist ein professionell abgesicherter Teil organisatorischer Infrastrukturen mit idealerweise klar definierten, häufig durch Open-Access-Policies festgelegten Regelungen sowie einer längerfristigen finanziellen Absicherung. Manche der Repositorien ohne institutionelle Einschränkungen entsprechen aufgrund mangelnder Ressourcen oder schwach definierter Verantwortlichkeiten nicht immer dem Stand der Technik oder können oft nicht flexibel auf Serviceanforderungen reagieren. Institutionen, die ein Repositorium als Schaufenster ihrer wissenschaftlichen Leistungen betreiben, können sich eine mangelhafte Umsetzung hingegen kaum leisten. Eine gute institutionelle Absicherung jeder Art von Repositorium, idealerweise in Verbindung mit einer entsprechenden Zertifizierung, kann hierbei zwar ein gewisses Maß an Sicherheit schaffen; doch selbst dann können sich – wie im Fall Zenodo – Herausforderungen hinsichtlich der Skalierbarkeit und letztlich Finanzierbarkeit stellen, da einzelne Institutionen ohne spezielle Förderung kaum den stets steigenden Bedarf an Archivierungsleistungen von außerhalb ihrer Trägerinstitution befriedigen können[9].
- Systemintegration: institutionelle Repositorien können mittels Schnittstellen leichter in die lokale IT-Systemlandschaft eingebunden werden bzw. können lokale Anforderungen (Stammdatenverwaltung, IT-Sicherheitsrichtlinien, spezielle Vorgaben zur Langzeitarchivierung etc.) von vornherein berücksichtigt werden.
- Rechtliche Rahmenbedingungen: Nicht nur technischen, auch rechtlichen Aspekten kann durch eine institutionelle Archivierungslösung oftmals besser begegnet werden. Hier wären etwa unterschiedliche nationale Urheberrechte oder Anforderungen wichtiger Fördergeber an Repositorien zu nennen, etwa das Vorliegen bestimmter Lizenzen für Metadaten, das Vorhandensein eines persistenten Identifikators, Angabe bestimmter Informationen zum Projekt bzw. Fördergeber etc.[10] Auch erlauben manche Verlage in

9 Vgl. hierzu Pujol Priego, L.; Wareham. J. (2019), S. 8f.
10 Für einen Überblick hierzu siehe Rücknagel, J. (2021).

ihren Open-Access Policies das Archivieren in institutionellen Repositorien häufiger als in themenspezifischen.

2.2. Akademische soziale Netzwerke

Akademische soziale Netzwerke (ASN) stellen seit einigen Jahren eine bedeutende Herausforderung für Open-Access-Repositorien dar. Unter ASN werden Online-Netzwerke verstanden, die sich primär an Wissenschaftler:innen richten. Sie erlauben wie andere soziale Netzwerke auch das Erstellen von Profilen und ermöglichen eine Vernetzung zwischen den Teilnehmenden. Darüber hinaus können auch wissenschaftliche Publikationen, Forschungsdaten etc. zu den Profilen hinzugefügt und mit anderen Wissenschaftler:innen geteilt bzw. frei verbreitet werden. Während institutionelle Repositorien das Schaufenster einer Institution darstellen, fungieren die ASN also als Schaufenster der einzelnen Wissenschaftler:innen. Die am weitesten verbreiteten ASN sind die jeweils 2008 gegründeten Plattformen Academia.edu[11], ResearchGate[12] und die auch als Literaturverwaltungsprogramm dienende Software Mendeley[13]. Die Funktionalitäten der ASN umfassen üblicherweise u. a. Anfragemöglichkeiten für Forschungsergebnisse (wenn sie nicht ohnehin frei angeboten werden), Aufgabe von Stellenanzeigen, Suche nach Kooperationspartner:innen, Bereitstellen von Zitationsmetriken etc. Diese Plattformen stellen auch ein Beispiel für sogenanntes Guerilla-Open-Access-Publishing dar, da urheberrechtlich geschützte Materialien oftmals informell geteilt werden, was allerdings schon zu Konflikten mit etablierten wissenschaftlichen Verlagen geführt hat[14].

Das Angebot an Funktionalitäten steht im Fokus des Interesses von Forschenden – was aber bedeutet das für deren Bereitschaft, ihre Forschungsergebnisse zusätzlich zur Nutzung von ASN auch in institutionellen Repositorien abzulegen? Empirische Studien kommen zum Ergebnis, dass Forschende häufiger Dokumente in ASN ablegen als in den Repositorien an ihren Institutionen[15]. Interessanterweise argumentieren zwei Studien[16], dass ASN und institutionelle Repositorien nicht unbedingt in Konkurrenz zueinander stehen müssen, zeige sich doch, dass jene Forschenden, die ihre Ergebnisse in ASN ablegen, dies auch verstärkt in den Repositorien ihrer Institutionen tun – sie ziehen also mehrere Kanäle zum Teilen der Forschungsergebnisse heran. Die ASN könnten demnach aus Sicht der Repositorien-Betreiber

11 https://www.academia.edu
12 https://www.researchgate.net
13 https://www.mendeley.com
14 Vgl. Jordan, K. (2019)
15 Vgl. ebd. S. 4f.
16 Lovett, J. A. et al. (2017) und Eva, N. C.; Wiebe, T. A. (2019)

dazu dienen, open-access-affine Forschende zu identifizieren, die dann gezielt für das Archivieren ihrer Forschungsergebnisse geworben werden.

Selbst wenn institutionelle Repositorien über diesen Umweg befüllt werden können, stellt sich immer noch die Frage, welchen Zweck sie besser als ASN erfüllen und worin ihr spezifischer Nutzen liegt. In diesem Zusammenhang können durchaus einige Problemfelder von ASN genannt werden, die allerdings nicht im Zentrum der Aufmerksamkeit der Forschenden liegen dürften[17]:

- Es ist ungewiss, ob diese kommerziellen Unternehmen in Zukunft kostenpflichtig werden oder wie lange sie überhaupt existieren werden. Dies wirft auch Fragen zur Langzeitverfügbarkeit der dort befindlichen Dokumente auf.
- Es wird zumeist weniger Augenmerk auf korrekte Metadaten und die Organisationszugehörigkeit der Forschenden gelegt.
- Es gibt in ASN in der Regel keine Prüfung, ob eine Veröffentlichung überhaupt rechtlich zulässig ist.

2.3. Die Rolle von Repositorien im Rahmen derzeitiger Open-Access-Geschäftsmodelle

Als das Subskriptionsmodell das gängige Geschäftsmodell am Zeitschriftenmarkt darstellte, war die Zweitveröffentlichung wissenschaftlicher Aufsätze in Repositorien das Mittel der Wahl, um Open Access zu verwirklichen. Mittlerweile hat sich Open Access als Geschäftsmodell kommerzieller Verlage etabliert – immer mehr Zeitschriftenartikel erscheinen nach Bezahlung einer Publikationsgebühr in Open-Access-Zeitschriften oder können aus traditionellen subskriptionspflichtigen Zeitschriften freigekauft werden und erscheinen dann ebenfalls unmittelbar in der Originalfassung Open Access. Zwar ist in den Richtlinien bedeutender Fördergeber mitunter die Auflage oder Empfehlung enthalten, dass Forschungsergebnisse, die in Open-Access-Publikationsorganen erscheinen oder freigekauft wurden, zusätzlich und ohne zeitliche Verzögerung auch in Repositorien archiviert werden müssen[18]; allerdings scheint es davon abgesehen fragwürdig, Kopien dieser Volltexte oder deren Vorversionen (Fassungen vor dem Peer-Review, sogenannte „Pre-Prints“) in (institutionellen) Repositorien abzulegen – zumindest dann, wenn die betreffenden Verlage die Langzeitarchivierung garantieren können. Derzeit scheint sich die Transformation zu Open Access vorwiegend über kommerzielle,

17 Vgl. auch Eva, N. C.; Wiebe, T. A. (2019), S. 14f.
18 Vgl. Rücknagel, J. (2021)

von Verlagen getriebene Geschäftsmodelle zu vollziehen, allerdings gibt es weiterhin Ansätze von Forschungsförderern und auf politischer Ebene, die Zweitveröffentlichung bzw. Archivierung in Repositorien als (zumindest ergänzenden) Weg zu verfolgen[19]. Aktuelle Zahlen zur Entwicklung der Open-Access-Quote für verschiedene Formen von Open Access liegen für Deutschland vor und unterstreichen die wachsende Bedeutung von kommerziell betriebenem Open Access: Im Zeitraum 2005-2019 weisen die hybriden Publikationen (also Open Access durch „Freikauf" von Artikeln aus Subskriptionszeitschriften) eine durchschnittliche jährliche Wachstumsrate von 30 % auf, beim goldenen Weg zu Open Access (also das Publizieren in Open-Access-Zeitschriften, zumeist verbunden mit Publikationsgebühren) sind es 25 %. Hingegen nimmt sich die Wachstumsrate beim grünen Weg zu Open Access (also Zweitveröffentlichung in Repositorien) mit nur 2 % vergleichsweise bescheiden aus[20]. Für Monographien, Buchbeiträge, Forschungsdaten, graue Literatur oder Lehrmaterialien lassen sich aufgrund fehlender Daten keine belastbaren Aussagen zur Open-Access-Quote machen; es ist allerdings zu vermuten, dass für diese Publikationsformen Repositorien (allerdings nicht zwingend institutionelle) weiterhin eine zentrale Rolle in der Realisierung von Open Access zukommen dürfte.

3. Integration von Informationssystemen an Hochschulen und Lock-In-Effekte

Die Frage der Anbindung an andere Informationssysteme einer Institution ist seit jeher mit dem Betrieb von institutionellen Repositorien verknüpft. Insbesondere Forschungsinformationssysteme (in der Fachliteratur zumeist abgekürzt als CRIS für Current Research Information Systems), die alle Forschungsergebnisse einer Institution erfassen und für das Berichtswesen aufbereiten, stehen hierbei häufig im Mittelpunkt der Betrachtung. Immerhin verzeichnen sowohl CRIS als auch institutionelle Repositorien bibliographische Daten und bilden Forschungsleistungen einer Institution ab, wobei die Daten häufig von den Forschenden selbst in die Systeme eingegeben oder gepflegt werden.

Um hierbei Synergien zu finden, bieten sich drei Möglichkeiten an: Erstens können institutionelle Repositorien zusätzlich zu den Open-Access-Objekten samt deren Metadaten auch alle anderen bibliographischen Daten von Forschungsergebnissen und die für das Berichtswesen erforderlichen Daten halten. Aufgrund der äußerst

19 Vgl. Deppe, A.; Beucke, D. (2017)
20 Vgl. Barbers, I.; Pollack, P. (2021), S. 5f.

komplexen und laufend steigenden Anforderungen an das Berichtswesen im Bereich des Forschungsmanagements ist dies jedoch eine zunehmend schwieriger herzustellende Variante. Zweitens können CRIS neben der Bibliographie der Forschungsleistungen auch Open-Access-Objekte enthalten und zur freien Nutzung anbieten und die Metadaten über eine geeignete Schnittstelle in diversen Suchdiensten des Internet verbreiten. Drittens können beide Systeme weiterbestehen, aber über geeignete Schnittstellen sicherstellen, dass Daten nur in eines der beiden Systeme eingegeben und anschließend an das andere weitergereicht werden[21]. Aufgrund der in einem CRIS reichhaltigeren und stärker ausdifferenzierten Metadaten ist es in dieser dritten Variante sinnvoll, dieses als datenführendes System zu verwenden. Das angebundene Repositorium würde die Objekte und ggf. auch die Metadaten speichern, die aus dem CRIS generiert würden[22].

Ein weitreichender und zukunftsträchtiger Ansatz im Sinne einer Integration ist die Etablierung eines institutionellen Informationssystems (IIS), das nicht nur die Funktionalitäten eines institutionellen Repositoriums und eines CRIS in sich vereint, sondern darüber hinaus auch weitere Dienste anbietet, die die Bedürfnisse der Forschenden in den Mittelpunkt rücken. Hier wären etwa Profilseiten mit den Expertisen, Lebensläufen und vollständigen Publikations- und Tätigkeitslisten zu nennen, auch wenn diese an anderen Institutionen ihren Ursprung haben. Dabei ist es im Falle von Open-Access-Publikationen hinsichtlich der Verfügbarkeit unerheblich, ob die frei verfügbaren Dokumente der Forschenden lokal an der Institution, in einem themenspezifischen Repositorium oder direkt bei den Verlagen archiviert sind, solange sie aus dem IIS heraus korrekt verlinkt sind. Die dadurch erreichte Fokussierung auf Forschende dient dabei nicht nur dazu, die Akzeptanz eines IIS zu befördern, sondern diese Systeme können auch auf Augenhöhe mit den ASN konkurrieren, die sich ebenfalls dadurch auszeichnen, den Forschenden eine umfängliche Präsentationsmöglichkeit unabhängig allfälliger institutioneller Zugehörigkeiten zu bieten[23].

Ein Aspekt, der bei allen Entscheidungen im Zusammenhang mit Repositorien, insbesondere aber bei einer Integration von Systemen Beachtung finden sollte, ist der sogenannte Lock-In-Effekt[24]. Darunter versteht man Wechselkosten, die einen allfälligen System- oder Anbieterwechsel in Zukunft erschweren. Zwar sind Lock-In-Effekte in der Informationsbranche der Normalfall, allerdings können zukünftige

21 Vgl. Joint, N. (2008)
22 Vgl. dazu Jeffery, K.; Asserson, A. (2009)
23 Vgl. Rybinski, H. et al. (2017)
24 Vgl. dazu Shapiro, C.; Varian, H. R. (1999), S. 139-228.

Wahlmöglichkeiten bzw. die Höhe der damit verbundenen Kosten ganz entscheidend durch heutige Investitionsentscheidungen beeinflusst werden:

- Generell stellt sich bei Informationssystemen bzw. Datenbanken die Kernfrage, inwieweit die enthaltenen Daten später auf ein anderes System ohne Verluste übertragen werden können und welche Kosten bei einem Datentransfer entstehen. Vor diesem Hintergrund sind möglichst offene Schnittstellen und offene, nicht-proprietäre Datenformate zu bevorzugen, wie sie etwa in auf Open-Source-Software basierenden Systemen Anwendung finden.
- Es sollte überlegt werden, wie zukünftige Erweiterungen oder Anpassungen des Systems erfolgen sollen. Durch vertragliche Verpflichtungen beim Kauf eines kommerziellen Produktes können Anbieter zu bestimmten Leistungen verpflichtet werden. Bei auf Open-Source-Software basierenden Systemen ist auch in diesem Zusammenhang generell ein geringeres Lock-In zu erwarten.
- Sollte ein Informationssystem umfangreiche produkt- oder markenspezifische Trainings erfordern, so steigt das Ausmaß des Lock-In, je mehr die Anwender:innen auf das neue System trainiert werden müssen.
- Der Verkauf von Komplementärprodukten führt häufig zu einer Prozessintegration und ist eine beliebte Strategie von Anbietern, ein ausgeprägtes Lock-In zu erzeugen. Wenn beispielsweise sowohl das Forschungsinformationssystem als auch die Software zur Forschungsevaluation sowie allfällige lizenzpflichtige bibliographische Datenbanken, die die Metadaten für das Forschungsinformationssystem liefern, das Produktportfolio eines Anbieters bei einem Kunden ausmachen, ist zukünftig ein Wechsel einzelner Komponenten dieses Systemverbunds oder auch des Gesamtsystems nur erschwert möglich.

4. Einsatzmöglichkeiten und Ausgestaltung zeitgemäßer institutioneller Repositorien

Aufgrund der Richtlinien von Fördergebern sowie für bestimmte Materialien, die nicht im tradierten und von Verlagen organisierten Publikationskanälen erscheinen (Forschungsdaten, graue Literatur, digitalisierte ältere Literatur, Lehrmaterialien etc.) werden Repositorien weiterhin benötigt. ASN stellen aufgrund der fehlenden Langzeitarchivierung bzw. der generell unsicheren Zukunftsperspektive keine gleichwertige Alternative dazu dar.

Doch müssen Repositorien deshalb institutionell sein? Institutionelle Repositorien werden zumindest dann gebraucht, wenn keine geeigneten, mit den erforderlichen Funktionalitäten ausgestatteten und langfristig abgesicherten anderweitigen Repositorien zur Verfügung stehen. Den aktuellen Stand der Technik stellen dabei die oben erwähnten IIS dar, die neben diversen Einsatzmöglichkeiten im Bereich des Forschungsmanagements auch die Funktion eines institutionellen Repositoriums übernehmen können. Sie können auch – besser als die traditionellen institutionellen Repositorien – als Schaufenster der Institution dienen, da sie nicht nur die open access verfügbaren Objekte zeigen, sondern alle wissenschaftlichen Leistungen der Institution bzw. der Forschenden auflisten.

Die erforderlichen Funktionalitäten der Software unterscheiden sich zum Teil je nach Einsatzgebiet, gespeicherten Inhalten und Nutzungsanforderungen. Folgende Aspekte sind jedoch jedenfalls zu berücksichtigen, unabhängig davon, ob es sich um Eigenentwicklungen oder um kommerzielle oder unter Open-Source-Bedingungen verfügbare Softwarepakete handelt[25]:

- Eine eindeutige Referenzierung der Inhalte ist für die Zitierfähigkeit sicherzustellen, wozu in der Regel sogenannte persistente Identifikatoren (etwa DOI – Digital Object Identifier[26] oder URN – Uniform Resource Name[27]) herangezogen werden. Das bedeutet, dass Objekte auch im Zuge einer inhaltlichen Aktualisierung als Version erhalten bleiben und mit der neueren Version verknüpft werden müssen.
- Langzeitarchivierung: eine an das Repositorium angeschlossene Archivierungssoftware ist wünschenswert, um die digitalen Dokumente dauerhaft zu sichern.

25 Vgl. dazu Deinzer, G. (2017)
26 https://www.doi.org/
27 Vgl. https://www.dnb.de/DE/Professionell/Services/URN-Service/urn-service_node.html

- Die IT-Sicherheit stellt Anforderungen u. a. hinsichtlich der Authentizität und Integrität der Dokumente. Hierbei sind eine verschlüsselte Datenübertragung, die Möglichkeit einer differenzierten Rechtevergabe für einzelne Nutzergruppen sowie die Authentifizierung der Autor:innen zu nennen.
- Eine gute Usability ist wichtig für die Akzeptanz des Systems. Hierzu zählt u. a. ein einfacher Datenupload, eine einfache redaktionelle Bearbeitbarkeit von Einträgen, Möglichkeiten zur Nachnutzung bzw. Weiterverarbeitung der Metadaten mit Literaturverwaltungssystemen etc.
- Interoperabilität ist seit Anbeginn ein zentrales Element von Repositorien. Neben der OAI-PMH[28]-Schnittstelle (Open Archives Initiatives – Protocol for Metadata Harvesting) zum Auslesen der Metadaten als Basisanforderung sind auch Anbindungen an bestimmte Suchdienstleister und deren spezielle Metadatenschemata, die Anbindung an die lokalen IT-Systeme der Hochschule (etwa Zugriff auf die Personalstammdaten, um ein erleichtertes Login zu ermöglichen), Optimierung für Suchmaschinen, Schnittstellen zu ASN etc. zu nennen.
- Die Zertifizierung von Repositorien stellt sicher, dass der Stand der Technik hinsichtlich Betrieb und Funktionalität eingehalten wird. Ein Erwerb eines anerkannten Zertifikates, z. B. das für Deutschland anwendbare DINI-Zertifikat[29] der deutschen Initiative für Netzwerkinformation oder das international verbreitete CoreTrustSeal[30], ist ein wichtiger Schritt zur Sicherstellung eines professionellen institutionellen Repositoriums.

28 https://www.openarchives.org/pmh/
29 https://dini.de/dienste-projekte/dini-zertifikat/
30 https://www.coretrustseal.org/

5. Fazit

Trotz der in diesem Beitrag beschriebenen Herausforderungen werden institutionelle Repositorien zumindest in näherer Zukunft ein wichtiger Bestandteil der Informationsinfrastruktur an Hochschulen bleiben: entweder in ihrer traditionellen Form zur langfristigen Archivierung und Verbreitung all jener Dokumente, die einen starken institutionellen Bezug aufweisen (z. B. Hochschulschriften) oder für die es keine andere passende Speichermöglichkeit gibt; oder in veränderter Form als Teilfunktion eines IIS. Letzteres stellt den derzeitigen Stand der technologischen Entwicklung für all jene Hochschulen dar, die willens und in der Lage sind, eine Integration ihrer Informationssysteme zu betreiben.

Jegliche Grundsatzentscheidung im Zusammenhang mit institutionellen Repositorien – z. B. Eigenentwicklung der Software, Zukauf eines Produktes, Auslagerung der Dienstleistung, Überführung der Funktionalität in ein IIS etc. – ist mit Lock-In-Effekten verbunden. Kommerzielle Anbieter haben ein Interesse an einem möglichst starken Lock-In, um eine langfristige Geschäftsbasis mit ihren Kunden sicherzustellen. Hochschulen sollten sich dessen bewusst sein und diesen Aspekt in der Entscheidungsfindung im Zusammenhang mit Repositorien gebührend berücksichtigen.

Bibliografie

Barbers, Irene; Pollack, Philipp (2021): Open Access in Deutschland. Entwicklung in den Jahren 2005–2019. Jülich: Forschungszentrum Jülich. http://hdl.handle.net/2128/27849

Crow, Raym (2002): The Case for Institutional Repositories. A SPARC Position Paper. Washington, DC: SPARC. https://www.researchgate.net/publication/215993546 (abgerufen am 26.01.2024)

Deinzer, Gernot (2017): Repositoriensoftware. In: Bernhard Mittermaier und Konstanze Söllner (Hg.): Praxishandbuch Open Access. Berlin, Boston: De Gruyter, S. 290–298. https://doi.org/10.1515/9783110494068-034

Deppe, Arvid; Beucke, Daniel (2017): Ursprünge und Entwicklung von Open Access. In: Mittermaier, Bernhard; Söllner, Konstanze (Hg.): Praxishandbuch Open Access. Berlin, Boston: De Gruyter, S. 12–20. https://doi.org/10.1515/9783110494068-002

Eva, Nicole C.; Wiebe, Tara A. (2019): Whose Research Is It Anyway? Academic Social Networks Versus Institutional Repositories. In: Journal of Librarianship and Scholarly Communication 7 (1). https://doi.org/10.7710/2162-3309.2243

Jeffery, Keith; Asserson, Anne (2009): Institutional Repositories and Current Research Information Systems. In: New Review of Information Networking 14 (2), pp. 71–83. https://doi.org/10.1080/13614570903359357

Joint, Nicholas (2008): Current Research Information Systems, Open Access Repositories and Libraries. In: Library Review 57 (8), pp. 570–575. https://doi.org/10.1108/00242530810899559

Jones, Richard; Andrew, Theo; MacColl, John A. (2006): The Institutional Repository. Oxford: Chandos Publishing.

Jordan, Katy (2019): From Social Networks to Publishing Platforms. A Review of the History and Scholarship of Academic Social Network Sites. In: Frontiers in Digital Humanities 6. https://doi.org/10.3389/fdigh.2019.00005

Lovett, Julia A.; Rathemacher, Andrée J.; Boukari, Divana; Lang, Corey (2017): Institutional Repositories and Academic Social Networks. Competition or Complement? A Study of Open Access Policy Compliance vs. ResearchGate Participation. In: Journal of Librarianship and Scholarly Communication 5 (1). https://doi.org/10.7710/2162-3309.2183

Novotny, Gertraud; Seyffertitz, Thomas (2018): Institutionelle Repositorien. Traum und Wirklichkeit. In: Mitteilungen der Vereinigung Österreichischer Bibliothekarinnen und Bibliothekare 71 (1), S. 87–106. https://doi.org/10.31263/voebm.v71i1.2002

Pujol Priego, Laia; Wareham, Jonathan (2019): Zenodo. Open Science Monitor Case Study. Luxembourg: Publications Office of the European Union. https://doi.org/10.2777/298228

Rücknagel, Jessika (2021): Fördererauflagen zu Open Access. Was gilt es zu beachten? Vortrag in der Reihe Open Access Talk, 15.04.2021. https://doi.org/10.5281/zenodo.4694320

Rybinski, Henryk; Skonieczny, Lukasz; Koperwas, Jakub; Struk, Waclaw; Stepniak, Jolanta; Kubrak, Weronika (2017): Integrating IR with CRIS. A Novel Researcher-Centric Approach. In: Program: Electronic Library and Information Systems 51 (3), pp. 298–321. https://doi.org/10.1108/PROG-04-2017-0026

Shapiro, Carl; Varian, Hal R. (1999): Online zum Erfolg. Strategie für das Internet-Business. Langen Müller/Herbig: München.

Michael Katzmayr ist Fachreferent für Wirtschaftswissenschaften an der Universitätsbibliothek der Wirtschaftsuniversität Wien und Leiter der Abteilung Bestandsmanagement. Er ist Vortragender zu den Themengebieten „Bestandsmanagement“ und „Wissensmanagement“ im Universitätslehrgang Library and Information Studies an der Österreichischen Nationalbibliothek bzw. der Universität Wien.

Susanne Blumesberger

Die Rolle von Repositorien im Forschungsdaten-management aus unterschiedlichen Perspektiven

Eine abwechslungsreiche und fordernde Tätigkeit

Handbuch Repositorienmanagement, Hg. v. Blumesberger et al., 2024, S. 61–90
https://doi.org/10.25364/97839033742325

Susanne Blumesberger, Universität Wien, Universitätsbibliothek, susanne.blumesberger@univie.ac.at |
ORCID iD: 0000-0001-9018-623X

Zusammenfassung

Repositorien spielen eine große Rolle im Forschungsdatenmanagement, denn sie können nicht nur für die langfristige Sicherung von Daten eingesetzt werden und damit als Möglichkeit dienen, Forschungsoutput langfristig offen zur Verfügung zu stellen, sondern sie werden auch genutzt, um Forschungsergebnisse während der Laufzeit von Forschungsprojekten mit anderen teilen und gemeinsam bearbeiten zu können. In diesem Beitrag werden die unterschiedlichen Rollen von Repositorien im Forschungsdatenmanagement aus verschiedenen Perspektiven betrachtet: aus der Sicht der jeweiligen Forschungsinstitutionen, der Fördergeber, der forschungsunterstützenden Stellen an den Universitäten und der Forschenden selbst. Anhand aktueller praktischer Beispiele wird die derzeitige Repositorienlandschaft kurz umrissen, abstrahierte Use-Cases ermöglichen einen Einblick in die Anforderungen von Forschungsprojekten hinsichtlich der Speicherung und Archivierung der Daten. Die aktuellen Angebote an der Universität Wien werden ebenso beleuchtet wie derzeitige Desiderata im Bereich Forschungsdatenmanagement.

Schlagwörter: Repositorien; Forschungsdatenmanagement; Langzeitarchivierung; Datenspeicherung

Abstract

The Role of Repositories in Research Data Management from Different Perspectives. A Varied and Challenging Job

Repositories play a major role in research data management, because they are not only used for the long-term preservation of data and thus serve as a way to make research output openly available in the long term. They may also be used to share and collaborate on research results during the lifetime of research projects. In this paper, the different roles of repositories in research data management are considered from various perspectives: from the points of view of the respective research institutions, the funding bodies, the research support agencies and the researchers themselves. Current practical examples will be used to briefly outline the present repository landscape, and abstracted use cases will provide an insight into the requirements of research projects with regard to data storage and archiving. The current offerings at the University of Vienna will be highlighted as well as current desiderata in the area of research data management.

Keywords: Repositories; research data management; long-term archiving; data storage

1. Definition von Repositorien

Repositorien werden unterschiedlich definiert, wie folgende zwei Beispiele zeigen: „Repositorien sind Dokumentenserver, auf denen Materialien archiviert und entgeltfrei zugänglich gemacht werden können“[1]. Eine etwas allgemeinere Definition lautet: „Repositorien sind Speicherorte für digitale Objekte, die diese für einen öffentlichen oder beschränkten Nutzerinnen- oder Nutzerkreis zur Verfügung stellen.“[2]

Hier soll der Begriff „Repositorium“ allgemeiner als Ort zur Speicherung von Daten verstanden werden.

Repositorien lassen sich nach folgenden Kriterien unterscheiden:

- nach der Art der zu speichernden Objekte (beispielsweise Publikationen oder Forschungsdaten),
- nach der Domäne der enthaltenen Daten (institutionell, fachlich oder generisch),
- nach der Speicherfrist der Daten (z. B. zehn Jahre, um den Regeln der guten wissenschaftlichen Praxis zu genügen, oder dauerhaft) oder
- nach den Policies, mit denen die Daten abgerufen und nachgenutzt werden dürfen.[3]

Repositorien garantieren die (Langzeit-)Verfügbarkeit von Forschungsdaten und sind damit ein wesentlicher Baustein für ein umfassendes Forschungsdatenmanagement. Sie begleiten im Idealfall den gesamten Forschungsprozess, stellen einen Pool an wiederverwendbaren Daten, wie z. B. Open Educational Resources (offene Bildungsressourcen), am Anfang der Forschung zur Verfügung, begleiten die Forschungsarbeit, um beispielsweise Publikationen oder Zwischenergebnisse zu archivieren, und sind unerlässlich, um am Ende für die langfristige Sicherung des Forschungsprozesses zu sorgen.

Wenn man sich ein klassisches Forschungsprojekt ansieht, kann man, grob gesehen, sechs Schritte im Forschungsdatenmanagement unterscheiden, wobei sowohl die einzelnen Schritte als auch die Reihenfolge je nach Forschungsdisziplin voneinander abweichen können:

- Planung der Forschung
- Datenerhebung, Datengenerierung
- Analyse der Daten

1 https://open-access.network/informieren/publizieren/repositorien
2 https://forschungsdaten.info/themen/veroeffentlichen-und-archivieren/repositorien/
3 Ebd.

- Teilen von Daten
- Datenarchivierung und
- Publikation und Visualisierung der Ergebnisse

Betrachtet man diese Schritte im Detail, erkennt man die jeweils unterschiedlichen Anforderungen an Beratung, technischen Lösungen und Services.

Idealerweise beginnt das Forschungsdatenmanagement bereits in der Planungsphase.

1.1. Projektplanung

Bei den Projektvorbereitungen werden Fragen gestellt, die auch in einem Datenmanagementplan zu finden sind, etwa: „Welches Ziel verfolgt die Forschungsarbeit, mit welchen Daten wird gearbeitet?“ Eventuell können Forschende auf bereits vorhandene Daten, die in einem Repositorium liegen, zurückgreifen. Dieser Re-Use der Daten ist nicht nur von den Fördergebern erwünscht, sondern für viele Fachbereiche nahezu unerlässlich, denn Daten selbst zu generieren, ist zeitaufwändig und teuer. Will man Daten wiederverwenden, muss man auf die Rechtslage achten und berücksichtigen, unter welcher Lizenz die Daten stehen, denn die Lizenz regelt die Weiternutzung. Aus den Metadaten, also den Beschreibungen, die ebenfalls im Repositorium gespeichert sind, erfährt man im besten Fall, unter welchen Bedingungen und in welchem Kontext die Daten jeweils entstanden sind. Diese Informationen über bereits vorhandene Daten sind wesentlich für die eigene Forschung und müssen selbstverständlich in die Beschreibung des Forschungsprozesses einfließen. Zusätzlich verfügen die Daten in einem Repositorium, das für die Langzeitarchivierung vorgesehen ist, im Regelfall über einen permanenten Identifier, der ein Zitieren und ein gesichertes Wiederauffinden erlaubt. Repositorien werden in dieser ersten Projektphase vor allem als Datenpool genutzt.

Gleichzeitig greifen Forschende während ihrer Arbeit auch auf Publikationen zurück, die idealerweise Open Access, mit einer freien Lizenz[4], in Repositorien zur Verfügung stehen. In diesem Fall wird das Repositorium als Volltextdatenbank genutzt. Sind Daten und Publikationen, die nicht unbedingt die eigenen sein müssen, miteinander verknüpft, kann man bereits aus diesen Verbindungen einen Mehrwert generieren, da Zusammenhänge deutlich gemacht werden können.

---

4 Siehe etwa die Creative Common-Lizenzen: https://creativecommons.org/licenses/?lang=de

1.2. Generieren und Nachnutzung von Daten

In der nächsten Projektphase werden Daten entweder selbst hergestellt, durch Experimente, Mess- oder Digitalisierungsverfahren, Audio- oder Videoaufnahmen, Feldnotizen usw., oder aus anderen Quellen zusammengetragen. Das Archivieren dieser Daten erfolgt ebenfalls in Repositorien, eventuell in unterschiedlichen Systemen, denn es sollen in der Regel nicht alle Daten sofort langzeitarchiviert werden, einige müssen sogar nach einer gewissen Zeit wieder gelöscht werden. Für diese Phase werden zusätzlich Speicherorte benötigt, die eine Löschung der Daten zulassen, zugleich aber die Sicherheit bieten, dass nichts verloren geht, befugte Personen sicher Zugriff haben, diesen aber, wenn nötig, anderen auch verwehren können. In dieser Phase ist es wichtig, die Daten strukturiert abzulegen und sie nach gewissen Regeln zu benennen.

1.3. Analyse der Daten

Um Daten gemeinsam mit den Projektpartner:innen analysieren zu können, wird ebenfalls ein sicherer, aber kurzfristiger Speicherplatz benötigt, der unter Umständen auch große Mengen an Daten bzw. auch große Datensets aufnehmen kann. Zugleich ist es notwendig, dass die am Projekt beteiligten Forschenden darauf raschen Zugriff haben.

1.4. Sichern und Teilen der Daten

Für die Sicherung der Daten reicht eine kurzfristige Speicherung nicht aus, die Daten sollen in einem Repositorium verwahrt werden, wo sie längerfristig archiviert werden und eventuell auf die Langzeitarchivierung vorbereitet werden können. Im besten Fall können hier auch Metadaten strukturiert gespeichert werden. Wichtig ist auch in dieser Phase, dass mehrere Personen, auch aus unterschiedlichen Institutionen und Ländern, möglichst ohne großen Aufwand rasch miteinander arbeiten können. Zusätzlich zu einem regelmäßigen Backup mit einem genauen Plan, wie und von wem dieses durchgeführt wird, müssen die Daten auch jederzeit bearbeitbar bleiben.

Wie und welche Daten generiert werden, hängt stark von der jeweiligen Fachdisziplin ab. In einem ersten Schritt geht es vor allem um eine Speicherung der (Roh-)Daten, so unterschiedlich diese auch in den jeweiligen Fächern definiert werden. An der Universität Wien werden dafür gemeinsam nutzbare Speicherbereiche auf der zentralen Infrastruktur (Share), Cloudlösungen, Versionskontrolle-Tools (etwa GitLab) und weitere Systeme angeboten, die einzeln verwendet werden können, aber im Rahmen eines größeren Forschungsprojekts meist miteinander kombiniert verwendet werden. Spätestens jetzt müssen die ethischen und juristischen Fragen geklärt sein, wenn die Daten über Projektgrenzen hinweg geteilt werden sollen. Unerlässlich ist auch die Frage, wem die Daten gehören und wer in Zukunft dafür verantwortlich sein wird. Außerdem ist ein gut regelbarer Zugriff nötig. Auch die Beschreibung der Daten ist von großer Wichtigkeit, da diese bereits in diesem Projektabschnitt weiter- und nachgenutzt werden. Welches System dafür genutzt wird, hängt stark von den Rahmenbedingungen ab. Sensible Daten müssen selbstverständlich gänzlich anders behandelt werden als beispielsweise automatisch generierte Messdaten, die keinem Urheberrecht unterliegen und, wenn es keine anderen Vereinbarungen gibt, bedenkenlos frei genutzt werden können.

1.5. Datenarchivierung

Die längerfristige oder langfristige Datenarchivierung findet meist am Ende des Forschungsprojekts statt, wenn alle Rechte geklärt sind, die Metadaten vorhanden sind und auch die Wahl eines geeigneten Repositoriums getroffen wurde. Je nach Art der Daten, Vorgaben der Fördergeber und der jeweiligen Institutionen muss ein fachliches, institutionelles oder generisches Forschungsdatenrepositorium gewählt werden. Selbstverständlich kann es auch sinnvoll sein, mehre Repositorien für unterschiedliche Daten zu wählen. Ebenso ist es eventuell aus rechtlichen oder ethischen Gründen nicht möglich, alle Daten sofort Open Access zu stellen. In vielen Repositorien ist es möglich, eine Embargofrist einzustellen und damit den Zugang zunächst einzuschränken und später erst zu öffnen. Ebenso differenziert muss mit den Lizenzen umgegangen werden, dabei gilt die Regel, die Daten so offen wie möglich und so geschlossen wie nötig zur Verfügung zu stellen.

1.6. Publikation und Visualisierung der Ergebnisse

Abschließend erfolgt die Publikation der Ergebnisse in Fachzeitschriften mit Verknüpfung zu diversen Repositorien. Die permanenten Links zu den Veröffentlichungen und zu den Forschungsdaten können dann auf Projektwebseiten sichtbar gemacht werden. Schnittstellen zwischen Content-Management-Systemen und Repositorien lassen weitere Optionen der Darstellung zu.

2. Repositorien aus der Sicht der Fördergeber

In seiner Open-Access Policy schreibt der Wissenschaftsfonds (FWF), dass für Forschungsdaten, die den wissenschaftlichen Publikationen des bewilligten Projekts zu Grunde liegen, der offene Zugang verpflichtend ist.[5] Darunter werden alle Daten verstanden, die zur Reproduktion und Überprüfbarkeit der Ergebnisse der Publikationen erforderlich sind, einschließlich der zugehörigen Metadaten. Diese Daten sollten möglichst schnell veröffentlicht werden, spätestens aber mit der Publikation. Wenn das aus rechtlichen oder ethischen Gründen nicht möglich ist, müssen die Forschenden dies im Datenmanagementplan nachvollziehbar machen. Alle anderen Daten müssen zwar im Datenmanagementplan beschrieben werden, es obliegt jedoch der jeweiligen Projektleitung, die Daten verfügbar zu machen. Alle Forschungsdaten müssen zusätzlich den FAIR-Prinzipien[6] entsprechen und über institutionelle, disziplinspezifische oder disziplinübergreifende Repositorien verfügbar gemacht werden. Grundvoraussetzungen sind, dass das gewählte Repositorium im Registry of Research Data Repositories re3data[7] gelistet ist, dass die Daten permanente Identifier erhalten und mit einer Lizenz versehen werden, die eine uneingeschränkte Wiederverwendbarkeit ermöglicht, wobei hier CC BY oder ähnlich offene Lizenzen genannt werden. Zertifizierte Repositorien (z. B. Core Trust Seal)[8] sind zu bevorzugen.

Die 2012 von der DFG, der Deutschen Forschungsgemeinschaft, ins Leben gerufene Datenbank re3data, auf die sich auch die Guidelines to the Rules on Open Access to Scientific Publications and Open Access to Research Data in Horizon 2020 beziehen, beschreibt sich selbst als

> a global registry of research data repositories that covers research data repositories from different academic disciplines. It includes repositories that enable permanent storage of and access to data sets to researchers, funding bodies, publishers, and scholarly institutions. re3data promotes a culture of sharing, increased access and better visibility of research data.[9]

---

5 FWF: Open Access für Forschungsdaten: https://www.fwf.ac.at/ueber-uns/aufgaben-und-aktivitaeten/open-science/open-access-policy/open-access-policy-fuer-forschungsdaten (abgerufen am 01.02.2024).

6 Ebd.

7 https://www.re3data.org/

8 CoreTrustSeal ist eine internationale, gemeinschaftsbasierte, nichtstaatliche und gemeinnützige Organisation zur Förderung nachhaltiger und vertrauenswürdiger Dateninfrastrukturen: https://www.coretrustseal.org/.

9 https://www.re3data.org/about

Repositorienmanager:innen können das Repositorium in diese Datenbank eintragen lassen, es müssen jedoch drei Voraussetzungen erfüllt sein:

„a research data repository must

- be run by a legal entity, such as a sustainable institution (e.g. library, university)
- clarify access conditions to the data and repository as well as the terms of use
- have focus on research data.“[10]

Derzeit sind 41 österreichische Repositorien[11] in re3data gelistet. Interessierten Personen stehen zahlreiche Filter zur Verfügung, nach denen sie ein passendes Repositorium wählen können. Zu den Auswahlkriterien zählen Fachrichtungen, Datentypen, wie beispielsweise Bilder, Texte, Audio- und Videofiles, Datenbanken, aber auch Rohdaten. Man kann nach Ländern suchen, nach vorhandenen Schnittstellen, nach Zertifikaten und nach dem Zugang zu den Daten. Dabei werden auch jene Repositorien angezeigt werden, die Daten enthalten, die mit einer Embargofrist versehen sind. Zusätzlich besteht die Möglichkeit, nach verfügbaren Lizenzen zu recherchieren, nach der Möglichkeit, ob man Daten mit oder ohne Registrierung hochladen kann, ob es sich um kommerzielle oder non-profit-Repositorien handelt, welche Metadatenschemata verwendet und welche persistenten Identifier vergeben werden, und nach Keywords. Die Sprache, die dahinter liegende Software und der Repositorientyp, also disziplinär oder institutionell, sind ebenfalls mögliche Suchkriterien.[12]

Damit steht den Forschenden eine Möglichkeit zur Verfügung, ein geeignetes Repositorium zu finden.

In den Vorlagen für Datenmanagementpläne des FWF und der von der EU geförderten Forschungsprogramme wird an mehreren Stellen Bezug auf Repositorien genommen, nicht erst bei der Frage nach der langfristigen Archivierung, sondern bereits zu Beginn, wenn es um die eventuelle Nutzung von bereits vorhandenen Daten geht. Im Wesentlichen sind diese Fragen auch in den Vorgaben anderer Fördergeber vorhanden.[13] Der FWF startete am 01.01.2019 mit einer ersten Version

10 Ebd.
11 Stand 20.11.2022.
12 https://www.re3data.org/suggest
13 Siehe auch Spichtinger, D.; Blumesberger, S. (2020)

eines Templates für Datenmanagementpläne, am 01.01.2022 wurde eine überarbeitete Version publiziert.[14]

2.1. Beschreibung der Daten sowie der Erhebung neuer oder der Nachnutzung bestehender Daten

Im FWF-Template werden folgende Fragen an die Forschenden gestellt: Wie werden neue Daten erhoben oder erstellt und/oder wie werden bestehende Daten nachgenutzt? Welche Daten (Art, Format und Menge) werden erhoben oder erstellt? Um den Forschenden das Ausfüllen des Templates zu erleichtern, wurden die Fragen, die sich dahinter verbergen, nach und nach ausführlicher und spezifischer. Gefragt wird u. a. nach den Methoden bzw. nach der Software, die verwendet werden, wenn neue Daten erhoben oder erstellt werden. Die Antragsteller:innen werden aufgefordert, etwaige Einschränkungen für die Nachnutzung vorhandener Daten zu beschreiben, die Datenherkunft zu dokumentieren und Einzelheiten über die Art der Daten anzugeben, konkret, ob es sich um numerische Daten, textbasierte Dokumente, Bild-, Audio- oder Videodaten handelt. Diese Fragen sind in zweifacher Hinsicht hilfreich für Forschende: Erstens werden sie sich bewusst, dass es sich bei ihrem Forschungsoutput um Daten handelt, und zweitens bekommen sie einen Impuls, sich über mögliche Speicherungs- und Archivierungsmaßnahmen Gedanken zu machen. Auch die Wahl des passenden Datenformats für die Archivierung soll begründet werden. „Die Entscheidung kann beispielsweise auf einer Präferenz für offene Formate, auf Standards von Datenarchiven, der weit verbreiteten Verwendung in einer Disziplin oder der verwendeten Software oder Equipment beruhen“[15], so der FWF. Die weitere Ausführung bezieht sich bereits eindeutig auf Repositorien: „Nutzen Sie bevorzugt offene und standardisierte Formate, da sie die gemeinsame Nutzung und langfristige Nachnutzung von Daten erleichtern (mehrere Repositorien bieten Listen solcher ‚bevorzugten Formate‘ an)“[16]. Ebenso zielt die Frage nach der Angabe zur Datenmenge auf die später verwendeten Systeme ab, wie auch die Aussage: „Auch die Verwendung von Metadatenstandards hängt eng mit dem gewählten Repositorium zusammen“[17].

Der Abschnitt „III. Dokumentation und Datenqualität“ enthält den Punkt „3.1. Metadaten und Dokumentation“. Die zentrale Frage in Abschnitt III lautet: Welche Metadaten und Dokumentationen (z. B. die Methodik der Datenerhebung und die Art

14 https://www.fwf.ac.at/ueber-uns/aufgaben-und-aktivitaeten/open-science/forschungsdatenmanagement
15 FWF (2022b), S. 2.
16 Ebd.
17 Ebd.

der Organisation der Daten) werden erstellt? Hier ist anzugeben, welche Metadaten erstellt und welche Metadatenstandards verwendet werden. Um diese Fragen verständlicher zu machen, folgt die Vertiefung: „Konsistente, gut organisierte Forschungsdaten sind leichter zu finden, zu verstehen und wiederzuverwenden. Geben Sie an, wie die Daten während des Projekts organisiert werden sollen, und nennen Sie beispielsweise Konventionen, Versionsverwaltung und Ordnerstrukturen.“[18] Auch der Hinweis „Überlegen Sie, wie diese Informationen erfasst und wo sie dokumentiert werden sollen, z. B. in einer Datenbank mit Links zu den einzelnen Elementen, einer ‚Readme‘-Textdatei oder Laborbüchern“[19] verweist auf Services im Bereich des Forschungsdatenmanagements. Für die geforderte Kontrolle der Daten wird ebenfalls Speicherplatz, also in einem weiten Sinne ein Repositorium benötigt. Unter dem Punkt IV sind die Themen Speicherung, gemeinsame Nutzung und Langzeitarchivierung von Daten zusammengefasst. Im Punkt „IV.1 Datenspeicherung und Backup während des Forschungsprozesses“ soll beschrieben werden, wo die Daten und Metadaten während der Forschungstätigkeit gespeichert und deren Backups erstellt werden und wie oft Backups durchgeführt werden, wobei empfohlen wird, die Daten an mindestens zwei verschiedenen Orten zu speichern. Auch wird in dieser neuen Version des Datenmanagementplans darauf verwiesen, bevorzugt einen robusten, verwalteten Datenspeicher mit automatischen Backups zu verwenden, der vom IT-Support der jeweiligen Forschungsstätte bereitgestellt wird. Die Speicherung von Daten auf Laptops, externen Festplatten oder Speichergeräten wie USB-Sticks wird explizit nicht empfohlen. Hingewiesen wird auch darauf, die Datenschutzrichtlinien der jeweiligen Forschungsstätte zu beachten.

Bei „IV.2 Gemeinsame Nutzung und Langzeitarchivierung von Daten“ gibt es selbstverständlich die stärksten Bezüge zu Repositorien. Es folgen Fragen, wie und wann Daten zur Verfügung gestellt werden, ob es Einschränkungen für die gemeinsame Nutzung von Daten oder Gründe für ein Embargo gibt. Der FWF verlangt auch die Entscheidung, welches Repositorium verwendet, welcher persistenter Identifier und welche Nutzungslizenzen gewählt werden. Auch soll beschrieben werden, wie die zu archivierenden Daten ausgewählt, und wo die Daten langfristig aufbewahrt werden. Zu beachten ist auch, dass der sofortige offene Zugang (Open Access) zu Forschungsdaten für Daten, die Publikationen zugrunde liegen, verpflichtend ist,

18 Ebd.
19 Ebd.

sofern es keine rechtlichen, ethischen oder anderen Gründe gibt, die dagegensprechen. Wenn es Gründe gibt, sind diese zu erläutern. Auch die nächsten Fragen beziehen sich direkt auf das Repositorium:

Erläutern Sie, wie die Daten auffindbar und für die Nachnutzung verfügbar gemacht werden sollen, und gehen Sie dabei auf die Wahl des Repositoriums, den Persistent Identifier (z. B. DOI[20]) und die Nutzungslizenz (siehe How to License Research Data[21]) ein. Beachten Sie bei der Wahl des Repositoriums die Science Europe Criteria for the selection of trustworthy repositories und nutzen Sie www.re3data.org zur Repositorien-Suche.[22]

Es ist auch anzugeben, wer die Daten nutzen kann, und wenn nötig ist eine Vereinbarung über eine gemeinsame Datennutzung zu verfassen. Bzgl. der Nachnutzung der Daten soll auch beschrieben werden, ob dafür spezielle Werkzeuge nötig sind. Auch eine etwaige Verpflichtung zur Langzeitarchivierung oder zur Löschung soll festgehalten und genau beschrieben werden.

Auch bei „V.1. Rechtliche Aspekte" spielen Repositorien eine große Rolle. Hier wird an erster Stelle gefragt, wer im Projekt das Recht hat, über die Daten zu verfügen und den Zugang zu regeln. Bei mehreren Partner:innen ist darüber ein Konsortialvertrag zu unterzeichnen. Bei sensiblen Daten, z. B. bei Interviews, sollen Einverständniserklärungen eingeholt werden. Wenn nötig, müssen die Daten pseudonymisiert, anonymisiert, bzw. dekontextualisiert werden.

Im Abschnitt „V.2. Ethische Aspekte" verweist der FWF vor allem auf die Dokumente Ethics for researchers[23] und European Code of Conduct for Research Integrity.[24] Neu seit 01.01.2022 ist die Evaluationsmatrix[25], die Beispiele enthält, wann ein DMP ausreichend ausgefüllt ist und wann nicht.

In diesem beispielhaften Datenmanagementplan des FWF wurde also deutlich, welch große Rollen Repositorien während des Forschungsprozesses spielen. Ein Blick aus der Sicht von einzelnen Institutionen folgt.

20 Digital Object Identifier
21 Vgl. Ball, A. (2014)
22 FWF (2022b), S. 3.
23 European Commission (2013)
24 ALLEA (2023)
25 FWF (2022a)

3. Repositorien aus der Sicht der Forschungsinstitutionen

Eine zusätzliche Perspektive gibt es von diversen Institutionen, an denen geforscht und gelehrt wird, u. a. Universitäten und Fachhochschulen, aber auch von jenen, die eher Archive oder Museen im Blick haben und die ihre digitalisierten Objekte auch der interessierten Öffentlichkeit zur Verfügung stellen möchten. Festmachen lässt sich die Bewertung von Repositorien einerseits durch diverse Angebote, aber auch durch die jeweiligen Bestimmungen und Vorgaben, wie etwa Forschungsdatenpolicies der einzelnen Institutionen, denn eine nationale Policy zum Forschungsdatenmanagement gibt es derzeit (noch) nicht. Sieben Universitäten haben bereits eine solche Policy verabschiedet, einige bereiten diese eben vor.[26]

3.1. Repositorien in Forschungsdatenpolicies

Die „Policy für Forschungsdatenmanagement" der Medizinischen Universität Wien wurde am 13.1.2021, die der Medizinischen Universität Graz am 19.1.2021 unterfertigt und am 17.2.2021 im Mitteilungsblatt der Medizinischen Universität Graz veröffentlicht.[27] Darin werden Repositorien folgendermaßen definiert:

> Ein Repositorium ist eine Datenbank bzw. ein Datenarchiv zur Speicherung und Publikation von digitalen Forschungsdaten mit dem primären Zweck, diese für einen begrenzten oder unbegrenzten Zeitraum aufzubewahren sowie verfügbar, zitierbar und nachnutzbar zu halten.[28]

Es wird jedoch kein spezielles Repositorium empfohlen, denn

> [a]ufgrund der Vielgestaltigkeit von Forschungsdaten und -prozessen ist es nicht möglich, einheitliche Vorgaben für das Management von Forschungsdaten im Detail zu definieren (z. B. hinsichtlich Dateistrukturen, Repositorien, Software, Metadaten etc.).[29]

Allerdings wird Folgendes gefordert:

> Das Forschungsdatenmanagement muss an jeder Organisationseinheit so organisiert sein, dass nicht nur einzelne Personen bestimmte Daten auffinden und darauf zugreifen können, sondern dass – auch in Abwesenheit einzelner am Forschungsprozess beteiligter Personen – die Auffindbarkeit und Zugänglichkeit gewährleistet sind. [...] Sofern von Dritten (z. B. Fördergebern oder

---

26 Siehe https://www.forschungsdaten.info/fdm-im-deutschsprachigen-raum/oesterreich/fdm-policies/
27 Medizinische Universität Graz (2021)
28 Medizinische Universität Graz (2021), S. 8.
29 Ebd., S. 4.

> Herausgebern von Journalen) diesbezügliche Anforderungen gestellt werden, müssen Forschungsdaten unter Berücksichtigung des Datenschutzes in einem geeigneten Repositorium abgelegt und zugänglich gemacht werden.[30]

An der Medizinischen Universität Wien sind folgende Vorgaben zu berücksichtigen:

> Forschungsdaten müssen im Verfügungsbereich der MedUni Wien zugänglich gemacht werden. Sofern von Dritten (z. B. Fördergebern oder Herausgebern von Journalen) diesbezügliche Anforderungen gestellt werden, müssen Forschungsdaten unter Berücksichtigung des Datenschutzes in einem geeigneten Repositorium abgelegt und zugänglich gemacht werden. Die Nutzung eines externen Repositoriums ist mittels Datenmanagementplan (DMP) an die MedUni Wien zu melden. An der MedUni Wien tätige Personen (z. B. ForscherInnen, MitarbeiterInnen und Studierende) und andere Befugte (z. B. forschungsunterstützende Einrichtungen, Behörden) müssen Zugang zu den Originaldaten haben, um auftretende Fragestellungen beantworten zu können (z. B. zu Validierung, Nachvollziehbarkeit und Qualitätssicherung).[31]

Die Universität für Musik und darstellende Kunst Wien (mdw) veröffentlichte die „Richtlinie des Rektorats zum Forschungsdatenmanagement"[32] am 05.12.2017. Unter der Überschrift „Umgang mit Forschungsdaten" heißt es:

> Forschungsdaten sollen in einem geeigneten Repositorium aufbewahrt und angeboten werden. Die mdw bietet ihren Forschenden zu diesem Zweck mit einem eigenen institutionellen Repositorium eine robuste, internationalen Standards entsprechende Infrastruktur für das Forschungsdatenmanagement an (mdw Repository)[33]. Die Nutzung anderer Repositorien ist in begründeten Fällen möglich, insbesondere wenn Daten speziellen rechtlichen Regulierungen unterliegen (z. B. medizinische Patientendaten) oder wenn das die Verbreitung von Daten fördert (z. B. in fachspezifischen Repositorien) bzw. wenn die Nutzung bestimmter Repositorien vertraglich geregelt ist (z. B. durch Drittmittelgeber). Eine solche Nutzung ist von der/vom betreffenden Forschenden der für Forschungsförderung zuständigen Abteilung der mdw zur Kenntnis zu bringen.[34]

---

30 Ebd., S. 6.
31 Medizinische Universität Wien (2021), S. 5.
32 Universität für Musik und darstellende Kunst Wien (2017)
33 https://www.mdw.ac.at/repository/
34 Universität für Musik und darstellende Kunst Wien (2017), S. 2.

Die „Framework Policy für Forschungsdatenmanagement an der TU Graz“ stammt vom 11.12.2019. „Das vorliegende Policy-Papier listet erstrebenswerte Ziele. Die Implementierung wird einige Jahre in Anspruch nehmen und nicht zuletzt von der Verfügbarkeit entsprechender Ressourcen abhängen“[35], heißt es darin. Von der Bibliothek wird erwartet, dass sie „in Zusammenarbeit mit dem ZID sowie dem Team ‚Chancenfeld Forschung‘ zertifizierte Services bereitstellt, die die Datenkuratierung/Langzeitarchivierung von Daten für mindestens 10 Jahre sicherstellen“.[36]

Zum Thema Datenrepositorium heißt es an der TU Graz:

> Jegliche Form von Daten für die langfristige Speicherung vorgesehen ist, gleich ob öffentlich oder nicht, sollte in einem vertrauenswürdigen digitalen Repositorium hinterlegt werden. Den Forscher:innen wird empfohlen, Repositorien zu verwenden, die in ihren Communities Standard sind. Eine Übersicht von Repositories ist bei Re3data abrufbar: www.re3data.org. Wo es kein geeignetes externes Repositorium gibt, wird die TU Graz eine lokale Infrastruktur zur Verfügung stellen.[37]

Am 26.04.2021 veröffentlichte die TU Graz eine zusätzliche „Fakultätsspezifische Implementierungsstrategie Maschinenbau und Wirtschaftswissenschaften“, wo es u. a. heißt: „Die Fakultäten müssen fakultätsspezifische Umsetzungsstrategien entwickeln“[38]. Darunter fallen beispielsweise: die „Erfassung, Dokumentation und Speicherung von Forschungsdaten während des Forschungsprozesses“, die „Sicherstellung, dass Forschungsdaten, die begutachtete Publikationen stützen, angemessen dokumentiert und in einem Forschungsdaten-Repository in Übereinstimmung mit den FAIR-Prinzipien (Findable, Accessible, Interoperable, Reusable) für mindestens zehn Jahre ab dem Datum der Veröffentlichung der Forschungsergebnisse freigegeben werden, es sei denn, es gibt triftige Gründe, dies nicht zu tun.“[39]

In dieser speziellen Richtlinie wird vor allem auf die unterschiedlichen Rollen der Stakeholder:innen hinsichtlich der Implementierung eines Data-Stewardship-Modells eingegangen. Dabei handelt es sich um Wissenschafter:innen, die Forschende aus dem eigenen Fach unterstützen, mit ihrer fachlichen Expertise und ihrem Wissen im Bereich Forschungsdatenmanagement unterstützen und zugleich ein Bindeglied zwischen dem Bereich Datenmanagement und Forschung darstellen. Je

35 Technische Universität Graz (2019), S. 1.
36 Ebd., S. 2.
37 Ebd., S. 3.
38 Technische Universität Graz (2021), S. 1.
39 Ebd.

nach Größe der Organisation werden unterschiedliche Formen von Data Stewardship eingesetzt.[40]

Die „Policy für Forschungsdatenmanagement an der TU Wien“ wurde am 3.7.2018 unterzeichnet und ging am 4.7.2018 online.[41] Die Policy basiert auf der englischsprachigen LEARN-Muster-Policy[42]. „Forschungsdaten sind von Anfang an in geeigneten Systemen zu speichern und pflegen und in einem geeigneten Repositorium zur Verfügung zu stellen“, heißt es darin.[43]

Die „Forschungsdatenmanagement-Policy der Universität Graz“[44] wurde vom Rektorat am 14.02.2019 beschlossen. Darin heißt es:

> Um die Integrität der Forschungsdaten zu erhalten, müssen diese korrekt, vollständig, unverfälscht und zuverlässig gespeichert werden. Darüber hinaus müssen sie auffindbar, zugänglich, nachverfolgbar, interoperabel und nach Möglichkeit für die Wiederverwendung nach den FAIR-Prinzipien der EU verfügbar sein. Die Speicherung muss mit Datum versehen sein, spätere Änderungen sind möglichst getrennt von den Originaldaten zu speichern.[45]

Dabei wird detaillierter eingegangen:

> Sofern keine Rechte Dritter, gesetzliche Verpflichtungen, ethische Aspekte oder Eigentumsvorschriften dem entgegenstehen, sollen Forschungsdaten mit einer freien Lizenz versehen werden. Die Mindestarchivierungsdauer für Forschungsdaten beträgt 10 Jahre nach der Vergabe eines persistenten Identifikators oder der Veröffentlichung eines zugehörigen Werkes nach Abschluss einer Forschungsaktivität, je nachdem, welcher Zeitpunkt später liegt. Die die Forschungsaktivitäten begleitenden Verwaltungsunterlagen sind ebenfalls zu archivieren.[46]

Dabei ist die Universität Graz zuständig für „die Bereitstellung und den Betrieb eines Repositoriums für die Aufbewahrung, Sicherung und Zugänglichmachung von Forschungsdaten“ und beinhaltet auch die „Bereitstellung geeigneter finanzieller Mittel und Ressourcen für forschungsunterstützende Maßnahmen zur Aufrechterhaltung von Dienstleistungen für die Ablage, Auffindbarkeit und Registrierung von

40 Vgl. Hasani-Mavriqi, I. (2021)
41 TU Wien (2018)
42 https://doi.org/10.14324/000.learn.26
43 Ebd., S. 3.
44 Universität Graz (2019)
45 Ebd., S. 2.
46 Ebd.

Forschungsdaten und zur Aus- und Weiterbildung der MitarbeiterInnen".[47] Die Forschenden sind zur „Übergabe der Forschungsdaten an ein Repositorium spätestens zum Abschluss der Forschungsaktivität" verpflichtet.[48]

Die Wirtschaftsuniversität Wien (WU) publizierte die Policy „WUPOL Forschungsdatenmanagement"[49] am 08.05.2019. Unter dem Abschnitt „Umgang mit Forschungsdaten" ist zu lesen:

> Forschungsdaten sind vollständig und unverfälscht aufzubewahren. Dies sollte elektronisch und den jeweils aktuellen Sicherungsstandards entsprechend erfolgen. Der Speicherort ist so zu wählen, dass eine allfällige Einsichtnahme in die Forschungsdaten durch befugte Personen technisch und organisatorisch sichergestellt ist. Eine Speicherung ausschließlich auf lokalen Datenträgern ist daher i.d.R. nicht ausreichend. Bei der Veröffentlichung von Forschungsdaten sind Identifizierbarkeit, Auffindbarkeit, Verfügbarkeit, Nachnutzbarkeit und Interoperabilität anzustreben. Die WU empfiehlt, Forschungsdaten frei zugänglich zu veröffentlichen, sofern keine Rechte Dritter, gesetzliche Verpflichtungen, ethische Aspekte oder Eigentumsregelungen dem entgegenstehen.[50]

Wie auch in anderen Universitäten, sind derzeit noch nicht alle Tools verfügbar, deshalb wird angekündigt: „Die WU verpflichtet sich, die Voraussetzungen zur Erfüllung der vorliegenden Policy zu schaffen."[51] Darunter fällt das „Bereitstellen eines entsprechend abgesicherten Speicherortes für besonders schützenswerte oder sensible Forschungsdaten" und das Bereitstellen „von Informationen über bzw. Zugang zu Dienstleistungen und Infrastrukturen für die Speicherung und Archivierung von Forschungsdaten und Aufzeichnungen."[52] Die WU lässt aber auch Ergänzungen in Abstimmung mit dem Rektorat zu, „um ihren jeweiligen forschungsdisziplinären Besonderheiten Rechnung zu tragen".[53]

Die „Policy für Forschungsdatenmanagement an der Universität Wien"[54] wurde am 08.09.2021 vom Rektorat unterschrieben. Unter „Anforderung an die Verarbeitung von Forschungsdaten" ist zu lesen:

---

47 Ebd.
48 Ebd.
49 Wirtschaftsuniversität Wien (2019)
50 Ebd., S. 2.
51 Ebd., S. 3.
52 Ebd., S. 4.
53 Ebd.
54 Universität Wien (2021)

> Archiviert werden sollen mindestens alle Forschungsdaten, die einer Publikation zugrunde liegen und für die Nachvollziehbarkeit der Ergebnisse erforderlich sind, sofern diese nicht bereits anderweitig dauerhaft zur Verfügung gestellt werden und genutzt werden dürfen. Forschungsdaten, an deren Archivierung ein öffentliches Interesse oder ein fortgesetztes wissenschaftliches oder historisches Forschungsinteresse besteht oder durch welche statistische Zwecke verfolgt werden, sollen ebenfalls archiviert werden.[55]

Die Speicherung und Zurverfügungstellung von Forschungsdaten soll in einem geeigneten Repositorium oder Archivierungssystem, wie einem etablierten fachspezifischen (z. B. AUSSDA in den Sozialwissenschaften), einem institutionellen (z. B. PHAIDRA an der Universität Wien) oder einem allgemeinen kostenlosen erfolgen.[56]

Die zwischen 2017 und 2021 veröffentlichten Forschungsdatenpolicies zeigen bzgl. der Rolle von Repositorien im Forschungsdatenmanagement sehr viele Gemeinsamkeiten. So werden in allen bisher vorliegenden Policies Repositorien als wünschenswerte Archivierungsorte erwähnt, wenn auch nicht alle Institutionen über ein eigenes Forschungsdatenrepositorium verfügen. Die Einhaltung der FAIR-Prinzipien, wie auch die Möglichkeit der eigenen Institution, auf die Daten der Forscher:innen zugreifen zu können, stehen im Mittelpunkt.

4. Repositorien in Österreich

Das Angebot im Bereich des Forschungsdatenmanagements korreliert nicht unbedingt mit dem Betreiben eigener Repositorien. Jene Institutionen, die bereits über eine Forschungsdatenpolicy verfügen, haben meist bereits Services im Bereich FDM aufgebaut.

Die Medizinische Universität Wien stellt beispielsweise auf ihrer Website ein Glossar über die wichtigsten Begriffe[57] zur Verfügung. Das Forschungsservice der Medizinischen Universität Wien bietet Unterstützung bei der Einreichung und bei der Durchführung ihrer Forschungsprojekte, verfügt jedoch über kein eigenes Forschungsdatenrepositorium.

55 Ebd., S. 2.
56 Ebd.
57 https://www.meduniwien.ac.at/web/rechtliches/policy-fuer-forschungsdatenmanagement/

An der Universität für Musik und darstellende Kunst Wien bietet das Projektservice der Stabstelle Forschungsförderung Erstberatung im Bereich des Forschungsdatenmanagements an.[58] Dazu gehören u. a. Unterstützung bei der Nutzung des mdw Repository[59], das über einen frei zugänglichen und einen internen Bereich verfügt, die Datenmanagementplanung und Unterstützung bei Anforderungen von fördergebenden Stellen an die Datenmanagementpläne bzgl. Open Access. Interessierte finden zahlreiche weiterführende Links und auch das regelmäßig stattfindende mdw-Forum „Forschung & Digitalisierung", eine Plattform zum Informations- und Erfahrungsaustausch für Forschende, Archiv- und Projektmitarbeiter:innen der mdw.[60]

Die TU Graz bietet auf einer eigenen Website zum Thema Forschungsdatenmanagement[61] eine Übersicht ihrer umfangreichen Angebote an. Forschende finden Informationen über die von den Fördergebern verlangten Datenmanagementpläne, auch die Entwicklung von machine-actionable DMPs wird vorgestellt. Das TU Graz Repository (invenioRDM) wird erklärt und ebenso das Forschungsdatenanalysetool CAT-CyVerse Austria. Die Seite informiert darüber hinaus auch zu den Themen FAIR Data Principles, Metadaten und Lizenzen und bietet ein Glossar sowie eine Übersicht über anfallende Kosten für das Datenmanagement. Die TU Graz ist auch eine Vorreiterin in Sachen Data Stewardship[62], drei Data Stewards aus unterschiedlichen Disziplinen sind bereits an der TU Graz beschäftigt. Auch bzgl. Data Champions[63], also Personen, die sich sehr gut im Bereich Forschungsdatenmanagement auskennen, bzgl. Datenmanagement Vorreiter:innen auf ihrem Gebiet sind und dieses Wissen mit Kolleg:innen teilen, gibt es Veranstaltungen. Gemeinsam mit der TU Wien und der Universität Wien, mit denen gemeinsam das Projekt FAIR Data Austria[64] durchgeführt wurde, werden regelmäßig Webinare und andere Veranstaltungen durchgeführt.

Die Universität Graz bietet an der Universitätsbibliothek im Bereich Publikationsservice umfangreiche Unterstützung an.[65] Man findet außerdem Informationen zu

58 Siehe https://www.mdw.ac.at/forschungsf%C3%B6rderung/?PageId=4264
59 https://www.mdw.ac.at/repository/
60 https://www.mdw.ac.at/forschungsfoerderung/?PageId=4374
61 https://www.tugraz.at/sites/rdm/home/
62 https://www.tugraz.at/sites/rdm/support-service/data-stewards
63 https://www.tugraz.at/sites/rdm/support/data-champions/
64 https://forschungsdaten.at/fda/
65 Universität Graz: Merkblatt Forschungsdaten. Planung, Sicherung und Nachnutzung: https://forschungsdatenmanagement.uni-graz.at/de/

Datenmanagementplänen und Vorlagen. FAIR Data und Open Data werden ebenfalls thematisiert, bzgl. Repositorien wird auf AUSSDA für die Sozialwissenschaften, bzw. auf Zenodo[66] oder für die Geisteswissenschaften auf GAMS[67] verwiesen.

Die Wirtschaftsuniversität Wien bietet unter Forschungsdatenmanagement an der Universitätsbibliothek der WU Beratungen u. a. auch zu Repositorien an. Das Forschungsservice hilft, die Anforderungen der Fördergeber zu erfüllen, und unterstützt bei Datenmanagementplänen, und das IT-Service bietet Lösungen für die sichere Archivierung und Speicherung von Daten an. An der WU steht mit WU Research seit 2022 ein umfassendes Research Management System zur Verfügung, das auch die Funktion eines Institutionellen Repositoriums innehat.[68]

Die Universität Wien verfügt zwar erst seit 2021 über eine Forschungsdatenpolicy, jedoch bereits seit 2008 mit PHAIDRA[69] über ein institutionelles Repositorium, das von Beginn an auch für Forschungsdaten konzipiert war. Die Seite „Forschungsdatenmanagement an der Universität Wien“[70] informiert über die Forschungsdatenpolicy, die durch ausführliche FAQ[71] ergänzt wird, allgemein über Forschungsdatenmanagement, die FAIR-Prinzipien und diverse Services, die von der Universitätsbibliothek Wien und dem Zentralen Informatikdienst angeboten werden, sowie über Beratungs- und Schulungsmöglichkeiten. Die Webseiten der Abteilung Repositorienmanagement PHAIDRA-Services geben Auskunft über das Langzeitarchivierungssystem PHAIDRA, über das lokale PHAIDRA, das im Netz der Universität Wien nutzbar ist, die PHAIDRA-Testumgebung und über das österreichweit angebotene PHAIDRA-Depot[72], das kleineren Institutionen oder Vereinen zur Verfügung steht. Die PHAIDRA-Webseiten geben einen breiten Überblick über die Funktionalitäten der Systeme, Uploadmöglichkeiten, Formatempfehlungen und diverse Netzwerke, Schulungsangebote usw. Zusätzlich wird auf relevante Publikationen und Links hingewiesen.

Ähnlich wie die Universität Wien haben auch andere Forschungseinrichtungen begonnen, Repositorien zu implementieren, ohne zunächst eine Forschungsdatenpolicy zu haben. Die Bibliothek des Institute of Science and Technology (IST) betreibt

66 https://zenodo.org/
67 https://gams.uni-graz.at/
68 https://research.wu.ac.at/
69 https://phaidra.univie.ac.at/
70 https://rdm.univie.ac.at/de/
71 https://rdm.univie.ac.at/de/
72 https://depot.phaidra.at/

beispielsweise den IST Austrian Research Explorer[73]. Die Fachhochschule St. Pölten[74] und die Veterinärmedizinische Universität Wien sind beide Kooperationspartner von PHAIDRA an der Universität Wien und haben beide mit einem Repositorium für Hochschulschriften begonnen und es schließlich für Forschungsdaten[75] geöffnet. Auch die Kunstuniversität Graz[76], die Kunstuniversität Linz[77], die Anton Bruckner Privatuniversität in Oberösterreich[78] und die Donau Universität Krems, die ihr Repositorium unter dem Namen DOOR betreibt, haben sich aufgrund des raschen und verlässlichen Service und der inzwischen großen Community für PHAIDRA entschieden, 2022 wurde ein Partnerschaftsvertrag mit der Akademie der Bildenden Künste Wien unterzeichnet.

Die Bibliothek des IST berät u. a. zu Fragen über Open Access, Identifikatoren für Autor:innen und Datenmanagementpläne. Die Bibliothek der FH St. Pölten bietet u. a. Schulungsvideos für das Repositorium PHAIDRA an. An der Kunstuniversität Graz wird neben PHAIDRA auch, analog zur Universität Wien, KUG-scholar angeboten, das Repositorium für Open Access Veröffentlichungen.

Forschungsdatenmanagement beinhaltet, wie auch bereits bei den oben diskutierten Datenmanagementplänen ersichtlich, auch die Speicherung bzw. langfristige Archivierung von Forschungsdaten. Deshalb sind Repositorien essenziell, unabhängig davon, ob es sich um Repositorien aus der eigenen Institution oder um generische, wie beispielsweise Zenodo, bzw. fachspezifische Repositorien handelt. So wichtig die Langzeitverfügbarkeit von Daten auch ist, es darf darüber nicht vergessen werden, dass die Forschenden auch Speichermöglichkeiten für Daten benötigen, die eventuell nach einiger Zeit wieder gelöscht werden müssen oder nur während der Projektlaufzeit Bedeutung für die Arbeit haben und aus rechtlichen und/oder ethischen Gründen nicht für die Öffentlichkeit bestimmt sind. Größere Institutionen, an denen zu unterschiedlichen Themen geforscht wird und die mit sehr vielfältigen Speicherdaten zu tun haben, benötigen ein breit gefächertes Angebot an Speicher- und Archivierungsmöglichkeiten.

---

73 https://research-explorer.app.ist.ac.at/
74 https://phaidra.fhstp.ac.at/
75 https://phaidra.vetmeduni.ac.at/
76 https://phaidra.kug.ac.at/
77 https://phaidra.ufg.at/#?page=1&pagesize=10
78 https://www.bruckneruni.at/de/bibliothek/phaidra-repositorium

5. Die Rahmenbedingungen an der Universität Wien

An der Universität Wien wurde 2006 ein Digital Asset Management System an der Historisch-Kulturwissenschaftlichen Fakultät namens UNIDAM[79] etabliert, um vor allem den Lehrenden die Möglichkeit zu geben, Studierenden rasch Materialien, meist Bilder, für die Lehrveranstaltungen zur Verfügung zu stellen. Gleichzeitig bereitete eine vom Rektorat initiierte Arbeitsgruppe den Aufbau eines institutionellen Repositoriums vor, das sämtliche digitale Objekte, die im Rahmen von Forschung, Lehre und Verwaltung entstehen, langfristig verfügbar halten sollte.[80] Sowohl bereits digitalisierte Objekte jeglichen Formats, auch jene die in Zukunft mittels Retrodigitalisierung erzeugt werden, sollten hier sicher archiviert werden können. Da es zu dieser Zeit noch kein fertiges Produkt gab, das allen Anforderungen entsprach, plante man eine Eigenentwicklung auf Basis der Open Source Software Fedora. Von Anfang an zeichnete sich PHAIDRA durch einige Alleinstellungsmerkmale aus, wie beispielsweise die Offenheit für alle Angehörigen der Universität Wien, auch Studierende und Personen aus der Verwaltung dürfen Objekte hochladen. Es wurde ein ausgeklügeltes Zugriffssystem implementiert, das sowohl eine völlige Öffnung des Zugangs zu den Objekten als auch die – temporäre oder grundsätzliche – Sperre erlaubt, wobei der/die Eigentümer:in der Objekte jederzeit bestimmen kann, welche Institute, Departments, Forscher:innengruppen oder Einzelpersonen Zugriff haben dürfen. Jedes Objekt kann außerdem lizenziert werden. Schon damals wurde auf größtmögliche Transparenz geachtet, indem beispielsweise auch die Metadaten der gesperrten Objekte in Suchmaschinen gefunden werden. Schnittstellen waren ebenfalls von Anfang an eingeplant, sodass ein Austausch mit anderen Systemen möglich war. Im Laufe der Zeit wurde ein Teil von PHAIDRA zum institutionellen Repositorium u:scholar, über das vor allem Zweitveröffentlichungen verfügbar gemacht werden können. PHAIDRA wurde durch ein Testsystem und eine lokale Variante für die Universität Wien ergänzt und darüber hinaus auch von anderen Institutionen genutzt, sodass derzeit ein Netzwerk von 23 Partner:innen besteht.[81] Für sozialwissenschaftliche Daten wurde das Repositorium The Austrian Social Science Data Archive (AUSSDA) an der Universitätsbibliothek Wien etabliert: „Aufgrund der neuen Herausforderungen wurde die Architektur von einem Repositorium hin zu einem Ökosystem aus Repositorien und Daten-Services geändert."[82]

79 https://datamanagement.univie.ac.at/ueber-phaidra-services/unidam/
80 Siehe dazu auch Blumesberger, S. (2020a), S. 500-508 und Blumesberger, S.; Ganguly, R. (2019), S. 193-200.
81 https://phaidra.org/
82 Blumesberger, S.; Ganguly, R. (2019), Anm. 63, S. 195.

Zusätzlich zu den Tools, die in den letzten Jahren durch beispielsweise GitLab ergänzt wurden, wurden auch die Beratungen ausgeweitet. Ging es am Anfang fast ausschließlich um den Hochladeprozess und die Beschreibung der Objekte, spezialisierten sich die Fragen später auf ein die Archivierung übersteigendes umfassendes Forschungsdatenmanagement. Vor allem die Einführung der Datenmanagementpläne, am FWF verpflichtend seit 1.1.2019, trugen zu einer Ausweitung der Schulungen, Workshops und Vorträge bei. Derzeit reichen die Anfragen von der Bitte um Speicherplatz auf Shares, über den Zugang zu Tools, technische Beratung bzgl. Formaten oder Schnittstellen, bis zu Visualisierung von Forschungsdaten und Vorbereitung eines Datenmanagementplans. Diese Anfragen ermöglichen den forschungsunterstützenden Stellen, tiefere Einblicke in das Forschungsgeschehen zu nehmen. Bibliothekar:innen und Personen aus dem IT-Bereich erfahren so unmittelbarer von den Bedürfnissen der Forschenden, ihre Daten so professionell wie möglich zu erstellen, zu teilen, zu sichern, sichtbar und langfristig verfügbar zu machen.

Forschenden an der Universität Wien stehen für den gesamten Forschungsdatenzyklus mehrere Tools für die Speicherung von Daten zur Verfügung:

Name	Dauer der Speicherung	Kostenlos	Für Studierende	PI[83]	Sichtbarkeit
PHAIDRA[84]	LZA[85]	ja	ja	ja	OA[86] möglich, Metadaten immer OA
U:scholar[87]	LZA	ja	ja	ja	OA möglich, Metadaten immer OA
AUSSDA[88]	LZA	ja	ja	ja	OA möglich
UNIDAM[89]	langfristig	ja	ja	nein	nur nach Anmeldung
GitLAB[90]	langfristig	ja	ja	nein	nur nach Anmeldung
PHAIDRA-local	langfristig	ja	ja	nein	nur nach Anmeldung

83 Persistenter Identifier
84 Für sämtliche Daten aus allen Fachrichtungen offen.
85 Langzeitarchivierung
86 Open Access
87 Für Zweitveröffentlichungen; u:scholar ist technisch gesehen ein Teil von PHAIDRA.
88 Für (quantitative) Daten aus den Sozialwissenschaften
89 Vor allem für Daten der Digital Humanities
90 Wird für das Managen von Forschungsdaten innerhalb der Universität Wien angeboten.

Shares	mittelfristig	nein	nein	nein	nur nach Anmeldung
U:cloud/ u:cloud pro[91]	mittelfristig	ja/nein	nein	nein	nur nach Anmeldung
Temp-Space[92]	kurzfristig	ja	nein	nein	nur nach Anmeldung
PHAIDRA-Sandbox[93]	kurzfristig	ja	ja	nein	innerhalb der Uni Wien möglich

6. Anwendungsfälle an der Universität Wien

Um den unterschiedlichen Umgang mit den angebotenen Services zu verdeutlichen, sollen hier fingierte, aber durchaus realitätsnahe Use-Cases gezeigt werden.

6.1. Beispiel A – Einzelforscherin im Fachbereich Geschichte

Planung der Forschung

Die Forscherin findet offen lizenzierte Daten in AUSSDA und in PHAIDRA, die sie für ein vom FWF gefördertes Projekt im Fachbereich Geschichte benötigt. Im vom FWF verlangten Datenmanagementplan beantwortet sie nach einem Gespräch mit Kolleg:innen aus dem Bereich Forschungsdatenmanagement sämtliche Fragen und erhält auch gleich Tipps, welche Tools zur Verfügung stehen und welche Formate für ihre Daten für die Langzeitarchivierung günstig sind. Außerdem dokumentiert sie sämtliche Forschungsschritte in einem eigenen Dokument auf der u:cloud, das sie später auch anderen Forscher:innen zur Verfügung stellen möchte.

Datenerhebung, Datengenerierung

Daten, die sie in anderen Repositorien gefunden hat, bzw. die sie durch eigene Recherchen selbst generiert hat, stellt sie auf einen Share, den sie beim Zentralen Informatikdienst über den Institutsvorstand beantragt hat.

91 Bis zu 50 GB sind kostenlos; für alles darüber hinaus fallen bei der u:cloud pro-Version Kosten an.
92 Mitarbeiter:innen der Universität Wien können Daten bis zu 100 GB kurzfristig speichern. Nach sieben Tagen können die Daten jederzeit gelöscht werden.
93 Dabei handelt es sich um ein Testsystem, das innerhalb des Netzes der Universität Wien verwendet werden kann.

Analyse der Daten

Daten, die am Share-Laufwerk liegen, werden analysiert und nach und nach mit Beschreibungen und Metadaten versehen. Zu diesem Zweck hat die Forscherin schon einige unterschiedliche Daten, z. B. Bilder, Texte und Audiofiles, in die PHAIDRA-Testumgebung hochgeladen, um sich mit dem dort vorhandenen Metadatenschema vertraut zu machen.

Teilen von Daten

Da die Forschende in der Lehre tätig ist, beschließt sie, auch UNIDAM zu nutzen. So kann sie beispielsweise ihre Bilder, die sie in der Vorlesung zeigen möchte, auch ihren Studierenden zur Verfügung stellen. Für Daten, die sie mit Kolleg:innen teilen möchte, vergibt sie entsprechende Zugriffsrechte auf dem Share-Ordner.

Datenarchivierung

Nicht alle Daten, die die Forschende verwendet oder generiert hat, darf sie aus rechtlichen Gründen mit anderen teilen. Scans aus Archiven darf sie beispielsweise nur als Arbeitsgrundlage verwenden, aber nicht weitergeben. Die anderen Daten, vor allem jene, die sie für zukünftige Publikationen benötigt, werden für die Langzeitarchivierung vorbereitet und mit den Metadaten gemeinsam in PHAIDRA hochgeladen. Die Forscherin lädt auch die Dokumentation hoch und bildet aus all diesen Objekten eine Collection, die sie umfassend beschreibt und mit einem Link an interessierte Kolleg:innen weitergeben kann. Bei einigen Forschungsdaten möchte sie zusätzlich zum automatisch in PHAIDRA vergebenen handle-Link[94] einen DOI verwenden. Diesen bestellt sie beim DOI-Service der Universität Wien.[95]

Publikation und Visualisierung der Ergebnisse

Das Projekt ist abgeschlossen, die Daten sind, soweit rechtlich und ethisch möglich, mit einer offenen Lizenz in PHAIDRA verfügbar. Inzwischen hat die Forscherin einen Beitrag in einer Open-Access-Fachzeitschrift veröffentlicht und ihre mit einer DOI versehenen Forschungsdaten in ihrem Text verlinkt. Nun möchte sie ihre Publikation auch an der Universität Wien sichtbarer machen. Dafür plant sie, den Artikel in u:scholar hochzuladen. Da der Verlag bereits eine DOI für ihren Beitrag vergeben hat, werden die Metadaten automatisch übernommen. Am Ende fügt sie die

94 Eine eindeutige permanente Signatur
95 https://doi-service.univie.ac.at/

Publikation noch ihrer Collection hinzu, in der schon die Forschungsdaten gesammelt sind.

Um ihre Arbeit noch sichtbarer zu machen, beschließt die Forschende, ihre Ergebnisse auch auf ihrer eigenen Homepage öffentlich zugänglich zu machen. Nach einem Gespräch mit Kolleg:innen vom Zentralen Informatikdienst erhält sie Unterstützung bei der Visualisierung ihrer Ergebnisse. Bilder und Videos werden beispielsweise direkt in die Homepage mittels permanenten Links eingebunden. So kann sie sicher sein, dass keine Daten verloren gehen, auch wenn ihre Homepage in Zukunft nicht mehr weiter betreut werden sollte.

6.2. Beispiel B – Forscher:innengruppe im Bereich der Biologie

Planung der Forschung

Drei Forscher:innen von der Universität Wien sind beteiligt an einem EU-Forschungsprojekt mit Partner:innen aus vier weiteren Ländern. Die Studie ist transdisziplinär geplant, es werden mikroskopische Bilder erzeugt, aber auch gleichzeitig Interviews mit unterschiedlichen Personen zum Thema Klimaschutz geführt, Videos aufgenommen und quantitative Umfragen erstellt. Die Projektleitung liegt an der Universität Wien, die anderen beteiligten Personen verfügen an ihren Universitäten nur zum Teil über ein geeignetes Repositorium. Nach einem Beratungsgespräch mit Personen aus dem Forschungsdatenmanagement sieht sich die Projektgruppe als Beispiele Datenmanagementpläne von EU-Projekten an und geht mit Mitarbeiter:innen der Universitätsbibliothek Wien und dem ZID die Fragen eines Datenmanagementplanes im Detail durch. So erfahren sie nicht nur, welche Tools ihnen an der Universität Wien zur Verfügung stehen, sondern auch, welche Formate für ihre Daten für die Langzeitarchivierung günstig sind. Außerdem erhalten sie Hinweise, wo sie eventuell bereits publizierte Daten zu ihrem Thema finden können. Es wird in der Gruppe geklärt, wem die erhobenen Daten gehören, wer von der Forschungsgruppe für Sicherheit und Backup zuständig ist und wer als Ansprechpartner:in für das Datenmanagement gelten soll.

Datenerhebung, Datengenerierung

Die Forscher:innengruppe hat sich entschieden, als Tool für die gemeinsame Arbeit mit den generierten Daten GitLab zu verwenden. Dort sind ihre Daten sicher gespeichert und es steht ihnen auch ein Tool für agiles Projektmanagement zur Verfügung.

Analyse der Daten

Zusätzlich verwendet die Gruppe Temp-Space, um einen Platz für analysierte Daten zu haben, und die u:cloud, um die Forschungsschritte zu dokumentieren und miteinander zu teilen.

Teilen von Daten

In dieser Phase entscheidet die Gruppe, welche Daten in Zukunft miteinander geteilt werden sollen und dürfen und wenn ja, mit welcher Lizenz sie versehen werden sollen. Personenbezogene Daten, die nicht mehr benötigt werden, werden gelöscht.

Datenarchivierung

Für die Langzeitarchivierung werden sowohl AUSSDA als auch PHAIDRA gewählt. Die quantitativen Umfrageergebnisse werden dem Team von AUSSDA übergeben. Die Daten werden überprüft, sicher archiviert und mit einem DOI versehen. Da alle Daten einen DOI erhalten sollen, werden diese vor dem Hochladen in PHAIDRA beim DOI-Service der Universität Wien reserviert. Bilder, Interviews und Videos werden auf einen Share gestellt, mit Metadaten versehen und in Zusammenarbeit mit dem ZID in PHAIDRA hochgeladen. Einige der Interviews wurden davor auf Wunsch der befragten Personen anonymisiert. Bei einigen Videos wurden nicht alle Rechte sofort freigegeben, sie sind vorerst nur für einen bestimmten Nutzer:innenkreis verfügbar. Die eingestellte Embargozeit erlaubt jedoch die Öffnung nach einem gewissen Zeitraum. Die anderen Daten können mit Projektende Open Access gestellt werden.

Publikation und Visualisierung der Ergebnisse

Im Rahmen des Projekts entstanden mehrere Publikationen in unterschiedlichen Open-Access-Fachzeitschriften, die über u:scholar verfügbar gemacht und gemeinsam mit den archivierten Daten in einer Collection zusammengefasst werden. Die Projektergebnisse werden mittels ihrer permanenten Links auf der Projekthomepage publiziert.

So oder so ähnlich könnte das Datenmanagement für Forschungsprojekte ablaufen. Selbstverständlich sind die einzelnen Schritte von zahlreichen Faktoren abhängig, wie beispielsweise von der Größe der Studie, von der Anzahl der Kooperationspartner:innen, vom Fachgebiet, von der Art der Daten, ob es sich um sensible Daten handelt oder nicht, ob mit Firmen zusammengearbeitet wird und natürlich, welche

Verbindlichkeiten es gibt. So müssen natürlich auch immer wirtschaftliche Interessen berücksichtigt werden.

7. Fazit

Repositorien sind wesentliche Bausteine im Forschungsdatenmanagement. Wie sich an den Universitäten, u. a. an der Universität Wien, zeigt, reicht der Aufbau eines einzigen Repositoriums nicht aus, um die Daten während ihres gesamten Lebenszyklus managen zu können.[96] Forschende benötigen neben der Langzeitarchivierung auch Möglichkeiten der kurzfristigeren Speicherung. Es werden Tools für Daten unterschiedlicher Größe, Struktur und Komplexität eingesetzt. Auch der Zugriff auf die Daten muss flexibel sein – im Idealfall sollte jederzeit entschieden werden können, ob die Daten eingeschränkt oder uneingeschränkt zugänglich sein sollen. Zusammenfassend lässt sich sagen, dass Repositorien effizientes Datenmanagement in unterschiedlichen Phasen unterstützen. Sie müssen, ebenfalls wie die zugehörigen Services, mit den Bedürfnissen der Forschenden mitwachsen und sich entwickeln.[97] Dafür ist die Zusammenarbeit mit den IT-Abteilungen wichtig, mit den Forschenden und den anderen Stakeholdern im Bereich Forschungsdatenmanagement, wie beispielsweise Mitarbeite:innen von Forschungsservices und Jurist:innen. Es müssen geeignete Rahmenbedingungen, beispielsweise mittels Policies, und Services bereitgestellt werden, sowie genügend Ressourcen zur Verfügung stehen. Am wichtigsten ist aber die Kommunikation mit allen beteiligten Personen, denn nur so können Repositorien user:innengerecht weiterentwickelt, Information über bestehende Services verbreitet und Hilfestellungen angeboten werden.[98] Datenmanagement wird an der Universität Wien als Teamwork betrachtet.[99]

Durch den ständigen Wandel in der Technik wird es in Zukunft wichtig werden, die Bandbreite der technischen Möglichkeiten immer wieder zu ergänzen, u. a. mit 3-D-Modellen oder auch mit der Möglichkeit, Datenbanken mit sämtlichen Funktionalitäten langfristig über das Projektende hinaus verfügbar zu machen. Aber auch auf der organisatorischen Seite kommen neue Aufgaben für Repositorien dazu. So sollen beispielsweise Repositorien in Zukunft miteinander verknüpft werden, sodass eine Metasuche möglich wird, oder es kommen neue persistente Identifier dazu. Ein Beispiel dafür ist die ORCID-iD (Open Researcher and Contributor-iD), eine ID für Forschende, die ihnen u. a. die Pflege ihrer Publikationsliste erleichtert. Wissenschafter:innen können sich mit ihren Publikationen, Forschungsdaten und

96 Siehe auch Blumesberger, S. (2020a), Anm. 63, S. 506 und Blumesberger, S. (2020b), S. 503-511.
97 Blumesberger, S. (2020b), S. 510.
98 Ebd.
99 Siehe Blumesberger, S.; Ganguly, R. (2019), Anm. 63, S. 198.

anderem Forschungsoutput eindeutig vernetzen.[100] Kann das Repositorium ORCID-iDs verarbeiten, kann man sich eventuell direkt mit der ORCID-iD einloggen und Daten hochladen und muss diese nicht händisch mit der ORCID-iD verknüpfen. Es werden ständig neue Herausforderungen auf die Repositorienlandschaft und das Forschungsdatenmanagement zukommen, in Kooperation mit den Forschenden und Nutzer:innen bleibt das Arbeitsfeld für alle Mitarbeiter:innen in diesem Bereich spannend. Wichtig ist, technische und strategische Entwicklungen stets zu beobachten und möglichst rasch auf neue Anforderungen zu reagieren.

Bibliografie

ALLEA (2023): The European Code of Conduct for Research Integrity. Revised Edition 2023. Berlin: ALLEA All European Academies. http://www.doi.org/10.26356/ECOC

Ball, Alex (2014): How to License Research Data. A Digital Curation Centre and JISC Legal "Working Level" Guide. https://www.dcc.ac.uk/guidance/how-guides/license-research-data (abgerufen am 12.07.2023)

Bauer, Bruno; Ferus, Andreas (2018): Österreichische Repositorien in OpenDOAR und re3data.org. Entwicklung und Status von Infrastrukturen für Green Open Access und Forschungsdaten. In: Mitteilungen der VÖB 71 (1), S. 70-86. https://doi.org/10.31263/voebm.v71i1.2037

Blumesberger, Susanne (2020a): Forschungsdatenmanagement gestern, heute und morgen zwischen FAIR, CARE und EOSC. Ein Praxisbericht der Universität Wien. In: b.i.t. online 23 (5), S. 500-508. https://www.b-i-t-online.de/heft/2020-05-fachbeitrag-blumesberger.pdf (abgerufen am 12.07.2023)

Blumesberger, Susanne (2020b): Repositorien als Tools für ein umfassendes Forschungsdatenmanagement. Am Beispiel von PHAIDRA an der Universitätsbibliothek Wien. In: Bibliothek Forschung und Praxis 44 (3), S. 503-511. https://doi.org/10.1515/bfp-2020-2026

Blumesberger, Susanne; Ganguly, Raman (2019): Der Umgang mit heterogenen (Forschungs-)daten an einer wissenschaftlichen Bibliothek. Use Cases und Erfahrungen aus technischer und nicht technischer Sicht an der Universität Wien. In: Forschungsdaten – Sammeln, sichern, strukturieren. 8. Konferenz der Zentralbibliothek, Forschungszentrum Jülich, WissKom 2019, Jülich, Germany, June 4-6, 2019. (Schriften des Forschungszentrums Jülich. Reihe Bibliothek/Library 23). Jülich: Verlag des Forschungszentrums Jülich, S. 193-200. http://hdl.handle.net/2128/22274

Blumesberger, Susanne; Gänsdorfer, Nikos; Ganguly, Raman; Gergely, Eva; Gruber, Alexander; Hasani-Mavriqi, Ilire; Kalová, Tereza; Ladurner, Christoph; Macher, Therese; Miksa, Tomasz; Sanchez Solis, Barbara; Schranzhofer, Hermann; Stork, Christiane; Stryeck, Sarah und Thöricht, Heike (2021): FAIR Data Austria – Abstimmung der Implementierung von FAIR Tools und Services 2021. In: Mitteilungen der VÖB 74 (2), S. 102-120. https://doi.org/10.31263/voebm.v74i2.6379

100 Siehe https://www.orcid-de.org/

European Commission (2013): Ethics for Researchers. Facilitating Research Excellence in FP7. Brussels: European Commission. http://ec.europa.eu/research/participants/data/ref/fp7/89888/ethics-for-researchers_en.pdf (abgerufen am 11.07.2023)

FWF (2022a): FWF-Datenmanagementplan (DMP). Evaluationsmatrix. https://www.fwf.ac.at/fileadmin/files/Dokumente/Open_Access/FWF_DMPMatrix_d.pdf (abgerufen am 12.07.2023)

FWF (2022b): FWF-Datenmanagementplan (DMP). Leitfaden und Vorlage. https://www.fwf.ac.at/fileadmin/files/Dokumente/Open_Access/FWF_DMP-Template_d.docx (abgerufen am 12.07.2023)

Hasani-Mavriqi, Ilire (2021): Professionalising Data Stewardship in the Netherlands. Competences, Training and Education. Dutch Roadmap Towards National Implementation of FAIR Data Stewardship. Webinar Video Recording. https://hdl.handle.net/11353/10.1188966

Medizinische Universität Graz (2021): Mitteilungsblätter. https://online.medunigraz.at/mug_online/wbMitteilungsblaetter.display?pNr=1108449 (abgerufen am 12.07.2023)

Medizinische Universität Wien (2021): Policy für Forschungsdatenmanagement. Version 1.1, 13.01.2021. https://www.meduniwien.ac.at/web/fileadmin/content/serviceeinrichtungen/itsc/it4science/Policy_fuer_Forschungsdaten-Management_v1.1.pdf (abgerufen am 12.07.2023)

Open Access Network (2022): Intro. Publizieren in Repositorien. https://open-access.network/informieren/publizieren/repositorien (abgerufen am 12.07.2023)

Spichtinger, Daniel; Blumesberger, Susanne (2020): FAIR Data and Data Management Requirements in a Comparative Perspective: Horizon 2020 and FWF Policies. In: Mitteilungen der VÖB 73 (2), S. 207-216.

Technische Universität Graz (2019): Framework Policy für Forschungsdatenmanagement an der TU Graz. https://www.tugraz.at/fileadmin/user_upload/tugrazExternal/0c4b9c02-50a6-4a31-b5fd-24a0f93b69c5/Framework_Policy_fuer_Forschungsdatenmanagement.pdf (abgerufen am 12.07.2023)

Technische Universität Graz (2021): TU Graz RDM Policy. Fakultätsspezifische Implementierungsstrategie Maschinenbau und Wirtschaftswissenschaften. v1.3 (26.4.2021). https://www.tugraz.at/fileadmin/user_upload/tugrazExternal/0c4b9c02-50a6-4a31-b5fd-24a0f93b69c5/TUG_Faculty-specific_RDM_Policy_MBWW_v1_3_de.pdf (abgerufen am 12.07.2023)

Technische Universität Wien (2018): Policy für Forschungsdatenmanagement (FDM) an der TU Wien. https://www.tuwien.at/index.php?eID=dms&s=4&path=Richtlinien%20und%20Verordnungen/Forschungsdatenmanagement%20Policy.pdf

Universität für Musik und darstellende Kunst Wien (2017): Richtlinie des Rektorats zum Forschungsdatenmanagement. https://www.mdw.ac.at/upload/MDWeb/forschungsfoerderung/downloads/FDM_Policy_mdw_DE_20171128endR_MB.pdf (abgerufen am 12.07.2023)

Universität Graz (2019): Forschungsdatenmanagement-Policy der Universität Graz. https://static.uni-graz.at/fileadmin/strategische-entwicklung/Dateien/FDM-Policy_DE_FINAL_Layout.pdf (abgerufen am 12.07.2023)

Universität Wien (2021): Policy für Forschungsdatenmanagement an der Universität Wien. https://rdm.univie.ac.at/fileadmin/user_upload/p_forschungsdatenmanagement/Dokumente/RDM_Policy_UNIVIE_v1_de.pdf (abgerufen am 12.07.2023)

Wirtschaftsuniversität Wien (2019): WUPOL Forschungsdatenmanagement. Policy für Forschungsdatenmanagement an der Wirtschaftsuniversität Wien. https://www.wu.ac.at/fileadmin/wu/s/library/images_forschungsdatenmanagement/WUPOL_Forschungsdatenmanagement.pdf (abgerufen am 12.07.2023)

Susanne Blumesberger hat das Studium der Medien- und Kommunikationswissenschaft und Germanistik an der Universität Wien absolviert. Sie arbeitet als wissenschaftliche Bibliothekarin im Bereich Forschungsdatenmanagement an der Universität Wien. Von 1999 bis 2014 war sie als Koordinatorin und Principal Investigator mehrerer wissenschaftlicher Forschungsprojekte am Institut für Wissenschaft und Kunst, Wien, tätig. Seit 2007 ist sie Repositorienmanagerin an der Universität Wien, seit 2016 Leiterin der Abteilung Repositorienmanagement PHAIDRA-Services an der Universitätsbibliothek Wien. Seit 2007 ist sie Lehrbeauftragte für Kinder- und Jugendliteratur an der Universität Wien und seit 2013 Vorsitzende der Österreichischen Gesellschaft für Kinder- und Jugendliteraturforschung. Ihre Forschungsschwerpunkte liegen auf Kinder- und Jugendliteraturforschung und Exilliteratur. Sie ist Mitherausgeberin der Zeitschrift „libri liberorum“ und veröffentlichte zahlreiche Fachbeiträge in nationalen und internationalen Fachzeitschriften im Bereich Kinder- und Jugendliteraturforschung und Bibliothekswissenschaft.

Elisabeth Steiner

Das OAIS-Referenzmodell

Grundlage für das Repositorienmanagement

Handbuch Repositorienmanagement, Hg. v. Blumesberger et al., 2024, S. 91–102
https://doi.org/10.25364/97839033742326

Elisabeth Steiner, Universität Graz, ZIM-ACDH, elisabeth.steiner@uni-graz.at | ORCID iD: 0000-0001-9116-0402

Zusammenfassung

Das OAIS-Referenzmodell bildet die Grundlage für das Management von digitalen Repositorien, unabhängig von der Art der enthaltenen Daten oder den verwendeten Technologien. Es beschreibt die beteiligten Akteur:innen und ihre Interessen sowie sämtliche Arbeitsabläufe für die digitale Langzeitarchivierung. Daraus sind Merkmale von Repositorien ableitbar, die weiterführend in Kriterienkatalogen bzw. Zertifizierungsrichtlinien münden können. Der Beitrag beschreibt das OAIS-Referenzmodell sowie seine wichtigsten Implikationen für das praktische Repositorienmanagement.

Schlagwörter: Repositorium; Langzeitarchivierung; Referenzmodell

Abstract

The OAIS Reference Model. A Foundation for Repository Management

The OAIS reference model forms the basis for managing digital repositories, regardless of the type of data contained or the technologies used. It describes the actors involved, their interests, and all workflows for long-term digital preservation. Based on the reference model, characteristics of repositories can be derived, which further lead to criteria catalogues or certification guidelines. The contribution outlines the OAIS reference model and its most important implications for practical repository management.

Keywords: Repository; long-term preservation; reference model

1. Einleitung

Repositorienmanagement und Langzeitarchivierung sind komplexe Aufgaben, bei denen unterschiedliche Akteur:innen und Funktionseinheiten zusammenarbeiten müssen. Die dafür notwendigen Arbeitsabläufe und Planungsprozesse können vereinfacht in Modellen abgebildet werden, die eine Abstraktion von konkreten technischen Umsetzungen erlauben und einen gemeinsamen Bezugspunkt für Terminologie und Definitionen bieten.

Für die Langzeitarchivierung von digitalen Ressourcen hat sich die Verwendung des Open Archival Information System-Referenzmodells[1] (OAIS-RM), welches vom Consultative Committee for Space Data Systems (CCSDS) entwickelt wurde, als de facto konkurrenzloser Standard etabliert.[2]

Ergänzend stehen für den gesamten Datenlebenszyklus weitere Modelle wie das Curation Life Cycle Model[3] des Digital Curation Centre zur Verfügung. Ebenso können für das Umfeld relevante Standards der International Organization for Standardization (ISO), beispielsweise zum Thema Dokumentenmanagement, herangezogen werden.[4]

Im Folgenden werden die wesentlichen Funktionen und Rollen in einem digitalen Langzeitarchiv nach OAIS vorgestellt und einige sich daraus ergebenden praktischen Implikationen für Repositorien beschrieben.

1 The Consultative Committee for Space Data Systems (2012)

2 Projekte mit ähnlicher Zielsetzung wie das IMS Digital Repositories Interoperability - Core Functions Information Model (https://www.imsglobal.org/digitalrepositories) konnten sich nicht für ein breites Publikum durchsetzen. Trotzdem muss auch das OAIS-RM mit sich verändernden Umständen Schritt halten und sich gegebenenfalls einer Revision unterziehen, vgl. die Diskussion in Wilson, T. C. (2017), S. 128-136.

3 Higgins, S. (2008), S. 134-140.

4 Eine Übersicht hierzu bietet die Digital Preservation Coalition unter https://www.dpconline.org/handbook/institutional-strategies/standards-and-best-practice

2. Das Referenzmodell und seine zentralen Konzepte

Das Open Archival Information System-Referenzmodell wurde vom CCSDS in den 90er Jahren des letzten Jahrhunderts entwickelt. Die erste Version wurde 2002 publiziert und weiterführend in eine ISO-Richtlinie überführt (2003). Die derzeit aktuelle Version stammt aus dem Jahr 2012, das Kompetenzzentrum für Langzeitarchivierung nestor[5] hat 2013 eine deutsche Übersetzung der Spezifikation publiziert.[6]

Das Dokument besteht aus Definitionen von Konzepten und Verantwortlichkeiten sowie aus darauf aufbauenden Empfehlungen, welche die verlässliche und langfristige Sicherung von digitaler Information zum Ziel haben. Das OAIS-RM ist ein abstraktes Modell, das keinerlei Aussagen über die konkrete technische Umsetzung seiner Empfehlungen enthält. Systeme zur Langzeitarchivierung können auf unterschiedlichen technischen Architekturen basieren, aber trotzdem mit den Prinzipien des Referenzmodells im Einklang stehen (OAIS Conformance/Compliance). Deswegen bildet das OAIS-RM den wichtigsten Bezugspunkt für die Planung und Durchführung von Langzeitarchivierung, unabhängig vom archivierten Material oder der wissenschaftlichen Disziplin. Auch die Benennung der betroffenen Akteur:innen und die Festlegung von wichtigen Definitionen stellt ein wesentliches Verdienst des Dokumentes dar.

Ein OAIS-konformes digitales Langzeitarchiv zielt auf die Erhaltung des Informationsgehalts[7] seiner Ressourcen. Diese Inhaltsinformation wird gemeinsam mit weiteren Daten in einem Informationspaket (Information Package) gebündelt. In diesen konzeptuellen Containern werden Inhalte, Metadaten und Identifizierungsinformationen zusammengefasst[8]. Je nach Funktion unterscheidet man Übergabeinformationspaket (Submission Information Package, SIP), Archivinformationspaket (Archival Information Package, AIP) und Auslieferungsinformationspaket (Dissemination Information Package, DIP).

5 Der Kooperationsverbund nestor wurde 2002 gegründet und bis 2009 in zwei Perioden vom Bundesministerium für Bildung und Forschung (Deutschland) gefördert. Seit 2009 wird der Verbund von den Partnern (Bibliotheken, Archive, Universitäten, etc.) getragen und engagiert sich im Themenbereich Langzeitarchivierung mit Veranstaltungen, Arbeitsgruppen und Publikationen (vgl. dazu die Website www.langzeitarchivierung.de für viele nützliche Materialien zum Thema).

6 Nestor (2013)

7 Bestehend aus der Information selbst und zugehörigen Repräsentationsinformationen (vgl. CCSDS: OAIS (Anm. 1), S. 2-3).

8 Genauer: Provenance, Context, Reference, Fixity, Access Rights (vgl. CCSDS: OAIS (Anm. 1), S. 2-6 - 2-7).

Im Folgenden werden die funktionalen Einheiten des OAIS-RM vorgestellt und ihre wichtigsten Aufgaben skizziert. Die Abbildung zeigt die wichtigsten Aufgaben des OAIS-konformen Archivs grafisch zusammengefasst:

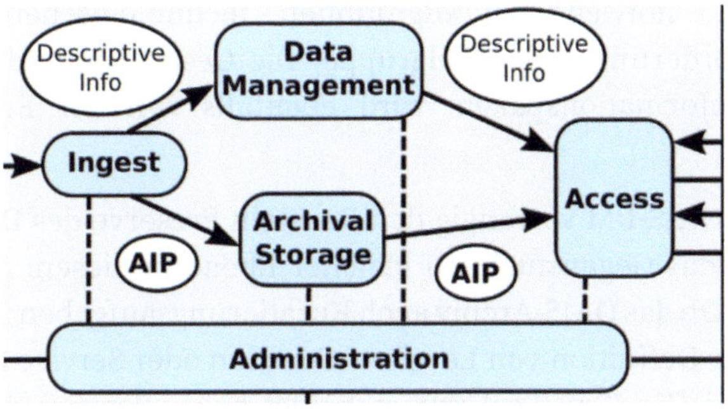

OAIS-Referenzmodell[9]

Das SIP wird von Produzent:innen der Information an das Archiv übergeben. Es gelangt in die Einheit Übernahme (Ingest), wo es verarbeitet wird. Zu den Aufgaben dieser Einheit gehören die Qualitätskontrolle des SIP, Generierung des AIP nach den Richtlinien des Archivs (beispielsweise Formatkonvertierungen und -validierungen) und die Extraktion relevanter deskriptiver Information zur Verwaltung der Ressource (beispielsweise administrative und technische Metadaten).

Die Datenverwaltung (Data Management) verwaltet die Erschließungsinformationen der Ressourcen und ermöglicht ihre Ergänzung, Erhaltung und Abfrage.

Das aus dem Ingest resultierende AIP wird in den Archivspeicher (Archival Storage) übernommen und langfristig gespeichert. Diese Funktionseinheit sorgt für die Verwaltung des Speichers und der Datenträger, für periodische Fehlerkontrollen und bei Bedarf für die Notfallwiederherstellung (Disaster Recovery).

Die Zurverfügungstellung des DIP an die Nutzer:innen erfolgt durch die Einheit Zugriff (Access). Diese ermöglicht die Auffindung, Bestellung und Auslieferung der gewünschten Ressourcen. DIPs können in unterschiedlichen Formaten generiert und bei Bedarf Zugriffskontrollen implementiert werden.

Die Administration (Administration) sichert den Betrieb des Repositoriums und stellt alle dafür notwendigen Services und Dienste bereit. Diese Einheit ist für den

9 Nach CCSDS: OAIS (Anm. 1), S. 4-1, grafisch aufbereitet von Gunter Vasold.

Abschluss von Verträgen und Vereinbarungen zuständig und entwickelt und pflegt Standards und Richtlinien.

Alle Aktivitäten des Archivs werden durch die Erhaltungsplanung (Preservation Planning) begleitet. Die Einheit beobachtet das Umfeld des OAIS-Archivs und gibt Empfehlungen zu notwendigen Migrationen, technologischen Veränderungen oder neuen Anforderungen der Zielgruppe. Die Gestaltung und Evaluierung der Vorgaben für Informationspakete wird ebenfalls von der Erhaltungsplanung durchgeführt.[10]

Damit deckt das OAIS-RM vorrangig den Baustein Preserve des DCC Curation Life Cycle Model ab, das Gegenstück auf gleicher Ebene in diesem Modell bildet der Baustein Curate. Ob das OAIS-Archiv auch Kuratierungsaufgaben übernimmt, kann (und soll) in einer Definition von Levels of Curation oder Service Levels kommuniziert werden. Das CoreTrustSeal unterscheidet beispielsweise vier Levels unterschiedlicher Kuratierungsaufgaben (A bis D).[11]

3. Praktische Implikationen

Aus dem abstrakten Funktionsmodell lassen sich zahlreiche praktische Erfordernisse und notwendige Services von Repositorien ableiten. Einige zentrale Komponenten werden im Folgenden an Hand konkreter Beispiele aus dem Repositorienmanagement genauer beschrieben.

3.1. Persistente Identifikation

Identifikationsinformation wird in der Referenzinformation (Reference Information) der Erhaltungsmetadaten (Preservation Description Information) und der Paketbeschreibung (Package Description) gespeichert und bei der Erstellung des AIP im Ingest erzeugt.[12] Identifikation bezieht sich dabei meist auf mehrere Ebenen. Die erste Ebene liegt innerhalb des Archivs, wo eine Relation zwischen dem Namen der Ressource und dem tatsächlichen Speicherort der Inhaltsinformation auf dem Datenträger hergestellt wird. Die zweite Ebene liegt in der Vergabe eines externen persistenten Identifikators (PID).

10 Vgl. CCSDS: OAIS (Anm. 1), S. 4-1 – 4-3.

11 Vgl. CoreTrustSeal Standards and Certification Board: CoreTrustSeal Trustworthy Data Repositories Requirements 2020–2022 (v02.00-2020-2022). 2019. https://doi.org/10.5281/zenodo.3638211, S. 3. Vertrauenswürdige digitale Langzeitarchive können sich mit dem CoreTrustSeal zertifizieren lassen. Wichtigste Grundlage für die Richtlinien ist einmal mehr das OAIS-RM.

12 Vgl. CCSDS: OAIS (Anm. 1), S. 4-30.

PIDs identifizieren das digitale Objekt auch unabhängig vom physischen Speicherort (Server) oder vom Archiv. Das Objekt kann also in ein anderes Archiv mit einem anderen Server „umziehen“ und behält den gleichen „Namen“. Um die Relation zwischen Name und Ort herzustellen, wird ein Verzeichnisdienst (Resolver) benötigt, der diese Information verwaltet. Es gibt verschiedene Systeme zur persistenten Identifikation, beispielsweise DOI[13], URN[14], Handle[15] oder ARK[16]. Die Verwendung eines PID stellt eine wesentliche Voraussetzung für dauerhaft zitierbare und verlässlich auffindbare Information dar.

3.2. Festlegung von Archivformaten

Jedes Repositorium sollte eine Liste von akzeptierten Formaten (möglich im SIP) und Archivformaten (zur Archivierung der Inhaltsinformation im AIP geeignet) festlegen. Nicht alle Dateiformate eignen sich zur Langzeitarchivierung. Die Reduktion auf eine beschränkte Anzahl von ausgewählten und geeigneten Formaten ermöglicht erst die dauerhafte Wartung der Infrastruktur und der darin enthaltenen Daten. Das Archiv kann, falls nötig, bei der Umwandlung vom SIP ins AIP (Format-)Konvertierungen vornehmen. Für jeden Datentyp gibt es unterschiedliche präferierte Formate, allerdings gibt es auch gemeinsame Kriterien: Sie sollten möglichst quelloffen, menschen- und maschinenlesbar sein, Metadaten enthalten und ausreichend standardisiert und dokumentiert sein.[17] Die Durchführung von Formaterkennungs- und Validierungsprozessen[18] wird in den Arbeitsablauf des Archivs integriert und anlassbezogen (z. B. beim Ingest) oder periodisch durchgeführt.

3.3. Erfassung und Modellierung von Metadaten

Das OAIS-RM verlangt eine ausreichende Beschreibung der relevanten Information mit deskriptiven, technischen, administrativen und rechtlichen Metadaten in Form von Strukturstandards, Wertstandards, Inhaltsstandards und Formatstandards[19].

13 Digital Object Identifier (DOI) https://www.doi.org

14 Uniform Resource Name (URN), in Österreich vergeben von der OBVSG https://www.obvsg.at/services/urn-resolver

15 Handle http://hdl.handle.net

16 Archival Resource Key (ARK: https://arks.org)

17 Siehe zu den Datenformaten die Beiträge in diesem Band. Eine umfangreiche und strukturierte Liste ist zu finden bei Böker, E. (2021).

18 Dafür stehen unter anderem frei verfügbare Tools und Bibliotheken wie FITS (https://projects.iq.harvard.edu/fits), JHOVE (https://jhove.openpreservation.org) oder DROID (https://www.nationalarchives.gov.uk/information-management/manage-information/preserving-digital-records/droid/) zur Verfügung.

19 Vgl. Gilliland, A. J. (2008)

Die Kriterien für die Metadatenformate ähneln jenen für die Datenformate, besonders ist hier auch der domänenspezifische Aspekt der Beschreibung für die vorgesehene Zielgruppe zu bedenken.[20] Hervorzuheben sind hierbei Strukturstandards, die explizit für die Anwendung im Archivierungsprozess entwickelt wurden (beispielsweise PREMIS[21] für Archivierungsmetadaten oder METS[22] als Containerformat zur Beschreibung und zum Austausch digitaler Objekte).

3.4. Dokumentation aller Prozesse und rechtliche Rahmenbedingungen

Alle Arbeitsabläufe im OAIS-Archiv sollen ausreichend dokumentiert, nachvollziehbar und begründbar sein. So wird im gesamten Ablauf Transparenz gewährleistet. Welche Ressourcen aufgenommen werden können und welche nicht dem Sammelfokus entsprechen, wird in einer Policy festgehalten (collection policy). Ebenso können Beziehungen zu Einheiten außerhalb des Archivs (Trägerinstitution, Öffentlichkeit, etc.) etwa durch ein mission statement oder die Einbettung in eine institutionelle Forschungsdatenpolicy klar dargelegt werden.

Jede Datenübergabe, an der das Archiv beteiligt ist, soll rechtlich durch Vereinbarungen gesichert werden. Das betrifft sowohl die Abgabe der Daten durch Produzent:innen ins Archiv wie auch die Zurverfügungstellung der Ressourcen an die Konsument:innen (vgl. dazu Kap. 5 Rollen).

3.5. Schnittstellen und Interoperabilität

Definierte und standardisierte technische Schnittstellen (application programming interfaces – APIs) gewährleisten die Austauschbarkeit von Information unter Archiven oder mit Produzent:innen und Nutzer:innen. Beispiele dafür sind OAI-PMH[23] für Metadaten oder IIIF[24] für Bilddateien. Vor allem OAI-PMH hat sich mit Hinblick auf Datenaustausch und -aggregation als Grundlage etabliert. Um eine bestmögliche Weiternutzung und Dissemination zu erreichen, müssen sowohl Services wie auch die (Meta-)Daten selbst möglichst interoperabel gestaltet sein. Das

---

20 Für mehr Informationen zu Metadaten und FAIR Data siehe die Beiträge in diesem Band.

21 Preservation Metadata: Implementation Strategies (PREMIS) http://www.loc.gov/standards/premis. PREMIS definiert Metadaten, die für die Langzeitarchivierung und -verfügbarkeit von digitalen Objekten notwendig sind, und stellt hierfür ein Datenmodell zur Verfügung.

22 Metadata Encoding and Transmission Standard (METS) http://www.loc.gov/standards/mets. METS wurde als Containerstandard explizit für das Management von digitalen Objekten in Repositorien und ihren Austausch konzipiert und kann für die Modellierung von SIP, AIP und DIP zur Anwendung kommen.

23 The Open Archives Initiative: Protocol for Metadata Harvesting. https://openarchives.org/pmh

24 International Image Interoperability Framework (IIIF) https://iiif.io

bezieht sich sowohl auf die technische Schnittstelle wie auch auf die tatsächliche Verwendung und Befüllung der verwendeten Metadatenfelder.

3.6. User focus und designated community

Im OAIS-RM ist die Festlegung der vorgesehenen Zielgruppe (designated community) des Repositoriums vorgesehen. Dazu wird häufig eine bestimmte wissenschaftliche Domäne als Kriterium herangezogen.[25] Die Erfüllung der Bedürfnisse und Erwartungen dieser Zielgruppe stellt ein zentrales Anliegen für ein OAIS-Archiv dar. Diese Art des user focus wird auch in anderen Richtlinien wie den FAIR-Data-Prinzipien[26] eingemahnt. Daher spielen community-spezifische Standards sowohl beim Punkt 3.3 Metadaten wie auch beim Punkt 3.5 Interoperabilität eine wichtige Rolle, gerade wenn Metadaten aus unterschiedlichen Archiven gesammelt (geharvestet) und zum Zweck der Suche oder Analyse zu einem größeren Verbund zusammengeschlossen werden. Für die Weiterverwendung der Daten in solchen Aggregationen sollte vor allem die Verwendung von community-spezifischen Vokabularen und URIs im Sinne von Linked Open Data[27] Berücksichtigung finden. Metadatenaggregationsservices sammeln tatsächlich immer nur die Metadaten der Forschungsdaten, der Zugriff auf die damit beschriebene Ressource erfolgt dann beim jeweiligen Datenprovider unter dem PID, der in den Metadaten vermerkt ist.

4. Strategien: Preservation Planning und Migration

Das OAIS-RM begreift die Erhaltungsplanung (Preservation Planning)[28] als Teil des Archivs. In dieser Funktionseinheit wird der Kontext des Archivs überwacht und notwendige Änderungen werden evaluiert: Müssen die Speichermedien getauscht werden? Gibt es neue Datenformate, die besser zur Langzeitarchivierung geeignet sind? Stellen Nutzer:innen neue Anforderungen an die Ressourcen?

Die Erhaltungsplanung kann solchen veränderten Anforderungen begegnen, indem die Daten oder Teile der Infrastruktur einer Migration unterzogen werden.

Eine Migration kann auf mehreren Ebenen erfolgen. Die unterste Ebene stellt die Verfügbarkeit auf dem Datenträger sicher (Bitstream Preservation). Datenträger werden periodisch geprüft und gegebenenfalls durch neue ersetzt. Eine größere Herausforderung ist die Daten- bzw. Formatmigration: Hier werden Daten in neue Formate konvertiert oder in neue Umgebungen überführt. Dies soll möglichst ohne

---

25 Vgl. CCSDS: OAIS (Anm. 1), S. 1-11.
26 Vgl. Wilkinson, M. D. et al. (2016)
27 Berners-Lee, T. (2006)
28 Vgl. CCSDS: OAIS (Anm. 1), S. 4-14 – 4-15.

Verlust der signifikanten Eigenschaften des Informationsobjektes vor sich gehen, bedeutet für das Repositorium jedoch oft einen erheblichen technischen und personellen Aufwand.[29] Nichtsdestotrotz macht die technische Evolution solche Prozesse immer wieder notwendig.

5. Rollen

Das OAIS-Archiv interagiert mit drei externen Gruppen: den Produzent:innen, den Konsument: innen und dem Management[30]. Bei Produzent: innen und Konsument: innen kann es sich sowohl um natürliche Personen oder Organisationen wie auch um technische Systeme (Clients) handeln.

Zum Zwecke der Übergabe von Daten gehen Produzent:innen und OAIS-Archiv eine Übergabevereinbarung (deposition/submission agreement) ein. Darin werden Art und Umfang der Daten, rechtliche Rahmenbedingungen, Zeitpläne und generell die Rechte und Pflichten der Beteiligten festgehalten. Der Informationsfluss zwischen Archiv und Nutzer:innen kann unterschiedlich gestaltet sein: Neben dem Online-Zugriff auf Ressourcen können auch klassische Bestellungen erfolgen, wobei der Trend hier in Richtung direkte und teilweise auch automatische Abfrage im Web geht. Auch hier findet eine – wenn auch implizite – Abmachung statt, nämlich durch die Zurverfügungstellung der Ressourcen unter Angabe der Rechte. Um die bestmögliche Nutzung zu sichern, müssen die Angebote auf die Anforderungen der vorgesehenen Zielgruppe abgestimmt sein.

Das Management muss von der internen Administration des OAIS-Archivs unterschieden werden. Die Administration beschäftigt sich mit dem operativen Tagesgeschäft des Repositorienmanagements, das Management ist auf höherer Ebene angesiedelt. Es evaluiert und steuert das Repositorium, häufig stellt es die Finanzierung.

Von zentraler Bedeutung ist die explizite Regelung von Zuständigkeiten innerhalb und außerhalb des OAIS-Archivs.

29 Vgl. Funk, Stefan E. (2010), Kap.8:10-15.
30 Vgl. CCSDS: OAIS (Anm. 1), S. 2-9. – 2-11.

6. Fazit

Das OAIS-Referenzmodell bildet die Grundlage für die Arbeit jedes Repositoriums und auch die Basis für viele Zertifizierungen als Trusted Digital Repository[31]. Es definiert die notwendigen Konzepte, charakterisiert die beteiligten Akteur:innen und legt standardisierte Arbeitsabläufe fest. Seine Bedeutung für die theoretische und praktische Beschäftigung mit Langzeitarchivierung über alle Disziplinen hinweg kann daher nicht hoch genug eingeschätzt werden.

Der zunehmende Umfang und die vermehrte Anzahl von digitalen Forschungsdaten verlangt eine entsprechende Infrastruktur, daher steigt auch der Bedarf an geeigneten Repositorien und Archivierungsanbietern. Diese bilden dabei allerdings nur einen Baustein im größeren Bild des Forschungsdatenmanagements. Um die Weiternutzung der publizierten Ressourcen zu gewährleisten, kommt vor allem der Interoperabilität von (Meta-)Daten und Services immer mehr Bedeutung zu.

Infrastrukturen zur Archivierung sollen zwar nachhaltig und langzeitorientiert sein, gleichzeitig führen technische und organisatorische Einflüsse sowie neue Anforderungen aus Sicht der Community zu ständigem Veränderungsdruck. Diese Änderungen transparent, nachvollziehbar und geplant ablaufen zu lassen und ein Gleichgewicht zwischen Beständigkeit und Flexibilität zu erreichen, bleibt die große Herausforderung für Repositorien. In diesem Prozess bildet das OAIS-RM eine Entscheidungsgrundlage und einen Rahmen für die notwendige Evolution von technischer und organisatorischer Infrastruktur.

Bibliografie

Berners-Lee, Tim (2006): Linked Data. https://www.w3.org/DesignIssues/LinkedData.html (abgerufen am 15.06.2022)

Böker, Elisabeth (2021): Formate erhalten. https://www.forschungsdaten.info/themen/veroeffentlichen-und-archivieren/formate-erhalten (abgerufen am 15.06.2022)

CoreTrustSeal Standards and Certification Board (2019): CoreTrustSeal Trustworthy Data Repositories Requirements 2020–2022 (v02.00-2020-2022). https://doi.org/10.5281/zenodo.3638211

The Consultative Committee for Space Data Systems (2012): Reference Model for an Open Archival Information System (OAIS). https://public.ccsds.org/pubs/650x0m2.pdf (abgerufen am 15.06.2022)

31 Siehe den Beitrag zum Konzept der Vertrauenswürdigkeit und zur Zertifizierung von Repositorien in diesem Band.

Funk, Stefan E. (2010): Migration. In: Neuroth, Heike; Oßwald, Achim; Scheffel, Regineet al. (Hg.): nestor Handbuch. Eine kleine Enzyklopädie der digitalen Langzeitarchivierung. Version 2.3 [online], S. 10-15. http://nbn-resolving.de/urn/resolver.pl?urn:nbn:de:0008-2010071949

Gilliland, Anne J. (2016): Setting the Stage. In: Baca, Murtha (ed.): Introduction to Metadata. 3rd edition. Los Angeles: Getty Publications http://www.getty.edu/publications/intrometadata/setting-the-stage (abgerufen am 15.06.2022)

Higgins, Sarah (2008): The DCC Curation Lifecycle Model. In: International Journal of Digital Curation 3 (1), pp. 134-140. https://doi.org/10.2218/ijdc.v3i1.48.

Metadata Encoding and Transmission Standard (METS). http://www.loc.gov/standards/mets/ (abgerufen am 15.06.2022)

Nestor (2013): Referenzmodell für ein Offenes Archiv-Informations-System. Deutsche Übersetzung 2.0. (nestor-materialien 16). https://nbn-resolving.org/urn/resolver.pl?urn=urn:nbn:de:0008-2013082706

Wilkinson, Mark D.; Dumontier, Michel; Aalbersberg, IJsbrand Jan et al. (2016): The FAIR Guiding Principles for Scientific Data Management and Stewardship. In: Scientific Data 3, 160018. https://doi.org/10.1038/sdata.2016.18.

Wilson, Thomas C. (2017): Rethinking Digital Preservation: Definitions, Models, and Requirements. In: Digital Library Perspectives 33 (2), pp. 128-136. https://doi.org/10.1108/DLP-08-2016-0029

Elisabeth Steiner studierte Linguistik, Germanistik und Digital Humanities in Graz (AT), Aarhus (DK) und Köln (DE). Seit 2012 verstärkt sie das Team des ZIM-ACDH an der Universität Graz in den Bereichen Metadatenmanagement und Repositorienmanagement. Sie beschäftigt sich dabei praktisch und theoretisch mit der Langzeitarchivierung und -verfügbarkeit von geisteswissenschaftlichen Forschungsdaten und lehrt zu diesen Themengebieten.

Raman Ganguly

Workflow-Modell für das Datenmanagement

Handbuch Repositorienmanagement, Hg. v. Blumesberger et al., 2024, S. 103–120
https://doi.org/10.25364/97839033742327

Raman Ganguly, Universität Wien, Zentraler Informatikdienst, raman.ganguly@univie.ac.at |
ORCID iD: 0000-0002-9837-0047

Zusammenfassung

Das Workflow-Modell wurde an der Universität Wien entwickelt und dient der Unterstützung des Forschungsdatenmanagementsupports. Es soll darstellen, wie die Daten in eine zentrale Infrastruktur zur Aufbewahrung gelangen und wo welche Aufgaben und Verantwortungen der handelnden Personen liegen. Die Darstellung ist so generisch wie möglich, damit möglichst viele Anwendungsfälle abgedeckt werden können. Es soll keine konkreten Anforderungen darstellen, die umzusetzen wären, sondern wesentlichen Punkte, die das Datenmanagement an die Datenlieferant:innen stellt und umgekehrt. Die im Modell verwendeten vier Phasen können weiter differenziert werden. So kann dieses Modell auch als Basis für eine Workflowdarstellung im Bereich Open Educational Resources eingesetzt werden.

Schlagwörter: Forschungsdatenmanagement; Support; Datenaufbewahrung; Digitale Objekte; Langzeitarchivierung

Abstract

A Workflow Model for Data Management

The workflow model was developed at the University of Vienna with the purpose to support research data management. It is primarily used to show how the data are preserved in a central infrastructure and where which tasks and responsibilities lie. The representation is as generic as possible so that as many use cases as possible can be covered with it. It does not serve to implement a specific requirement, but is intended to represent the essential requirements of data management on the data suppliers and vice versa. The four phases used in the model can be further differentiated for specific use cases. This model has also served as the basis for a workflow representation in the area of open educational resources.

Keywords: Research data management; support; data preservation; digital objects; long-term preservation

1. Entstehung des Workflow-Modells

Seit dem Start des Repositoriums PHAIDRA an der Universität Wien 2008 können alle Mitarbeiter:innen und Student:innen dieses Service nutzen. Damals wurde angenommen, dass die meisten Personen Daten mittels Einzelupload über das Webinterface von PHAIDRA hochladen und diese Daten ebenfalls Objekt für Objekt mit den entsprechenden Metadaten beschreiben würden. Bei der Einführung des Services entstanden zwei Herausforderungen in der Kommunikation mit den Benutzer:innen: Erstens war vielen Benutzer:innen der Begriff Metadaten nicht geläufig, auch die Frage, wie die Daten am besten beschrieben werden können, war nicht gelöst. Zweitens war die Annahme falsch, dass das Webinterface für den Upload ausreichend sein würde. Schon bald zeigte sich, dass besonders an der Schnittstelle zwischen Datenproduzent:innen und Datenmanagement ein großer Aufwand an zusätzlichen Entwicklungen nötig ist.

Im weiteren Verlauf der Beratungen und Durchführung von Projekten stellte sich zusätzlich heraus, dass die Kommunikation schwierig ist. Das Team vom Datenmanagement kann sich teilweise nur bedingt den Prozess der Datenerstellung vorstellen bzw. weiß sehr wenig darüber, wie die Daten aussehen, die in das Repositorium gelangen sollen. Die Forscher:innen ihrerseits haben ein ähnliches Problem damit. Sie verstehen nur bedingt, was der Forschungsdatensupport von ihnen benötigt und wie die Daten an das Repositorium geliefert werden sollen, damit die Daten langfristig aufbewahrt werden können. Es war daher notwendig, eine anschauliche Methode für die Beratung zu entwickeln, die auf möglichst viele Bereiche anwendbar ist.

2. Anforderungen an das Workflow-Modell

Das Modell dient der Kommunikation mit den Personen, die keine bzw. nur wenig Vorerfahrung mit Datenmanagement haben, daher müssen in den Beratungen alle wichtigen Terminologien erklärt bzw. damit in Einklang gebracht werden. Weiters muss es, wie schon angesprochen, möglichst generisch sein, damit alle wissenschaftlichen Disziplinen und unterschiedlichen Fälle für die Übertragung der Daten in das Repositorium abgebildet werden können. Zusätzlich zur Einfachheit und Allgemeingültigkeit sollte das Modell auch alle entstehenden Aufwände transparent machen, damit diese klar sind und von beiden Seiten zeitlich und budgetär geplant werden können.

Zusammengefasst sind die Anforderungen an dieses Modell:

- Verständlichkeit
- generisch sein
- Transparenz
- Vollständigkeit

3. Entwicklung des Modells

Die erste Orientierung bietet das Open Archival Information System (OAIS)-Modell, das ein Referenzmodell für die Archivierung von Daten ist. Genau beschrieben ist es im sogenannten Magenta Book von Consultative Committee for Space Data Systems (CCSDS), welches ein Beratungskomitee für Weltraumdatensysteme ist.

In diesem Magenta Book wird Folgendes definiert:

> An OAIS is an Archive, consisting of an organization, which may be part of a larger organization, of people and systems that has accepted the responsibility to preserve information and make it available for a Designated Community. It meets a set of such responsibilities as defined in this document, and this allows an OAIS Archive to be distinguished from other uses of the term 'archive'. The term 'Open' in OAIS is used to imply that this Recommendation, as well as future related Recommendations and standards, are developed in open forums, and it does not imply that access to the Archive is unrestricted.[1]

Es stehen hier die Organisation und die Personen im Vordergrund, die für die Datenarchivierung verantwortlich sind. Das Modell beschränkt sich nicht nur auf offene Daten, sondern das Open im Namen bezieht sich auch auf die Implementierung des Modells und nicht auf die Daten selbst. Das Workflow-Modell selbst ist sehr komplex und eher an Expert:innen des Datenmanagements gerichtet. Es ist sehr generisch und zeichnet den Datenfluss gut nach.

Das Fundament für das Workflow-Modell basiert auf diesem OAIS-Modell, es muss nur noch vereinfacht und auf den Bedarf der Kommunikation beim Support umgelegt werden. Es ist ein Modell für die Implementierung von Archivsystemen in einer Organisation und die Basis einer ISO-Norm, daher auch komplex und an ein Fachpublikum gerichtet. Das Workflow-Modell hat eine geringere Granularität, also eine höhere, abstraktere Sichtweise auf das Datenmanagement. Dennoch werden wichtige Begriffe übernommen wie z. B. Ingest und Data Management, beide werden im Folgenden noch genau beschrieben. Im OAIS-Modell wird zwischen

1 CCSDS (2012), S. 1.

Submission Information Package (SIP), Archival Information Package (AIP) und Dissemination Information Package (DIP) unterschieden[2], die wichtig für die Implementierung des Archivsystems sind, aber nicht für den Datenfluss eines im Einsatz befindlichen Archivsystems.

Beim OAIS-Modell werden drei Phasen oder Organisationseinheiten definiert: Producer, Management und Consumer[3]. Beim Workflow-Modell, das mehr den Fluss der Daten und nicht die Organisation widerspiegeln soll, wurde zusätzlich der Ingest als eigene Phase eingeführt. Hier soll insbesondere auf den Aufwand, der beim Ingest entsteht, hingewiesen werden.

4. Das Workflow-Modell

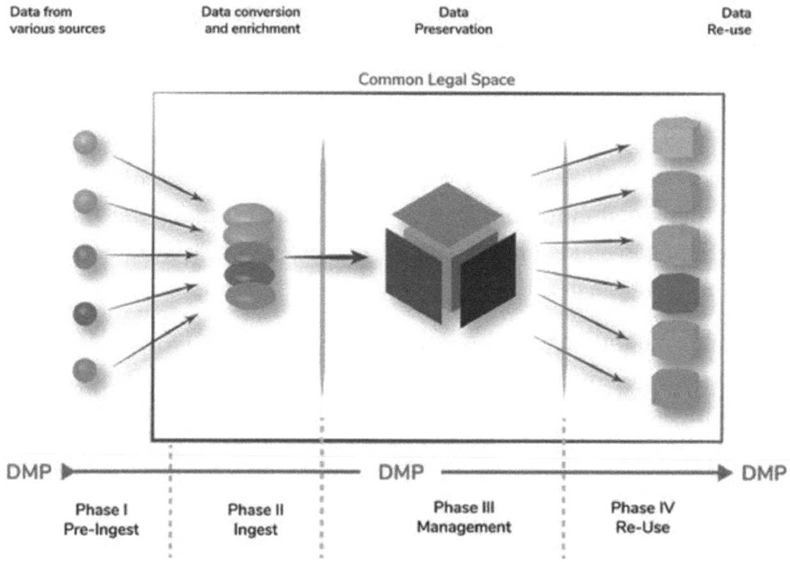

Abbildung 1: Workflow-Modell[4]

2 Ebd., S. 4-35.
3 Ebd. S. 2.
4 https://hdl.handle.net/11353/10.527220

Abbildung 1 zeigt das gesamte Workflow-Modell. Der Kern besteht aus vier Phasen: Pre-Ingest, Ingest, Management und Re-Use. Bei den Phasen gibt es unterschiedliche handelnde und zuständige Personen. Die Pre-Ingest-Phase wird von den Datenproduzent:innen durchgeführt und liegt auch in deren Verantwortlichkeit, die Management-Phase vom Datenmanagementteam. Die Phasen I (Ingest) und IV (Re-Use) sind jene Phasen, in denen die Daten dem System übergeben bzw. aus dem System geholt werden. Im Idealfall werden die abgerufenen Daten erneut verwendet und wieder in den Workflow eingespeist.

Sämtliche Prozessschritte umfassen das Datenmanagement. Hier muss zwischen dem Prozess und der Rolle des Datenmanagements unterschieden werden. Die Rolle des Datenmanagements wird üblicherweise von einer zentralen Einrichtung übernommen, die Daten langfristig zur Verfügung stellen kann. Der Prozess hingegen erstreckt sich über den gesamten Daten-Lifecycle, also von der Erstellung, über die Nachnutzung bis zum eventuellen Löschen von Daten. Viele Daten sollen jedoch für die Ewigkeit aufbewahrt werden, da entfällt natürlich die Löschung.

Im Workflow-Modell ist auch der Data-Management-Plan (DMP) eingezeichnet, der bereits vor der ersten Phase beginnt und nach der letzten Phase andauert. Der DMP umspannt den gesamten Zeitraum, vom Beginn, also der Planung der zu generierenden Daten, der Entstehung der Daten, bis zur Nachnutzung der Daten. Ein DMP wird aus Sicht eines Projekts erstellt und beschreibt auch, wie Daten über das Ende des Projekts aufbewahrt, geteilt und verwaltet werden müssen.

Ein gemeinsamer rechtlicher Rahmen, der Common Legal Space der Daten, wird durch das Viereck gekennzeichnet, das sich vom Ingest bis zur Nachnutzung erstreckt. Beim Ingest sollen die Rechte so geklärt werden, dass die Daten ohne weiteres durch die anderen Phasen durchlaufen können. Besonders wichtig ist dies bei der Nachnutzung, denn es muss für die Nachnutzer:innen klar und eindeutig sein, in welcher Form sie die Daten nutzen können.

4.1. Pre-Ingest

In der Pre-Ingest-Phase werden die Daten erzeugt, daher sind in dieser Phase die handelnden und verantwortlichen Personen die Datenproduzent:innen. Meistens werden die Daten im Rahmen eines Forschungsprojekts erstellt, daher kann es sich auch um ein längeres Vorhaben handeln, wie zum Beispiel die Digitalisierung von Sammlungen. Der Fokus liegt auf der Erstellung von hochqualitativen Daten. Hier wird in der Regel noch keine Rücksicht auf eine spätere Datenaufbewahrung gelegt.

Die Aufbewahrung wird relevant, wenn bei der Erfassung gewisse Rahmenbedingungen erfüllt werden können, die einen späteren Ingest ermöglichen, aber keinen Einfluss auf die Qualität der Daten haben.

Einem DMP entsprechend ist es wie bereits oben vermerkt sinnvoll, bereits bei der Datenerfassung auf die rechtlichen Rahmenbedingungen für eine spätere Aufbewahrung zu achten. So können bei der Erhebung gleich die entsprechenden Einverständniserklärungen oder Rechte eingeholt werden, die bei einem späteren Zeitpunkt vermutlich mit einem erheblich höheren Aufwand erbracht werden müssten.

Auch kann beim Pre-Ingest auf die Dokumentation und Beschreibung (später als Metadaten verwendbar) sowie auf das Datenformat geachtet werden. Die Metadaten gleich bei der Entstehung zu erfassen, spart Aufwand und man sollte außerdem Formate verwenden, die für die langfristige Aufbewahrung geeignet sind, sofern dies möglich ist. All diese Maßnahmen können den Aufwand beim Ingest von Seiten der Datenproduzent:innen verringern. Der Ingest findet aus Sicht des Projekts meist gegen Ende statt, da meist erst dann die Daten zur Verfügung stehen. Gegen Ende des Projekts sind eingeplante Zeitpuffer jedoch meist schon aufgebraucht und manche Projektmitarbeiter:innen haben bereits Verpflichtungen in neuen Projekten. Dadurch werden die Ressourcen knapp.

4.2. Ingest

Beim Ingest werden die Daten von den Produzent:innen an das Datenmanagement übergeben. Die Daten werden dabei für die Aufbewahrung aufbereitet. Konkret bedeutet das, dass aus den Daten digitale Objekte werden. Nachdem Format und Rechte geprüft wurden, erfolgt eine Datenanreicherung.

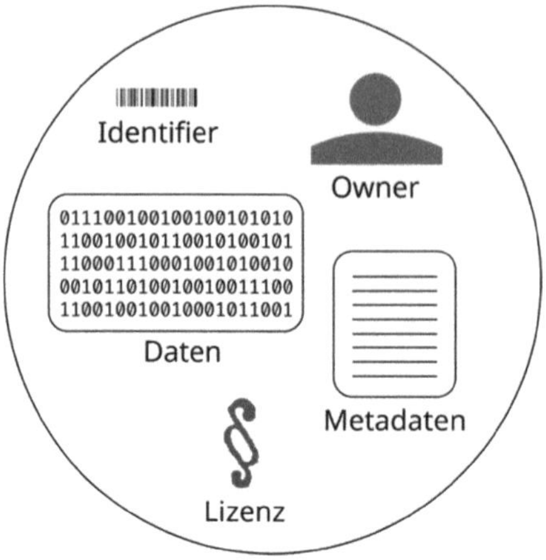

Abbildung 2: Digitales Objekt

Ein Digitales Objekt besteht aus den folgenden Teilen:

- den Daten selbst
- Persistenten Identifikatoren (PI)
- Metadaten, also der Beschreibung der Daten
- der Lizenz
- der/dem Rechteinhaber:in

Für jedes Objekt müssen möglichst früh die Urheberrechte geklärt und die Art der Nutzung klargestellt werden. Die eingeschränkteste Form für die Nachnutzung ist „alle Rechte vorbehalten", damit gelten die Regelungen des verankerten Urheberrechts. Von den meisten Forschungsförderern werden offene Lizenzen gefordert, sofern dies möglich ist. Hier werden in den meisten Fällen die Creative-Commons-Lizenzen vergeben. Die offenste Form, CC0, lässt Nachnutzer:innen alle Freiheiten, sogar ohne die Nennung des/der Urheber:in[5]. Nach dem österreichischen Urheberrecht ist diese Form der Nutzung nur bedingt möglich[6], somit ist CC BY die offenste Form. Hier gilt gleiches wie bei CC0, nur dass die Quelle der Daten, also die Namensnennung der Datenerfasser:innen gefordert ist.

5 Amini, S.; Blechl, G. et al. (2016)
6 Kucsko, G.; Zemann, A. (2017)

4.3. Management

Die Management-Phase ist die Kernphase der Aufgabe der langfristigen Aufbewahrung der Daten. Dabei werden die Daten über die geforderte Zeit in der geforderten Qualität aufrechterhalten und den Personen zur Verfügung gestellt, die das Recht haben, die Daten zu nutzen.

Mit dieser Phase ist der langfristige Betrieb einer Infrastruktur verknüpft, mit der die Daten aufbewahrt werden können. In den meisten Fällen handelt es sich um Repositorien, in denen Daten vorgehalten werden. Diese Repositorien müssen für die Datenintegrität sorgen und eine Landingpage zur Verfügung stellen, über die die Metadaten permanent auffindbar sind. Eine Landingpage ist eine Webseite, die mit dem Persistenten Identifier verknüpft ist und somit die Persistenz des Ortes im Netz garantiert. Es ist die Seite, auf die verlinkt wird und die den Zugang zu den Daten ermöglicht. Diese Seite soll auch für Personen erreichbar sein, die keinen direkten Zugang zu den Daten haben dürfen, damit ist eine Zitierbarkeit in Publikationen gewährleistet, auch wenn es sich um geschlossene Daten handelt. Dies ist ein wichtiges Kriterium zur Erfüllung der FAIR-Data-Prinzipien.[7]

Die Infrastruktur geht weit über ein Repositorium hinaus, da es einerseits Daten geben kann, die nicht in Form von Dateien gespeichert sind, und andererseits auch die Langzeitarchivierung betrachtet werden muss. Mehr dazu im Kapitel 5.

4.4. Re-Use

In der Re-Use-Phase findet die zweite Übergabe statt. Hier werden die Daten an die Personen übergeben, die diese nachnutzen wollen. Es ist jene Phase, die die Notwendigkeit für das Datenmanagement begründet. Ohne potentiellen Re-Use ist der gesamte Aufwand für das Datenmanagement nutzlos, weil sonst nur Daten gesammelt werden. Oft sind die möglichen Re-Use-Szenarien am Ende eines Projekts nicht vollumfänglich erkennbar, dennoch sollte man bei der Auswahl der Daten für die Aufbewahrung an die Nachnutzung denken. Natürlich gibt es offensichtliche und/oder vorgeschriebene Szenarien, wie etwa die Nachvollziehbarkeit und/oder Reproduzierbarkeit der Ergebnisse.

7 Die FAIR-Data-Prinzipien sind ein Akronym für Findable, Accessible, Interoperable, Reuseable und bilden das Grundprinzip für das Datenmanagement bei der European Open Science Cloud (EOSC).

Im Lauf der Zeit können die Daten auch in einem ganz anderen Kontext wiederverwendet werden. So werden z. B. heute Jahrhunderte alte Logbücher aus der Schifffahrt für die Klimaforschung verwendet[8]. Niemand konnte damals den Wert der Daten für die heutige Forschung erkennen.

Werden Daten an Nachnutzer:innen übergeben, so werden Kopien der Daten weitergegeben. Das eigentliche Digitale Objekt verbleibt im Repositorium. Dies ist von der Art und Weise zwar völlig logisch, da im digitalen Raum immer Kopien weitergegeben werden, es entstehen daraus aber verschiedene Probleme: Da es sich um eine Kopie handelt, kann nicht mehr nachvollzogen werden, was mit dieser Kopie alles passiert, z. B. die Verbreitung der Kopie auf anderen Kanälen. Hier ist die Lizenz besonders wichtig, da diese bestimmt, was erlaubt ist und was nicht. Aus Sicht des Repositorien-Managements muss darauf vertraut werden, dass sich die Nachnutzer:innen entsprechend der Lizenz rechtskonform verhalten. Es liegt nicht in der Verantwortung des Managements, die Einhaltung zu kontrollieren.

Da es sich um eine Kopie der Daten handelt, kann nicht verhindert werden, dass die Daten außerhalb des Repositoriums verbreitet werden, falls dies die Lizenz zulässt. Daher ist eine nachträgliche Änderung der Lizenz nicht zulässig, da nicht nachvollziehbar ist, wann die Lizenzen geändert wurden und unter welcher Lizenz dann die jeweilige Kopie steht.

Ein weiteres Thema ist die Authentizität der Daten. Wird die Kopie der Daten, die außerhalb des Repositoriums liegt, geändert, so kann dies nicht nachvollzogen werden. Nur durch eine korrekte Zitierung der Daten, die wieder auf das Original im Repositorium verweist, kann die Korrektheit überprüft werden.

5. Die Phasen aus Sicht der Daten

Nun betrachten wir dieses Modell aus Sicht der Daten und was mit den Daten in den jeweiligen Phasen geschieht. Zunächst wird geklärt, welche Daten in das Datenmanagement überführt werden können und wie die Daten im Ingest zu digitalen Objekten werden. Anschließend wird beschrieben, welche Maßnahmen getroffen werden müssen, damit die Qualität der Daten erhalten bleibt. Der Re-Use wird in dieser Darstellung nur am Rande betrachtet, da es sich aus Sicht des Modells um eine reine Kopie handelt. Dennoch wird hier unabhängig vom Modell noch dargestellt, wie Infrastrukturen des Datenmanagements den Re-Use erleichtern können.

8 Becker, R. (2019)

5.1. Pre-Ingest: Art von Daten, die entstehen

In einem Forschungsprozess kann jede erdenkliche Art von Daten entstehen bzw. verwendet werden. Erst der Kontext der Forschung definiert das Forschungsdatum. Besonders gut kann man das im Datenmanagement von institutionellen Infrastrukturen an Universitäten beobachten. Mit der großen Vielzahl an unterschiedlichen Disziplinen kommt es auch zu einer hohen Variation an unterschiedlichen Arten von Daten.

Daten können in Form von Textdokumenten, Bildern, Audio/Video-Daten, Messreihen, 3D-Objekten, Software, Datenbanken usw. vorliegen. Alle diese Daten sind unterschiedlich komplex und müssen teilweise in verschiedenen Infrastrukturen aufbewahrt werden. Dabei können erfahrungsgemäß diese drei Typen unterschieden werden: Dateien, Software und Datenbanken. Bei der folgenden Betrachtung handelt es sich um eine modellhafte Vereinfachung, bei der Big Data zunächst einmal ausgeblendet wird. Beim Thema Big Data entstehen neue Anforderungen an die Infrastruktur, die den Rahmen hier sprengen würden.

5.1.1. Dateien

Bei Daten kann es sich um Texte, Bilder, Audio oder Video-Daten handeln. Worum es sich genau handelt, bestimmt das Format und kann meist über die Dateiendung erkannt werden. So sind Textdateien, die mit Microsoft Word geschrieben wurden, mit der Endung .docx gekennzeichnet. Auch .pdf ist ein sehr übliches und bekanntes Format, das für das Datenmanagement wichtig ist.

Wesentlich ist die Abgeschlossenheit der Datei. Sie kann mit einer entsprechenden Software geöffnet und verarbeitet werden. Hier gilt es zu unterscheiden, ob Daten in einem offenen oder geschlossenen Format gespeichert werden. Bei einem offenen Format ist allgemein einsehbar, wie die Spezifikation, also die Struktur der Datei, ist. Unterschiedliche Hersteller:innen von Software können und dürfen entsprechende Programme schreiben, die eine Datei in diesem Format verarbeiten kann. Bei geschlossenen Formaten handelt es sich meist um Formate von Firmen, die oft nur mit der Software des Herstellers verarbeitet werden dürfen. Die Wahl des Formats hat eine direkte Auswirkung auf die Interoperabilität und wie einfach oder schwierig es ist, die Daten nachzunutzen.

5.1.2. Software

Bei der Software stellt sich die Frage, ob der Software-Code archiviert werden soll, oder ob die Software selbst in Betrieb gehalten werden soll. Aus der Praxis gesprochen, ist diese Frage früh zu klären, da unter dem abstrakten Begriff Archivierung oder sogar langfristige Zurverfügungstellung sehr unterschiedliche Dinge verstanden werden.

Soll nur der Software-Code aufbewahrt werden, kann die Software wie Dateien behandelt werden. Im Prinzip handelt es sich bei Software-Code nur um Text, der in einem offenen Dateiformat gespeichert ist. Wichtig ist, dass neben dem Code auch noch eine umfangreiche Dokumentation abgelegt wird. Diese geht in den meisten Fällen über die klassischen Metadaten hinaus, da erklärt werden muss, welche Schritte und welche Infrastrukturen notwendig sind, um die Software in Betrieb zu nehmen. Dafür haben sich in der Software-Entwicklung gängige Praktiken etabliert (z. B. Versionierung), die vom Datenmanagement übernommen werden sollten. Es ist auch ratsam, ein Tool für die Versionskontrolle zur Verfügung zu stellen. Nach derzeitigem Stand der Technik ist Git[9] am sinnvollsten einzusetzen. Auf dem Versionskontrolle-Tool Git aufbauend gibt es Tools mit Webinterfaces, die sich gut für das Datenmanagement eignen. GitHub[10], GitLab[11] und Bitbucket[12] sind die drei bekanntesten Tools, wobei GitLab auch unter einer Open-Source-Lizenz zur Verfügung steht.

Von klassischen Repositorien aus kann man eine Verbindung mit einem Git-Repositorium herstellen, in dem auch die Dokumentation zur Software vorhanden sein kann. Der Begriff Repositorium wird bei der Versionskontrolle anders verwendet als im Datenmanagement. Repositorium wird hier als Einheit verstanden, die eine Software vorhält, und nicht als übergeordnetes System, in dem die Objekte liegen. Im Repositorium kann es dann zu mehreren Versionen einer Software kommen und jede Version hat einen eindeutigen Identifikator, der wiederum die Basis für ein digitales Objekt in einem klassischen Datenrepositorium sein kann. Somit können die Vorteile aus beiden Bereichen miteinander verknüpft werden. Es gibt eine Landingpage mit Metadaten, DOI (falls gewünscht), Owner usw. und man kann den Source-Code so nutzen, wie es in der Software-Entwicklung üblich ist. Man findet im Internet viele Beispiele zur Funktionsweise von Git. Einen guten Überblick über den Aufbau und die Möglichkeiten von Git findet sich auf Developer-Info-Seiten von IBM[13].

---

9 git – fast-version-control; Webseite des Projekts: https://git-scm.com/
10 https://github.com/
11 https://about.gitlab.com/
12 https://bitbucket.org/
13 https://developer.ibm.com/tutorials/d-learn-workings-git/

Soll die Software in Betrieb gehalten werden, wird es kompliziert. Eine Software ist nie abgeschlossen und fehlerfrei, und hängt sie auch von anderen Software-Elementen ab. Sie benötigt ein Ökosystem, in dem sie laufen kann. Das Ökosystem besteht aus Software und Hardware, die sich wiederum im Laufe der Zeit ändert. Erfahrungsgemäß sind die Zyklen der Änderungen von Hard- und Software, die die Infrastruktur des Ökosystems bilden, teilweise sehr kurz (ein bis zwei Jahre). Daher entsteht ein hoher Aufwand, die Software in Betrieb zu halten, da Änderungen im Ökosystem sich auf die Software auswirken können. Dieser Aufwand kann nicht mehr vom Projekt getragen werden, da es weit über das Projektende hinausreicht. Für eine zentrale Einheit des Datenmanagements, die die Software noch nie zuvor gesehen hat, ist es ein sehr hoher Aufwand, den Betrieb zu übernehmen. Es kann auch nur schwer die Qualitätssicherung übernommen werden, wenn das Domänenwissen der Software, also das Wissen, wofür die Software eingesetzt wurde, nicht mehr vorhanden ist.

5.1.3. Datenbanken

Datenbanken sind noch komplexer als Software. Auch hier stellt sich vorrangig die Frage, ob die Datenbank in Betrieb gehalten werden soll oder nicht. Zusätzlich muss geklärt werden, was genau unter dem Begriff Datenbank verstanden wird und welches Datenbankkonzept verwendet wird.

Grundsätzlich sind Datenbanken Systeme, in denen Daten nach einer bestimmten Struktur, dem Datenmodell, abgelegt werden. Oft sind die Datenbanken mit einer Software verknüpft, die für die Eingabe und Darstellung der Daten verantwortlich ist. Nicht nur die Datenbank als solche, sondern auch die dazugehörige Software für die Ein- und Ausgabe von Daten muss in Betrieb gehalten werden. Auch wenn es nur die Datenbank betrifft, muss hierfür die Betreuung des Betriebs mit eingerechnet werden.

5.2. Ingest

Beim Ingest wird die Art der Daten geprüft und, wie diese aufbewahrt werden können. Hierbei ist die Expertise des Datenmanagements gefragt. Beim Datenmanagement kommt es auf eine Balance zwischen technischen und nicht-technischen Aufgaben an. Nur wenn beide Bereiche gemeinsam betrachtet werden, können Lösungen für Infrastrukturen gefunden werden. Der Ingest sorgt nun dafür, dass Daten in die Infrastrukturen für die Aufbewahrung überführt werden. Das Knowhow des nicht-technischen Bereichs kommt aus dem Bibliotheks- und Archivwesen, das eine lange Tradition hat, Wissen zu bewahren. Dieses muss nun mit den neuen digitalen Techniken kombiniert werden, um digitale Daten aufzubewahren. Erst die Kombination schafft die Möglichkeit, der Flüchtigkeit von digitalen Daten entgegenzuwirken, damit diese auch nach mehreren Generationen nachnutzbar sind.

Daten haben ihren Ursprung in den jeweiligen wissenschaftlichen Domänen. Nur mit ihrer Hilfe können aus den Daten digitale Objekte erstellt werden, da das Datenmanagement selbst keine Beschreibung und notwendigen Informationen für die Metadaten hat bzw. erstellen kann. Wenn verstanden wird, wie die Daten der einzelnen Domänen entstehen und wie deren Prozesse ausgestaltet sind, können die Infrastrukturen, in denen die Daten entstehen, mit den Infrastrukturen zusammengeführt werden, in denen die Daten aufbewahrt werden. Auch können so automatisiert Metadaten erstellt werden. Ziel ist es, beim Ingest einen möglichst geringen Aufwand zu haben und bereits bestehende Metadaten bei der Erzeugung des digitalen Objektes zu nutzen.

Die große Herausforderung hierbei ist, dass sowohl Bibliotheken und IT-Services als auch die Fachdomain ihre ganz eigenen Traditionen und Arbeitsweisen haben. Nur durch eine intensive Zusammenarbeit kann Verständnis für die jeweils andere Tradition entwickelt und eine gemeinsame Sprache gefunden werden, die das Fundament für die Entwicklung von kombinierten Infrastrukturen für die Entstehung, Analyse und Aufbewahrung von Forschungsdaten ist.

5.3. Datenmanagement

Was die Daten anbelangt, geht es beim Datenmanagement um die Erhaltung der Qualität über eine definierte Zeit. Der Zeitraum kann kurz, aber auch sehr lang sein. Dabei stellt sich die Frage, welche Qualität über einen gewissen Zeitraum aufrechterhalten werden soll. Je länger dieser Zeitraum ist, umso komplexer ist die Aufgabe. Das liegt daran, dass das digitale Zeitalter noch sehr jung ist und wir noch nicht erahnen können, wie die Daten in hundert oder mehr Jahren gespeichert und gelesen werden, und wir auf keine Erfahrungen aus einer längeren Vergangenheit zurückgreifen können. Von einer Stabilität wie bei der geschriebenen Informationsweitergabe auf Papier, Tontafeln oder sonstigen Trägermaterialien können wir im digitalen Raum nicht ausgehen. Es kommt auch zu permanenten Veränderungen bei der Software und bei der Hardware, mit denen digitale Daten genutzt und abgerufen werden.

Auch bisher mussten wir die Träger der Information erhalten, damit die Qualität der Daten stabil bleibt. Übertragen auf die digitale Welt ist die Hard- und Software das Medium, das es zu bewahren gilt. Nur sind die Daten nun unabhängig von deren

Medium und müssen daher getrennt betrachtet werden. Anders als im analogen Raum können sich die Daten verlustfrei von Medium zu Medium im virtuellen Raum bewegen. Es kommt immer darauf an, ob der Zielort die Daten auch verarbeiten und deren Inhalt preisgeben kann. Die Auflösung von Raum bedeutet aber nicht eine völlige Lösung von physikalischen Rahmenbedingen. Auf der physikalischen Ebene sind die 0 und 1, in denen Daten gespeichert werden und auf der Hardware vorliegen, die Basis der Daten. Die Formate definieren logische Sinneinheiten, die der Serie von 0 und 1 eine Struktur verleihen. Erst durch das Format können wir wissen, ob es sich bei der 0 und 1 um ein Dokument, ein Bild, ein Video usw. handelt. Mit Hilfe von Software werden dann die Inhalte dargestellt. Nur Software, die das jeweilige Format auch kennt, kann dies leisten. Dazu braucht es die entsprechenden Programme.

5.3.1. Bitstream

Die Reihe von 0 und 1, die in einer Hardware gespeichert ist und die Basis der Sinneinheiten bildet, wird Bitstream genannt. Für eine Aufbewahrung der Daten muss sichergestellt werden, dass dieser Bitstream nicht verändert wird. Die Library of Congress spricht sogar davon, dass die Erhaltung des Bitstreams ein Eckpfeiler der digitalen Aufbewahrung[14] ist.

Veränderungen können durch Prozesse passieren, etwa durch das Kopieren oder die Übertragung von Daten. Auch durch Fehler in Speichermedien kann es zum sogenannten „Bit-Rot" kommen. Dies sind Fehler im Bitstream, die sich bei der Speicherung auf dem physikalischen Medium im Lauf der Zeit einschleichen können[15].

Bei der Bitstream Preservation geht es darum, den Bitstream regelmäßig daraufhin zu prüfen, ob es zu Veränderungen gekommen ist. Dies kann mittels eines Hashwerts[16] geprüft werden. Ein Hashwert kann als Prüfsumme verwendet werden, da er eindeutig ist. Verändert sich der Bitstream, so verändert sich auch der Hashwert und Fehler können erkannt werden. Die Integrität muss anschließend wieder hergestellt werden. Daher ist es notwendig, bei der Bitstream Preservation Kopien der Daten zu haben, die in unterschiedlichen Datenpools gehalten werden. Alle Datenpools müssen dahingehend regelmäßig geprüft werden, ob die Integrität der Daten noch vorhanden ist.

14 Library of Congress (n.d.)
15 https://en.wikipedia.org/wiki/Data_degradation
16 https://de.wikipedia.org/wiki/Hashfunktion

5.3.2. Formate

Genauso wie die Software verändern sich auch die Formate. Es werden nicht nur neue Formate entwickelt, sondern auch alte Formate werden obsolet, oder es kommt zu neuen Versionen bestehender Formate. Z. B. gibt es die Dateiendung .doc, die für das Dokumentenformat von Microsoft Word steht, schon sehr lange. Das Format selbst hat sich im Laufe der Zeit stark verändert, da neue Funktionen in das Programm Word aufgenommen wurden, die auch im Format abgebildet werden mussten. Ein Beispiel wäre die Library of Congress, welche die Änderungen dokumentiert, da sie es für ihr eigenes Datenmanagement benötigt[17].

Die alten Formate können von neuerer Software oft nicht mehr gelesen werden. Damit man auf die Inhalte der Daten zugreifen kann, muss man entweder die alte Software erhalten oder das Format auf die neue Version migrieren. Beides ist mit einem erheblichen Aufwand verbunden.

Bei der Erhaltung der Software muss berücksichtigt werden, dass alte Software auch ein altes Betriebssystem benötigt. Es muss das gesamte alte Ökosystem erhalten werden. Mit neuen Technologien funktioniert es schon recht gut, dies zu erhalten. Z. B. helfen sogenannte Virtuelle Maschinen dabei, ein altes Softwaresystem zu betreiben. Eine Virtuelle Maschine simuliert eine Hardware[18] und man kann auf einem Computer mehrere Betriebssysteme gleichzeitig laufen lassen. Auch kann man diese Technik dazu nutzen, um ein Betriebssystem zum Laufen zu bringen, das schon älter ist. Nur geht dies nicht uneingeschränkt: Die alten Apple-Computer beispielsweise hatten einen anderen Prozessor und in solchen Fällen wird es schon sehr schwierig, das Betriebssystem in einer virtuellen Maschine zum Laufen zu bringen.

Formate in eine aktuellere Version zu migrieren, ist eine weitere Möglichkeit, die Lesbarkeit der Datei aufrecht zu erhalten. Damit das möglich ist, muss das Format offen sein, so dass das Ausgangsformat auch vollständig in seiner Struktur bekannt ist. Außerdem muss bei der langfristigen Aufbewahrung darauf geachtet werden, dass möglichst nur offene Formate verwendet werden. Damit kann man die Abhängigkeit von Format und Softwarehersteller trennen. Ansonsten kann es passieren, dass es keine Software mehr gibt, die das Format lesen kann, falls der Hersteller die Software aufgibt oder in Konkurs geht.

Neben einem offenen Format ist auch wichtig zu wissen, ob das Format die Daten komprimiert hat. Falls die Daten komprimiert sind, ist es notwendig zu wissen, ob

17 Vgl. https://www.loc.gov/preservation/digital/formats/fdd/fdd000509.shtml
18 https://de.wikipedia.org/wiki/Virtuelle_Maschine

diese verlustfrei oder verlustbehaftet komprimiert sind. Für die Aufbewahrung wird empfohlen, wenn möglich, ein offenes und unkomprimiertes (bzw. verlustfrei komprimiertes) Format zu wählen. Da dies nicht immer möglich ist, muss das Datenmanagement Kompromisse in diesem Bereich eingehen, vor allem bei Videodaten.

5.4. Re-Use

Beim Re-Use wird dem/der Nachnutzer:in eine Kopie der Daten zur Verfügung gestellt. Bei Dateien in einer Größe, die leicht über das Internet verbreitet werden kann, ist dies ein einfaches Verfahren. Es wird meistens über Download-Links geregelt. Bei Software und Datenbanken ist das schon etwas schwieriger.

Wenn die Daten in einer Software integriert sind, muss entweder die Software so zur Verfügung gestellt werden, dass sie den/die Nachnutzer:in auf einer eigenen Infrastruktur in Betrieb nehmen kann, oder die Software ist in einer lauffähigen Version vorhanden, die auch die Nachnutzer:innen verwenden können.

Bei Datenbanken ist es ähnlich, auch hier sind die Daten nicht direkt über eine Datei erreichbar. Es werden das Datenbanksystem benötigt, die Struktur, in der die Daten abgelegt sind, und natürlich die Daten selbst. Auch hier gibt es die Möglichkeit, die Struktur und Daten zur Verfügung zu stellen. Dann müssen die Nachnutzer:innen das Datenbanksystem selbst betreiben und die Struktur sowie die Daten in das Datenbanksystem importieren. Natürlich kann auch das Datenmanagement die Datenbank im Betrieb halten und Nachnutzer:innen direkt auf die Daten zugreifen lassen.

Das Team des Datenmanagements muss sich Wege überlegen, wie die Daten von den Archivsystemen zu den Computersystemen übertragen werden können. Hier bedarf es einer Integration zu den Forschungsinfrastrukturen. Im Idealfall hat man für den Ingest der Daten bereits die Schnittstellen aufgebaut.

6. Conclusio

Das Workflow-Modell ermöglicht die Kommunikation mit den Forscher:innen und ist ein Werkzeug für den Support und die Beratung. Forscher:innen sind mit den neuen Anforderungen der Forschungsförderer zum Teil überfordert und sie wissen nicht, wie Datenmanagement funktioniert und was im Bereich Datenmanagement von ihnen erwartet wird. Das Modell erklärt sehr gut, wo und wann die Aufwände für die Aufbewahrung von Daten entstehen und wer dafür verantwortlich ist. Dabei ist es wesentlich, die Anforderungen von ihnen auf dieses Modell zu übertragen. Es kommt immer darauf an, wie die Daten entstehen und wohin sie fließen. Das Modell nimmt, wie bereits beschrieben, die Perspektive der Daten ein und dokumentiert ihren Fluss von der Entstehung bis zur Nachnutzung. Das Modell kann auch als Grundlage zur Vermittlung der Anforderungen des Datenmanagements herangezogen werden.

Bibliografie

Amini, Seyavash; Blechl, Guido; Hamdi, Djawaneh et al. (2015): Cluster E: FAQs zu Creative-Commons-Lizenzen unter besonderer Berücksichtigung der Wissenschaft. https://phaidra.univie.ac.at/o:459183

Becker, Rachel (2019): Why Century-Old Ship Logs Are Key to Today's Climate Research. The Verge, 03.05.2019. https://www.theverge.com/2019/5/3/18528638/southern-weather-discovery-ship-logs-climate-change (abgerufen am 08.03.2023)

CCSDS. The Consultative Committee for Space Data Systems (ed.) (2012): Recommendation for Space Data System Practices. Reference Model for an Open Archival Information System (OAIS). Recommended Practice CCSDS 650.0-M-2. Magenta Book. https://public.ccsds.org/pubs/650x0m2.pdf (abgerufen am 08.03.2023)

Kucsko, Guido; Zemann, Adolf (2017): CC0 1.0 Universal – Beurteilung der Verzichtserklärung und der Lizenzerteilung im Rahmen der Fallback-Klausel nach österreichischem Recht. https://phaidra.univie.ac.at/o:528411

Library of Congress (n.d.): Bit Level Preservation and Long Term Usability. In: Digital Collections Management Compendium. https://www.loc.gov/programs/digital-collections-management/digital-formats/bit-level-preservation-and-long-term-usability/ (abgerufen am 10.02.2023)

Raman Ganguly hat seinen fachlichen Hintergrund in der Softwareentwicklung und Medientechnik. Er leitet die Abteilung IT Support für Research am Zentralen Informatikdienst der Universität Wien und ist für die Entwicklung und den Betrieb von Datenmanagement-Infrastruktur verantwortlich. Seit 2011 beschäftigt er sich mit der Archivierung von digitalen Daten aus der Forschung und Lehre mit dem Schwerpunkt der langfristigen Verfügbarhaltung. Er ist der technische Leiter des an der Universität Wien entwickelten Open-Source-Archivierungssystems PHAIDRA und der technischen Koordination für den internationalen Verbund von PHAIDRA bestehend aus 21 Institutionen. Raman Ganguly berät wissenschaftliche Bibliotheken bei technischen Fragen zum Datenmanagement und ist Vortragender bei den Universitätslehrgängen Data Librarian und Data Steward.

Herbert Hrachovec

OAI-PMH

Grundstein und Prüfstein der Open-Access-Bewegung

Handbuch Repositorienmanagement, Hg. v. Blumesberger et al., 2024, S. 121–132
https://doi.org/10.25364/97839033742328

Herbert Hrachovec, Universität Wien, Institut für Philosophie, herbert.hrachovec@univie.ac.at |
ORCID iD: 0000-0003-4778-014X

Zusammenfassung

Die technischen Voraussetzungen des freien Austausches wissenschaftlicher Fachliteratur, den die „Budapester Erklärung“ 2002 promulgierte, wurden bereits 1999 durch eine Forschungsgruppe angeregt. Ein HTML-Übertragungsprotokoll (OAI-PMH) sollte die Verbreitung bibliographischer Metadaten standardisieren. Dieser Regelsatz erwies sich als nachhaltiger Erfolg und wurde zum Kernstück der „Open Access Initiative“ (OAI). Er wird skizzenhaft dargestellt und in seiner Geschichte verfolgt. In der weiteren Entwicklung digitaler bibliographischer Informationsbehelfe zeigten sich Schwachstellen und Erweiterungsmöglichkeiten des Protokolls. Durch die Entwicklung mächtiger Suchmaschinen und leistungsfähiger Big-Data-Algorithmen wird es in eine neue, in ihren Auswirkungen noch ungewisse, soziopolitische Umgebung versetzt.

Schlagwörter: Metadaten; technische Infrastruktur; Bibliotheksparadigma; Suchmaschinen

Abstract

OAI-PMH. Cornerstone and Touchstone of the Open-Access Movement

The technical requirements of the free exchange of scientific literature, which the “Budapest Declaration” promulgated in 2002, had already been suggested by a research group in 1999. An HTML transfer protocol (OAI-PMH) was to standardise the dissemination of bibliographic metadata. This rule set proved to be a lasting success and became the core of open-access technology. It will be outlined and its history traced. As it progressed, weaknesses and the extensibility of the protocol became apparent. The development of powerful search engines and powerful big-data algorithms put it in a new socio-political environment, still uncertain in its implications.

Keywords: Metadata; technical infrastructure; library paradigm; search engines

1. Einleitung

Das „Open Archives Initiative Protocol for Metadata Harvesting“[1] legt Prozesse fest, die zwischen digitalen Archiven und Servicestellen, welche deren Metadaten sammeln, ablaufen. Es wurde ursprünglich entworfen, um den Austausch zwischen bibliographischen Datenquellen unterschiedlichen Formates zu standardisieren und eine einheitliche Grundlage zur Weiterverarbeitung ihrer Inhalte anbieten zu können. Softwarepakete, die im Anschluss an die „Open Access Initiative“ (OAI) entwickelt wurden, implementieren die sechs Abfragemuster, aus denen das knappe Protokoll besteht. Zunächst ist ein Blick auf diese Festlegungen zu werfen. Zwanzig Jahre nach seiner Veröffentlichung ist OAI-PMH einerseits nicht aus der Infrastruktur des offenen Datenaustausches wegzudenken, andererseits aber durch nachfolgende Entwicklungen teilweise überholt worden. Das heißt jedoch keineswegs, es wäre von bloß historischem Interesse. Gerade seine Rolle im Verlauf der letzten beiden Dezennien lässt erkennen, wo wir heute stehen. Diesem Aspekt gilt der zweite Abschnitt des vorliegenden Beitrags. Im dritten Teil wird, anknüpfend an die Geschichte dieser technischen Mustervorgabe, ein tiefgreifendes Dilemma der Politik von Open Access angesprochen. Institutionell vorgegebene Regeln zur Förderung des gemeinschaftlichen Zugangs zu Ressourcen stehen in Konkurrenz zu weniger kanonisch festgelegten Prozeduren, deren Effektivität ihr Defizit an Gemeinnutzen aufzuwiegen verspricht. Im Klartext: Die Informationsbürokratie der Archivverwaltung steht gegen kommerzielle Big-Data-Algorithmen.

2. Technik

Ein OAI-Archiv sammelt Publikationen und deren Metadaten, um sie zur Abfrage über das Internet zur Verfügung zu stellen. Das dazu verwendete Protokoll gliedert sich in Anfragen zur Archivstruktur und Anweisungen zur Übermittlung der angebotenen Inhalte. Konzeptuell wird zwischen einer Ressource („resource“), deren Eintragung im Archiv („item“) und den mit ihr verbundenen Datensätzen („records“) unterschieden. Einträge erfassen ein Objekt in Datensätzen, die möglicherweise verschiedenen metasprachlichen Standards folgen. Der digitale Informationstransfer besteht in Kommandos, die intuitiv gebräuchlichen „Verben“ nachgebildet sind. Drei Eingaben ermitteln die Archivstruktur. Dem in HTML abgesandten Anforderungstyp „identify“ antwortet eine Kurzbeschreibung des Archivs. „ListMetadataFormats“ gibt an, in welchen Formaten es seine Metadaten bereitstellt, und „ListSets“ dokumentiert, in welche inhaltlichen Gruppen sie allenfalls gegliedert

1 http://www.openarchives.org/pmh/

sind. Der eigentlichen Datenübertragung dienen drei weitere Ausdrücke. „ListIdentifiers“ bietet eine Kurzfassung der archivierten Ressourcen, während sie durch „ListRecords“ vollständig angeführt werden. „GetRecord“ liefert schließlich die Metadaten einer einzelnen Ressource. Alle Verben besitzen optionale Parameter, die es erlauben, die Abfragen unter anderem nach Kategorien, Datum und Zeitspanne der Archivierung einzuschränken.[2]

Der geordneten Erfassung von Metadaten kommt im Wissenschaftsbetrieb besondere Bedeutung zu. Das weltweite Netz akademischer Institutionen bedarf einer Infrastruktur, welche den digitalen Austausch der Information über vorhandene wissenschaftliche Ressourcen steuert. Aus diesem Grund haben sich gegen Ende des vergangenen Jahrhunderts diverse Zitiermuster zur informationstechnischen Erfassung wissenschaftlicher Publikationen entwickelt. Ein frühes Beispiel ist das seit 1999 etablierte MARC21, ein Digitalformat zur Erfassung computerisierter Bibliothekskataloge.[3] Der „Metadata Encoding and Transmission Standard“ (METS)[4] wiederum dient der Beschreibung unterschiedlicher Perspektiven auf eine bestimmte Ressource (z. B. jener der Drucktechnik und der eines Inhaltsverzeichnisses). Die „Digital Item Declaration Language“ (DIDL)[5], um noch ein Beispiel zu nennen, definiert eine Struktur von Mengeninklusionen zwischen „Containern“, „Items“, „Components“ und „Resources“. Diese Formate sind, entsprechend lokalen Bedürfnissen, noch immer in Gebrauch. Die bedeutsame Neuerung von OAI-PMH besteht nun darin, solche Spezifikationen optional zuzulassen (sie werden durch „ListMetadataFormats“ abgefragt), jedoch für eine obligatorische Datenstruktur zu sorgen. Dazu wird die Erfassung der Bestände mittels einer Basisversion von „Dublin Core“[6] vorgeschrieben. Dieses weit verbreitete Format stellt 15 gebräuchliche bibliographische Attribute zur Verfügung. Zu diesen Angaben gehören u. a. Titel und Autor:innen der Ressource, eine Kurzbeschreibung des Inhalts, der Verlag und das Publikationsdatum. Die genannten Metadaten sind durch OAI-PMH für den allgemeinen Gebrauch über das WWW zugänglich und werden in einer XML-Struktur ausgeliefert. Die Form der Dateneinträge ist allerdings stellenweise nicht exakt normiert, was zu Problemen führen kann. Es ist nicht unerheblich, ob der erste Eintrag in ein Namensfeld als Vor- oder Nachname zu interpretieren ist

2 Eine Übersicht zur Terminologie und Verwendung von OAI-PMH gibt Warner, S. (2001). Die Präsentation von Naravaran, N. (2010) enthält eine hilfreiche Visualisierung der Zusammenhänge. Siehe die vergleichbaren Folien von Brungai, L. (2011). Gaudinat, A.; Beausire, J.; Fuss, M. et al. (2017) haben eine Studie zur Reichweite und Überschneidung der gebräuchlichsten OAI-PMH konformen Meta-Kataloge vorgelegt.

3 https://www.loc.gov/marc/bibliographic/

4 http://www.loc.gov/standards/mets/

5 http://xml.coverpages.org/mpeg21-didl.html

6 https://dublincore.org/

(„Berthold Ludwig", „Elisabeth Anne").[7] Die Festschreibung eines Minimalkonsenses zur Formalisierung von Informationen im bibliographischen Datentransfer war wohl entscheidend für den eindrucksvollen Erfolg von OAI-PMH. Er wird durch zahlreiche informationstechnische, praxisorientierte und medientheoretische Publikationen belegt, die sich die Umsetzung der Deklarationen von Budapest und Berlin zum Ziel gesetzt haben.[8]

Die offizielle Registrierungsstelle[9] meldet zum unten angeführten Datum 5.318 protokoll-konforme Repositorien („data providers"), der „Bielefeld Academic Research Engine" (BASE)[10] nennt 9.101 „Datenlieferanten". Die Zahlen alleine geben allerdings nur ein ungefähres Bild. Das Volumen der erfassten Archive variiert, manche stagnieren oder sind verwaist. Dennoch ist mit OAI-PMH ein Instrument geschaffen worden, das die Vorstellung einer transparenten Organisation der verfügbaren Kenntnisse über wissenschaftliche Forschungsergebnisse exemplarisch zu realisieren hilft. Die Bedeutung dieses Umstands ist im Vergleich mit den in weiterer Folge entwickelten proprietären Angeboten des „social web" zu ermessen, auf die im dritten Abschnitt dieses Beitrags zurückgekommen wird. Ebenso wichtig wie die Archive „vor Ort" sind die im Protokoll vorgesehenen „Harvesters", denen die Aufgabe zufällt, das Datenmaterial gesammelt in einer konsistenten, benutzer:innenfreundlichen Form zur Verfügung zu stellen (BASE, CORE[11], OpenAIRE[12], Zenodo[13]). Die erwähnte unvollständige Operationalisierung von Dublin Core erfordert z. B. Korrekturarbeiten seitens der Aggregatoren[14]. Die Auslieferung großer Datenmengen läuft außerdem nicht immer störungsfrei, doch solche Schwierigkeiten scheinen die Verbreitung des Protokolls nicht behindert zu haben. Als Beispiel der anhaltenden Attraktivität der beschriebenen Infrastruktur kann eine kürzlich unternommene Recherche dienen. Seit dem Jahr 2000 wurden weltweit etwa 50 neue Open Access e-Journals aus dem Bereich der Philosophie gegründet[15]. Die

---

7 Vgl. zum Problem https://de.comm.infosystems.www.authoring.misc.narkive.com/P8ihO9lz/dublic-core-autoren.

8 Siehe die Budapester und Berliner Open-Access-Deklarationen: https://www.budapestopenaccessinitiative.org/read/german-translation/ und https://openaccess.mpg.de/Berliner-Erklaerung. Zur Entwicklung der Open-Access-Bewegung: Suber, P. (2016). Die Deutsche Initiative für Netzwerkinformation hat eine Informationsbroschüre herausgegeben: Deutsche Initiative für Netzwerkinformation e. V. (2005). Zur deutschen Diskussion der Open-Archives-Initiativen: Herb, U. (2012).

9 https://www.openarchives.org/Register/BrowseSites

10 https://www.base-search.net/

11 https://core.ac.uk/

12 https://www.openaire.eu/

13 https://zenodo.org/

14 Müller, S. (2020)

15 Hrachovec, H. (2021)

Mehrzahl ihrer Inhalte stehen über eine OAI-PMH-Schnittstelle zum Abruf zur Verfügung, sodass die Journalseiten gleichzeitig als frei zugängliche Archive fungieren. Über die genannten „Harvesters" sind die Beiträge dem interessierten Publikum zugänglich.

3. Geschichte

Als OAI-PMH entwickelt wurde[16], war das Protokoll darauf ausgelegt, „Service Providers" mit den Grunddaten zur bibliometrischen und bibliothekarischen Aufbereitung zu versorgen. Zu ihren Aufgaben sollten nicht bloß die Erfassung wissenschaftlicher Publikationen, sondern auch die Dokumentation ihrer Verbreitung durch Abfragen und Zitationen gehören. Die direkte Zugänglichkeit der faktischen Dokumente fehlte allerdings, wie auch im traditionellen Katalogeintrag die verzeichneten Bücher selbst nicht enthalten waren. Dementsprechend bezeichnet das Ensemble von Informationen, welches im Rahmen von OAI-PMH transportiert wird, die betreffenden Ressourcen nicht mit einer URI. „ListIdentifiers" gibt eine archivinterne Adresse an, Weblinks sind fakultativ. Zur Jahrtausendwende war noch nicht absehbar, dass in Zukunft hocheffektive Suchmaschinen wissenschaftlich relevante Texte mit Hilfe ausgefeilter Algorithmen (ziemlich) präzise aus einer Unmenge von Webseiten herausfiltern könnten. Dieses Defizit von OAI-PMH motivierte verschiedene Vorschläge zu Protokollerweiterungen. Im Rahmen der OAI-Initiative selbst entwickelten Carl Lagoze und Herbert Van de Sompel „Open Archives Initiative – Open Reuse and Exchange" (OAI-ORE) zur protokollkonformen Erfassung medial komplexer digitaler Objekte (2007)[17]. Die Verteilung und Wiederverwertung der Einträge soll danach durch ihre Definition als Aggregate gewährleistet werden. Sie bestehen aus sachlich zusammengehörigen Komponenten, die im Unterschied zu OAI-PMH durch eine „Resource Map" erschlossen werden. Durch sie wird ein Zugang zum semantischen Web geschaffen, also zur Möglichkeit einer Charakteristik solcher Aggregation in gängigen Datenformaten (z. B. RDF/XML, RDFa oder AtomXML).[18] Andere Ansätze zur Ausweitung der Kapazitäten von OAI-PMH sind im Rahmen externer Projekte verfolgt worden. „Linked Data" bezeichnet eine Anzahl von Konventionen zur maschinen-lesbaren Verknüpfung von Informationsbeständen des WWW. Bezogen auf frei zugängliche Daten bilden sie einen Teil

---

16 Den Ausgangspunkt bildete die Einladung zu einem Treffen in Santa Fe (Juli 1999), bei dem die Kompatibilität der zu diesem Zeitpunkt aktuellen e-prints-Formate zur Debatte stand. Federführend waren Paul Ginsparg, Rick Luce und Herbert Van de Sompel. Zur Geschichte vgl. das instruktive Tutorium: http://www.ukoln.ac.uk/metadata/oa-forum/tutorial/page2.htm

17 http://www.openarchives.org/ore/

18 Siehe https://www.w3schools.com/xml/xml_rdf.asp; https://rdfa.info/; http://www.atomenabled.org/developers/syndication/

des „semantischen Webs“, das sich aus derartigen heterogenen Inhalten knüpfen lässt. OAI-PMH Datensätze können systematisch durch Bestände der „Linked Open Data Cloud“ (LOD-Cloud) ergänzt werden[19]. Dabei werden die OAI-PMH „Identifiers“ durch gängige URLs ergänzt, die auf semantisch angereicherte Ressourcenbeschreibungen verweisen. Sie binden die Metadaten in eine LOD-Cloud ein[20].

Anders als OAI-PMH zeigten dessen Ergänzungen durch semantische Zusätze relativ wenige Folgewirkungen. Einer Umfrage aus dem Jahr 2018 zufolge publizieren 65 % von 142 erfassten Institutionen „linked data“ zu experimentellen Zwecken „to demonstrate what could be done with datasets as linked data“; 45 % geben an, dass sie das Konzept an hauseigenen Daten ausprobieren wollten[21]. Eine Breitenwirkung des Konzepts ist nicht festzustellen, wohl aber einige Versuche, in diese Richtung weiter zu forschen. So konvertiert das OntoOAI-Modell Ergebnisse von OAI-PMH-Sammlungen nach RDF, reichert sie mit LOD-Daten an und produziert nach einer Validierung in LOD-Tripeln semantische Graphen, aus denen neue Wissensbestände extrahiert werden können[22]. Einen weiteren eigenständigen Ansatz zur Datenverbreitung verfolgt das „ResourceSync Framework“[23]. Die Idee dahinter ist, dass die Synchronisation über den Abgleich der Seitenverzeichnisse geeigneter Portale („sitemaps“) die Bereitstellung gemeinsamer Informationen und ihrer Aktualisierungen mit einem Schlag auf elegante Art lösen soll. Julien A. Raemy analysierte in einer Studie 2020 mit Blick auf die Zielvorstellungen des Europeana-Projektes das Angebot an Alternativen zu OAI-PMH. 71,2 % (von 37 Teilnehmer:innen an der Umfrage) verwenden dieses Format zur Aggregation von Metadaten[24]. Angesichts des Aufwands, der mit der Einrichtung dieser Informationsarchitektur verbunden war, äußerten sich einige Befragte skeptisch gegenüber einer Veränderung des status quo[25]. Raemy rechnet nicht damit, dass die Sammlung von Metadaten in der Betreuung des kulturellen Erbes in absehbarer Zeit auf alternative Formate wechseln wird[26]. Seine Untersuchung steuert (ungewollt) eine wichtige zusätzliche Erklärung dafür bei. Unter den angeführten Optionen ist kein Vorschlag, der auch nur in die Nähe der Standardisierung, Akzeptanz und Verbreitung von OAI-PMH käme. Weder die Schwachstellen des 20 Jahre alten Protokolls noch die Aussichten

19 Linked Open Data. Europeana Pro: https://pro.europeana.eu/page/linked-open-data
20 Haslhofer, B.; Schandl, B. (2008). Der 2008 vorgestellte Ansatz wurde nicht weiter verfolgt.
21 Raemy, J. A. (2020), S. 96.
22 Becerril-García, A.; Aguado-López, E. (2018)
23 ResourceSync Framework Specification – Table of Contents: http://www.openarchives.org/rs/toc
24 Raemy, J. A. (2020), S. 34.
25 Raemy, J. A. (2020), S. 39.
26 Raemy, J. A. (2020), S. 54.

auf erweiterte Funktionalitäten scheinen seine Hauptrolle in der Branche gefährden zu können.

Debatten über OAI-PMH sind eng mit der Operationsweise institutionell verankerter Archive („institutional repositories") verbunden. Richard Poynder hat deren, aus der Sicht mancher Skeptiker enttäuschende, Entwicklung mit Unzulänglichkeiten in Verbindung gebracht, die sich bis zum programmatischen Beginn der Initiative in der richtungsweisenden Santa-Fe-Tagung (1999) zurückverfolgen lassen[27]. Die halbherzige Einbeziehung des HTML-Linkmechanismus und die mangelnde Koordination der Zusatzdienste sind durch die Eigenschaften der kontextarmen, teilstandardisierten Konvention zum Metadaten-Austausch mitverursacht. Die „Confederation of Open Access Repositories" (COAR), eine 2009 gegründete Interessensgemeinschaft von 156 Partnern aus allen Bereichen der wissenschaftlichen Infrastruktur, setzt mit der Initiative „Next Generation Repositories" bei dieser Diagnose an[28]. Sie greift die Ziele des Santa-Fe-Treffens in verändertem Kontext auf. Repositorien sollen die Grundlage einer global vernetzten Infrastruktur wissenschaftlicher Kommunikation werden. Das System soll stärker an der Forschung orientiert und innovationsoffen von der „scholarly community" selbst verwaltet werden. Die programmatische Beschreibung eines umfassenden Organisationsrahmens – von der Ebene wissenschaftlicher Inhalte über deren Publikation bis hin zur Dissemination – aus dem Jahr 2022 liegt vor[29]. Sie enthält allerdings keine technischen oder organisatorischen Details, an denen sich die Umsetzung des Entwurfes orientieren könnte.

4. Politik

Der beschriebene status quo von OAI-PMH[30] in der Aufbereitung und Verbreitung wissenschaftlicher Fachliteratur ist durch Hinweise auf parallele Entwicklungen der Informations- und Kommunikationstechnologie in dieser Sache zu ergänzen. Technische Fortschritte beruhen auf sozialen Vorgaben, die ihre Richtung bestimmen und umgekehrt von ihnen affiziert werden. Herbert Van de Sompel, ein prominenter Akteur innerhalb der meisten hier dargestellten Initiativen, hat die Voreingenommenheit für den Fall von OAI-PMH retrospektiv und selbstkritisch formuliert:

---

27 https://poynder.blogspot.com/2016/09/q-with-cnis-clifford-lynch-time-to-re_22.html
28 https://www.coar-repositories.org/news-updates/what-we-do/next-generation-repositories/
29 https://www.coar-repositories.org/news-updates/pubfair-version-2-now-available/
30 Den Versuch einer Einschätzung unternimmt Poynder, R. (2019). Siehe auch Hrachovec, H. (2018).

> It is a perspective in which a repository resembles a brick and mortar library, a library that one can go visit and that allows such visits subject to policies – the protocol – that may simultaneously be well intended and idiosyncratic. This kind of repository, although it resides on the web, hinders seamless access to its content because it does not fully embrace the ways of the web.[31]

Institutionen (Universitäten, Forschungsinstitute, Museen) administrieren ihre Ressourcen nach biblio-bürokratischen Richtlinien. Sie schaffen Hierarchien und garantieren dadurch weitgehende Konsistenz. Dazu benötigen sie normierte Erhebungsbögen und ein vormodelliertes Datenmanagement. Im Gegensatz dazu ist das WWW eine unübersichtliche Mega-Kollektion unterschiedlichster Inhalte, die mit solchen Mitteln nicht zu bändigen sind. Der erfolgreichen Weiterentwicklung institutioneller Archive steht im Weg, dass sich die Orientierungsmöglichkeiten im Angebot der Wissensgesellschaft verlagert haben.

Die traditionserprobten bibliographischen Metadaten, die OAI-PMH erfasst und transportiert, sind ein Instrument, Nadeln im Heuhaufen zu finden, den die Datenexpansion fortwährend vergrößert. Die mächtigen Suchmaschinen, allen voran Google, sind auf diese Situation eingestellt. Sie operieren, soweit man weiß, nicht auf der Grundlage konventioneller Datenbanken, sondern mit Big-Data-Algorithmen, die sich dem Untersuchungsfeld kontinuierlich anpassen[32]. Anders als OAI-PMH sind sie in der Lage, einem allenfalls vorhandenen Link auf eine Ressource automatisch zu folgen. Google hat, wie Stevan Harnad treffend bemerkt, genügend Zeit und Geld, um daraus eine hocheffektive Wissenschaftsplattform zu entwikkeln, während die betroffenen Institutionen im ständigen Konkurrenzkampf um knappe öffentliche Mittel und Sponsorengelder stehen[33]. Peter Suber, ein Open-Access-Verfechter der ersten Stunde, kommt schon 2004 im Vergleich zwischen der Archivierung in kuratierten digitalen Archiven und der Indizierung durch Suchmaschinen zum Ergebnis, „that putting an eprint on your personal web site won't always be worse, or won't be much worse, than depositing it in an OA-OAI archive."[34] Das Hauptargument für seine ernüchterte Einschätzung ist wie bei Harnad, dass

---

31 Van de Sompel, H.; Nelson, M. L. (2015), S. 3.

32 Stephens, O. (2012)

33 „The biggest Quasitory of all is the Virtual Quasitory called Google Scholar (GS). GS has mooted most of the fuss about interoperability because it full-text-inverts all content. It's a nuclear weapon, but it is in no hurry. Unlike institutions and funders, GS is under no financial pressure. And unlike publishers, it does not have the ambition or the need to capture and preserve publishers' obsolete, parasitic functions (even though, unlike publishers, GS is in an incomparably better position to maximise functionality on the web). GS is waiting patiently for the research community to get its act together." Comment von Stevan Harnad: https://poynder.blogspot.com/2016/10/institutional-repositories-response-to.html.

34 Suber, P. (2016), S. 6.

kontinuierlich verbesserte Lernalgorithmen den riesigen Datenmengen besser gewachsen sein könnten als die in OAI-PMH implementierten, von der Erfahrung von Bibliothekar:innen ausgehenden, in Gremien standardisierten Protokolle. Einem Weltkonzern steht die heterogene, hochspezialisierte, administrativ weitgehend autonome Vielfalt kultureller und wissenschaftlicher Sammlungen gegenüber. Der künftige Verlauf dieser Konstellation kann an dieser Stelle nicht prognostiziert werden.

Metadaten sind gegenüber den Inhalten, die sie kennzeichnen, neutral – keineswegs aber im sozio-ökonomischen Gebrauch. Sie sind ein Mittel, um Übersicht zu bewahren und Abläufe zu lenken. In der Praxis ist OAI-PMH ein Instrument zum standardisierten Datenaustausch zwischen Institutionen, überwiegend in extrakommerziellem Interesse – ein transparenter, unveräußerlicher Regelsatz zur Aufbereitung geteilter Informationen. Bekanntlich gelten diese Prinzipien weder für die global agierenden Suchmaschinen noch für die Serviceanbieter in privater Hand, die sich freier (und freiwillig bereitgestellter) Inhalte bedienen, um verkäuflichen Mehrwert zu gewinnen. Ihre Produkte basieren auf einer Infrastruktur, die im Prinzip für alle zugänglich, im Effekt jedoch von einschränkenden proprietären Interessen überlagert ist. Die Herkunft von OAI-PMH aus der selbstverwalteten Organisation kultureller und wissenschaftlicher Produkte bedingt auch seine Grenzen. Gary Hall hat darauf aufmerksam gemacht, dass die gegenwärtige mediale Umgebung tendenziell nicht mehr durch den „Besitz“ von Inhalten, sondern zunehmend durch die Ausübung von Datenkontrolle gekennzeichnet ist:

> In this world who gate-keeps access to (and so can extract maximum value from) content is less important, because that access is already free, than who gate-keeps (and so can extract maximum value from) the data generated around the use of that content, which is used more because access to it is free.[35]

Die von G. Hall angesprochene institutionelle Verwaltung von Inhalten mit Hilfe von OAI-PMH ist eine Reminiszenz aus der Gelehrtenrepublik, die ihre Arbeitsergebnisse an Universitäten, Akademien und Archiven in eigener Machtvollkommenheit pflegte. Das Protokoll ist, wie diese Aufbewahrungsstätten selbst, im Datenuniversum ernsthafter Konkurrenz ausgesetzt. Die Transparenz und Abwesenheit von privatwirtschaftlichen Eingrenzungen, die OAI-PMH motiviert und maßgeblich ermöglicht, steht auf dem Prüfstand. Stabile Ordnungsmuster von branchenspezifischer Bedeutung finden sich, davon ist auszugehen, eingelagert in eine Unübersichtlichkeit, an der eine solche Orientierung sich zu bewähren hat.

---

35 Hall, G. (2012)

Orientierungshilfen

Registrierung, Validierung

Directory of Open Access Repositories: https://v2.sherpa.ac.uk/opendoar/

OAI-PMH Registered Data Providers: https://openarchives.library.cornell.edu/Register/BrowseSites

OAI-PMH Validator & Data Extractor: https://validator.oaipmh.com/

Open Archives Initiative - Repository Explorer: http://oai.clarin-pl.eu/

Tutorials

OAI for Beginners - the Open Archives Forum Online Tutorial: http://www.ukoln.ac.uk/metadata/oa-forum/tutorial/

OAI-PMH Implementation: http://eprints.rclis.org/4586/1/tutorial3muller.pdf

OSTI OAI Repository Manual: https://www.osti.gov/sites/www.osti.gov/files/public/OSTI OAI Repository Manual 1_1_0.pdf

Das Open Archives Initiative Protocol for Metadata Harvesting: Zielsetzung, Funktionalität, Einsatzgebiete: https://zenodo.org/record/1253735/files/Diederichs Wuttke OAI PMH Term Paper 2018.pdf

Bibliografie

Becerril-García, Arianna; Aguado-López, Eduardo (2018): A Semantic Model for Selective Knowledge Discovery over OAI-PMH Structured Resources. In: Information 9 (6), p. 144. https://doi.org/10.3390/info9060144

Brungai, Lena (2011): OAI and OAI-PMH. https://www.slideshare.net/LenaBruncaj/oai-and-oaipmh (abgerufen am 12.01.2022)

Gaudinat, Arnaud; Beausire, Jonas; Fuss, Megan et al. (2017): Global Picture of OAI-PMH Repositories through the Analysis of 6 Key Open Archive Meta-Catalogs. https://arxiv.org/abs/1708.08669 (abgerufen am 12.01.2022)

Deutsche Initiative für Netzwerkinformation e.V. (Hg.) (2005): Elektronisches Publizieren an Hochschulen. Inhaltliche Gestaltung der OAI-Schnittstelle – Empfehlungen. https://edoc.hu-berlin.de/bitstream/handle/18452/2131/2-de2.pdf (abgerufen am 14.01.2022)

Hall, Gary (2012): Has Critical Theory Run Out of Time for Data-Driven Scholarship? In: Debates in the Digital Humanities. https://dhdebates.gc.cuny.edu/read/untitled-88c11800-9446-469b-a3be-3fdb36bfbd1e/section/1a9b138c-eb51-4f48-bcb8-039505f88ff8 (abgerufen am 14.01.2022)

Haslhofer, Bernhard; Schandl, Bernhard (2008): The OAI2LOD Server. Exposing OAI-PMH Metadata as Linked Data. http://events.linkeddata.org/ldow2008/papers/03-haslhofer-schandl-oai2lod-server.pdf (abgerufen am 14.01.2022)

Herb, Ulrich (Hg.) (2012): Open Initiatives. Offenheit in der digitalen Welt und Wissenschaft – Onlineversion. https://publikationen.sulb.uni-saarland.de/bitstream/20.500.11880/30534/1/OnlineversionOpenInitiativesUlrichHerb.pdf (abgerufen am 14.01.2022)

Hrachovec, Herbert (2018): Zugang für alle? Rhetorik und Realität der Open Access-Initiativen. In: Information Wissenschaft & Praxis 69 (4), S. 161-170. https://doi.org/10.1515/iwp-2018-0022

Hrachovec, Herbert (2021): Jüngere Open Access Journale in Philosophie. https://doi.org/10.5281/zenodo.5140827

Müller, Stefan (2020): Datenaustausch schwer gemacht. Das Beispiel OAI-PMH-Schnittstellen. https://dhmuc.hypotheses.org/2827 (abgerufen am 14.01.2022)

Naravaran, Nikesh (2010): Open Archives Initiatives for Metadata Harvesting. https://www.slideshare.net/nikeshn/open-archives-initiatives-for-metadata-harvesting (abgerufen am 12.01.2022).

Poynder, Richard (2019): Open Access. Could Defeat Be Snatched from the Jaws of Victory? https://richardpoynder.co.uk/Jaws.pdf (abgerufen am 06.04.2023)

Raemy, Julien Antoine (2020): Enabling Better Aggregation and Discovery of Cultural Heritage Content for Europeana and Its Partner Institutions. https://julsraemy.github.io/assets/doc/Mastersthesis_europeana_raemyjulien_FV.pdf (abgerufen am 14.01.2022)

Stephens, Owen (2012): What Does Google Do? CORE Blog. https://blog.core.ac.uk/2012/03/ (abgerufen am 14.01.2022)

Suber, Peter (2016): Knowledge Unbound. Selected Writings on Open Access, 2002–2011. Cambridge, MA: MIT Press. http://nrs.harvard.edu/urn-3:HUL.InstRepos:26246071

Van de Sompel, Herbert; Nelson, Michael L. (2015): Reminiscing About 15 Years of Interoperability Efforts. In: D-Lib Magazine 21 (11/12). https://doi.org/10.1045/november2015-vandesompel

Warner, Simeon (2001): Exposing and Harvesting Metadata Using the OAI Metadata Harvesting Protocol. A Tutorial. In: High Energy Physics Libraries Webzine 4. https://webzine.web.cern.ch/4/papers/3/ (abgerufen am 12.01.2022)

Herbert Hrachovec ist ao. Univ.-Prof. i.R. an der Universität Wien. Lehraufträge für Technik- und Medienphilosophie. Publikationen aus Analytischer Philosophie, Ästhetik, Medienphilosophie und Metaphysik. http://hrachovec.philo.at

Anwendungsfelder

Anna Bellotto, Cristiana Bettella, Linda Cappellato,
Yuri Carrer, Giulio Turetta

Modelling (Meta)Data in a Digital Repository

Methodological Tips in Practice

Handbuch Repositorienmanagement, Hg. v. Blumesberger et al., 2024, S. 135–161
https://doi.org/10.25364/97839033742329

Anna Bellotto | ORCID iD: 0000-0003-1148-5456
Cristiana Bettella, University of Padua, Library Centre | ORCID iD: 0000-0001-5268-9522
Linda Cappellato, University of Padua, Library Centre | ORCID iD: 0000-0002-8649-4691
Yuri Carrer, University of Padua, Library Centre | ORCID iD: 0000-0002-1823-1646
Giulio Turetta, University of Padua, Library Centre | ORCID iD: 0000-0002-5430-6852

Abstract

Metadata play an essential role in making a digital object discoverable, accessible, usable, and interpretable. By adopting the conflation of data and metadata in the expression (meta)data modelling, the key aim of the contribution is to properly highlight the multi-layer dimension of the descriptive representation levels informed by a digital object, showing how this constitutes the foundational basis on which a (meta)data model is grounded. The contribution offers insights into the essential principles of shaping a (meta)data model, their applicability and interoperability challenges, with the aim to serve as an entry point for anyone interested in the field looking for good practices.

Keywords: (Meta)data modelling; digital object; FAIRness; metadata standards; interoperability; metadata application profile

Zusammenfassung

Modellierung von (Meta)Daten in einem digitalen Repository. Methodische Tipps für die Praxis

Metadaten spielen eine wesentliche Rolle dabei, ein digitales Objekt auffindbar, zugänglich, nutzbar und interpretierbar zu machen. Durch die Verschmelzung von Daten und Metadaten im Begriff der (Meta-)Datenmodellierung besteht das Hauptziel des Beitrags darin, die mehrschichtige Dimension der beschreibenden Repräsentationsebenen eines digitalen Objekts angemessen hervorzuheben und zu zeigen, wie diese die grundlegende Basis für ein (Meta-)Datenmodell bildet. Der Beitrag bietet Einblicke in die wesentlichen Prinzipien der Gestaltung eines (Meta-)Datenmodells, ihre Anwendbarkeit und die Herausforderungen der Interoperabilität, mit dem Ziel, als Einstiegspunkt für jeden zu dienen, der sich für dieses Gebiet interessiert und nach bewährten Verfahren sucht.

Schlagwörter: Metadaten; Datenmodellierung; Digitales Objekt; FAIRness; Metadatenstandards; Interoperabilität; Metadaten-Anwendungsprofil

1. Introduction

The theoretical and methodological decisions in modelling (meta)data lay the foundation of a digital repository while involving a substantial, and often challenging, combination of critical thinking, domain expertise, computational knowledge, user requirements, and therefore an evaluation of several heterogeneous aspects. The present contribution is a step towards this vast landscape by offering a holistic but practice-driven overview of what is meant by (meta)data modelling, delineating complementary benefits and complexities that may arise.

The reader will be accompanied through a hands-on agenda that reflects the key areas of the process of creating, implementing, managing, evaluating and disseminating (meta)data in digital repositories. The contribution opens with a preliminary orientation on basic concepts and definitions aiming to frame the discourse on common ground. Following this contextual introduction, the text then leads to an analytical exploration of the first topics of crucial priority: which theoretical decisions need to be made when defining a (meta)data model; to what extent the descriptive representation of data determines the richness of metadata; and which practical steps its implementation entails. The paper will raise awareness of existing methodological approaches, the primary role of community standards and the identification of the designated community. Simultaneously, it will seek to anchor a deep understanding of the model as a binomial of syntax and semantics, meant, on the one hand, as the language and structure of the model, or the design model tout court; on the other hand, as the capacity of formal representation provided by the model itself. Another section of the paper covers the central topics of interoperability and FAIRness of both human- and machine-actionable (meta)data. It will be shown how these principles have direct and profound relevance to the accessibility, quality, and discoverability of a digital repository while offering the concurrent benefit of enhancing its trustworthiness. Finally, the significance of tools and practices will be discussed by presenting specific examples of their use in order to efficiently and systematically analyse and evaluate the quality of the outcomes.

Placed within the layered but interrelated framework of digital repository management, this contribution will offer insights into the essential principles of shaping a (meta)data model, their applicability and technical challenges, with the aim to serve as an entry point for anyone interested in the field looking for good practices.

2. “Setting the stage”[1]

Metadata plays an essential role in making a digital object discoverable, accessible, usable, and interpretable. According to Berg-Cross, Ritz, and Wittenburg, if a digital object is defined as a complex entity that is “represented by a bitstream, is referenced and identified by a persistent identifier and has properties that are described by metadata”, metadata “contains descriptive, contextual and provenance assertions about the properties of a digital object”[2]. By adopting the conflation of data and metadata in the expression (meta)data modelling, the multi-layer dimension of the descriptive representation levels informed by a digital object is properly highlighted, showing how this constitutes the foundational basis of a (meta)data model.

So what do we mean by (meta)data modelling and what is its context? Borrowing the definition offered by Flanders and Jannidis, we could state that “data modeling refers to the activity of designing a model of some real (or fictional) world segment to fulfill a specific set of user requirements using one or more of the metamodels available in order to make some aspects of the data computable and to enable consistency constraints”[3]. The next few paragraphs will attempt to dissect the cornerstones of the modelling process wholly encompassed in this definition, providing a foundational overview of what is considered one of the research practices at the heart of the Digital Humanities, and in a broader sense of the Digital Scholarship tout court[4].

In an integrated view that combines the “two cultures”[5] of humanities – here, philosophy and formal logic – and science – here, database design and software engineering –, data modelling emerges as an intellectual and computational activity, pushing towards what Willard McCarty claims to be a “Philosophy of modelling”:

> the manipulatory essence of modelling, with its connotation of embodied action, physically or metaphorically; the mediating role and ternary relationship modelling establishes between knower and known; the directed, vector-like engagement of the inquirer’s attention, through the model he or she has made to the object of study; and the model’s consequent function as an artificial agent of perception and instrument of thought[6].

---

1 Gilliland, A. J. (2016)
2 Berg-Cross,G.; Ritz, R.; Wittenburg, P. (2015). For a further discussion on the concept of Digital Object, see below, p. 6f.
3 Flanders, J.; Jannidis, F. (2015), p. 15.
4 Ciula, A.; Eide, Ø.; Marras, C.; Sahle, P. (2018), pp. 7–29.
5 Snow, C. P. (1959)
6 McCarty, W. (2005), p. 55.

At its first step, as stated by Eide and Ore[7], the development of a data model cannot preclude an ontological analysis of the field or objects we are intended to describe in the digital realm. Within this context, the usage of the word "modelling" refers to the identification and description of the entities that form the part of the world a modeller is modelling, along with their relevant properties as well as their relationships[8].

On the one hand, this operation necessarily involves a substantial level of subjectivity. A model does not have the purpose of being a copy of the object it represents, capturing all the features it may depict[9]. Rather, it should just select the ones that are considered relevant, allowing "questions about the one [the object] to be answered by examining the other [the model]"[10]. The act of selection and implicit reduction inherently holds both the modeller's point of view and assumptions about that universe of discourse, as well as the intended usage of the objects being represented. Indeed, when modelling has a utilitarian as opposed to a pedagogical or self-reflexive goal[11], the most significant aspect that impacts the complexity and richness of the data model is its function[12]. The discussion around this factor will be unfolded below by illustrating the two main types of approaches – curation-driven as opposed to research-driven – arising from the different digitization communities.

On the other hand, by considering the dimensions of "adequacy" and "robustness", the task of modelling may still embed a form of objectivity. "Modeling does not simply mirror an external reality" – Jannidis and Flanders[13] comment – "but is an active process that depends on the social construction of a segment of the world". Having "a body of pre-existence knowledge" in common with their specific community of reference[14], modellers have the possibility to operate a negotiation of meaning between their own interpretations and the expectations of the community of peers. Aligning project-specific models with the community's understanding through the use of standard reference models, models can overcome the mere private context and reach mutual agreement and social consensus, while potentially

7 Eide, Ø.; Smith Ore, C.-E. (2019), p. 184.
8 Flanders, J.; Jannidis, F. (2019b), p. 28, p. 82.
9 Flanders, J.; Jannidis, F. (2019b) p. 28.
10 Sperberg-McQueen, C. M. (2019), note 8, p. 286.
11 Sperberg-McQueen, C. M. (2019), note 10, p. 286.
12 Flanders, J.; Jannidis, F. (2019b), p. 84.
13 Flanders, J.; Jannidis, F. (2019b), p. 90.
14 Pierazzo, E. (2019), p. 129.

successfully performing also across diverse settings and applications[15]. The relevance of standardisation in the realm of data modelling is another main topic that the following section will examine.

A conceptual model per se, however, cannot be treated and processed by a computer without first further operations. The features of the observed reality and its assumptions need to be formally and explicitly specified in a language that could be understood not only by humans but also by machines. At this subsequent stage of the developmental workflow, the word modelling enters the sphere of the technical implementation.

The codification of the abstract model in a machine-readable and actionable form distinguishes two levels of analysis to which two components of formal data modelling correspond: the metamodel and the data model. The metamodel refers to the formally defined syntax selected as an encoding format for the model representation. This syntax works as an organisational construct for the data structure, informing about the relationships and the information properties entities can hold, such as "hierarchy, inheritance, one-to-one vs. many-to-one relationships, cyclicality, nesting, sequencing, and so forth"[16]. The most widely used metamodels are the relational models used in database systems, the eXtensible Markup Language (XML) and the Resource Description Framework (RDF). All three model information in a different way: a relational database structures it as a table, XML as a tree, and RDF as a graph[17]. At this layer of analysis, formats and encodings serve as technical agreements that influence the potential exchange and reuse of data represented by the model. Their differences across multiple systems bear pivotal responsibility towards interoperability issues: as stressed by Zeng, "[w]ithout syntactic interoperability, data and information cannot be handled properly [...]"[18].

At the next level, independent of any encoding syntax selected at the layer below[19], the data model – also called schema – is the machine-processable translation of the ontological representation of the universe of discourse[20]. In these terms, a data model is a set of rules and constraints that express information about which data elements the modelled object is allowed or required to include, which attributes each element can have, how they must be ordered and how many times they can

15 Flanders, J.; Jannidis, F. (2019b), note 8, p. 90.
16 Flanders, J.; Jannidis, F. (2019a), p. 322.
17 Riley, J. (2017)
18 Zeng, M. L. (2019a), pp. 122–146.
19 Zeng, M. L. (2019b), note 18.
20 Tomasi, F. (2018), pp. 170-179.

appear, while concurrently providing data typing information[21]. The reference to community standards at this tier greatly benefits its corresponding layer of interoperability – i.e. the "structural layer" – illustrated by Zeng[22].

Within the paradigm of digital repositories, along with the key principles of data modelling, a clear understanding of the meaning of the concept of Digital Object (DO) should be offered to the reader. Digital objects, at a level of abstraction, can be considered as artefacts, encapsulating and virtualizing atomic elements that afford the online distribution of digital assets in terms of storage, dissemination, management, exchange and reuse. Starting from the seminal conceptualization given by Robert Kahn and Robert Wilensky in 1995's A framework for distributed digital object services, where the authors formally define a digital object as

> an instance of an abstract data type that has two components, data and key-metadata. The data is typed [...]. The key-metadata includes a handle, i.e., an identifier globally unique to the digital object; it may also include other metadata, to be specified[23],

we have been witnessing the evolution of the concept towards what the FAIR Digital Object Forum calls now "[a] technical essence of a 'thing' in cyberspace" binding "all critical information about an entity in one place and creat[ing] a new kind of actionable, meaningful and technology independent object that pervades every aspect of life today"[24]. A FAIR digital object (FDO), according to the technical definition[25], is therefore

> a unit composed of data that is a sequence of bits, or a set of sequences of bits, each of the sequences being structured (typed) in a way that is interpretable by one or more computer systems, and having as essential elements an assigned globally unique and persistent identifier (PID), a type definition for the object as a whole and a metadata description (which itself can be another FAIR digital object) of the properties of the object, making the whole findable, accessible, interoperable and reusable both by humans and computers for the reliable interpretation and processing of the data represented by the object[26].

21 Flanders, J.; Jannidis, F. (2019a), note 16, p. 328; note 17, p. 16.
22 Zeng, M. L. (2019b), note 18.
23 Kahn, R.; Wilensky, R. (2006), pp. 115–123.
24 https://fairdo.org/, where FAIR stands for Findable, Accessible, Interoperable, and Reusable.
25 https://fairdo.org/library/
26 Within the context of the Reference Model for an Open Archival Information System (OAIS), it might also be worth mentioning, it is the information object that yields the information represented by the data object – either a physical and a digital object as well –, and it is properly the

3. Transitioning from one generation to another

Digital innovations that occurred in the past few decades are exerting pressure on institutions to pursue their transition "to the next generation of metadata"[27]. Changes in standards, infrastructures and tools are having an impact on the way metadata are modelled and created, pushing forward a semantic evolution of the concept of metadata to Linked Open Data[28]. The outline of this current framework and its evolving modelling practices will be the topic of the next few paragraphs.

According to the Organization for the Advancement of Structured Information Standards (OASIS), a reference model is "an abstract framework for understanding significant relationships among the entities of some environment, and for the development of consistent standards or specifications supporting that environment"[29]. In other words, a reference model represents a conceptual formalisation of a certain domain of knowledge, providing a common semantics that can be used unambiguously across and between different implementations[30]. As stressed already, a data model informs the design, as well as the conceptual structure of the data, from the double point of view of the syntax and the semantics assumed with respect to the reference information context. The degree of openness of a data model is expressed through the inherent capacity of being adaptable to different information contexts, and for information purposes and needs that might be diverse and unpredictable in principle. "By nature", Willard McCarty explains, "modelling defines a ternary relationship in which it mediates epistemologically, between modeller and modelled, between researcher and data or between theory and

---

knowledge representation of data content which the information system must guarantee to preserve, hence "data" provide "[a] reinterpretable representation of information in a formalized manner suitable for communication, interpretation, or processing" (CCSDS 650.0-M-2, 2012, p. 10 and ISO 14721:2012: Space data and information transfer systems – Open archival information system (OAIS). Geneva, ISO 2012). Examples of data include a sequence of bits, a table of numbers, the characters on a page, the recording of sounds made by a person speaking, or a moon rock specimen. OAIS identifies four parts to the digital object, i.e. an object composed of a set of bit sequence, described by them as the information package. These are the content information and the preservation description information, which are packaged together with packaging information, and which is discoverable by virtue of the descriptive information.

27 Smith-Yoshimura, K. (2020); Bahnemann, G.; Carroll, M.; Clough, P. et al (2021). Both reports served as background reading and inspiration for the eight virtual round table discussions promoted by OCLC Research, and held in six different European languages, throughout the month of March 2021. "How do we make the transition to the next generation of metadata happen at the right scale and in a sustainable manner, building an interconnected ecosystem, not a garden of silos?" was the primary question to lead the whole discussion among participants. An overview of the discussion series, accompanied by summary reports and recordings, is available from https://www.oclc.org/go/en/events/next-generation-of-metadata.html

28 Bellotto, A.; Bettella, C. (2019), pp. 167-184.

29 ISO 14721:2012, note 26.

30 Bekiari, C.; Bruseker, G.; Doerr, M. et al. (2021). Riva, P.; Le Bœuf, P.; Žumer, M. (2017).

the world"[31]. Hence, following Jannidis and Flanders[32], modelling data might be characterised by two main approaches: the curation-driven approach "which emphasizes the open-ended usefulness of the data", and the research-driven approach "where data is being created to support the creator's own research needs", both affecting and affected by the semantic extent from which the data model seeks to be elicited through the manipulative, iterative, and interactive process of modelling.

Such adaptive compliance – between modeller and model, and between data modeller and data model – defines the edge of the so-called data profile[33], by establishing a set of rules and constraints that should be declared into a documented schema, and certified by the adoption of community standards[34]. In these terms, a data profile formally translates the reference model into a (meta)data specification, becoming as such potentially applicable to other information contexts and for other information purposes, enabling the meaningful information integration and exchange. It acts as a Metadata Application Profile (abridged MAP) – the notion of which has been coined by the Dublin Core Community in 2000[35]: "a metadata design specification that uses a selection of terms from multiple metadata vocabularies, with added constraints, to meet application-specific requirements"[36]. Sliding over

31 McCarty, W. (2005), note 6, p. 24.

32 Flanders, J.; Jannidis, F. (2019b), note 8, p. 86.

33 "A profile identifies a set of base standards, together with appropriate options and parameters necessary to accomplish identified functions for purposes including: (a) interoperability, and (b) methodology for referencing the various uses of the base standards, meaningful both to users and suppliers" (ISO/IEC TR 10000-1:1998, quoted at https://www.loc.gov/z3950/agency/profiles/about.html by the Library of Congress, designated as Maintenance Agency and Registration Authority for ANSI/NISO Standard Z39.50 and ISO 23950:1998).

34 By way of example, and partially drawn from the typology of metadata standards outlined by Anne J. Gilliland (Gilliland: Setting the Stage (Note 1), based on the classification by Karim Boughida, 2005), we can distinguish: standards related to data structure, e.g.: MARC/BIBFRAME, Dublin Core Metadata Elements Set, MODS, VRA Core, EAD, TEI; to data content, e.g.: AACR2, RDA; to data value, e.g.: semantic artefacts such as subjects, classifications, thesauri, controlled vocabularies, ontologies; or standards for data exchange, e.g.: ISO 2709-2008, MARCXML, RDF, JSON-LD. A Metadata Standards Catalog applicable to scientific data, and maintained by the RDA Metadata Standards Catalog (MSC) Working Group, is available from https://rdamsc.bath.ac.uk/. For a graphic representation of the metadata landscape, it is well worth citing Riley, Jenn (2010): Seeing Standards. A Visualization of the Metadata Universe. Graphic design funded by the Indiana University Libraries White Professional Development Award: http://www.jennriley.com/metadatamap.

35 The coinage of MAP is by Rachel Heery and Manjula Patel, firstly introduced at the 8th Dublin Core™ workshop of October 2000 (http://www.ariadne.ac.uk/issue/25/app-profiles/). See also: Baker, Thomas (2011): Dublin Core™ Application Profiles at eleven years (2011). DCMI Blog posts: https://www.dublincore.org/blog/2011/application_profile/, and Coyle, Karen; Baker, Thomas (2013): Application Profiles as an alternative to OWL ontologies. In: DC-2013, Lisbon, Portugal.

36 https://www.dublincore.org/resources/glossary/application_profile/, ideally based on, or compatible with, vocabularies defined in RDF, and Coyle, Karen; Baker, Thomas (2009): Guidelines for Dublin Core™ Application Profiles. Dublin Core Metadata Initiative (DCMI): https://www.dublin-

the past two decades of history of data, the Program for Cooperative Cataloging (PCC) Task Group on Metadata Application Profiles has recently framed a comprehensive definition of MAP:

> A metadata application profile (MAP) is a set of recorded decisions about a shared data target for a given community. MAPs declare what models are employed (what types of entities will be described and how they relate to each other), what controlled vocabularies are used, the cardinality of fields/properties (what fields are required and which fields have a cap on the number of times they can be used), data types for string values, and guiding text/scope notes for consistent use of fields/properties. A MAP may be a multipart specification, with human-readable and machine-readable aspects, sometimes in a single file, sometimes in multiple files (e.g., a human-readable file that may include input rules, a machine-readable vocabulary, and a validation schema)[37].

From this perspective, we can argue that MAPs function as a crucial construct that performs and enhances semantic interoperability in its broadest sense[38]. Let us describe closely how this takes place in the contemporary landscape of modelling data.

Assuming that any data model is created with the goal of meeting local functional requirements, a schema that fulfils solely this necessity is usually of little use outside the specific implementation. When integration and interoperability across heterogeneous systems and applications are listed as additional targets, machine-readable meaning and context of structured data play a pivotal role. The disclosure of the intended meaning of data is what is needed by computers to decode data into knowledge and from the very beginning, computational ontologies and Linked Data technologies were conceived with this goal in mind.

Adapting it from the philosophical field to the digital environment, the computer science community started to use the term ontology to describe an engineering ar-

---

core.org/specifications/dublin-core/profile-guidelines/. It is worth mentioning at least the Europeana Data Model (EDM): https://pro.europeana.eu/page/edm-documentation (retrieved 07.01.2022), on which it is based the Metadata Application Profile of the Digital Public Library of America: https://pro.dp.la/hubs/metadata-application-profile (retrieved 07.01.2022); the DCAT Application Profile for Data Portals in Europe, based on the specification of the Data Catalog Vocabulary (DCAT) of 16 January 2014 and the Data Catalog Vocabulary (DCAT) – Version 2, W3C Recommendation, 04 February 2020: https://joinup.ec.europa.eu/solution/dcat-application-profile-data-portals-europe. Linked Art based on CIDOC CRM: https://linked.art/

37 https://www.loc.gov/aba/pcc/taskgroup/Metadata-Application-Profiles.html

38 Zeng, M. L. (2019b), note 18.

tefact, which can be defined as a "formal, explicit specification of a shared conceptualisation"[39]. This specification commonly takes the form of a set of classes and properties representing concepts and relationships of that piece of the world, expressed through logical axioms usually based on the so-called Description Logics, i.e. a formal language for the knowledge representation that gives the capability of deducing new information from an explicated group of data[40]. As stressed by Eide and Ore, although there is sometimes some fuzziness when discussing models of the real world versus implementations of these models, ontologies should denote "a special kind of data model dealing with formalized conceptualizations rather than implementation issues"[41].

Thanks to their nature, ontologies have played a fundamental role in the development of the Semantic Web, an extension of the World Wide Web able to automatically read and process data and information without human intervention[42]. Providing context, i.e. a clearly expressed description of concepts, terms, and relationships within a knowledge domain, and serving as sources of shared meaning, ontologies affirmed their main significance towards this goal. Alongside, the new extension of the Web needed a set of established standards and technologies - what the term Linked Data collectively refers to - to create relationships among different datasets and formally explain to computers how to access and associate information[43]. Key standards for encoding and connecting data are the Resource Description Framework (RDF)[44], Web Ontology Language (OWL)[45] and Simple Knowledge Organization System (SKOS)[46], while Simple Protocol And RDF Query Language (SPARQL)[47] is the most used language to query and retrieve data.

---

39 Studer, R.; Benjamins, R. V.; Fensel, D. (1998), pp. 161-198. p. 184. For a detailed account of the notions of "conceptualization" and explicit "specification" according to Gruber's definition of ontology (Gruber, Thomas R. (1993): A translation approach to portable ontology specifications. In: Knowledge Acquisition 5 (2), pp. 199–220), while discussing the importance of *shared* explicit specifications introduced by Borst (Borst, Willen Nico (1997): Construction of Engineering Ontologies, PhD thesis, Institute for Telematica and Information Technology, University of Twente, Enschede, The Netherlands), see: Guarino, Nicola; Oberle, Daniel; Staab, Steffen (2009): What Is an Ontology? In: Staab, S.; Studer, R. (2009).

40 Biagetti, M. T. (2016), pp. 49–50.

41 Eide, Ø.; Ore, S. (2019), note 7, p. 182.

42 Berners-Lee, T.; Hendler, J.; Lassila, O. (2001)

43 https://www.w3.org/standards/semanticweb/data. Yoose, B.; Perkins, J. (2013), pp. 197-211.

44 https://www.w3.org/TR/rdf11-concepts/

45 https://www.w3.org/TR/owl2-overview/

46 https://www.w3.org/TR/skos-reference/

47 https://www.w3.org/TR/sparql11-query/

Given the possible outcomes of the use of Linked Data technologies, such as powerful data sharing and integration, efficient communication and meaningful information discovery, many repositories are currently investing time and efforts in the process of semantic enrichment, i.e. a procedure which consists in providing metadata of "more contextualized meanings" by expressing various types of relationship[48].

On the one hand, RDF gives the possibility to uncover the semantics of the data model by providing shareable and machine-processable definitions of metadata elements. Expressing information through the use of assertions called statements[49], the RDF format would require the components of a triple to be unambiguously identified through unique identifiers (URIs). In this context, using URIs that refer to external formal ontologies created by discipline-specific communities – to cite some examples: BIBFRAME[50] (for library resources), CIDOC CRM[51] (for cultural heritage data) or FRAPO[52] (for research project administrative information) – or developed with more general purposes – such as DCMI Metadata Terms[53] or Schema.org[54] –, is the key to enable computers to identify what the URI is and to understand the concept the metadata field refers to. The vast range of options that modellers deal with when selecting ontologies for the local data model requires a careful examination of the assumptions and agreements left implicit in the preliminary ontological analysis.

On the other hand, the link to thesauri, controlled vocabularies and classification schemes that adhere to the principles of Linked Open Data and are expressed in a standardised formal language (such as SKOS) allow metadata values populating the local datasets to gain substantial benefits. Namely, these are a more efficient interlinking with heterogeneous external resources described with the same concepts, an increased visibility and accessibility, and a potential supplementation of (multilingual) information, such as translated labels or broader labels. The use of standardised URI-values coming from authoritative and well-established LOD reference resources[55] – such as the Art & Architecture Thesaurus (AAT) by The Getty Research

48 Zeng, M. L. (2019b), p. 7.
49 In RDF each statement takes the form of a triple made of three elements: subject, i.e. the thing that is described; predicate, i.e. the property, attribute or relationship that is attributed to that thing in order to describe it; object, i.e. the value of that property.
50 https://www.loc.gov/bibframe/
51 https://www.cidoc-crm.org/Version/version-7.1.1
52 Shotton, D. (2017)
53 https://www.dublincore.org/specifications/dublin-core/dcmi-terms/
54 https://schema.org/
55 https://id.loc.gov/

Institute[56] or the Resource Type vocabulary by COAR[57] – facilitate semantic interoperability, assuring that the meaning of the language and terminology used is correctly understood. As for the choice of ontologies illustrated before, the selection of the targets for the semantic enrichment at the value metadata level is far from trivial. It requires "a good knowledge of the source data in terms of topic coverage, gaps, quality issues" as well as a rigorous analysis to assure a matching granularity and coverage between sources and targets[58].

4. Metadata as a FAIR enabler

Metadata is key when dealing with the interoperability of digital objects managed, curated and archived in a repository. The data model of the digital repository should consider from the outset what characteristics of the metadata elements are necessary for effective interoperability. The semantics of the data model plays a fundamental role in ensuring the interoperability of digital assets so that they can be shared and reused by the user community.

Semantic interoperability "ensures that the precise format and meaning of exchanged data and information is preserved and understood throughout exchanges between parties, in other words 'what is sent is what is understood'"[59] and can be defined as "the ability of computer systems to transmit data with unambiguous, shared meaning. Semantic interoperability is a requirement to enable machine computable logic, inferencing, knowledge discovery, and data federation between information systems"[60].

Semantic networks[61] – a network of semantic relations – are the lowest common level of strong semantic interoperability. Well-known thesauri can be used to achieve basic semantic interoperability[62]. Machine-actionability further strengthens interoperability allowing to query and aggregate relations from existing semantic networks, thus improving or even creating novel networks. According to this framework, adherence to community-driven standards enables a robust representation of domain-relevant data and metadata.

56 https://www.getty.edu/research/tools/vocabularies/aat/
57 https://vocabularies.coar-repositories.org/resource_types/
58 https://pro.europeana.eu/page/europeana-semantic-enrichment
59 https://joinup.ec.europa.eu/collection/nifo-national-interoperability-framework-observatory/glossary/term/semantic-interoperability
60 Corcho, O.; Eriksson, M.; Kurowski, K. et al. (2021).
61 Pirnay-Dummer, P.; Ifenthaler, D.; Seel, N. M. (2012).
62 Hugo, W.; Le Franc, Y.; Coen, G. (2020), p. 14.

An advantageous and operative strategy to enable semantic interoperability in the context of digital repositories is the uptake of FAIR principles for data and metadata management, first introduced in the article The FAIR Guiding Principles for scientific data management and stewardship[63] in 2016. The FAIR principles consist of 15 high-level principles[64], providing guidelines to improve the findability, accessibility, interoperability and reuse of digital assets. Data and metadata can hardly be separated from each other when dealing with FAIR guidelines, although some principles state specifically what characteristics metadata should hold to be considered FAIR. As an example, Principle F3, which concerns the findability of data, states that metadata must explicitly mention the global and persistent identifier assigned to the described data. Therefore, if the data is assigned a DOI, Handle, or ARK identifier[65], the identifier must be encoded in the metadata. Letter I of the FAIR principles targets the interoperability of digital assets, and hence metadata plays a substantial role in it. The three principles involved are:

1. (Meta)data use a formal, accessible, shared, and broadly applicable language for knowledge representation
2. (Meta)data use vocabularies that follow the FAIR principles
3. (Meta)data include qualified references to other (meta)data

Principle I1 states that the knowledge representation language of the metadata must be readable by humans and machines. To ensure machine readability, the RDF knowledge representation model and at least a subset of RDF serialisation formats, namely Turtle, RDF/XML, and Javascript Object Notation for Linked Data (JSON-LD) should be utilised. Principle I2 concerns the findability and documentation of Knowledge Organization Systems (KOS) used by the data model of the digital repository. The BARTOC.org registry[66], a database of KOS resources, is a well-established and reliable resource for finding FAIR vocabularies and ontologies. Finally, Principle I3 prescribes the use of qualified relationships in the digital repository. Relationships must be captured in the metadata so that meaningful links between digital objects (or parts of the objects) can be established. The more specific the meaning of the relationships, the greater the interoperability of the related digital assets. Suitably qualified relationships may come from general-purpose metadata schemas – such as the DCMI Metadata Terms isPartOf relationship – or discipline-specific ontologies – such as the Europeana Data Model has Type relationship.

---

63 Wilkinson, M. D.; Dumontier, M.; Aalbersberg, I. J. et al. (2016).

64 https://www.go-fair.org/fair-principles/

65 The Library of Congress maintains the Standard Identifier Schemes list at https://id.loc.gov/vocabulary/identifiers.html

66 https://bartoc.org/

When considering the adoption of FAIR principles, it should be clear from the start who the designated community of the digital repository is. According to the CoreTrustSeal glossary[67], the designated community is

> an identified group of potential consumers who should be able to understand a particular set of information. The designated community may be composed of multiple user communities. A designated community is defined by the repository and this definition may change over time.

Namely, the designated community for a disciplinary research data repository consists of researchers, students, and scholars who interact with the repository (e.g. by depositing a dataset or making use of the data) or the end user of the data, or someone who should be able to use the data applying disciplinary standards.

Adhering to the FAIR principles also means understanding the level of FAIRness the digital repository aims to achieve. The FAIRness of a digital object can be defined as the measure of the extent to which the object is FAIR. A possible way to achieve the desired FAIRness level is by adopting the FAIR principles incrementally: the most useful and straightforward principles (concerning the repository needs) should be taken into account first. Identifying digital objects using globally unique and persistent identifiers (Principle F1) could be a starting point. Furthermore, recording repository details on re3data.org[68] and FAIRsharing.org[69] registries of data repositories and indexing the metadata of the objects in discovery tools such as OpenAIRE Explore[70] (Principle F4) are low-effort tasks that can improve the findability of digital objects and help pinpoint the strengths and weaknesses of the repository. Principle F4 could also include the use of custom search engines for FAIR datasets[71] and tools for FAIR metadata to be “presented on the Web”[72]. The I (Interoperability) subset of the principles can be addressed by exposing metadata elements through metadata crosswalks. Schema.org metadata schema for structured data could be a possible choice to ensure improvements in the interoperability of digital assets without modifying the underlying data model of the repository. To this end, a subset of entities and relationships, serialised as JSON-LD, from the Schema.org vocabulary can be easily embedded in the HTML source code of the landing page of the digital object. The subsequent and more challenging step would

67 CoreTrustSeal Standards and Certification Board (2022)
68 https://doi.org/10.17616/R3D
69 Sansone, S. A.; McQuilton, P.; Rocca-Serra, P. et al. (2019), pp. 358-367.
70 https://explore.openaire.eu/
71 https://www.dtls.nl/fair-data/find-fair-data-tools/
72 https://www.fairdatapoint.org/

be to design the repository data model using a comprehensive RDF representation of the metadata of the digital assets.

Several initiatives and projects have been initiated among the stakeholder community since the publication of the FAIR guiding principles. GO FAIR[73] is one of them. GO FAIR is an initiative that aims to promote the implementation of FAIR principles and the coherent development of a network of FAIR services. GO FAIR also proposes technical solutions for metadata that are not natively FAIR: metadata can undergo a FAIRification process[74] by means of FAIRification tools[75], or they can be exposed on FAIR Data Points[76]. A digital repository data model that needs to maintain backward compatibility with legacy metadata can consequently become FAIR without losing any previous feature.

To evaluate progress in adopting FAIR principles, the use of metrics and assessment tools should be considered. For this purpose, the FAIRsFAIR project[77] has developed the FAIRsFAIR Data Object Assessment Metrics and two practical tools, FAIR-Aware and F-UJI[78]. It is worth noting that the FAIRsFAIR object metrics and tools assume the assessment of research data objects as a subset of the possible digital objects that a repository can manage; therefore, the results of the assessment should be tailored to the specific use case of digital objects.

FAIR-Aware[79] is a disciplinary-agnostic self-assessment tool intended to raise awareness about FAIR principles. It consists of a questionnaire comprising ten questions provided with practical tips. Comprehensive understanding and adoption of the FAIR principles are key for the designated community; FAIR-Aware can help create a liaison between the community and the repository managers. The self-assessment tool could be included as part of the repository deposit workflow to improve data and metadata quality and user community awareness.

The FAIRsFAIR metrics are mainly drawn from the set of indicators provided by the RDA FAIR Data Maturity Model Working Group[80]. The FAIRsFAIR metrics focus on what and how these indicators can be evaluated in practice[81].

---

73 https://www.go-fair.org/
74 https://www.go-fair.org/fair-principles/fairification-process/
75 https://github.com/FAIRDataTeam/OpenRefine-metadata-extension/
76 https://www.go-fair.org/how-to-go-fair/fair-data-point/
77 https://fairsfair.eu/
78 Devaraju, A.; Mokrane, M.; Cepinskas, L. et al. (2021), pp. 1-14.
79 https://fairsfair.eu/fair-aware
80 RDA FAIR Data Maturity Model Working Group (2020)
81 Devaraju, A.; Mokrane, M.; Cepinskas, L. et al. (2021), note 78.

F-UJI[82] is an automated assessment tool for programmatically assessing published digital objects for their level of FAIRness. Provided an identifier of the object, the tool performs practical tests on the FAIRsFAIR Data Object Assessment Metrics. As an example, to check compliance with Principle I3 involving the FsF-I3-01M metric, F-UJI performs the following tests:

- Related resources are explicitly mentioned in the metadata
- Related resources are indicated by machine-readable links or identifiers

The first test succeeds if at least one relationship is found in the metadata. For instance, the test checks whether the is Part Of relationship, which might state that an object belongs to a collection of objects, is listed in the object metadata. The second test checks if the identifier of the related resource points to the resource through a resolvable URI. F-UJI allows one to set up an iterative workflow to incrementally adopt the FAIR principles by using the tool to test the improvements made to the repository data model after every implementation step.

In the process of adopting the FAIR principles, the foundational elements of knowledge representation in the Semantic Web and Linked Data landscape come into play, namely RDF and triples, especially when interoperability, FAIRness, and long-term preservation are the main objectives. RDF is a way to represent the world using triples that comprise a subject, a predicate, and an object. Asserting that 'Beethoven is the author of the Ninth Symphony', a suitable triple could be:

- Subject: the Symphony No. 9
- Predicate: has author
- Object: Beethoven

This approach is formal enough for a consistent representation of knowledge[83]. Once a set of triples is created, an RDF graph is generated. The graph consists of subjects and objects of the triples as vertices and predicates as edges. This kind of graph is known as the graph of knowledge. Metadata and relationships become triples as well. Furthermore, controlled vocabularies, ontologies, and classification schemes can be represented as triples.

A knowledge graph does not offer by itself a way to query it or retrieve data from it. To query a knowledge graph, the SPARQL query language is needed. SPARQL is a semantic query language that can be used by humans and automated agents to query a SPARQL endpoint. For example, if a 'title' property exists in the metadata of a digital object – i.e. the 'has title' predicate of an RDF triple – the endpoint can

82 Devaraju, A.; Huber, R. (2021)
83 Oldman, D.; Doerr, M.; Gradmann, S. (2016)

be queried for that metadata element using an SQL-like syntax. More complex queries can be built, for instance, to list the titles of objects belonging to a collection or to find the depositors of a set of objects alongside the number of objects they have deposited. The repository should provide a public SPARQL endpoint for querying the metadata elements that describe the digital assets. A well-known example of a public SPARQL endpoint is the Wikidata Query Service[84].

RDF is suitable for exposing metadata of digital objects as well as for their internal representation by the Digital Asset Management System (DAMS)[85] of the repository. Metadata are internally represented as documents, usually stored in RDF/XML or JSON-LD serialisation formats. The DAMS transforms the metadata elements into RDF triples, usually stored in a database. These triples can then be indexed by search engine software[86] for internal repository functionality or external uses that could comprise end-user searches and queries by agents on machine-readable endpoints.

As the internal representation of metadata may not be unique, repositories should support bulk uploads of digital objects, data manipulation tasks, and external data services queries on common ground. Therefore, repositories should develop an Application Programming Interface (API). An HTTP REST API[87] uses the HTTP protocol to send data to or retrieve data from the repository, enabling a simple interface to exchange and operate the data in the repository. It is best practice to detail the support level (timespan, rate limits) for each published version of the API specifications and the standards being implemented. The URL of the API endpoint should also be recorded on the aforementioned public repository registries. API responses return metadata depending on the metadata serialisation formats available in the repository. XML and JSON are commonly used formats that ensure a high degree of interoperability. A repository that models metadata following RDF specifications could benefit from exposing metadata in the JSON-LD format, an RDF serialisation format that encodes linked data by means of the JSON format. A reliable repository API can enhance the confidence of the designated community in the repository and increase the use and reuse of digital assets by external data services.

---

84 https://query.wikidata.org/. Several example queries can be found at https://www.wikidata.org/wiki/Wikidata:SPARQL_query_service/queries/examples

85 Fedora is a DAMS platform commonly utilised by digital repositories. Fedora documentation can be found at https://duraspace.org/fedora/

86 Digital repositories often use Solr https://solr.apache.org/ or ElasticSearch https://www.elastic.co/elasticsearch/ as search engine software

87 https://csrc.nist.gov/glossary/term/rest

Generally, digital assets stored in a repository must remain unchanged for a prolonged period of time to ensure long-term preservation. Metadata again comes into play in the form of an integrity check indicator. These metadata values are not usually disclosed to end users, but doing so can improve the trustworthiness of the repository. A nearly effortless approach is to compute a fingerprint of the data and metadata of the digital object in the form of short sequences of alphanumeric characters using Message-Digest 5 (MD5) checksums. The result of the computation is 32-character sequences that uniquely represent the content of the data and metadata. The computed fingerprint is stored and recomputed when users modify the metadata[88]. Whenever something unexpected occurs to the data or metadata, the recomputed checksums will differ from the stored ones. Secure Hash Algorithm (SHA) is a more advanced hash algorithm and a common alternative to the MD5 algorithm, but can serve the same purpose. An automated procedure should be set up to periodically check if data and metadata undergo any unexpected change by recalculating the checksums and comparing them to the stored ones. As periodic recalculation might be computationally expensive, especially when a large number of objects are involved, the procedure can be scheduled weekly or monthly or even performed offline on data backups. A digital repository should choose the best approach for its use case, but managing integrity check metadata is a cornerstone to ensure the long-term preservation and reliability of archived data and metadata.

5. Quality of metadata

Metadata quality is a fundamental aspect of a digital repository, but it is not so simple to deal with it since no general consensus has been reached on 'what metadata quality is': it is a multidimensional and context-specific concept[89], so it is not possible to provide universally valid indications on how to manage metadata quality. An efficient metadata quality control is essential to realise a good repository. It helps to ensure the ease of finding the desired objects, user satisfaction, data interoperability, and increase the possibility of data sharing and reuse. The presence of quality metadata, in fact, allows the user to find digital objects that respond correctly to his request, to interpret them, to understand their context and consequently to reuse the data.

Metadata errors are more common than one might think. For this reason, it is necessary to provide control and verification systems and try to provide the necessary

88 The same MD5 checksum could potentially have the same value for different binary contents, but it is very rare (from a statistical point of view) that if an unexpected error occurs in the data the MD5 checksum remains the same.

89 Tani, A.; Candela, L.; Castelli, D. (2013), pp. 1194-1205.

tools to metadata creators to reduce such errors as much as possible. The errors generally concern typing or spelling mistakes, inconsistency in the formatting of dates, fields in the metadata editor that are incomplete or left blank, incorrect use of punctuation and separators, inaccuracies in the attribution of keywords and entering values in the wrong fields.

Thinking about the quality of metadata means taking into consideration different aspects, in particular: criteria for assessing the quality of metadata, quality control procedures and mechanisms to ensure quality.

The parameters that can be used to evaluate the quality of metadata are many, and each author who has dealt with this topic has identified different characteristics to be evaluated and different metrics to be used. The main ones are as follows[90]:

- Completeness: each digital object should be accompanied by all the metadata necessary to be found and correctly interpreted. There is no degree of completeness that is generally valid because it may depend on the type of resources and some choices of the repository managers.
- Accuracy: the metadata must be accurate both in terms of content and in terms of form.
- Logical consistency and coherence: this is the most difficult element to ensure, especially when several people create metadata in the same repository. Having consistent metadata within the repository means that the same value is always used to express the same concept and that each value is used with the same meaning for different objects; it also means consistently using the different fields of the metadata set, always inserting the same type of value in a given field.
- Conformance to expectations: this parameter is very strictly related to context and depends on the characteristics of the repository and of the user community.
- Timeliness
- Accessibility
- Provenance: refers to the origin of the metadata (who created them or, in case of machine-derived metadata, how they were generated)
- Shareability: it depends on the interoperability of the repository (e.g. use of standard communication protocol). For a single digital object to be shareable, it should also have consistent and complete metadata, thus providing context.

90 Park, J.-R.; Tosaka, Y. (2010), pp. 696-715. Hillmann, D. I.; Dushay, N.; Phipps, J. (2004). Tani, A.; Candela, L.; Castelli, D. (2013). McCarthy, K. (2015).

Creating good quality metadata means ensuring that they remain meaningful even outside the local context, for example, when (meta)data are shared with other repositories. Interoperability plays a fundamental role: when metadata exit from the original context, the difficulty of maintaining high metadata quality grows exponentially (the purpose can change, some information can get lost, etc.).

Quality control can take place before or after the ingest phase of the data (to also check the display of the data) and can be[91]:

Primary (by those who create the metadata, also through batch mechanisms):

- Fill in all required fields
- Filling the fields with the correct values
- Absence of typing and spelling errors
- Correct formatting, for example in the use of separators or date formats
- Secondary (by those who create the metadata or other experts):
- The ability of entered values to accurately describe digital objects
- Consistency of metadata
- Completeness

Some measures can help improve the quality of metadata. Repository staff should, for example, ensure accurate training of the staff in charge of metadata creation, provide tools for requesting support, regularly update the staff, and also carry out recurring checks and report any inaccuracies found to the creator of the metadata to avoid repetition.

Also, some tools can be useful to guarantee metadata quality, in particular:

- Clear guidelines and examples
- An intuitive metadata editor, with drop-down menus and links to thesauri, which can help improve data consistency
- Mandatory fields to ensure at least a basic completeness of metadata
- Use of widespread and well-established vocabularies, ontologies, standards, both to reach data consistency and to improve interoperability of data into the Semantic Web
- Templates and other tools that make compilation easier, for instance, tools for automatic creation of metadata and conversion scripts that transform metadata already created and checked (for example, for bibliographic catalogue) into the format required by the repository

91 UCLA Library (2015)

- Data quality checklists, to facilitate self-analysis of data quality by the creator of the metadata

Writing guidelines is especially important when there are multiple people depositing digital objects in the repository and compiling metadata. Two different people, in fact, can interpret the meaning of the fields in a slightly different way or decide to enter the same information in different fields. In addition, some formal aspects, such as the formatting of the dates or the use of separators, can differ according to the preferences and habits of those who compile (for example, a date can be expressed as 06 September 2021 or 09/06/21 or even 6th September 21). To maintain uniformity within the repository, it is therefore necessary to have a certain rigidity in the metadata editor or to provide clear indications through guidelines or contextual help. Furthermore, the existence of guidelines is an excellent reminder for those who upload digital objects only occasionally. It is much easier to create high-quality metadata from the beginning than to intervene in existing metadata to improve its quality, so it is important that tools to ensure quality and control mechanisms are planned from the beginning. To give a practical example, you can think of a repository with digital objects uploaded by several subjects, where the field to enter the keywords is a free text field. In the absence of clear indications (e.g. guidelines), we will easily have differences in the use of separators and inconsistency/incoherence in the use/meaning of terms. This situation may confuse users and represents a problem with interoperability.

Measures to clean up and harmonise pre-existing content are long and complex, they involve many manual interventions, object-by-object, and require getting in touch with formal metadata creators one by one. Additionally, some inaccuracies may get out of control and remain excluded from the corrections made.

It is much easier (and much more efficient) to design a repository with clear guidelines and practical examples, links to widespread thesauri and ontologies and 'stricter' fields to enter values (in this example, if each keyword were to be entered in a different field, there would be no problem with separators). However, providing quality tools and control mechanisms is not enough: the process of FAIRification of (meta)data, together with continuous technical improvements of the repository and of other databases related to it, implies recurring updates of the guidelines, tools and existing data. It is also necessary that the repository manager knows as much as possible about the content of the repository to ensure a rapid update of tools and workflows and to understand which objects need to be intervened with from time to time and what types of improvements are necessary. A reasoned work of metadata reconciliation should be considered to enrich metadata and improve their quality[92].

6. Final remarks

The reader has been accompanied through a hands-on agenda that reflects the key areas of the process of creating, implementing, managing, evaluating, and disseminating (meta)data in digital repositories. In this analytical exploration, the viewpoint of the model as a binomial of syntax and semantics, meant as the design model tout court and the capacity of formal representation provided by the model itself, has been stressed. Additionally, technical implementations towards the improvement of semantic interoperability and FAIRness have been described, highlighting how they can have a direct and profound relevance to the accessibility, quality and discoverability of a digital repository.

Grounded on the direct experience in managing repositories dealing with a heterogeneity of digital assets, the strategies and approaches illustrated throughout this contribution have been drawn from the acknowledgement to sharpen a needed balance between machine and human actionability in the process of modelling data. By way of practical expertise, it has also been demonstrated that the awareness of semantic interoperability, the increment of FAIRness, and the trustworthiness of data and metadata are fundamental to pave the way for meeting the requirements for repository certification. Among the various existing certifications, achieving the CoreTrustSeal[93] certification can build stakeholder trustfulness in the repository while ensuring a core-level standardisation of processes and good practices. The repository will then become a trustworthy digital repository capable of fulfilling data management mandates from national and international funding bodies.

Bibliography

Bahnemann, Greta; Carroll, Michael; Clough, Paul et al. (2021): Transforming Metadata into Linked Data to Improve Digital Collection Discoverability: A CONTENTdm Pilot Project. Dublin, OH: OCLC Research. https://doi.org/10.25333/fzcv-0851

Bekiari, Chryssoula; Bruseker, George; Doerr, Martin et al. (eds.) (2021): ISO 21127. Information and Documentation – A Reference Ontology for the Interchange of Cultural Heritage Information, Geneva: ISO 2014; ISO/IEC 21838-1:2021: Information Technology – Top-Level Ontologies (TLO) – Part 1: Requirements. Geneva: ISO 2021; ICOM/CIDOC: Definition of the CIDOC Conceptual Reference Model. Produced by the ICOM/CIDOC

92 Khalid, H.; Zimanyi, E.; Wrembel, R. (2018). Tillman, R. K. (2016). See also https://freeyourmetadata.org/reconciliation/

93 https://www.coretrustseal.org/

Documentation Standards Group, Continued by the CIDOC CRM Special Interest Group. Version 7.1.1. https://www.cidoc-crm.org/version/version-7.1.1 (retrieved 07.01.2022)

Bellotto, Anna; Bettella, Cristiana (2019): Metadata as Semantic Palimpsests. The Case of PHAIDRA@unipd. In: Manghi, Paolo; Candela, Leonardo; Silvello, Gianmaria (eds.) (2019): Digital Libraries: Supporting Open Science. IRCDL 2019. (Communications in Computer and Information Science 988). Cham: Springer, pp. 167–184. https://doi.org/10.1007/978-3-030-11226-4_14

Berg-Cross, Gary; Ritz, Raphael; Wittenburg, Peter (2015): Data Foundation and Terminology Work Group Products. https://doi.org/10.15497/06825049-8CA4-40BD-BCAF-DE9F0EA2FADF

Berners-Lee, Tim; Hendler, James; Lassila, Ora (2001): The Semantic Web. A New Form of Web Content That Is Meaningful to Computers Will Unleash a Revolution of New Possibilities. In: Scientific American 284 (5), pp. 1–5.

Biagetti, Maria Teresa (2016): An Ontological Model for the Integration of Cultural Heritage Information: CIDOC-CRM. In: JLIS.it 7 (3), pp. 49–50. http://dx.doi.org/10.4403/jlis.it-11930

Ciula, Arianna; Eide, Øyvind; Marras, Cristina et al. (2018): Modelling. Thinking in Practice. An Introduction. In: Historical Social Research, Supplement 31, pp. 7–29. https://doi.org/10.12759/hsr.suppl.31.2018.7-29. The authors have collected the results of their combined efforts to clarify the use and role of models in humanities research supported by computational methods in: Ciula, Arianna; Eide, Øyvind; Marras, Cristina et al. (2023): Modelling Between Digital and Humanities. Thinking in Practice. Cambridge: Open Book Publishers. https://doi.org/10.11647/OBP.0369

Corcho, Oscar; Eriksson, Magnus; Kurowski, Krzysztof et al. (2021): EOSC Interoperability Framework. Report from the EOSC Executive Board Working Groups FAIR and Architecture. Luxembourg: Publications of the European Union. https://data.europa.eu/doi/10.2777/620649

CoreTrustSeal Standards and Certification Board. (2022). CoreTrustSeal Trustworthy Data Repositories Requirements: Glossary 2023-2025. https://doi.org/10.5281/zenodo.7051125

Devaraju, Anusuriya; Huber, Robert (2021): An Automated Solution for Measuring the Progress Toward FAIR Research Data. In: Patterns 2 (11) 100370. https://doi.org/10.1016/j.patter.2021.100370

Devaraju, Anusuriya; Mokrane, Mustapha; Cepinskas, Linas et al. (2021): From Conceptualization to Implementation. FAIR Assessment of Research Data Objects. In: Data Science Journal 20 (4), pp. 1–14. https://doi.org/10.5334/dsj-2021-004

Eide, Øyvind; Ore, Christian-Emil Smith (2019): Ontologies and Data Modeling. In: Flanders, Julia; Jannidis, Fotis (eds.): The Shape of Data in the Digital Humanities. Modeling Texts and Text-based Resources. New York: Routledge, pp. 178–196.

Flanders, Julia; Jannidis, Fotis (2019a): Glossary. In: Flanders, Julia; Jannidis, Fotis (eds.): The Shape of Data in the Digital Humanities: Modeling Texts and Text-based Resources. New York: Routledge, pp. 331–351.

Flanders, Julia; Jannidis, Fotis (2019b): A Gentle Introduction to Data Modeling. In: Flanders, Julia; Jannidis, Fotis (eds.): The Shape of Data in the Digital Humanities: Modeling Texts and Text-Based Resources. New York: Routledge, pp. 26–98.

Flanders, Julia; Jannidis, Fotis (2015): Knowledge Organization and Data Modeling in the Humanities. White paper. urn:nbn:de:bvb:20-opus-111270

Gilliland, Anne J. (2016): Setting the Stage. In: Baca, Murtha (ed.): Introduction to Metadata. 3rd ed. Los Angeles: Getty Publications. https://www.getty.edu/publications/intro-metadata/ (retrieved 04.04.2023)

RDA FAIR Data Maturity Model Working Group (2020): FAIR Data Maturity Model: specification and guidelines. Research Data Alliance. https://doi.org/10.15497/RDA00050

Hillmann, Diane I.; Dushay, Naomi; Phipps, Jon (2004): Improving Metadata Quality. Augmentation and Recombination. In: DC-2004--Shanghai Proceedings. https://dcpapers.dublincore.org/pubs/article/view/770 (retrieved 17.08.2023)

https://www.library.ucla.edu/help/services-resources/digital-projects-for-special-collections/ (retrieved 25.01.2024)

Hugo, Wim; Le Franc, Yann; Coen, Gerard et al. (2020): D2.5 FAIR Semantics Recommendations Second Iteration (1.0). https://doi.org/10.5281/zenodo.5362010

Kahn, Robert; Wilensky, Robert (2006): A Framework for Distributed Digital Object Services. In: International Journal on Digital Libraries 6 (2), pp. 115–123. https://doi.org/10.1007/s00799-005-0128-x

Khalid, Hiba; Zimanyi, Esteban; Wrembel, Robert (2018): Metadata Reconciliation for Improved Data Binding and Integration. In: Kozielski, Stanisław; Mrozek, Dariusz; Kasprowski, Pawel et al. (eds.): Beyond Databases, Architectures and Structures. Facing the Challenges of Data Proliferation and Growing Variety. 14th International Conference, BDAS 2018, Held at the 24th IFIP World Computer Congress, WCC 2018, Poznan, Poland, September 18-20, 2018, Proceedings. (Communications in Computer and Information Science 928). Cham: Springer, pp. 271–282. https://doi.org/10.1007/978-3-319-99987-6_21

McCarthy, Kate (2015): Guide to Metadata Quality Control (2015–2019). Digital Repository of Ireland. https://doi.org/10.7486/DRI.sj13pg68d-1

McCarty, Willard (2005): Humanities Computing. New York: Palgrave Macmillan.

Oldman, Dominic; Doerr, Martin; Gradmann, Stefan (2016): Zen and the Art of Linked Data. In: Schreibman, Susan; Siemens, Ray; Unsworth, John (eds.): A New Companion to Digital Humanities. 2nd ed. Chichester: Wiley-Blackwell, pp. 251–273. https://doi.org/10.1002/9781118680605.ch18

Park, Jung-Ran; Tosaka, Yuji (2010): Metadata Quality Control in Digital Repositories and Collections. Criteria, Semantics, and Mechanisms. In: Cataloging & Classification Quarterly 48 (8), pp. 696–715. https://doi.org/10.1080/01639374.2010.508711

Pierazzo, Elena (2019): How Subjective Is Your Model? In: Flanders, Julia; Jannidis, Fotis (eds.): The Shape of Data in the Digital Humanities: Modeling Texts and Text-Based Resources. New York: Routledge.

Pirnay-Dummer, Pablo; Ifenthaler, Dirk; Seel, Norbert M. (2012): Semantic Networks. In: Seel, Norbert M. (ed.): Encyclopedia of the Sciences of Learning. Boston: Springer. https://doi.org/10.1007/978-1-4419-1428-6_1933

Riley, Jenn (2017): Understanding Metadata. What is Metadata, and What Is It For? Baltimore: National Information Standards Organization. https://www.niso.org/publications/understanding-metadata-2017 (retrieved 04.04.2023)

Riva, Pat; Le Bœuf, Patrick; Žumer, Maja (2017): IFLA Library Reference Model. Den Haag: IFLA 2017. https://repository.ifla.org/handle/123456789/40

Sansone, Susanna Assunta; McQuilton, Peter; Rocca-Serra, Philippe et al. (2019): FAIRsharing as a Community Approach to Standards, Repositories and Policies. In: Nature Biotechnology 37, pp. 358–367. https://doi.org/10.1038/s41587-019-0080-8

Shotton, David (2017): FRAPO, the Funding, Research Administration and Projects Ontology. https://sparontologies.github.io/frapo/current/frapo.html (retrieved 04.04.2023)

Smith-Yoshimura, Karen (2020): Transitioning to the Next Generation of Metadata. Dublin, OH: OCLC Research. https://doi.org/10.25333/rqgd-b343

Snow, Charles Percy (1959): The Two Cultures. Cambridge: Cambridge University Press (= The Rede Lecture).

Sperberg-McQueen, C. Michael (2019): Playing for Keeps: The Role of Modeling in the Humanities. In: Flanders, Julia; Jannidis, Fotis (eds.): The Shape of Data in the Digital Humanities: Modeling Texts and Text-based Resources. New York: Routledge.

Staab, Steffen; Studer, Rudi (eds.) (2009): Handbook on Ontologies. International Handbooks on Information Systems. Berlin, Heidelberg: Springer. https://doi.org/10.1007/978-3-540-92673-3

Studer, Rudi; Benjamins, Richard V.; Fensel, Dieter (1998): Knowledge Engineering. Principles and Methods. In: Data & Knowledge Engineering 25 (1–2), pp. 161–198. https://doi.org/10.1016/S0169-023X(97)00056-6

Tani, Alice; Candela, Leonardo; Castelli, Donatella (2013): Dealing With Metadata Quality. The Legacy of Digital Library Efforts. In: Information Processing & Management 49 (6), pp. 1194–1205. https://doi.org/10.1016/j.ipm.2013.05.003

Tillman, Ruth Kitchin (2016): Extracting, Augmenting, and Updating Metadata in Fedora 3 and 4 Using a Local OpenRefine Reconciliation Service. In: The Code4lib Journal 31. https://journal.code4lib.org/articles/11179 (retrieved 04.04.2023)

Tomasi, Francesca (2018): Modelling in the Digital Humanities. Conceptual Data Models and Knowledge Organization in the Cultural Heritage Domain. In: Historical Social Research. Supplement 31, pp. 170–179. https://doi.org/10.12759/hsr.suppl.31.2018.170-179

Wilkinson, Mark D.; Dumontier, Michel; Aalbersberg, IJsbrand Jan et al. (2016): The FAIR Guiding Principles for Scientific Data Management and Stewardship. In: Scientific Data 3, 160018. https://doi.org/10.1038/sdata.2016.18

Yoose, Becky; Perkins, Jody (2013): The Linked Open Data Landscape in Libraries and Beyond. In: Journal of Library Metadata 13 (2-3), pp. 197–211.

Zeng, Marcia Lei (2019a): Interoperability. In: Knowledge Organization 42 (2), pp. 122-146. Also available in: Hjørland, B.; Claudio Gnoli, C. (eds.): Encyclopedia of Knowledge Organization. https://www.isko.org/cyclo/interoperability (retrieved 04.04.2023)

Zeng, Marcia Lei (2019b): Semantic Enrichment for Enhancing LAM Data and Supporting Digital Humanities. In: El profesional de la información 28 (1) e280103, p. 7. https://doi.org/10.3145/epi.2019.ene.03 (retrieved 25.01.2024)

Anna Bellotto graduated in Italian Philology and Digital Humanities, has been focusing on topics of data curation, metadata modelling and controlled vocabularies. She previously worked with the team of Europeana Foundation and the digital repositories of the University of Padova and University of Vienna.

Cristiana Bettella graduated in Romance Philology and Digital Humanities, works at the Digital Library Office of the University of Padua Library Centre as Metadata and Electronic Resources Services coordinator. She is engaged in digital scholarship, data modelling and curation of the digital repository Phaidra.

Linda Cappellato graduated in Archival and Library Science at the University Ca' Foscari of Venice, works at the Digital Library Office of the University of Padua Library Centre. She is involved in services related to digital collections, institutional archives, open science, virtual exhibitions and information literacy.

Yuri Carrer graduated in Computer Engineering at the University of Padua, in his thesis dealt with digital objects, an activity he prosecuted since 2003 at the Library System of the University of Padua. He has developed the Padua@ institutional research and research data archives and manages Phaidra as technical manager, dealing with the FAIRification of the repository.

Giulio Turetta graduated in Telecommunications Engineering, works as Digital Services Librarian at the Digital Library Office of the University of Padua Library Centre. He is a manager of the library discovery service and the Phaidra digital repository.

Moritz Strickert

Metadaten und kontrollierte Vokabulare

Handbuch Repositorienmanagement, Hg. v. Blumesberger et al., 2024, S. 163–184
https://doi.org/10.25364/978390337423210

Moritz Strickert, Humboldt-Universität zu Berlin, Universitätsbibliothek, moritz.strickert@ub.hu-berlin.de |
ORCID iD: 0000-0001-9626-5932

Zusammenfassung

Metadaten sind ein zentraler Bestandteil heutiger Wissensorganisation und werden bei der Bewältigung von permanent wachsenden Informationsmengen zusehends wichtiger. Der vorliegende Artikel arbeitet heraus, was unter dem Terminus „Metadaten“ zu verstehen ist, welche Standards existieren und wozu Metadaten(-standards) gebraucht werden. Des Weiteren liegt der Fokus auf der Erschließung, die auf eine strukturierte Beschreibung von analogen und digitalen Ressourcen abzielt. Um die Austauschbarkeit zwischen verschiedenen Institutionen bzw. Datenquellen sicherzustellen, bedarf es dabei gemeinsamer Standards. Wichtig ist in diesem Zusammenhang der Rückgriff auf kontrollierte Vokabulare und Normdateien, insbesondere die im deutschsprachigen Raum zentrale Gemeinsame Normdatei (GND).

Schlagwörter: Forschungsdaten; Metadaten; Dublin Core; Inhaltserschließung; Thesaurus; Normdatei

Abstract

Metadata and Controlled Vocabularies

Metadata are a central component of today’s knowledge organization and are becoming increasingly important in the management of permanently growing amounts of information. This article elaborates on what is meant by the term metadata, which standards exist, and what metadata (standards) are used for. Furthermore, the focus is on indexing, which aims at a structured description of analog and digital resources. In order to ensure exchangeability between different institutions or data sources, common standards are required. In this context, it is important to have reference to controlled vocabularies and authority files, especially the Gemeinsame Normdatei (GND), which is key in the German-speaking world.

Keywords: Research data; metadata; Dublin Core; subject cataloging; thesaurus; authority file

1. Einleitung

Der vorliegende Beitrag zielt auf die Einführung und Diskussion der Bereiche Metadaten, Erschließung und kontrollierte Vokabulare sowie Normdaten ab. Er gliedert sich folgendermaßen: Zu Beginn erfolgt eine allgemeine Einführung in den Bereich der Metadaten und Metadatenschemata, die mit konkreten Beispielen aus der Praxis angereichert ist. Im Anschluss werden verschiedene Formen der Erschließung von Ressourcen dargestellt, die diese für Nutzer:innen auffindbar und nutzbar machen sollen. Hierzu werden die Prozesse der Formal- und Sacherschließung vorgestellt und die Unterschiede zwischen Stichwörtern, Schlagwörtern und kontrollierten Vokabularen herausgearbeitet. Darauf aufbauend wird das Konzept der Normdaten und deren Vorteile in der Informationsverarbeitung erörtert und gleichzeitig die im deutschsprachigen Raum wichtige Gemeinsame Normdatei (GND) vorgestellt. Eine Kritik an kontrollierten Vokabularen sowie ein Fazit samt Ausblick runden den Beitrag ab.

2. Metadaten und Metadatenschemata

Metadaten dienen der Beschreibung von Ressourcen, um diese auffindbar und weiterverwendbar zu machen. Diese Ressourcen beinhalten u. a. digitale und nicht-digitale Literatur in Bibliotheken, Forschungsdaten sowie Objektdaten in Museen. Richard Gartner unterscheidet drei Metadatentypen: deskriptive, administrative und strukturelle Metadaten.[1] Deskriptive Metadaten – zentraler Inhalt dieses Beitrags – beschreiben die Ressourcen, auf die sie sich beziehen, so dass sie gefunden und mit anderen verknüpft werden können.[2] Strukturelle Metadaten sind Hintergrundinformationen, die sicherstellen, dass Ressourcen gespeichert, aufbewahrt, angezeigt und abgerufen werden können. Sie enthalten Informationen bezüglich des Aufbaus der Ressource und stellen die Funktionalität dieser sicher.[3] Ein Teilbereich struktureller Metadaten sind technische Metadaten, die mitunter auch als gesonderter Datentyp beschrieben werden[4]: Diese umfassen alles, was ein System über ein digitales Objekt, z. B. eine Bild- oder Textdatei, wissen muss, um es korrekt darzustellen und nutzbar zu erhalten, bspw. die Pixelzahl oder das Dateiformat. Ferner enthalten administrative Metadaten Informationen darüber, welche Eigentumsrechte an Daten bestehen und welche Arten der Nutzung gestattet werden, z. B. in Form von Lizenzen.

1 Gartner, R. (2016), S. 6-8.
2 Sugimoto, S.; Nagamori, M.; Mihara, T.; Honma, T. (2015), S. 105.
3 Joudrey, D.; Taylor, A. (2018), S. 139.
4 Dierkes, J. (2021), S. 314.

Die meisten Metadaten besitzen drei Hauptkomponenten, die zumeist durch Standards definiert werden. Die Semantik definiert die Bedeutungen der Metadatenelemente. Das Datenmodell gibt an, welche inhaltliche Struktur die Daten annehmen sollen. Die Syntax strukturiert die Art und Weise, in der die Metadaten dargestellt sind z. B. in Tabellenform.[5] Durch Metadaten ist es möglich, dass die lokale Objekterschließung, die beispielsweise durch Bibliotheken geleistet wird, mittels übergreifender Datenverzeichnisse anderen zugute kommt und Fremddaten, die von anderen Institutionen (erschlossen) bereitgestellt werden, übernommen werden können. Um einen reibungslosen Austausch zwischen verschiedenen Datenbeständen sicherzustellen, sind Metadatenstandards notwendig. Diese Standards sind auf verschiedenen Ebenen angesiedelt und oft fachspezifisch. Es existieren konzeptionelle Modelle für einzelne Domänen, beispielsweise das IFLA Library Reference Model (LRM), das die logische Struktur bibliografischer Erschließung beschreibt, oder das CIDOC Conceptual Reference Model als Modell zum Austausch von Information für das Feld des kulturellen Erbes. Daneben existieren Strukturstandards wie Dublin Core, die einfach gehaltene und einheitliche Standards für Metadatenelemente zur Beschreibung von Ressourcen liefern. Des Weiteren gibt es Standards, die die strukturierte Erschließung von Inhalten, beispielsweise bezüglich Schreibkonventionen, regeln (Resource Description and Access, RDA; Regeln für die Schlagwortkatalogisierung, RSWK), Wertestandards (Gemeinsame Normdatei, GND; Open Researcher and Contributor iD, ORCID iD), sowie Standards, die den Datenaustausch zwischen Institutionen regulieren (Machine-Readable Cataloging, MARC bzw. MARC21; Lightweight Information Describing Objects, LIDO). Jens Dierkes nennt als Gütekriterien für die Metadatenqualitität folgende Parameter: „Vollständigkeit, Genauigkeit, Provenienz, Erwartungskonformität, logische Konsistenz und Kohärenz, Aktualität und Zugänglichkeit."[6]

Jedes Metadatenschema beinhaltet als standardisierte Beschreibungskonvention verschiedene Metadatenelemente (Kategorien oder Felder), die die einzelnen Teile einer Ressourcenbeschreibung (z. B. Titel, Erstellungsdatum) umfassen. Dafür ist es wichtig, standardisiert festzulegen, auf welche Art und Weise die Elemente erfasst werden (z. B. Schreibweisen von Daten).[7] Zur Beschreibung von Dokumenten und anderen Ressourcen ist Dublin Core als Standard sehr weit verbreitet. Gartner bezeichnet diesen gar als „lingua franca"[8] für deskriptive Metadaten im Internet.

---

5 Joudrey, D.; Taylor, A. (2018), Anm. 3, S. 133.
6 Dierkes, J. (2021), Anm. 4, S. 322.
7 Joudrey, D.; Taylor, A. (2018), Anm. 3, S. 132.
8 Gartner, R. (2016), Anm. 1, S. 33.

Die Entwicklung des Dublin-Core-Standards hatte das Ziel, einen Kern von Elementen zu identifizieren, der auf jedes physische oder digitale Objekt angewendet werden kann. Dublin Core besteht in seiner einfachsten Form (Simple Dublin Core) aus lediglich 15 Elementen, von denen jedes so weit definiert ist, dass es für alle Anwender:innen verständlich und umfassend nutzbar sein sollte.[9] Mit diesem Standard – der ursprünglich aus dem Bereich der Bibliotheken kam – lassen sich nunmehr grundsätzlich unterschiedliche elektronische Dokumente beschreiben, recherchieren und austauschen. Problematisch ist jedoch, dass bei Simple Dublin Core solche Elemente wie Schöpfer:in („Creator") sehr weit gefasst sind: Sie sind so vage definiert, dass bei Auffinden zweier Datensätze mit dem gleichen Element nicht sicher ist, dass diese Elemente auch das Gleiche bedeuten.[10] Als Beispiel nennt Gartner den Film „Rebecca", in welchem sowohl Alfred Hitchcock (der Regisseur) als auch David O. Selznick (der Produzent) als „Creator" gelistet werden. Nutzende haben aber oftmals ein Interesse daran, genauer zu wissen, welche Rolle eine Person einnahm. Für diesen präziseren Informationsbedarf wurden verschiedene Lösungen entwickelt. Ein früher Lösungsansatz ist Qualified Dublin Core, dabei werden Dublin-Core-Elemente mit weiteren Tags versehen, um sie durch zusätzliche Informationsanreicherung präziser zu machen.[11]

Um die semantische Bedeutung von Elementen eindeutig verstehen und einordnen zu können, ist es notwendig, klar zu identifizieren, auf welcher Metadatendefinition diese basieren. Das Mapping, das als Prozess der Beziehungen zwischen Metadatenbegriffen verschiedene Schemata erkennt, abgleicht und verknüpft, ist eine entscheidende Aufgabe, um die Metadaten interoperabel zu machen.[12] Natürlichsprachige Termini wie beispielsweise „Titel" sind zu unpräzise. Aus diesem Grund wird auf Uniform Resource Identifier (URI) zurückgegriffen. Diese bestehen aus Zeichenketten (Buchstaben, Zahlen, Satzzeichen) und können eindeutige Auskunft darüber geben, dass z. B. der Titel in der vorliegenden Ressource nach den Maßgaben von Dublin Core definiert ist.[13] Da sich die Beschreibungselemente von Dublin Core in der Hauptsache auf Textdokumente beziehen, ist der Standard jedoch beispielsweise für Museen nur begrenzt geeignet, weil die Bedarfe für eine umfassende Objektdokumentation, z. B. in Hinblick auf relevante physische Objekteigenschaften, nicht erfüllt werden können.[14]

9 Gartner, R. (2016), Anm. 1, S. 31f.
10 Gartner, R. (2016), Anm. 1, S. 35.
11 Gartner, R. (2016), Anm. 1, S. 32-34.
12 Sugimoto, S.; Nagamori, M.; Mihara, T. et al. (2015), Anm. 2, S. 105.
13 Gartner, R. (2016), Anm. 1, S. 52.
14 Team MusIS im BSZ (2020), S. 3f.

Darüber hinaus werden für die Beschreibung von Forschungsdaten auch disziplinspezifische Metadatenstandards verwendet. Ein Beispiel aus der sozialwissenschaftlichen Forschung stellt der DDI-Standard (Data Documentation Initiative Standard) dar. Er dient zur Beschreibung z. B. von Umfragen, Fragebögen oder statistischen Datensätzen und ermöglicht, Forschungsdaten über ihren gesamten Lebenszyklus hinweg zu beschreiben sowie effizient und nachhaltig zu verwalten, einschließlich der Veröffentlichung und Nachnutzung der Daten. Der Standard ist interoperabel mit anderen Standards wie DataCite und Dublin Core. Durch die Verwendung des DDI-Standards ist es möglich, Forschungsdaten für Sekundärnutzende verständlich zu erschließen. Zugleich sollen die Maschinenlesbarkeit sowie die Auffindbarkeit und der Austausch zwischen verschiedenen Organisationen sichergestellt werden. Von Wissenschaftsseite wurde an diesem Schema jedoch kritisiert, dass die Erfassung von audio-visuellen Ressourcen weitestgehend unmöglich ist.[15]

Da bei der Vergabe von Metadaten zwischen minimalen und umfassenden Anforderungen eine große Spannweite existiert, ist es notwendig abzuwägen, ob im Einzelfall eher generische oder spezifische bzw. stark kontextgebundene Beschreibungen für Forschungsdaten gebraucht werden sollen. Metadatenschemata, welche stark auf die jeweilige Forschungscommunity bezogen sind, erleichtern die Aufnahme wichtiger fachspezifischer Bedarfe. Deren Übertragbarkeit auf andere Disziplinen ist jedoch oft problembehaftet. Die Interoperabilität von Metadaten(-Schemata) benötigt darüber hinaus Pflege, um ihre Konsistenz dauerhaft sicherzustellen.[16]

Als Beispiel dient die qualitative sozialwissenschaftliche Forschung: Hier ist oft das Verstehen von Sinnzusammenhängen essenziell. Da Sekundärnutzende von Forschungsdaten nicht an der ursprünglichen Forschungssituation beteiligt waren, sind einfache Metadaten oft nicht ausreichend und eine zusätzliche Kontextualisierung ist notwendig.[17] Diese verschafft Klarheit bezüglich des Forschungsprozesses

15 Imeri, S.; Sterzer, W.; Harbeck, M. et al. (2019), S. 25.

16 Sugimoto, S.; Nagamori, M.; Mihara, T. et al. (2015), Anm. 2, S. 107.

17 Doris Bambey, Alexia Meyermann, Maike Porzelt und Marc Rittberger differenzieren bei der Kontextualisierung die Makro-, Mikro- und Objektebene. Die Makroebene gibt Auskunft über Studienhintergründe und den Erstellungskontext, die in der Forschung verwendeten Methoden und Forschungsprozesse sowie rechtliche Aspekte. Die Mikroebene beschreibt das Setting der Forschung, beispielsweise die Interviewsituation oder zusätzliche biografische Informationen der Beforschten. Die Objektebene gibt Auskunft über das Vorgehen bei der Datenaufbereitung (z. B. Transkriptionsregeln), ob verschiedene Versionen bestehen, den Umfang der einzelnen Datensätze und in welcher Beziehung diese zueinander stehen, siehe dazu Bambey, D.; Meyermann, A.; Porzelt, M. et al. (2018), S. 63. Grundsätzlich ist ebenfalls abzuwägen, wie viele Ressourcen für die Kontextualisierung eingesetzt werden sollen, um analytisches Potenzial sicherzustellen.

auf verschiedenen Ebenen: dem institutionellen Hintergrund, dem theoretisch-methodischen Studienansatz, der Art und Weise, wie Daten erhoben, aufbereitet und analysiert wurden, welche strategischen Entscheidungen durch die Primärforschenden getroffen wurden und schließlich welche Bedingungen bei einer Nutzung zu beachten sind.[18] Neben der inhaltlich-thematischen Übereinstimmung sind auch „Aktualität, Zugangsmöglichkeiten, Versionierung, Datenqualität, Erhebungsmethoden, Provenienz und Untersuchungsbereich“[19] wichtige Auswahlkriterien für Forschende, die diese Daten nachnutzen wollen. Nachhaltige und standardisierte Erschließung mittels Metadaten ist mit Blick auf Forschungsdaten unverzichtbar, die erst so auffindbar werden und für eine potenzielle Nachnutzung bereitstehen. Überdies können Forschungsdaten durch die Erschließung zusehends als eigenständige Publikationsform angesehen werden.[20] Die Anwendung von persistenten Identifikatoren (z. B. Digital Object Identifier, DOI) ermöglicht, dass Verknüpfungen zu Dateien, Dokumenten oder Webseiten, trotz sich mitunter wandelnder Speicherorte, dauerhaft sichergestellt werden können. Fremddaten, die aus externen Quellen bezogen werden, können den eigenen Datenbestand ergänzen und überdies zur Vermeidung doppelter Erschließungsarbeit beitragen. Darüber hinaus ist es sinnvoll, dass Forschungsdaten in fachrelevante Bibliothekskataloge, Portale und Nachweissysteme (z. B. da|ra, Registrierungsagentur für Sozial- und Wirtschaftsdaten) eingespeist werden und auf diesem Wege zu finden sind.[21]

Grundsätzlich ist innerhalb des Erschließungsprozesses zwischen der Formalerschließung und der Sach- bzw. Inhaltserschließung zu unterscheiden. Erstere greift nur auf Informationen zurück, die sich unmittelbar ermitteln lassen. Bei einem gedruckten Buch sind dies beispielsweise Autor:in, Titel, Verlag, Seitenanzahl. Diese Informationen sind als Metadaten durch Standardisierung, z. B. durch das Standardisierungsregelwerk Resource Description and Access (RDA), mit anderen Einrichtungen austauschbar. Jenseits der genuin bibliothekarischen Sphäre ist die Formalerschließung weniger stark mittels Regelwerken strukturiert. Bei Forschungsdaten ist die Erschließung deshalb oftmals abhängig von den Anforderungen der entsprechenden Repositorien.

Einen konkret ausformulierten Ansatz für die durchzuführende Kontextualisierung beschreibt das Forschungsdatenzentrum Qualiservice in ihrer Handreichung zur Kontextualisierung qualitativer Forschungsdaten mit besonderem Fokus auf den sogenannten Studienreport, siehe dazu Heuer, J.-O.; Kretzer S.; Mozygemba, K. et al. (2020).

18 Smioski, A. (2011), S. 228f.

19 Friedrich, T.; Recker, J. (2021), S. 414.

20 Queckbörner, B. (2019), S. 66.

21 Klump, J. (2010), S. 112.

Die Sacherschließung dient der Erschließung der Ressourcen nach inhaltlich-thematischen Kriterien. Dies kann durch die verbale Erschließung mittels Schlagwörtern geschehen, hauptsächlich auf Grundlage der Regeln für die Schlagwortkatalogisierung (RSWK) oder durch die Zuordnung in Klassifikationen wie der Regensburger Verbundklassifikation (RVK) oder der Dewey-Dezimalklassifikation (DDC). Die Vergabe von Schlagwörtern findet zumeist noch auf intellektueller Ebene statt, wobei derzeit bereits Verfahren (weiter-)entwickelt werden, um dies mittels (semi-)automatisierter Text- und Datenanalyse maschinell durchzuführen.[22]

3. Recherche auf Basis von Stichwörtern, Schlagwörtern und kontrollierten Vokabularen

Der Erschließungsprozess umfasst bestenfalls eine detaillierte und einheitliche Beschreibung von analogen und digitalen Ressourcen auf Grundlage von strukturierten Metadaten und kontrollierten Vokabularen. Die Erschließung soll Nutzer:innen gesuchte Ressourcen und Informationen möglichst umfassend zur Verfügung stellen. Es sind hierbei grob fünf Ziele zu unterscheiden: Sie soll 1.) zuverlässiges Auffinden ermöglichen; 2.) helfen, Verschiedenes zu unterscheiden; 3.) zusammenführen, was zusammengehört; 4.) Gefundenes übersichtlich machen; 5.) das Ausgewählte zugänglich machen.[23] An mögliche Suchergebnisse sind zwei zentrale Anforderungen zu richten, die als „Precision" (Genauigkeit) und „Recall" (Vollständigkeit) beschrieben werden. Die Genauigkeit ist ein Indikator, wie viele der abgerufenen Dokumente relevant sind; die Vollständigkeit ist ein Indikator, wie viele der relevanten Dokumente in einem System tatsächlich abgerufen werden. Es gilt: Suchergebnisse sollen möglichst präzise sein und das Suchmaschinensystem soll nur die tatsächlich interessanten Treffer finden. Gleichzeitig sollen jedoch auch alle für die Nutzer:innen relevanten Dokumente aufgefunden werden.[24]

Im Prozess der Recherche wird von Suchenden vielfach auf Stichwörter und Schlagwörter zurückgegriffen. Das Stichwort wird dem Dokument, beispielsweise aus dem Titel, entnommen, das Schlagwort der Ressource auf Grundlage seines Inhalts

22 So erschließt die Deutsche Nationalbibliothek seit 2010 in zunehmendem Maße den stark wachsenden Anteil von digitalen Ressourcen mittels maschineller Verfahren. Dieses Verfahren wurde 2017 auch für physische Medien erweitert, siehe dazu Mödden, E.; Schöning-Walter, C.; Uhlmann, S. et al. (2018), S. 30. Für die klassifikatorische Erschließung wird dabei auf maschinelle Lernverfahren zurückgegriffen; bei der Vergabe von Schlagwörtern finden linguistische Verfahren Anwendung, eine kompakte Verfahrensbeschreibung findet sich in Uhlmann, S. (2013). Die Ergebnisse dieser Abgleichsverfahren sind derzeit jedoch noch fehleranfällig und oft unpräzise, siehe dazu Wiesenmüller, H. (2018), S. 28. Zur grundsätzlichen Kritik an diesen Entwicklungen siehe Ceynowa, K. (2017).

23 Joudrey, D.; Taylor, A. (2018), Anm. 3, S. 207f.

24 Joudrey, D.; Taylor, A. (2018), Anm. 3, S. 121ff.

hinzugefügt. Die Recherchepraxis mit Stichwörtern, z. B. in Form einer Volltextsuche, ist problematisch, da diese in den sprachlichen Formulierungen der Autor:innen verhaftet bleibt, jedoch ist sie gleichzeitig weit verbreitet. Es werden mitunter Wörter verwendet, die wenig nützlich zur inhaltlichen Beschreibung der Ressourcen sind. Auf diese Weise liefern Suchanfragen einerseits nicht relevante Ergebnisse und andererseits werden Ressourcen, die ähnliche Inhalte haben, nicht gefunden, wenn diese von den Verfasser:innen nicht mit denselben Begriffen benannt worden sind. Inhalte sind nur auffindbar, wenn sie explizit als Begriff in der Ressource auftauchen. Das Vorkommen eines Begriffs bedeutet nicht notwendigerweise, dass ein Text den gesuchten Themenkomplex tatsächlich behandelt. Insbesondere bei der Volltextsuche im Internet treten Probleme bei der Suche nach abstrakten Themen wie etwa Ethik oder Gesundheit auf, da sie eine viel zu große und wenig fokussierte Ergebnismenge liefern.[25] Die Ergänzung durch Inhaltsverzeichnisse und andere Informationen z. B. in Bibliothekskatalogen erhöht zwar den Suchtrefferumfang, die Treffer sind aber oft wenig präzise.[26] Die Art der Suche kann das Vorkommen von Wörtern in den gesuchten begrifflichen Zusammenhängen nicht vom Auftauchen der gleichen Wörter in nicht gesuchten Zusammenhängen trennen. Es können nur Ergebnisse mit den Suchbegriffen erzielt werden, die die Suchenden kennen - verwandte oder unbekannte Begriffe fallen weg.[27]

Eine Stichwortsuche auf Grundlage von Titeln ist ebenfalls problembehaftet: Viele Titel geben zu wenig Aufschluss über den Inhalt. Es fehlen vielfach Informationen darüber, welchen zeitlichen oder räumlichen Bezug der Text besitzt. Personennamen, aber auch Körperschaften und Geografika sind durch Mangel an Kontrolle bei dieser Form der Recherche nicht eindeutig voneinander abgrenzbar und somit auch nicht zuordenbar. Vergebene Titel nutzen zudem oft bildliche Sprache, deren Metaphorik nicht durch eine Stichwortsuche in ihrem Bedeutungsgehalt erkannt bzw. übersetzt werden kann.[28] Des Weiteren können Stichwörter die Probleme von Synonymen/Homonymen, abweichenden Ausdrücken und verschiedenen Sprachen, die für dieselben Themen verwendet werden, nicht lösen. Oftmals gibt es mehrere Arten, ein vorhandenes Konzept zu bezeichnen. Dies umfasst verschiedene Schreibweisen desselben Sachverhalts (z. B. BE/AE „harbour" / „harbor"), Abkürzungen und Initialen, das Problem veralteter Termini, die heute für Sachverhalte nicht mehr gebräuchlich sind oder in unterschiedlichen Disziplinen unter-

25 Beall, J. (2008), S. 442.
26 Gross, T.; Taylor, A. G.; Joudrey, D. N. (2015), S. 17f.
27 Mann, T. (2008), S. 163-165.
28 Flachmann, H. (2004), S. 767.

schiedlich verwendet werden. Bei Homonymen, also Wörtern mit mehreren Bedeutungen (z. B. „Tau"), wird eine Stichwortsuche das Wort in allen seinen verschiedenen Bedeutungen zurückliefern, obgleich die Suche nur auf eine bestimmte Bedeutung abzielt. Ein ähnliches Problem besteht darüber hinaus, wenn ähnlich oder identisch geschriebene Wörter in unterschiedlichen Sprachen, jedoch mit verschiedenen Bedeutungen, existieren. Die Folge ist auch hier eine sehr große unpräzise Ergebnismenge.[29] Die Recherche via Freitextfeldern sowie Stichworten und ohne Rückgriff auf kontrollierte Termini liefert somit eher dürftige Resultate.

Für die beschriebenen Probleme der Stichwortsuche bieten (Sach-)Schlagwörter eine Lösung. Schlagwörter können sowohl für die inhaltliche Erschließung von Ressourcen als auch als Grundlage für Recherchen verwendet werden. Bei der inhaltlichen Erschließung mit Schlagwörtern muss grob zwischen freien Termini, beispielsweise in Form von Folksonomien (z. B. durch Social Tagging[30]), und genormten Schlagwörtern unterschieden werden. Dieser Erschließungsprozess ist ressourcenintensiv, ermöglicht jedoch eine tiefergehende inhaltliche Recherche, indem auch Ressourcen ohne das Wissen um bibliografische oder formale Angaben (z. B. Autor:in, Verlag etc.) auffindbar gemacht werden. Manche Ressourcen nicht textueller Art wie Bilder oder Grafiken brauchen bislang eine weitergehende Beschreibung, damit sie überhaupt recherchierbar werden können.[31] Auch nichtdeutschsprachige Titel können nach Verschlagwortung mit Rückgriff auf deutsche Schlagwörter gefunden werden. Dies ist deshalb wichtig, da Recherchekompetenzen in einer Fremdsprache beispielsweise in Hinblick auf die Kenntnis relevanter Suchtermini oftmals deutlich schlechter ausgeprägt sind als bei einer Suche in der Erstsprache.[32] Gleichzeitig liefern Suchanfragen weniger Treffer, die für die Nutzenden nicht von Relevanz sind. Tina Gross et al. kommen in ihrer Metastudie zu folgendem Ergebnis:

29 Beall, J. (2008), Anm. 25, S. 439f.

30 Soziales oder kollaboratives Tagging umfasst die Verschlagwortung von Ressourcen durch die Nutzenden selbst, wobei keine umfassenden Regelwerke zur Anwendung kommen. Die Begriffssammlung, die im Zuge dessen erstellt wird, wird als „Folksonomie" bezeichnet. Vorteile dieses Vorgehens bestehen darin, dass bislang wenig bekannte bzw. bearbeitete Ressourcen und Themengebiete, die zu speziell für die Aufnahme in kontrollierte Vokabulare sind, präzise beschrieben werden können. Das große Problem bei dieser Art von Beschreibung ist jedoch, dass sie ungeordnet ist. Beispielsweise werden weder Schreibweisen kontrolliert noch Synonyme miteinander verknüpft sowie die vergebenen Tags nicht auf ihre Sinnhaftigkeit hin überprüft. Dies führt dazu, dass die Suchergebnisse große Lücken aufweisen, da Hinweise auf relevante Ressourcen fehlen, die zwar einen ähnlichen Inhalt besitzen, aber mit einer alternativen Schreibweise oder Begrifflichkeit versehen sind, siehe dazu Gartner, R. (2016), S. 96ff.; Gross, T.; Taylor, A. G.; Joudrey, D. N. et al. (2015), S. 14.

31 Gross, T.; Taylor, A. G.; Joudrey, D. N. et al. (2015), Anm. 26, S. 11.

32 Flachmann, H. (2004), Anm. 28, S. 767.

> The 2005 study of the effect of controlled vocabulary on the results of keyword searching found that an average of 35.9 % of hits in keyword searches would be lost if subject headings were to be removed from or no longer included in catalog records. The current study found that with the addition of tables of contents and summaries or abstracts, an average of 27 % of hits would be lost if the subject headings were not present in the records.[33]

Für die intellektuelle Erschließung durch Menschen und für maschinelle Verfahren, die eine automatisierte Erschließung auf Grundlage von Abstracts, Inhaltsverzeichnissen oder Volltextanalysen ermöglichen sollen, ist der Rückgriff auf zeitgemäßes und kontrolliertes Vokabular unersetzlich. Für zukünftige Entwicklungen im Bereich des Text- und Data-Minings[34], wie es beispielsweise im Bereich der Digital Humanities bereits erprobt wird, ist dies ebenfalls bedeutsam. Ein solches Vokabular, z. B. in Form eines Thesaurus, soll sicherstellen, dass die Schlagwortvergabe konsistent und mit präzisen Termini erfolgt. Dies macht eine terminologische Kontrolle notwendig, die auf die Mehrdeutigkeit von Begriffen reagiert und klar ausweist, was auf welche Weise bezeichnet werden soll. Es werden begriffliche Beziehungen nachgewiesen, indem eine Vorzugsbenennung (Deskriptor) festgelegt wird, die im Anschluss zur Verschlagwortung verwendet werden kann. Gleichzeitig müssen Synonyme möglichst vollständig aufgenommen und mittels Verweisen mit der Benennung verknüpft werden. Des Weiteren müssen die Bedeutungen bei allen Homonymen (siehe oben), Polysemen – dies sind Wörter gleichen etymologischen Ursprungs (z. B. „Flügel“: Körperteil und Instrument) – eindeutig identifiziert werden. Diese Erfassung ermöglicht, dass bei einer späteren Recherche Synonyme als Sucheinstiege fungieren können, die wiederum auf die entsprechende Vorzugsbenennung verweisen. Dies verbessert die Recherche, da bei der Suche mit Synonymen ebenfalls die vergebenen Vorzugsbenennungen und weitere Synonyme gefunden werden können. Zugleich sind formale Konventionen notwendig, die unter anderem die Schreibweise sowie die Verwendung im Singular oder Plural reglementieren. Für den deutschsprachigen Raum basiert dieser Festlegungsprozess auf den Regeln der Schlagwortkatalogisierung (RSWK). Außerdem existiert eine sogenannte „Zerlegungskontrolle“, die sehr lange Wortkomposita vermeiden will. An ihre Stelle tritt eine Kombination aus bereits existenten Deskriptoren der Schlagwortsammlung, die den Bedeutungsinhalt des zusammengefügten Wortes umfasst.

---

33 Gross, T.; Taylor, A. G.; Joudrey, D. N. et al. (2015), Anm. 26, S. 31.

34 Diese Verfahren zielen darauf ab, mittels Algorithmen Bedeutungsstrukturen in umfangreichen, wenig bis gar nicht strukturierten Textmengen zu erkennen und für eine tiefergehende Analyse nutzbar zu machen.

Es lassen sich zwei Verschlagwortungsprinzipien unterscheiden: Das gleichordnende Prinzip sieht vor, dass Schlagwörter einzeln nebeneinander stehen und eine Kombination mittels Suchoperatoren erfolgt. Beim syntaktischen Indexieren werden Schlagwörter hingegen in eine sinnhafte Beziehung zueinander gesetzt, sodass eine Art Kurzabstract gebildet wird.

Ein Thesaurus unterscheidet sich von einer alphabetisch geordneten Schlagwortliste darin, dass dessen Termini gleichzeitig in eine Hierarchie eingefügt werden. Hierarchische Relationen verbinden somit spezifischere Unter- und umfassendere Oberbenennungen: Äquivalenzrelationen umfassen Synonyme, wohingegen Assoziationsrelationen verwandte Deskriptoren beinhalten können. Vielfach sind Thesauri polyhierarchisch aufgebaut, sodass sie eine Benennung über mehrere Über- bzw. Unterbenennungen besitzen. Wichtig ist, dass sowohl diejenigen, die die Verschlagwortung vornehmen, als auch die Nutzenden passende Deskriptoren einfach und zuverlässig finden können.[35]

Normierte Sucheinstiege sind auch für die Suche nach Personen relevant, da hierbei der bevorzugte Name einer Person festgelegt wird. Gleichzeitig können Verweisungen zu alternativen Schreibweisen angelegt werden. Das Ziel ist die eindeutige Referenzierung und Auffindbarkeit von Personen. Dies kann beispielsweise sichergestellt werden, indem Personendatensätze durch biografische Daten ergänzt werden und der einzelnen Person im Anschluss ein Identifikator zugeordnet werden kann.[36]

4. Normdaten

Eine wichtige Rolle kommt sogenannten Normdaten zu, die verwendet werden, wenn eine eindeutige Benennung von Entitäten gewünscht wird. In einer Normdatei (authority file) werden diese dann gesammelt. Eine Entität ist in diesem Zusammenhang eine Informationseinheit, die eindeutig identifizierbar und abgrenzbar

35 Eine gute Möglichkeit, um relevante Terminologien zu recherchieren, bietet das von der Universität Basel entwickelte Nachschlageinstrument Basic Register of Thesauri, Ontologies & Classifications (BARTOC).

36 Neben der weiter unten beschriebenen Gemeinsamen Normdatei (GND) spielt hier das Virtual International Authority File (VIAF) als ein gemeinschaftliches Projekt zahlreicher Nationalbibliotheken und Verbünde eine wichtige Rolle. Insgesamt werden dort die Bestände für Personendaten von 25 Normdateien zusammengebracht und regelmäßig aktualisiert. Die Datenbestände sind miteinander verlinkt und können online recherchiert und genutzt werden. Jeder Datensatz erhält dabei eine eindeutig identifizierbare Normdatennummer in Form eines Uniform Resource Identifiers (URI). Darüber hinaus ist die Orcid iD bedeutsam, die von der Open Researcher Contributor Identification Initiative (ORCID) initiiert wurde und einen nicht-proprietären Code umfasst, mit welchem sich wissenschaftliche Autor*innen ebenfalls eindeutig identifizieren lassen.

ist, wie beispielsweise eine Bezeichnung für eine Sache, eine Person oder ein Ort. Diese Entitäten können durch Begriffsdefinitionen und eindeutige Identifikationsnummern, sogenannte persistente Identifikatoren (z. B. Digital Object Identifier, DOI), Begriffsdefinitionen sowie Quellenangaben angereichert werden. Auf dieser Grundlage können Ressourcen weitere semantische Beziehungen zugewiesen werden, die sie wiederum mit anderen verknüpfbar machen und ein Netz von verbundenen Datensätzen (linked data) ermöglichen, das sich im Web vielfältig nutzen lässt.[37] Die Verknüpfung und eindeutige Referenzierung von Ressourcen ermöglichen damit eine erhöhte Sichtbarkeit, Verfügbarkeit und Zitierbarkeit in heterogenen und neuen Anwendungskontexten.[38]

Kontrollierte Vokabulare schaffen ein höheres Maß an Konsistenz in Hinblick auf die Erschließung, indem sie auf eine einheitliche Benennung von Sachverhalten, Personen und Körperschaften zurückgreifen. Damit ermöglichen sie eine präzisere und qualitativ hochwertigere Metadatenbeschreibung. Metadaten können auf diese Weise harmonisiert und vernetzt werden. Zugleich kann auf individualisierte Personen oder andere Entitäten referenziert und so Informationen angereichert werden. Das liefert bei der Recherche verlässlichere Ergebnisse und erhöht die Auffindbarkeit von Publikationen und verteilten Datenbeständen. Im deutschsprachigen Raum verknüpft beispielsweise Kalliope als überregionales Nachweisinstrument für Nachlässe, Autographen und Verlagsarchive diese Bestände mit den Normdaten der Gemeinsamen Normdatei (GND). Ein Darstellungsformat, das sich für Anwendungen jenseits des reinen Lesens von elektronischen Texten eignet, ist die Extensible Markup Language (XML). Als Auszeichnungssprache kann sie hierarchisch strukturierte Daten darstellen, die auch maschinenlesbar sind. Die Vorteile von XML sind, dass sie nicht an eine spezielle Software gebunden ist, sich leicht zwischen verschiedenen Systemen austauschen lässt und sich gut für die Datenarchivierung eignet.[39]

---

37 Das Semantic Web, als erweitertes Netz von Webressourcen und Datensätzen, ermöglicht die Verlinkung von verschiedenen Ressourcen aus unterschiedlichen Fachcommunities, die sich auch maschinell verarbeiten lassen. Menschen und Computer könnten auf diese Weise besser interagieren. Dazu müssen die Ressourcen mit eindeutigen Uniform Resource Identifiers (URIs) identifiziert und beschrieben werden, siehe dazu Joudrey, D.; Taylor, A. (2018), S. 32. Auf Grundlage dessen ermöglicht beispielsweise das Resource Description Framework (RDF), verschiedene Ressourcen als linked data mittels logischer und maschinenlesbarer Aussagen miteinander zu verbinden. Dabei sind die sogenannten Tripel wie ein einfacher Satz aufgebaut, der ein Subjekt, ein Prädikat und ein Objekt enthält, siehe dazu Haffner, A. (2012), S. 5. Auf diese Weise können Aussagen getroffen werden, z. B. „Berlin ist die Hauptstadt von Deutschland". Mittels Abfragesprachen wie SPARQL ist es dann auf Grundlage der Datenverknüpfung möglich, umfangreiche und komplexe Suchanfragen zu stellen.

38 Lill, J. (2019), S. 18.

39 Gartner, R. (2016), Anm. 1, S. 56.

Mit kontrollierten Vokabularen erschlossene Ressourcen stellen somit grundlegende Qualitätskriterien für eine standardisierte Datenerfassung und einen standardisierten Datenaustausch sicher. Bezüglich des Ressourcenteilbereichs der Forschungsdaten befördert dies auch die in den FAIR-Prinzipien formulierten Ziele – „Findable, Accessible, Interoperable, Reusable"[40] –, die ein nachhaltiges Forschungsdatenmanagement, eine erhöhte Interoperabilität und umfassendere Zugänglichmachung der Ressourcen einfordern.

Es besteht jedoch Weiterentwicklungsbedarf auf der Ebene der Recherchesysteme, um die Möglichkeiten des Schlagwortnetzes[41] umfassend als Filter und Verweisung nutzen zu können. Wiesenmüller weist darauf hin, dass es in vielen Online-Katalogen nicht problemlos möglich ist, sich bei der Schlagwortrecherche ebenfalls verwandte bzw. unter- und obergeordnete Bezeichnungstreffer darstellen zu lassen, obgleich diese Informationsrelationen in den Normdateien verzeichnet sind.[42] Dies würde ermöglichen, dass die Nutzenden auf zusätzliche, ebenfalls relevante Ressourcen aufmerksam gemacht werden könnten. Die Entwicklung von „navigierbare[n] Visualisierungen von Fachgebieten (mit Wikipedia-Anbindung, Diensten zur direkten Übernahme von Definitionen und Ähnliches) und den damit assoziierten Beständen"[43] würde den weiteren Nutzungsmehrwert ebenfalls erhöhen.

5. Die Gemeinsame Normdatei (GND)

Im deutschsprachigen Raum ist insbesondere die GND ein zentraler Referenzpunkt für kontrolliertes Vokabular.[44] Sie ist ein Zusammenschluss aus verschiedenen, bereits zuvor existenten Normdateien. Deren Pflege wird durch ein Redaktionssystem

40 Wilkinson, M. D.; Dumontier, M. et al. (2016)

41 Dieses Schlagwortnetz entsteht durch die Verknüpfung verschiedener Begriffsdatensätze beispielsweise in Form von abstrakteren Oberbegriffen mit präziseren Unterbegriffen. Bei der Recherche könnte bei zu vielen Suchtreffern auf die detaillierteren Unterbegriffe zurückgegriffen werden. Gibt es wenig Suchtreffer, könnten die allgemeineren Oberbegriffe genutzt werden, um den Ergebnismenge zu erweitern.

42 Wiesenmüller, H. (2018), S. 29.

43 Kasprzik, A.; Kett, J. (2018), S. 138.

44 In der 2016 durchgeführten Befragung zum Thema Objekterschließung in Bibliotheken, Museen und Archiven antworteten 75 % der Befragten (insbesondere in Bibliotheken und Museen), dass sie auf kontrollierte (normierte) Vokabulare zurückgriffen. Folgende Vokabulare wurden verwendet: „Neben der Gemeinsamen Normdatei / GND (35) und einem eigenen Thesaurus (27) wurden folgende Thesauri genannt: Wikipedia (7), GeoNames (4), VIAF (3), Icon-Class (2), Library of Congress Authorities (1), RDA (1), Eine eigene Klassifikation (1), TU Systematik (1), Catalogue of Life (1), Index Kewensis (1), id.loc.gov (1), ethnologue.com (1), RVK (1), OBZ (1)." Vgl. Marković, B.; Kmyta, O. et al. (2016), S. 418f.
Im englischsprachigen Raum nehmen die Library of Congress Subject Headings als präkombiniertes, kontrolliertes Vokabular eine zentrale Rolle ein. Für eine dahingehende Übersicht siehe Stone, A. T. (2000), S. 1-15.

übernommen, das sich aus verschiedenen deutschsprachigen Bibliotheksverbünden rekrutiert. In der GND selbst sind derzeit circa neun Millionen Datensätze angelegt. Diese umfassen normierte Datensätze für Geografika, Körperschaften, Kongresse, Personen, Sachschlagwörter sowie Werktitel. Bislang wurden diese hauptsächlich zur Medienkatalogisierung in Bibliotheken genutzt. Zusehends finden sie aber auch umfassendere Anwendung zur Kulturgutvernetzung in Archiven, Museen und verschiedenen Projekt- und Webkontexten.

Hier ist für den deutschsprachigen Raum insbesondere das von der Deutschen Forschungsgemeinschaft (DFG) geförderte Projekt GND für Kulturdaten (GND4C) zu nennen, das auf einen Ausbau und eine Vernetzung verschiedener Institutionstypen abzielt. Der Fokus liegt dabei bislang auf Geografika, Personen, Sachbegriffen und Werken (Bau- und Kunstwerke).[45] Die vier Hauptziele sind: 1. Nachhaltiger Aufbau einer sparten- und fächerübergreifenden Organisation, 2. Weiterentwicklung des Datenmodells und der Regeln im Hinblick auf nicht-bibliothekarische Anwendungskontexte, 3. Bereitstellung von Schnittstellen und Werkzeugen zur Unterstützung nicht-bibliothekarischer Anwendungskontexte, 4. Stärkung der Kommunikation mit den verschiedenen Interessengruppen über verschiedene Kommunikationskanäle und Sichtbarmachen des GND-Netzwerks.[46]

Die Datensätze basierten lange auf dem literary warrant (gedruckten Publikationsaufkommen). Das heißt, ein Schlagwort wurde nur dann angelegt, wenn es nachweislich Literatur gab, die nicht mit den bereits vorhandenen Begrifflichkeiten beschrieben werden konnte und somit ein neues Schlagwort zur Beschreibung forderte. Heute können Datensatze sowohl proaktiv als auch auf Grundlage anderer Bedarfe aus unterschiedlichen Bereichen des GLAM-Sektors angelegt werden. Innerhalb der GND wird einzelnen Entitäten jeweils eine eindeutige Identifikationsnummer zugewiesen. Bei Personen werden neben der normierten Hauptbenennung auch abweichende Namensformen im Datensatz hinterlegt. Datensätze können mit zusätzlichen biografischen Informationen angereichert werden, was eine eindeutige Zuordnung von Personen und eine Vernetzung mit anderen Datensätzen möglich macht.[47] Dies umfasst Lebensdaten, Geburts- und Sterbeorte, Berufe, Affiliationen, aber auch die Verknüpfung mit publizierten Werken. Bei Körperschaften (z. B. Universitätsinstituten) können auch ehemalige Bezeichnungen, Nachfolge- und Vorgängereinrichtungen und die Einbettung in größere Verwaltungseinheiten

45 Lill, J. (2019), Anm. 38, S. 19.
46 Kett, J. (2019), S. 62.
47 Ohne diese zusätzlichen Informationen ist es nicht möglich, Personen mit gleichem Namen zu unterscheiden; beispielsweise: Beck, Kurt; Ethnologe, 1952- | 134285603, Beck, Kurt; Politiker, Elektromechaniker, 1949- | 120301342, Beck, Kurt; Werkzeugmacher, Fotograf, 1909-1983 | 1027234143.

dargestellt werden. Vielfach besitzt die GND zudem Verknüpfungen mit anderen Normdateien wie die der Library of Congress, sodass auch viele Ressourcen, die mit englischsprachigen Schlagwörtern versehen worden sind, mittels GND-Begriffen auffindbar sind. Die GND basiert dabei auf dem Prinzip der Postkoordination: Auf das Zusammensetzen von langen, festen Terminiketten wird verzichtet. Es werden vielmehr mehrere Schlagworte vergeben, die den komplexen Sachverhalt darstellen. Nutzende können dies bei der Suche im Bibliothekskatalog durch die Verwendung von booleschen Operatoren anwenden. Die GND kann darüber hinaus auch als Nachschlagewerk genutzt werden, um zu eruieren, welche Vorzugsbenennungen für die Recherche und die eigene Verschlagwortung geeignet sein könnten.[48] Jens Lill weist darauf hin, dass für den deutschsprachigen Museumsbereich weiterhin verschiedenste Erfassungssysteme genutzt werden, die gängige Datenmodelle und Metadatenstandards häufig nicht ausreichend einbeziehen. Die GND ist, bedingt durch ihre hohe Verbreitung, grundsätzlich gut geeignet zur Normdatenanreicherung. Einschränkend ist jedoch zu beachten, dass zahlreiche für Museen relevante Begriffe noch nicht Teil der GND sind.[49]

6. Kritik an kontrollierten Vokabularen

Der weiter oben beschriebene Rekurs auf das Publikationsaufkommen, Einschränkungen durch bibliothekarische Regelwerke und mangelnde Ressourcen für eine kontinuierliche Datenanreicherung und -pflege sowie die unterschiedliche Güte einzelner Datensätze via Fremddatenübernahme führen dazu, dass die GND für einige Anwendungsbereiche unzureichend ist. Es fehlen Personen – beispielsweise relevante Personen aus dem Archiv- oder Museumsbereich, die teilweise im bibliothekarischen Kontext bislang nicht erwähnt wurden – oder die dazu gehörigen Datensätze verfügen über nicht ausreichende Angaben. Außerdem mangelt es an umfassenden Verknüpfungen zwischen Begriffen, sodass keine durchgängige Thesaurusstruktur vorhanden ist.

Neben diesen Leerstellen existiert eine politisch-ethische Kritik an Normdaten.[50] Kritiker:innen weisen darauf hin, dass Klassifikationssysteme nach Möglichkeit

---

48 Es existieren verschiedene Recherchemöglichkeiten, die einen Online-Zugriff auf die GND ermöglichen, beispielsweise die Homepage der OGND, die vom Bibliotheksservice-Zentrum Baden-Württemberg betreut wird. Lobid.org, gehostet vom Hochschulbibliothekszentrum des Landes NRW, besitzt neben einer Rechercheoberfläche auch Schnittstellen (APIs), mit denen ein automatisierter Abgleich und eine Harmonisierung von Daten mit der GND möglich ist.

49 Lill, J. (2019), Anm. 38, S. 20.

50 Für eine weitergehende Betrachtung dieses Komplexes siehe: Strickert, M. (2021). Für den deutschsprachigen Raum wurden zudem viele dieser Fragestellungen im Rahmen des digitalen Denkla-

vieldeutig und flexibel sein sollten, kontrollierte Vokabulare hingegen zu statisch seien. Die angestrebte Universalsprache hätte nur eine Scheinneutralität, wohingegen Wissen und Kategorien notwendigerweise (historisch) situiert sind. Die verwendeten Ausdrucksweisen zur Beschreibung von Themen sind unweigerlich ideologisch gefärbt[51] und privilegieren bestimmte Subjektpositionen und -perspektiven.[52] Es steht dabei in Frage, inwiefern eine Normierung die historische und kulturelle Perspektivität von Wissen berücksichtigen und trotz universellen Anspruchs gleichzeitig Diversität und Multiperspektivität in sich aufnehmen kann. Zugleich wird die Vorstellung von einem bzw. einer „neutralen Durchschnittsleser:in" kritisiert, an die sich die Erschließungsarbeit richten soll.[53]

Die Untersuchung von Bias in kontrollierten Vokabularen findet in den USA bereits seit den späten 1960ern statt.[54] Ein Diskussionsansatz stellt die demokratische Teilhabe mittels Folksonomien und anderen kooperativen Praktiken, wie der Integration von Suchtermini von Nutzer:innen in (kontrollierte) Vokabulare, dar.[55] Einige Autor:innen weisen zudem darauf hin, dass eine schlichte Umbenennung die Spuren von Historizität und Ideologie unsichtbar machen würde und dass vielmehr die Brüche in der Benennung deutlich gemacht werden sollten.[56] Dies gilt umso mehr,

---

bors Critical Library Perspectives (https://lab.sbb.berlin/events/critical-library-perspectives/#programm) erörtert. Eine Dokumentation der Projektergebnisse findet sich unter: 027.7 Zeitschrift für Bibliothekskultur. Critical Library Perspectives 9 (4) (2022).

51 Gartner, R. (2016), Anm. 1, S. 42.

52 Adler, M. (2017), S. 2.

53 Knowlton, S. A. (2005), S. 124.

54 Sanford Berman veröffentlichte mit „Prejudices and Antipathies. A Tract on the LC Subject Heads Concerning People" die erste umfassende Auseinandersetzung mit problematischen Begrifflichkeiten im Hinblick auf die Library of Congress Subject Headings. Neben Bermans jahrzehntelanger Arbeit in diesem Feld gibt es auch immer wieder Interventionen zu einzelnen Termini, siehe hier exemplarisch die Arbeit zum Terminus „East Indians" von Biswas, P. (2018), S. 1-18. Oder der Streit um die Ersetzung der Benennung „Illegal Aliens" durch die Bezeichnung „Undocumented Immigrants", der eine politische Debatte auslöste, in die sich sogar US-Senatsmitglieder einbrachten, siehe dazu Aguilera, J. (2016); Lo, G. (2019), S. 170-196.
Siehe für grundsätzliche (queer-)theoretische Erwägungen zu diesem Thema: Drabinski, E. (2013), S. 94.
Auch im deutschsprachigen Raum gibt es Kritik: So wird der Androzentrismus innerhalb der GND bemängelt, der nicht nur politisch problematisch sei, sondern gleichzeitig auch präzise Suchanfragen erschwere und zusätzlichen Rechercheaufwand schaffe (vgl. Aleksander, K. (2014), S. 15; Marković, B.; Kmyta, O. et al. (2016); Sparber, S. (2016)). Eine weitere Möglichkeit stellt die projektbezogene Anpassung von kontrollierten Vokabularen dar. Ein Beispiel ist die AMA MAIN-LCSH Working Group, die die Library of Congress Subject Headings mit Bezug auf indigene Gruppen für den kanadischen Archivkontext anpasste und dabei kulturell unsensible Begriffe durch solche ersetzte, die dem indigenen Sprachgebrauch mehr entsprechen, siehe dazu Bone, C.; Lougheed, B. (2018), S. 84.

55 Olson, H. A. (2002)

56 Drabinski, E. (2013), Anm. 54, S. 101.

zumal jede Kategorisierung notwendigerweise Ausschlüsse schafft und Änderungen immer Kontingenz aufweisen sowie zeitlich unabgeschlossen sind.[57]

7. Fazit und Ausblick

Metadaten spielen eine zentrale Rolle bei der Archivierung, Erschließung und Auffindbarkeit von Ressourcen. Eine Recherche über verschiedene Bestände und Portale hinweg ist dabei auf eine homogene Erschließung basierend auf konsistenten und aktuell gehaltenen, kontrollierten Vokabularen angewiesen. Einzelnen Forscher:innen helfen kontrollierte Vokabulare und Normdateien insofern, als sie der Orientierung dienen können, was gebraucht wird, wenn diese z. B. selbst Schlagwörter vergeben müssen, sodass eine größere Qualität der Ressourcenbeschreibung möglich ist.[58] Gleichzeitig erhöht eine präzise Begriffssammlung die Beschreibungsqualität bei der inhaltlichen Erschließung. Dies schafft ergänzende Sucheinstiege und liefert passendere Rechercheergebnisse, die das Potenzial einer höheren Auffindbar- und Sichtbarkeit der Ressourcen bieten.

Kontrollierte Vokabulare und ein darauf basierender Austausch von Metadaten ermöglichen eine Stärkung der Kooperation zwischen verschiedenen Institutionen sowohl aus dem universitären als auch außeruniversitären Bereich (Museen, Archive, Spezialbibliotheken etc.). Dies gilt trotz der berechtigten Kritik an jenen und ihrer zu reflektierenden politisch-historischen Perspektivität und Eingebundenheit. In Hinblick auf zukünftige Entwicklungen liegt ein großes Innovationspotenzial von Normdaten darin, dass diese die Grundlage für ein internationales semantisches Netzwerk sein können, das bislang voneinander getrennte Ressourcen aus den verschiedensten Institutionen maschinenlesbar zusammenführt und für weitere Anwendungen nutzbar macht. Auf diese Weise können neue Verbindungen etabliert, Bestände umfassender zugänglich gemacht und schließlich neues Wissen gewonnen werden. Um dies zu realisieren, müssen Ressourcen jedoch tatsächlich auf (aktuelle) Normdaten zurückgreifen und mit diesen durchgängig erschlossen werden.

57 Adler, M. (2017), Anm. 52, S. 157.

58 Für eine Anleitung, die Interessierten zeigt, wie sie bei der Recherche nach Normdaten vorgehen können, die als Schlagwörter z. B. bei der Einreichung eigener Artikel oder der Datenabgabe an Repositorien, aber auch zur Recherche verwendet werden können, siehe: Strickert, M. (2023).

Bibliografie

027.7 Zeitschrift für Bibliothekskultur (2022), 9 (4): Critical Library Perspectives. https://doi.org/10.21428/1bfadeb6.2d09bc20

Adler, Melissa (2017): Cruising the Library. Perversities in the Organization of Knowledge. 1st edition. New York: Fordham University Press.

Aguilera, Jasmine (2016): Another Word for "Illegal Alien" at the Library of Congress: Contentious. The New York Times, 23.07.2016. https://www.nytimes.com/2016/07/23/us/another-word-for-illegal-alien-at-the-library-of-congress-contentious.html (abgerufen am 17.05.2023)

Aleksander, Karin (2014): Die Frau im Bibliothekskatalog. In: LIBREAS 25. https://libreas.eu/ausgabe25/02alexander/ (abgerufen am 17.05.2023)

Bambey, Doris; Meyermann, Alexia; Porzelt, Maike et al. (2018): Bereitstellung und Nachnutzung qualitativer Daten in der Bildungsforschung. Das Forschungsdatenzentrum (FDZ) Bildung am DIPF. In: Hollstein, Betina; Strübing, Jörg (Hg.): Archivierung und Zugang zu qualitativen Daten. 1. Aufl. Berlin: Rat für Sozial- und Wirtschaftsdaten (RatSWD Working Paper 267/2018), S. 59-68.

Beall, Jeffrey (2008): The Weaknesses of Full-Text Searching. In: Journal of Academic Librarianship 34 (5), pp. 438-444.

Berman, Sandford (1971): Prejudices and Antipathies. A Tract on the LC Subject Heads Concerning People. Lanham: Scarecrow Press Books.

Biswas, Paromita (2018): Rooted in the Past: Use of "East Indians" in Library of Congress Subject Headings. In: Cataloging & Classification Quarterly 56 (1), pp. 1-18.

Bone, Christine; Lougheed, Brett (2018): Library of Congress Subject Headings Related to Indigenous Peoples. Changing LCSH for Use in a Canadian Archival Context. In: Cataloging & Classification Quarterly 56 (1), pp. 83-95. https://doi.org/10.1080/01639374.2017.1382641

Ceynowa, Klaus (2017): In Frankfurt lesen jetzt zuerst Maschinen. Frankfurter Allgemeine Zeitung, 31.07.2017. https://www.faz.net/aktuell/feuilleton/buecher/maschinen-lesen-buecher-deutsche-nationalbibliothek-setzt-auf-technik-15128954.html?printPagedArticle=true#pageIndex_4 (abgerufen am 17.05.2023)

Dierkes, Jens (2021): Planung, Beschreibung und Dokumentation von Forschungsdaten. In: Putnings, Markus; Neuroth, Heike; Neumann, Janna (Hg.): Praxishandbuch Forschungsdatenmanagement. 1. Aufl. Berlin: De Gruyter Saur, S. 303-326.

Drabinski, Emily (2013): Queering the Catalog. Queer Theory and the Politics of Correction. In: Library Quarterly: Information, Community, Policy 83 (2), pp. 94-111.

Flachmann, Holger (2004): Erschließung. Zur Effizienz bibliothekarischer Inhaltserschließung. Allgemeine Probleme und die Regeln für den Schlagwortkatalog (RSWK). In: Bibliotheksdienst 38 (6), S. 745-791.

Friedrich, Tanja; Recker, Jonas (2021): Auffindbarkeit und Nutzbarkeit von Daten. In: Putnings, Markus; Neuroth, Heike; Neumann, Janna (Hg.): Praxishandbuch Forschungsdatenmanagement. 1. Aufl. Berlin: De Gruyter Saur, S. 405-426.

Gartner, Richard (2016): Metadata. Shaping Knowledge from Antiquity to the Semantic Web. 1st edition. Basel: Springer.

Gross, Tina; Taylor, Arlene G.; Joudrey, Daniel N. (2015): Still a Lot to Lose. The Role of Controlled Vocabulary in Keyword Searching. In: Cataloging & Classification Quarterly 53 (1), pp. 1-39.

Haffner, Alexander (2012): Internationalisierung der GND durch das Semantic Web. https://wiki.dnb.de/download/attachments/43523047/20120716_internationalisierung-DerGndDurchDasSemanticWeb.pdf (abgerufen am 17.05.2023)

Heuer, Jan-Ocko; Kretzer, Susanne; Mozygemba, Kati et al. (2020): Kontextualisierung qualitativer Forschungsdaten für die Nachnutzung. Eine Handreichung für Forschende zur Erstellung eines Studienreports. Bremen: Universität Bremen. (Qualiservice Working Papers 1).

Imeri, Sabine; Sterzer, Wjatscheslaw; Harbeck, Matthias (2019): Forschungsdatenmanagement in den ethnologischen Fächern. Berlin: Zentraleinrichtung Universitätsbibliothek. (Schriftenreihe der Universitätsbibliothek der Humboldt-Universität zu Berlin 67).

Joudrey, Daniel; Taylor, Arlene (2018): The Organization of Information. 1st edition. Santa Barbara, California: Libraries Unlimited. (Library and Information Science Text Series).

Kasprzik, Anna; Kett, Jürgen (2018): Vorschläge für eine Weiterentwicklung der Sacherschließung und Schritte zur fortgesetzten strukturellen Aufwertung der GND. In: o-bib. Das offene Bibliotheksjournal 5 (4), S. 127-140.

Kett, Jürgen; Balter, Detlev; Fischer, Barbara K. et al. (2019): Content kuratieren. Das Projekt „GND für Kulturdaten" (GND4C). In: o-bib. Das offene Bibliotheksjournal 6 (4), S. 59-97.

Klump, Jens (2010): Digitale Forschungsdaten. In: Neuroth, Heike; Oßwald, Achim; Scheffel, Regine; Strathmann, Stefan; Huth, Karsten (Hg.): nestor-Handbuch. Eine kleine Enzyklopädie der digitalen Langzeitarchivierung, S. 104-115. http://nestor.sub.uni-goettingen.de/handbuch/nestor-handbuch_23.pdf (abgerufen am 17.05.2023)

Knowlton, Steven A. (2005): Three Decades since Prejudices and Antipathies. A Study of Changes in the Library of Congress Subject Headings. In: Cataloging & Classification Quarterly 40 (2), pp. 123-145.

Lill, Jens (2019): Gemeinsam neu definiert. Das Projekt „GND für Kulturdaten (GND4C)". In: AKMB-news 25 (1), S. 18-23.

Lo, Grace (2019): "Aliens" vs. Catalogers. Bias in the Library of Congress Subject Heading. In: Legal Reference Services Quarterly 38 (4), pp. 170-196.

Mann, Thomas (2008): Will Google's Keyword Searching Eliminate the Need for LC Cataloging and Classification? In: Journal of Library Metadata 8 (2), pp. 159-168.

Marković, Barbara; Kmyta, Olga; Sucker, Irina (2016): Objekterschließung an Bibliotheken, Museen und Archiven in Österreich. Ergebnisse einer Erhebung. In: Mitteilungen der VÖB 69 (3/4), S. 414-421.

Mödden, Elisabeth; Schöning-Walter, Christ; Uhlmann, Sandro (2018): Maschinelle Inhaltserschließung in der Deutschen Nationalbibliothek. Breiter Sammelauftrag stellt hohe

Anforderungen an die Algorithmen zur statistischen und linguistischen Analyse. In: Bub Forum Bibliothek und Information 70 (1), S. 30-35.

Olson, Hope A. (2002): The Power to Name. Locating the Limits of Subject Representation in Libraries. 1st edition. Dordrecht: Springer Netherlands.

Queckbörner, Boris (2019): Forschungsdaten und Forschungsdatenmanagement in der Geschichtswissenschaft. Gegenwärtige Praxis und Perspektiven am Beispiel ausgewählter Sonderforschungsbereiche. 1. Aufl. Berlin: Institut für Bibliotheks- und Informationswissenschaft der Humboldt-Universität zu Berlin. (Berliner Handreichungen zur Bibliotheks- und Informationswissenschaft 441).

Smioski, Andrea (2011): Wegweiser qualitative Datenarchivierung. Infrastruktur, Datenakquise, Dokumentation und Weitergabe. In: SWS-Rundschau 51 (2), S. 219-238.

Sparber, Sandra (2016): What's the frequency, Kenneth? - Eine (queer)feministische Kritik an Sexismen und Rassismen im Schlagwortkatalog. In: Mitteilungen der VÖB 69 (2), S. 236-243.

Stone, Alva T. (2000): The LCSH Century: A Brief History of the Library of Congress Subject Headings, and Introduction to the Centennial Essays. In: Cataloging & Classification Quarterly 29 (1-2), pp. 1-15.

Strickert, Moritz (2021): Zwischen Normierung und Offenheit. Potenziale und offene Fragen bezüglich kontrollierter Vokabulare und Normdateien. In: LIBREAS. Library Ideas 40. https://doi.org/10.18452/23807

Strickert, Moritz (2023): Vom Suchen und Finden. Handreichung zur Arbeit mit kontrollierten Vokabularen und Normdateien. https://doi.org/10.18452/26390

Sugimoto, Shigeo; Nagamori, Mitsuharu; Mihara, Tetsuya et al. (2015): Metadata in Cultural Contexts. From Manga to Digital Archives in a Linked Open Data Environment. In: Ruthven, Ian; Chowdhury, Gobinda (eds.): Cultural Heritage Information. Access and Management. 1st edition. London: Facet Publishing, pp. 89-112.

Team MusIS im BSZ (2020): Regelwerke, Thesauri, Klassifikationen, Systematiken und Begriffslisten. https://wiki.bsz-bw.de/display/MUSIS/Regelwerke%2C+Thesauri%2C+Klassifikationen%2C+Systematiken+und+Begriffslisten (abgerufen am 17.05.2023)

Uhlmann, Sandro (2013): Automatische Beschlagwortung von deutschsprachigen Netzpublikationen mit dem Vokabular der Gemeinsamen Normdatei. In: Dialog mit Bibliotheken 25 (2), S. 26-36.

Wiesenmüller, Heidrun (2018): Maschinelle Inhaltserschließung in der Deutschen Nationalbibliothek. Breiter Sammelauftrag stellt hohe Anforderungen an die Algorithmen zur statistischen und linguistischen Analyse. In: Bub Forum Bibliothek und Information 70 (1), S. 26-29.

Wilkinson, Mark D.; Dumontier, Michel; Aalbersberg, IJsbrand Jan et al. (2016): The FAIR Guiding Principles for Scientific Data Management and Stewardship. In: Scientific Data 3, 160018.

Moritz Strickert ist Ethnologe, Soziologe und wissenschaftlicher Bibliothekar. Derzeit ist er Mitarbeiter des Fachinformationsdienstes Sozial- und Kulturanthropologie (FID SKA) an der Universitätsbibliothek der Humboldt-Universität zu Berlin. Er arbeitet in einem Projekt zur GND aus ethnologischer Perspektive und ist in der Arbeitsgruppe Thesauri des Netzwerks für nachhaltige Forschungsstrukturen in kolonialen Kontexten aktiv.

Sonja Fiala

Schritt-für-Schritt-Anleitung: Metadatenmapping

Handbuch Repositorienmanagement, Hg. v. Blumesberger et al., 2024, S. 185–195
https://doi.org/10.25364/978390337423211

Sonja Fiala, Universität Wien, Fachbereichsbibliothek Philosophie und Psychologie, sonja.fiala@univie.ac.at | ORCID iD: 0000-0002-5492-8934

Zusammenfassung

Metadaten sind die Basis der Informationsgesellschaft. Nur wenn sie vollständig und korrekt angegeben werden, ist ein präzises Wiederauffinden der Objekte, die sie beschreiben, möglich. In dem folgenden Beitrag werden die verschiedenen Vorgehensweisen beim Metadatenmapping erörtert. Es wird auf die wichtigsten Punkte beim Mappingvorgang hingewiesen.

Schlagwörter: Metadatenmapping; Phaidra; MODS; RDF

Abstract

A Step-By-Step Tutorial: Metadata Mapping

Metadata form the fundament of the information society. The objects they describe can only be retrieved if the data are complete and precise. In the following paper different possible procedures in metadata mapping will be discussed, highlighting the most important points in the mapping process.

Keywords: Metadata mapping; phaidra; MODS; RDF

1. Einleitung

Die folgende Anleitung schildert die Erfahrungen, die während eines gemeinsamen Projekts der Universität Wien mit der Universität Padua gewonnen wurden. Seit einiger Zeit werden im „Universitätslehrgang Library and Information Studies“ das Wahlfach „Data Librarian“ und der Teilbereich Metadatenmapping unterrichtet. Als Beispiel der Ausführungen dient das Repositorium der Universität Wien (Phaidra[1]). Die Datenstruktur von Phaidra wurde über die letzten zehn Jahre durch verschiedene Fremdelemente, wie z. B. um die Angabe der ORCID iD, konstant erweitert und adaptiert. Um für die Zukunft gerüstet zu sein, kann es notwendig sein, bestehende Datensätze in international übliche Datenformate zu konvertieren und neue Datensätze nach internationalen Standards einzupflegen. Besonders wichtig wird dies, um verlässliche Suchergebnisse zu erhalten.

Metadaten spielen seit jeher im Bibliothekswesen eine wichtige Rolle. Früher waren es die Zettelkataloge, heute sind es die Daten über Daten, die im Zentrum der Arbeit stehen. Es ist von größter Bedeutung, dass die Erschließung der Daten nach Richtlinien erfolgt, um die Qualität der Suchergebnisse garantieren zu können. So wird es notwendig, zwischen den unterschiedlichen Beschreib- und Erschließungssystemen Parallelen herzustellen und die einzelnen Kategorien in Verbindung zu bringen. Die Metadaten müssen operabel sein, um in Zukunft von Nutzen sein zu können.

> Mapping is an important operation for data migration from legacy systems, a database model system, to other modern web technology or semantic system that computers can understand meaning of data. These are in many application domains, such as semantic web, schema or ontology integration, data integration etc. The methodology of mapping can distinguish three ways are: (1) database schema mapping, (2) Ontology mapping, and (3) database to RDF mapping [...][2] [sic!]

Metadaten werden zunehmend zum entscheidenden Faktor in der Informationsgesellschaft. Nur wenn die Metadaten eines Objektes exakt erfasst sind, werden Datensätze auffindbar und präzise recherchierbar. Man kann somit Metadaten als die Basis der Informationsgesellschaft bezeichnen[3]. Neben den Kernelementen (z. B. Metadata Object Description Schema (MODS): titleInfo, name, typeofResource,

1 https://phaidra.univie.ac.at/
2 Thangsupachai, N. et al. (2014), S. 123.
3 Als allgemeine Einführung in das Thema Metadaten ist folgendes Buch sehr empfehlenswert: Pomerantz, J. (2015).

genre, originInfo, language, physicalDescription, abstract, identifier, …)[4] enthalten Metadaten viele weitere Informationen, die auch immer im Auge behalten werden müssen. Alle Ebenen müssen korrekt verwaltet und gewartet werden – so beispielsweise die deskriptiven Metadaten, strukturellen Metadaten, Erhaltungsmetadaten, Herkunftsmetadaten, Nutzungsmetadaten und administrativen Metadaten.

Metadaten entscheiden über die Wiederauffindbarkeit, die präzise Suchbarkeit und letztendlich über die Möglichkeit des korrekten wissenschaftlichen Arbeitens. Hierbei spielen verschiedene Komponenten zusammen: Es müssen die Metadaten in den richtigen Feldern eingetragen sein, sie müssen vollständig sein und sie müssen die Daten ausreichend beschreiben.

2. Metadatenmapping

Eine adäquate Herangehensweise beim Metadatenmapping ist, dass man sich zunächst die Datenstruktur ansieht: Es ist wichtig zu verstehen, wie ein Datensatz in sich aufgebaut ist. Oftmals sind die einzelnen Kategorien in den unterschiedlichen Beschreibsystemen verschieden benannt. Jeder Datensatz folgt einer Logik, die nach bestimmten Regeln aufgebaut ist. Die Bedeutung der einzelnen Kategorien erschließt sich im Gebrauch. Das strukturierte Verstehen der einzelnen Kategorien zeichnet den Mappingvorgang aus. Die Problematik, dass die Eingabe der Daten z. B. in einem Repositorium wie Phaidra von verschiedenen Personen und mit unterschiedlicher Erschließungsgenauigkeit erfolgt, führt zu einem Herantasten an die Verwendung der Kategorien. Hier ist in Zukunft auf genaue Anleitungen für Personen, die Daten hochladen, zu achten. Das Metadatenmapping erinnert an das Zitat von Ludwig Wittgenstein, der zum Gebrauch der Wörter Folgendes sagt: „So lerne ich nach und nach verstehen, welche Dinge die Wörter bezeichnen, die ich wieder und wieder, an ihren bestimmten Stellen in verschiedenen Sätzen, aussprechen hörte.“[5] Und weiter „Was sie bezeichnen, wie soll sich das zeigen, es sei denn in der Art ihres Gebrauchs?“[6] Es werden auch Angaben sichtbar, die nicht in ein neues Schema überführbar sind. Für sie muss dann nach einer anderen Lösung gesucht werden (z. B. Notizfeld etc.).

4 MODS Elements and Attributes: https://www.loc.gov/standards/mods/userguide/generalapp.html#top_level

5 Wittgenstein, L. (2019), S. 237.

6 Ebd. S. 242.

3. Mappingvorgang

Das Mapping gleicht einer Drehbewegung, die an verschiedenen Stellen Halt sucht. Man beginnt mit jeweils einem Beispiel der unterschiedlichen Beschreibungsarten. Diese stellt man einander gegenüber und versucht Verbindungen herzustellen. Dann überprüft man die gewonnenen Erkenntnisse auch in den darauffolgenden Beispieldatensätzen. Hier kommt noch ein ganz wichtiger Aspekt dazu, nämlich die Frage, wie tief man die Datensätze in Zukunft erschließen möchte. Das heißt, an diesem Punkt muss man sich die Frage stellen, wie die Verbesserung in Zukunft aussehen soll. Man sieht sich das zugrundeliegende Schema genau an und entscheidet, welche Kategorien wichtig sind. Hier kann auch das probeweise Erfassen des Objekts in dem neuen Schema ein hilfreicher Vorgang sein. So werden die unterschiedlichen Kategorien schnell sichtbar und der Fokus wird auf die zu klärenden Unterschiede gelegt.

4. Dokumentation

Der Dokumentation der Kategorienverwendung kommt eine große Bedeutung zu. Alle Überlegungen sollten dokumentiert und kommentiert werden. Je mehr Personen den Mappingvorgang begleiten und mitdenken, desto verlässlicher wird das Ergebnis. Auch die Kommunikation zwischen den Datenbankbetreiber:innen, den Nutzer:innen und den Wissenschaftler:innen bekommt hier eine besondere Bedeutung. Welche Suchanfragen werden von den Nutzer:innen benötigt und verwendet? Wie aufwendig soll die Dateneingabe gestaltet sein? Gibt es Anleitungen und Schulungen?

5. Metadatenmanager:innen

Die Aufgaben des/der Metadatenmanager:in[7] umfassen nicht nur die korrekte Beschreibung der Metadatensätze, sondern auch die Kommunikation. Diese rückt ins Zentrum der Aufgabe, je weiter die Arbeit voranschreitet. Ebenso bedeutsam ist die Fähigkeit, auf Basis großer Erfahrung strukturiert zu arbeiten. Eine Kategorie nach der anderen muss bewertet und analysiert werden. Es sind viele unterschiedliche Darstellungsweisen möglich und potenziell sinnvoll, aber letztlich entscheidet der Erfolg darüber, welche Darstellungsweise man wählt.

Das Metadatenmapping wird somit zu einer spannenden und herausfordernden Arbeit, die wohl zu den gefragtesten bibliothekarischen Tätigkeiten der Zukunft werden wird. Viele Datenbanken entwickeln sich über viele Jahre und müssen ständig

7 Blumesberger, S.; Traub, I. D.; Schubert, B. et al. (2016)

gepflegt und gewartet werden. Neue Dateitypen entstehen und das kontrollierte Vokabular muss laufend gepflegt werden. Ein aktuelles Thema ist zum Beispiel die Beschreibung von barrierefreien Dateien[8]. Viele Normen müssen berücksichtigt und in der Dokumentation festgehalten werden. Diese Dokumentation ist wichtig für die nachkommende Generation, denn nur dann ist der Datenbankaufbau nachvollziehbar. Dieser Punkt wurde gerade in den Anfängen der Digitalisierung nicht ausreichend berücksichtigt. So sind viele Eingabemöglichkeiten historisch gewachsen und bei einem Mapping schwer zuordenbar. Die Kategorien von Dublin Core haben oft in der Praxis nicht ausgereicht und so wurden viele Angaben im Laufe der Zeit ergänzt.

> As mentioned above, Dublin Core was developed to be a lowest common denominator metadata element set. The problem with the lowest common denominator, however, is that sometimes it's too low.[9]

Auch die neue Architektur der Linked Data macht eine Überarbeitung der Datenstruktur notwendig. Am Beispiel Phaidra lassen sich die unterschiedlichen Entwicklungsstadien gut ablesen. Es gibt UWMETADATA-Datensätze (Universität-Wien-Metadatensätze)[10], Dublin-Core-[11] , JSON-LD-[12] („JavaScript Object Notation for Linked Data") und MODS-Datensätze[13]. MODS wird von der Library of Congress zur Verfügung gestellt.[14] Von MODS soll dann der Weg zu Resource Description Framework (RDF) geebnet sein.[15]

Besonders erwähnenswert sind auf der Seite der Library of Congress die verschiedenen MODS-Beispiele für unterschiedliche Medienarten[16] und die verschiedenen Versionen[17], da MODS laufend aktualisiert wird: So kommen neue Eingaben hinzu, wie zum Beispiel ORCID iD[18]:

---

8 Siehe auch Fiala, S. (2019).
9 Pomerantz, J. (2015), S. 81.
10 Z. B. https://fedora.phaidra.univie.ac.at/fedora/objects/o:740497/methods/bdef:Asset/getUWMETADATA
11 Z. B. https://services.phaidra.univie.ac.at/api/object/o:740497/index/dc
12 Z. B. https://services.phaidra.univie.ac.at/api/object/o:1192264/jsonld
13 Z. B. https://services.phaidra.univie.ac.at/api/object/o:950749/mods?format=xml
14 http://www.loc.gov/standards/mods/
15 https://www.loc.gov/standards/mods/modsrdf/
16 https://www.loc.gov/standards/mods/userguide/examples.html
17 https://www.loc.gov/standards/mods/mods-schemas.html
18 https://orcid.org/

Beispiel ORCiD iD:

```
<name>
  <namePart type="given">Wilhelmina</namePart>
  <namePart type="family">Randtke</namePart>
  <nameIdentifier type="orcid">https://orcid.org/0000-0002-7439-
8205</nameIdentifier>
 </name>
```

Wenn man die UWMETADATA nun auf MODS-Niveau bringen möchte, ist ein Metadatenmapping notwendig. In Zusammenarbeit mit der Universität Padua ist ein solches bereits vorbereitet worden[19]. Besonders dann, wenn es sich um eine gemeinsame Suchoberfläche (z. B. u:search der Universitätsbibliothek Wien) handelt, führt eine korrekte Datenstruktur zu qualitativ hochwertigeren Ergebnissen.

Die Bedeutung einer ausreichenden Dokumentation kann an dieser Stelle nicht genug betont werden. Die Festlegung der Reihenfolge der Kategorien, ihre Wiederholbarkeit, die zugrundeliegenden Standards und Normen müssen dokumentiert und erklärt werden.

6. Dokumentation der Verwendung

Es gibt bereits einige Beispiele für praxisnahe MODS-Dokumentationen. Hier seien z. B. die Dartmouth College Library MODS Documentation, die Princeton University MODS Documentation und die Swepub MODS format specification erwähnt.[20]

Aufbauend auf der Kenntnis beider Metadatenschemata und der Gegenüberstel lung verschiedener Beispiele rückt nun in einem nächsten Schritt die Datensatzkohärenz in den Mittelpunkt.

19 Fiala, S.; Huggle, C. (2019)

20 Dartmouth College Library MODS Documentation: https://www.dartmouth.edu/library/catmet/metadata_nonmarc/mods_docs/; Princeton University Library MODS Documentation: https://library.princeton.edu/departments/tsd/metadoc/mods/index.html; National Library of Sweden: https://www.kb.se/namespace/swepub/mods-format-specification/SWP_MODS_3.pdf

</mods:subject> <subject> <topic authority="gnd" authorityURI="http://d-nb.info/gnd/" valueURI="http://d-nb.info/gnd/4039902-3">Mönch</topic> <topic authority="gnd" authorityURI="http://d-nb.info/gnd/" valueURI="http://d-nb.info/gnd/4008690-2">Buddhismus</topic> <genre authority="gnd" authorityURI="http://d-nb.info/gnd/" valueURI="http://d-nb.info/gnd/4006568-6">Bild</genre> </subject>	
<classification authority="ddc" edition"13">930: Geschichte des Altertums bis ca. 499, Archäologie</classification> <classification authority="ÖFOS 2012">601010: Klassische Archäologie</classification> <classification authority="ÖFOS 2012">601026: Virtuelle Archäologie</classification>	<ns1:classification> <ns7:taxonpath> <ns7:source>13</ns7:source> <ns7:taxon seq="0">1072220</ns7:taxon> <ns7:taxon seq="1">1072233</ns7:taxon> <ns7:taxon seq="2">1068322</ns7:taxon> </ns7:taxonpath> <ns7:taxonpath> <ns7:source>16</ns7:source> <ns7:taxon seq="0">1072240</ns7:taxon> <ns7:taxon seq="1">1072397</ns7:taxon> <ns7:taxon seq="2">1073639</ns7:taxon> <ns7:taxon seq="3">1072400</ns7:taxon> </ns7:taxonpath> <ns7:taxonpath> <ns7:source>16</ns7:source> <ns7:taxon seq="0">1072240</ns7:taxon> <ns7:taxon seq="1">1072397</ns7:taxon> <ns7:taxon seq="2">1073639</ns7:taxon>

Beispiel 1: Prüfung der gebräuchlichen Elemente (Metadatenmapping, Universitätsbibliothek Wien, Frühjahr 2018)

Eine Analyse der fehlenden Kategorien ist unumgänglich, um korrekte und vollständige Datensätze zu erhalten.

Man kann die bisherigen Schritte wie folgt zusammenfassen und im letzten Schritt gemeinsam anwenden:

- Gegenüberstellung von Beispieldatensätzen
- Kenntnis und Erlernen beider Metadatenschemata
- Analyse der fehlenden Kategorien
- Prüfung der Metadatenkohärenz
- Probemapping mit Anmerkungen und weiteren Bearbeitungsschritten (z. B. Festlegung des kontrollierten Vokabulars etc.)

Das Mapping erfolgt von den Kernelementen hin zu den Randelementen.

1 MAPPING UWMETADATA --> MODS 3.6 erstellt von Sonja Fiala und Christina Huggle Stand: 05. Juni 2018

Beispiel 1 (Artikel, Text): o:685260

<ns0:uwmetadata xmlns:ns0="http://phaidra.univie.ac.at/XML/metadata/V1.0" xmlns:ns1="http://phaidra.univie.ac.at/XML/metadata/lom/V1.0" xmlns:ns10="http://phaidra.univie.ac.at/XML/metadata/provenience/V1.0"xmlns:ns11="http://phaidra.univie.ac.at/XML/metadata/provenience/V1.0/entity" xmlns:ns12="http://phaidra.univie.ac.at/XML/metadata/digitalbook/V1.0" xmlns:ns13="http://phaidra.univie.ac.at/XML/metadata/etheses/V1.0"xmlns:ns2="http://phaidra.univie.ac.at/XML/metadata/extended/V1.0" xmlns:ns3="http://phaidra.univie.ac.at/XML/metadata/lom/V1.0/entity" xmlns:ns4="http://phaidra.univie.ac.at/XML/metadata/lom/V1.0/requirement"xmlns:ns5="http://phaidra.univie.ac.at/XML/metadata/lom/V1.0/educational" xmlns:ns6="http://phaidra.univie.ac.at/XML/metadata/lom/V1.0/annotation" xmlns:ns7="http://phaidra.univie.ac.at/XML/metadata/lom/V1.0/classification"xmlns:ns8="http://phaidra.univie.ac.at/XML/metadata/lom/V1.0/organization" xmlns:ns9="http://phaidra.univie.ac.at/XML/metadata/histkult/V1.0">	<?xml version="1.0" encoding="UTF-8"?> <mods xmlns="http://loc.gov/mods/v3" xsi:schemaLocation="http://www.loc.gov/mods/v3 http//www.loc.gov/standards/mods/v3/mods-3-6.xsd" xmlns:xsi=http://www.w3.org/2001/XMLSchema-instance" version="3.6">
<ns1:general> <ns1:identifier>o:685260</ns1:identifier> <ns1:title language="de"> Digitale Archäologie und Molino San Vincenzo: Kein "Digital Dark Age" in der Toskana </ns1:title>	<titleInfo lang="de"> <title>Digitale Archäologie und Molino San Vincenzo: Kein "Digital Dark Age" in der Toskana</title> </titleInfo>
<ns1:language>de</ns1:language>	<language> <languageTerm type="code" authority="iso639-2b">ger</languageTerm> </language>
<ns1:description language="de"> Um den verschiedenen Prinzipien offener Wissenschaftskommunikation – wie auch dem ganzen Konzept »open science« als solchem – gerecht zu werden, ist eine	<abstract> Um den verschiedenen Prinzipien offener Wissenschaftskommunikation – wie auch dem ganzen Konzept »open science« als solchem – gerecht zu werden, ist eine nachhaltige Disseminations- und

Beispiel 2: Mapping der Datensätze (Metadatenmapping, Universitätsbibliothek Wien, Frühjahr 2018)

Hierfür kann eine Statistik hilfreich sein. Diese Statistik erfasst die Verwendungshäufigkeit einer Kategorie. Am Beispiel Phaidra kann diese Statistik dann für die Bewertung unterschiedlicher Kategorien herangezogen werden.

7. Gegenüberstellung

Für die weitere Vorgehensweise sind nun die Top-Level Elements[21] in MODS wichtig. Am besten eignen sich zwei Spalten in einem Textverarbeitungs- oder Tabellenkalkulationsprogramm mit Kommentaren für die Analyse der Datensätze.

In den Kommentaren werden die Sachverhalte, die noch geklärt werden müssen, erläutert. Um eine bessere Vorstellung des Mappingvorgangs zu bekommen, empfiehlt es sich, ein Probemapping durchzuführen. Alle Probleme und Fragestellungen werden in Kommentaren festgehalten. Ins Zentrum der Aufmerksamkeit rükken die Punkte, die noch weiter diskutiert und besprochen werden müssen.

Seit dem Sommersemester 2020 wird der Fachbereich Metadatenmapping im Universitätslehrgang Library and Information Studies unterrichtet. Die Studierenden

21 https://www.loc.gov/standards/mods/userguide/generalapp.html#top_level

erhalten die Aufgabe, ein Mapping (UWMETADATA >> MODS) durchzuführen, gemeinsam zu diskutieren und alle Überlegungen ausführlich zu dokumentieren und zu kommentieren.

Die Schritt-für-Schritt-Anleitung dient als Ausgangspunkt für die Studierenden, die dann gemeinsam ein breites Spektrum an Herangehensweisen erarbeiten. Diese praxisnahen Erkenntnisse sollen die Studierenden auf ihre zukünftigen Aufgaben als Metadatenspezialist:innen vorbereiten.

Bibliografie

Blumesberger, Susanne; Traub, Imola Dora; Schubert, Bernhard; Hudak, Rastislav; Gründhammer, Veronika (2016): Jobprofil von MetadatenmanagerInnen. https://phaidra.univie.ac.at/o:441513

Fiala, Sonja (2019): Kennzeichnung barrierefreier Dateien – eine Zusammenstellung am Beispiel MARC21 und MODS. https://resolver.obvsg.at/urn:nbn:at:at-ubi:3-6007

Fiala, Sonja; Huggle, Christina (2019): Metadatenmapping. Die Gegenüberstellung verschiedener Metadatenschemata am Beispiel UWMETADATA >> MODS 3.6. https://resolver.obvsg.at/urn:nbn:at:at-ubi:3-6020

Pomerantz, Jeffrey (2015): Metadata. (The MIT Press essential knowledge series). Cambridge, Mass.: The MIT Press.

Thangsupachai, Noppol; Niwattanakul, Suphakit; Chamnongsri, Nisachol (2014): Learning Object Metadata Mapping for Linked Open Data. In: Kulthida Tuamsuk, Adam Jatowt, Edie Rasmussen (eds.): The Emergence of Digital Libraries – Research and Practices. 16th International Conference on Asia-Pacific Digital Libraries, ICADL 2014, Chiang Mai, Thailand, November 5-7, 2014 Proceedings. (Lecture Notes in Computer Science 8839). Cham: Springer.

Tuamsuk, Kulthida; Jatowt, Adam; Rasmussen, Edie (eds.) (2014): The Emergence of Digital Libraries – Research and Practices. 16th International Conference on Asia-Pacific Digital Libraries, ICADL 2014, Chiang Mai, Thailand, November 5-7, 2014, Proceedings. (Lecture Notes in Computer Science 8839). Cham: Springer.

Wittgenstein, Ludwig (2019): Tractatus logico-philosophicus, Tagebücher 1914-1916, Philosophische Untersuchungen, 23. Auflage. (Ludwig Wittgenstein: Werkausgabe 1) Frankfurt am Main: Suhrkamp.

Sonja Fiala ist Leiterin der Fachbereichsbibliothek Philosophie und Psychologie der Universität Wien. Sie unterrichtet das Wahlfach Informationsethik im Universitätslehrgang Library and Information Studies und den Fachbereich Metadatenmapping im Wahlfach „Data Librarian" bzw. im gleichnamigen Zertifikatskurs. Sie veröffentlichte zum Thema Informationsethik und Bibliotheken sowie zum Thema

Metadatenmapping. Zuletzt: Sonja Fiala (2019): Kennzeichnung barrierefreier Dateien – eine Zusammenstellung am Beispiel MARC21 und MODS, https://resolver.obvsg.at/urn:nbn:at:at-ubi:3-6007.

Kristina Andraschko

Dateiformate in der Langzeitarchivierung

Handbuch Repositorienmanagement, Hg. v. Blumesberger et al., 2024, S. 197–213
https://doi.org/10.25364/978390337423212

Kristina Andraschko, Universität Wien, DLE Raum- und Ressourcenmanagement, kristina.andraschko@univie.ac.at

Zusammenfassung

Die verwendeten Dateiformate spielen eine wesentliche Rolle in der Langzeitspeicherung von digitalen Objekten. Durch die ständige Weiterentwicklung unterschiedlicher Technologien lässt sich immer nur eine aktuelle Empfehlung abgeben, die ihre Gültigkeit schnell verlieren kann. Es lassen sich jedoch Kriterien für Dateiformate definieren, durch die eine lange Speicherung begünstigt wird. Verschiedene Arten von Objekten, wie Videos, Tonaufnahmen, Bilder oder Texte stellen dabei unterschiedliche Anforderungen an die Wahl des geeigneten Dateiformats. Auch wenn ein Format alle Voraussetzungen für eine lange Archivierung erfüllt, ist es notwendig, neue Entwicklungen stets zu verfolgen und vorhandene Dateien möglichst verlustfrei anzupassen. Um digitale Objekte über einen langen Zeitraum aufzubewahren, ist es wichtig zu überlegen, in welcher Form sie gespeichert werden sollen. Nicht alle Dateiformate erweisen sich in dieser Hinsicht als zuverlässig. Der vorliegende Text soll einerseits für die Beurteilung von Formaten wichtiges Wissen vermitteln und andererseits einen Überblick über die aktuell häufig empfohlenen Formate bieten, sodass auch nicht genannte oder neue Formate auf ihre Eignung für die Langzeitarchivierung beurteilt werden können.

Schlagwörter: Dateiformat; Langzeitarchivierung

Abstract

Digital Formats for Long-Term Preservation

Deciding which file formats to use in a repository is a crucial task in the long-term preservation of digital objects. Due to constant changes in technology, one can only give recommendations that can very well be outdated quickly. However, there are criteria for file formats that support long-term-preservation. Various types of objects, such as video, audio, images or texts need different considerations to determine the appropriate file format. Even if a format meets all prerequisites for long-term preservation, it is important to be aware of new developments and to adapt existing file formats if necessary. In order to preserve digital objects over a long period of time, it is important to consider in which form they should be stored. Not all file formats prove to be reliable in this respect. On the one hand, this text is intended to provide important knowledge for the evaluation of formats. On the other hand, it provides an overview of the currently frequently recommended formats so that even formats not mentioned or new formats can be evaluated for their suitability for long-term archiving.

Keywords: File format; digital preservation

1. Formate für die Langzeitarchivierung

In der digitalen Langzeitarchivierung spielen Dateiformate eine wichtige Rolle, da sie den Zeitraum der Nutzbarkeit von Objekten mitbestimmen. Ist das Format nicht mehr aktuell, lässt sich eine Datei im schlimmsten Fall nicht mehr öffnen und ist so für das Archiv unbrauchbar.

Durch neue technische Anforderungen und Möglichkeiten kommen kontinuierlich neue Formate hinzu, während andere ihre Bedeutung verlieren und nicht mehr verwendet werden – bis zu dem Zeitpunkt, an dem sie gar nicht mehr verwendet werden *können*, weil beispielsweise die nötigen Programme fehlen. Solche Entwicklungen können schnell passieren, sodass es eine gewisse Herausforderung darstellt, sich unter den verfügbaren Formaten zurechtzufinden. Erschwerend kommt hinzu, dass im alltäglichen Sprachgebrauch und in unwissenschaftlichen Quellen unterschiedliche Begriffe häufig synonym verwendet werden. So spricht man beispielsweise häufig von PDF, auch wenn das Objekt als PDF/A – eine für die Langzeitarchivierung besser geeignete Unterart von PDF – vorliegt.

Je komplexer der Objekttyp, desto mehr scheiden sich auch die Geister darüber, welches „das beste Format" für diesen Typus ist.

Aufgrund der Vielschichtigkeit dieser Thematik ist ein Verständnis davon, was Dateiformate sind und worauf man achten sollte, wichtig. Daher wird im ersten Teil des vorliegenden Beitrags die Frage behandelt, was Dateiformate sind und welche Kriterien für die Auswahl von Formaten für die Langzeitarchivierung zu beachten sind. Im zweiten Teil werden aktuelle Formatempfehlungen für unterschiedliche Objekttypen beschrieben und mit Anmerkungen ergänzt. Zur besseren Übersichtlichkeit und für die Benutzung in der Praxis sind die Formatempfehlungen am Ende dieses Abschnitts in einer Tabelle zusammengefasst.

2. Was sind Dateiformate?

Um auch bei neuen oder unbekannten Dateiformaten eine Entscheidung im Hinblick auf die Eignung zur Langzeitspeicherung treffen zu können, ist es wichtig zu verstehen, was Dateiformate überhaupt sind und was diese tun. Die Antwort auf diese Fragestellung ist so komplex, dass sie selbst ganze Bücher füllen kann.[1] Da es

1 Eine verständliche Erklärung der Grundlagen bietet das Einführungskapitel in Gumm, H.-P. (2013), S. 4ff. oder Kersken, S. (2021), S. 55ff. Zu in Bibliotheken bzw. bei der Digitalisierung gebräuchlichen Formaten sei auch der Abschnitt Einstellungen, Formate und spezielle Verfahren empfohlen in: Lang, E. (2019), S. 169ff.

hier nur darum gehen soll, ein generelles Verständnis für die Thematik zu schaffen, wird im Folgenden eine vereinfachte Darstellung vorgenommen.

Damit ein Computer mit unseren digitalen Objekten umgehen kann, werden diese als Signale übertragen und gespeichert. Die Einheiten dieser Signale sind Bytes bzw. Bits, die als sogenannter Bitstream in einer Reihenfolge vorliegen, die von Programmen interpretiert und dadurch in der intendierten Form präsentiert werden können, z. B. als Bild oder Text.

Das Dateiformat gibt vor, wie die Bits im Bitstream einer Datei angeordnet sein müssen, damit ein Betriebssystem sie der richtigen Anwendung zuweisen kann, und wie das Programm weiter damit verfahren soll. Dazu gibt es gewisse Regeln, die die jeweiligen Programme kennen müssen, um mit der Datei zu arbeiten. Kennen sie diese Richtlinien nicht, können die Daten nicht korrekt wiedergegeben werden. Dieses Problem zeigt sich in der Praxis oft in Form von Fehlermeldungen, die vermutlich hinreichend bekannt sind („Diese Datei kann nicht geöffnet werden, dieses Format wird nicht unterstützt.“).

Diese Regeln, die definieren, wie die Daten codiert und angeordnet sein müssen, sind in der Spezifikation eines Dateiformats beschrieben. Es ist übrigens ein wichtiges Kriterium für ein Format in der Langzeitarchivierung, dass diese Spezifikation einsehbar ist.

Wie die Speichermedien selbst, können auch Dateiformate mit der Zeit obsolet werden, wenn es kein Gerät oder Programm mehr gibt, das mit ihnen umgehen und sie richtig interpretieren kann. Ein Objekt kann dadurch für das Archiv unbrauchbar werden. Um der Obsoleszenz vorzubeugen, ist ein Monitoring der verwendeten Formate wichtig, aber bereits bei der Auswahl der zu akzeptierenden Formate sollte dieser Fall mitbedacht werden.

3. Kriterien für die Auswahl von Formaten für die Langzeitarchivierung

Eine Gefahr in der Langzeitarchivierung in Bezug auf die Dateiformate ist also, dass es kein Programm mehr gibt, das in der Lage ist, eine Datei zu öffnen und korrekt darzustellen. Aber auch häufige Migration oder eine sich verändernde Rechtslage können dazu führen, dass Formate – und im schlimmsten Fall die digitalen Objekte selbst – unbrauchbar werden. Daher sollten bei der Wahl geeigneter Dateiformate verschiedene Faktoren in Betracht gezogen werden. Es gibt gewisse Kriterien, die dabei als Orientierung dienen:

- Offenheit
- Verbreitung
- Transparenz/Verlustfreiheit
- Selbstdokumentation/Metadaten
- Freiheit von Kopierschutz und Verschlüsselungen
- Externe Abhängigkeiten/Portabilität
- Patentfreiheit

Im Folgenden werden die Kriterien zusammen mit den Fragen, die man sich bei der Wahl eines geeigneten Datenformats stellen kann, näher erläutert.

Offenheit

Ist eine Spezifikation des Formates zugänglich?

Im Idealfall sollte die Spezifikation eines Dateiformats offen einsehbar und dokumentiert sein. Dadurch wird ermöglicht, ein Programm zum Lesen eines Formats nachzubauen, wenn beispielsweise die ursprüngliche Software nicht mehr verfügbar ist. Zu beachten ist auch, ob das Dateiformat urheberrechtlich geschützt (proprietär) ist. Nicht-proprietäre Dateiformate haben meistens eine offene Dokumentation. Es gibt aber auch proprietäre Formate, deren Spezifikationen durch den Rechteinhaber veröffentlicht wurden.

Verbreitung

Wie weit verbreitet ist das Format? Wird es häufig genutzt oder handelt es sich eher um ein Nischenprodukt? Gibt es ein anderes Format im selben Bereich, das hier deutlich mehr genutzt wird?

Je weiter verbreitet ein Format ist, desto mehr Möglichkeiten gibt es in der Regel, Dateien in diesem Format zu lesen. Eine hohe Verbreitung beugt auch einer Obsoleszenz des Formates vor.

Transparenz/Verlustfreiheit

Welche Codierung wird innerhalb des Formats verwendet? Welcher Komprimierungsalgorithmus wird bei diesem Format eingesetzt?

Für die Langzeitarchivierung geeignete Formate sollten möglichst direkt analysiert werden können, z. B. durch die Lesbarkeit in einem Text-Editor. Der Inhalt sollte nach bestehenden Standards codiert sein, so empfiehlt sich z. B. für Text Unicode oder UTF-8.

Für Bilder, Audios und Videos gibt es verlustfreie und verlustbehaftete Formate, wobei man sich dabei in den meisten Fällen auf den verwendeten Komprimierungsalgorithmus bezieht. In vielen Bereichen ist Datenverlust durchaus hinnehmbar, z. B., wenn eine geringe Dateigröße erzielt werden soll. Das kann der Fall sein, wenn nur wenig Speicherplatz zur Verfügung steht, mit dem sparsam umgegangen werden muss. In der Langzeitarchivierung sind Formate mit möglichst verlustfreier Kompression die bessere Wahl. Eine Speicherung ganz ohne Datenverlust bzw. -komprimierung ist nicht immer möglich, da die Dateigrößen bei multimedialen Objekten in vielen Fällen nicht zu bewältigen wären.

Wenn eine Umwandlung in ein anderes Format notwendig wird, ist ebenso eine verlustfreie Umwandlung zu wählen, sofern eine solche umsetzbar ist.

Selbstdokumentation/Metadaten

Welche Arten von Metadaten werden in diesem Format gespeichert, wie kann darauf zugegriffen werden oder wo werden sie dargestellt?

Verschiedene Dateiformate können in unterschiedlichem Maße zusätzliche Informationen speichern, die die Lesbarkeit und Dokumentation eines Objekts vereinfachen. Technische Metadaten können auch mit unabhängigen Tools generiert und vom digitalen Objekt getrennt gespeichert werden, jedoch ist es für die Zukunft eines Objekts wesentlich günstiger, wenn es diese Daten direkt selbst enthält. Zusätzlich können auch deskriptive Metadaten direkt in einer Datei enthalten sein, was ihre Auffindbarkeit und den Umgang mit ihr langfristig erleichtern kann. Sofern das vorliegende Dateiformat eine Speicherung der Metadaten unterstützt, kann diese automatisch, z. B. direkt durch das Aufnahmegerät, oder manuell erfolgen.

Freiheit von Kopierschutz und Verschlüsselungen

Enthält ein Objekt einen Kopierschutz und/oder ist es verschlüsselt?

Der Gedanke, ein Objekt durch integrierte Mechanismen vor dem Kopieren zu schützen, widerspricht der Langzeitarchivierung grundsätzlich. Um Dateien dauerhaft für die Zukunft zu sichern, wird man sie kopieren müssen. Ein Kopierschutz darf auch nicht ohne Weiteres entfernt oder umgangen werden. Daher sollte sichergestellt werden, dass die zu archivierenden Objekte nach Möglichkeit in einem Format ohne Kopierschutz oder Digital-Rights-Management-Systeme (DRM) vorliegen. Ein Format muss allerdings nicht ausgeschlossen werden, nur weil es die Möglichkeit bietet, einen solchen Kopierschutz zu implementieren.

Externe Abhängigkeiten/Portabilität

Mit welchem Gerät wird die Datei geöffnet? Kann ich sie auf anderen Geräten öffnen? Welche Software wird dafür benötigt und gibt es mehr als ein Programm zum Öffnen dieser Datei?

Für die Langzeitarchivierung geeignete Dateiformate sollten nicht an eine bestimmte Hard- oder Software gebunden sein. Mit Blick auf die Zukunft ist immer denkbar, dass die benötigten Geräte oder Programme nicht mehr zur Verfügung stehen.

Patentfreiheit

Ist ein Format patentiert? Wer ist der Patentinhaber? Welche Firmen stehen dahinter, wie positioniert sich der Patentinhaber zu Forschung und Open-Source-Projekten usw.?

Patente verhindern sowohl die Weiterentwicklung von Software, die mit einem Format in Zusammenhang steht, als auch die Planbarkeit in Bezug auf die Nutzung eines Objekts. So können sich beispielsweise Lizenzbedingungen in eine Richtung ändern, die aus unterschiedlichen Gründen von Archiven nicht mehr toleriert wird. Durch zeitlich begrenzte Lizenzierung oder für die Freischaltung benötigte externe Quellen kann nicht garantiert werden, dass eine Datei oder eine Software nach mehreren Jahren immer noch zur Verfügung stehen.

Durch eine genaue Analyse vor der Auswahl eines Datenformats werden gute Bedingungen geschaffen, um die Daten auch in Zukunft noch verwenden zu können. Dass auch mit Bedacht ausgewählte Formate obsolet werden können und daher die Arbeit hier noch nicht getan ist, wird im Abschnitt „Migration und Emulation“ thematisiert.

4. Dateiformate – aktuelle Empfehlungen

Im Folgenden sind die derzeit empfohlenen Formate für Objekte der Typen Text, Bild, Audio und Video beschrieben, da diese momentan am häufigsten archiviert werden sollen. Die Empfehlungen ergeben sich aus den bereits beschriebenen Kriterien, sowie bestehenden Empfehlungen namhafter Bibliotheken und Institute.[2] Häufige Dateiendungen der jeweiligen Formate sind dabei angegeben, es sei aber

2 Informationsquellen und Anlaufstellen werden in Abschnitt 6 „Nutzen verschiedener Quellen und Vernetzung“ angegeben.

darauf hingewiesen, dass die Dateiendung allein nicht automatisch einen Rückschluss auf das tatsächlich vorliegende Datenformat zulässt.

In diesem Kapitel wird in einigen Bereichen ein breiteres Basiswissen vorausgesetzt. In den Fußnoten finden sich zusätzliche Informationen und Links zur Einführung bzw. Vertiefung in das jeweilige Thema. Für die Formate selbst sei an dieser Stelle auf die Formatbeschreibungen der Library of Congress[3] hingewiesen.

Text

Genau genommen sind Textdateien codierte Textzeichen, die nacheinander interpretiert werden. Dem Objekt liegt ein standardisierter Zeichensatz zugrunde, anhand welchem der Inhalt decodiert werden kann.[4] Zusätzlich kann in einer Textdatei auch die Information zu einer Schriftart gespeichert sein. Hier ist Vorsicht geboten, da diese Schriftarten außerhalb der Datei gespeichert sind. Entscheidet man sich für die Speicherung in Form einer Textdatei, sollten verbreitete und standardisierte Zeichensätze (UTF[5] oder ASCII) verwendet werden. Geht es nicht nur um den Text, sondern auch um die Darstellungsform, muss die Information zur Schriftart in den Metadaten gespeichert werden.

Generell sollten nur Formate verwendet werden, die die Informationen zu Zeichensatz und Schriftart enthalten.

Meist handelt es sich bei den zu archivierenden Dateien aber nicht um reine Textdokumente. Es kann daher sinnvoll sein, Formate zu wählen, die auch mit einer komplexeren Darstellung von Tabellen und Bildern umgehen können. Auch Spreadsheets und Tabellen können in diese weiter gefasste Definition von Textdateien fallen.

Selbstverständlich ist es auch möglich, Texte als Bilder zu speichern. Umgangssprachlich werden auch solche Dateien als Textdateien bezeichnet.

<u>Empfohlen (Text)</u>: **unformatierter Text** (z. B.: *.txt, *.asc, *.c), **PDF/A** (*.pdf), **PDF/UA** (*.pdf), sowie **XML-basierte Formate** (z. B.: EPUB3 *.epub)

<u>Empfohlen (Tabellen, Spreadsheets)</u>: **CSV** (*.csv)

<u>Bedingt geeignet:</u> **PDF** (*.pdf) LaTeX, TeX (*.tex)

---

3 https://www.loc.gov/preservation/digital/formats/fdd/descriptions.shtml

4 Eine gute Einführung in die Zeichencodierung bietet das W3C (World Wide Web Consortium): https://www.w3.org/International/questions/qa-what-is-encoding.de

5 Unicode Transformation Format. Der Unicode-Standard findet sich auf der Website des Unicode Consortiums: https://www.unicode.org/versions/Unicode14.0.0/

Nicht geeignet: **Word** (*.doc), **Powerpoint** (*.ppt)

Anmerkungen

Unformatierter Text soll nach Möglichkeit als ASCII, UTF-8 oder UTF-16 codiert sein. Bei UTF muss die Byte-Order Mark angegeben sein, die die Reihenfolge beschreibt, in der die Bytes gelesen werden müssen. Bei Bedarf kann auch ISO 8859-1[6] verwendet werden.

Bei PDF/A handelt es sich um eine Spezialisierung des PDF-Standards, die für die Archivierung empfohlen wird. Verglichen mit dem PDF-Standard wurde hier eine Reduzierung vorgenommen und es wurden Funktionen eliminiert, die der Archivierung nicht förderlich wären. So wurde z. B. die Möglichkeit entfernt, externe Elemente einzubinden.

Eine weitere Spezialisierung des PDF-Standards, PDF/UA, definiert den Umgang mit unterschiedlichen Unterstützungstechnologien und damit den barrierefreien Zugang zu einer Datei.

Bei der Verwendung von auf XML[7] basierenden Formaten ist darauf zu achten, dass keine externen Links verwendet werden und dass die Buchstabencodierung und die Dokumenttypdefinition (DTD) in der Datei angegeben sind.

LaTeX[8] bzw. TeX-Dateien sind für die Langzeitarchivierung geeignet, wenn sie die empfohlenen Codierungen verwenden. Zusätzlich sollten aber auch die erzeugte PDF-Datei sowie gegebenenfalls verwendete Pakete z. B. mit Schriftarten gespeichert werden.

In Bezug auf die nicht geeigneten Formate ist festzuhalten, dass zu den beliebten, aber proprietären Formaten aus der Microsoft-Office-Familie zwar teilweise bereits Dateiformatspezifikationen veröffentlicht wurden, diese aber nicht zwingend vollständig sind.

Bild

Es gibt eine große Anzahl von Bild- bzw. Grafikformaten. Viele verfolgen unterschiedliche Zwecke wie schnelle Implementierbarkeit oder möglichst wenig benötigten Speicher. In vielen Fällen enthalten die Formate einen Komprimierungsalgorithmus, mit dem Bildpunkte zusammen gespeichert werden. Je nach Art der

---

6 https://www.iso.org/standard/28245.html

7 XML (Extensible Markup Language) Essentials mit Beispielen: https://www.w3.org/standards/xml/core

8 The LaTeX-Project: https://www.latex-project.org/

Komprimierung ist die Datei verlustbehaftet oder verlustfrei. Verlustfreiheit bedeutet in den meisten Fällen eine größere Datei und damit mehr benötigten Speicher. Zusätzlich unterscheidet man zwischen Vektor- und Rastergrafiken. Eine Rastergrafik besteht aus Bildpunkten in unterschiedlichen Farben, während eine Vektorgrafik aus grafischen Elementen wie Linien und Pfaden besteht.[9] Für beide Varianten gibt es unterschiedliche Verwendungen und Dateiformate, weshalb sie im Folgenden separat behandelt werden.

Rastergrafik

Empfohlen: **TIFF** (*.tif), **JPEG2000** (*.jp2), **PNG** (*.png)

Bedingt geeignet: **Digital Negative Format** (*.dng), **GIF** (*.gif), **JPEG/JFIF** (*.jpg), **BMP** (*.bmp)

Nicht geeignet: proprietäre Rohdatenformate verschiedener Kamerahersteller, deren Dateiformatspezifikationen nicht offen sind

Anmerkungen

Viele der angegebenen Formate unterstützen unterschiedliche Stufen der Komprimierungen. Für die Langzeitarchivierung empfiehlt sich, eine möglichst verlustfreie Komprimierung zu wählen.

Bei dem Digital Negative Format handelt es sich um ein Rohdatenformat von Adobe Inc., dessen Dateiformatspezifikation offen ist. Da es mit einem Patent belegt ist, ist es nur bedingt für die Langzeitarchivierung geeignet. Möchte man aber die Rohdaten eines Bildes speichern, empfiehlt sich dieses Format wegen seiner Verbreitung und der Offenheit der Spezifikation.

Vektorgrafik

Empfohlen: **Scalable vector graphics** (*.svg)

Nicht geeignet: **InDesign Grafik** (*.indd), **Photoshop** (*.psd, *.psb), **Encapsulated Postscript** (*.eps, *.epsf, *.ps)

Audio

Eine Audiodatei enthält die digitale Form einer Audioaufzeichnung. Wie bei Bildern wird auch bei Audiodateien häufig ein Algorithmus zur Komprimierung angewendet, um eine geringere Dateigröße zu erzielen. Das kann zu Datenverlusten führen, die in der Langzeitarchivierung vermieden werden sollen.

---

9 Als niederschwelliger Einstieg in die Computergraphik sei hier empfohlen: Eck, D. (2021).

Häufig kommen für Audiodateien sogenannte Containerformate zum Einsatz. Der Container beinhaltet dabei verschiedene Daten, die durch einen Codec entschlüsselt werden. Genau genommen kommen durch Container und Codec zwei Formate zum Einsatz.

Empfohlen: **WAVE** (*.wav), **BMF,** FLAC [Codec] (Audiodaten als LPCM)

Bedingt geeignet: **Advanced Audio Coding** (*.mp4), **MP3** (*.mp3)

Nicht geeignet: z. B.: **AIFF** (*.aif), **Windows Media Audio** (*.wma), **Ogg** (*.ogg)

Anmerkungen

Das WAVE Format ist eigentlich ein von Microsoft und IBM entwickeltes proprietäres Format. Da die Dokumentation offen und die Verbreitung sehr hoch sind, hat es sich dennoch als Standard durchgesetzt.

Bei WAVE handelt es sich um ein Containerformat, das für die Langzeitarchivierung im Idealfall eine unkomprimierte Tonspur in LPCM-Codierung[10] enthalten sollte.

Broadcast Wave ist eine Unterkategorie des empfohlenen WAVE Formats, das die Speicherung von Metadaten möglich macht. Es wird überwiegend im Rundfunkbereich eingesetzt.

Video

Eine Videodatei ist komplex, da sie neben auditiven auch visuelle Inhalte enthält. Sie besteht meist aus einer Containerdatei, in der unter anderem die Audio- und Video- Streams enthalten sind. Diese Streams haben ein Format, das durch einen Codec (de-)codiert wird.

Meistens ist mit dem Format jenes der Containerdatei gemeint. Die Bezeichnungen für Container, Videoformat und Codec werden häufig synonym verwendet oder manchmal schlicht verwechselt, was die Informationsbeschaffung erschweren kann.[11]

---

10 Pulse-Code Modulation beschreibt ein Verfahren, bei welchem analoge Signale in digitale umgewandelt werden. PCM und die spezielle Form LPCM (Linear Pulse-Code Modulation) werden in den Formatbeschreibungen der Library of Congress geführt: https://www.loc.gov/preservation/digital/formats/fdd/fdd000016.shtml, https://www.loc.gov/preservation/digital/formats/fdd/fdd000011.shtml

11 Für eine vertiefende Auseinandersetzung mit dem Thema Video eignet sich z. B. Weynand, D. (2016).

Die Überlegung, ob ein Format geeignet ist, muss für Videodateien noch weitergehen als bei den bisher behandelten Objekttypen, da nicht nur der Codec, sondern auch das Containerformat für die Langzeitspeicherung geeignet sein muss. Dass nicht alle Containerformate mit jedem Codec verwendbar sind, macht die Aufgabe, Videodateien längerfristig zu speichern, noch komplexer.

Daher ist es im Falle von Videodateien besonders wichtig, sich bei der Formatwahl an die eingangs definierten Kriterien zu halten und z. B. nur standardisierte und offene Codecs zu verwenden. Unkomprimierte Videodateien erfordern meist zu viel Speicherplatz, weshalb man Codecs mit verlustfreier Kompression wählen sollte.

Betrachtet man die Komplexität von Videodateien, ist es nicht verwunderlich, dass es in diesem Bereich unterschiedliche Meinungen und Richtungen in Bezug auf empfohlene Formate gibt. In den meisten Fällen lässt sich das Format gar nicht so einfach wählen, da manche Aufnahmegeräte bereits ein bestimmtes Format ausgeben oder eine Datei bereits vorliegt. Wenn es die Umstände erlauben, ist es empfehlenswert, auch andere Formate, z. B. die bedingt geeigneten, zu akzeptieren und eine größere Formatanzahl in Kauf zu nehmen. Eine Migration in ein empfohlenes Format ist oft nur eingeschränkt sinnvoll, da sie einen Datenverlust bedeuten kann. Aufgrund dessen und in Hinblick auf die sich schnell entwickelnde Technik in diesem Bereich sollte zu häufiges Migrieren von Videodateien besser vermieden werden.

Empfohlen: **Matroska** (*.mkv) [Container] mit den Codecs: FFV1 (Version 3) und FLAC, **MXF** (*.mxf) [Container]

Bedingt geeignet: **Quick Time** (*.mov) [Container] mit den Codecs: 444 (XQ), 4444 oder 444 HQ, **Motion JPEG 2000** (*.mj2, *.mjp2) [Container] mit Codec JPEG 2000, MPEG-2 [Codec], **MPEG-4** (*.mp4)

Nicht geeignet: **Windows Media Video** (*.wmv) **RealVideo** (*.rm, *.rv), **Flash Video** (*.flv),

Anmerkungen

Die Moving Pictures Experts Group (MPEG) ist als Arbeitsgruppe der ISO und der IEC für die Standardisierung von Video- und Audiokompression verantwortlich. In den Standards der MPEG sind sowohl Videoformate als auch -Codecs beschrieben.[12]

12 https://www.mpegstandards.org/standards/

Von der Library of Congress wird das Containerformat Quick Time zusammen mit den Codecs 4444 (XQ), 4444 oder 444 HQ empfohlen.[13] Allerdings handelt es sich dabei um ein proprietäres Format der Firma Apple, dessen Dokumentation jedoch offen ist.

Motion JPEG 2000 ist ein Containerformat für den Codec JPEG 2000. Beides ist nicht völlig lizenzfrei. Der Codec JPEG 2000 bietet die Möglichkeit, sowohl verlustbehaftet als auch verlustfrei zu komprimieren.

Da FFV1 eine vergleichbare Kompression bietet und damit häufig die bessere Alternative darstellt, ist JPEG 2000 nur bedingt empfehlenswert.

Neben den genannten Objektarten gibt es eine Vielzahl weiterer, die in der Langzeitarchivierung eine Rolle spielen. So können abhängig vom Forschungsfeld ganz andere Formate relevant sein. Durch die fortschreitende technologische Entwicklung entstehen auch neue Elemente, die archiviert werden müssen. Zunehmend gewinnen dynamische Objekttypen wie Datenbanken, Programme oder Computerspiele für die Langzeitarchivierung an Bedeutung. Ein Format kann dann vielleicht nicht mehr vorgeschrieben werden und der Fokus muss darauf liegen, möglichst viele Informationen und Möglichkeiten zum langen Erhalt zusätzlich zu archivieren. Software muss z. B. mit genauen Angaben zur benötigten Umgebung (Betriebssystem, Hardware) und mitsamt Sourcecode gespeichert werden. Auch das Betriebssystem selbst muss unter Umständen archiviert werden, um sicherzustellen, dass das archivierte Objekt für die Zukunft erhalten werden kann.

5. Migration und Emulation

Eingangs wurde die Schnelllebigkeit digitaler Inhalte und Formate bereits thematisiert. Laufend werden neue Formate und Standards entwickelt und neue Technologien verändern immer öfter den Umgang mit Medien.

Für die Langzeitarchivierung bedeutet das, dass die Arbeit nicht beendet ist, wenn ein geeignetes Format für ein Objekt gewählt wurde. Neue Entwicklungen und ihre Verbreitung unter den Endbenutzer:innen müssen beständig verfolgt werden.

Wenn sich die Dateien in einem bestimmten Format nicht mehr verwenden lassen, weil es z. B. keine Programme mehr dafür gibt, spricht man von einem obsoleten Format. Droht ein Format obsolet zu werden, lässt es sich nicht vermeiden, dass

13 LoC recommended formats statement 2021/2022: https://www.loc.gov/preservation/resources/rfs/RFS%202021-2022.pdf

ein Objekt von einem Dateiformat in ein anderes migriert, also umgewandelt werden muss. Dabei muss sichergestellt werden, dass so wenig Datenverlust wie möglich auftritt. Wenn Ausgangs- und Zielformat hinreichend dokumentiert sind, lässt sich anhand der technischen Gegebenheiten entscheiden, ob eine verlustfreie Migration möglich ist. Gerade bei komplexen Objekten, z. B. mit audiovisuellen Inhalten, ist eine Umwandlung ohne Informationsverlust nur schwierig zu realisieren. Zu häufiges Migrieren sollte in diesen Fällen daher vermieden werden.

Als Alternative zur Migration kann immer öfter eine Emulation in Erwägung gezogen werden. Dabei wird ein System nachgebildet, um Inhalte wieder verfügbar zu machen, die auf einem aktuellen System nicht mehr abspielbar sind. Mit einer wachsenden Zahl an dynamischen digitalen Objekten gewinnt die Emulation zunehmend an Bedeutung.

6. Nutzen verschiedener Quellen und Vernetzung

Derzeit herrscht im Wesentlichen eine gewisse Einigkeit bei den empfohlenen Formaten für die Objekttypen Text, Bild und Ton. Bei Videodateien, die mehrere Formattypen umfassen, bilden sich unterschiedliche Präferenzen aus. Ein Abweichen von einem empfohlenen Format kann unter gewissen Voraussetzungen auch sinnvoll sein.

Zum Abschluss sei an dieser Stelle noch einmal darauf hingewiesen, dass sich Empfehlungen für geeignete Formate schnell ändern können und dass das passende Format – besonders bei komplexen multimedialen Objekttypen – von vielen unterschiedlichen Faktoren abhängig ist. Es ist daher notwendig, kontinuierlich Recherche zu betreiben. Viele Bibliotheken und Archive geben regelmäßig Formatempfehlungen oder Statements ab, die eine gute Orientierungshilfe darstellen. Bestehende File Format Registries können zurate gezogen und in die eigenen Archive eingebunden werden. Um vorliegende Formate erkennen und besser beurteilen zu können, lassen sich unterschiedliche Tools einsetzen. Einige hilfreiche Informationsquellen sind im Folgenden gelistet. Diese ersetzen nicht die eigene Recherche, denn auch die genannten Quellen können veralten und bilden daher nur eine Momentaufnahme ab.

Formatempfehlungen und Informationssammlungen

Library of Congress Recommended Formats Statement[14]

Die amerikanische Library of Congress gibt jährlich Formatempfehlungen aus, die auf der genannten Website abrufbar sind. Dort finden sich neben Empfehlungen für digitale Objekte auch Angaben zu analogen Werken.

Formatpolicy der Universitätsbibliothek Bern[15]

Als Beispiel für die Empfehlungen einer deutschsprachigen Bibliothek sei hier die Formatpolicy der Universitätsbibliothek Bern genannt, die zuletzt 2020 auf der Website der Bibliothek veröffentlicht wurde. Die Koordinationsstelle für die dauerhafte Archivierung elektronischer Unterlagen[16] wird dabei als einschlägige Quelle angegeben.

Sustainability of Digital Formats[17]

Die Library of Congress bietet zudem eine große Informationssammlung zu nachhaltigen Formaten in der Langzeitarchivierung, wo auch detaillierte Formatbeschreibungen zu finden sind.

IANUS[18]

Das Forschungsdatenzentrum Archäologie und Altertumswissenschaften des Deutschen Archäologischen Instituts enthält Formatbeschreibungen von für die Fachrichtung relevanten Formaten. Neben den auch in dem vorliegenden Kapitel behandelten Objekttypen finden sich dort auch Informationen zu Datenbanksystemen und Geoinformationssystemen. Da die angeführten Formatbeschreibungen besonders detailliert sind, sind die Informationen auch außerhalb der angegebenen Fachrichtung hilfreich.

Tools und File Format Registries

PRONOM[19] – File Format Registry des National Archives of the United Kingdom

14 https://www.loc.gov/preservation/resources/rfs/
15 https://www.ub.unibe.ch/unibe/portal/unibiblio/content/e6304/e583799/e791542/e791788/files955270/UBBerndLZAFormatpolicy_ger.pdf
16 https://kost-ceco.ch/
17 https://www.loc.gov/preservation/digital/formats/index.html
18 https://ianus-fdz.de/it-empfehlungen/inhalt
19 https://www.nationalarchives.gov.uk/PRONOM/Default.aspx

DROID[20] – Formatanalysetool des National Archives of the United Kingdom

JHOVE[21] – Tool zur Formatanalyse und -validierung

Durch das optimale Ausnutzen solcher bestehenden Informationsquellen sowie durch den Austausch mit anderen Institutionen wird die Beschäftigung mit Dateiformaten für alle erheblich erleichtert und muss keine Aufgabe darstellen, die fast unbewältigbar ist.

7. Empfohlene Dateiformate – Überblick

	Empfohlen	**Bedingt geeignet**	**Nicht empfohlen**
Text	unformatierter Text (z. B: *.txt, *.asc, *.c), PDF/A (*.pdf), PDF/UA (*.pdf) sowie XML-basierte Formate (z. B.: EPUB3 *.epub), CSV (*.csv)	PDF (*.pdf), LaTeX, TeX (.*tex)	Word (*.doc), Powerpoint (*.ppt)
Bild	TIFF (*.tif), JPEG2000 (*.jp2), PNG (*.png), Scalable vector graphics (*.svg)	Digital Negative Format (*.dng), GIF (*.gif), JPEG/JFIF (*.jpg), BMP (*.bmp)	proprietäre Rohdatenformate verschiedener Kamerahersteller, deren Dateiformatspezifikationen nicht offen sind, InDesign Grafik (*.indd), Photoshop (*.psd, *.psb), Encapsulated Postscript (*.eps, *.epsf, *.ps)
Audio	WAVE (*.wav), BMF, FLAC [Codec] (Audiodaten als LPCM)	Advanced Audio Coding (*.mp4), MP3 (*.mp3)	AIFF (*.aif), Windows Media Audio (*.wma), Ogg (*.ogg)
Video	Matroska (*.mkv) [Container] mit den Codecs: FFV1 (Version 3) und FLAC, MXF (*.mxf) [Container]	Quick Time (*.mov) [Container] mit den Codecs: 444 (XQ), 4444 oder 444 HQ, Motion JPEG 2000 (*.mj2, *.mjp2) [Container] mit Codec JPEG 2000, MPEG-2 [Codec], MPEG-4 (*.mp4)	Windows Media Video (*.wmv) RealVideo (*.rm, *.rv), Flash Video (*.flv)

20 https://www.nationalarchives.gov.uk/information-management/manage-information/preserving-digital-records/droid/

21 https://jhove.openpreservation.org/

Bibliografie

Drümmer, Olaf; Chang, Bettina (2013): PDF/UA in a Nutshell. Accessible Documents With PDF. Berlin: Association for Digital Document Standards e.V. https://www.pdfa.org/wp-content/until2016_uploads/2013/08/PDFUA-in-a-Nutshell-PDFUA.pdf (abgerufen am 17.05.2022)

Eck, David (2021): Introduction to Computer Graphics. https://math.hws.edu/eck/cs424/downloads/graphicsbook-linked.pdf (abgerufen am 17.05.2022)

El Idrissi, Bouchra (2019): Long-term Digital Preservation. A Preliminary Study on Software and Format Obsolescence. In: Proceedings of the ArabWIC 6th Annual International Conference Research Track 2019. New York: Association for Computing Machinery, Article 13, pp. 1-6. https://doi.org/10.1145/3333165.3333178

Gumm, Heinz-Peter (2013): Einführung in die Informatik. 10. vollständig überarbeitete Auflage. München: Oldenbourg Verlag.

Ishida, Richard (2015): Zeichencodierung für Anfänger. Übers. Gunnar Bittersmann (2016). https://www.w3.org/International/questions/qa-what-is-encoding.de (abgerufen am 17.05.2022)

Kersken, Sascha (2021): IT-Handbuch für Fachinformatiker*innen. Der Ausbildungsbegleiter. 10., aktualisierte und überarbeitete Auflage. Bonn: Rheinwerk Computing.

Lang, Elke; Bohne-Lang, Andreas (2019): Praxishandbuch IT-Grundlagen für Bibliothekare. Berlin/Boston: Walter De Gruyter GmbH.

Neuroth, Heike; Oßwald, Achim et al. (Hg.) (2010): Nestor Handbuch. Eine kleine Enzyklopädie der digitalen Langzeitarchivierung. Version 2.3. Glückstadt: vwh – Verlag Werner Hülsbusch, Fachverlag für Medientechnik und -wirtschaft.

Rudnik, Pia (2020): Video: Crashkurs Digitale Langzeitarchivierung – Dateiformate. https://doi.org/10.5281/zenodo.3985075

Schelkens, Peter; Touradj, Ebrahimi et al. (2009): The JPEG 2000 Suite. Chichester, West Sussex, U.K.: Hoboken, N.J.

SLUB Dresden (2021): Langzeitarchivfähige Dateiformate. Version 2.0, 2021-10-01. https://slubarchiv.slub-dresden.de/fileadmin/groups/slubsite/slubarchiv/SLUBArchiv_langzeitarchivfaehige_Dateiformate_v2.0.pdf (abgerufen am 17.05.2022)

Watkinson, John (2004): The MPEG Handbook. MPEG-1, MPEG-2, MPEG-3, MPEG-4, 2nd ed. Oxford: Elsevier/Focal Press.

Weynand, Diana (2016): How Video Works. From Broadcast to the Cloud, 3rd ed. New York, London: Focal Press.

Kristina Andraschko ist IT-Administratorin der DLE Raum- und Ressourcenmanagement an der Universität Wien. Sie erarbeitete 2018 die Formatempfehlungen für das Repositorium zur Sicherung von digitalen Beständen an der Universität Wien (PHAIDRA) im Zuge des Grundlehrgangs Library and Information Studies.

Joachim Losehand

Creative Commons im Repositorien-Management

Handbuch Repositorienmanagement, Hg. v. Blumesberger et al., 2024, S. 215–231
https://doi.org/10.25364/978390337423213

Joachim Losehand, joachim@losehand.at | ORCID iD: 0000-0002-6039-6372

Zusammenfassung

Creative-Commons-Lizenzen sind nicht mehr aus dem Alltag wissenschaftlichen Publizierens und Archivierens wegzudenken. Waren bis vor wenigen Jahren Vortragstitel wie „Keine Angst vor Creative Commons“ noch berechtigt, stehen heute zunehmend die Zeichen auf Normalisierung, auch wenn es in manchen Disziplinen nach wie vor vereinzelt „Gallische Dörfer“ gibt. Der Beitrag gibt einen Überblick über Creative Commons im Rahmen des Urheberrechts und zeigt Möglichkeiten, aber auch Grenzen und Problemzonen auf. Die Lizenzen werden in der neuesten Fassung (4.0) in einem zweiten Schritt dargestellt. Schließlich werden dann einzelne Fragen der „usability“ im Rahmen eines Repositoriums und eine nutzungsfreundliche Praxis behandelt.

Schlagwörter: Creative Commons; Open Access; Offene Lizenzen; Open Education; Lizenzmanagement

Abstract

Repository Management and Creative Commons

Creative Commons licenses have become an integral part of everyday academic publishing and archiving. Until a few years ago, the question “Who’s afraid of Creative Commons?” seemed to be justified, but today the signs are increasingly pointing to normalization, even if there are still isolated “Gallic villages” in some disciplines. The article gives an overview of Creative Commons in the context of copyright law and points out their possibilities, but also limits and problem areas. The licenses are presented in the latest version (4.0) in a second step. Finally, individual questions of „usability“ in the context of a repository and a user-friendly approach are addressed.

Keywords: Creative Commons; open access; open licenses; open education; license management

Creative-Commons-Lizenzen sind von Anfang an und seit nunmehr neunzehn Jahren[1] sog. „Jedermann-Lizenzen", das heißt: Lizenzen, die von allen (Urheber:innen wie Nutzer:innen) genutzt werden können. Auch wenn es im Sinne dieses Beitrags im Handbuch Repositorienmanagement wäre: Creative-Commons-Lizenzen (CC-Lizenzen) sind, anders als das World Wide Web, leider nicht insbesondere mit Blick für die Bedürfnisse der Wissenschaftskommunikation entwickelt worden. CC-Lizenzen waren eine Reaktion auf die Digitalisierung und die Verbreitung von Daten und Informationen im World Wide Web, die bekanntermaßen in allen Gesellschaften und Ökonomien seit Ende des 20. Jahrhunderts bis heute einen disruptiven Paradigmenwechsel eingeläutet haben. Das erklärte Ziel von Creative Commons war und ist es einerseits, Lizenzverträge besonders für den digitalen Raum im Rahmen des bestehenden Urheberrechts kostenlos anzubieten, die von allen Urheber:innen und Rechteinhaber:innen genutzt werden können, um ihre Werke digital zu verbreiten. Andererseits aber bietet Creative Commons auch eine Alternative zu den bis dahin geltenden Vorstellungen von (rechtlicher und kreativer) Urheberschaft und Werkherrschaft.

Angesichts der notwendigen Knappheit der folgenden Ausführungen sei für weitere, detailliertere und umfassendere Informationen ausdrücklich der Praxis-Leitfaden zur Nutzung von Creative-Commons-Lizenzen (dt. ²2016, engl. 2014) von Till Kreutzer empfohlen[2], ebenso der weitaus kürzere englischsprachige Guide to Creative Commons for Scholarly Publications and Educational Resources.[3] Einen verdichteten Überblick über die häufigsten Fragen und Antworten zu Creative-Commons-Lizenzen unter besonderer Berücksichtigung der Wissenschaft gibt das gleichnamige Dokument, das 2015 im Rahmen des Clusters E (Legal and Ethical Issues) des Projektes e-Infrastructures Austria erstellt wurde.[4]

1. Allgemeine Bemerkungen zum Urheberrecht

Jeder Mensch, der ein Werk schafft, ist Urheber:in im Sinne des Urheberrechts. Anders als im Patent- oder Markenrecht entsteht das Recht von Urheber:innen an ihrem Werk automatisch mit und im kreativen Prozess – und sobald sich ein Werk als „eigenständig" identifizieren lässt. Einzige Anforderung an Urheber:innen ist,

1 Während die Creative Commons Foundation im Jahr 2021 tatsächlich ihr 20. Gründungsjahr feiern kann, wurde das erste Set an Lizenzen erst ein Jahr später, 2002, offiziell veröffentlicht.
2 Kreutzer, T. (2014)
3 Braak, P. et al. (2020)
4 Amini, S. et al. (2015)

„natürliche Person" im Sinne des Rechts zu sein, d. h., ein Mensch.[5] Die Rechte und damit die Herrschaft der Urheber:innen über ihr Werk sind am Anfang umfassend und absolut. Grundlegend sind die Rechte auf Veröffentlichung (das Werk überhaupt in die Öffentlichkeit zu bringen), das Recht der namentlichen Anerkennung der Urheberschaft und das Recht auf Unversehrtheit des Werkes selbst. Im europäischen Urheberrecht sind diese drei Grundrechte von Urheber:innen („Urheberpersönlichkeitsrechte") an die Person gebunden und somit generell nicht aufgebbar oder veräußerbar. Alle anderen Rechte am Werk – Nutzungsrechte oder Verwertungsrechte – können von den Urheber:innen vertraglich auf Dritte übertragen werden. Urheberrechte sind also Eigentumsrechte und werden wie bei Eigentum an beweglichen oder unbeweglichen Sachen regelmäßig privatrechtlich organisiert und durchgesetzt. Das Urheberrecht ist somit konzipiert als ein mit dem Werk automatisch entstehender Rundumschutz, der die Urheber:innen des Werkes ermächtigt, jede Nutzung ihrer Werke zu kontrollieren.

Zu den eigentlichen Urheberrechten treten bei manchen Werkarten noch Leistungsschutzrechte hinzu (bei Audiowerken, Lichtbildwerken, Filmwerken inkl. Video, neuerdings bei Presseerzeugnissen). Diese schützen Investitionen und Leistungen, die auch von Institutionen oder kommerziellen Unternehmen (juristischen Personen) erbracht werden können. Im wissenschaftlichen Kontext ist durch ein Leistungsschutzrecht die Erstveröffentlichung (editio princeps) von Werken geschützt, deren urheberrechtlicher Schutz eigentlich abgelaufen ist (§ 76b öUrhG) oder – weil „avant la lettre" – niemals bestand.

Dem deutschen Rechtswissenschaftler Rudolf von Jhering (1818-1892) wird das Bonmont zugeschrieben: „In Deutschland ist alles verboten, was nicht erlaubt ist; in England ist alles erlaubt, was nicht verboten ist; in Russland ist alles verboten, auch was erlaubt ist; in Italien ist alles erlaubt, auch was verboten ist".[6] In Anlehnung an diese Einsicht ließe sich für das Urheberrecht formulieren: „Im Urheberrecht ist alles verboten, was nicht ausdrücklich erlaubt ist."

Wie bei jeder Regel gibt es auch hier entscheidende Ausnahmen. Der Konsum eines Werkes ist jedenfalls erlaubt; wer ein Buch auf einer Parkbank findet, darf es immer erlaubterweise lesen, wer ein Bild oder ein Video in den sozialen Medien findet

5 In manchen Rechtssystemen wie dem US-amerikanischen Copyright-Regime kann auch eine juristische Person (Kapitalgesellschaft usw.) Urheber:in sein. Im kontinentaleuropäischen und damit österreichischen Kontext ist Urheber:in jedoch immer eine natürliche Person.

6 Der Aphorismus zirkuliert in unterschiedlichen Ausgestaltungen, es fehlt jedoch jede Quellenangabe und lässt sich somit nicht sicher mit Rudolph von Jhering in Verbindung bringen. Jedoch lässt sich von Jhering ein „scheinbar mühelos aus ihm hervorsprudelnder Aphorismen- und Anekdotenschatz" zuschreiben, der „einer Reihe von eigens zu diesem Zweck angelegten Notizbüchern entstammte", vgl. Behrends, O. et al. (1993), S. 22.

und ansieht, begeht aus urheberrechtlicher Perspektive niemals eine Rechtsverletzung. Immer vorausgesetzt, man hat sich nicht widerrechtlich Zugang zu dem Werk verschafft, aber auch hier ist nicht der Konsum eine Verletzung des Urheberrechts, sondern der (digitale) Einbruch in einen geschützten Raum. Auch notwendige technische Erfordernisse wie das Zwischenspeichern einer Datei im Cache des Browsers als Voraussetzung, ein Werk überhaupt konsumieren zu können, sind immer genehmigungsfrei.

Als andere Ausnahmen („Schranken", „freie Werknutzungen", „fair use") können das (nicht unumschränkt geltende) Recht auf Privatkopie und das Zitatrecht sowie die in vielen Rechtsordnungen bestehenden Regelungen für Wissenschaft, Bildung und Unterricht genannt werden. Alle Nutzungen, die nicht vom jeweiligen Katalog an freien Werknutzungen erfasst sind (z. B. Vervielfältigung außerhalb der Privatkopie, Bearbeitung, Zurverfügungstellung im World Wide Web usw.), sind jedenfalls nur dann erlaubt, wenn der Urheber oder der Rechteinhaber diese Rechte ausdrücklich einräumen. In gewisser Weise signalisiert das „Copyright"-Symbol ©, dass Urheber:innen bzw. Rechteinhaber:innen jedes Mal gefragt werden wollen, wenn man ein Werk über den reinen Konsum und die bestehenden gesetzlichen Schrankenregelungen hinaus nutzen will.

2. Creative-Commons-Lizenzen im Kontext des Urheberrechts

2.1 Vorbemerkungen

Das Symbol von Creative Commons 🅭 signalisiert, dass Urheber:innen bzw. Rechteinhaber:innen nicht jedes Mal gefragt werden wollen, wenn man ein Werk über den reinen Konsum und die bestehenden gesetzlichen Schrankenregelungen hinaus nutzen will. In Anlehnung an Rudolf von Jhering könnte man formulieren: „Mit einer CC-Lizenz ist alles erlaubt, was nicht ausdrücklich verboten ist". In gewisser Weise erweitern Urheber:innen den Katalog der gesetzlich bestehenden Ausnahmen, die nicht notwendigerweise für alle gelten, durch einen privatrechtlich begründeten Akt für ein bestimmtes Werk und für alle Nutzer:innen. Das ist zwar rechtstheoretisch bzw. systematisch nicht zutreffend, jedoch ist die Wirkung dieses Rechtsakts bzw. der CC-Lizenzierung nach außen faktisch dieselbe.[7] CC-Lizenzen sind darauf ausgelegt, dass Werke von allen genutzt werden können. Sie sind gedacht, der größtmöglichen Menge an Nutzer:innen die größtmöglichen Freiheiten zu gewährleisten.

---

7 HG Wien 39 Cg 65/14y

Creative Commons stellt hierfür vorgefertigte, nicht abänderbare Lizenzvertragstexte kostenlos in drei Darstellungsweisen oder Komponenten zur Verfügung. Diese richten sich jeweils an alle Menschen ("commons deed"), an Maschinen ("machine readable version") und an Jurist:innen ("legal code"). Die Vertragstexte sind darauf ausgelegt, in allen Rechtsordnungen rechtssicher und rechtsgültig urheberrechtliche Nutzungen zu lizenzieren. Mit der aktuellen Version 4.0 aller Lizenzen werden keine für bestimmte Rechtsordnungen angepassten („portierten") Lizenzen mehr angeboten. Damit wird das Ziel verfolgt, Barrieren für die legale Nutzung und Verbreitung von Werken im digitalen Raum zu verringern.

Es muss jedoch betont werden, dass CC-Lizenzen nicht für alle Anwendungsfälle geeignet sind und sein können. Auch muss man manchen Versprechungen oder Zielen, die im weiteren Zusammenhang von Creative Commons von Befürworter:innen einer Vergesellschaftung von kreativem Schaffen, Gemeinfreiheit oder Public Domain geäußert werden, kritisch gegenüberstehen. CC-Lizenzen bewirken keinen paradiesischen Rechtszustand für Lizenzgeber:innen wie Lizenznehmer:innen, weder in der Abwesenheit von Recht („rechtsfreier Raum"), noch in einer garantierten Rechtssicherheit und rechtlichen Klarheit in allen Aspekten. Trotz allen Bemühens gibt es Lücken und Schwierigkeiten, und wahrscheinlich „steckt in jeder Lösung ein neues Problem, das verzweifelt versucht, herauszukommen". Mit Blick auf Repositorien kann jedenfalls gesagt werden, dass CC-Lizenzen Werkzeuge sind, um effektive Wissenschaftskommunikation zu garantieren.

2.2 Grundprinzipien der Creative-Commons-Lizenzen

Bei der Wahl von CC-Lizenzen sind folgende Grundprinzipien zu beachten:

a) Die Entscheidung, ein Werk mit CC zu lizenzieren, kann nicht widerrufen werden: es ist möglich, von restriktiveren CC-Lizenzen zu freieren CC-Lizenzen zu wechseln, jedoch nicht umgekehrt. Es besteht sozusagen ein „Zwang zur Freiheit": Was eine einmal gewählte Lizenz nicht verbietet, ist dauerhaft und unabänderlich allen erlaubt;
b) Keine zeitliche Befristung und keine geographische Begrenzung: CC-Lizenzen sind immer global und immer zeitlich unbefristet gültig, das heißt, solange ein gesetzlicher Urheberrechtsschutz für ein Werk besteht (in der Regel bis 70 Jahre nach dem Tod der Urheber:innen);
c) CC-Lizenzen richten sich immer an alle, man kann mit einer CC-Lizenz individuelle Nutzer:innen oder Nutzergruppen nicht privilegieren oder ausschließen;

d) Keine individuelle Steuerung von erlaubten Nutzungen über die Module der Lizenz hinaus („Kontrahierungszwang“);
e) Restriktionen gelten nur für die Nutzenden (Lizenznehmer:innen), die Urheber:innen (Lizenzgeber:innen) unterliegen nicht den Restriktionen der Lizenz;
f) Keine Abänderung der CC-Lizenz. Der Text einer CC-Lizenz ist fix vorgegeben und darf weder von Lizenzgeber:in noch Lizenznehmer:in verändert werden.

Darüber hinaus machen CC-Lizenzen keine Unterschiede zwischen den einzelnen Medienarten und -formaten, d. h., es gibt nicht verschiedene Lizenzen für Text, Bild, Ton usw. CC-Lizenzen umfassen immer Urheber- und (wo zutreffend) Leistungsschutzrechte. CC-Lizenzen sind – als privatrechtliche Lizenz- oder Nutzungsverträge – dem bestehenden Regelwerk des jeweils national geltenden Urheberrechts unterworfen, d. h., was ein nationales Urheberrechtsgesetz allgemein verbietet oder erlaubt (siehe Schrankenregelungen bzw. freie Werknutzungen), wird durch eine CC-Lizenz nicht erlaubt oder verboten.

Allgemein muss natürlich immer sichergestellt sein, dass bei der Verwendung von Werken Dritter im Rahmen eines anderen Werkes, z. B. von Abbildungen, einerseits die hierzu entsprechenden Nutzungsrechte vorliegen bzw. durch die jeweilige Nutzung bestehende Lizenzen nicht verletzt werden, andererseits die entsprechende Abgrenzung zwischen den einzelnen eigenen und fremden Materialien deutlich kenntlich gemacht wird.

2.3 Creative-Commons-Lizenzen im Detail

CC-Lizenzen sind modular aufgebaut und bestehen aus wenigstens einem Lizenz-Modul:

1) Das Modul „BY“ („von“) ist Bestandteil aller Lizenzen und verpflichtet dazu, den Namen der Urheber:innen und den Titel des Werkes in einer vorgegebenen Weise zu nennen. Diese Pflicht wird in der Version 4.0 auch durch die Verlinkung auf eine Seite mit den gesammelten vollständigen Angaben erfüllt.

2) das Modul „SA“ („same attribution“ = „gleiche Bedingungen“) verpflichtet dazu, z. B. im Fall einer Bearbeitung oder ähnlichen Nutzung das neue Werk mit derselben Lizenz wie das ursprüngliche Werk zu lizenzieren, das heißt, unter denselben Bedingungen wie das Ausgangswerk weiterzugeben; mit der Version 4.0 wird damit die letzte vergebene Lizenz angesprochen.

3) Das Modul „NC“ („non commercial“ = „nicht kommerziell“) verpflichtet dazu, das Werk ohne Gewinnerzielungsabsicht zu verbreiten; Gewinnerzielungsabsicht wird bei kommerziellen Nutzer:innen (Unternehmen) immer angenommen, bei nicht-kommerziellen Nutzer:innen wird auf den jeweiligen Kontext abgehoben (z. B. Bannerwerbung auf Webseiten gemeinnütziger Vereine oder Privatpersonen usw.). Beim Einsatz einer Lizenz mit NC-Modul muss vonseiten der Lizenzgeber:innen bedacht werden, dass dieses Modul folglich nicht nur kommerziell ausgerichtete Wirtschaftsunternehmen betrifft. Das NC-Modul schließt auch gemeinnützig orientierte Institutionen wie soziale Hilfseinrichtungen oder Stiftungen, die Einnahmen auch anders als durch Spenden oder öffentliche Finanzierung erhalten, aus, ebenso Privatpersonen, die einen „gofundme“-Spendenaufruf für einen guten Zweck initiieren.[8]

4) Das Modul „ND“ („no derivatives“ = „keine Bearbeitungen“) verbietet, das lizenzierte Werk in bearbeiteter bzw. veränderter Weise zu verbreiten. Eine Veränderung des Dateiformats und mit der Version 4.0 auch Data Mining werden dabei nicht als Bearbeitung im Sinne der Lizenz verstanden. Eine Änderung des Formats, der Auflösung, Größe, Farbgebung, grammatikalische Korrektur in Texten, Verbreitung von Auszügen aus Sammelbänden usw. werden hingegen immer als Bearbeitung im Sinne der Lizenz verstanden.

Diese vier Lizenzmodule werden zu insgesamt sechs[9] verschiedenen Lizenzen kombiniert:

- „CC-BY“ (Namensnennung),
- „CC-BY-SA“ (Namensnennung, Weitergabe unter gleichen Bedingungen),
- „CC-BY-ND“ (Namensnennung, keine Bearbeitung),
- „CC-BY-NC“ (Namensnennung, nicht kommerziell),
- „CC-BY-NC-SA“ (Namensnennung, nicht kommerziell, Weitergabe unter gleichen Bedingungen) und
- „CC-BY-NC-ND“ (Namensnennung, nicht kommerziell, keine Bearbeitung).

Von diesen sechs Lizenzen gelten als „offene Lizenzen“ bzw. „freie Lizenzen“ nur „CC-BY“ und „CC-BY-SA“.

8 Einen ausführlichen Überblick über CC-Lizenzen mit NC-Modul gibt Klimpel, P. (2012).
9 Zur CC0 vgl. Abschnitt 2.7.

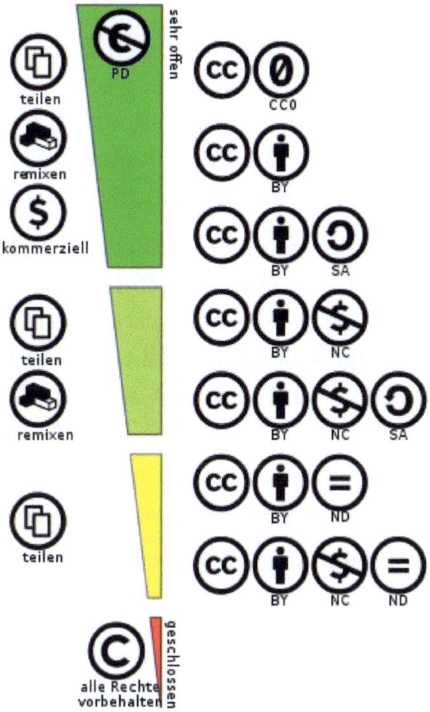

Abbildung 1: Creative-Commons-Lizenzspektrum[10]

10 Creative commons licence spectrum.svg. by Shaddim CC BY 4.0; https://de.wikipedia.org/wiki/Datei:Creative_commons_license_spectrum.svg

2.4 Lizenz-Versionen

Seit der Veröffentlichung der ersten Lizenzen im Jahr 2002 (Version 1.0) wurden verschiedene Verbesserungen und Adaptierungen durch weitere Versionen vorgenommen, letztens 2013 durch die Version 4.0, wobei vorangegangene Versionen (1.0 bis 3.0) durch eine neuere Version nicht automatisch ersetzt oder sogar ungültig werden (keine „Update“-Funktion). Das bedeutet, dass zumindest grundsätzlich alle Versionen gleichzeitig im Umlauf sind und jede Version gewählt werden kann.

Die aktuelle Version 4.0 bietet gegenüber der Vorgänger-Version 3.0 Veränderungen: Datenbankrechte lassen sich nun mit CC lizenzieren, Data Mining gilt ausdrücklich nicht als Bearbeitung (ND-Modul), etwaige bestehende Leistungsschutzrechte werden allgemein eingeschlossen, es gibt neue „Heilungsfristen“ bei versehentlichen Lizenzverletzungen, im Fall des SA-Moduls gilt die letzte vergebene Lizenz.[11]

2.5 Angabe und Erläuterung von Bearbeitungen

Sofern an einem Werk Bearbeitungen vorgenommen wurden (und die jeweilige Lizenz Bearbeitungen auch zulässt), sehen die verschiedenen Lizenz-Versionen unterschiedliche Vorgehensweisen vor:

- Die Versionen 1.0 und 2.0 bzw. 2.5 kennen keine ausdrücklichen Regelungen, d. h., die Angabe über eine Bearbeitung und Art und Umfang der Bearbeitung ist aufgrund der Lizenz nicht notwendig, der Hinweis, dass es sich bei einem neuen Werk gegebenenfalls um eine Adaption bzw. Abwandlung des lizenzierten Werkes handelt ist jedoch verpflichtend.
- Bei den Lizenzen der Version 3.0 besteht die ausdrückliche Verpflichtung, darauf hinzuweisen, dass Bearbeitungen am lizenzierten Werk vorgenommen wurden bzw. dass ein neues Werk (Adaptierung, Abwandlung) aufgrund der Bearbeitung des lizenzierten Werkes entstanden ist.
- Die aktuelle Lizenz-Version 4.0 verlangt, dass angegeben werden muss, dass und auch welche Änderungen bzw. Bearbeitungen an einem Werk vorgenommen wurden[12], und es müssen bestehende Angaben von Änderungen, die zuvor durch Dritte vorgenommen wurden, weiterhin angegeben werden.

---

11 Vgl. Weitzmann, J. (2013)

12 Vgl. https://wiki.creativecommons.org/wiki/Best_practices_for_attribution#This_is_a_good_attribution_for_material_you_modified_slightly und https://wiki.creativecommons.org/wiki/Best_practices_for_attribution#This_is_a_good_attribution_for_material_from_which_you_created_a_derivative_work

Die bestehenden jeweiligen Verpflichtungen, insbesondere bei Bearbeitungen von lizenzierten Werken, gehören erfahrungsgemäß nicht zum Allgemeinwissen von Nutzer:innen der CC-Lizenzen. Inwieweit die mit der Version 4.0 eingeführten umfassenderen „Berichtspflichten" (auch mit Blick auf die Akkumulierung von Bearbeitungsangaben) praktikabel sind und auch umgesetzt werden, ist offen.

2.6 Ältere, inzwischen ausgelaufene Lizenzen

In der Anfangsphase von Creative Commons wurden weitere Lizenzen bzw. Lizenzmodule entwickelt und eingeführt, z. B. CC-BY-DevNations, die, entgegen der heute geltenden Prinzipien, geographisch nur in Entwicklungsländern ("developing nations") galten. Diese und andere Lizenzen sind nicht über das Stadium der Version 1.0 hinausgelangt und wurden im Laufe der Zeit in der Regel aufgrund fehlender Nachfrage zurückgezogen und eingestellt.[13]

2.7 CC0 („CC Zero")

Ein gewisses Unikum aus europäischer Sicht stellt die siebte CC-„Lizenz" dar, die sog. "public domain dedication", abgekürzt mit „CC0" („CC Zero"). Ihrem Wesen und ihrer Absicht nach ist CC0 keine Lizenz, sondern eine (umfassende) Verzichtserklärung. Der Wortlaut der Verzichtserklärung besagt, „[d]ie Person, die ein Werk mit dieser Deed [d. h., Erklärung] verknüpft hat, hat dieses Werk in die Gemeinfreiheit - auch genannt Public Domain - entlassen, indem sie weltweit auf alle urheberrechtlichen und verwandten Schutzrechte verzichtet hat, soweit das gesetzlich möglich ist." Die CC0 wird wie die Lizenzen CC-BY und CC-BY-SA zu den „offenen" oder „freie Lizenzen" gezählt (auch "approved for free cultural works").

Die Existenz von CC0 erklärt sich daher, dass das US-Copyright keinen gesetzlich verankerten allgemeinen und unaufgebbaren Schutz von Verwertungsrechten und Urheberpersönlichkeitsrechten kennt, sondern alle Rechte kommerziell verwertbar und verzichtbar sind. Die Wirkung der Verzichtserklärung CC0 auf den Status eines Werkes ist im US-amerikanischen Rechtsraum also identisch mit dem gesetzlichen Ablauf der urheberrechtlichen Schutzfrist oder dem Status von Werken, die vor Einführung des Verlags- und Urheberrechts seit dem 18. Jahrhundert geschaffen wurden. Eine solche umfassende Verzichtserklärung sieht das europäische Urheberrecht jedenfalls für die Urheberpersönlichkeitsrechte nicht vor und wäre darum auch ungültig. Den Schöpfer:innen der CC0 waren diese grundsätzlichen Unterschiede natürlich bekannt und darum wird die Lizenz auch um das caveat „...

13 Vgl. https://de.wikipedia.org/wiki/Creative_Commons#Ältere_Lizenzen

soweit das gesetzlich möglich ist …", d. h., um eine „Fallback-Bestimmung" im Erklärungstext ergänzt.[14]

Der Frage, ob eine solche umfassende Erklärung, die einen Verzicht auf Verwertungsrechte und Urheberpersönlichkeitsrechte beinhaltet, in Österreich möglich ist, gehen Guido Kucsko und Adolf Zemann in ihrem Gutachten aus dem Jahr 2017[15] nach. Für Kucsko/Zemann bestehen „gute Argumente dafür, dass ein Verzicht auf Verwertungsrechte nach österreichischem Recht möglich ist. Ein derartiger Verzicht würde die umfassende Nutzung eines Schutzgegenstandes durch Dritte möglich machen. Dazu gehört insbesondere auch die Bereitstellung in Repositorien zum Abruf durch Dritte. Einschränkungen bestünden allenfalls bei Nutzungen, die in unverzichtbare Urheberpersönlichkeitsrechte eingreifen."[16] Wenn jedoch „ein Verzicht [auf die Verwertungsrechte, Anm. d. A.] nach österreichischem Recht nicht möglich wäre und (nur) die Fallback-Bestimmung der CC0 anwendbar wäre", würde das bedeuten, dass mit der Lizenz CC0 entweder eine „Erteilung einer Werknutzungsbewilligung im Sinne des § 24 [ö]UrhG" oder eine „(schlichte) Einwilligung" zur Werknutzung vorliegt. Ungeklärt ist dabei einerseits, ob und inwieweit eine Werknutzungsbewilligung oder schlichte Einwilligung zur Werknutzung (zumindest für die Zukunft) gegebenenfalls widerrufen werden könnten,[17] und andererseits ergeben sich Fragen der Haftung für Betreiber:innen von Repositorien bei der Verwendung von fremden Inhalten, also Materialien und Dokumenten, die nicht von Angehörigen der eigenen Institution erstellt wurden.[18]

Nach österreichischem Recht würde die „Fallback-Klausel" der Lizenz CC0 im Grunde die Wirkung einer „CC-BY sans BY" entfalten, einer CC-BY-Lizenz, bei der man auf die Namensnennung verzichten kann.[19] Denn das Recht auf die Urheberbezeichnung gemäß § 21 Abs. 1 öUrhG stellt keine „Bezeichnungspflicht" dar, sondern obliegt in freiem Ermessen dem/der Urheber:in und kann, wie einschlägige Judikatur bereits mehrfach bestätigt hat, nach dem Willen des Urhebers auch ganz unterlassen werden.[20] Die „Fallback-Klausel" der Lizenz CC0 sieht jedoch nicht vor, dass die anderen Bedingungen der CC-Lizenzen und der CC-BY hinsichtlich der verschiedenen Hinweise auf die Lizenz, Lizenztext usw. eingehalten werden müssen.

---

14 "Should any part of the Waiver for any reason be judged legally invalid or ineffective under applicable law, then the Waiver shall be preserved to the maximum extent permitted taking into account Affirmer's express Statement of Purpose." https://creativecommons.org/publicdomain/zero/1.0/legalcode

15 Kucsko, G. et al. (2017)

16 Kucsko, G. et. al. (2017), S. 22.

17 Kucsko, G. et. al. (2017), S. 22.

18 Kucsko, G. et. al. (2017), S. 23.

19 Kucsko, G. et. al. (2017), S. 27.

20 Kucsko, G. et. al. (2017), S. 14.

Wenn die Nutzung eines mit CC0 lizenzierten Werkes keinerlei Bedingungen unterliegt, d. h., auch nicht die Lizenz und die Lizenzbedingungen angegeben werden müssen, hat das gravierende Folgen: Denn, wenn die Lizenz-Kennzeichnung eines mit CC0 lizenzierten Werkes nicht zwingend erfolgen muss, kann damit allgemein nicht mehr rechtssicher unterschieden werden zwischen einem sich in tatsächlicher Gemeinfreiheit befindlichen Werk (einem Werk, das nicht mit einer CC0 Lizenz lizenziert wurde) und einem Werk, das von Rechteinhaber:innen mit CC0 lizenziert wurde. Ein Umstand, der dem inhärenten Ziel, Barrieren durch Rechtssicherheit abzubauen, nicht unbedingt gerecht wird.

Problematisch ist jedenfalls, dass in der deutschsprachigen „einfachen Darstellungsweise“ des „deed“[21] dieser überschrieben ist mit „kein Urheberrechtsschutz“, einer falschen oder wenigstens sehr missverständlichen Aussage, da für Werke, die von europäischen Urheber:innen geschaffen wurden und deren gesetzliche Schutzfrist nicht abgelaufen ist, immer wenigstens der Urheberrechtsschutz der Urheberpersönlichkeitsrechte besteht.

2.8 Die „Qual der Wahl“ der „richtigen“ CC-Lizenz

Sofern nicht eine bestimmte CC-Lizenz z. B. durch Plattformbetreiber:innen oder Verlage vorgegeben ist, steht es den Urheber:innen frei, eine CC-Lizenz aufgrund eigener Präferenzen zu wählen. Es wird allgemein seitens Creative Commons empfohlen, zunächst jeweils die aktuellste Version zu verwenden, das heißt, Version 4.0 (international). Es kann aber auch Gründe geben, die dafür sprechen, auch heute noch eine frühere Version bzw. eine ältere länderspezifisch angepasste („portierte“) Version wie 3.0 AT einzusetzen.

Es gibt verschiedene Online-Werkzeuge, z. B. von Creative Commons[22], und Schaubilder, die die Präferenzen des potentiellen Lizenzgebers abfragen und die jeweils daraus resultierende Lizenz vorschlagen, z. B.:

21 https://creativecommons.org/publicdomain/zero/1.0/deed.de
22 https://creativecommons.org/choose/

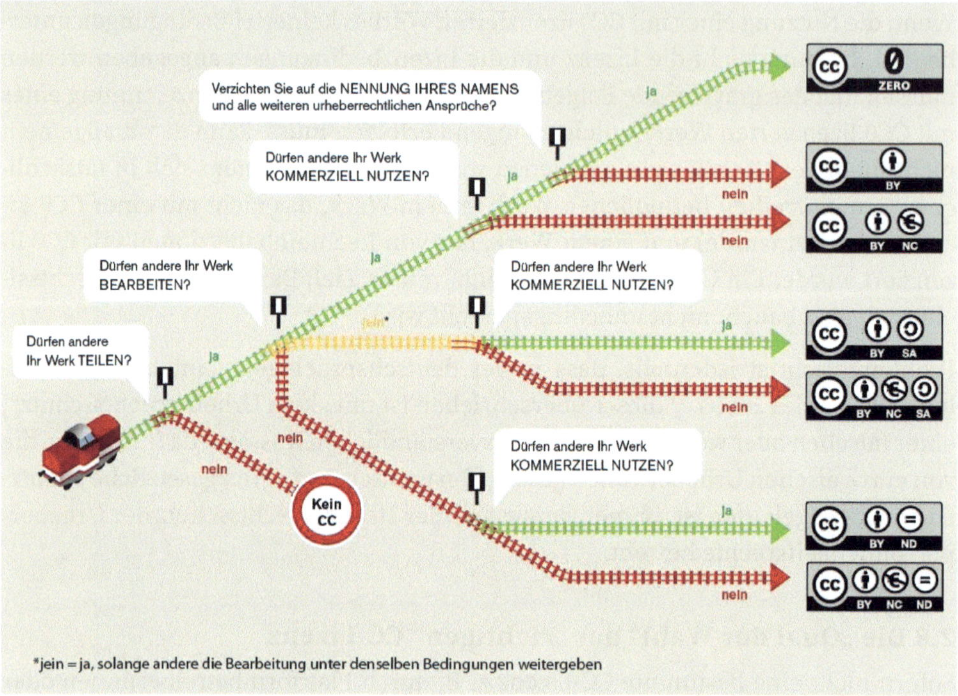

Abbildung 2: Infografik: Welche CC-Lizenz ist die richtige für mich?[23]

3. Creative Commons im Repositorienmanagement

Beim Betrieb eines Online-Repositoriums sind naturgemäß verschiedene umfängliche rechtliche Vorgaben und Aspekte zu beachten und zu berücksichtigen. Die Entscheidung, (nur) mit einer CC-Lizenz lizenzierte Werke in einem Repositorium online zur Verfügung zu stellen, hat vor allem positive Auswirkungen auf die Nutzung der Werke bzw. stellt einen Vorteil für die Nutzer:innen des Repositoriums dar. Für die Betreiber:innen bzw. rechtlich Verantwortlichen („provider") ändert sich hinsichtlich der gesetzlichen Haftung als „Content-Provider" oder „Host-Provider" und damit hinsichtlich der Sorgfaltspflichten und der Rechteverwaltung nichts Wesentliches. Die Betreiber:innen müssen wie auch bei der Verfügung von nicht mit CC lizenzierten Werken im Rahmen der geltenden gesetzlichen Vorgaben sicherstellen, dass die Zurverfügungstellung eines Werkes im Repositorium nicht die Rechte Dritter verletzt. Das kann insbesondere im Fall einer Zweitverwertung eines

23 CC-BY-SA 3.0 by Jöran Muuß-Merholz und Susanne Witt für wb-web, aktualisiert am 30.03.2021 (https://wb-web.de/material/medien/die-cc-lizenzen-im-uberblick-welche-lizenz-fur-welche-zwecke-1.html).

bereits veröffentlichten Werkes der Fall sein, bei dem in der Regel die originalen Autor:innen bzw. Urheber:innen bereits sämtliche Verwertungsrechte an den erstpublizierenden Verlag übertragen haben und die Zweitverwertung in einem Online-Repositorium nicht ohne ausdrückliche Zustimmung des jeweiligen Verlages erfolgen kann, ganz zu schweigen von einer späteren Lizenzierung dieses Werkes mit einer CC-Lizenz.

Im Idealfall sind die Werke, die ein Repositorium bereithält, entweder sicher gemeinfrei, oder die Werke sind eigene Werke der Betreiber:innen des Repositoriums, oder die Werke sind bereits bei ihrer Erstveröffentlichung mit einer CC-Lizenz lizenziert worden (unabhängig davon, ob das Repositorium oder ein anderes Medium der Ort der Erstveröffentlichung ist).

Aus Sicht der Nutzer:innen eines Online-Repositoriums sollten die Betreiber:innen nicht nur das „bare minimum" an verpflichtenden Informationen über die jeweilige Lizenz oder Rechtesituation eines Werkes geben, sondern sie deutlich kennzeichnen, z. B. durch die Nutzung der von Creative Commons bereitgestellten grafischen „Icons". Und es sollte auch immer in kurzen Schlagworten der Umfang der Lizenz, wie er im „commons deed" dargestellt wird, erläutert werden, da erfahrungsgemäß Nutzer:innen selbständig eher selten die von CC bereitgestellten Lizenzinformationen aufrufen. Das Vorgesagte gilt umso mehr, wenn ein Repositorium nicht nur eine einzige Lizenz bzw. eine einzige Lizenz-Version (mit oder ohne Portierung) verwendet, sondern eine Vielzahl von Lizenzen und gegebenenfalls auch „all rights reserved" verwendet werden. Hier wäre jedenfalls wünschenswert, wenn auf die jeweils zutreffende Lizenz oder Rechtesituation ausdrücklich und grafisch auffällig hingewiesen wird. Online-Repositorien sollen sich in dieser Hinsicht nach wie vor auch ihrer didaktischen Funktion bewusst sein, d. h., bei unerfahrenen oder gänzlich unkundigen Nutzer:innen Sichtbarkeit und Aufmerksamkeit für die verschiedenen CC-Lizenzen und ihren regelgerechten Gebrauch in der Wissenschaftskommunikation schaffen.

Die Frage, welche CC-Lizenzen von Repositorien unterstützt werden sollten, lässt sich nur hinsichtlich der Lizenz-Versionen eindeutig beantworten: Ein aktives Repositorium sollte jedenfalls die jeweils neuesten Lizenz-Versionen (2022: Version 4.0) unterstützen, parallel zu allen Lizenz-Versionen, die bisher im Repositorium in Gebrauch waren. Ob ein Repositorium nur internationale Lizenzen oder auch nationale, d. h. portierte Lizenzen unterstützt, hängt vom Nutzungskontext und der geographischen Herkunft der Zielgruppen ab. Auch was die Lizenzarten anlangt, d. h. ob ein Repositorium nur sog. „freie Lizenzen" oder alle aktiven CC-Lizenzen unterstützen sollte, lässt sich auch mit Blick auf die garantierte Vertragsfreiheit nicht allgemein beantworten. Hier werden die Betreiber:innen selbst am besten wissen, wie sie entsprechend der eigenen, gegebenenfalls auch politischen Prämissen, im Kontext von bestehenden Usancen sowie von Erfahrungen und Erwartungen von allen Beteiligten abwägen. Es sollte aber vermieden werden, neue Barrieren und Einschränkungen insbesondere für die Urheber:innen einzuführen, die das CC-Lizenzsystem ja eigentlich verringern soll.

Bibliografie

Amini, Seyavash; Blechl, Guido; Losehand, Joachim (2015): FAQs zu Creative-Commons-Lizenzen unter besonderer Berücksichtigung der Wissenschaft. https://phaidra.univie.ac.at/detail/o:408042 (abgerufen am 03.03.2022)

Behrends, Otto; von Jhering, Rudolf (1993): Beiträge und Zeugnisse aus Anlass der einhundertsten Wiederkehr seines Todestages am 17.9.1992. 2. Aufl. Wallstein: Göttingen.

Braak, Pascal; de Jonge, Hans; Trentacosti, Giulia; Verhagen, Irene; Woutersen-Windhouwer, Saskia (2020): Guide to Creative Commons for Scholarly Publications and Educational Resources. https://doi.org/10.5281/zenodo.4741966

Klimpel, Paul (2012): Folgen, Risiken und Nebenwirkungen bei nichtkommerziellen CC-Lizenzen.https://irights.info/2012/05/02/folgen-risiken-und-nebenwirkungen-von-nc/4002 (abgerufen am 03.03.2022)

Kreutzer, Till (2016): Open Content Praxis-Leitfaden zur Nutzung von Creative Commons Lizenzen. 2. Aufl. engl. Fassung 2014. https://irights.info/artikel/neue-version-open-content-ein-praxisleitfaden-zu-creative-commons-lizenzen/26086 (abgerufen am 03.03.2022)

Kucsko, Guido; Zemann, Adolf (2017): CC0 1.0 Universal – Beurteilung der Verzichtserklärung und der Lizenzerteilung im Rahmen der Fallback-Klausel nach österreichischem Recht. https://phaidra.univie.ac.at/o:528411

Plotkin, Hal (2002): All Hail Creative Commons / Stanford Professor and Author Lawrence Lessig Plans a Legal Insurrection. https://www.sfgate.com/news/article/All-Hail-Creative-Commons-Stanford-professor-2874018.php (abgerufen am 03.03.2022)

Weitzmann, John (2013): Creative Commons in Version 4.0 verfügbar. Was sich ändert und was nicht. https://irights.info/artikel/creative-commons-in-version-4-0-verfugbar-was-sich-andert-und-was-nicht/19528 (abgerufen am 03.03.2022)

Bildquellen

CC BY SA 3.0 by Jöran Muuß-Merholz für wb-web aktualisiert am 30.03.2021, CC BY SA 3.0 by Susanne Witt für wb-web

https://de.wikipedia.org/wiki/Datei:Creative_commons_license_spectrum.svg

Joachim Losehand ist Altertumswissenschaftler, Kirchenrechtler und Theologe. Er war beruflich bislang tätig u. a. als Berater des VFRÖ und arbeitet seit 2008 zu den rechtlichen Rahmenbedingungen digitalen Publizierens. Er war Mitglied der AG Future of Scholarly Communication in der OANA und im Projekt e-Infrastructures Austria. Er ist u. a. lead science commons bei Creative Commons Austria.

Adelheid Mayer

Hochschulschriften-Repositorien

Begriffsdefinitionen und rechtliche Aspekte

Handbuch Repositorienmanagement, Hg. v. Blumesberger et al., 2024, S. 233–258
https://doi.org/10.25364/978390337423214

Adelheid Mayer, Universität Wien, Universitätsbibliothek, adelheid.mayer@univie.ac.at |
ORCID iD: 0000-0001-7923-5256

Zusammenfassung

Seit 1997 besteht in Österreich die Veröffentlichungspflicht für wissenschaftliche Abschlussarbeiten zur Erlangung eines akademischen Grades. Wurde diesem Auftrag bislang durch Aufstellen der Arbeiten in der jeweiligen Hochschulbibliothek und bei Dissertationen in der Nationalbibliothek nachgekommen, verlagerte sich in den letzten 15 Jahren die Veröffentlichung zunehmend in den digitalen Raum. Im Beitrag werden zu Beginn die verschiedenen Begriffe wie Hochschulschriften und wissenschaftliche Arbeiten betrachtet sowie die Frage geklärt, welche Materialien unter diese Bezeichnungen fallen. Spezifisch österreichische rechtliche Aspekte spielen nicht nur diesbezüglich eine Rolle, sondern definieren auch die Grenzen, denen Universitäten bei der Sammlung wissenschaftlicher Abschlussarbeiten unterworfen sind. Es wird gesondert auf die Situation an Universitäten, Kunstuniversitäten, Privatuniversitäten und Fachhochschulen eingegangen. Weiters werden studienrechtliche Aspekte beleuchtet, die Auswirkungen auf die systematische Sammlung von Hochschulschriften in einem Repositorium haben. Zuletzt wird der Zusammenhang zwischen der Einrichtung von Hochschulschriften-Repositorien und wissenschaftlicher Integrität aufgezeigt.

Schlagwörter: Hochschulschriften; Repositorien; wissenschaftliche Abschlussarbeiten; Studienrecht; Urheberrecht

Abstract

University Theses Repositories. Definitions and Legal Aspects

Since 1997, there has been an obligation to publish academic theses for the award of an academic degree in Austria. While this obligation was previously fulfilled by placing the theses in the respective university libraries and, in the case of dissertations, in the National Library, publication has increasingly shifted to the digital space in the last 15 years. This contribution starts with looking at the various terms and clarifies the question of which materials fall under these designations. Specific Austrian legal aspects not only play a role in this regard, but also define the limits to which universities are subject when collecting academic theses. The situations at universities, art universities, private universities and universities of applied sciences are dealt with separately. Furthermore, aspects of study law are examined that have an impact on the systematic collection of university theses in a repository. Finally, the connection between the establishment of university repositories and academic integrity is shown.

Keywords: Theses; repositories; academic theses; study law; copyright

1. Einleitung

Die Sammlung von Hochschulschriften in einem Repositorium ist facettenreicher, als es zunächst scheinen mag. Zahlreiche Aspekte studienrechtlicher und urheberrechtlicher Natur machen aus dem Unterfangen, „einfach“ die wissenschaftlichen Abschlussarbeiten einer Hochschule systematisch sammeln zu wollen, in der Regel ein Großprojekt.

Wissenschaftliche Abschlussarbeiten dienen ausschließlich dem Zweck, dass Hochschulabsolvent:innen die Befähigung zu selbstständigem wissenschaftlichem Arbeiten nachweisen und so einen akademischen Grad bzw. eine Lehrbefugnis erlangen können. Sie weisen in der Form, wie wir sie heute kennen, seit ihrer Einführung im Lauf des 19. Jahrhunderts einen hohen Grad an inhaltlicher und äußerer Formalisierung auf.

Der Ursprung wissenschaftlicher Arbeiten liegt in den sogenannten Thesenblättern des Mittelalters.[1] Mit der Entstehung und Verbreitung des Modells der europäischen Universität, die von Bologna im 11. Jahrhundert ausging, nahm auch das Muster der Graduierung der Absolventen zu Bakkalaureaten, Magistern und Doktoren seinen Ausgang. Bis ins 18. Jahrhundert war dieser Vorgang bestimmt durch die Abfolge von Zulassung zur Graduierung - mündlicher Prüfung - öffentlicher Verteidigung aufgestellter Thesen zu einer wissenschaftlichen Fragestellung (Disputation) - und schließlich der feierlichen Inauguration in den akademischen Rang.[2]

Auf Thesenblättern wurde die jeweilige Disputation angekündigt. Sie enthielten Angaben zu Ort, Zeit und den Hauptbeteiligten Präses und Respondent.[3] Sie konnten auch die wichtigsten Thesen selbst enthalten und wurden im Lauf der Jahrhunderte immer aufwändiger gestaltet. Mit der Verbreitung des Druckwesens entwickelte sich die wissenschaftliche Argumentation weg von der öffentlich ausgetragenen Disputation hin zur Verschriftlichung in Form der Dissertation, die im 17. und 18. Jahrhundert eine Erweiterung des Thesenblatts darstellte.[4] Diese wurden jedoch oft von den Präses verfasst und nicht von den Disputenten, was die Zuordnung der Autorenschaft historischer Dissertationen mitunter schwierig macht.

Die Rigorosenordnung von 1872 verankerte an den philosophischen Fakultäten in den Ländern der Habsburger Monarchie die Dissertation in der heutigen Form als

1 Zur Geschichte von Graduierungen an europäischen Hochschulen siehe ausführlicher Mayer, A. (2015), S. 13-30.

2 Mayer, A. (2015), S. 14.

3 Mayer, A. (2015), S. 19.

4 Mayer, A. (2015), S. 21.

geschriebene oder gedruckte Abhandlung über ein frei gewähltes Thema.[5] Ab der Wende zum 20. Jahrhundert wurden auch erstmals Frauen zur Promotion zugelassen. In der zweiten Hälfte des 20. Jahrhunderts wurde das verpflichtende Verfassen von Diplomarbeiten für die meisten Studienfächer eingeführt, ab 2002 hielt mit der Umsetzung des Bologna-Prozesses schließlich auch der „Bachelor" wieder Einzug an den europäischen Universitäten. Die 1997 eingeführte Veröffentlichungspflicht für Diplom- und Masterarbeiten sowie Dissertationen bedingt, dass an allen Hochschulen Workflows existieren, wie die Abschlussarbeiten von den jeweils für die Beurteilung zuständigen Studienabteilungen in die Bibliothek gelangen. Seit Beginn des 21. Jahrhunderts findet die Sammlung der Arbeiten auch – und zunehmend ausschließlich – in elektronischer Form statt.

Im Folgenden werden die wichtigsten Aspekte wie Definitionen, gesetzliche Vorgaben und mögliche daraus resultierende Problemfelder bei der systematischen Sammlung von Hochschulschriften erörtert.

2. Begriffsdefinitionen

2.1 Hochschulschriften

Das *Lexikon des gesamten Buchwesens Online* definiert Hochschulschriften (HSS) als „bibliothekarische[n] Fachausdruck für Schriften, die unter dem Namen der Hochschule oder ihrer Fakultäten veröff. werden." Er entstand zu Beginn des 20. Jahrhunderts für Verzeichnisse aller von Hochschulen herausgegebenen Schriften, worunter auch Vorlesungsverzeichnisse und Studienführer angeführt wurden.[6] Damit ist bereits klar umrissen, dass dies ein Begriff ist, der im Wesentlichen und fast ausschließlich im Bibliothekswesen gebräuchlich ist.

Das Katalogisierungshandbuch des österreichischen Bibliothekenverbunds schränkt den Begriff weiter ein als „ein Werk, das zur Erlangung eines akademischen Grades präsentiert wird"[7]. Dazu zählen „Bachelorarbeit, Diplomarbeit, Dissertation, Habilitationsschrift, Lizenziatsarbeit, Magisterarbeit". Kernelement der Erfassung in Bibliothekskatalogen ist der sogenannte „Hochschulschriftenvermerk". Er enthält „Informationen über den akademischen Grad, für den das Werk präsentiert wurde, über die Institution oder Fakultät, die den Grad verleiht, und das Jahr, in dem der Grad verliehen wurde"[8].

5 Mayer, A. (2015), S. 28.
6 Pflug, G. (2017), § 89 UG: Widerruf inländischer akademischer Grade oder akademischer Bezeichnungen (Anm. 9).
7 https://wiki.obvsg.at/Katalogisierungshandbuch/ArbeitsunterlagenFEHochschulschriftenALMA
8 Ebd.

2.2 Wissenschaftliche Arbeit / Abschlussarbeit / wissenschaftliche Abschlussarbeit

Der Sammelbegriff „wissenschaftliche Arbeit“ entzieht sich einer genauen Definition, da sich nicht exakt festlegen lässt, was darunter zu verstehen ist. Gemeinhin wird unter dem Begriff „wissenschaftliche Arbeit“ sowohl die Tätigkeit selbst, also die Forschung, als auch deren schriftliches oder immaterielles Ergebnis verstanden. Im administrativen universitären Alltag hingegen ist mit diesem Begriff meist eine schriftliche studentische Abschlussarbeit gemeint. Mitunter ist für letzteres zur Begriffseinengung auch von „wissenschaftlicher Abschlussarbeit“ oder nur „Abschlussarbeit“ die Rede. Die korrekte Bezeichnung wäre „wissenschaftliche Arbeit zur Erlangung eines akademischen Grades“. Aufgrund der Sperrigkeit wird dieser Begriff jedoch nicht wirklich verwendet.

Selbst der Gesetzgeber bietet keine eindeutige Definition, was er unter „wissenschaftlicher Arbeit“ versteht. Wahlweise werden „Diplomarbeit, Masterarbeit oder Dissertation“,[9] der schriftliche Teil der Habilitation[10], Forschung von Universitätsangehörigen ganz allgemein[11] oder auch die (schriftlichen) Ergebnisse dieser Forschung[12] mit diesem Begriff belegt.

Im Folgenden werden die Begriffe Hochschulschrift, wissenschaftliche Arbeit und wissenschaftliche Abschlussarbeit zwecks besserer Lesbarkeit gleichbedeutend verwendet.

3. Gesetzliche Bestimmungen

3.1 Universitäten

Für die 22 öffentlichen Universitäten Österreichs sind alle Bestimmungen zu wissenschaftlichen Arbeiten im *Bundesgesetz über die Organisation der Universitäten und ihre Studien (Universitätsgesetz 2002 – UG)* festgehalten.

3.1.1 Bachelorarbeiten

„Bachelorarbeiten sind die im Bachelorstudium anzufertigenden eigenständigen schriftlichen oder künstlerischen Arbeiten, die im Rahmen von Lehrveranstaltungen abzufassen sind.“[13] Die näheren Bestimmungen wie Art der Arbeit, Umfang,

---

9 § 72 Abs. 1 Universitätsgesetz 2002 – UG
10 § 103 Abs. 5 UG
11 § 105 UG
12 § 106 Abs. 1 UG
13 § 51 Abs. 2 S. 7 UG

Themenwahl etc. sind in den jeweiligen Curricula festzulegen.[14] Sie können auch aus mehreren Teilen bestehen. Bachelorarbeiten dienen zwar dem Erwerb eines akademischen Titels,[15] sind jedoch vom Gesetzgeber von der Bezeichnung „wissenschaftliche Arbeit“ ausgenommen.[16] Daher werden sie an vielen Universitäten nicht systematisch gesammelt und finden kaum Eingang in Bibliotheken.

3.1.2 Diplom- und Masterarbeiten

Dagegen werden Diplom- und Masterarbeiten ausdrücklich als „wissenschaftliche[...] Arbeiten in den Diplom- und Masterstudien, die dem Nachweis der Befähigung dienen, wissenschaftliche Themen selbstständig sowie inhaltlich und methodisch vertretbar zu bearbeiten“[17], definiert. „Nähere Bestimmungen über Betreuung und Beurteilung von Diplom- oder Masterarbeiten sind in der Satzung, nähere Bestimmungen über das Thema der Diplom- oder Masterarbeit sind im jeweiligen Curriculum festzulegen.“[18] Dabei ist die Aufgabenstellung „so zu wählen, dass für eine Studierende oder einen Studierenden die Bearbeitung innerhalb von sechs Monaten möglich und zumutbar ist.“[19] Das gemeinsame Bearbeiten eines Themas ist gestattet.[20] Des Weiteren gilt, dass in „besonders berufsorientierten Studien mit Ausnahme von Lehramtsstudien“ im Curriculum festgelegt werden kann, dass anstelle der Diplom- oder Masterarbeit ein „gleichwertiger Nachweis“ erbracht werden kann.[21]

In künstlerischen Studien sind laut Universitätsgesetz künstlerische Diplom- oder Masterarbeiten zu schaffen. Sie dienen dem Nachweis der Befähigung, „im Hinblick auf das Studienziel des Studiums selbstständig und wissenschaftlich fundiert künstlerisch zu arbeiten.“ Den Schwerpunkt der Arbeit bildet ein künstlerischer Teil. Daneben hat ein schriftlicher Teil den künstlerischen zu erläutern. Alternativ haben Studierende aber das Recht, eine wissenschaftliche Arbeit „aus einem im Curriculum festgelegten wissenschaftlichen Prüfungsfach zu verfassen.“ Bestimmungen über Betreuung und Beurteilung sind auch hier in der Satzung festzulegen, Bestimmungen zu Themen im jeweiligen Curriculum.[22] Allerdings ist hier weder

14 § 80 Abs. 1 UG
15 § 51 Abs. 10 UG: „Bachelorgrade sind die akademischen Grade, die nach dem Abschluss der ordentlichen Bachelorstudien verliehen werden. Sie lauten ‚Bachelor‘ mit einem im Curriculum festzulegenden Zusatz, wobei auch eine Abkürzung festzulegen ist.“
16 Siehe § 72 Abs. 1 sowie § 51 Abs. 2 S. 7 UG.
17 § 51 Abs. 2 S. 8 UG
18 § 81 Abs. 1 UG
19 § 81 Abs. 2 UG
20 § 81 Abs. 3 UG
21 § 81 Abs. 1 UG
22 § 82 Abs. 1 und 2 UG

eine zeitliche Limitierung noch die Möglichkeit der gemeinsamen Bearbeitung eines Themas vorgesehen.[23]

3.1.3 Masterarbeiten aus Universitätslehrgängen (ULG)

Universitätslehrgänge sind außerordentliche Studien, die der Weiterbildung dienen.[24] Auf die Abschlussarbeiten von außerordentlichen Studien treffen die gleichen Bestimmungen zu wie auf alle anderen Studien.[25] Daher kann indirekt abgeleitet werden, dass Masterarbeiten aus Universitätslehrgängen als wissenschaftliche Arbeiten zu betrachten sind. Das Abfassen einer schriftlichen Arbeit kann, muss aber nicht, im Curriculum festgelegt werden.[26]

3.1.4 Dissertationen

„Dissertationen sind die wissenschaftlichen Arbeiten, die anders als die Diplom- und Masterarbeiten dem Nachweis der Befähigung zur selbstständigen Bewältigung wissenschaftlicher Fragestellungen dienen."[27] Mit dieser Definition „grenzt der Gesetzgeber Dissertationen als *qualifizierte wissenschaftliche Arbeiten* von Diplom- und Masterarbeiten ab".[28]

> Im Doktoratsstudium und im kombinierten Master- und Doktoratsstudium ist eine wissenschaftliche oder künstlerische Dissertation abzufassen. Nähere Bestimmungen über Betreuung und Beurteilung von Dissertationen und künstlerischen Dissertationen sind in der Satzung, nähere Bestimmungen über das Thema der Dissertation oder künstlerischen Dissertation sind im jeweiligen Curriculum festzulegen.[29]

Weiters ist festgehalten, dass auch Dissertationsthemen durch mehrere Studierende bearbeitet werden dürfen.[30]

---

23 Perthold-Stoitzner, B. (Stand: 1.12.2018), § 82 UG, Kommentar 5.

24 Vgl. § 51 Abs. 20, 21, 22, 23 und 23a UG.

25 Dies geht aus einem Kommentar zum Universitätsgesetz hervor: „die Qualifikation als akademischer Grad hat insb. die Anwendbarkeit der §§ 87 ff UG zur Folge." Perthold-Stoitzner, B. (Stand: 1.12.2018), § 51 UG. Begriffsbestimmungen. Zu Z 23 (Mastergrade).
Die Gleichbehandlung mit ordentlichen Studien geht z. B. auch aus dem Studienrechtlichen Teil der Satzung der Universität Wien hervor.

26 Vgl. § 87 Abs. 2 UG

27 § 51 Abs. 13 UG

28 Perthold-Stoitzner, B. (Stand: 1.12.2018), § 83 UG.

29 § 83 Abs. 1 UG

30 § 83 Abs. 2 UG

3.1.5 Kumulative Arbeiten

Dieser Begriff findet im Universitätsgesetz keinen Niederschlag. Diese Form von Arbeiten entstanden vielmehr aus der Praxis einzelner Wissenschaftsbereiche heraus, speziell der Naturwissenschaften. Kumulative Dissertationen bestehen nicht aus einer in sich geschlossenen Abhandlung in Art einer Monografie, sondern aus mehreren bereits veröffentlichten oder sich in Begutachtung befindenden wissenschaftlichen Artikeln. Diese müssen jedoch „in einem fachlichen Zusammenhang stehen und durch eine übergeordnete Fragestellung verbunden sein“.[31]

3.1.6 Habilitationen

Anders als alle bisher aufgezählten Hochschulschriften dienen Habilitationsschriften nicht der Erlangung einer Graduierung, sondern dem Erwerb der Lehrbefugnis (venia docendi). Als „Habilitation“ wird eigentlich nur das Verfahren, das zur Erteilung der Lehrbefugnis führt, bezeichnet.[32] Neben dem Nachweis didaktischer Fähigkeiten sind auch schriftliche Arbeiten vorzulegen[33], sie können entweder als Monografie oder kumulative Arbeiten eingereicht werden. Da die schriftlichen Teile von Habilitationen in der Regel ohnehin in Verlagen veröffentlicht werden bzw. aus bereits veröffentlichten Artikeln bestehen, unterliegen sie nicht der Veröffentlichungspflicht durch Bibliotheken (siehe unten) und werden meist auch nicht in Hochschulschriften-Repositorien gesammelt.

Künstlerische Habilitationsanträge bestehen hingegen nicht zwingend aus schriftlichen wissenschaftlichen Texten, sondern können

> entsprechend der schier unerschöpflichen Anzahl künstlerischer Betätigungs- und Schaffensfelder von unterschiedlichster Ausgestaltung sein, ein Gemälde, eine Skulptur, ein musikalisches Werk wie eine Komposition, eine musikalische Ausführung im Bereiche von Instrumenten, Opern oder Gesang, schriftstellerische Werke aller Art, Rezitationen etc. Zu klären ist, ob das vorgelegte künstlerische Werk die hervorragende Qualifikation des Bewerbers/der Bewerberin dokumentieren kann.[34]

31 Universität Wien, Büro Studienpräses (2015), S. 1. Ähnlich lautende Bestimmungen finden sich an den anderen österreichischen Universitäten.

32 Perthold-Stoitzner, B. (Stand: 1.12.2018), Rainer, J. M.: § 103 UG. Habilitation. 1. Begriff.

33 § 103 Abs. 3 UG

34 Perthold-Stoitzner, B. (Stand: 1.12.2018), Rainer, J. M.: § 103 UG. Habilitation. V. Publikationen, 12.

3.1.7 Studienrecht

§ 19 Abs. 1 des UG legt fest, dass jede Universität die für die Durchführung notwendigen Vorschriften durch Verordnung (Satzung) selbst erlässt. Weiters ist dort neben den Rahmenbedingungen auch ein monokratisches Organ festzulegen, das für die Vollziehung der studienrechtlichen Bestimmungen zuständig ist.[35] Das kann z. B. ein/e Studiendirektor:in (Universität Innsbruck[36], Universität Graz[37]) oder die/der Studienpräses (Universität Wien[38]) sein. Das jeweilige Organ hat in studienrechtlichen Verfahren das Allgemeine Verwaltungsverfahrensgesetz (AVG) anzuwenden.[39] Die Entscheide des studienrechtlichen Organs gelten somit als amtlicher Bescheid. Dagegen kann das Rechtsmittel der Beschwerde eingelegt werden. Die nächsthöhere Instanz ist das Bundesverwaltungsgericht.[40]

Sämtliche Durchführungsbestimmungen zu wissenschaftlichen Arbeiten sind in der jeweiligen Satzung der Universität zu verankern. Dies betrifft insbesondere Themenwahl und Betreuung. Hinsichtlich des Workflows der Einreichung und Sammlung von Hochschulschriften können die dort ebenfalls festgelegten Fristen, innerhalb derer die Beurteilung der Arbeit ab Einreichung erfolgt sein muss, relevant sein.

3.2 Privatuniversitäten

Bestimmungen zu wissenschaftlichen Arbeiten an Privatuniversitäten finden sich im *Bundesgesetz über Privathochschulen (Privathochschulgesetz – PrivHG)*[41]. Hier ist festgelegt, dass Privatuniversitäten berechtigt sind, akademische Grade gleichlautend zum Universitätsgesetz zu vergeben. Die Studien müssen „mit den entsprechenden Studien an öffentlichen Universitäten in Bezug auf das Ergebnis der Gesamtausbildung gleichwertig sein."[42]

> Die Absolventin oder der Absolvent hat vor der Verleihung des akademischen Grades der Privathochschule, an welcher der akademische Grad verliehen wird, jeweils ein vollständiges Exemplar der positiv beurteilten Diplom- oder Masterarbeit, Dissertation oder künstlerischen Diplom- oder Masterarbeit bzw. der vergleichbaren wissenschaftlichen oder künstlerischen Arbeit oder

35 § 19 Abs. 2 Z. 2 UG
36 Leopold-Franzens-Universität Innsbruck (2003), S. 59.
37 Universität Graz (2004), S. 4.
38 Siehe Universität Wien (2015b)
39 § 46 Abs. 1 UG
40 § 46 Abs. 4 UG
41 Bundesgesetz über Privathochschulen (Privathochschulgesetz – PrivHG), BGBl. I Nr. 77/2020
42 § 8 Abs. 1 PrivHG

der Dokumentation der künstlerischen Diplom- oder Masterarbeit zu übergeben.[43]

Die „Regelungen hinsichtlich der Abfassung von Bachelorarbeiten, Master- oder Diplomarbeiten sowie Dissertationen und Betreuung von wissenschaftlichen Arbeiten“ sind ebenso wie Berufungs- und Habilitationsverfahren in der Satzung festzulegen.[44]

Auch Privathochschulen sind nach § 5 PrivHG verpflichtet eine Satzung zu erstellen und zu veröffentlichen. Grimberger und zu Hohenlohe halten diesbezüglich allerdings fest, dass, anders als Satzungen von Universitäten, Satzungen von Privathochschulen „in der Regel mangels hoheitlicher Zuordnung keine (Rechts-)Verordnungen [sind]. Vielmehr handelt es sich dabei nach herrschender Lehre im Verhältnis zu den Studierenden um mit AGBs vergleichbare Akte des Privatrechts.“[45]

3.3 Fachhochschulen

Das *Bundesgesetz über Fachhochschulen (Fachhochschulgesetz – FHG)*[46] erteilt das Recht zur Graduierung für Fachhochschul-Bachelorstudiengänge und Fachhochschul-Masterstudiengänge, nicht jedoch für Dissertationsstudien.[47] Im Gegensatz zum UG finden sich im FHG keine näheren Definitionen der schriftlichen Abschlussarbeiten. Nach Werner Hauser ist davon auszugehen, „dass auch die im Fachhochschul-Bereich zu verfassenden Bachelorarbeiten gleich denen des Universitätsbereiches als bloße ‚vorwissenschaftliche Arbeiten‘“ und „Diplom- bzw. Masterarbeiten als wissenschaftliche Arbeiten anzusprechen sind.“[48]

Im Gegensatz zu Universitäten ist für Fachhochschulen keine Möglichkeit der Substituierung der schriftlichen Arbeit durch einen „gleichwertigen Nachweis“ vorgesehen.[49] Das FHG gibt auch keinen zeitlichen Rahmen vor, innerhalb dessen die Diplom- oder Masterarbeit zu bewältigen ist. Allerdings ist davon auszugehen, dass die Vorgaben so zu gestalten sind, dass die Arbeit innerhalb der ordentlichen Studienzeit abgeschlossen werden kann.[50]

---

43 § 11 Abs. 4 PrivHG
44 § 12 Abs. 1 S. 5 und § 5 Abs. 1 S. 7 PrivHG
45 Grimberger, M.; zu Hohenlohe, D. (2021), S. 26.
46 Bundesgesetz über Fachhochschulen (Fachhochschulgesetz – FHG), StF: BGBl. Nr. 340/1993
47 § 3 FHG
48 Hauser, W. (2019), S. 284.
49 Hauser, W. (2019), S. 285.
50 Hauser, W. (2019), S. 285.

Das gemeinsame Bearbeiten eines Themas bei Bachelor- und Masterarbeiten wird als zulässig erachtet[51] und soll teamorientiertes (vor)wissenschaftliches Arbeiten trainieren und damit die sozialen Kompetenzen der Studierenden verbessern.[52]

Auch an Fachhochschulen sind nach § 10 Abs. 3 S. 10 FHG Satzungen festzulegen. Studienrechtliche Entscheidungen obliegen der jeweiligen Studiengangsleitung.[53] Beschwerde dagegen kann beim Kollegium, dem Leitungsgremium der Fachhochschule, und in weiterer Folge beim Bundesverwaltungsgericht eingelegt werden.[54]

3.4 Pädagogische Hochschulen

Das *Bundesgesetz über die Organisation der Pädagogischen Hochschulen und ihre Studien (Hochschulgesetz 2005 – HG)*[55] ist die Rechtsgrundlage für staatliche pädagogische Hochschulen und regelt die Anerkennung privater pädagogischer Hochschulen. In § 48 bzw. 48a finden sich die Regelungen zu Bachelorarbeiten und Masterarbeiten. Für beide sind nähere Bestimmungen im jeweiligen Curriculum festzulegen. Die Bearbeitung der Aufgabenstellung für eine Masterarbeit muss innerhalb von sechs Monaten möglich sein, die „gemeinsame Bearbeitung eines Themas durch mehrere Studierende ist zulässig“ und künstlerische Masterarbeiten „haben neben einem künstlerischen Teil, der den Schwerpunkt bildet, auch einen schriftlichen Teil zu umfassen“, der den künstlerischen Teil zu erläutern hat.[56]

Derzeit gibt es 14 Pädagogische Hochschulen in Österreich. Sie bieten „Lehramtsstudien für die Primarstufe (Volksschule), für die Sekundarstufe (Allgemeinbildung) und für die Sekundarstufe (Berufsbildung) an“.[57] Lehramtsstudien für die Volksschule werden ausschließlich von den Pädagogischen Hochschulen angeboten. Lehramtsstudien für allgemeinbildende Fächer an Mittelschulen, Allgemeinbildenden Höheren Schulen, Polytechnischen Schulen, Mittleren und Höheren Berufsbildenden Schulen werden gemeinsam mit öffentlichen Universitäten durchgeführt.[58]

---

51 § 19 Abs. 1 FHG

52 Hauser, W. (2019), S. 286.

53 § 10 Abs. 5 S. 4 FHG

54 § 10 Abs. 6 FHG

55 Bundesgesetz über die Organisation der Pädagogischen Hochschulen und ihre Studien (Hochschulgesetz 2005 – HG), BGBl. I Nr. 30/2006

56 § 48a HG

57 https://www.bmbwf.gv.at/Themen/schule/fpp/ph.html

58 https://www.bmbwf.gv.at/Themen/schule/fpp/ausb/pbneu.html

4. Veröffentlichung

4.1 Veröffentlichungspflicht

Da bis in die 80er-Jahre des 20. Jahrhunderts wissenschaftliche Arbeiten häufig nicht publiziert wurden[59], führte der österreichische Gesetzgeber 1981 ein, dass nach Approbation der Arbeit jeweils ein Exemplar der Diplomarbeit bzw. Dissertation an die Bibliothek der jeweiligen Hochschule und an die Österreichische Nationalbibliothek abzuliefern ist.[60] Diese sogenannte „Ablieferungspflicht" bedingte allerdings nicht automatisch die Zugänglichkeit der Arbeiten, da die Bereitstellung der Werke nur „in Hinblick auf berücksichtigungswürdige wissenschaftliche oder wirtschaftliche Interessen des Autors, des Betreuers oder von Einrichtungen, die die Abfassung der Diplomarbeit oder Dissertation durch die Bereitstellung von Mitteln ermöglicht haben", sowie nach Zustimmung der Autor:innen erfolgte.[61] Im Jahr 1997 wurde mit der sogenannten „Veröffentlichungspflicht" die bisherige Freiwilligkeit gekippt.[62] Da dem Gesetzgeber der Eingriff in die bis dahin geltenden Urheberrechte der Verfasser:innen wissenschaftlicher Arbeiten bewusst war[63], wurde vorangehend das Urheberrechtsgesetz dahingehend erweitert, dass Bibliotheken von veröffentlichten, aber nicht erschienenen Werken Vervielfältigungsstücke ausstellen und verleihen dürfen.[64]

Divergent zu anderen Ländern, wie z. B. Deutschland, wurde vom Gesetzgeber bewusst von der verpflichtenden Drucklegung von Dissertationen Abstand genommen, um Studierende nicht finanziell zu belasten.[65] Neben dem gewünschten Zugang zu Forschungsergebnissen war ein weiterer Aspekt der Einführung der Veröffentlichungspflicht, „wirksame Maßnahmen gegen Plagiate setzen zu wollen".[66]

Die verpflichtende Veröffentlichung von wissenschaftlichen Arbeiten ist in den entsprechenden Bundesgesetzen festgelegt. Dies gilt für Diplom-, Magister- und Masterarbeiten, Master-Thesen (ULG) sowie Dissertationen. Da, wie oben erwähnt,

59 Staudegger, E. (2018), S. 6.

60 § 25 Abs. 4 Bundesgesetz vom 15. 7. 1966 über die Studien an den wissenschaftlichen Hochschulen (Allgemeines Hochschul-Studiengesetz), BGBl 1966/177 idF BGBl 1981/332

61 § 1 Abs. 4 Verordnung des Bundesministers für Wissenschaft und Forschung vom 26. August 1979 über die Bibliotheksordnung für die Universitäten, BGBl 1979/410

62 § 65 Abs. 1 Bundesgesetz über die Studien an den Universitäten (Universitäts-Studiengesetz – UniStG), BGBl I 1997/48

63 Staudegger, E. (2018), S. 7.

64 Vervielfältigung zum eigenen Gebrauch von Sammlungen, § 42 Abs. 4 Bundesgesetz, mit dem das Urheberrechtsgesetz und die Urheberrechtsgesetznovelle 1980 geändert werden (Urheberrechtsgesetz-Novelle 1996 – UrhG-Nov. 1996) BGBl. Nr. 151/1996

65 Mayer, A. (2015), S. 39.

66 Staudegger, E. (2018), S. 7.

Bachelorarbeiten nicht explizit als wissenschaftliche Arbeiten bezeichnet werden, gilt für sie diese Pflicht nicht.[67]

> Die Absolventin oder der Absolvent hat vor der Verleihung des akademischen Grades jeweils ein vollständiges Exemplar der positiv beurteilten wissenschaftlichen oder künstlerischen Arbeit oder der Dokumentation der künstlerischen Arbeit durch Übergabe an die Bibliothek der Universität, an welcher der akademische Grad verliehen wird, zu veröffentlichen. Für diese Übergabe kann in der Satzung festgelegt werden, dass diese ausschließlich in elektronischer Form zu erfolgen hat. Weiters kann in der Satzung festgelegt werden, dass die Veröffentlichung elektronisch in einem öffentlich zugänglichen Repositorium erfolgen muss.[68]

Im fast gleichlautenden Passus des Privathochschulgesetzes ist der allgemeine Terminus „wissenschaftliche[...] oder künstlerische[...] Arbeit oder [...] Dokumentation der künstlerischen Arbeit“ durch „Diplom- oder Masterarbeit, Dissertation oder künstlerische[...] Diplom- oder Masterarbeit bzw. [...] vergleichbare[...] wissenschaftliche[...] oder künstlerische[...] Arbeit oder [...] Dokumentation der künstlerischen Diplom- oder Masterarbeit“ ersetzt.[69]

Von der Veröffentlichungspflicht ausgenommen sind sowohl an Universitäten als auch an Privatuniversitäten „die wissenschaftlichen oder künstlerischen Arbeiten oder deren Teile, die einer Massenvervielfältigung nicht zugänglich sind.“[70] Dies betrifft vor allem die künstlerischen Teile von Abschlussarbeiten, die ob ihrer Beschaffenheit (Installationen, Bilder, Skulpturen etc.) unikal sind.

Für Fachhochschulen lautet der Passus zur Veröffentlichungspflicht: „Die positiv beurteilte Masterarbeit ist durch Übergabe an die Bibliothek der Fachhochschule zu veröffentlichen.“[71] Für Pädagogische Hochschulen heißt es dementsprechend „durch Übergabe an die Bibliothek der Pädagogischen Hochschule, an welcher der akademische Grad verliehen wird“.[72]

---

67 Perthold-Stoitzner, B. (Stand: 1.12.2018), § 86 UG. Veröffentlichungspflicht.
68 § 86 Abs. 1 UG
69 § 11 Abs. 4 PrivHG
70 § 86 Abs. 3 UG und § 11 Abs. 4 PrivHG
71 § 19 Abs. 3 FHG
72 § 49 Abs. 1 HG

4.2 Veröffentlichung ohne akademischen Grad

Die positive Beurteilung einer wissenschaftlichen Arbeit durch geeignete Person(en), abhängig von der Art der Hochschulschrift, ist Voraussetzung für die Zulassung zu den Abschlussprüfungen bzw. der Defensio. Allerdings muss nach Einreichung und Beurteilung der schriftlichen Arbeit der Studienabschluss nicht notgedrungen erfolgen. Die Veröffentlichungspflicht bezieht sich lediglich auf die beurteilte Arbeit und ist nicht daran gebunden, ob die Graduierung letztendlich stattfindet.

4.3 Ausschluss der Benützung

Seit 1997 wird einhergehend mit der Veröffentlichungspflicht den Studierenden die Möglichkeit der zeitlich befristeten Sperre der Nutzung der wissenschaftlichen Arbeit eingeräumt. Dadurch sollen potenzielle Nachteile der zwangsweisen Veröffentlichung für die Autor:innen – insbesondere hinsichtlich einer Verlagsveröffentlichung – gemildert werden.[73]

Das UG besagt diesbezüglich, dass „die Verfasserin oder der Verfasser berechtigt [ist], den Ausschluss der Benützung der abgelieferten Exemplare für längstens fünf Jahre nach der Übergabe zu beantragen. Dem Antrag ist vom für die studienrechtlichen Angelegenheiten zuständigen Organ stattzugeben, wenn die oder der Studierende glaubhaft macht, dass wichtige rechtliche oder wirtschaftliche Interessen der oder des Studierenden gefährdet sind.“[74]

Die entsprechenden Abschnitte des Privathochschulgesetzes, des Fachhochschulgesetzes und des Hochschulgesetzes 2005 sind nahezu gleichlautend.[75]

4.4 Elektronische Veröffentlichung

Im Universitätsgesetz findet sich seit 2017 ausdrücklich ein Passus, der besagt, dass in der Satzung der jeweiligen Hochschule festgelegt werden kann, dass sowohl die Übergabe der wissenschaftlichen Arbeit ausschließlich in elektronischer Form als auch die Veröffentlichung elektronisch in einem öffentlich zugänglichen Repositorium zu erfolgen hat.[76] Gleiches gilt für die Veröffentlichung von Dissertationen

---

73 Staudegger, E. (2018), S. 8.
74 § 86 Abs. 4 UG
75 § 11 Abs. 5 PrivHG, § 19 Abs. 3 FHG und § 49 Abs. 3 HG
76 § 86 Abs. 1 UG

durch Übergabe an die Nationalbibliothek.[77] Wie diese Bestimmungen genau auszulegen sind, ist umstritten, da die Vorgaben und Erläuterungen genauer betrachtet „ungenau und unklar“ sind.[78]

Im Privathochschulgesetz hingegen wird bezüglich der Übergabe an die Hochschule oder der Veröffentlichung kein Bezug auf elektronische Exemplare genommen. Nur hinsichtlich der Veröffentlichung von Dissertationen in der Nationalbibliothek ist festgelegt: „Positiv beurteilte Dissertationen sind überdies durch Übergabe an die Österreichische Nationalbibliothek zu veröffentlichen. Sofern vorhanden, kann die Übergabe auch in elektronischer Form erfolgen.“[79]

Im Fachhochschulgesetz findet sich keine explizite Erwähnung der elektronischen Form von wissenschaftlichen Abschlussarbeiten.

Pädagogische Hochschulen hingegen sind wie Universitäten berechtigt, in der Satzung festzulegen, dass die Übergabe der wissenschaftlichen Arbeit „ausschließlich in elektronischer Form zu erfolgen hat. Weiters kann in der Satzung festgelegt werden, dass die Veröffentlichung elektronisch in einem öffentlich zugänglichen Repositorium erfolgen muss.“[80]

4.5 Titelblatt – ÖNORM

Ob auf die Gestaltung der jeweiligen Titelblätter wissenschaftlicher Arbeiten besonderer Wert gelegt wird, ist von Hochschule zu Hochschule verschieden. Wenig bekannt ist die Tatsache, dass dazu eine ÖNORM existiert. Sie dient der bibliographischen Erfassung von Diplomarbeiten, Masterarbeiten und Dissertationen durch Bibliotheken.[81] Demnach hat die Titelseite folgende Angaben zu enthalten: Name des Verfassers/der Verfasserin, Titel und, falls vorhanden, Untertitel, Gesamttitel, falls die Arbeit aus mehreren Bänden besteht, Gesamtzahl der Bände, Art der Abschlussarbeit, Studienrichtung, Name der Hochschule, Ort der Hochschule, Name(n) des/der Betreuenden, Name(n) des/der Beurteilenden, Jahr der Einreichung.[82] Darüber hinaus ist vorgesehen, dass auf einer eigenen Seite ein Abstract enthalten sein soll.[83]

77 § 86 Abs. 2 UG
78 Pribas, S. (2019), S. 72.
79 § 11 Abs. 4 PrivHG
80 § 49 Abs. 1 HG
81 ÖNORM A 2662: Wissenschaftliche Abschlussarbeiten - Angaben für den bibliographischen Nachweis. Ausgabedatum: 2023-11-01.
82 ÖNORM A 2662: 2023-11-01, S. 5 f.
83 ÖNORM A 2662: 2023-11-01, S. 6.

5. Urheberrechtliche Aspekte

5.1 Urheberrecht

Im Universitätsgesetz ist für alle Formen der hier definierten Arbeiten explizit festgehalten: „Bei der Bearbeitung des Themas und der Betreuung der Studierenden sind die Bestimmungen des Urheberrechtsgesetzes, BGBl. Nr. 111/1936, zu beachten.“[84] Der gleiche Wortlaut findet sich auch für Bachelor- und Masterarbeiten an Pädagogischen Akademien.[85] Aus der Tatsache, dass sich weder im Fachhochschulgesetz noch im Privathochschulgesetz ein ähnlicher Hinweis findet, kann jedoch nicht geschlossen werden, dass hier das Urheberrecht nicht Geltung haben sollte.

Tatsächlich räumt das Urheberrecht auch Autor:innen wissenschaftlicher Werke als „Werke der Literatur“ (§ 2 Z. 3 Urheberrechtsgesetz) zahlreiche Rechte wie Urheberpersönlichkeitsrechte und Verwertungsrechte ein, die uneingeschränkt auch für Hochschulschriften gelten.

Die Urheberpersönlichkeitsrechte bieten einen umfassenden Schutz gegen die Entstellung des Werkes, seine Veränderung, Kürzung, Übersetzung oder Bearbeitung. Unter die im Zusammenhang mit Hochschulschriften relevanten Verwertungsrechte fallen das Recht der Vervielfältigung, der Verbreitung, der Zurverfügungstellung (z. B. im Internet) sowie das Werknutzungsrecht. Daher ist es bei der Anzeige von wissenschaftlichen Arbeiten in einem Repositorium notwendig, dass der/die Urheber:in der Institution die Werknutzungsbewilligung einräumt.

5.2 Elektronische Veröffentlichung versus verpflichtender Open Access

Mit der Änderung des Universitätsgesetzes 2017 wurde den Universitäten die Kompetenz eingeräumt, in der Satzung festzulegen, dass die Veröffentlichung wissenschaftlicher Arbeiten „in elektronischer Form zu erfolgen hat. Weiters kann in der Satzung festgelegt werden, dass die Veröffentlichung elektronisch in einem öffentlich zugänglichen Repositorium erfolgen muss.“[86] Ob dies tatsächlich als Ermächtigung zu einer verpflichtenden Open-Access-Veröffentlichung verstanden werden kann, ist umstritten. Open-Access-Veröffentlichung bedeutet „dass die Arbeit weltweit ohne erkennbare Restriktionen, ohne Anfrage, ohne Registrierung o.Ä. genutzt werden kann.“[87] Tatsächlich ist jedoch der Gesetzestext hinsichtlich der „Veröffentlichung elektronisch in einem öffentlich zugänglichen Repositorium“ vage

84 § 80 Abs. 2, § 81 Abs. 4, § 82 Abs. 3, § 83 Abs. 2 UG
85 § 48 Abs. 2 und § 48a Abs. 5 HG
86 § 86 Abs. 1 UG
87 Staudegger, E. (2018), S. 6.

und besagt lediglich, dass bei verpflichtender elektronischer Veröffentlichung das entsprechende Repositorium *öffentlich zugänglich* sein muss. Dies trifft prinzipiell auf alle öffentlichen Bibliotheken, also auch Universitätsbibliotheken, zu. Mit dieser Formulierung kann also auch ein Repositorium gemeint sein, auf das ausschließlich innerhalb der Bibliotheksräume zugegriffen werden kann.

Elisabeth Staudegger kommt in ihrer rechtswissenschaftlichen Untersuchung zur Frage der Open-Access-Veröffentlichung zu folgendem Fazit:

> Hingegen ist die ohne weitere Erklärung gesetzlich eingeräumte Satzungskompetenz der Universitäten, die Veröffentlichung wissenschaftlicher Abschlussarbeiten ‚in einem öffentlich zugänglichen Repositorium' verpflichtend vorzusehen, rechtlich kritisch. Zunächst ist die Ermächtigungsnorm selbst äußerst vage, sodass fraglich ist, ob sie dem verfassungsrechtlichen Bestimmtheitsgebot genügt. Inhaltlich würde mit einer OA-Veröffentlichungspflicht tief in persönlichkeitsrechtliche und verwertungsrechtliche Interessen der wissenschaftlichen bzw. künstlerischen UrheberInnen eingegriffen und karrierebestimmende, unwiderrufliche Maßnahmen gesetzt, die die VerfasserInnen der Werke einseitig belasten und nachhaltig beeinträchtigen können. Sollte eine Universität tatsächlich entsprechende Satzungsbestimmungen vorsehen wollen, wäre jedenfalls eine ausreichend deutliche Beschreibung des Modells unter ausreichender Berücksichtigung der Interessen der UrheberInnen erforderlich.[88]

Die Diskussion, ob die zwangsweise weltweite und uneingeschränkte Veröffentlichung in einem Open-Access-Repositorium für wissenschaftliche Arbeiten, insbesondere von Dissertationen, den im Urheberrechtsgesetz festgelegten Rechten widerspricht, ist mit Stand im Jahr 2022 keineswegs eindeutig entschieden. An den meisten Hochschulen Österreichs ist die Sammlung von Hochschulschriften in elektronischer Form längst Usus. Ob und wie die Arbeiten im Internet angeboten werden, ist jedoch bei Weitem nicht einheitlich. Ausschlaggebend ist hier neben der technischen Realisierung vor allem die Frage, wie die Hochschule die gesetzlichen Vorgaben interpretiert und diese als ausreichend ausformuliert erachtet, um einer verpflichtenden Veröffentlichung im Internet auch im Klageweg standzuhalten.

Daher ist an österreichischen Hochschulen derzeit die Art und Weise, wie Hochschulschriften zugänglich sind, mannigfaltig. Die Bandbreite liegt zwischen zwangsweiser weltweiter Open-Access-Veröffentlichung, der Anzeige für einen

88 Staudegger, E. (2018), S. 24.

eingeschränkten Nutzungskreis innerhalb der Bibliothek mit mehr oder weniger ausgeklügeltem Access-Rights-Management bis zur elektronischen Veröffentlichung ausschließlich auf freiwilliger Basis.

5.3 Vergabe von CC-Lizenzen

Ebenso divers wird an Hochschulen die Vergabe von Creative-Commons-Lizenzen (CC) für wissenschaftliche Arbeiten gehandhabt. Die Problematik liegt hier vor allem in der Tatsache, dass einmal unter einer Lizenz veröffentlichte Arbeiten nicht mehr von der Veröffentlichung zurückgezogen werden können, da die Vergabe der Lizenz nicht widerrufbar ist. Besonders Hochschulen, die keine verpflichtende Open-Access-Veröffentlichung vorsehen, ihren Nutzer:innen jedoch die Vorteile eines Repositoriums bieten, ermöglichen ihren Nutzer:innen bewusst das Zurückziehen der Arbeit von der Verbreitung im Internet.

Die Vergabe einer Lizenz muss auf jeden Fall mit ausdrücklicher Zustimmung durch den/die Autor:in erfolgen, da davon auszugehen ist, dass mit der „Veröffentlichung in einem Repositorium“ vom Gesetzgeber keinesfalls auch die institutionelle Vergabe von CC-Lizenzen gemeint ist.

Abhängig vom jeweiligen Workflow, wie die Arbeiten ins Repositorium gelangen, ist hier eine geeignete Stelle zu finden, an der die ausdrückliche Einwilligung gegeben werden kann. Erfolgt die Abfrage aller Kenntnisnahmen und Einwilligungen (siehe unten) während des Hochladevorgangs zur Einreichung der Abschlussarbeit, eventuell auch in Zusammenhang mit einer eventuellen Plagiatsprüfung, könnte eine unwiderrufbare Zustimmung von den Studierenden als Überrumpelung betrachtet werden, da sie zu diesem Zeitpunkt den Studienabschluss im Fokus haben und nicht den weltweiten Zugriff auf ihre Arbeit. Abhilfe könnte hier die nachträgliche Vergabe von CC-Lizenzen für bereits veröffentlichte Arbeiten im Repositorium durch die Studierenden selbst schaffen. Allerdings erfordert dies unter Umständen einen beträchtlichen zusätzlichen administrativen Aufwand.

Die Gründe, wissenschaftliche Abschlussarbeiten vom Internet-Zugriff zurückzuziehen, sind vielfältig. So kann z. B. die Verwendung von Bildern, deren Urheberschaft nicht eindeutig geklärt ist, zu Klagsdrohungen führen. Auch die Verwendung von Daten Dritter z. B. in Interviews kann die Absolvent:innen dazu veranlassen, ihre Arbeit von der Verbreitung im Internet zurückzuziehen, besonders, wenn dadurch Leib und Leben der betreffenden Personen gefährdet wären.

Inwiefern das Zugeständnis der Weitergabe, Veränderung und/oder kommerziellen Nutzung einer wissenschaftlichen Abschlussarbeit durch eine CC-Lizenz der

Förderung der Wissenschaft dienlich ist oder ob die Veröffentlichung unter den Bedingungen des Urheberrechts für diesen Zweck durchaus ausreichend sind, wird wohl noch länger kontrovers diskutiert werden.

6 Aspekte des Workflows

6.1 Beilagen

Wissenschaftlichen Abschlussarbeiten liegen oftmals diverse ergänzende bzw. erklärende Anhänge unterschiedlichster Inhalte und Gestaltungen bei. Da sie nicht die wissenschaftliche Arbeit selbst darstellen und oftmals „einer Massenvervielfältigung nicht zugänglich sind"[89], unterliegen sie nicht der Veröffentlichungspflicht. Werden sie dennoch von der Bibliothek gesammelt, ist im Einzelfall zu entscheiden, ob sie der Öffentlichkeit zur Verfügung gestellt werden.

6.2 Retrodigitalisierung

An manchen Universitäten wird auch Alumni die Möglichkeit geboten, ihre wissenschaftlichen Abschlussarbeiten im Hochschulschriften-Repositorium online zu stellen. Hier muss unbedingt darauf geachtet werden, dass eine schriftliche Zustimmungserklärung des/der Autor:in zur Online-Veröffentlichung vorliegt und die Identität des/der Hochladenden bekannt ist. Ohne Zustimmungserklärung dürfen Arbeiten gemäß Urheberrecht erst 70 Jahre nach dem Tod des/der Urheber:in einer Hochschulschrift digitalisiert und online gestellt werden.[90]

6.3 Beurteiltes Exemplar

Positiv beurteilte Hochschulschriften sind die Voraussetzung für die Erlangung eines akademischen Grades. Daher gelten die Originale – das sind die beurteilten Exemplare – als rechtsgültige Dokumente. Es ist davon auszugehen, dass zur Beurteilung eingereichte schriftliche Arbeiten lediglich den die Arbeit betreuenden und beurteilenden Personen vorgelegt werden. Im Fall, dass das elektronische Exemplar als das offizielle eingestuft wird, müsste das hochgeladene Dokument eindeutig als das originäre Dokument gekennzeichnet (z. B. mit einer digitalen Signatur versehen) werden, damit spätere Veränderungen, z. B. durch Beurteiler:innen,

89 § 86 Abs. 3 UG

90 § 60 Abs. 1 Bundesgesetz über das Urheberrecht an Werken der Literatur und der Kunst und über verwandte Schutzrechte (Urheberrechtsgesetz), BGBl. Nr. 111/1936.

nicht möglich sind. Jedenfalls müsste sichergestellt werden, dass ein rein elektronischer Workflow DSGVO-konform abläuft und Dokumente nicht unverschlüsselt verschickt werden.

6.4 Veränderung der Arbeit

> Wird ein Werk auf eine Art, die es der Öffentlichkeit zugänglich macht, benutzt oder zum Zweck der Verbreitung vervielfältigt, so dürfen auch von dem zu einer solchen Werknutzung Berechtigten an dem Werke selbst, an dessen Titel oder an der Urheberbezeichnung keine Kürzungen, Zusätze oder andere Änderungen vorgenommen werden, soweit nicht der Urheber einwilligt oder das Gesetz die Änderung zuläßt.[91]

Das bedeutet, dass eine Institution, der mittels Werknutzungsbewilligung das Recht zur Speicherung und zum Onlinestellen übertragen wurde, sicherstellen muss, dass Arbeiten nach der Beurteilung nicht nachträglich verändert werden können. Erfolgt eine Veränderung inhaltlicher Natur, z. B. durch Schwärzen von Bildern, muss dies zwingend in den Metadaten angeführt werden.

Da aber die dauerhafte Speicherung und Archivierung elektronischer Dokumente die Migration auf aktuelle Systeme und/oder Speichermedien bedingen kann, sollte die Institution in der Satzung bzw. einer ergänzenden Verordnung festhalten, dass an den elektronischen Versionen von Hochschulschriften aus technischen Gründen Veränderungen technologischer Art zum Zweck der Langzeitarchivierung vorgenommen werden können.[92]

6.5 Verbindliche Erklärungen

Abhängig davon, durch welchen Workflow die Hochschulschriften in das Repositorium gelangen und welche Rechtsauffassung die Institution gegenüber einer eventuellen verpflichtenden Veröffentlichung vertritt, sollte die Institution entsprechende rechtsverbindliche Erklärungen von den Urheber:innen einfordern. Damit stellt die Institution trotz Verankerung in der Satzung oder nachfolgenden Verordnungen sicher, dass der/die Studierende die jeweiligen Konditionen zur Kenntnis genommen hat. Durch eine schriftliche Erklärung wird der Anspruch auf Beweisbarkeit erfüllt.

---

91 § 21 Abs. 1 Urheberrechtsgesetz.

92 Vgl. 260. Verordnung über die Formvorschriften bei der Einreichung wissenschaftlicher Arbeiten: Universität Wien (2015a), S. 4.

Im Fall der Verknüpfung der Einreichung und/oder Plagiatsprüfung mit der Sammlung und Speicherung der Arbeiten in einem Repositorium sind rechtsverbindliche Erklärungen zur Urheberschaft (Bestätigung der Urheberschaft), zur Identität der Version (Übereinstimmung der elektronischen mit der Druckversion), zur Einhaltung der guten wissenschaftlichen Praxis und – falls implementiert – zur Kenntnisnahme der Plagiatsprüfung einzuholen.

Bezüglich der Speicherung in einem Repositorium sollen rechtsverbindliche Erklärungen zur Langzeitarchivierung (Veränderungen technologischer, nicht inhaltlicher Art), zur Veröffentlichung von Metadaten, zur Veröffentlichung des Abstracts sowie eine Erklärung zur Schad- und Klagloshaltung gegenüber der Institution im Fall der Verletzung der Rechte Dritter vorliegen.

Sollte die Institution die Freiwilligkeit der Veröffentlichung der Arbeiten am Hochschulschriftenserver vorsehen, ist unbedingt eine Werknutzungsbewilligung einzuholen.

7. Wissenschaftliche Integrität

Seit den 90er Jahren des 20. Jahrhunderts ist die Diskussion der wissenschaftlichen Integrität von Hochschulschriften in der Mitte der Gesellschaft angekommen. Daher war es eine wesentliche Intention des Gesetzgebers bei der Einführung der Veröffentlichungspflicht wissenschaftlicher Arbeiten 1997, die Aufdeckung von Plagiaten zu erwirken.[93] Ein Jahrzehnt später war die Aufdeckung mehr oder weniger prominenter Plagiatsfälle auch medial sehr präsent und veranlasste die ersten österreichischen Universitäten, mit der Einführung von Plagiatsprüfungen zu beginnen.[94]

An den meisten österreichischen Hochschulen werden wissenschaftliche Abschlussarbeiten routinemäßig auf Textgleichheiten überprüft. Vielfach geschieht dies auch im gleichen Workflow wie das Sammeln der Arbeiten durch die Bibliothek. Es sind verschiedene Softwaresysteme im Einsatz, die die Texte gegen andere im Internet verfügbare Texte prüfen, aber auch gegen Verlagsdatenbanken, um sie gegen Monografien und Zeitschriften abzugleichen.

Die Überprüfung wird immer nur eine Momentaufnahme sein und es kann sich eventuell zu einem späteren Zeitpunkt herausstellen, dass eine Arbeit abgeschrieben wurde. Im Allgemeinen hinkt die Entwicklung der Tools immer ein wenig dem

93 588 der Beilagen zu den Stenographischen Protokollen des Nationalrates XX. GP, zu § 65, S. 99.
94 An der Universität Wien wurde z. B. im Jahr 2006 mit der Plagiatsprüfung begonnen.

Erfindungsreichtum von Menschen, die betrügen wollen, hinterher. Übersetzungen aus in Europa nicht sehr gängigen Sprachen, Verwendung von Homoglyphen, um die Software auszutricksen, oder der Einsatz von Paraphrasierungs-Tools sind hier als Beispiele zu nennen.

Das Phänomen der Bezahlung von Ghostwritern (im Englischen als "Contract Cheating" bezeichnet), um die wissenschaftliche Arbeit, oft aber bereits auch schon die „Vorwissenschaftliche Arbeit" im Gymnasium[95] erstellen zu lassen, ist inzwischen weit verbreitet. Ihnen kann mittels Plagiatsprüfung kaum auf die Schliche gekommen werden, da die Arbeiten methodisch meist einwandfrei gemacht sind. Technologien, die auf deren Erkennung abzielen, konzentrieren sich auf die Analyse und/oder (langfristige) Beobachtung des Schreibstils von Studierenden (Stilometrie) sowie die Analyse von Metadaten. Obwohl auch hier einzelne Hersteller bereits Tools anbieten, ist die Technologie noch nicht für einen breiten Einsatz geeignet. Darüber hinaus muss noch geklärt werden, ob die Analyse des persönlichen Schreibstils von Autor:innen datenschutzrechtlich unbedenklich ist.

Der durch die Veröffentlichung von ChatGPT (Generative Pre-trained Transformer) Ende 2022 hervorgerufene Hype um die Verwendung von Künstlicher Intelligenz (KI) für alle Arten von Texterzeugung, hat auch die Beurteilung wissenschaftlicher Arbeiten nachhaltig verändert. Software-Firmen arbeiten intensiv an Tools zur Erkennung möglicher Beteiligung von KI an der Textproduktion und Hochschulen passen fieberhaft ihre Leitlinien für Forschung und Lehre den neuen Gegebenheiten an. Dabei zeichnet sich ab, dass die Empfehlungen in Richtung „Potentiale von KI-Tools nutzen und Integrität wahren"[96] gehen, das heißt Studierenden ein verantwortungsbewusster Umgang mit den KI-Tools gelehrt werden soll.

Die Gesetzeslage ist recht eindeutig. War das Plagiieren von Arbeiten bisher schon kein Kavaliersdelikt, wurde mit der UG-Novelle 2021, die am 27.05.2021 veröffentlicht wurde, das Plagiieren unter Verwaltungsstrafe gestellt. Plagiate können damit laut § 116 Abs. 3 UG den „Tatbestand des unberechtigten Führens eines [akademischen] Titels erfüllen, was die Aberkennung des akademischen Grades und eine Geldstrafe bis zu 15.000 Euro nach sich ziehen kann."[97]

Weiters wurde mit der Strafbarkeit für unentgeltliches Ghostwriting mit einer Geldstrafe bis zu 25.000 € und für professionelle Ghostwriter:innen und Ghostwriting-Agenturen mit einer Geldstrafe bis zu 60.000 € einer langjährigen Forderung der Universitäten nachgekommen. Bis dahin erfüllte lediglich das Verwenden einer

95 Siehe z. B. Anders, T. (2021)
96 Universität Wien (2023)
97 Bundesministerium für Bildung, Wissenschaft und Forschung (2021), S. 3.

nicht selbst erstellten Arbeit den Tatbestand der Vortäuschung. Professionelle Ghostwriter:innen konnten hingegen ungeniert ihre Dienste selbst an Schwarzen Brettern der Universitäten anbieten.

Wurde ein akademischer Grad nachweislich „durch gefälschte Zeugnisse oder durch das Vortäuschen von wissenschaftlichen oder künstlerischen Leistungen erschlichen", so ist der Verleihungsbescheid vom studienrechtlich zuständigen Organ aufzuheben und einzuziehen.[98]

Erfolgt eine technische Plagiatsprüfung im Rahmen der Sammlung von Hochschulschriften, so ist jedenfalls sicherzustellen, dass dieses Procedere in der Satzung verankert ist und Studierende die Kenntnisnahme der Plagiatsprüfung schriftlich bestätigen.

8. Datenschutz

Der Datenschutz gilt nicht nur für alle im Repositorium gespeicherten und veröffentlichten Daten der Studierenden. Hier ist gemäß DSGVO vor allem das Prinzip der Datenminimierung zu beachten, also nur so viele Daten anzuzeigen, wie unbedingt notwendig. Daher sollten personenbezogene Daten wie Matrikelnummern, Adressen, Geburtsdaten, Lebensläufe oder auch Unterschriften nach Möglichkeit nicht veröffentlicht werden. Für alle im Repositorium angezeigten Daten-Kategorien ist jedenfalls die Prüfung durch den/die jeweilige:n Datenschutzbeauftragte:n der Hochschule notwendig.

Ein anders gelagertes, weiteres Problemfeld eröffnet sich, wenn in wissenschaftlichen Arbeiten Persönlichkeitsrechte Dritter tangiert werden. Dies kann beispielsweise bei der Verwendung von Interviews der Fall sein, die so wiedergegeben werden, dass der/die Interviewte erkennbar ist. Die Wiedererkennbarkeit der Interviewten kann auch durch Beschreibung von Personen oder Szenen in Krisengebieten dieser Erde gegeben sein und könnte so zur politischen Verfolgung der genannten Personen führen. Die Möglichkeiten sind vielfältig. Derartige Arbeiten sollten jedenfalls unbedingt zumindest von der Online-Veröffentlichung ausgenommen werden.

98 § 89 UG: Widerruf inländischer akademischer Grade oder akademischer Bezeichnungen (Anm. 9)

9. Fazit

Bei der Sammlung von Hochschulschriften in einem Repositorium ist darauf zu achten, dass alle gesetzlichen Bestimmungen, die durch die Hochschulgesetze und das Urheberrecht festgelegt sind, eingehalten werden. Erfolgt die Sammlung systematisch und flächendeckend, ist das Prozedere sowie Formvorschriften in einer entsprechenden Verordnung festzuhalten. Von Studierenden ist die Bestätigung der Kenntnis dieser Vorschriften aktiv in einem entsprechenden Dokument einzuholen. Es empfiehlt sich bei der Ausarbeitung der entsprechenden Texte, unbedingt juristische Expertise in Anspruch zu nehmen. Um die Integrität der Arbeiten zu gewährleisten, sollen nach der Abgabe weder durch die Urheber:innen noch durch die Institution inhaltliche Veränderungen an den Dokumenten vorgenommen werden können. Bei der technischen Umsetzung sind mögliche Schnittstellen zu anderen administrativen Systemen und eine einwandfreie Dokumentation aller Bearbeitungsschritte zu bedenken.

Zu guter Letzt ist festzuhalten, dass für einen gelungenen Workflow die enge Kooperation zwischen Bibliothek und den studienrechtlich verantwortlichen Organen unerlässlich ist. Sie fördert gegenseitiges Verständnis und ermöglicht die reibungslose Sammlung der wissenschaftlichen Abschlussarbeiten.

Bibliografie

588 der Beilagen zu den Stenographischen Protokollen des Nationalrates XX. https://www.parlament.gv.at/PAKT/VHG/XX/I/I_00588/index.shtml (abgerufen am 29.09.2023)

Anders, Theo (2021): Ghostwriterin. „Bei mir melden sich die verzweifelten Eltern“. In: Der Standard, 21.03.2021. https://www.derstandard.at/story/2000125046984/ghostwriterin-bei-mir-melden-sich-die-verzweifelten-eltern (abgerufen am 29.09.2023)

Bundesgesetz über Fachhochschulen (Fachhochschulgesetz – FHG), StF: BGBl. Nr. 340/1993. https://www.ris.bka.gv.at/GeltendeFassung.wxe?Abfrage=Bundesnormen&Gesetzesnummer=10009895 (abgerufen am 29.09.2023)

Bundesgesetz über die Organisation der Pädagogischen Hochschulen und ihre Studien (Hochschulgesetz 2005 – HG), BGBl. I Nr. 30/2006. https://www.ris.bka.gv.at/GeltendeFassung.wxe?Abfrage=Bundesnormen&Gesetzesnummer=20004626 (abgerufen am 29.09.2023)

Bundesgesetz über die Organisation der Universitäten und ihre Studien (Universitätsgesetz 2002 – UG), BGBl. I Nr. 120/2002. https://www.ris.bka.gv.at/GeltendeFassung.wxe?Abfrage=Bundesnormen&Gesetzesnummer=20002128 (abgerufen am 29.09.2023)

Bundesgesetz über Privathochschulen (Privathochschulgesetz – PrivHG), BGBl. I Nr. 77/2020. https://www.ris.bka.gv.at/GeltendeFassung.wxe?Abfrage=Bundesnormen&Gesetzesnummer=20011248 (abgerufen am 29.09.2023)

Bundesgesetz über das Urheberrecht an Werken der Literatur und der Kunst und über verwandte Schutzrechte (Urheberrechtsgesetz), BGBl. Nr. 111/1936. https://www.ris.bka.gv.at/GeltendeFassung.wxe?Abfrage=Bundesnormen&Gesetzesnummer=10001848 (abgerufen am 29.09.2023)

Bundesministerium für Bildung, Wissenschaft und Forschung (2021): Eckpunkte der UG-Novelle 2021. https://www.bmbwf.gv.at/dam/jcr:e45c9d16-e3a0-47e9-a6d5-cc47f3d9dcbd/20210216_Presseunterlage_Eckpunkte%20der%20UG_Novelle_2021.pdf (abgerufen am 29.09.2023)

Grimberger, Markus; zu Hohenlohe, Diana (2021): Der neue Rechtsrahmen für Privathochschulen und -universitäten. In: Zeitschrift für Hochschulrecht, Hochschulmanagement und Hochschulpolitik 20 (1), S. 20–26. https://doi.org/10.33196/zfhr202101002001

Hauser, Werner (2019): FHStG Kurzkommentar Fachhochschul-Studiengesetz. 8. Aufl. Wien: Verlag Österreich. https://doi.org/10.33196/9783704681911

Leopold-Franzens-Universität Innsbruck (2003): Mitteilungsblatt, Studienjahr 2003/2004, Ausgegeben am 11. November 2003, 8. Stück, S. 59. https://www.uibk.ac.at/universitaet/mitteilungsblatt/2003/08/mitteil.pdf (abgerufen am 29.09.2023)

Mayer, Adelheid (2015): Wissenschaftliche Abschlussarbeiten. Historische, technische, organisatorische und ethische Aspekte der Sammlung sowie des Plagiarismus von Dissertationen, Diplom-, Magister- und Masterarbeiten an österreichischen Universitäten unter besonderer Berücksichtigung der Universität Wien. Master Thesis (ULG). Universität Wien. https://doi.org/10.25365/thesis.40071

ÖNORM A 2662:1993 05 01 – Äußere Gestaltung von Hochschulschriften.

Perthold-Stoitzner, Bettina (Hg.): Kommentar zum Universitätsgesetz, Update 3.01 (Stand: 01.12.2018). Abrufbar in: RDB – Rechtsdatenbank. Wien: Manz. https://rdb.manz.at/nachschlagen?execution=e4s1#/1145_2_ug_p0085 (abgerufen am 10.07.2022)

Pflug, Günther (2017): Hochschulschriften (HSS). In: Corsten, Severin et al. (Hg.): Lexikon des gesamten Buchwesens Online. 1. Aufl. Leiden. http://dx-doi-org.uaccess.univie.ac.at/10.1163/9789004337862__COM_080747

Pribas, Sebastian (2019): Einreichung und Veröffentlichung wissenschaftlicher Arbeiten in elektronischer Form. In: Zeitschrift für Hochschulrecht 18, S. 72–78. https://doi.org/10.33196/zfhr201903007201

Staudegger, Elisabeth (2018): Open-Access-Veröffentlichungspflicht für Dissertationen? Eine rechtswissenschaftliche Untersuchung aus Anlass der Ergänzung von § 86 Abs. 1 UG durch BGBl I 2017/129. In: Austrian Law Journal 5 (1), S. 1-25. https://doi.org/10.25364/01.5:2018.1.1

Universität Graz (2004): Satzungsteil Studienrechtliche Bestimmungen. Mitteilungsblatt der Karl-Franzens-Universität Graz, 17. Sondernummer, ausgegeben am 1.4.2004, 12.c Stück. https://mitteilungsblatt.uni-graz.at/de/2003-04/12.c/pdf/ (abgerufen am 29.09.2023)

Universität Wien, Büro Studienpräses (2015): Leitfaden für kumulative Dissertationen. (Stand 01.10.2015). https://studienpraeses.univie.ac.at/fileadmin/user_upload/p_studienpraeses/Studienpraeses_Neu/Info-Bl%C3%A4tter/Leitfaden_fuer_kumulative_Dissertationen_011015.pdf (abgerufen am 29.09.2023)

Universität Wien (2015a): Mitteilungsblatt. Studienjahr 2014/15, Ausgegeben am 24.09.2015, 39. Stück. https://mtbl.univie.ac.at/storage/media/mtbl02/02_pdf/20150924.pdf (abgerufen am 29.09.2023)

Universität Wien (2015b): Studienpräses. https://satzung.univie.ac.at/alle-weiteren-satzungsinhalte/studienpraeses/ (abgerufen am 29.09.2023)

Universität Wien (2023): OK mit KI?! Potentiale von KI-Tools nutzen und Integrität wahren. univie Blog, 14. September 2023. https://blog.univie.ac.at/studium/ok-mit-ki/ (abgerufen am 29.09.2023)

Adelheid Mayer ist Leiterin der Stabstelle Innovation an der Universitätsbibliothek Wien. Von 2006 bis 2008 leitete sie den Aufbau des gemeinsamen Workflows von Büro Studienpräses und Universitätsbibliothek zur Plagiatsprüfung und flächendeckenden Sammlung von Hochschulschriften in elektronischer Form an der Universität Wien und ist nach wie vor koordinierend in diesem Bereich tätig.

Andreas Jeitler

Repositorium? Ja, aber bitte barrierefrei!

Handbuch Repositorienmanagement, Hg. v. Blumesberger et al., 2024, S. 259–282
https://doi.org/10.25364/978390337423215

Andreas Jeitler, Universität Klagenfurt, Universitätsbibliothek, andreas.jeitler@aau.at

Zusammenfassung

Nicht zuletzt rechtliche Vorgaben erfordern es, dass Repositorien sowie deren Inhalte und die sie beschreibenden Metadaten auch von Menschen mit Behinderung barrierefrei genutzt werden können. Die meisten Repositorien bieten heute einen Web-Zugang, wofür mit den Web Content Accessibility Guidelines schon sehr gute Richtlinien existieren. Die Inhalte selbst können vielfältig sein, häufig kommen im wissenschaftlichen Kontext jedoch PDF-Dokumente zum Einsatz. Diese so zu erstellen, dass sie möglichst barrierefrei nutzbar werden, erfordert bestimmte Vorgehensweisen. Ein gutes System an Metadaten bildet die Grundlage, um in einem Repositorium Inhalte gut auffinden zu können. Auch diese müssen barrierefrei gestaltet werden und können ihrerseits die Barrierefreiheit von Inhalten beschreiben.

Schlagwörter: Barrierefreiheit; Behinderung; Richtlinien; Metadaten; Inklusion

Abstract

A Repository? Yes, but Please without Access Barriers!

Not only legal requirements demand that repositories, their content and the metadata describing it can also be used barrier-free by people with disabilities. Most repositories today offer web access, for which very good guidelines already exist in the form of the Web Content Accessibility Guidelines. The content itself can be diverse, but often PDF documents are used in a scientific context. Creating them in such a way that they are as accessible as possible requires certain procedures. A good system of metadata forms the base for being able to find content easily in a repository. Metadata must also be designed to be accessible and can in turn describe the accessibility of content.

Keywords: Accessibility; disability; guidelines; metadata; inclusion

1. Einleitung

Digitale Medien erlauben Menschen mit Behinderungen grundsätzlich ein bisher nicht dagewesenes Maß an Teilhabe am Wissen der Welt. Nur ein verschwindend kleiner Teil an Literatur war bis vor Kurzem z. B. in Braille (der taktilen Blindenschrift) verfügbar, weshalb blinden Menschen ein Großteil des Wissens verborgen blieb. Gehörlose Menschen haben erst durch Video-Telefonie eine Möglichkeit erhalten, digital in ihrer Muttersprache (der Gebärdensprache) adäquat remote zu kommunizieren.

Ein Großteil der heute publizierten Werke erscheint, zumindest auch, in digitaler Form. Digital bedeutet nun aber noch nicht a priori, dass diese Werke für Menschen mit diversen Behinderungen auch gebrauchstauglich nutzbar sind. Häufig entstehen Barrieren, die Menschen mit diversen Beeinträchtigungen bei der Nutzung von Medien *behindern*.

Repositorien, als Speicher dieser digitalen Medien, spielen eine wesentliche Rolle dabei, ob Menschen mit Behinderungen die Vorteile digitaler Dokumente auch selbständig und möglichst ohne fremde Hilfe nutzen können. Von zentraler Bedeutung ist dabei die Möglichkeit, die Suchfunktion, sowie die daraus entstehenden Ergebnisse möglichst barrierefrei nutzen zu können, um Werke überhaupt aufzufinden. Maaß und Rink beschreiben daher *Auffindbarkeit* als ersten Schritt im Prozess barrierefreier Kommunikation.[1] Schlussendlich müssen auch die Werke selbst in einer Art vorliegen, die eine möglichst barrierefreie Nutzung erlaubt.

Nachfolgend wird daher näher darauf eingegangen, welche Überlegungen und Handlungen bei der Umsetzung eines möglichst barrierefreien Repositoriums beachtet werden sollten.

Um ein Verständnis dafür zu entwickeln, welche Faktoren dabei zu berücksichtigen sind, macht es Sinn, zunächst ein Verständnis für Termini wie Barrierefreiheit oder Behinderung zu entwickeln, sowie die Anforderungen kennenzulernen, die Menschen mit diversen Behinderungen an digitale Medien stellen.

Barrierefreiheit ist heute nicht mehr nur ein Akt der Nächstenliebe. Menschen mit Behinderungen haben vielerorts einen rechtlichen Anspruch darauf, an allen Aspekten des Lebens barrierefrei teilnehmen zu können. Daher wird auch die rechtliche Situation im Fokus der Barrierefreiheit zu beleuchten sein.

1 Maaß, C.; Rink, I. (2018), S. 24.

Grundsätzlich werden an dieser Stelle drei Aspekte eines Repositoriums identifiziert, bei denen Barrieren für die Nutzung durch Menschen mit diversen Behinderungen auftreten können: Die Benutzerschnittstelle des Repositoriums selbst, die Barrierefreiheit der darin gespeicherten Daten und die Barrierefreiheit der Metadaten. Jedem dieser drei Aspekte wird nachfolgend ein Abschnitt gewidmet.

In diesem Text werden Sie viele Verweise auf Dokumente des World Wide Web Consortium (W3C) finden. Der Grund dafür ist, dass die World Accessibility Initiative (WAI) sich dem Motto verschrieben hat: "If you have a question about an aspect of accessibility, then we have a document for it." Um ein Verständnis dafür zu erhalten, wie Menschen mit diversen Behinderungen das Web nutzen, empfiehlt sich die Lektüre von "How People with Disabilities Use the Web" auf der W3C Website[2].

2. Was bedeutet barrierefrei?

Wenn der Zugang zu etwas für einzelne Menschen erschwert wird, sprechen wir vom Vorhandensein von Barrieren. Eine Stufe stellt für rollstuhlfahrende Personen, aber natürlich auch für Personen mit Kinderwagen, eine erschwerte Zugänglichkeit und somit eine Barriere dar. Auch bei der Nutzung von Medien können Barrieren entstehen. Wird Kommunikation nach dem von Shannon und Weaver eingeführten Kommunikationsmodell[3] als der Prozess des Sendens einer Nachricht oder der Übertragung von einer sendenden Partei über ein Medium zu einer empfangenden Partei verstanden, so empfängt ein Mensch in der Rolle der empfangenden Partei Information über seine fünf Sinne. Ist ein Sinn eingeschränkt oder fällt dieser sogar gänzlich aus (beispielsweise, wenn die Person blind ist und somit keine visuellen Informationen empfangen kann), so ist die Wahrnehmung von gesendeten Informationen nur mangelhaft oder gar nicht möglich. In diesem Fall ist es hilfreich, alternative Kommunikationskanäle oder Medien zur Verfügung zu haben, damit ein Sinn durch einen anderen ersetzt werden kann.

Eine blinde Person wird aus einem klassischen Printmedium mit Hilfe der verbliebenen anderen Sinne keine brauchbaren Informationen entnehmen können. Als Alternative könnte das Werk in Brailleschrift (also taktil) oder als Audiobuch (auditiv) angeboten werden. Der visuelle Kanal wird durch den Tastsinn oder das Gehör kompensiert. Im Fokus steht hier das Prinzip der Wahrnehmung. Aber auch wenn eine Person in der Lage ist, Informationen über die eigenen Sinne aufzunehmen, kann es sein, dass die Person die Information in einem kognitiven Sinn nicht richtig versteht (z. B. Menschen mit Lernschwierigkeiten) oder die Information vom Sinn

---

2 https://www.w3.org/WAI/people-use-web/
3 Shannon, C. E.; Weaver, W. (1949)

zum Hirn verloren geht oder verändert wird (z. B. Dyslexie). Dies wären dann Barrieren, die aus dem Prinzip der mangelnden Verständlichkeit folgen. Aber auch wenn die Information über die Sinne wahrgenommen und entsprechend weiterverarbeitet werden kann, so kann es sein, dass eine Person nicht in der Lage ist, mit einem Medium zu interagieren, es zu bedienen. Eine Person mit motorischen Beeinträchtigungen könnte beispielsweise nicht in der Lage sein, ein Buch zu halten, oder die Seiten darin umzublättern. Diese Barrieren entstehen aus dem Prinzip mangelnder Bedienbarkeit. Die Prinzipien Wahrnehmbarkeit, Bedienbarkeit und Verständlichkeit bilden die oberste Ebene (Dimension) der später besprochenen Web Content Accessibility Guidelines (WCAG).

Bei mangelnder Barrierefreiheit wird der Zugang zu einem Medium für bestimmte Personen in bestimmten Situationen eingeschränkt, und eine *Barriere* entsteht. Andere Termini für Barrierefreiheit sind daher auch „Zugänglichkeit" oder das englische Wort „Accessibility". In diesem Kontext kann auch der Begriff „Behinderung" entsprechend dem Slogan der Selbstbestimmt Leben-Bewegung „Wir sind nicht behindert, wir werden behindert" verstanden werden. Das soziale Modell von Behinderung nach Michael Oliver[4] geht davon aus, dass nicht die Beeinträchtigung (die physischen Eigenschaften eines Körpers), sondern das soziale Umfeld für den Grad der Behinderung verantwortlich ist, die eine Person erfährt. Je barrierefreier ein Repositorium für eine bestimmte Person ist, desto weniger wird sie bei der Nutzung desselben *behindert*.

Barrierefreiheit kann aber auch als eine Erweiterung von *Gebrauchstauglichkeit* verstanden werden. Die Internationale Organisation für Normung (ISO) definiert Gebrauchstauglichkeit (Usability) folgendermaßen: „[...] das Ausmaß, in dem ein System, ein Produkt oder eine Dienstleistung durch bestimmte Benutzer in einem bestimmten Nutzungskontext genutzt werden kann, um bestimmte Ziele effektiv, effizient und zufriedenstellend zu erreichen."[5]

Bei der Prüfung, ob ein System gebrauchstauglich ist, werden also bestimmte Personengruppen untersucht. Meist werden hier demografische Daten wie Alter, Geschlecht, Vorkenntnis, Bildungsgrad etc. herangezogen. Menschen mit diversen Behinderungen werden dabei meist nicht berücksichtigt.

Auch der Kontext, in dem ein System genutzt wird, ist für die Evaluierung von Gebrauchstauglichkeit von Relevanz. Nutze ich es am Desktop, auf einem mobilen Endgerät, im Auto oder auf der Straße? Wie sieht die Nutzung jedoch z. B. im Kontext eines Screen Readers oder nur mit der Tastatur – ohne Maus – aus? Sind die

---

4 Oliver, M. (1996)
5 Siehe DIN EN ISO 9241-11

Informationen für Menschen mit Lernschwierigkeiten oder gehörlose Personen verständlich?

Barrierefreiheit kann vor dieser Definition als Gebrauchstauglichkeit für mehr Menschen (eben auch Menschen mit Behinderung) in mehr Situationen (beispielsweise durch Nutzung mit einem Screen Reader) gesehen werden.

3. Anforderungen von Menschen mit Behinderung an digitale Medien

Grundsätzlich soll an dieser Stelle festgehalten werden, dass jede Form von Behinderung individuell ist und nicht einfach davon ausgegangen werden kann, dass für zwei Personen, die eine ähnliche Form der Beeinträchtigung haben, Vermeidungsstrategien für Barrieren gleichermaßen wirksam sind. Zum besseren Verständnis sollen hier jedoch einige archetypische Behinderungsformen vorgestellt werden sowie eine Erklärung gegeben werden, wie im jeweiligen Fall mit digitalen Medien häufig gearbeitet wird.

Blinde Personen verwenden Screen Reader, um den Inhalt des Bildschirmes am Rechner erfassen zu können. Es handelt sich dabei um Software, die den visuell angezeigten Text entweder mittels Sprachsynthese vorliest (auditiv) oder über ein Braille-Terminal ausgibt (taktil).

Eine Eigenart dieser beiden Ausgabe-Methoden besteht darin, dass die Ausgabe sequenziell erfolgt. Während sehende Personen in der Lage sind, den Inhalt des Bildschirms „auf einen Blick" zu erfassen, kennen blinde Personen den Inhalt erst dann, wenn sie das Ende des Textes erreicht haben.

Im Hinblick auf die Interaktion mit Computersystemen beschränken sich blinde Personen in der Regel auf die Tastatur. Die Maus als visuelles Eingabegerät kommt nicht zum Einsatz. Auf mobilen Geräten kann gut mit Touch-Gesten gearbeitet werden. Hierfür ist jedoch die Aktivierung eines speziellen Screen-Reader-Modus nötig, der das Interaktionsschema ändert.

Personen mit Sehbehinderung, deren Visus zwar eingeschränkt ist, die aber dennoch über ausreichend Restsehvermögen verfügen, um visuell am PC oder mit mobilen Geräten zu arbeiten, verwenden meist eine Kombination aus Bildschirm-Vergrößerungssoftware und Screen Reader. Im Gegensatz zu blinden Personen kommt häufig noch die Maus zum Einsatz. Viele Aktionen lassen sich jedoch mit Hilfe der Tastatur weitaus schneller erledigen. Ein Braille-Terminal kommt hier eher selten zum Einsatz.

Viele Menschen unterliegen dem Trugschluss, dass *gehörlose Personen* bei der Verwendung von elektronischen Medien bis auf die Nichtwahrnehmung von auditiven Informationen eigentlich auf keine weiteren Barrieren stoßen würden. Texte, Bilder und Animationen sind für sie ja *wahrnehmbar*. Da für viele gehörlose Personen die Gebärdensprache und nicht die gesprochene/geschriebene Sprache als Muttersprache anzusehen ist, verhält sich die Wahrnehmung der deutschen Sprache ähnlich wie bei Personen mit Migrationshintergrund oder Personen mit Lernschwierigkeiten. Eine möglichst einfache Sprache erleichtert das Verständnis. Angebote in der Muttersprache (in diesem Fall der Gebärdensprache) würden sich empfehlen, sind meist aber schwer umzusetzen, da hierfür gebärdensprachkompetente Personen benötigt werden. Auch für dynamische Inhalte ist dies meist nur sehr schwer umzusetzen, da Videos immer wieder neu erzeugt oder angepasst werden müssen.

Schwerhörige Personen sind, ähnlich wie sehbehinderte Menschen im Kontext des visuellen Sinns, noch in der Lage, Audio gut genug wahrzunehmen, um Sprache zu verstehen. Die Lautsprache ist für sie meist die Muttersprache, das Verständnis derselben daher besser als bei vielen gehörlosen Menschen. Barrieren entstehen am häufigsten bei der Wahrnehmung audiovisueller Medien, da gesprochene Sprache oft schlecht wahrgenommen wird. Schwerhörigkeit bedeutet in der Regel nicht, nur leise zu hören. Meist ist die Wahrnehmung einzelner Frequenzbänder eingeschränkt. Für die Lautsprache sehr ungünstig ist eine Einschränkung jener Frequenzen, die für Zischlaute verwendet werden. Um das Verständnis von Lautsprache zu kompensieren, bieten sich Text-Alternativen für Audio als alternativer Kanal an (Transkriptionen, Untertitelung etc.).

Die Gruppe der Personen mit kognitiven Beeinträchtigungen bezeichnet sich selbst als Menschen mit Lernschwierigkeiten, um damit anzuzeigen, dass sie alle Inhalte verstehen können, dafür möglicherweise nur mehr Zeit sowie zusätzliche Erklärungen etc. benötigen. Menschen mit Lernschwierigkeiten profitieren, wie auch gehörlose Personen oder all jene Personen, für die (z. B.) Deutsch nicht die Muttersprache ist, von einer möglichst einfachen Sprache. Auch der Einsatz von Piktogrammen, nach dem Motto „Ein Bild sagt mehr als tausend Worte“, erleichtert das Verständnis. Hierbei sollte jedoch Vorsicht geboten sein, da die Semantik von Piktogrammen auch falsch verstanden werden kann.

Für Personen mit motorischen Beeinträchtigungen, die Extremitäten nicht oder nur eingeschränkt für die Arbeit mit Medien nutzen können, existieren heute unterschiedlichste assistive Technologien, die ihnen die Mediennutzung erlauben oder diese erleichtern. Exemplarisch wären hier Mund-Mäuse, spezielle Tastaturen sowie Spracherkennungs- und Sprachsynthesesysteme zu nennen. Barrieren entstehen meist nicht durch Mangel an Wahrnehmung oder Verständnis, sondern durch Bedienbarkeit.

Wie anfangs festgehalten wurde, ist jede Form der Behinderung sehr individuell, und die genannten Beispiele sollen nur zu einem grundsätzlichen besseren Verständnis beitragen. Die Liste ist demzufolge auch keineswegs vollständig, sondern nur exemplarisch.

4. Rechtliche Rahmenbedingungen

Die Gleichstellung von Menschen mit Behinderung wird in Österreich in diversen Rechtsnormen geregelt. Bereits die Bundesverfassung stellt fest: „Alle Staatsbürger sind vor dem Gesetz gleich. [...] Niemand darf wegen seiner Behinderung benachteiligt werden.“[6]

Auch die Österreichische Gebärdensprache als Muttersprache vieler gehörloser Menschen wird als „eigenständige Sprache“ anerkannt.[7]

Das Bundesbehindertengleichstellungsgesetz (BGStG) definiert u. a. auch „Systeme der Informationsverarbeitung“ als barrierefrei, „wenn sie für Menschen mit Behinderungen in der allgemein üblichen Weise, ohne besondere Erschwernis und grundsätzlich ohne fremde Hilfe zugänglich und nutzbar sind“.[8] Fühlt sich eine Person mit Behinderung bei der Benützung eines Repositoriums oder der darin gespeicherten Objekte aufgrund der Behinderung diskriminiert, so kann sie im Rahmen dieses Gesetzes ein Schlichtungsverfahren einleiten (BGStG §14). Im Rahmen von Mediationsgesprächen unter Aufsicht des Sozialministeriumservices sollen die Schlichtungsparteien versuchen, eine Lösung im Kontext der geschehenen Diskriminierung zu finden. Gelingt dies, so wird das Schlichtungsverfahren positiv abgeschlossen. Wird keine Einigung erzielt, so endet dieses negativ, und die schlichtende Person erhält vom Sozialministeriumservice einen Bescheid, mit dem sie bei Gericht eine Zivilrechtsklage auf Schadenersatz einbringen kann. Grundsätzlich kann im Sinne des BGStG nur ein Schadenersatz für eine erbrachte Diskriminierung eingefordert werden, ein Beseitigungsanspruch für die Diskriminierung ist nicht vorgesehen.

Auch das Behinderteneinstellungsgesetz (BEinstG) kann für den Betrieb eines Repositoriums von Relevanz sein, wenn begünstigt behinderte Personen im Betrieb

---

6 B-VG Artikel 7 Abs. 1
7 B-VG Artikel 8 Abs. 3
8 Siehe BGStG § 6 Abs. 5

beschäftigt sind. Diese müssen dann nämlich in der Lage sein, neben dem Frontend auch das Backend des Repositoriums barrierefrei nutzen zu können. Da potenziell in allen Betrieben begünstigt behinderte Personen beschäftigt werden könnten, empfiehlt es sich, das Backend eines Repositoriums, genauso wie das Frontend, möglichst barrierefrei zu gestalten, um für den Bedarfsfall gerüstet zu sein.

Für „Websites und mobile Anwendungen des Bundes“ gilt seit 2019 das Web-Zugänglichkeitsgesetz (WZG). Websites und Anwendungen, die unter das WZG fallen, müssen jedenfalls eine „Erklärung zur Barrierefreiheit“ beinhalten, die einen umfassenden Status über die Umsetzung der Barrierefreiheit angibt. Weiters muss eine Möglichkeit zur Meldung von Barrieren angeboten werden. Bei der Österreichische Forschungsförderungsgesellschaft (FFG) wurde eine eigene Monitoring-Stelle eingerichtet, die für die Überwachung der Barrierefreiheit der Ziel-Websites zuständig ist. Das Gesetz fordert dabei in der aktuellen Fassung die Umsetzung der Web Content Accessibility Guidelines in der Version 2.1 auf Level AA[9]. Als Fristen für die Umsetzung der Barrierefreiheit für Webinhalte gelten im Kontext dieses Gesetzes:

- Webinhalte, die vor dem 23. September 2018 veröffentlicht worden sind, müssen ab dem 23. September 2020 dem Gesetz entsprechen.
- Webinhalte, die nach dem 23. September 2018 veröffentlicht werden, müssen bereits seit dem 23. September 2019 barrierefrei gestaltet sein.
- Auf mobilen Anwendungen sind die Vorschriften ab dem 23. Juni 2021 anzuwenden.

Die Umsetzung möglichst barrierefreier Repositorien und deren Inhalte wird somit in Österreich von diversen Rechtsnormen geboten und sollte daher unbedingt fixer Bestandteil von Planung und Implementierung sein.

Um die möglichst barrierefreie Nutzung von Repositorien für möglichst viele Menschen gewährleisten zu können, werden nachfolgend drei Faktoren eines Repositoriums identifiziert, die in weiterer Folge näher betrachtet werden sollen, und zwar die Barrierefreiheit von Benutzerschnittstellen, die Barrierefreiheit von Metadaten sowie die Barrierefreiheit der eigentlichen Inhalte des Repositoriums.

9 Vgl. dazu die Ausführungen zu den Web Content Accessibility Guidelines weiter unten im Text.

5. Barrierefreiheit von Benutzerschnittstellen

Je nachdem, ob es sich um ein Web-Interface, eine Desktopanwendung oder eine mobile App handelt, existieren unterschiedliche Richtlinien, die bei der Umsetzung Beachtung finden sollten.

Im Fall eines Web-Interfaces existieren mit den Web Content Accessibility Guidelines (WCAG) sehr ausführlich dokumentierte Handlungsvorschläge für die Erzeugung möglichst barrierefreier Schnittstellen. Den WCAG kommt insofern eine Sonderstellung unter den Guidelines zu, da sie eigentlich „Inhalte“ beschreiben, und Webseiten wiederum selbst Inhalte sind.

Die WCAG sind so abstrakt gehalten, dass sie auf unterschiedliche Technologien angewendet werden können. Neben der Spezifikation selbst helfen Dokumente wie “How to meet WCAG”[10] beim Verständnis der einzelnen Prüfpunkte und der möglichen Umsetzung. Eine Übersicht der Dokumente findet sich auf der WCAG-2-Overview[11]-Seite.

Die Web Accessibility Initiative (WAI)[12] hat sich vor ein paar Jahren für eine schrittweise Erweiterung der Richtlinien entschieden. Nach den WCAG 2.0[13] aus dem Jahr 2008, die 2008 den Status einer Empfehlung erhalten haben, ist die derzeit gültige Fassung Version 2.1[14], die 2018 zur Empfehlung wurde. Die künftigen WCAG 2.2[15] liegen zur Zeit der Erstellung dieses Textes als Empfehlungskandidat vor, sind sozusagen in der BETA-Phase. Ziel der zusätzlichen Ergänzungen soll eine Verbesserung der Gebrauchstauglichkeit für Personen mit kognitiven Beeinträchtigungen, blinde und sehbehinderte Personen sowie all jene sein, die Schwierigkeiten mit mobilen Endgeräten haben. Während die WCAG 2.1 z. B. neue Prüfpunkte in Bezug auf Touch-Gesten aufnahmen, befassen sich die WCAG 2.2 mit Fragestellungen der Authentifizierung. Kognitive Funktionstests wie das Erinnern an ein Passwort oder das Lösen eines Rätsels sollen künftig vermieden werden, da diese Methoden für Menschen mit kognitiven Beeinträchtigungen möglicherweise zu kompliziert sein können (Erfolgskriterium 3.3.7 – Accessible Authentication). Parallel wird bereits an den WCAG 3.0[16] gearbeitet, die jedoch einen neuen Ansatz verfolgen und nicht mehr rückwärtskompatibel sein sollen.

---

10 https://www.w3.org/WAI/WCAG21/quickref/
11 https://www.w3.org/WAI/standards-guidelines/wcag/
12 https://www.w3.org/WAI/
13 http://www.w3.org/TR/WCAG20/
14 https://www.w3.org/TR/WCAG21/
15 https://www.w3.org/TR/WCAG22/
16 https://www.w3.org/TR/wcag-3.0/

Die WCAG sind pyramidenartig auf verschiedenen Ebenen aufgebaut, die nachfolgend kurz beschrieben werden.

- Prinzipien: Die höchste Ebene bilden vier Prinzipien, welche die Grundlage für Barrierefreiheit von Inhalten darstellen sollen:
    - Wahrnehmbarkeit: Informationen und Bestandteile der Benutzerschnittstelle müssen den Benutzenden so präsentiert werden, dass diese sie wahrnehmen können.
    - Bedienbarkeit: Bestandteile der Benutzerschnittstelle und Navigation müssen bedienbar sein.
    - Verständlichkeit: Informationen und Bedienung der Benutzerschnittstelle müssen verständlich sein.
    - Robustheit: Inhalte müssen robust genug sein, damit sie zuverlässig von einer großen Auswahl an Benutzeragenten einschließlich assistierender Technologien interpretiert werden können.
- Richtlinien: Richtlinien geben die wesentlichen Ziele vor, auf die Autor:innen hinarbeiten sollten, um Inhalte für Benutzende mit verschiedenen Behinderungen barrierefreier zu gestalten. Jede Richtlinie ist dabei einem Prinzip zugeordnet. Die WCAG 2.1 umfassen 13 Richtlinien. Die Richtlinien selbst sind nicht testbar.
- Erfolgskriterien: Für jede Richtlinie wurden testbare Erfolgskriterien definiert, um prüfen zu können, ob die Richtlinien richtig angewendet wurden oder Inhalte mit der WCAG-Spezifikation in welchem Ausmaß konformgehen. Konformitätstests sind z. B. dann nötig, wenn die Einhaltung von Rechtsnormen oder Vereinbarungen im Kontext von Beschaffung oder Verträgen geprüft werden soll. Die Erfolgskriterien sind somit auch jene Ebene der WCAG, die bei der Umsetzung von Repositorien im Kontext der Barrierefreiheit am meisten Beachtung finden wird. Um den Bedarfen verschiedener Personengruppen gerecht zu werden, wurden drei Stufen der Konformität festgelegt: A (niedrigste), AA sowie AAA (höchste). Jedem Erfolgskriterium wird dabei eine der Konformitätsklassen zugewiesen. Um beispielsweise konform mit WCAG A zu sein, müssen alle A-Erfolgskriterien erfüllt worden sein. Die meisten Rechtsnormen fordern eine AA-Konformität. AAA ist nur schwer umsetzbar, meist werden einzelne AAA-Erfolgskriterien realisiert, wenn besonderes Augenmerk auf bestimmte Formen von Behinderungen gelegt werden soll. Die WCAG 2.1 definieren 78 Erfolgskriterien.
- Ausreichende und empfohlene Techniken: Für die Richtlinien und Erfolgskriterien wurden informative Techniken dokumentiert, die entweder ausrei-

chend sind, um Erfolgskriterien zu erfüllen, oder empfohlen werden. Empfohlene Techniken gehen über das hinaus, was von den einzelnen Erfolgskriterien verlangt wird.

Im Rahmen der WCAG wird darauf hingewiesen, dass sogar Inhalte mit der höchsten Konformitätsstufe (AAA) nicht für Menschen mit allen Arten, Ausprägungen oder Kombinationen von Behinderungen barrierefrei sind. Eine Barrierefreiheit für alle Menschen ist folglich in der Praxis nur schwer bis gar nicht umsetzbar. Es sollte daher eher von möglichst barrierefreien Inhalten gesprochen werden.

Um die Konformität des eigenen Repositoriums zu den WCAG festzustellen, bietet es sich an, eigens dafür spezialisierte Expert:innen für die Analyse zu beauftragen. Natürlich kann auch ein Selbsttest durchgeführt werden. Im Kontext des WZG, oder wenn ein WACA-Zertifikat[17] angestrebt wird, empfiehlt sich im Sinne der Transparenz jedoch eine unabhängige externe Prüfung. Zur Durchführung eines Selbsttests bietet es sich an, der Website Accessibility Conformance Evaluation Methodology (WCAG-EM) 1.0[18] zu folgen. Sehr hilfreich kann dabei das WCAG-EM Report Tool[19] sein, das bei der Erstellung eines strukturierten Prüfberichts unterstützt. Es ersetzt jedoch nicht ein fundiertes Wissen über die WCAG oder das Verständnis, wie Menschen mit diversen Beeinträchtigungen das Web nutzen. Die Selbsterfahrung ist immer noch eine der zielführendsten Methoden für ein gutes Verständnis der Problematik. Erst wer selbst einmal mit einem Screen Reader gearbeitet hat, ohne dabei auf den Bildschirm zu sehen, oder die eigene Sicht mittels Simulationsbrillen oder Software so eingeschränkt hat, wie eine Person mit einer bestimmten Augenerkrankung, kann sich etwas in die Situation einfühlen. Der Österreichische Blinden- und Sehbehindertenverband[20] bzw. die einzelnen Landesgruppen und andere Organisationen bieten beispielsweise Simulationsbrillen an, mit denen einzelne Augenerkrankungen simuliert werden können. Ein Tool der Hilfsgemeinschaft der Blinden und Sehschwachen[21] bietet die Möglichkeit, mit einem Handy oder Tablet Augenerkrankungen zu simulieren. Auch die Selbsterfahrung durch die eigenständige Nutzung von Screen Readern ist empfehlenswert. Für Windows gibt es den kostenlosen Screen Reader NVDA[22], und auch kostenpflichtige Tools wie Jaws[23] bieten einen Demo-Modus, der für Testzwecke völlig ausreichend ist. Auf Apple-Geräten

17 https://waca.at/
18 https://www.w3.org/TR/WCAG-EM/
19 https://www.w3.org/WAI/eval/report-tool/#/
20 http://www.blindenverband.at/
21 https://www.hilfsgemeinschaft.at/
22 http://www.nvaccess.org/
23 http://www.freedomscientific.com/fs_products/JAWS_HQ.asp

ist der hauseigene Screen Reader VoiceOver[24] vorinstalliert, der nur aktiviert werden muss.

Erfolgt die Bedienung über eine Desktop-Anwendung oder eine mobile App, so bieten alle modernen Betriebssysteme Accessibility-APIs an, die von den Anwendungen genutzt werden sollten. Für die Entwicklung von Apple-Anwendungen empfiehlt sich die Lektüre des Accessibility-Bereichs auf den Entwicklungsseiten des Herstellers[25]. Microsoft bietet mit Microsoft Active Accessibility (MSAA) ebenfalls eine Schnittstelle für Windows.[26] Auch Google stellt Informationen zur möglichst barrierefreien App-Entwicklung unter Android bereit[27]. Technisch gesehen werden bei allen Accessibility-APIs die Elemente des User Interfaces in einer Baumstruktur abgebildet. Die einzelnen Objekte dieses Baums werden mit Metadaten wie Beschreibungstexten etc. versehen, die dann von assistiven Technologien wie Screen Readern ausgelesen werden. Befinden sich in einer Eingabemaske beispielsweise mehrere Buttons, deren Beschreibungstexte nicht befüllt wurden, so sieht die Anwendung für sehende Personen zwar verständlich und in Ordnung aus, blinde Personen bekommen oft jedoch nur „Button, Button, Button" vorgelesen, ohne Hinweis darauf, welche Funktion die einzelnen Schaltflächen haben. Für die Entwicklung interaktiver Web-Anwendungen empfiehlt es sich, Accessible Rich Internet Applications (WAI-ARIA) näher kennenzulernen.[28]

6. Handlungsempfehlungen

Es sollte sichergestellt werden, dass die Schnittstellen des von Ihnen angebotenen Repositoriums sowohl im Frontend wie auch im Backend den jeweils für die jeweilige Anwendungsform geltenden Richtlinien entsprechen. Bei Ausschreibungen für die Erstellung oder den Ankauf eines Repositoriums muss überprüft werden, dass dort explizit die Konformität zur jeweils gültigen Fassung, z. B. der WCAG, gefordert wird, bzw. die Einhaltung der aktuell gültigen Rechtsnormen genannt wird. Es reicht nicht aus, sich darauf zu verlassen, dass Unternehmen oder Personen a priori die Rechtsnormen einhalten. Eine explizite Forderung ist wichtig, es muss festgehalten werden, dass die Nichteinhaltung einem Vertragsbruch entspricht.

24 https://www.apple.com/accessibility/vision/
25 https://developer.apple.com/accessibility/
26 https://learn.microsoft.com/en-us/windows/win32/winauto/microsoft-active-accessibility
27 https://developer.android.com/guide/topics/ui/accessibility
28 Siehe ARIA Authoring Practices Guide https://www.w3.org/WAI/ARIA/apg/ bzw. WAI-ARIA Overview https://www.w3.org/WAI/standards-guidelines/aria/

7. Barrierefreiheit von Inhalten

Neben der Nutzungsschnittstelle des Repositoriums selbst ist auch die Barrierefreiheit der im Repositorium gespeicherten Objekte zu berücksichtigen. Da diese Objekte sehr mannigfaltig sein können, wird an dieser Stelle nur auf die Problematiken bei der Erstellung von PDF-Dokumenten aus Office-Anwendungen wie Word eingegangen, um häufige Problemfelder und Lösungsansätze zu veranschaulichen.

Obwohl es aus juristischen Gründen eigentlich schon Usus sein sollte, nur noch barrierefreie Dokumente anzubieten, sind noch immer eine Vielzahl an elektronischen Publikationen für viele Menschen mit Behinderung nicht nutzbar. Woran liegt das?

Ein Grund ist sicher, dass viele Tools, mit denen Office-Dokumente erstellt werden, es uns sehr leicht machen, nicht-barrierefreie Inhalte zu erstellen. Um Dokumente für Screen Reader gut navigierbar zu gestalten, empfiehlt es sich beispielsweise, Formatvorlagen für Überschriften einzusetzen. Word schreibt uns dies jedoch nicht vor. Viele Textschreibende formatieren Überschriften einfach händisch, indem sie den Text fett formatieren und mit einem größeren oder anderen Zeichensatz versehen. Damit ist der Text optisch als *Überschrift* erkennbar, jedoch nicht semantisch. Ein Screen Reader liest den Text als Fließtext vor.

Oft werden Hervorhebungen in Texten derart gestaltet, dass zwischen den einzelnen Buchstaben mehr Abstand eingefügt wird. Der klassische Weg, den wir aus der Zeit der Schreibmaschinen kennen, besteht darin, zwischen den einzelnen Buchstaben einfach ein Leerzeichen einzufügen. Ein Screen Reader wird die einzelnen Buchstaben des Wortes buchstabieren, da er diese nicht als zusammenhängend, sondern als für sich alleinstehende Buchstaben interpretiert. In der Regel kann der Abstand zwischen Zeichen in den Zeichenformat-Einstellungen beliebig gewählt werden. Wörter bleiben dann bestehen.

Mit Tools wie Latex werden Textschreibende eher dazu erzogen, Überschriften, Hervorhebungen etc. auch semantisch als solche auszuzeichnen, da es vergleichsweise umständlich ist, dies anders zu bewerkstelligen. Das Aussehen der Elemente wird durch Style-Dateien für das gesamte Dokument gewählt. Ähnlich funktioniert die Trennung zwischen Inhalt und Layout auch in HTML. Word bietet mit Formatvorlagen zwar ein ähnliches Feature, das aber häufig nicht im genannten Sinn eingesetzt wird.

Grundsätzlich führen die folgenden zehn Handlungsvorschläge dazu, dass in Word oder anderen Textverarbeitungsprogrammen erstellte Texte deutlich barrierefreier nutzbar werden. Diese Punkte haben sich in der Praxis über die letzten Jahre als für viele Personen leicht umsetzbar erwiesen, und werden daher im Kontext der Accessibility Services an der Universitätsbibliothek Klagenfurt empfohlen.[29]

- Formatvorlagen (Überschriften) dienen der Textstrukturierung. Diese semantische Struktur wird dann beim Export in Formate wie PDF beibehalten. Bei längeren Dokumenten ist ein Inhaltsverzeichnis, das sich aus diesen Vorlagen generiert, sinnvoll.
- Textalternativen für alle Nicht-Text-Inhalte wie Grafiken bieten sich an, sofern deren Inhalt für das Textverstehen relevant ist. Grafiken können ansonsten als Ziergrafik ausgezeichnet werden. Diagramme und komplexe Abbildungen sind mit Hilfe von Beschriftungen oder im Fließtext zu beschreiben. Als Entscheidungshilfe, ob ein Objekt für den Text inhaltlich relevant ist, sollte überlegt werden, ob der Text noch Sinn macht, wenn das Objekt weggelassen werden würde.
- Listen und Nummerierungen für Auflistungen erleichtern die Navigation mit Screen Readern.
- Links und Textmarken ermöglichen eine leichtere Navigation. Dies hilft dabei, schnell innerhalb eines Dokuments umherspringen zu können.
- Ausgefallene Schriftarten sind zu vermeiden. Für eine bessere Lesbarkeit sollten eher einfache, serifenlose Schriften ohne Schnörkel etc. eingesetzt werden. Seit kurzem existiert mit Atkinson ein Font, der für schlecht sehende Personen optimiert wurde.[30]
- Der logische Textfluss (z. B. Spalten) sollte beachtet werden. Spalten oder Formulare werden häufig mit Hilfe von Layout-Tabellen implementiert. Tabellen haben ihre Berechtigung bei der Repräsentation relationaler Daten im Sinn von Datentabellen, sollten im Layout jedoch vermieden werden. Textverarbeitungsprogramme wie Word bieten eine eigene Spalten-Funktion. Der Screen Reader liest die Spalten dann einfach nacheinander, für ihn ist dies ein Fließtext.
- Tabellen sind richtig einzusetzen. Im Sinne relationaler Daten müssen Tabellen immer entweder Zeilen- oder Spaltenüberschriften enthalten. Diese müssen auch semantisch als solche ausgezeichnet werden, da Screen Reader sie dann zur jeweiligen Zelle, in der sie sich befinden, dazu lesen. In Word ist dies derzeit nur über die Funktion „Gleiche Kopfzeile auf jeder Seite" in den Tabelleneigenschaften erreichbar und gilt somit nur für die erste Zeile der Tabelle. Komplexere Tabellen sind in Word derzeit generell nicht möglich,

29 https://www.aau.at/universitaetsbibliothek-klagenfurt/benuetzung-und-service/accessibility-services/barrierefreie-medien/
30 https://brailleinstitute.org/freefont

was die Verwendung im wissenschaftlichen Kontext sehr erschwert. Befinden sich in einer Tabelle verbundene Zellen, kann dies ebenfalls zu Problemen beim Export in ein PDF führen.

- Wichtig ist auch, auf ausreichend Kontrast zwischen Vorder- und Hintergrundfarbe zu achten. Die Textfarbe sollte sich vom Hintergrund möglichst gut abheben. Das Optimum sind natürlich Schwarz und Weiß. Schrift vor Hintergrundgrafiken, auch wenn diese blass oder durchscheinend sind, sollte vermieden werden.
- Metadaten ergänzen das Dokument. Auch in Word und anderen Textverarbeitungsprogrammen können Zusatzinformationen wie Titel, Autor:in, Tags etc. angegeben werden. Wenigstens ein Titel muss angegeben werden, da dieser für den Export in z. B. PDF/UA zwingend notwendig ist. Metadaten helfen bei der leichten Auffindung des Dokuments und sind daher insbesondere bei der Verwendung im Kontext von Repositorien ohnehin wünschenswert.
- Die Textsprache muss entsprechend definiert werden. Die meisten Screen Reader sind in der Lage, verschiedene Stimmen auf Texte in verschiedenen Sprachen anzuwenden. Dieser Wechsel funktioniert meist sogar automatisch. Wenn in einem deutschen Text also englische Wörter vorkommen, sollten diese als solche ausgezeichnet sein. Ein englisches *Menu* wird dann auch als *Menju* vorgelesen und nicht mit einem *u* am Ende. Es kann dabei sowohl die generelle Dokument-Sprache als auch die Sprache einzelner Wörter, Sätze, Absätze etc. geändert werden.

Wer nun die zuvor genannten zehn Punkte beherzigt, ist auf einem guten Weg, barrierefreiere elektronische Textdokumente zu erstellen. Leider verhalten sich manche Tools (wie eben auch Word) beim Export in andere Formate oft nicht so, wie man es erwarten würde und wie es für die Generierung barrierefreier Dateien nötig wäre. Beim Export in ein PDF sollte unbedingt beachtet werden, nicht die „in ein PDF drucken“-Funktion, sondern „speichern als PDF“ zu nutzen. Bei ersterem gehen die zuvor extra erstellten semantischen Informationen wie Textstruktur, Alternativtexte etc. verloren.

Ein weiterer oft kritisierter Mangel ist auch, dass derzeit kein Workflow existiert, um mit Word oder anderen Textverarbeitungsprogrammen barrierefreie PDF-Formulare zu erstellen.

7.1. Fallbeispiel PDF

Das PDF-Format an sich bietet eigentlich gute Voraussetzungen, barrierefreie Inhalte bereitzustellen. Grundsätzlich ist PDF jedoch nur ein Container, in dem z. B. auch nur ein Bild abgelegt werden kann. Aus einem Bild (als Bitmap) kann ein Screen Reader Inhalte jedoch ohne vorherige Aufbereitung nicht extrahieren und vorlesen.

Die Problematik von PDF liegt in der Tatsache begründet, dass Inhalte in der Regel in Software wie MS Word, Libre Office oder InDesign erstellt und erst dann in PDF umgewandelt werden. Und dieser Umwandlungsprozess geschieht mit jeder aktuell gängigen Software mehr oder weniger schlecht.

Posselt und Frölich bieten einen sehr detaillierten Überblick über die Erstellung möglichst barrierefreier PDF-Dokumente aus diversen Quelldokumenten.[31]

Ob eine PDF-Datei von Screen Readern vorgelesen werden kann, würde natürlich am besten mit Hilfe eines Screen Readers überprüft werden können, es kann jedoch auch die Barrierefreiheitsprüfung in Adobe Acrobat dafür herangezogen werden.

7.2. PDF/UA

PDF/UA (für „Universal Accessibility") ist eine Einschränkung des PDF-Formats hinsichtlich seiner Merkmale für die Nutzung durch Personen mit Behinderung. Es handelt sich um einen technischen Standard, dementsprechend werden durch die diversen Prüftools auch nur technische Aspekte analysiert. Zur Prüfung eignen sich zum einen die kostenlose Windows Software PDF Accessibility Checker (PAC)[32], der ebenfalls kostenlose Web-Service PDF Accessibility Validation Engine (PAVE)[33] sowie das Preflight Tool des Adobe Acrobat. Anzumerken bleibt, dass Word bis heute nicht in der Lage ist, in PDF/UA zu exportieren und beim Export in PDF oft Syntax generiert, die bei den Prüftools Fehler verursacht. Wer trotzdem in PDF/UA exportieren möchte, muss entweder viel Ahnung über die Interna des PDF-Formates mitbringen und z. B. in Acrobat selbst Hand anlegen oder teure Zusatztools wie axesPDF for Word[34] kaufen, die diese Funktionalität automatisieren.

Der Vollständigkeit halber soll an dieser Stelle neben textbasierten Dokumenten auf die Wichtigkeit hingewiesen werden, auch die Barrierefreiheit bei zeitbasierten

31 Posselt, K.; Frölich, D. (2019)
32 https://www.access-for-all.ch/ch/pdf-accessibility-checker-pac.html
33 https://pave-pdf.org/
34 https://www.axes4.com/axespdf-for-word-ueberblick.html

Medien nicht zu vergessen. Das W3C hat auch hierfür eine Anleitung mit dem Titel „Making Audio and Video Media Accessible“[35] erstellt.

8. Gendergerechte Schreibweise und Barrierefreiheit

Eine nicht-binäre gendergerechte Schreibweise ist heute – insbesondere im akademischen Umfeld – unverzichtbar. Obwohl sie nicht dem Regelwerk der deutschen Rechtschreibung entsprechen, und der Rat für die deutsche Rechtschreibung von der Nutzung abrät[36], finden sich Schreibweisen wie der Gender-Stern (*), der Unterstrich (_) oder der Doppelpunkt (:) als Verkürzungsformen für genderneutrale Schreibweisen in immer mehr Texten wieder.

Im Kontext der Barrierefreiheit müssen diese Schreibweisen jedoch als problembehaftet angesehen werden. Bei der Nutzung mit Screen Readern werden diese Sonderzeichen beispielsweise explizit vorgelesen, was im einfachsten Fall sehr irritierend sein kann und insbesondere nicht der intendierten gesprochenen Sprache entspricht.

Auch für Menschen mit Lernschwierigkeiten, gehörlose Personen oder grundsätzlich all jene Menschen, deren Muttersprache nicht Deutsch ist, können Genderstern und Co. das Textverständnis erschweren.

Leider existieren zu diesem Zeitpunkt noch fast keine wissenschaftlichen Arbeiten, die sich mit der Problematik beschäftigen. Aufgrund der persönlichen Erfahrungswerte aus der praktischen Arbeit im Kontext der Accessibility Services der UB Klagenfurt ist dort gerade eine neue Schreibweise in Erprobung, die sowohl schriftlich als auch mündlich gleich klingt. Ähnlich der binären Doppelnennung von männlich und weiblich wird das binäre *und* durch ein offeneres *bis* ersetzt, und somit ein Raum aufgespannt. Wir sprechen also von Kolleginnen *bis* Kollegen.

Momentan ist nicht absehbar, wo uns die Zukunft im Kontext einer barrierefreien gendergerechten Sprache hinführen wird. Es sollte jedoch im Hinterkopf behalten werden, dass manche Formulierungen aus Sicht der Barrierefreiheit problematisch sein könnten.

---

35 https://www.leichte-sprache.org/leichte-sprache/die-regeln/

36 Vgl. Rat für deutsche Rechtschreibung (2021)

9. Barrierefreiheit und Metadaten

Metadaten sind ein zentraler Aspekt von Repositorien zur Strukturierung und Auffindbarkeit von Inhalten. Insbesondere Menschen mit Behinderung profitieren von aussagekräftigen Metadaten. Es stellt sich daher die Frage, wie barrierefrei Metadaten selbst sind (Metadata Accessibiliy). Auf der anderen Seite können Metadaten auch dazu verwendet werden, die Barrierefreiheit der Objekte zu beschreiben, auf die sie referenzieren (Accessibility Metadata), um es Menschen mit Behinderung erleichtern zu prüfen, ob die verfügbaren Objekte für sie a priori nutzbar sein werden. Beides soll nachfolgend diskutiert werden.

9.1. Metadata Accesssibility

Auch wenn Metadaten theoretisch nicht-textueller Natur sein könnten, beispielsweise eine Grafik, die den Zustand eines Objektes darstellt, kommt dies in der Praxis eher selten vor, da Metadaten meist maschinen-verarbeitbar sein sollen. Erst im User Interface wird die textuelle Form dann möglicherweise durch eine Grafik dargestellt. Die Metadaten selbst bleiben dabei Text ohne Farbe, Formatierung oder andere visuelle Ausdrucksformen. Der wichtigste Faktor zur Beurteilung der Barrierefreiheit von Metadaten scheint daher das Prinzip der Verständlichkeit zu sein. Von leicht verständlichen Formulierungen profitieren nicht nur Menschen mit Lernschwierigkeiten, sondern auch Personen, für die Deutsch nicht die Muttersprache ist, einschließlich gehörloser und fachfremder Personen. Es darf nicht davon ausgegangen werden, dass alle User:innen Fachtermini oder repositorien-übliche Begrifflichkeiten a priori verstehen. Ein Glossar oder die Möglichkeit, sich Erklärungen anzeigen zu lassen, sollten daher bei der Planung berücksichtigt werden. Die Regeln für Leichte Sprache[37] vom deutschen Netzwerk Leichte Sprache sind ein guter Einstieg, um sich mit den Grundlagen der Leichten Sprache zu beschäftigen.

Erst wenn Metadaten im Kontext eines User Interfaces zum Einsatz kommen, spielen Wahrnehmbarkeit, Bedienbarkeit oder Robustheit wie aus den WCAG bekannt entsprechend wieder eine Rolle. Einen Einblick in die möglichst barrierefreie Darstellung von Metadaten gibt der User Experience Guide for Displaying Accessibility Metadata 1.0[38], der von der Publishing Community Group des W3C herausgegeben wurde. Dieser bezieht sich zwar auf die im nächsten Abschnitt besprochenen Accessibility Metadata, fördert jedoch das Verständnis in Hinblick auf alle Formen

37 http://www.leichtesprache.org/index.php/startseite/leichte-sprache/die-regeln
38 https://www.w3.org/2021/09/UX-Guide-metadata-1.0/principles/

von Metadaten. In dem im Rahmen des Projektes e-Infrastructures Austria[39] entstandenen Papers Metadata and Accessibility[40] werden drei Beispiele genannt, an denen die Barrierefreiheit der Repräsentation von Metadaten veranschaulicht wird. Soll beispielsweise ein Objektzustand mit Hilfe einer Ampel grafisch repräsentiert werden, so empfiehlt es sich, nicht nur ein gelbes, rotes oder grünes Farbfeld zu verwenden, sondern eine komplette Ampel, wie aus dem Straßenverkehr bekannt. Wie bei einer realen Ampel wird nur das jeweils entsprechende Licht angezeigt, nicht jedoch die anderen beiden. Damit wird der Forderung nachgekommen, Information nicht nur durch Farbe allein zu kommunizieren, um auch Personen mit einer Farbenblindheit die korrekte Wahrnehmung zu erlauben. Per Konvention ist das oberste Licht einer Ampel rot, das mittlere gelb und das unterste grün.

Werden Metadaten oder eine transformierte Repräsentation von ihnen also im Rahmen einer Benutzerschnittstelle angezeigt, muss diese Repräsentation den für diese Schnittstelle anzuwendenden Richtlinien (z. B. den WCAG) entsprechen.

9.2. Accessibility Metadata

Metadaten können auch dazu verwendet werden, die Gebrauchstauglichkeit von in Repositorien gespeicherten Objekten für bestimmte Personen auszuzeichnen. Einer blinden Person würden somit z. B. nur Medien, die für Screen Reader auch nutzbar sind, angezeigt werden bzw. gleich der Verweis auf ein alternatives Medium mit demselben Inhalt, das nutzbar wäre. Im Umkehrschluss könnte sich eine blinde Person den Download von Dateien ersparen, die für sie nicht nutzbar sind.

Der Wunsch vieler Repositorien-Betreibenden wäre natürlich, für ein Werk einfach ein Flag zu setzen, also zu kennzeichnen, ob es barrierefrei ist oder nicht. So trivial ist diese Fragestellung aber leider nicht zu beantworten. Generell sollte von Pauschalaussagen, wie z. B. ein Hörbuch wäre für blinde Personen a priori barrierefrei, Abstand genommen werden. Ein Hörbuch ist eine Medienform, die – wie auch andere – bestimmte Sinneskanäle bedient, andere eben nicht. Generell zu argumentieren, dass ein Hörbuch, weil ich es als hörende Person rezipieren kann, für diesen Kanal barrierefrei ist, bezieht sich nicht nur auf blinde Personen, sondern ist ein *Feature* dieses Objektes, von dem alle profitieren, die den Kanal rezipieren können. Analog könnten wir auch argumentieren, dass ein gedrucktes Buch für alle, die sehen können, barrierefrei ist.

39 https://e-infrastructures.univie.ac.at/
40 Jeitler, A.; Blumesberger, S. (2016), S. 13.

Komplizierend kommt noch hinzu, dass es nur schwer möglich ist, einer Medienform pauschal bestimmte Eigenschaften zuzuordnen. Sowohl eine Word- wie auch eine PDF- oder eine ePub-(Daisy-)Datei sind nur Container, in die verschiedene Inhalte gepackt werden können. Ob nun ein strukturierter Text oder nur ein Bild abgelegt werden, führt zum Ergebnis, für welche Personengruppen der Inhalt nutzbar ist. Selbst wenn nur reiner Text vorliegt, dieser aber nicht strukturiert wurde, ist er zwar grundsätzlich für beispielsweise blinde Personen *rezipierbar*, aber möglicherweise nicht *gebrauchstauglich*. Niemand möchte gerne ein 500-Seiten-Werk ohne Inhaltsverzeichnis, Seitenzahlen, Abbildungen, nur im Fließtext ohne visuell hervorgehobene Kapitel lesen müssen. Lesen könnten wir das Werk, Vergnügen wäre es aber keines. Selbst ePub[41] ist im Prinzip nichts anderes als eine Zip-Datei, in die eine lokale Website abgelegt wurde. Dort gelten dieselben Anforderungen an Barrierefreiheit wie für Webseiten (also die WCAG).

Nehmen wir ein Hörbuch als Beispiel: Dieses kann als gut ausgezeichnetes Daisy Book implementiert worden sein, bei dem ich nach Text suchen lassen kann und dann direkt an die entsprechende Stelle springe, ein Inhaltsverzeichnis habe etc. Es kann aber auch als eine große WAVE-Datei vorliegen, die ich mir zwar anhören kann, gebrauchstauglich ist das aber nicht, da ich in der Zeitleiste nur vor- und zurückspulen kann. Insbesondere dann ist dies unpraktisch, wenn es sich um wissenschaftliche Literatur handelt, bei der ich viel im Text umherspringen muss. Für Belletristik ist dies meist ausreichend. Für Personen mit Lernschwierigkeiten, gehörlose Personen oder einfach Menschen, die Deutsch nicht als Muttersprache haben, kann der Komplexitätsfaktor des enthaltenen Textes von Relevanz sein, also entscheidend dafür, ob sie das Werk rezipieren können.

Es wird also für jedes individuelle konkrete Objekt, das in einem Repository abgelegt wird, zu bestimmen sein, welche Accessibility Features, aber auch welche Hürden es anbietet. Und hier kommen Accessibility Metadata ins Spiel, denn mit ihnen können diese Sachverhalte abgebildet werden. Wären alle Werke für alle Menschen barrierefrei nutzbar, könnten wir auf derartige Konstrukte verzichten.

Accessibility Metadata liegen in verschiedenen Markups, jeweils für bestimmte Anwendungsformen vor.[42] Die Metadaten von Schema.org werden in Webinhalte eingebunden und erlauben somit die Suche in einer Vielzahl von Anwendungsfällen,

41 https://www.w3.org/TR/epub/
42 Rothberg, M. (2020)

sogar ePub. Sie können dabei in Microdata[43], RDFa[44], oder JSON-LD[45] ausgedrückt werden.

Schema.org und Co. definieren u. a. folgende Arten von Accessibily Metadata:

- accessibilityFeature: Funktionen, welche die Barrierefreiheit unterstützen, wie Textalternativen, Audiodescription, Untertitel etc.
- accessibilityHazard: Hürden, welche die Nutzung durch bestimmte Personengruppen erschweren wie Blitze, unerwartete Geräusche etc.
- accessibilitySummary: Eine textuelle Zusammenfassung der Barrierefreiheits-Eigenschaften des Objektes
- accessMode: Primäre Art der Rezeption – visuell, auditiv, textuell, taktil
- accessModeSufficient: Genauere Angaben zu möglichen Kombinationen der accessModes, um den Inhalt rezipieren zu können.

Für ein fundiertes Verständnis der Accessibility Metadata empfiehlt sich ein Blick auf die Creative-Work-Klasse von Schema.org[46].

Der User Experience Guide for Displaying Accessibility Metadata 1.0[47] schlägt eine bestimmte Reihenfolge vor, in der Accessibility Metadata dargestellt werden sollen, um sicherzustellen, dass die wichtigsten Informationen gleich zu Beginn angezeigt werden. Der Guide identifiziert Screen Reader Friendly und Full Audio, gefolgt von der Accessibility Summary als am meisten bedeutend.

Sowohl die Barrierefreiheit der Metadaten selbst, wie auch ihre Fähigkeit, die Barrierefreiheit von in Repositorien gespeicherten Objekten zu beschreiben, sind daher wichtige Komponenten, die bei der Planung eines Repositoriums mitbedacht werden sollten.

---

43 https://html.spec.whatwg.org/
44 http://www.w3.org/TR/xhtml-rdfa-primer/
45 https://www.w3.org/TR/json-ld/
46 http://schema.org/CreativeWork
47 https://www.w3.org/publishing/a11y/UX-Guide-metadata/techniques/epub-metadata/

10. Konklusion

Zusammenfassend kann festgehalten werden, dass es sich bei Fragen der Barrierefreiheit um ein komplexes Themenfeld handelt, das nicht einfach mit ein paar Prüfschritten abgehakt werden kann. Bei der Planung von Repositorien sollte neben Überlegungen hinsichtlich der Gebrauchstauglichkeit auch von Beginn an die Barrierefreiheit im Fokus stehen, denn immerhin kann Barrierefreiheit als *Gebrauchstauglichkeit für mehr Personen in mehr Situationen* gesehen werden. Auch rechtlich führt heute kein Weg mehr an barrierefreien Repositorien vorbei. Um den rechtlichen Rahmenbedingungen zu entsprechen, sollte im Fall von Web-Inhalten und Anwendungen jedenfalls eine AA-Konformität der jeweils aktuell gültigen WCAG-Version eingehalten werden. Auch Repositorien-Inhalte wie Office-Dokumente sollten den aktuell geltenden Accessibility-Standards wie z. B. PDF/UA entsprechen.

Wenn Barrierefreiheit schon in den grundlegenden Anforderungen eingebettet wurde, zieht sich dies durch das gesamte Projekt, und die Wahrscheinlichkeit für spätere unerwartete Kosten zur Behebung mangelnder Barrierefreiheit wird deutlich geringer. Um ein möglichst hohes Maß an Barrierefreiheit zu erreichen, müssen alle drei hier vorgestellten Faktoren eines Repositoriums bedient werden (die Schnittstelle zu den User:innen, die Metadaten sowie die Inhalte selbst). Wer für einen dieser Teile zuständig ist, sollte entsprechend geschult werden bzw. angemessene Unterlagen sowie Unterstützung erhalten.

Wünschenswert wäre es für viele Organisationen, sich strukturiert an das Thema Barrierefreiheit heranzuwagen. Empfehlenswert ist dabei die Umsetzung eines Accessibility-Maturity-Models, wie jenes des W3C[48]. Für die Umsetzung von Repositorien ist hier insbesondere die Dimension ICT Development Lifecycle interessant; die Barrierefreiheit des Repositoriums und seiner Inhalte profitiert aber auch von allen anderen Dimensionen wie Kommunikation, Beschaffung, Kultur etc. Ein Ziel dieses Prozesses sollte sein, dass Barrierefreiheit zur gelebten Normalität wird.

48 https://www.w3.org/TR/maturity-model/

Bibliografie

Bundes-Verfassungsgesetz (B-VG) (2024). Fassung vom 12.03.2024. Republik Österreich. https://www.ris.bka.gv.at/GeltendeFassung.wxe?Abfrage=Bundesnormen&Gesetzesnummer=10000138

Jeitler, Andreas; Blumesberger, Susanne (2016): Metadata and Accessibility. e-infrastructures Austria Deliverable. https://doi.org/11353/10.459817

Jeitler, Andreas; Gergely, Eva; Blumesberger, Susanne (2022): FAIRe Daten sind barrierefrei. Folien und Aufzeichnung des Webinars „FAIRe Daten sind barrierefrei" der Veranstaltungsreihe „Forschungsdatenmanagement in Österreich" am 19.09.2022. https://phaidra.univie.ac.at/o:1604426

Maaß, Christiane; Rink, Isabel (Hg.) (2018): Handbuch Barrierefreie Kommunikation. (Kommunikation – Partizipation – Inklusion 3). Berlin: Frank & Timme. https://library.oapen.org/handle/20.500.12657/43216

Oliver, Michael (1996): Understanding Disability. London: Macmillan Education UK. https://doi.org/10.1007/978-1-349-24269-6

Posselt, Klaas; Frölich, Dirk (2019): Barrierefreie PDF-Dokumente erstellen. Das Praxishandbuch für den Arbeitsalltag – mit Beispielen zur Umsetzung in Adobe InDesign und Microsoft Office/LibreOffice. Heidelberg: dpunkt.verlag GmbH.

Rat für deutsche Rechtschreibung (2021): Geschlechtergerechte Schreibung. Empfehlungen vom 26.03.2021. Pressemitteilung. https://www.rechtschreibrat.com/geschlechtergerechte-schreibung-empfehlungen-vom-26-03-2021/ (abgerufen am 08.06.2021)

Rothberg, Madeleine (2020): Accessibility Metadata Statements. Presented at Balisage: The Markup Conference 2020, Washington, DC, July 27 - 31, 2020. In: Proceedings of Balisage: The Markup Conference 2020. (Balisage Series on Markup Technologies 25). https://doi.org/10.4242/BalisageVol25.Rothberg01

Shannon, Claude E.; Weaver, Warren (1949): The Mathematical Theory of Communication. Urbana: University of Illinois Press.

Andreas Jeitler ist an der UB Klagenfurt für die Accessibility Services verantwortlich und unterstützt in diesem Kontext bei der Umsetzung von Barrierefreiheit und Gleichstellung von Menschen mit Behinderungen. Als Informatiker sowie Medien- und Kommunikationswissenschaftler lehrt und publiziert er in den Feldern barrierefreie Informations- und Kommunikationstechnologien sowie Disability Studies.

Daniel Beucke, Christian Hauschke, Sebastian Herwig, Kathrin Höhner, Jochen Schirrwagen

Synergien und Herausforderungen bei der Integration von Repositorien mit Forschungsinformationssystemen

Handbuch Repositorienmanagement, Hg. v. Blumesberger et al., 2024, S. 283–303
https://doi.org/10.25364/978390337423216

Daniel Beucke, Niedersächsische Staats- und Universitätsbibliothek Göttingen, beucke@sub.uni-goettingen.de |
ORCID iD: 0000-0003-4905-1936
Christian Hauschke, Technische Informationsbibliothek (TIB), christian.hauschke@tib.eu |
ORCID iD: 0000-0003-2499-7741
Sebastian Herwig, Universität Münster, sebastian.herwig@uni-muenster.de | ORCID iD: 0000-0003-0488-386X
Kathrin Höhner, Technische Universität Dortmund, kathrin.hoehner@tu-dortmund.de |
ORCID iD: 0000-0002-3988-7839
Jochen Schirrwagen, Universität Bielefeld, schirrwagen@ub.rwth-aachen.de | ORCID iD: 0000-0002-0458-1004

Zusammenfassung

Im bibliothekarischen Bereich haben Repositorien zur Verwaltung von Volltexten und Metadaten eine lange Tradition, wohingegen sich in den letzten Jahren Forschungsinformationssysteme als Werkzeug in der Forschungsberichterstattung herausgebildet haben. Publikationen, als ein Teil des wissenschaftlichen Outputs, spielen in beiden Systemen eine entscheidende Rolle und so gibt es immer mehr Überschneidungen bei Publikationen und weiteren Forschungsaktivitäten, die in den Systemen vorgehalten werden. Auf der einen Seite wird es immer wichtiger, dass die beiden Systeme Daten miteinander austauschen, und auf der anderen Seite übernehmen die Systeme zunehmend Aufgaben des jeweiligen anderen Systems.

Schlagwörter: CERIF; Forschungsinformationssystem; Interoperabilität; KDSF; Publikationsmanagement; Repositorium

Abstract

Synergies and Challenges in Combining Repositories with Current Research Information Systems

In the context of libraries, repositories for the management of full texts and metadata have a long tradition, whereas research information systems have emerged in recent years as a tool for research reporting. Publications, as a part of the scientific output, play a key role in both systems and so there is more and more overlap in publications and other research activities that are held in the systems. On the one hand, it is becoming increasingly important for the two systems to exchange data with each other, and on the other hand, the systems are increasingly handling tasks of the respective other system.

Keywords: CERIF; current research information system; interoperability; KDSF; publication management; repository

1. Forschungsinformationen zwischen zwei Welten

Publikationen sind eine der wichtigsten Arten der Kommunikation von wissenschaftlichen Ergebnissen. Und Bibliotheken sind seit jeher der Ort, an dem diese Publikationen gesammelt, systematisiert, katalogisiert, archiviert und zugänglich gemacht werden. Mit der Zeit hat sich die Art der Publikationen stark verändert. Und so ist es aktuell der Fall, dass eine Vielzahl von Publikationen in digitalen Versionen entstehen bzw. hybrid veröffentlicht werden. Für diese Art der Veröffentlichungen haben sich sogenannte Repositorien[1] in Bibliotheken etabliert, die die zuvor genannten Aufgaben übernehmen und digitale Publikationen beinhalten. In der Regel sind in diesen Systemen die Open-Access-Volltexte direkt mit den beschreibenden Daten - den Metadaten - verbunden.

Die Art der Publikationen kann je nach Sammelauftrag der Einrichtung variieren[2]: So gibt es fachliche Bibliotheken, die ihren Nutzenden ein Repositorium anbieten, auf dem fachspezifische Dokumente unterschiedlicher Herkunft zu finden sind. Beispielsweise sind für die Wirtschaftswissenschaften eine große Anzahl von wissenschaftlichen Publikationen und Working-Papers auf dem fachbezogenen Repositorium EconStor[3] zu finden. Eine andere Art stellen institutionelle Repositorien dar, die umfänglich alle Dokumente einer Einrichtung verzeichnen und Abschlussarbeiten, Dissertationen, andere Primärpublikationen, aber auch Zweitveröffentlichungen einer Einrichtung erfassen.

Die Funktionalitäten von disziplinspezifischen Repositorien und institutionellen Repositorien können durchaus Unterschiede aufweisen. Während es in Fachrepositorien primär um das beste, zielgruppenspezifische Angebot von Fachinformationen geht, welches Funktionen wie Relevanzranking, Aktualität, Umfeldsuche oder den einfachen Export erforderlich machen, stehen in institutionellen Repositorien Funktionalitäten wie z. B. die korrekte Personenzuordnung oder Aspekte der Außendarstellung (Publikationslisten, Kontaktmöglichkeiten, Output bezogene Funktionen) im Vordergrund.

Das Ziel der Repositorien ist bei beiden Arten jedoch, möglichst umfänglich und ohne Beschränkungen Publikationen für die jeweilige Zielgruppe bereitzustellen. Dazu gehören neben den Volltexten die Metadaten. Zudem dienen die Repositorien als „Datenlieferanten" für dritte Dienste wie wissenschaftliche Suchmaschinen. Für

1 In diesem Artikel wird der Begriff „Repositorium" als Synonym für Publikationsrepositorium verwendet.

2 Vgl. für eine Definition der verschiedenen Repositorienarten Müller, U.; Scholze, F.; Vierkant, P. et al. (2019), S. 71f.

3 https://www.econstor.eu

diesen Zweck sind die technischen Systeme mit Schnittstellen ausgestattet, die die Daten in standardisierter Form anbieten.[4]

Publikationen nehmen nicht nur in der bibliothekarischen Praxis des Publikationsmanagements eine zentrale Rolle ein, sondern finden zunehmend Eingang in die Forschungsberichterstattung. Hochschulen und Forschungseinrichtungen sehen sich mehr denn je mit der Notwendigkeit einer umfassenden und fundierten Berichts- und Auskunftsfähigkeit über die eigenen Forschungsaktivitäten und -ergebnisse konfrontiert.[5] Forschungsbezogene Informationen unterschiedlicher Art, Herkunft und Güte werden daher verstärkt für die Abwicklung von gesetzlichen Berichts- und Auskunftserfordernissen, zur Unterstützung von Management- und Verwaltungsaufgaben oder auch zur Kommunikation und Verfügbarmachung von Forschungsaktivitäten und den daraus erwachsenen Erkenntnissen genutzt.

Der Blick auf bestehende Berichtsstandards und Datenformate wie beispielsweise den KDSF – Standard für Forschungsinformationen in Deutschland (vormals Kerndatensatz Forschung)[6], die Wissensbilanz in Österreich[7], das Strategy Evaluation Protocol for Research der niederländischen Universitäten[8] oder das Common European Research Information Format (CERIF)[9] macht deutlich, dass die verschiedenen Berichts- und Auskunftserfordernisse im Rahmen der Forschungsberichterstattung nicht allein auf Publikationsmetadaten abzielen, sondern darüber hinaus weitere Arten von Forschungsinformationen beispielsweise zum Personal, zu Projekten und Förderungen, zu Forschungsinfrastrukturen, zur Nachwuchsförderung, zum Transfer wie auch zur Internationalisierung der Forschung erfasst werden. Anders als beim Sammelauftrag der Repositorien für Publikationen zielt die Forschungsberichterstattung auf eine integrierte Betrachtung der verschiedenen Arten von Forschungsinformationen ab, um auf diese Weise auch die Kontexte der Forschungsaktivitäten und -ergebnisse in die Berichterstattung einzubeziehen. Beispielsweise gibt der KDSF vor, dass z. B. zu Publikationen mit unterschiedlichen Fokussen berichtet werden soll:

---

4 Vgl. Müller, U.; Scholze, F.; Vierkant, P. et al. (2019), S. 34–37.
5 Vgl. für einen Überblick zum Stand der Forschungsberichterstattung in Deutschland wie auch im Folgenden Herwig, S. (2018), S. 15–30.
6 Vgl. https://www.kerndatensatz-forschung.de
7 Vgl. https://www.bmbwf.gv.at/Themen/HS-Uni/Hochschulgovernance/Steuerungsinstrumente/Wissensbilanz.html
8 Vgl. https://www.universiteitenvannederland.nl/files/publications/SEP_2021-2027.pdf
9 Vgl. https://www.eurocris.org/services/main-features-cerif

- Wie viele und welche Publikationen sind im Rahmen eines Forschungsprojekts entstanden?
- Wie viele Publikationen wurden von einer bestimmten Förderorganisation gefördert?
- Unter Nutzung welcher Infrastruktur wurden die der Publikation zugrunde liegenden Erkenntnisse erworben?

Als ein Werkzeug zur Unterstützung und Abwicklung derartig überspannender und integrativer Anforderungen der Forschungsberichterstattung haben sich in der jüngsten Vergangenheit Forschungsinformationssysteme (FIS) herausgebildet. Unter einem FIS wird hierbei ein spezielles Informationssystem verstanden, welches der Bewältigung der Aufgaben der Forschungsberichterstattung dient und zu diesem Zweck die notwendigen informationstechnischen Mittel zur Erhebung, Verarbeitung und Bereitstellung von Forschungsinformationen umfasst sowie in die hierzu notwendigen organisatorischen Strukturen (z. B. Prozesse, Regeln, Zuständigkeiten) eingebettet ist.[10] Forschungsinformationssysteme bezeichnen somit nicht nur Werkzeuge zur Erfassung, Pflege und Qualitätssicherung von Forschungsinformationen, sondern können ebenfalls Funktionen zur Abwicklung von datenproduzierenden Prozessen sowie zur Auswertung und Darstellung von Forschungsinformationen umfassen. Hierzu greifen diese oft auf bereits verfügbare Informationen aus bestehenden Verwaltungssystemen wie z. B. Personal-, Finanz-, Campusmanagementsysteme und Publikationsrepositorien zurück, erlauben es, diese Informationen mit weiteren kontextbezogenen Informationen anzureichern, in einer einheitlich strukturierten und definitorisch aufeinander abgestimmten Datenbasis zusammenzuführen, wechselseitig in Beziehung zueinander zu setzen und wiederum für verschiedene Nutzungsszenarien zugänglich zu machen. Ein FIS muss hierbei nicht notwendigerweise als eine abgeschlossene Anwendung verstanden werden. Es kann ebenfalls als eine Sammlung integrierter Softwarelösungen betrachtet werden, wobei jede Lösung für sich spezifische Funktionalitäten wie beispielsweise eine Datenerfassungs- und Prozessabwicklungsumgebung, ein Forschungsportal zur Außendarstellung oder Berichts- und Auswertungswerkzeuge (z. B. Business Intelligence- und Data Warehouse-Lösungen) bereitstellt.

Publikationsdaten stehen somit zwischen zwei Welten – den Repositorien einerseits und FIS-Lösungen andererseits. Auf welches System soll die Wahl fallen? Oder lassen sich diese Welten nicht auch miteinander vereinen? Am Ende ist es den Nutzenden egal, in welchem System sie ihre Publikationsdaten erfassen.

10 Vgl. für eine Begriffsbestimmung wie auch im Folgenden Herwig, S.; Schlattmann, S. et al. (2016), S. 901–914 in Verbindung mit Herwig, S. (2018), S. 15-30 und Ebert, B.; Tobias, R.; Beucke, D. et. al. (2016).

Idealerweise erfolgt es jedoch nur einmal. Dabei verfolgen die unterschiedlichen Stakeholder:innen wie Forschende, Bibliothek und die Forschungsadministration Anforderungen, die im folgenden Abschnitt näher betrachtet werden. Die Eingabe dieser Daten (und Volltexte) ist aus technischer Sicht in beiden Systemen (FIS oder Repositorium) möglich. Je nachdem, welcher Weg gewählt wird, können sich die Datenflüsse bei einer Integration der beiden Systeme unterscheiden (darauf wird im Abschnitt 2.2. „Datenflüsse" eingegangen). Mittlerweile gibt es eine Vielzahl von technischen Systemen, die für die jeweiligen Anwendungsszenarien herangezogen werden können. Ein entscheidender Punkt ist jeweils die standardisierte Verwendung von Datenmodellen und Metadatenvokabularen. Darauf und auf weitere technische Fragestellungen wird der Abschnitt 2.3. „Technische Implementierung" eingehen. Abschließend wird auf die Gemeinsamkeiten und auch die Abgrenzungen der beiden Systeme eingegangen. Beide Systeme haben einen anderen Fokus auf die Publikation beziehungsweise verfolgen ein anderes Ziel bei der Erfassung und Darstellung einer Publikation.

2. Interoperabilität

2.1. Anforderungen von Stakeholder:innen

Während die Forschungsberichterstattung als relativ neues Feld in der Regel durch FIS-Lösungen unterstützt bzw. realisiert wird, sind Repositorien als Publikationsmanagementsysteme seit vielen Jahren etabliert. Sowohl Wissenschaftler:innen als auch Universitätsbibliotheken und -verwaltungen bewegen sich in beiden Welten: in der Forschungsberichterstattung und den Repositorien. Dabei können sie sowohl Daten nutzen als auch Daten liefern bzw. produzieren, was zu unterschiedlichen Anforderungen an beide Systeme führt.

2.1.1. Anforderungen von Wissenschaftler:innen

Repositorien bieten Wissenschaftler:innen als Nutzenden eine umfassende Möglichkeit für die Suche nach Publikationen. Für Wissenschaftler:innen in der Rolle als Autor:innen bieten sie eine niedrigschwellige Möglichkeit zum vollständigen Nachweis der eigenen Werke wie z. B. Publikationen, Dissertationen und grauer Literatur wie beispielsweise Arbeitsberichte, zunehmend aber auch von Preprints, Zweitveröffentlichungen und Forschungsdaten. Für jede einzelne Publikation, jeden Forschungsdatensatz müssen dann im Repositorium bibliographische Metadaten erfasst werden.

Mit Blick auf die Sichtbarkeit der eigenen Forschungsleistung erwarten Wissenschaftler:innen mithin, dass nicht nur die digitalen Objekte selbst leicht gefunden werden können, sondern dass diese auch eindeutig mit ihnen verknüpft sind. Auf diese Anforderung haben Repositorienbetreibende reagiert und ihre Systeme dahingehend weiterentwickelt, dass in den Repositorien selbst Personendaten zu den Autor:innen, idealerweise auch die Open Researcher and Contributor iD (ORCID iD) als eindeutige Identifikation für Personen erfasst sind.[11] Werden Wissenschaftler:innen in der Rolle von Datenlieferant:innen für die Forschungsberichterstattung aufgefordert, ihre Publikationen und Forschungsergebnisse an das FIS zu melden, entsteht aktuell ein Mehraufwand für die Forschenden, da sie mindestens zwei Systeme bedienen müssen. Wie schon im Positionspapier der DINI-AG FIS 2016 konstatiert, ist dies aus Sicht der Forschenden nur schwer nachvollziehbar.[12] Für die beteiligten Infrastrukturen ist es jedoch nicht leicht, diese organisationsinternen Datenerfassungsprozesse gut und auf die Bedürfnisse der Nutzenden abzustimmen.[13]

In Nordrhein-Westfalen befasst sich zur Zeit das Projekt CRIS.NRW[14] als landesweite Unterstützungsstruktur für die Einführung von FIS-Lösungen mit der Frage, auf welche Weise Repositorien an FIS angebunden werden können, um so den Mehraufwand für Forschende zu reduzieren. Denn Forschende möchten ihre Publikationen möglichst nur einmal erfassen, sie aber gleichzeitig in unterschiedlichen Systemen nachweisen. Dies können auch Systeme außerhalb des institutionellen Repositoriums und des FIS der eigenen Einrichtung sein.[15] 2018 wurde in einem DINI-Positionspapier zur ORCID die eindeutige Identifikation für Autor:innen über die ORCID iD als ein Lösungsansatz gesehen, den Mehraufwand für Forschende bei der Erfassung ihrer Publikationen zu verringern.[16] Ein solcher Mehrwert kann jedoch nur erzielt werden, wenn FIS wie Repositorien den automatisierten Datenaustausch via ORCID als Datenverteilplattform ermöglichen. Dabei erwarten Forschende zunehmend, dass bei einem Wechsel der institutionellen Zugehörigkeit ihre Publikationslisten einfach in die Systeme der neuen Institution übertragen werden können.[17]

Für die Erfassung wünschen sich Wissenschaftler:innen eine intuitiv zu bedienende Oberfläche, die den direkten Upload digitaler Objekte ermöglicht, d. h. dass

---

11 Dies trifft nicht auf alle Anbieter von Repositoriums-Software zu; eine differenzierte Betrachtung würde jedoch zu weit führen.
12 Ebert, B.; Tobias, R.; Beucke, D. et al. (2016), S. 13.
13 Jeffrey, K. (2012), S. 338.
14 https://www.uni-muenster.de/CRIS.NRW/
15 Ebert, B.; Tobias, R.; Beucke, D. et al. (2016), S. 17 („Zudem besteht der individuelle Bedarf an Forschungsinformationen nicht nur in einer institutionellen Präsenz auf der Webseite, sondern auch für Profile in Fachportalen und wissenschaftlichen sozialen Netzwerken“).
16 Vierkant, P.; Beucke, D.; Deinzer, G. et al. (2018), S. 10.
17 Vgl. Vierkant, P.; Beucke, D.; Deinzer, G. et al. (2018)

also bestenfalls der Datennachweis und die Datenspeicherung am selben Ort stattfindet. FIS und Repositorium müssen mithin zumindest soweit miteinander interagieren, dass Forschende die Metadaten zu ihren Forschungsergebnissen nur einmal eingeben müssen. Weiterhin sollte es nicht Aufgabe der Autor:innen sein, die Verknüpfung ihrer Werke mit Co-Autor:innen oder Organisationseinheiten vornehmen zu müssen – dies sollte idealerweise möglichst automatisiert erfolgen.

Eine wichtige Anforderung des KDSF kann jedoch nur durch die Wissenschaftler:innen selbst erfüllt werden: Hochschulen müssen u. a. auskunftsfähig über die aus bestimmten Projekten hervorgegangenen Publikationen sein – allein die beteiligten Forschenden können auf Ebene der einzelnen Publikation definieren, welche Veröffentlichung aus welchem Projekt hervorgegangen ist. Repositorien bieten diese Möglichkeit oft bereits, z. B. um die automatisierte Ablieferung an OpenAIRE[18] zu ermöglichen (Details siehe 2.3. „Technische Implementierung der Repositoriums-FIS-Integration"). Die Zuordnung von Publikationen zu Projekten sollte jedoch ebenso nur in einem System vorgenommen werden müssen. Hier kann durch die Verknüpfung von Repositorien und institutionellem FIS ein Synergieeffekt erzielt werden, welcher den Aufwand für die Forschenden deutlich verringert. Aus Sicht der Wissenschaftler:innen ist es zudem wünschenswert, dass persönliche oder organisationsbezogene Publikationslisten möglichst ohne zusätzlichen administrativen Aufwand aus einem der beiden Systeme heraus erstellt werden.[19] Bieten Repositorien oder FIS solche Mehrwerte, erhöht dies die Akzeptanz bei Wissenschaftler:innen, diese Systeme zu bedienen.[20]

2.1.2. Anforderungen von Bibliotheken

Bibliotheken als diejenigen Institutionen, die Repositorien betreiben, haben vornehmlich das Ziel, digitale Forschungsergebnisse der Angehörigen ihrer Hochschule oder Forschungseinrichtung verfügbar zu machen und für eine optimale Sichtbarkeit selbiger zu sorgen. Um Forschungsergebnisse direkt im Volltext oder als Datensatz bereitzustellen, bieten Repositorien Forschenden die Möglichkeit, ihre digitalen Objekte wie Dissertationen, Arbeitsberichte sowie Zweitveröffentlichungen von nicht im Open Access verfügbaren Verlagspublikationen als auch For-

---

18 OpenAIRE – pan-europäisches Forschungsinformationssystem, über das u. a. Forschungspublikationen aus EU-geförderten Projekten gemeldet werden: https://www.openaire.eu

19 Vgl. hierzu: „Entsprechend ist das Interesse an der persönlichen Publikationsliste und ihrer Präsentation im Internet in den letzten Jahren gewachsen, dem besonders Einrichtungen zuständig für die Webveröffentlichung, aber auch Bibliotheken und Forschungsdezernate Rechnung tragen wollen." Horstmann, W.; Jahn, N. (2010), S. 186.

20 Persönliche Erfahrungen aus dem Dialog mit Wissenschaftler:innen unterschiedlicher Disziplinen.

schungsdaten selbst hochzuladen (Selfdeposit). Zu diesem Zweck können erste Metadaten zu den digitalen Objekten erfasst und idealerweise das digitale Objekt direkt mit den Autor:innen oder Schöpfer:innen eindeutig verknüpft werden. Das hat jedoch zur Konsequenz, dass in den Repositorien explizit Personen als Entitäten erfasst werden müssen. Wie oben erwähnt, schafft die ORCID iD hier eine Erleichterung: Hat der/die Autor:in seine/ihre ORCID iD mit dem Repositorium verknüpft, können die Publikationen, die im Repositorium als Volltexte vorliegen, ebenso wie die Publikationen, zu denen nur bibliographische Metadaten in ORCID erfasst sind, im Repositorium mit der Entität des/der Autor:in verknüpft werden. Damit ist eine wichtige Voraussetzung für die Interoperabilität mit einem FIS geschaffen. Viele Bibliotheken bieten zudem aus ihrer Tradition der standardisierten Erschließung heraus den Service, die Metadaten bibliothekarisch aufzubereiten und bei Bedarf mit weiteren Daten zu verknüpfen, z. B. mit Stammdaten der Zeitschrift, in der ein Artikel erschienen ist, der nun als post-print veröffentlicht wird, oder auch mit Angaben zu Co-Autor:innen und deren Affiliationen. Die Anreicherung der Metadaten und die Verknüpfung mit z. B. Normdaten bedeutet eine Verringerung des Erfassungsaufwands für Bibliotheksbeschäftigte und erzielt im Kontext der Datensauberkeit oft schlankere Prozesse, vor allem, wenn die in den Repositorien erfassten Daten samt ihren qualitativ hochwertigen Metadaten für die Forschungsberichterstattung nachgenutzt werden können.

Um die Publikationen weltweit sichtbar zu machen, bedienen sich Repositorien dedizierter Schnittstellen, um Metadaten und zum Teil auch die digitalen Objekte selbst an andere Systeme weiterzugeben (Details siehe Abschnitt 2.2. „Datenflüsse"). Dies sind einerseits etablierte Suchmaschinen und zunehmend die Anbindung an Discovery-Dienste, andererseits aber auch die Deutsche Nationalbibliothek im Rahmen der Pflichtablieferung digitaler Dokumente, Software für die digitale Langzeitarchivierung oder auch persönliche oder organisationsbezogene Publikationslisten. Gerade der zuletzt genannte Service wird von Wissenschaftler:innen in den letzten Jahren verstärkt nachgefragt.[21] Und gerade hierdurch ergibt sich eine Synergie für die Forschungsberichterstattung: Pflegen Wissenschaftler:innen und Bibliotheken die Publikationen im Repositorium, können qualitativ hochwertige Metadaten zu Publikationen über die bereits vorhandenen Schnittstellen an FIS geliefert werden, womit ohne Mehraufwand valide Daten für diesen Bereich des Reportings zur Verknüpfung mit weiteren Daten bereitgestellt werden. Eine Herausforderung bleibt jedoch: die Zuordnung von Publikationen zu Projekten, Forschungsinfrastrukturen und anderen Aktivitäten. In welchem System – FIS oder Repositorium – dies erfolgt, sollte im Rahmen der etablierten Prozesse der einzelnen

21 Vgl. Horstmann, W.; Jahn, N. (2010), S. 186.

Hochschule individuell geprüft werden. Im Sinne der Verringerung des Aufwands für Bibliotheken wie auch für Forschende sollten beispielsweise Projektdaten nur einmal vorgehalten werden.

Gerade aufgrund ihrer langen Erfahrung in der systematischen Erfassung und Verarbeitung bibliographischer Metadaten wird die Expertise von Bibliotheken im Rahmen der Forschungsberichterstattung häufig für den Bereich der Publikationen herangezogen, wie die eigenen Erfahrungen der Autor:innen zeigen.[22] Da Metadaten zu den Publikationen der Angehörigen der eigenen Hochschule gemeinsam mit den digitalen Objekten selbst in Repositorien vorgehalten und bibliothekarisch aufbereitet werden, ist es ein Anliegen der Bibliotheken, diese Daten für ein FIS nachnutzbar zu machen. Gerade bei modular aufgebauten oder als Softwaresammlung konzipierten FIS kommt Repositorien als Datenquellen eine hohe Bedeutung zu. Die Interaktion zwischen FIS und Repositorium sollte über die bereits vorhandenen Schnittstellen erfolgen, um den manuellen Aufwand so gering wie möglich zu halten.

Voraussetzung für die Interoperabilität von FIS und Repositorium ist, dass es ein gemeinsames Verständnis und somit gemeinsame Definitionen von Bibliotheken und FIS-Betreibenden gibt.[23] Für Publikationsformen gibt es standardisierte Vokabulare, deren Ziel der automatisierte Austausch von Metadaten und teilweise auch digitalen Objekten ist. Im nationalen deutschen Kontext ist das bereits 2010 erarbeitete „Gemeinsame Vokabular für Publikations- und Dokumenttypen“[24] als de facto-Standard anzusehen. Für Publikationsdaten in FIS gibt es in Deutschland im Rahmen des „KDSF“[25] ebenfalls ein standardisiertes Vokabular. Aufgrund der unterschiedlichen Fokusse beider Standards – Austausch von Publikationsmetadaten bei Repositorien als auch Kontextualisierung von Forschungsinformation bei FIS – sind die beiden Vokabulare jedoch nicht deckungsgleich. Um die Interoperabilität beider Systeme zu verbessern, hat sich bereits 2018 eine Arbeitsgruppe aus den DINI-Arbeitsgruppen Elektronisches Publizieren (E-Pub), Forschungsinformationssysteme (FIS) und Kompetenzzentrum Interoperable Metadaten (KIM) gegründet, die in engem Austausch mit dem Helpdesk des KDSF eine Harmonisierung des

---

22 Im Rahmen des durch die Initiative CRIS.NRW initiierten Austauschs zu FIS in Nordrhein-Westfalen wurde häufig deutlich, dass Bibliotheken für diesen Bereich der Forschungsberichterstattung eine Schlüsselrolle einnehmen. Ebenso zeigte sich dies im Austausch innerhalb der DINI-AGs FIS und E-Pub.

23 Vgl. Herwig, S. (2018), S. 24.

24 Das Gemeinsame Vokabular (https://edoc.hu-berlin.de/handle/18452/2144) ist die Basis für das Harvesting digitaler Objekte durch die Deutsche Nationalbibliothek im Rahmen der Pflichtablieferung und Voraussetzung zur Erlangung des DINI-Zertifikats.

25 https://www.kerndatensatz-forschung.de/

Vokabulars mit dem „Gemeinsamen Vokabular für Publikations- und Dokumenttypen" der DINI anstrebt.[26] In diesem Rahmen wurde ein Mapping mit dem Ziel erstellt, die Datenlieferung aus Repositorien an FIS zu erleichtern.[27] Hierdurch können Synergien geschaffen werden, indem Mehrfacherfassung oder zusätzliche Nachbearbeitung von Metadaten zu Publikationen durch Beschäftigte in der Hochschulbibliothek und/oder zentraler Universitätsverwaltung vermieden wird. Ein weiteres Anliegen von Universitätsbibliotheken ist es, Auskunft für eigene Reportingzwecke geben zu können, von welchen Personen und in welchen Kontexten Forschungsergebnisse veröffentlicht wurden. Hierzu zählt z. B. das interne Monitoring von Kosten für Open-Access-Publikationen, die eine immer wichtigere Rolle im Erwerbungsbudget von Bibliotheken spielen.[28]

2.1.3. Anforderungen aus der Verwaltung

Verwaltungen von Forschungseinrichtungen hingegen kommen aus der Welt der Forschungsberichterstattung. Durch die Standardisierung, die mit der Einführung des KDSF aufkam, erhielten die Publikationen eine zunehmende Bedeutung als Forschungsergebnisse. Oft wurden schon qualitativ hochwertige bibliographische Daten in modernen Repositorien durch die Bibliotheken vorgehalten, die jedoch mit der Verwaltung oft keine Berührungspunkte hatten. Gibt es gleichzeitig beispielsweise etablierte Systeme für das Personal- und Projektmanagement, kann es zielführend sein, eine modulare FIS-Lösung, die eine Softwaresammlung darstellt, als FIS zu betreiben.[29] Sind solche Systeme nicht verfügbar oder bieten diese keine offenen oder nachnutzbaren Schnittstellen, kann es sinnvoller sein, eine monolithische FIS-Lösung zu wählen. Bei der Entscheidung sind alle beteiligten Stakeholder:innen zu involvieren: Neben der Hochschulleitung sind das die Drittmittel- und Personalverwaltung, Forschungstransfer, Förderberatung, Promotionsämter, Bibliotheken, Rechenzentren, IT-Abteilungen sowie nicht zuletzt die Forschenden selbst.[30] Dabei ermöglicht es der KDSF, ein gemeinsames Verständnis der einzelnen Elemente zu entwickeln, woraus im Idealfall Synergieeffekte für Datenlieferanten und Datennutzende geschaffen werden. Als Beispiel seien erneut die Publikationen genannt: Die Harmonisierung des Vokabulars für Publikationen des KDSF mit dem

---

26 Vgl. hierzu https://blog.dini.de/EPub_FIS/2020/02/17/empfehlung-kdsf/

27 DINI, Arbeitsgruppe Elektronisches Publizieren; DINI, AG Forschungsinformationssysteme (2022)

28 Gilt es z. B., Verträge zur Zeitschriftenlizenzierung abzuschließen, die eine Publikationskomponente beinhalten, muss die Bibliothek für die Kostenabschätzung und Bewertung wissen, in welchem Maße in welchen Fachgebieten bei dem jeweiligen Verlag publiziert wurde.

29 Herwig, S. (2018), S. 27.

30 Herwig, S. (2018), Tab. 1.

“Gemeinsamen Vokabular für Publikations- und Dokumenttypen”, das Repositorien verwenden, erleichtert die Sammlung und das Vorhalten bibliographischer Informationen zu Publikationen der eigenen Einrichtung. Da die Daten in Repositorien von Bibliotheksbeschäftigten kontrolliert und angereichert werden und der gesamte Prozess der Erfassung einschließlich der Auswahl der aufzunehmenden Publikationen in der Regel transparent dargestellt sind[31], wird gleichzeitig der Qualitätssicherung Rechnung getragen. Somit stellen Repositorien eine vertrauenswürdige Quelle dar und es liegt im Interesse der Universitätsverwaltung, auf Repositorien als Quelle für Publikationsdaten zurückgreifen zu können.[32]

2.2. Datenflüsse

Generell sind Datenflüsse sowohl vom Repositorium zum FIS als auch umgekehrt denkbar. Diese Integrationsvarianten können dabei unterschiedlich begründet sein. Wichtig ist, dass bei der Integration mehrerer Systeme spezifiziert wird, welches System als Quellsystem für Publikationen fungiert. Ein paar gängige Motivationen sind folgende:

2.2.1. Motivationen aus Sicht des Repositoriums

- Bereitstellen von Metadaten: Bedingt u. a. durch Mechanismen wie die Selbstarchivierung von Forschungsergebnissen durch Forschende ist die Qualität und Konsistenz der Metadaten in Repositorien oftmals nicht optimal, dennoch sind Repositorien eine wertvolle Datenquelle für Forschungsinformationssysteme, schon weil sie vielerorts als Ersatz für eine Hochschulbibliographie dienen.
- Erhöhung der Sichtbarkeit: Werden die Publikationen in einem (öffentlichen) Forschungsinformationssystem beschrieben und verlinkt, wird hierbei ein zusätzlicher Sucheinstieg geöffnet. Wer sich z. B. die Beschreibung eines Forschungsprojektes in einem Forschungsprofilsystem ansieht, kann durch die mit einem Projekt verknüpften Publikationen zu einem Repositoriumslink gelangen.

---

31 So fordert das DINI-Zertifikat, dass Repositorienbetreibende Leitlinien bereitstellen, die „den Dienst möglichst detailliert beschreiben und darin Aussagen über inhaltliche Kriterien und zum technischen Betrieb treffen – z. B. über die Art der veröffentlichten Dokumente, die angesprochenen Nutzungsgruppen und die Dauerhaftigkeit des Dienstes“. Vgl. Müller, U.; Scholze, F.; Vierkant, P. et al. (2019), S. 17.

32 Eigene Erfahrungen haben genau das gezeigt: Im Zuge der Diskussion der Einführung von FIS in Nordrhein-Westfalen ist zu beobachten, dass Bibliotheken als Expertinnen für Publikationsdaten und potentielle Datenlieferanten in den Einführungsprozess von FIS einbezogen werden.

- Kontextualisierung von Publikationen: In Repositorien werden Publikationen, Forschungsdaten und anderer Forschungsoutput veröffentlicht und mit Metadaten beschrieben. Es liegt nahe, diese Metadaten im FIS wiederzuverwenden und dort in Beziehung zu Personen, Organisationen, Projekten und anderen Entitäten aus der Welt der Forschungsinformationen zu setzen. Diese Kontextualisierung ist an verschiedene Voraussetzungen geknüpft.

2.2.2. Motivationen aus Sicht des Forschungsinformationssystems

- Anreicherung von Metadaten im Repositorium: Hierzu werden die in der Regel reicheren Metadaten aus dem FIS in das Repositorium importiert. Dies können z. B. Informationen über Forschungsprojekte oder mit dem Output in Zusammenhang stehende Organisationen (Forschungsinstitute, Förderer etc.) sein.
- Referenzierung von Publikationen: Durch Verlinkung eines Werkes im Repositorium wird Nutzenden des FIS ein persistenter Weg zu den beschriebenen Forschungsergebnissen aufgezeigt.
- Publikation von Forschungsergebnissen: Die Initiierung des Publikationsvorgangs kann aus einem FIS erfolgen, zum Beispiel via SWORD API (Simple Web-service Offering Repository Deposit, siehe unten) unter Verwendung der schon im FIS vorliegenden Metadaten des zu veröffentlichenden Werkes.

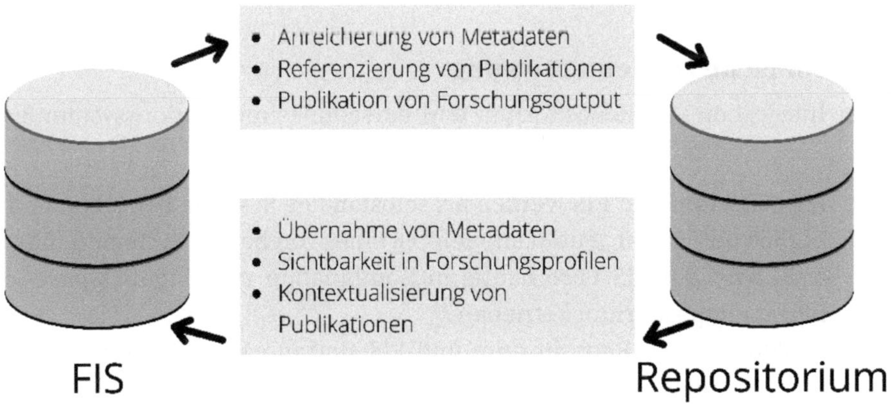

Abb. 1: Funktionale Verbindungen zwischen FIS und Repositorium

2.2.3. Integration mit übergeordneten Systemen

Datenflüsse finden nicht nur auf direktem Wege zwischen den beiden Systemtypen statt, es können auch Drittsysteme beteiligt sein. ORCID und OpenAIRE, die in unterschiedlicher Art und Weise Forschungsinformationen verwalten, können stellvertretend für weitere Dienste stehen, in denen institutionsübergreifend Forschungsinformationen aggregiert und über Schnittstellen zur Verfügung gestellt werden. ORCID stellt eine zurzeit nur seinen Mitgliedern zugängliche Schnittstelle bereit, die in die jeweiligen Systeme wie Repositorien oder Forschungsinformationssysteme integriert werden muss. Darüber lassen sich dann ORCID-Records nicht nur lesen und für den Datenimport nutzen, sondern auch aktualisieren, ergänzen und synchronisieren (push). Solche Profil-Informationen können Informationen über Affiliationen, Forschungsergebnisse und Projekte von Forschenden umfassen.

OpenAIRE als pan-europäisches Forschungsinformationssystem aggregiert bibliographische Informationen und damit in Zusammenhang stehende Fördergeber- und Projektinformationen von Schnittstellen datenbereitstellender Publikations- und Informationsinfrastrukturen (pull). Zudem reichert OpenAIRE Metadaten an, die von Repositorien und Forschungsinformationssystemen nachgenutzt werden können (brokering).

Sobald die genannten Dienste integriert sind und damit Publikationen aus Repositorien und FIS in den Diensten verzeichnet sind, ist so indirekt die Anreicherung und Nachnutzung von Metadaten über Schnittstellen im eigenen System möglich.

2.3. Technische Implementierung

Bei der Integration von Repositorium und Forschungsinformationssystem lassen sich folgende Konstellationen unterscheiden:

a) Repositorium und FIS werden als selbständige Systeme betrieben und bezüglich der Entität „Publikationen“ ist eines von beiden Systemen führend. Z. B. wird das FIS Pure häufig in Kombination mit einem DSpace- oder EPrints-Repositorium betrieben.[33]
b) Funktionen von Repositorium und FIS sind in einem System implementiert. Beispiele hierfür sind DSpace-CRIS[34] und Haplo[35].

33 Macgregor, G. (2019)
34 https://wiki.lyrasis.org/display/DSPACECRIS
35 https://www.haplo-services.com/docs/Haplo_Repository_Brochure.pdf

In beiden Fällen werden Anbindungen an externe Systeme (z. B. der Campus-IT, Identity Management (IDM), Zitationsdatenbanken) nötig sein und im Fall a) zusätzlich die Festlegung eines Metadatenmappings zwischen Repositorium und FIS und die Festlegung von Workflows und Datenflüssen zwischen beiden Systemen.

2.3.1. Standards für Datenmodelle und Metadatenvokabulare

Während Repositorien aufgrund ihrer Funktion für das Management von Publikationen primär bibliographischen Metadatenstandards (z. B. Dublin Core, MODS, MARC, DataCite) folgen, hat sich für FIS seit den 1990er Jahren der CERIF-Standard für die Erfassung, die Vorhaltung und den Transfer von Forschungsinformation auf europäischer Ebene herausgebildet. Auch der für Deutschland relevante KDSF orientiert sich an CERIF, wenngleich es konzeptionelle Unterschiede zwischen diesen Datenmodellen gibt.[36]

Mit dem KDSF lassen sich thematische Bereiche wie Beschäftigte, Nachwuchsförderung, Drittmittel und Finanzen, Patente, Ausgründungen, Publikationen sowie Forschungsinfrastrukturen beschreiben. Die wesentliche Schnittmenge zwischen FIS und Repositorium ist somit der Bereich Publikationen. Darüber hinaus unterstützen viele Repositorien in europäischen Ländern auch Attribute über drittmittelfinanzierte Projekte, nicht zuletzt im Zuge der Implementierung von Open-Access-Anforderungen und Berichtserfordernissen, z. B. über die OpenAIRE Infrastruktur an die Europäische Kommission.[37]

Ein besonderes Kennzeichen in den Datenmodellen von CERIF und KDSF ist die Ausprägung und granulare Beschreibung von Entitäten und die Verknüpfung der Entitäten untereinander. Demgegenüber sind die Datenmodelle von Repositorien häufig flach oder wenig hierarchisch definiert. Im Zuge einer Migration oder Integration bibliographischer Informationen zwischen Repositorium und FIS können deshalb Kurations- und Transformationsschritte notwendig werden. Das betrifft z. B. die Beschreibung von Zeitschriftenartikeln oder Sammelbandbeiträgen. Während im Repositorium das übergeordnete Werk, also Zeitschrift oder Sammelband, häufig nicht als digitales Objekt und nicht normiert angelegt ist, kann es hierfür im FIS eine eigene Entität geben, sodass Werk und übergeordnetes Werk verknüpfbar sind. Zudem ist zu beachten, dass wissenschaftliche Autor:innen in der Synchronisation zwischen beiden Systemen eindeutig über lokale (z. B. Uni-ID, LDAP) und externe Identifier (z. B. ORCID iD) identifizierbar sind.

36 Helpdesk Kerndatensatz Forschung (2020), S. 9.
37 Kaiser, O.; McNeill, G. (2019), S. 373–382.

Bei der Repositorium-FIS-Integration stellen sich aber neben der Harmonisierung und Synchronisierung bibliographischer Informationen weitere grundsätzliche Fragen, die im Folgenden diskutiert werden.

- Wie können Wissenschaftler:innen ihre Informationen zu Forschungsaktivitäten erfassen und verwalten?
- Lassen sich Systembrüche vermeiden, sodass die Erfassung und Verwaltung über ein System möglich ist?
- Kann die Erfassung von Publikationen im FIS erfolgen oder kann das Repositorium über die Erfassung von Publikationen hinaus erweitert werden?
- In welchem Umfang lassen sich aggregierte Informationen (Angaben zu Personen, Drittmitteln usw.) aus anderen Systemen der Verwaltung unter Vermeidung von Doppeleingaben nachnutzen?
- Welche Schnittstellen stehen zur Verfügung und welche Systeme sollen angebunden werden?
- Wie ist die Außendarstellung der Forschungsaktivitäten inklusive der Publikationen geplant?

Für einen möglichst komfortablen Zugriff sollte das System, welches Erfassung und Verwaltung von Publikationen und weiteren Forschungsinformationen übernimmt, eine Authentifizierung über Single Sign-On ermöglichen und an das Identity Management (IdM) der Einrichtung angebunden sein.

Je nach Festlegung, ob das Repositorium oder das FIS Quellsystem für Publikationen sein soll, ist die Frage zu klären, über welches System eine Anbindung an externe Zitationsdatenbanken (z. B. für automatisierte Importe von Metadaten), Registrierungsagenturen für Persistente Identifier (PID) und Normdatensysteme (ORCID, DOIs über DataCite oder Crossref, URNs und GNDs über die Deutsche Nationalbibliothek, Elektronische Zeitschriftenbibliothek, ...) erfolgen soll.

Werden Repositorium und FIS gekoppelt, gibt es für den Transfer der Publikationsdaten zwischen den Systemen mehrere Möglichkeiten:

- Das datenliefernde System stellt eine Web-API z. B. via REST[38] bereit. Die Schnittstelle des datenkonsumierenden Systems muss an die Abfragespezifikation der Web-API in der Regel angepasst werden. Sie legt auch ein oder mehrere Datenformate fest, z.B. XML oder JSON. Je nach Ausgestaltung der Web-API ist der Datenaustausch auf Metadaten beschränkt oder erfolgt für Metadaten und Volltext sukzessive in zwei Schritten.

38 https://restfulapi.net/

- Prinzipiell wäre auch ein Austausch über die OAI-PMH[39]-Schnittstelle zwischen Repositorium und FIS möglich, allerdings beschränkt auf XML-Formate und nur für die Metadaten.
- Über das SWORD-Protokoll[40] kann eine Übertragung von Metadaten und Volltext in einem Schritt erfolgen.

Die Außendarstellung der Forschungsaktivitäten einer Einrichtung kann über die öffentliche Weboberfläche des FIS oder über ein separates Forschungsportal erfolgen.

Je nach gewählter Art der Repositorium-FIS-Integration ist zu entscheiden, auf welches der beiden Systeme persistente Identifier der Publikationen verweisen und in welchem Umfang Publikationen im Forschungsportal repräsentiert werden sollen.

3. Fazit

Forschungsinformationssysteme und Repositorien sind unterschiedliche Typen von Systemen mit grundlegend anderen Zielvorgaben und Anwendungsfällen; dennoch gibt es Überschneidungspunkte und erste produktive Hybridlösungen am Markt.[41]

Entscheidend beim Betrieb der beiden Systeme ist es, ihre Nutzung gemeinsam zu denken, um aus den Stärken der beiden Systeme Synergien optimal ziehen zu können. Einer der wichtigsten Punkte ist, Datenstrukturen und Identifier aufeinander abzustimmen, um einen Austausch zwischen den Systemen überhaupt zu ermöglichen. Ein weiteres gemeinsames Thema für FIS und Repositorium sind Überlegungen, wie die Integration mit Aggregatoren wie OpenAIRE (wird zunehmend wichtiger für EU-Compliance und Sichtbarkeit sowie Kontextualisierung der Forschungsaktivitäten) erfolgen kann. In welchem System Publikationsdaten dauerhaft gepflegt werden, muss sorgfältig anhand der Zielvorgaben der Systeme und individueller Gegebenheiten abgewogen werden. Hier spielen viele Faktoren eine entscheidende Rolle. Ziel sollte es immer sein, dass die Daten möglichst nur einmal eingegeben werden müssen, in mehreren Systemen nachgenutzt und gegebenenfalls für singuläre Zwecke angereichert werden können. Ferner sollte im Sinne der Usability

39 https://www.openarchives.org/pmh/
40 https://swordapp.org/
41 Das Directory of Research Information Systems (DRIS; https://eurocris.org/services/dris), welches von der euroCRIS angeboten wird, gibt einen guten Überblick zu Forschungsinformationssystemen. Dort kann nach technischen Systemen gefiltert werden. Ein ähnliches Verzeichnis bietet die DINI mit der Liste der Publikationsdienste (https://dini.de/dienste-projekte/publikationsdienste/) an. Hier liegt der Schwerpunkt auf Repositorien. Diese Liste ist ebenso nach den technischen Systemen filterbar.

die Erfassung und Verwaltung von Daten durch Wissenschaftler:innen effizient und effektiv in einer einheitlichen Nutzeroberfläche erfolgen, selbst wenn es mehrere Quellsysteme für verschiedene Bereiche der Forschungsinformation gibt.

Es muss beim Austausch von Daten immer auf die rechtlichen Gegebenheiten, Bedingungen und Voraussetzungen Rücksicht genommen werden. Dies betrifft vor allem den Datenschutz bei personenbezogenen Daten und sicherlich weniger die Inhalte in den Repositorien als in den FIS, weil hier mehrere Entitäten und weitere Zusammenhänge wie z. B. Zeitspannen von Beschäftigungsverhältnissen und Projektzugehörigkeiten miteinander verknüpft werden. Im Repositorium hingegen, das die Publikation zum Ausgangspunkt der Präsentation der Daten hat, spielen Verknüpfungen zwischen Entitäten eine geringere Rolle. Erst mit der Verknüpfung zu einem FIS werden sie in höherem Maße relevant, jedoch ausschließlich innerhalb des Systems, nicht in der Außensicht, die bei Repositorien eine entscheidende Rolle spielt.

Beide Systeme haben gemeinsam, dass Publikationen als eine zentrale Ausprägung von Forschungsergebnissen eine wichtige Rolle spielen z. B. für die Nachnutzung der Publikationsdaten für die Darstellung selbiger auf den Webseiten der Forschenden. Dabei ist allerdings zu beachten, dass sich die Zielvorgaben der beiden Systeme sehr wohl unterscheiden können.

Repositorium:

- Vorhalten von Publikationsdaten und Verfügbarmachung (inkl. der Open-Access-Volltexte) je nach Sammlungsbeschreibung, wobei die institutionellen Repositorien einen Großteil der Repositorien ausmachen (87 %)[42],
- Nachnutzung der Metadaten und Volltexte durch Dritte,
- Langzeitarchivierung der elektronischen Publikationen,
- Weitergabe von Hochschulschriften als Pflichtabgabe an die DNB,
- Vergabe von PIDs für dauerhafte Findbarkeit und Zitationsfähigkeit.

Forschungsinformationssystem:

- Datengrundlage für Reports und Analysen. Dabei ist es zwingend erforderlich, dass die Daten nicht verändert werden können.
- Dient zusammen mit weiteren Forschungsinformationen (Projekte, Promotionen, Preisverleihungen etc.) zur Außendarstellung auf personen-, einrichtungs- oder projektbezogenen Webseiten.

42 Vgl. Schöpfel, J.; Azeroual, O. (2021), S. 20.

Unterschiedlich ist ebenso die Voraussetzung, wer die Daten in das jeweilige System eingibt und im Anschluss mit ihnen arbeitet. Je nach System kann ein (teil-) automatisierter Import der Daten erfolgen. Hier haben die kommerziellen Anbieter von FIS-Lösungen teilweise noch einen Vorteil, weil auf die jeweils im eigenen Portfolio umfangreiche Datenbasis zurückgegriffen werden kann und somit eine Integration erleichtert wird. Bei den Repositorien muss meist auf Schnittstellen zurückgegriffen werden, die erst angepasst werden müssen. In beiden Fällen ist jedoch immer die Voraussetzung, dass der Zugriff auf kostenpflichtige Datenpools lizenziert sein muss. Aus den Erfahrungen mit diesen Importen muss festgestellt werden, dass – je nach Anforderung im System – die Daten nach einem Import intellektuell überprüft werden sollten.

Letzten Endes ist es egal, wie die Daten in die Systeme kommen. Sicher ist es hilfreich, wenn die Einrichtung (hier meist die Bibliothek) einen Service für den Import von Daten anbietet, bei dem die Daten eine Anreicherung und Qualitätssicherung erhalten (z. B. eine Zuordnung zu Instituten oder die Anreicherung der Metadaten). Oft werden Daten, die in ein FIS eingespielt werden, noch einmal von einer prüfenden Stelle angescha und ggf. für weitere Bewertungen bearbeitet. Es bleibt aber abschließend zu sagen, dass eine Einrichtung, die Publikationen ihrer Forschenden selbst pflegt, eine umfangreiche Datengrundlage schafft. Erst diese kann eine qualitativ gute Aussage über das Publikationsverhalten der Einrichtung anbieten und stellt eine unabhängige Datensammlung in Bezug auf kommerzielle Anbieter dar.

Bibliografie

DINI, Arbeitsgruppe Elektronisches Publizieren; DINI, AG Forschungsinformationssysteme (2022): Mapping des Gemeinsamen Vokabulars für Publikations- und Dokumenttypen zum KDSF. https://doi.org/10.18452/24149.2

Ebert, Barbara; Tobias, Regine; Beucke, Daniel; Bliemeister, Andreas; Friedrichsen, Eiken; Heller, Lambert; Herwig, Sebastian; Jahn, Najko; Kreysing, Matthias; Müller, Daniel; Riechert, Mathias (2016): Forschungsinformationssysteme in Hochschulen und Forschungseinrichtungen. Positionspapier. Version 1.1. https://doi.org/10.5281/ZENODO.45564

Helpdesk Kerndatensatz Forschung (2020): Einführung in das CERIF-Datenmodell und Vergleich mit dem Datenmodell des Kerndatensatz Forschung (KDSF). https://kerndatensatz-forschung.de/version1/technisches_datenmodell/v_1_2/document/Einfuehrung%20Datenmodelle%20KDSF%20und%20CERIF.pdf (abgerufen am 12.04.2023)

Herwig, Sebastian (2018): Anforderungen an die Forschungsberichterstattung von Hochschulen in Deutschland – ein Überblick. In: Fuhrmann, Michaela; Güdler, Jürgen; Kohler, Jürgen; Pohlenz, Philipp; Schmidt, Uwe (Hg.): Handbuch Qualität in Studium, Lehre und Forschung. Berlin: DUZ Verlags- und Medienhaus GmbH, S. 15–30. https://nbn-resolving.de/urn:nbn:de:hbz:6-84149413979

Herwig, Sebastian; Schlattmann, Stefan (2016): Eine wirtschaftsinformatische Standortbestimmung von Forschungsinformationssystemen. In: Mayr, Heinrich C.; Pinzger, Martin (Hg.): Informatik 2016 – Informatik von Menschen für Menschen. Bonn: Gesellschaft für Informatik e. V., S. 901–914. http://subs.emis.de/LNI/Proceedings/Proceedings259/901.pdf (abgerufen am 12.04.2023)

Horstmann, Wolfram; Jahn, Najko (2010): Persönliche Publikationslisten als hochschulweiter Dienst – Eine Bestandsaufnahme. In: Bibliothek, Forschung und Praxis 34 (2). https://doi.org/10.1515/bfup.2010.032

Jeffrey, Keith G. (2012): CRIS in 2020. In: Jeffery, Keith G.; Dvořák, Jan (eds.): E-Infrastructures for Research and Innovation Linking Information Systems to Improve Scientific Knowledge Production: Proceedings of the 11th International Conference on Current Research Information Systems, pp. 333–342. http://hdl.handle.net/11366/119

Kaiser, Olivia; McNeill, Gerda (2019): OpenAIRE für Repository ManagerInnen – wie Repository ManagerInnen Open Science unterstützen können. In: Mitteilungen der Vereinigung Österreichischer Bibliothekarinnen und Bibliothekare 72 (2), S. 373–382. https://doi.org/10.31263/voebm.v72i2.2815

Macgregor, George (2019): Repository and CRIS Interoperability Issues within a 'Connector Lite' Environment. 14th International Conference on Open Repositories (OR2019), Hamburg, Germany. https://pureportal.strath.ac.uk/en/publications/repository-and-cris-interoperability-issues-within-a-connector-li (abgerufen am 12.04.2023)

Müller, Uwe; Scholze, Frank; Vierkant, Paul; Arning, Ursula; Beucke, Daniel; Blumtritt, Ute: Bove, Karolin; Braun, Kim; Deppe, Arvid; Deinzer, Gernot; Fenner, Martin; Klotz-Berendes, Bruno; Meinecke, Isabella; Pampel, Heinz; Schirrwagen, Jochen; Severiens, Thomas; Summann, Friedrich; Steinke, Tobias; Tullney, Marco; Voigt, Michaela; Walger, Nadine; Weimar, Alexander; Wolf, Stefan (2019): DINI-Zertifikat für Open-Access-Publikationsdienste 2019. Humboldt-Universität zu Berlin. https://doi.org/10.18452/20545

Schöpfel, Joachim; Azeroual, Otmane (2021): Current Research Information Systems and Institutional Repositories: From Data Ingestion to Convergence and Merger. In: Future Directions in Digital Information, pp. 19–37. https://doi.org/10.1016/b978-0-12-822144-0.00002-1

Vierkant, Paul; Beucke, Daniel; Deinzer, Gernot; Hartmann, Sarah; Herwig, Sebastian; Höhner, Kathrin; Müller, Uwe; Schirrwagen, Jochen; Summann, Friedrich (2018): Autorenidentifikation anhand der Open Researcher and Contributor ID (ORCID), Positionspapier. Humboldt-Universität zu Berlin. https://doi.org/10.18452/19528

Daniel Beucke arbeitet an der Niedersächsischen Staats- und Universitätsbibliothek Göttingen in der Gruppe Elektronisches Publizieren und ist am Göttingen Campus in der FIS-Gruppe vertreten. Eine Rolle ist die Koordination des Publikationsdatenmanagement GRO.publications. Er ist ein Sprecher der DINI-AG E-Pub und Mitglied in der DINI-AG FIS.

Christian Hauschke ist im Open Science Lab der Technischen Informationsbibliothek (TIB) im Themenfeld Forschungsinformationen und Forschungsinformationssysteme tätig. Seit 2020 leitet er dort die Lab Gruppe Offene Forschungsinformationen. Er ist Mitglied u. a. der DINI-AG FIS und des euroCRIS Technical Committee.

Sebastian Herwig ist seit 2011 Abteilungsleiter in der Universitätsverwaltung der Universität Münster und verantwortlich für Forschungsinformationen und Forschungsberichterstattung. Er leitete von 2016–2019 die Landesinitiative CRIS.NRW zur Umsetzung des KDSF an den Hochschulen in NRW. Er ist Sprecher der DINI-AG FIS und Board-Mitglied von euroCRIS.

Kathrin Höhner leitet seit 2017 den Geschäftsbereich Digitales Publizieren und Informationskompetenz an der UB Dortmund. In dieser Funktion ist sie u. a. die Open-Access-Beauftragte. Zu ihrem Bereich gehören neben Open Access auch strategische Beratungen zu Themen wie z. B. die Hochschulbibliographie und ORCID. Sie ist Mitglied der DINI-AG E-Pub.

Jochen Schirrwagen ist stellvertretender Leiter des Dezernats Publikationen an der UB der RWTH Aachen. Zuvor war er von 2017 bis 2023 Referent für Projektkoordination und Innovationsmanagement an der UB Bielefeld. Dort war er in der universitären Arbeitsgruppe zur Einführung eines Forschungsinformationssystems für den Bereich „Bibliothek“ zuständig. Er ist Mitglied u. a. in der DINI-AG E-Pub.

Tereza Kalová, Claudia Hackl

Kompetenzen rund um die Repositoriennutzung vermitteln

Ein Leitfaden zur Entwicklung von Schulungsmaßnahmen

Handbuch Repositorienmanagement, Hg. v. Blumesberger et al., 2024, S. 305–328
https://doi.org/10.25364/978390337423217

Claudia Hackl, Universität Wien, Center for Teaching and Learning, claudia.hackl@univie.ac.at |
ORCID iD: 0000-0002-0365-4400
Tereza Kalová, Universität Wien, Universitätsbibliothek, tereza.kalova@univie.ac.at |
ORCID iD: 0000-0002-1764-7228

Zusammenfassung

Forschende, Lehrende, aber auch Studierende können in Schulungen die Nutzung von Repositorien kennenlernen, sowie mehr über im Forschungs- und Lehrbetrieb relevante Themen wie Open Access, Open Research oder Management und Archivierung von Forschungsdaten erfahren. Ebenso können Repositorienmanager:innen über Schulungsmaßnahmen in den Austausch mit Zielgruppen treten und somit die Nutzung des institutionellen Repositoriums steigern, Services bewerben und regelmäßiges Feedback bekommen, das zur Weiterentwicklung genutzt werden kann. In diesem Beitrag werden aus dem bibliothekarischen Umfeld der Universität Wien Beispiele aus dem Schulungsbetrieb präsentiert und ein praxisorientierter Leitfaden für die Planung von Schulungskonzepten dargestellt.

Schlagwörter: Repositoriennutzung; Schulung; Schulungsentwicklung; Leitfaden; Train-the-Trainer; Universitätsbibliothek Wien

Abstract

Building Competencies Related to Repository Use. A Guide to the Development of Training Measures

Researchers, lecturers and students can learn about the use of repositories as well as related topics such as open access, open research or research data management in dedicated training courses. Repository managers can engage with their target groups through training to increase the use of the institutional repository, promote services and receive regular feedback that can be used for further development. This paper presents training examples from the Vienna University Library as well as a hands-on guideline for the planning of courses in the area of repository management.

Keywords: Repository use; training; training development; guideline; train-the-trainer; Vienna University Library

1. Einführung

Nicht nur im Zuge von Open Science bedingt die „digitale Revolution“ einen Wandel der Informationspraxis in wissenschaftlichen Institutionen, indem Repositorien immer mehr an Bedeutung innerhalb von Forschungsinstitutionen gewinnen, um u. a. die Langzeitarchivierung von Forschungsdaten, Lehr- und Lernobjekten oder auch Forschungssoftware zu gewährleisten. So wirft die Nutzung der Repositorien bei Nutzer:innen auf unterschiedlichen Ebenen Fragen auf, die sowohl den Umgang mit der jeweiligen Repositorien-Software betreffen, als auch den Archivierungsworkflow von unterschiedlichen Daten und Materialien, sowie das Anreichern dieser mit dementsprechenden aussagekräftigen Metadaten. In diesem Kontext sind Themenfelder wie das Entwickeln von Datenmanagementplänen, Open Science, das Forschungsdatenmanagement oder auch Publikationsstrategien ebenso relevant.

Um interessierte Angehörige der eigenen Institution im Umgang mit Repositorien zu schulen, Fragen von Nutzer:innen auf unterschiedlichen Ebenen abzufangen, und zugleich den Bekanntheitsgrad und die Nutzung des Repositoriums zu erhöhen, tritt eine Universitätsbibliothek für die Vermittlung von Informationskompetenz ein. Forschende sowie Studierende können in Schulungen die Nutzung von Repositorien kennenlernen und mehr über im Universitätsbetrieb relevante Themen wie Open Access, Open Research oder Management und Archivierung von Forschungsdaten erfahren.

Das Schulungsangebot kann zudem von Repositorienmanager:innen genutzt werden, um in den Austausch mit Zielgruppen zu treten und somit Anregungen dafür zu bekommen, wie die Nutzung des universitätsinternen Repositoriums zu steigern wäre. Hier kann regelmäßiges Feedback eingeholt werden, das zur Weiterentwicklung der Services genutzt werden kann. Auch sind diese Schulungsmaßnahmen eine Möglichkeit, bei der weitere Bibliotheksservices oder Services anderer Dienstleistungseinrichtungen beworben werden können, um das gesamtheitliche Wahrnehmen von Open Science an der Institution zu fördern. Dabei gilt es verschiedene Parameter zu beachten, die die Konzeption der zu planenden Schulung leiten können. Neben didaktischen Grundprinzipien, stellen Zielgruppenanforderungen und vorhandene bzw. nachnutzbare Ressourcen beispielsweise Grundelemente dar, die die jeweiligen zu entwickelnden Schulungskonzepte maßgeblich beeinflussen.

In diesem Beitrag werden aus dem bibliothekarischen Umfeld der Universität Wien Beispiele aus dem Schulungsbetrieb präsentiert und ein skalierbarer Leitfaden für die Planung von Schulungskonzepten zur Orientierung dargestellt.

2. Leitfaden zur Entwicklung einer Schulungsmaßnahme

Der im Rahmen dieses Beitrags erarbeitete Leitfaden, der als Orientierung für die Entwicklung einer Schulungsmaßnahme[1] im breit gefassten Kontext der Repositoriennutzung dient, gliedert sich in drei Phasen. Dieser Leitfaden basiert auf dem didaktischen Prinzip des „backward design“[2], das besagt, dass die Entwicklung einer Schulungsmaßnahme mit der Definition von Lernzielen starten sollte, um das bestmögliche Angebot im Sinne der Zielgruppenorientierung zu bieten. Darauf folgen dann die Festlegung auf die zum Einsatz kommenden Leistungsüberprüfungsmethoden sowie die Konzeption der Schulungseinheit(en).

In diesem Sinne startet die Konzeption eines Workshops mit der **Vorbereitungsphase**, bestehend aus der Bedarfsermittlung der Zielgruppen, der darauffolgenden Formulierung von ausdifferenzierten Lernzielen sowie ein Ressourcen-Check, um auszuloten, in welchem Ausmaß eine Schulungsmaßnahme entwickelt und durchgeführt werden kann. Darauf folgt die **Planungsphase** des konkreten Workshops bzw. der Trainingseinheit(en), mit der Erstellung eines zielgruppenorientierten Qualifizierungsangebots, gefolgt von der Erstellung oder Nachnutzung von begleitenden Materialien und der darauf startenden Bewerbung des Angebots. Zuletzt steht die **Erprobungsphase** des entwickelten Schulungskonzepts, mit der Durchführung der geplanten Einheit(en), sowie Evaluierung und Anpassung des Angebots, um das bestmögliche Service für die anvisierten Zielgruppen zu bieten.

Im Folgenden finden sich pro Phase zentrale Reflexionsfragen, die dabei helfen sollen, die Entwicklung von Schulungsmaßnahmen zu starten, gefolgt von weiteren Informationen, die im jeweiligen Schritt herangezogen werden können.

2.1. Vorbereitungsphase

In der Phase der Vorbereitung empfiehlt sich eine vorangestellte Bedarfsermittlung der Zielgruppen, gefolgt von der Formulierung der Lernziele sowie der Durchführung eines Ressourcen-Checks.

Bedarfsermittlung der Zielgruppen durchführen

- Welche Zielgruppe sollte mit dem Angebot erreicht werden?
- Welche Themen werden von der jeweiligen Zielgruppe gewünscht bzw. benötigt?

---

1 Für die Entwicklung eines umfassenden Schulungs- und Beratungskonzeptes siehe z. B. Helbig, K. (2021), S. 239-253.

2 Siehe McTighe, J. et al. (2005)

- Wo sieht die Institution bzw. sehen die Trainer:innen Bedarf bei der gewählten Zielgruppe?

Bei der Konzeption von Schulungsmaßnahmen sind Bedarfs- und Nachfrageorientierung aber auch Requirements Engineering[3] generalisierte Steuerungsmodi, die das zu erarbeitende Angebot richtungsweisend mitgestalten. Die Bedarfe der unterschiedlichen Zielgruppen sind jedoch auszudifferenzieren, sodass Angebote geschaffen werden können, die zielgruppenspezifisch orientiert sind. Auch allgemeine Einführungen in eine Software oder eine Thematik sind möglich.[4] Als Grundlage für diese vorangestellte Bedarfsermittlung der Zielgruppen können unterschiedliche Informationsquellen dienen. Neben klassischen Methoden zur Zielgruppenanalyse im Kontext der wissenschaftlichen Weiterbildung, wie Seitter diese zusammenfassend darstellt[5], können ebenso die eigene Beratungspraxis oder auch Schulungsmaßnahmen sowie niederschwelliges Feedback direkt von den betroffenen Personen herangezogen werden. Schulungskonzeption stellt – wie in diesem Beitrag dargelegt – einen Kreislauf mit drei Phasen dar, die ineinandergreifen können, sodass mögliche Evaluationen oder auch Erfahrungen aus der Erprobung der Schulungsmaßnahmen als erneute Basis für mögliche fokussierte Bedarfsermittlung der Zielgruppen dienen können. Ebenso können andere Dienstleistungseinrichtungen, die mit denselben Zielgruppen arbeiten, befragt werden, ob Trends erkennbar sind, die möglicherweise auch strategisch begründet den Bedarf der jeweiligen Zielgruppe konkretisieren. Typische Zielgruppen aus dem Feld der Repositoriennutzung stellen Wissenschaftler:innen, PhDs oder Projekt-Antragssteller:innen, (Master)-Studierende[6] sowie administratives Personal dar. Am Anfang „kann es sinnvoll sein, sich zunächst auf eine bestimmte Zielgruppe zu fokussieren und erst nach einer Etablierungsphase […] weitere Personen in den Blick zu nehmen“[7].

Ein wichtiges Thema hierbei stellt u. a. die Workshop-Sprache dar. Schulungen sollten, wenn möglich, die Sprachkenntnisse der Faculty widerspiegeln, um allen Zielgruppen an der Forschungseinrichtung Zugang zu Informationen zu gewährleisten. Demnach sollten Kurse neben der Landessprache auch auf Englisch als der lingua franca der Wissenschaft angeboten werden.[8] Dies gilt auch für allfällige

3 Siehe Blumesberger, S. (2018), S. 37-51.
4 Vgl. Seitter, W. (2019), S. 316 ff.
5 Vgl. Seitter, W. (2019), S. 320 ff.
6 Bzgl. Angebote für Studierende siehe z. B. Engelhardt, C. et al. (2021)
7 Helbig, K. (2021), S. 242.
8 Vgl. Kalová, T. (2020), S. 48.

asynchrone Kommunikation und Maßnahmen des Wissenstransfers, sowie Infomaterialien und Webseiten.

Lernziele formulieren

- Über welche Themen sollen Schulungsteilnehmer:innen (nicht) informiert werden?
- Mit welchen Inhalten sollen sich Schulungsteilnehmer:innen (nicht) aktiv auseinandersetzen?
- Welche konkreten Kompetenzen sollen Schulungsteilnehmer:innen (nicht) erlernen?

Um eine Schulung zielgruppenorientiert anbieten zu können, stellen formulierte Lernziele eine Grundvoraussetzung dar. Es sollte konkret festgehalten werden, welche Themen auf welchen Ebenen behandelt werden sollen. Schulungseinheit(en) können dazu genutzt werden, um über Themen zu informieren, sich aktiv mit Inhalten auseinanderzusetzen oder Kompetenzen zu erlernen. Bei der Formulierung von Lernzielen bietet die Lernzieltaxonomie – basierend auf Bloom et. al. (1956)[9], adaptiert durch Anderson et. al. (2001)[10] – eine gute Orientierung, da dabei das jeweilige kognitive Niveau des Unterrichts bewusst bestimmt wird und Aufgabenstellungen nach Komplexität ausdifferenziert werden können.

Lernzieltaxonomie – Stufen der Komplexität

1	Wissen	wiedergeben, nennen
2	Verstehen	beschreiben, erklären
3	Anwendung	anwenden, lösen
4	Analyse	analysieren, ermitteln, ableiten
5	Synthese	entwickeln, konstruieren
6	Evaluation	bewerten, beurteilen

Eine Abgrenzung der Lernziele schafft Klarheit und eine Basis für ein strukturiertes Schulungskonzept. Ein Beispiel hier wäre eine Schulung für Absolvent:innen: Da die Zielgruppe der Masterstudierenden mit Repositorien vor allem im Rahmen ihres Studienabschlusses in Berührung kommt, stehen hier beispielsweise der Upload von relevanten Forschungsdaten oder auch die Zurverfügungstellung der Abschlussarbeit über das dementsprechende institutionelle Service im Fokus. Lernziele wären demnach das Verstehen des Kontextwissens über Forschungsdaten und deren Archivierungsmöglichkeiten in Repositorien, mit Blick auf eine spätere aka-

9 Siehe Bloom, B. S. et al. (1956)
10 Siehe Anderson, L. (2001)

demische Karriere, sowie der Einstieg in die Diskussion rund um Datenmanagementpläne und deren Relevanz bei Projektanträgen, aber auch die praktisch orientierte Durchführung von korrektem Upload inklusive Anreicherung von Metadaten. Zur Formulierung von Lernzielen im Bereich Forschungsdatenmanagement kann zum Beispiel die Lernzielmatrix der DINI/nestor UAG-Schulungen verwendet werden[11].

Ressourcen-Check durchführen

Auf folgenden Ebenen empfiehlt sich ein Ressourcen-Check:

- personell
- zeitlich
- räumlich
- finanziell
- technisch

Nach dem Abstecken des Rahmens der zu planenden Schulung – Festlegen von Zielgruppe und zu erreichenden Lernzielen – empfiehlt sich ein Blick in Richtung der zur Verfügung stehenden Ressourcen. Fragen nach personellen, zeitlichen, aber auch räumlichen, finanziellen und technischen Rahmenbedingungen müssen geklärt werden. Es gilt zu klären, ob gesondertes Budget für die Planung, Durchführung und Evaluation einer Schulungsmaßnahme eingeplant werden kann, um beispielsweise externe Trainer:innen einzuladen oder Trainings im Rahmen der Regelarbeitszeit im Team untergebracht werden sollen.

Zusätzlich sollte der Kontakt mit im Kontext der gewählten Zielgruppe bereits aktiven Services oder Dienstleistungseinrichtungen an der eigenen Institution gesucht werden. Wenn es ein Teaching-and-Learning-Zentrum an der eigenen Institution gibt, ein Zentrum für Hochschuldidaktik, eine Personalentwicklungsabteilung oder anderweitige Forschungsunterstützungsservices, so wird sich ein Austausch und Abgleich des jeweiligen Angebots als hilfreich erweisen, da Forschende in den meisten Fällen auch Lehrende an der Institution sind, und somit in ihrer Doppelrolle Services von verschiedenen Einrichtungen in Anspruch nehmen werden, die für eine bestmögliche Unterstützung aufeinander abgestimmt sind.

Falls an der eigenen Institution diese verwandten Services nicht verankert sein sollten, so können bei einem Blick nach außen Unterstützungsmöglichkeiten entdeckt

11 Siehe Petersen, B. et al. (2022)

werden, die in der Phase der Vorbereitung der durchzuführenden Schulungsmaßnahme – u. a. für einen Erfahrungsaustausch – in Betracht gezogen werden können.

2.2. Planungsphase

Gefolgt auf die Vorbereitung umfasst die Planungsphase die Erstellung eines zielgruppenorientierten Qualifizierungskonzepts, das durch begleitende Materialien unterstützt wird und mit entsprechenden Bewerbungsmaßnahmen an die Zielgruppen getragen wird.

Zielgruppenorientiertes Qualifizierungskonzept erstellen

- Auf Basis der formulierten Lernziele sollen welche Themen von wem bearbeitet werden?
- Welchen zeitlichen Rahmen und Ablauf soll die Schulung aufweisen?
- Welche Schulungsform bzw. -modus eignet sich für die Themen und die Zielgruppe?
- In welcher Form ist eine Leistungserbringung an die Erlangung eines Teilnahmezertifikats geknüpft?

Zu Beginn empfiehlt sich das Abstecken der zu behandelnden Themen auf Basis der bereits formulierten Lernziele. Daraus – und aus dem bereits erfolgten Ressourcen-Check – lassen sich personelle Planungen anstellen, welche (hauseigenen oder externen) Trainer:innen in Frage kommen und gebucht werden müssen. Im Zusammenwirken mit den jeweiligen verfügbaren Ressourcen und den zu erreichenden Lernzielen lässt sich somit auch ein zeitlicher Rahmen sowie der Schulungsmodus für die geplante Schulungsmaßnahme abstecken. Hier steht es den Organisator:innen frei, ob in einem rein digitalen Setting Impulsvorträge mit nachfolgenden kurzen Diskussions- und Fragerunden mit einer Dauer von insgesamt etwa zwei Stunden veranstaltet werden oder ein rein präsenter Workshop zur Erarbeitung einer Themenstellung im Ausmaß eines Vormittags geplant wird. Weiters kann auch ein Training durchgeführt werden, das im Sinne des Flipped Classroom[12] asynchron vor der Schulungseinheit gelieferte Materialien zur Erarbeitung von Themenfeldern als Ausgangspunkt nimmt, um in einem hybriden Setting mit Teilnehmer:innen – sowohl vor Ort präsent als auch digital zugeschaltet – zentrale Fragestellungen in diesem Kontext zu diskutieren.

12 Für mehr Informationen zu diesem Konzept siehe https://www.flipped-classroom-austria.at/das-konzept/

Fest steht, dass sowohl bei Präsenz-Einheiten als auch virtuellen Veranstaltungen diverse interaktive Tools eingesetzt werden können, um Meinungsbilder einzufangen, Wissen abzufragen, oder Gruppenarbeiten zu ermöglichen. Dies sollte unter stetiger Beachtung des Nutzens dieser für die Erreichung der Lernziele erfolgen, um didaktisch reduziert zu arbeiten und keine Überforderung der Teilnehmer:innen hervorzurufen. Bei reinen Online-Schulungen ist es lohnend, sich zunächst mit den Interaktionsmöglichkeiten des jeweiligen verwendeten Videokonferenz-Tools auseinander zu setzen.[13] Tipp: Neben formalen Teilnahmebestätigungen können auch „open badges" vergeben werden![14]

Zu klären gilt es, ob das Ausstellen eines Teilnahmezertifikats angedacht ist. Dabei ist zu beachten, wer die ausstellende Einheit darstellt und – falls gewünscht – welche Formen der Leistungserbringungen an die Erlangung des Zertifikats geknüpft sind.[15] Diese müssen vorab definiert und im besten Fall direkt im Rahmen der Bewerbung transparent kommuniziert werden. Die Überprüfung dieser Leistungserbringungen ist ebenfalls einzuplanen. Beispielsweise könnte in einem einfachen Fall die Teilnahme an der Schulung bereits die Voraussetzung zur Erlangung des Zertifikats darstellen, aber auch eine Nachbereitungsaufgabe angepasst an die zu erreichenden Lernziele wäre möglich.

Begleitende Unterlagen nachnutzen bzw. entwickeln

- Kann auf bestehende Ressourcen (Open Educational Resources – OER) zurückgegriffen werden?
- Hat die Organisationseinheit (z.B. Bibliothek, Forschungsservice) Erfahrung oder Infrastruktur in diesem Bereich, die genutzt werden kann?

Für die geplante Qualifizierungsmaßnahme können begleitende Unterlagen entweder eigens erstellt und entwickelt, oder aber auch bereits vorhandene Materialien[16] nachgenutzt werden. Je nach verfügbaren Ressourcen wäre ebenso eine Kombinationslösung aus Nachnutzen und Produzieren sinnvoll. Ausgangspunkt für die Entwicklung von begleitenden Unterlagen ist die vorangestellte Planung der Schulungsmaßnahme. Es kann je nach Schulungsmodus beispielsweise mit Foliensätzen gearbeitet werden, mit Aufgabenstellungen für den Austausch in der Gruppe

13 Vgl. Hartmann, W. (2016), S. 133f.

14 Siehe https://openbadges.org/

15 Für mehr Information zu Richtlinien für Fortbildungen des Bundesministeriums für Arbeit, Soziales, Gesundheit und Konsumentenschutz siehe https://www.sozialministerium.at/dam/jcr:fb4fec5e-7566-48b5-a850-c27ac9109f48/Fortbildungsrichtlinie%20(2019-04).pdf

16 Siehe z. B. den „EOSC Pillar Training and Support Catalogue" unter https://eosc-pillar.d4science.org/web/eoscpillartrainingandsupport/home oder die „Offenen Bildungsressourcen Forschungsdatenmanagement" von FAIR Data Austria unter https://doi.org/10.5281/zenodo.6923344

oder Handouts für nachfolgenden Wissenstransfer, die darüber hinaus beispielsweise ebenfalls auf der Website verfügbar gemacht werden.

Open Educational Resources (OER) sind „Lehr-, Lern- und Forschungsressourcen in Form jeden Mediums, digital oder anderweitig, die gemeinfrei sind oder unter einer offenen Lizenz veröffentlicht wurden, welche den kostenlosen Zugang sowie die kostenlose Nutzung, Bearbeitung und Weiterverbreitung durch Andere ohne oder mit geringfügigen Einschränkungen erlaubt."[17] Sie stellen eine gute Ausgangsbasis dar, falls bereits vorhandenes Material wiederverwendet werden soll. OER können in ihrer Originalform entsprechend der jeweiligen Lizenz genutzt, aber auch weiterentwickelt werden. Ebenfalls gibt es unterschiedliche Ebenen, auf denen Material nachgenutzt werden kann, dies reicht von kurzen Texteinheiten, über Lehrvideos bis hin zu ganzen Kursen[18], die in die eigenen Trainings integriert werden können. Hierbei sollten die Anforderungen an OER beachtet werden. Wenn Materialien entwickelt[19] werden, ist es im Sinne der Open Science und Open Education zentral, diese unter einer entsprechenden freien Lizenz zu veröffentlichen, um eine Nachnutzung zu erlauben.

Bewerbung der Schulungsmaßnahmen verankern

- Welche Personen oder Organisationseinheiten sind für die Kommunikation und Öffentlichkeitsarbeit zuständig und können bei der Bewerbung unterstützen?
- Welche internen und externen Kommunikationskanäle stehen zur Verfügung?
- Welche von diesen eignen sich für die Zielgruppe?

Sobald ein neues Schulungsangebot entwickelt wurde, ist eine entsprechende Bewerbung bei den ausgewählten Zielgruppen für den Erfolg entscheidend. Im ersten Schritt ist dabei eine Überprüfung der zur Verfügung stehenden internen und externen Möglichkeiten wesentlich. Dabei können die formal Zuständigen wie Marketing- und Öffentlichkeitsarbeitsabteilungen der Organisationseinheit kontaktiert oder Kontakt zu Personen hergestellt werden, die mit den Zielgruppen vertraut sind. So können wertvolle Tipps für die Bewerbung gesammelt werden und die Schulung in übergreifende Schulungskonzepte verankert oder auch informell be-

17 Definition laut der UNESCO Pariser Erklärung zu OER (2012): https://unesdoc.unesco.org/ark:/48223/pf0000246687_ger

18 In Abschnitt 2.5 befindet sich eine aufbereitete Liste zu nachnutzbaren Kursen im Kontext der Repositorien-Nutzung, falls Repositorienmanager:innen trotz knapper Ressourcen auf bereits existierende Angebote hinweisen möchten.

19 Weitere Informationen zur Erstellung von OER unter https://www.openeducation.at/erstellen/

worben werden. Es kann sich dabei beispielsweise um interne Personalentwicklungsangebote für Mitarbeiter:innen oder Doktorand:innenzentren und Doctoral Schools für PhD-Studierende handeln[20]. Ebenfalls sollten neue Schulungsangebote zu Repositorien in Teaching Library-Konzepte einfließen. Mögliche interne und externe Kommunikationskanäle für die Bewerbung stellen E-Mail, Newsletter, Mailinglisten, Social Media, Webseiten, Intranet und thematisch relevante Veranstaltungen dar[21].

2.3. Erprobungsphase

Mit der abgeschlossenen Planungsphase kann das neue Schulungsangebot erprobt werden. Dabei werden hier einige Aspekte, die bei der Durchführung zu beachten sind, besprochen. Weiters werden Möglichkeiten zur Evaluation und Anpassung von Schulungen aufgezeigt.

Schulungsmaßnahme durchführen

- Sind alle notwendigen Rahmenbedingungen (z. B. Personal, (virtueller) Raum, Technik, Materialien, Anmeldung der Teilnehmer:innen, Tools, Verpflegung etc.) für die Durchführung geschaffen?
- Wurde eine Probeschulung bzw. ein Technik-Check (je nach Bedarf) durchgeführt?

Die Schulung ist geplant und für die erste Durchführung bereit. Zu diesem Zeitpunkt lohnt sich eine genaue Prüfung aller wichtigen Rahmenbedingungen. Der (virtuelle) Raum muss gebucht sein, das zuständige Personal sollte feststehen und bereit sein. Die Trainer:innen sollten mit allen technischen Lösungen wie Video-Konferenztools oder Projektoren, die verwendet werden wollten, vertraut sein und diese mehrmals im Vorfeld getestet haben. Neben den Tools sollten auch alle Materialien wie Präsentationsfolien, Feedbackbögen oder Handouts auf Vollständigkeit geprüft werden. Nicht zuletzt sollten die Anmeldungen der Teilnehmenden kontrolliert werden und alle wichtigen Informationen zur Vorbereitung bzw. dem Kurs an sie rechtzeitig im Voraus über passende Kanäle kommuniziert werden.

Tipp: Die angemeldeten Personen können im Voraus nach ihrem Fachgebiet und ihrer Motivation, am Kurs teilzunehmen, gefragt werden. So kann gegebenenfalls eine bedarfsgerechte Spezifizierung des Angebots vorgenommen werden!

20 Vgl. Schmidt, B. et al. (2016), S. 6.
21 Vgl. Helbig, K. (2021), S. 248.

Wenn Repositorienmanager:innen über wenig Erfahrung in der Abhaltung von Kursen verfügen oder eine neue Methode bzw. ein neues Tool zum ersten Mal ausprobieren möchten, kann darüber hinaus ein Probelauf der Schulung in der kompletten oder verkürzten Form bei der Vorbereitung helfen. Dabei kann die geplante Schulung mit Vertreter:innen der relevanten Zielgruppen oder mit Kolleg:innen durchgeführt werden. Idealerweise sollten im Voraus sinnvolle Möglichkeiten, welche Art von Feedback für sie hilfreich wäre, überlegt werden. Diese sollten an die Teilnehmenden des Probelaufs kommuniziert werden. Es kann dabei beispielsweise eine einfache Matrix[22] zur Anwendung kommen:

Probelauf **Peer Feedback Matrix**	Form (Präsentationsfolien, Präsentationsstil, Tools etc.)	Inhalt (konkret behandelte Themen)
Positiv		
Verbesserungswürdig (inkl. Verbesserungsvorschläge)		

Nun kann die Schulung zum ersten Mal durchgeführt werden.

Angebot evaluieren

- Wie wird das Angebot evaluiert, um die Qualität und Relevanz der Schulung langfristig zu sichern?
- Wie wird Feedback der Teilnehmenden gesammelt?
- Wie wird der Bedarf der Zielgruppen erhoben?

Schulungsangebote sollten regelmäßig und kontinuierlich auf Qualität, Relevanz und Auswirkungen auf die Nutzung weiterer Services überprüft werden. Dabei sollte bereits bei der Planung eines neuen Angebots festgehalten werden, wie dieses evaluiert wird. Relevant sind hier interne Standards und Richtlinien beispielsweise bezüglich der minimalen Anzahl an Teilnehmer:innen, die eine Durchführung rechtfertigt. Darüber hinaus können sich Repositorienmanager:innen selbst Kriterien überlegen, anhand derer sie den Erfolg der Schulung überprüfen werden, z. B.: Ist die Nutzung des Repositoriums gestiegen? Haben die Teilnehmenden nach dem Kurs Kontakt zu der durchführenden Stelle aufgenommen, um weitere Fragen zu klären?

Feedback von Teilnehmenden stellt einen wichtigen Aspekt der Evaluation dar und kann bei der Weiterentwicklung helfen. Das Sammeln von Rückmeldungen kann entweder synchron während des Trainings oder asynchron nach dem Kurs stattfin-

22 Adaptiert von dem Carpentries-Instructor-Training-Curriculum, Lizenz: CC-BY 4.0: https://carpentries.github.io/instructor-training/11-practice-teaching/

den. Trainer:innen sollten sich über die etablierten Möglichkeiten an ihrer Einrichtung – wie einheitliche Fragebögen – informieren. Diese können auch durch weitere Methoden wie die Erstellung einer Wordcloud, eine Blitzlichtrunde oder den Einsatz von Reaktionen/Emoticons direkt im Video-Konferenztool ergänzt werden.

Um die Bedürfnisse der Zielgruppen richtig einzuschätzen, sind gezielte Bedarfserhebungen wichtig. Beispielsweise können die Themen und häufige Fragen aus der Beratungs- und Schulungspraxis systematisch erfasst werden, um mögliche Wissenslücken oder Trends zu identifizieren. Qualitative oder quantitative Bedarfserhebungen in Form von Umfragen oder Interviews können ebenfalls wertvolle Erkenntnisse liefern. Diese können entweder selbst durchgeführt werden oder im Rahmen von größeren Befragungen der Serviceeinrichtung oder Institution inkludiert werden.

Anpassungen vornehmen

- Auf welchen Ebenen müssen Anpassungen vorgenommen werden (z. B. Präsentationsfolien, Bewerbung, Konferenz-Tool)?
- Wie kann auf die wachsenden/sich ändernden Bedürfnisse der Teilnehmenden bei der Weiterentwicklung adäquat reagiert werden?

Um das Schulungsangebot aktuell und bedarfsgerecht zu halten, sind Anpassungen und Aktualisierungen in (un)regelmäßigen Abständen wichtig. Die konkreten Impulse können aus dem gesammelten Feedback, den wachsenden Praxiserfahrungen mit der Durchführung, Änderungen im institutionellen Repositorium oder auch durch diverse Vorgaben der Forschungseinrichtungen kommen. Wichtig ist dabei zu beachten, auf welcher Ebene eine Anpassung notwendig ist und welche weiteren Personen und/oder Abteilungen betroffen sind. Beispielsweise können die Präsentationsfolien von Autor:innen direkt bearbeitet werden, während für eine bessere Bewerbung Kolleg:innen von der Öffentlichkeitsarbeit inkludiert werden sollten. Weiters empfiehlt es sich, den Bedarf der Zielgruppen an Informationen und Fähigkeiten z. B. im Bereich Green-Open Access oder Archivierung von Forschungsdaten zu beobachten. Die Zielgruppen können in die Weiterentwicklung und Aktualisierung von Schulungen eingebunden werden ebenso wie Personengruppen, die mit den Zielgruppen in engem Kontakt sind (z. B. Lehrende aus einschlägigen Lehrveranstaltungen bei der Zielgruppe Studierende).

2.4. Zielgruppenorientierte Einsatzszenarien aus der Praxis

Die Konzeption und Durchführung von Workshops und Schulungen gehört bei vielen Repositorienmanager:innen zu ihrem Alltag. Es kann sich dabei um praktische Anleitungen zu konkreten Repositorien und Datenarchiven handeln, die die eigene Institution betreibt oder zur Nutzung empfiehlt, oder um Kurse zu verwandten Themen, die mit der Verwendung von Repositorien einhergehen (wie Open Access, Open Research, Publikationsstrategien sowie Forschungsdatenmanagement).

Es werden nun drei ausgewählte Beispiele von Training im Kontext des institutionellen Repositoriums der Universität Wien geschildert, die aus dem Schulungsangebot des Forschungsdatenmanagement-Teams stammen. Diese können als Anregung für die Planung von Schulungsmaßnahmen dienen. Das Team setzt sich aus Mitarbeiter:innen der Universitätsbibliothek und des Zentralen Informatikdienstes zusammen. Die synchronen Kurse werden von jeweils zwei bis drei Hauptvortragenden vor Ort oder virtuell in einem Videokonferenztool abgehalten. Eine zusätzliche Person ist für die Betreuung des Chats und für den technischen Support zuständig.

Die folgenden ausgewählten Beispiele decken drei unterschiedliche Zielgruppen ab: Studierende auf Masterniveau, Doktorand:innen und Wissenschaftler:innen. Thematisch sind diese ebenso unterschiedlich verortet, sodass die Themenfelder Forschungsdatenmanagement sowie die praktische Einführung in das institutionelle Repositorium abgedeckt werden.

Forschungsdatenmanagement für Masterstudierende

Zielgruppe: Masterstudierende der Biologie

Dauer: ca. 4 Stunden Selbststudium

Teilnehmer:innenzahl: unbegrenzt

Format: E-Learning Kurs im Selbststudium (unbetreut)

Verwendete Tools: Moodle, Articulate

Sprache: Englisch

Kursbeschreibung: Der Kurs umfasst eine Einführung zum Thema Forschungsdatenmanagement mit einem besonderen Augenmerk auf die aktive Forschungsphase bei der Masterarbeit. Der Fokus liegt dabei auf Datenmanagement als Teil der guten wissenschaftlichen Praxis, der Organisation und Dokumentation von Daten, Open Science Praktiken und ethischen Aspekten von Data Sharing. Der Kurs ist in vier aufeinander aufbauende Abschnitte aufgeteilt: Einführung zum Forschungsdatenmanagement (1), Daten dokumentieren (2), Daten organisieren und beschreiben (3), Ethische Aspekte (4). Weiters wird auch auf die Vorteile der Nutzung von Repositorien eingegangen. Es werden interaktive spielerische Elemente wie Computer-Spiele, Quizze oder das Sortieren von Karten eingesetzt.

Angebot: Dieser Kurs wird als eine optionale Teilleistung im Rahmen einer Lehrveranstaltung für Masterstudierende der Biologie angeboten.

Einführung in das Forschungsdatenmanagement für Doktorand:innen

Zielgruppe: PhD-Studierende aus allen Disziplinen (besonders Angehörige der Universität Wien)

Dauer: 2 Stunden

Teilnehmer:innenzahl: 20 Personen

Vortragende: 2-3 Mitarbeiter:innen der Universitätsbibliothek und des Zentralen Informatikdienstes

Format: (virtueller) Workshop mit Impulsvorträgen und interaktiven Aktivitäten

Verwendete Tools: Moodle inklusive weiterer Funktionen wie H5P, Etherpad oder Wordcloud; Video-Konferenz-Tools wie BigBlueButton oder Zoom, anonyme Umfragen

Sprache: Deutsch, Englisch

Kurzbeschreibung: Dieser Kurs besteht aus einer Einführung zum Thema Forschungsdatenmanagement und Langzeitarchivierung sowie einer Vorstellung der Repositorien und unterstützenden Services, die die Universität Wien anbietet. Der Fokus liegt dabei auf praxisnahen Inhalten und Tipps. Im Sinne des „Flipped Classroom“-Konzeptes lernen die Teilnehmenden das Thema Forschungsdatenmanagement bereits vor dem Kurs in einem kurzen Video kennen. Der Workshopaufbau orientiert sich am Lebenszyklus von Forschungsdaten und den FAIR-Prinzipien. Der Großteil des Kurses vermittelt Kenntnisse für die aktive Forschungsarbeit: Dateibenennung, Ordnerstrukturen, Dokumentation, Metadaten und Datensicherung. Weiters lernen Studierende, wie sie ihre Daten archivieren und veröffentlichen können. Kurze Impulsvorträge werden zur Aktivierung der Teilnehmenden durch interaktive Elemente wie Umfragen und Gruppendiskussionen ergänzt. Die Studierenden können ihre Kompetenzen in einem weiteren Kurs „Forschungsdatenmanagement für Doktorand:innen: Tipps und Tricks“ vertiefen.

Angebot: Diese Fortbildung für PhD-Studierende der Universität Wien wird über das Doktorand:innenzentrum angeboten.

Praktische Einführung in das Repositorium PHAIDRA

Zielgruppe: Wissenschaftler:innen aus allen Disziplinen und allgemeines Personal (Angehörige der Universität Wien)

Dauer: 2-3 Stunden

Teilnehmer:innenzahl: 12 Personen

Vortragende: 2-3 Mitarbeiter:innen der Universitätsbibliothek

Format: (virtueller) Workshop

Verwendete Tools: Moodle-Kurs, Video-Konferenz-Tools BigBlueButton oder Zoom, anonyme Umfragen, PHAIDRA-Sandbox (Testsystem)

Sprache: Deutsch, Englisch

Kurzbeschreibung: In einem praktischen Workshop lernen die Teilnehmenden die wesentlichen Funktionen von PHAIDRA, dem institutionellen Repositorium der Universität Wien, kennen. Es werden in einer Eröffnungsdiskussion die Themen und Projekte der Teilnehmenden besprochen, die sie zur Teilnahme motiviert haben. Es werden sowohl die Suche als auch der gesamte Hochladeprozess Schritt-für-Schritt durchgespielt. Die Teilnehmenden können entweder zuschauen oder selber in der PHAIDRA-Sandbox[23]-Testumgebung die Schritte ausprobieren. Die kurzen Input-Abschnitte werden mit F&A-Blöcken ergänzt. Weiters bekommen die Teilnehmenden Links zu schriftlichen Anleitungen[24] zu den besprochenen Themen. Die Interaktion mit den Teilnehmenden wird darüber hinaus durch den Einsatz von Umfragen, z. B. zur Frage, für welche Objekte (wie Forschungsdaten oder Publikationen) das Repositorium hauptsächlich genutzt werden sollte, ergänzt.

Angebot: Diese Fortbildung für Mitarbeiter:innen der Universität Wien wird über die Kursdatenbank der universitätsinternen Personalentwicklung angeboten.

---

23 https://datamanagement.univie.ac.at/ueber-phaidra-services/phaidra-systeme/phaidra-sandbox-testseite/

24 https://datamanagement.univie.ac.at/ueber-phaidra-services/downloads-und-anleitungen/

2.5. Wenn Ressourcen knapp sind ...

Wenn zurzeit kein eigenes Schulungsangebot entwickelt werden kann, der Bedarf der Mitarbeiter:innen an Informationen und Training dennoch festzustellen ist, empfiehlt es sich, zumindest auf ausgewählte externe Angebote zu verweisen und diese an der eigenen Einrichtung zu bewerben. Eine Auswahl an relevanten kostenlosen E-Learning-Kursen und virtuellen Veranstaltungen:

Open Science, Open Research

- **FOSTER Open Science**[25]-Kurse (Englisch, Spanisch): Eine Plattform des abgeschlossenen EU-Projektes „FOSTER" mit E-Learning-Kursen zu verschiedenen Open-Science- und Forschungsdatenmanagement-Themen, die entweder direkt dort absolviert oder als SCORM-Pakete in die E-Learning-Lösung an der eigenen Einrichtung eingebettet werden können. Die Kurse werden derzeit auf die neue Training-Plattform „OpenPlato"[26] von OpenAIRE migriert (Stand Dezember 2022).

Forschungsdaten und -management

- Webinarreihe **„Forschungsdatenmanagement in Österreich"**[27] (Deutsch, Englisch) wurde von dem Projekt FAIR Data Austria[28], dem RepManNet und dem FWF 2020 gestartet. In 1-bis-2-stündigen Webinaren werden dort verschiedene Aspekte des Forschungsdatenmanagements behandelt und die Aufnahmen zur Nachnutzung bereitgestellt[29].
- E-Learning-Kurs **„Research Data Management"** (Englisch)[30] vermittelt in ca. einer Stunde die Grundlagen des Forschungsdatenmanagements inklusive der FAIR-Prinzipien und Datenmanagementpläne. Der Kurs wurde von dänischen Universitäten entwickelt.
- **Spielerische Zugänge**[31] (Englisch): virtueller Data Horror Escape Room[32], Research Data Management Adventure Game[33] oder ReproJuice[34] – ein Spiel zum Thema „Reproduzierbarkeit".

---

25 https://www.fosteropenscience.eu/
26 https://openplato.eu/
27 https://forschungsdaten.at/fda/materialien/
28 https://forschungsdaten.at/fda/
29 Videoaufzeichnungen und Präsentationsfolien im Repositorium Phaidra: https://hdl.handle.net/11353/10.1168881 bzw. auf YouTube: https://www.youtube.com/channel/UC6UGkAxSQDhL8fQ0WT48Icw
30 https://doi.org/10.11581/dtu:00000047
31 Siehe Capdarest-Arest, N. et al. (2019)
32 https://sites.google.com/vu.nl/datahorror/home
33 https://library.bath.ac.uk/research-data/training-advice-contact/rdm-adventure-game
34 https://reprojuice.gamelab.tbm.tudelft.nl/

Rechtliche Aspekte

- **„Rechtlich sicher forschen"**[35] (Deutsch) ist ein MOOC der Universität Wien, in dem in 8 Stunden Selbststudium für die Forschung in Österreich relevante rechtliche Themen, unter anderem datenschutzrechtliche, urheberrechtliche und vertragsrechtliche Fragen, erläutert werden.
- **„Rechtlich sicher publizieren"**[36] (Deutsch) ist ein weiterer MOOC der Universität Wien, in dem sich Teilnehmende in 8 Stunden Selbststudium mit rechtlichen Herausforderungen beim wissenschaftlichen Publizieren auseinandersetzen.

Diese Kurse können mit lokalen Beratungsangeboten oder offenen F&A-Sessions ergänzt werden, um allgemeine Inhalte mit lokalen Repositorienlösungen besser zu verbinden.

3. Train-the-Trainer

Die eigenen Kompetenzen in der Konzeption und Durchführung von Schulungen können neben der praktischen Erfahrung durch formale und informelle Weiterbildung gestärkt werden. Dabei können Repositorienmanager:innen thematisch-relevanten Netzwerken beitreten und Fortbildungen oder Zertifikatskurse absolvieren.

3.1. Netzwerke für den Austausch innerhalb der Community

Die Relevanz von Schulungs- und Fortbildungsmaßnahmen im Bereich Open Science äußert sich auch durch die zunehmende Anzahl von Initiativen und Netzwerken zum Austausch und Teilen von Erfahrungen und Expertise in diesem Bereich. Besonders Einsteiger:innen im Bereich „Training" können sich durch ihre Teilnahme an solchen Initiativen neues Wissen und neue Fähigkeiten auf einer informellen Art und Weise aneignen. Es wird häufig institutions- und landesunabhängig an Lösungen für gemeinsame Probleme gearbeitet. Die Teilnahme an öffentlichen Workshops und Konferenzen kann ebenso zur Erwerbung weiterer Kompetenzen beitragen.

35 https://imoox.at/course/RESIFO
36 https://imoox.at/course/RESIPU

Ausgewählte Netzwerke und Initiativen im D-A-CH Bereich:

- **Die VÖB-Kommission Informationskompetenz**[37] ist ein österreichweites Netzwerk von Bibliothekar:innen, die im Bereich der Vermittlung der Informationskompetenz tätig sind. Auch ohne Mitgliedschaft kann das hilfreiche „Starter Pack – Informationskompetenz für Teaching Librarians"[38] verwendet werden, um Schulungen zu entwickeln.
- **DINI/nestor UAG Schulungen/Fortbildung**[39] (Teil der DINI/nestor AG Forschungsdaten): Autor:innen des Train-the-Trainer-Programmes zum Thema Forschungsdatenmanagement (siehe 4.2) und der Lernzielmatrix zum Themenbereich Forschungsdatenmanagement (siehe 2.1). Treffen: monatlich
- **Netzwerk Tutorials in Bibliotheken**[40]: Ein Netzwerk für Beschäftigte aus Bibliotheken, die Interesse an der Erstellung von Tutorials wie Educasts haben. Treffen: monatlich

3.2. Möglichkeiten der Weiterbildung für das Schulungspersonal

Über formale Weiterbildungsmaßnahmen können ebenso relevante Kenntnisse für die eigene Schulungspraxis erworben werden. Dabei lohnt es sich, zunächst die Angebote der internen Personalentwicklung der eigenen Einrichtung im Bereich der Hochschuldidaktik und Kommunikation genau zu prüfen. Hier können besonders Kurse der Teaching-and-Learning-Zentren sowie die Personalentwicklungsabteilung in Betracht gezogen werden, da diese oft kostenlose oder vergünstigte Alternativen bieten. Auch Kurse zum Ausbau der Präsentationskompetenzen oder zum Umgang mit digitalen Kommunikationstools können für die Abhaltung von Schulungen behilflich sein. Im deutschsprachigen Raum stehen neben Studiengängen auch kostenpflichtige Zertifikatskurse (Dauer 1-2 Semester) oder kürzere Fortbildungen zur Verfügung.

37 http://www.informationskompetenz.or.at/
38 http://www.informationskompetenz.or.at/index.php/ik-praktisch/starter-pack
39 https://www.forschungsdaten.org/index.php/UAG_Schulungen/Fortbildungen
40 http://www.informationskompetenz.de/index.php/ik-praxis/netzwerk-tutorials/

Eine Auswahl an Fortbildungsangeboten (Stand März 2022):

- Zertifikatskurse
    - **Certificate of Advanced Studies (CAS) Bibliothekspädagogik[41].** Der CAS besteht aus drei Modulen des Masterstudiums Bibliotheks- und Informationsmanagements an der Hochschule der Medien in Stuttgart: Teaching Library, Lernort Bibliothek und Bibliothekspädagogik. Die Module können auch einzeln belegt werden.
      Dauer: 540 Zeitstunden, 18 ECTS
      Teilnahmegebühr: 2100 Euro
    - **Zertifikatskurs „E-Learning für Bibliotheken"[42].** Der Kurs der TH Köln vermittelt Grundlagen der Didaktik, sowie die Möglichkeiten bei der Erstellung von E-Learning-Angeboten.
      Dauer: 10 Monate, 8 ECTS
      Teilnahmegebühr: 1900 rein virtuell bzw. 2210 Euro hybrid
- Fortbildungen
    - **Wie vermitteln wir Informationskompetenz?** Didaktische Kompetenzen für die Vermittlung von Informationskompetenz[43]. Die Weiterbildung der Freien Universität Berlin vermittelt didaktische Grundlagen und verschiedene Methoden zur Konzeption und Durchführung von Schulungen.
      Dauer: 2 Tage
      Teilnahmegebühr: 250 Euro
    - **Train-the-Trainer der Österreichischen Agentur für wissenschaftliche Integrität[44] (ÖAWI).** Ein Kurs zu didaktischen Methoden und den Prinzipien guter wissenschaftlicher Praxis.
      Dauer: 2 Tage
      Teilnahmegebühr: Für Mitgliedsorganisationen kostenfrei

41 https://www.hdm-weiterbildung.de/zertifikatskurse/cas-bibliothekspaedagogik
42 https://www.th-koeln.de/weiterbildung/zertifikatskurs-e-learning-fuer-bibliotheken_75606.php
43 https://veranstaltung.weiterbildung.fu-berlin.de/Veranstaltung/importJPVeranstaltung60d2da977d365.html
44 https://oeawi.at/training-train-the-trainer/

- **Train-the-Trainer-Workshop für Open-Access-Multiplikator:innen[45].** Im Kurs werden didaktische Kompetenzen besonders für Open-Access-Beauftragte vermittelt.
  Dauer: 2 Halbtage
  Teilnahmegebühr: kostenfrei
- **Train-the-Trainer-Programm zum Thema Forschungsdatenmanagement[46].** In der im Rahmen des FDMentor-Projektes entwickelten Fortbildung werden die Grundlagen des Forschungsdatenmanagements erarbeitet und didaktische Kompetenzen erworben.
  Dauer: 2 Tage
  Teilnahmegebühr: von der durchführenden Organisation abhängig
- **Carpentries Instructor Training[47].** Den Teilnehmenden wird im Kurs eine Einführung zur Didaktik, der Methode des Live Coding und die Curricula der internationalen Carpentries Initiative nähergebracht.
  Dauer: 2 Tage
  Teilnahmegebühr: kostenfrei mit einer Wartezeit bzw. kostenpflichtig mit diversen Mitgliedschaftsstufen[48]
- **MOOC (Massive Open Online Course) „OER nutzen und erstellen“[49]:** Der E-Learning-Kurs gibt einen Überblick über theoretische Grundlagen und praktische Anwendungen von Open Educational Resources.
  Dauer: 8 Stunden Selbststudium
  Teilnahmegebühr: kostenfrei

45 https://open-access.network/fortbilden/train-the-trainer-workshop
46 https://doi.org/10.5281/zenodo.5773203
47 https://carpentries.org/become-instructor/
48 https://carpentries.org/membership/
49 https://imoox.at/course/oermooc

4. Zusammenfassung

Um bei den Zielgruppen der Forschenden, Lehrenden aber auch Studierenden ein gesamtheitliches Wahrnehmen von Open Science zu fördern, welches sich u. a. in einem reflektierten Umgang mit dem jeweiligen institutionellen Repositorium äußert, treten Schulungen aus dem bibliothekarischen Umfeld an eine zentrale Stelle. Diese Weiterbildungsmaßnahmen können beispielsweise in die Nutzung von Repositorien einführen, sowie Einblicke in im Forschungs- und Lehrbetrieb relevante Themen wie Open Access, Open Research oder Management und Archivierung von Forschungsdaten bieten. Repositorienmanager:innen können außerdem in den Austausch mit Zielgruppen treten und somit die Nutzung des institutionellen Repositoriums steigern, Services bewerben und regelmäßiges Feedback bekommen, das zur Weiterentwicklung genutzt werden kann.

In diesem Beitrag wurde ein praxisorientierter Leitfaden für die Planung von Schulungskonzepten dargestellt, der als Grundlage für die Entwicklung von Schulungsmaßnahmen dienen kann, um Nutzer:innen von Repositorien auf unterschiedlichen Ebenen bestmöglich zu unterstützen. Hierbei empfiehlt es sich, die Schulungsentwicklung anhand drei Phasen abzuhandeln: Vorbereitung, Planung, Durchführung. Der ausgearbeitete Leitfaden behandelt die Vorbereitungsphase – Bedarfsermittlung der Zielgruppen, Formulierung von Lernzielen und Ressourcen-Check. Darauf folgt die Planungsphase der Trainingseinheit(en) – Erstellung eines zielgruppenorientierten Qualifizierungsangebots, Erstellung oder Nachnutzung von begleitenden Materialien und Bewerbung des Angebots. Zuletzt steht die Erprobungsphase des entwickelten Schulungskonzepts – Durchführung der geplanten Schulung, Evaluierung und Anpassung des Angebots. Neben didaktischen Grundprinzipien, stellen so u. a. Zielgruppenanforderungen und vorhandene bzw. nachnutzbare Ressourcen Parameter dar, die die jeweiligen zu entwickelnden Schulungskonzepte maßgeblich beeinflussen.

Beispielhaft wurden ebenso Trainingsmaßnahmen aus dem bibliothekarischen Umfeld der Universität Wien präsentiert, die die unterschiedlichen Zielgruppen wie Studierende auf Masterniveau, Doktorand:innen und Wissenschaftler:innen im Allgemeinen abdecken.

Bibliografie

Anderson, Lorin W.; Krathwohl, David R. (2021): A Taxonomy for Learning, Teaching, and Assessing. A Revision of Bloom's Taxonomy of Educational Objectives. New York: Longman.

Bloom, Benjamin Samuel et. al. (1956): Taxonomy of Educational Objectives. The Classification of Educational Goals. Handbook 1. Cognitive Domain. New York: David McKay Company, Inc.

Blumesberger, Susanne (2018): Der Umgang mit Requirements-Engineering an wissenschaftlichen Bibliotheken. Young Information Scientist 3, S. 37-51. https://doi.org/10.25365/yis-2018-3-4

Blumesberger, Susanne (2021): PHAIDRA-Services an der Universität Wien. Mehr als Repositorienmanagement. In: Sustainability of Science in a Post-Covid World. Wien: IfII Institut für Intellektuelle Integration. https://hdl.handle.net/11353/10.1382635

Capdarest-Arest, Nicole et al. (2019): "Game On!" Teaching Gamification Principles for Library Instruction to Health Sciences Information Professionals Using Interactive, Low-Tech Activities and Design Thinking Modalities. In: JMLA Journal of the Medical Library Association 107 (4), pp.567-571. https://doi.org/10.5195/jmla.2019.636

Engelhardt, Claudia et al. (2021): D7.4 How to Be FAIR with Your Data. A Teaching and Training Handbook for Higher Education Institutions. https://doi.org/10.5281/zenodo.5787046

Hartmann, Werner (2016): Förderung von Informationskompetenz durch E-Learning: Wie viel Technik soll es sein? In: Handbuch Informationskompetenz. 2., überarbeitete Auflage. Berlin, Boston: De Gruyter, S. 127–136. https://doi.org/10.1515/9783110403367-014

Helbig, Kerstin (2021): Schulungs- und Beratungskonzepte. In: Praxishandbuch Forschungsdatenmanagement. Berlin, Boston: De Gruyter Saur, S. 239-253. https://doi.org/10.1515/9783110657807

Kalová, Tereza (2020): Metadaten für Forschungsdaten. Bedürfnisse und Anforderungen in den Naturwissenschaften. (Berliner Handreichungen zur Bibliotheks- und Informationswissenschaft 455). https://doi.org/10.18452/21536

McTighe, Jay; Wiggins, Grant (2005): Understanding by Design. Expanded 2nd edition. Alexandria, VA: Association for Supervision and Curriculum Development.

Petersen, Britta et al. (2022): Lernzielmatrix zum Themenbereich Forschungsdatenmanagement (FDM) für die Zielgruppen Studierende, PhDs und Data Stewards. Version 1. https://doi.org/10.5281/zenodo.7034478

Schmidt, Birgit et al. (2016): Stepping up Open Science Training for European Research. In: Publications 4 (2) 16. https://doi.org/10.3390/publications4020016

Seitter, Wolfgang (2019): Bedarfserfassung und Nachfrageorientierung in der wissenschaftlichen Weiterbildung. In: Handbuch Wissenschaftliche Weiterbildung. Wiesbaden: Springer Fachmedien, S. 315–328. https://doi.org/10.1007/978-3-658-17643-3_16

Tappenbeck, Inka (2016): Informationskompetenz im Wissenschaftssystem. In: Handbuch Informationskompetenz. 2., überarbeitete Auflage. Berlin, Boston: De Gruyter, S. 279–288. https://doi.org/10.1515/9783110403367-028

Claudia Hackl berät im Rahmen von „Open Education Austria Advanced“ – einem Digitalisierungsprojekt zur Schaffung attraktiver Lösungen für Open Educational Resources – als Projektmanagerin Hochschulen zur institutionellen Verankerung von Open Educational Resources. Ebenso ist sie Teil des Teams Digitale Lehre des Center for Teaching and Learning der Universität Wien, das mediendidaktische Qualifizierungs- und Unterstützungsangebote für Lehrende bietet.

Tereza Kalová arbeitet an der Universitätsbibliothek Wien als Data-Stewardship-Koordinatorin. Im Rahmen ihrer Tätigkeit beschäftigt sie sich mit der Konzeption und Durchführung von Trainingsangeboten zu Forschungsdatenmanagement und koordiniert den neuen Zertifikatskurs Data Steward.

Claudia Hackl, Christoph Ladurner, Andreas Parschalk, Julia Schindler, Markus Schmid, Raman Ganguly, Ortrun Gröblinger

An der Schnittstelle von E-Learning-Zentren, Zentralen IT-Services und Bibliotheken

Interdisziplinäre Zusammenarbeit zur Entwicklung einer nationalen Infrastruktur für Open Educational Resources (OER) aus dem österreichischen Hochschulraum

Handbuch Repositorienmanagement, Hg. v. Blumesberger et al., 2024, S. 329–352
https://doi.org/10.25364/978390337423218

Claudia Hackl, Universität Wien, Center for Teaching and Learning, claudia.hackl@univie.ac.at | ORCID iD: 0000-0002-0365-4400
Christoph Ladurner, TU Graz, Universitätsbibliothek, christoph.ladurner@tugraz.at | ORCID iD: 0000-0003-3653-7558
Andreas Parschalk, Universität Innsbruck, andreas.parschalk@uibk.ac.at | ORCID iD: 0000-0002-7114-1658
Julia Schindler, Universität Innsbruck, julia.schindler@uibk.ac.at | ORCID iD: 0000-0003-2957-2443
Markus Schmid | ORCID iD: 0000-0002-3952-7948
Raman Ganguly, Universität Wien, raman.ganguly@univie.ac.at | ORCID iD: 0000-0002-9837-0047
Ortrun Gröblinger, Universität Innsbruck, ortrun.groeblinger@uibk.ac.at | ORCID iD: 0000-0003-2982-3206

Zusammenfassung

Open Educational Resources (OER) etablieren sich in der Lehre aktuell analog zu offenen Praktiken in Wissenschaft und Forschung. Open Education Austria Advanced[1], ein Projekt österreichischer Universitäten, unterstützt diese Entwicklung mit dem gemeinsamen Aufbau eines Gesamtpakets für OER: der Ausbau lokaler OER-Repositorien und einer Meta-Suchmaschine (OERhub), sowie begleitende Maßnahmen wie Zertifizierung, Qualifizierung und der Wissenstransfer zwischen beteiligten und interessierten Hochschulen. Die erfolgreiche Umsetzung dieses Vorhabens bedingt die Zusammenarbeit von E-Learning-Zentren, Zentralen IT-Services und Bibliotheken. Der folgende Beitrag thematisiert die Arbeit an dieser Schnittstelle inklusive der unterschiedlichen Herangehensweisen und Anforderungen der Beteiligten.

Schlagwörter: Open Educational Resources; Schnittstellenarbeit; Open Science; Open Education; OER-Repositorien; Meta-Suchmaschine

Abstract

At the Intersection of E-Learning Centres, Central IT Services and Libraries. Interdisciplinary Cooperation for the Development of a National Infrastructure for Open Educational Resources (OER) in the Austrian Higher Education Area

Open educational resources (OER) are becoming established in the higher education area concurrently to open practices in science and research. Open Education Austria Advanced, a project of Austrian universities, supports this with the joint development of attractive solutions for OER: further development of local OER repositories and a meta search engine (OERhub), and accompanying measures such as certification, qualification and knowledge transfer between participating and interested universities. The successful implementation of this project requires an interdisciplinary team and the cooperation of e-learning centres, central IT services and libraries. The following contribution discusses the work at this intersection, including the different approaches and requirements of those involved.

Keywords: Open educational resources; interface work; open science; open education; OER repositories; meta search engine

1 Projekthomepage: http://www.openeducation.at

1. Einleitung

Analog zu institutionell bereits verankerten Aktivitäten im Bereich Open Access in der Forschung beginnen sich Open Educational Resources (OER – freie Bildungsressourcen) an Hochschulen zu etablieren. Diese stoßen bei Lehrenden, Studierenden und Leitungsebenen auf zunehmendes Interesse. Neben dem Kompetenzaufbau zur Verwendung und Erstellung von OER ist deren Verfügbarkeit und Auffindbarkeit von zentraler Bedeutung, um die Akzeptanz von OER nachhaltig zu sichern. Somit besteht die Anforderung, neben Publikationen und Forschungsdaten immer öfter auch Inhalte aus der Lehre langfristig verfügbar zu machen.

Open Educational Resources – offene Bildungsressourcen – als Ressourcen für das Lernen und Lehren mit möglichst offener Lizenzierung können nach der 5R-Typologie von Wiley (2014)[2] auf folgende Weisen genutzt werden: Einerseits können OER verwahrt und vervielfältigt werden (retain), aber auch direkt verwendet (reuse) und weiterverarbeitet (revise), somit auch vermischt (remix) und zuletzt verbreitet werden (redistribute).[3] Diese Freiheiten müssen bei der Verwendung von OER gewährleistet sein.[4]

In der EU-Open-Science Policy sind OER im Bereich der „Educational Skills" als eines der zentralen Ziele, die Forscher:innen beim Praktizieren von Open Science benötigen, verankert: "All scientists in Europe should have the necessary skills and support to apply open science research routines and practices"[5]. Das Etablieren dieser offenen Praktiken geht einher mit der digitalen Transformation des Hochschulsektors. Diese Open-Science-Praktiken umfassen Open Access, Open Data, Open Peer Review, Citizen Science und Open Education.[6]

Im Rahmen der aktuell durch das BMBWF geförderten Digitalisierungsprojekte[7] an öffentlichen Universitäten im Zeichen der digitalen und sozialen Transformation setzt das Projekt Open Education Austria Advanced auf die Zusammenführung der im österreichischen Hochschulraum produzierten OER durch den OERhub, der die nationale Meta-Suchmaschine für OER darstellt[8]. Kooperationspartner sind E-Learning-Zentren, Zentrale IT-Services und Universitätsbibliotheken der Projektpartner. Mit weiteren Initiativen zum Aufbau von technischen Infrastrukturen wird

2 Übersetzt von Muuß-Merholz (2015)
3 Vgl. Wiley, D. (2014)
4 Vgl. Muuß-Merholz, J. (2015)
5 European Commission (2021)
6 Vgl. O'Carroll, C.; Hyllseth, B. et al. (2017)
7 Weitere Informationen unter: https://pubshop.bmbwf.gv.at/index.php?article_id=9&sort=title&search%5Btext%5D=digitalisierungsvorhaben&pub=799
8 www.oerhub.at

u. a. mit Open Education Austria Advanced die EU-Open-Science Policy implementiert. So werden Repositorien für OER, Know-How z. B. im Umgang mit Metadaten oder Weiterbildungsangebote für das wissenschaftliche Personal von Seiten des Forschungsdatenmanagements aufgebaut. Es gilt, das Potenzial bereits intensiver Vorarbeiten beispielsweise des nationalen Netzwerks OANA (Open Science Network Austria)[9] und des interuniversitären Projekts e-Infrastructure Austria[10] zum koordinierten Aufbau von universitären Repositorien und Netzwerkstrukturen weiter zu entfalten.

Es wird im folgenden Beitrag ein Einblick in die Arbeit an der Schnittstelle zum Auf- und Ausbau der nationalen Infrastruktur für OER geboten. Daraufhin wird auf die Ebene der OER-Repositorien fokussiert. Es werden Anforderungen der unterschiedlichen Stakeholder einer Institution beleuchtet sowie zu beachtende Entscheidungsebenen aufgezeigt auf dem Weg zu einem institutionellen Repositorium, in das OER eingespeist werden. Darauf aufbauend wird beschrieben, wie eine Anbindung eines Repositoriums an den OERhub erfolgen kann und wie dieser funktioniert. Dieser Text richtet sich an Hochschulen, die ein institutionelles Repositorium für OER aufbauen und durch die Anbindung dieses an den OERhub ihre OER im österreichischen Hochschulraum sichtbar machen möchten. Dieser Weg wird stets aus den Perspektiven der unterschiedlichen Stakeholder beleuchtet: E-Learning-Zentren, zentrale IT-Services und Universitätsbibliotheken.

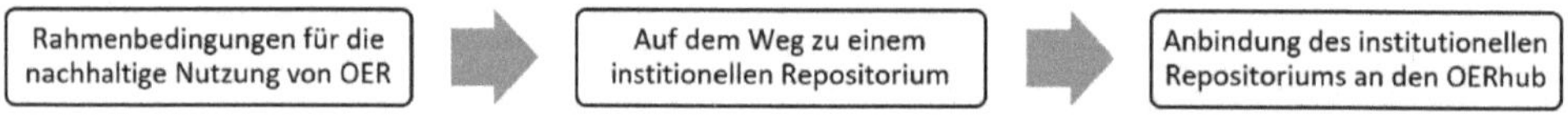

Abbildung 1: Von Rahmenbedingungen zu Anbindungen

9 https://www.oana.at
10 https://e-infrastructures.univie.ac.at/

2. Einblick in Rahmenbedingungen für nachhaltige Nutzung von OER

Im Folgenden findet sich ein kurzer Überblick über die sich im Rahmen des Projekts aktuell im Aufbau befindenden nationalen Lösungen für OER, die sogleich Rahmenbedingung für die nachhaltige Nutzung von OER im Kontext des österreichischen Hochschulraums darstellen.

Die technische Basis dieser nationalen Infrastruktur für OER im österreichischen Hochschulraum bildet die Weiterentwicklung des OERhub und der Aufbau lokaler Repositorien an den Partner-Hochschulen.

In diesem Kontext wurde bereits 2016 in der Roadmap „Open Educational Resources bis 2025“ darauf hingewiesen, dass es für Hochschulen notwendig ist, eine eigene OER-Strategie zu entwickeln, wenn das Thema national vorangebracht werden soll.[11] So arbeitet Open Education Austria Advanced einerseits an der Etablierung von Repositorien für OER bei allen am Projekt beteiligten Partner-Hochschulen, sowie andererseits an der Weiterentwicklung des OERhub.

Im Rahmen des Projekts wird nicht nur die Installation dieser lokalen Repositorien vollzogen, sondern auch deren Anbindung an die universitätseigenen Services, u. a. Learning-Management-Systeme, Benutzerverwaltung, Audio-Video-Portale etc. Hier begegnet das Projektteam der Herausforderung, dass die lokalen Infrastrukturen je nach Hochschule variieren und somit individuelle Setups entwickelt werden müssen. Ein Einblick in die unterschiedlichen Repositorien der Projektpartner, in denen OER archiviert werden:

Projektpartner	Repositorium im Einsatz
Universität Wien	PHAIDRA
Technische Universität Graz	TU Graz Repository (Invenio RDM)
Universität Graz	Edu-Sharing
Universität Innsbruck	Edu-Sharing

Der bereits 2016 im Projekt „Open Education Austria“ pilothaft gestartete OERhub stellt die zentrale OER-Meta-Suchmaschine für den österreichischen Hochschulraum dar, die einen offenen Zugang zu OER aus diesem schafft. Damals wurden erstmals E-Learning-Zentren, Bibliotheken und IKT-Services der Hochschulen als inneruniversitäre Dienstleistungen zur Implementierung des Fachportals (2020 umbenannt in OERhub) vernetzt.[12] Im Frühjahr 2020 wurde mit dem Projektstart

11 Vgl. Ebner, M.; Freisleben-Teutscher, C. F. et al (2016)
12 Vgl. Lingo, S.; Budroni, P. et al. (2019), S. 44.

von Open Education Austria Advanced die Arbeit am bereits entwickelten Prototyp fortgeführt.

Neben den technischen Aspekten der nationalen Infrastruktur stellen die Qualifizierung und Zertifizierung von Lehrenden und Hochschulen Arbeitsfelder von Open Education Austria Advanced dar. Gearbeitet wird zudem an einem Meta-OER-Erstellungsworkflow mit dem Ziel, gute Praxis in der Umsetzung von OER auf Lehrveranstaltungsebene offen zu legen und weiterzugeben.[13] Auch findet über die Projektlaufzeit hinweg ein durchgehender Wissenstransfer in die österreichischen Hochschulen an der Schnittstelle von Bibliotheken, Zentralen IT-Services und E-Learning-Zentren statt, der zur Sichtbarmachung und Nutzung von Synergien aus Open Science und Open Education beiträgt.

3. Anforderungen an ein OER-Repositorium

Im Kontext dieser sich im Ausbau befindenden nationalen technischen OER-Infrastruktur gilt es an den einzelnen Hochschulen, strategische Entscheidungen zu treffen. Nutzer:innen soll ein gut in die lokale Systemlandschaft integriertes, ansprechendes und nutzerfreundliches Repositorium zur Verfügung gestellt werden, in dem sie eigene OER publizieren und OER anderer Autor:innen finden und nutzen können.

Die grundlegenden Anforderungen an ein OER-Repositorium sind nahezu identisch zu Repositorien anderer Bereiche: In einer online zugänglichen Datenbank sollen Bildungsressourcen in unterschiedlichen Formaten mit möglichst aussagekräftigen Metadaten versehen, möglichst dauerhaft gespeichert und zur Anzeige bzw. zum Download zur Verfügung gestellt werden. Daten, die in OER-Repositorien vorgehalten werden, sollten laut den FAIR Prinzipien[14] für Open Access „auffindbar, zugänglich, interoperabel und wiederverwendbar“ sein. Wie für jedes Repositorium gelten die grundlegenden Anforderungen, welche im OAIS[15]-Referenzmodell ausführlich beschrieben sind.

13 Vgl. Breen-Wenninger, B.; Louis, B. (2020)
14 Weiterführende Informationen unter: https://www.openaire.eu/how-to-make-your-data-fair
15 Weiterführende Informationen unter: https://www.forschungsdaten.org/index.php/OAIS

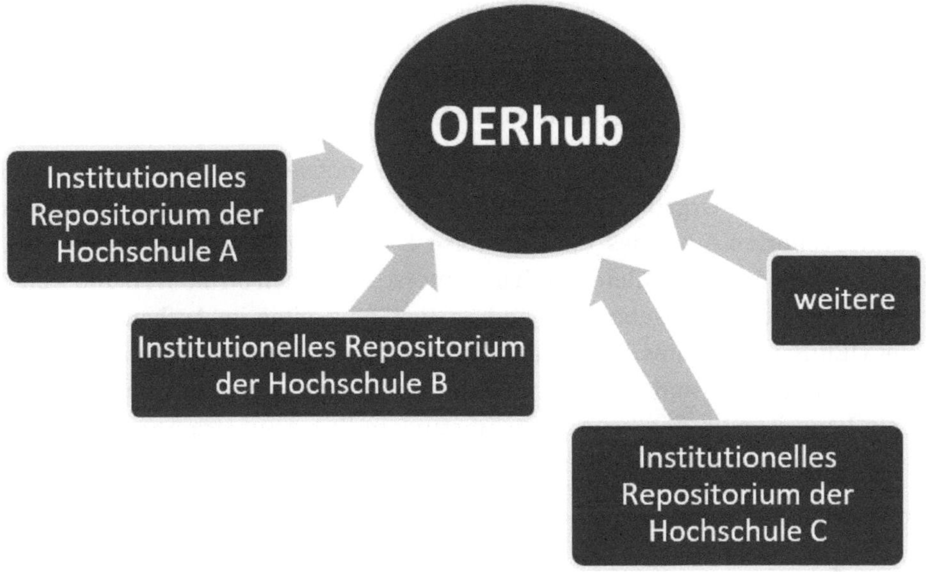

Abbildung 2: Anforderungen an ein institutionelles Repositorium

Der Vergleich zwischen den Anforderungen an Repositorien für Forschungsdaten und OER-Repositorien zeigt große Überschneidungen. Speziell hinsichtlich der Diversität der Formate der Materialien und der unterschiedlichen Metadaten in den verschiedenen Fächern und Fächergruppen sind die Anforderungen und auch Lösungen ähnlich. Bei der Archivierung von OER ist mit unterschiedlichsten Formaten zu rechnen: von einzelnen Arbeitsblättern im PDF-Format über interaktive Inhalte wie H5P[16], AV-Materialien, Tests im QTI-Standard[17] bis hin zu gesamten Kursen. Diese liegen in ebenso unterschiedlichen Archivformaten vor. Für manche dieser Formate existieren Viewer-Applikationen, welche in einem spezialisierten Repositorium für ein Preview der Materialien angeboten werden können. Wie die beispielhaft genannten Objekte nahelegen, ist auch die unterschiedliche Granularität der Objekte ähnlich der in Forschungsdatenrepositorien.

Im Metadatenbereich gibt es für Lernressourcen zwei verbreitete Standards: Learning Object Metadata (LOM)[18] und Learning Resource Metadata Initiative (LRMI)[19]. Die Verwendung von lernressourcenspezifischen Metadaten im eigenen

16 https://h5p.org/documentation/developers/h5p-specification
17 https://www.imsglobal.org/question/index.html
18 https://dini-ag-kim.github.io/hs-oer-lom-profil/latest/
19 http://lrmi.net/specifications/lrmi/

Repositorium ermöglicht es, Lernressourcen angemessen zu beschreiben. Die Definition eines repositoriumspezifischen Applikationsprofils, welches z. B. die verwendeten Taxonomien und kontrollierten Vokabularien klar beschreibt, erleichtert den Austausch mit anderen Repositorien und Metadaten-Hubs.

Die für Aufbau und Betrieb eines Repositoriums notwendigen Kompetenzen sind oft über mehrere Organisationseinheiten einer Institution verteilt. Im Falle von OER-Repositorien sind dies üblicherweise E-Learning-Zentren, Zentrale IT-Services und Bibliotheken. Allein durch die unterschiedlichen Strukturen und Abläufe an den Institutionen ergeben sich andere Zuständigkeiten im Aufbau und Betrieb eines OER-Repositoriums, wobei hier diese drei zentralen Bereiche im Zusammenspiel zu betrachten sind. Insbesondere bei der Formulierung der Anforderungen an ein Repositorium und bei der Abstimmung in Bezug auf strategische Entscheidungen sind ein intensiver Austausch und gute Kommunikation essentiell.

Ein Überblick der unterschiedlichen Anforderungen findet sich in der nachfolgenden Tabelle:

Anforderungen der		
E-Learning-Zentren	**Zentralen IT-Services**	**Universitätsbibliotheken**
nachhaltige Verankerung von OER in der Regellehre Weiterverwendung sowie didaktische Weiterentwicklung der freien Bildungsressourcen Services zur Unterstützung für Lehrende bei der Erstellung von OER: didaktische Beratung[20] niederschwellige Contentproduktion Sensibilisierung der Lehrenden für OER durch universitätsinterne Qualifizierungsangebote Schaffen von Zugängen zu den produzierten OER rechtliche Unterstützung der Lehrenden bei der Veröffentlichung von OER	Bereitstellen und Betreiben von zentralen IT-Infrastrukturen für die jeweils eigene Hochschule Planung, Schaffung, Sicherstellung und Koordination der Netz-, Kommunikations- und Rechnerinfrastruktur (IT-Infrastruktur) für Forschung, Lehre und Verwaltung Speicherung und Archivierung von Daten/OER Errichtung von entsprechender Infrastruktur für Forschung und Lehre → Repositorien[23] geeignete Software für ein Repositorium Integration des Repositoriums in die institutionelle Systemlandschaft	Publikationsberatung und -workflows Gewährleistung der Langzeitarchivierung von OER entsprechende Datenformate Standards bzw. Metadatenschemata (OER → LOM) Controlled Vocabularies, z. B. bezüglich der Verortung in einer Disziplin Verknüpfung der Services für Forschung und Lehre Infrastrukturen im Bereich des Forschungsdatenmanagements verantwortliche Data Stewards miteinbeziehen Open Education ↔ Open Access

20 Vgl. Lingo, S.; Budroni, P. et al. (2019), S. 48.

23 Exemplarisch wird hier auf den Abschlussbericht des Projekts e-Infrastructures Austria Plus verwiesen: Der Errichtung von Repositorien für Forschungsdaten kommt eine zentrale Bedeutung zu, denn hier können „Forschende [...] ihre Roh-/Masterdaten sichern und ihre aktiven, zitierfähigen und archivierten Forschungsdaten ablegen“. Siehe auch: Haselwanter, H.; Thöricht, H. (2019), S. 30.

(Creative Commons Lizenzen) [21] korrekte Darstellung der didaktisierten Lehr-/Lernmaterialien (u. a. Usability der Repositoriums und des OERhub) Diversität der OER: von Videos jeglicher Art, über Bilddateien und Textdokumente, bis hin zu ganzen Lernpfaden oder Learning-Management-System-Kursen oder gar MOOCs institutionelle OER-Policies[22]	Betrieb und Wartung des Repositoriums User:innenfreundliche Eingabemasken Auffindbarkeit der OER des lokalen Repositoriums in größeren Aggregatoren[24] Rechte- und Rollenmanagement Open Source ↔ Open Education	

4. Auf dem Weg zu lokalen OER-Repositorien: Entscheidungen auf verschiedenen Ebenen

Es sind also sehr unterschiedliche Stakeholder:innen, die unterschiedliche Anforderungen an ein Repositorium für OER herantragen: E-Learning-Zentren äußern den Wunsch nach guter Sichtbarkeit und Auffindbarkeit sowie der (Wieder-)Verwertbarkeit der gespeicherten Objekte, aus den Bibliotheken kommt die Forderung nach archivarischer Sorgfalt, angemessenen Metadaten und universalen Schnittstellen. Die Zentralen IT-Services hingegen bevorzugen gut in die Systemlandschaft integrierbare und nutzer:innenfreundliche Software.

21 Vgl. ebd., S. 48.

22 An der Karl-Franzens-Universität Graz gab es diese strategische Verankerung von OER im März 2020, an der Technischen Universität Graz im November 2020 sowie an der Universität Innsbruck im April 2022. Open Educational Resources Policy der Universität Graz: https://static.uni-graz.at/fileadmin/digitales-lehren-und-lernen/Dokumente/OER_Policy.pdf ; Richtlinie zu offenen Bildungsressourcen an der Technischen Universität Graz (OER-Policy): https://www.tu-graz.at/fileadmin/user_upload/tugrazExternal/02bfe6da-df31-4c20-9e9f-819251ecfd4b/2020_2021/Stk_5/RL_OER_Policy_24112020.pdf; Open Educational Resources Policy der Universität Innsbruck: https://www.uibk.ac.at/universitaet/mitteilungsblatt/2021-2022/32.html#h2-3

24 Vgl. Clements, K.; Pawlowski, J. M. et al (2014) S. 929-939.

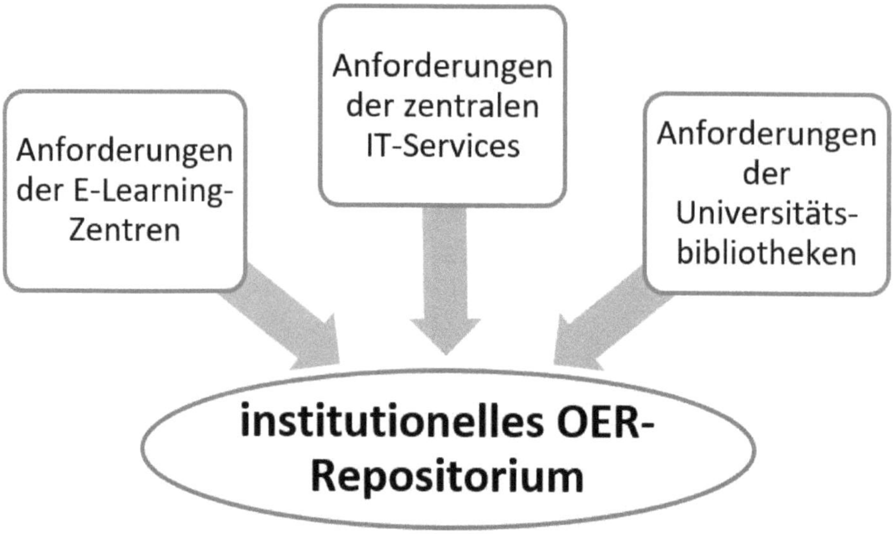

Abbildung 3: Entscheidungen auf dem Weg zu einem lokalen OER-Repositorium

Strategische Entscheidungen beeinflussen Anforderungen – nicht nur technischer Natur – an OER-Repositorien, welche großen Einfluss auf die technische Umsetzung, Wartung und den Betrieb derselben haben. So sind etwa die Wahl der Software und der Schnittstellen, die Art der Einbindung des Repositoriums in die Systemlandschaft, die gewünschten oder erwarteten Datentypen, die Abwägung der Rechte der Benutzer:innen und die Priorisierung der Ausfallsicherheit des Systems Faktoren, die sich sowohl auf organisatorischer Ebene als auch in der technischen Umsetzung niederschlagen. Idealerweise werden diese Entscheidungen gemeinsam von Techniker:innen und Repositorien-Manager:innen getroffen und die Verantwortlichkeit im Betrieb gemeinsam getragen. Die Ergebnisse dieser strategischen Überlegungen werden je nach Hochschule sehr unterschiedlich ausfallen, was aktuell sehr sichtbar ist an der vielfältigen Landschaft an OER-Repositorien, die im österreichischen Hochschulraum entsteht: „Da OER-Repositorien den individuellen Bedürfnissen einer Hochschule angepasst werden, entstehen sie lokal und sind dezentral organisiert.“[25]

Einige ausgewählte strategische Überlegungen, die es erlauben, unterschiedliche Schwerpunkte für das Repositorium zu setzen, sollen im Folgenden beleuchtet wer-

25 Vgl. Gröblinger, O.; Ganguly, R. et al. (2021), S. 39–44.

den. Da die verschiedenen Möglichkeiten miteinander vernetzt und teilweise voneinander abhängig sind, sind diese nie isoliert, sondern immer als Teil eines Systems zu betrachten.

Funktion	Intendierte Verwendung des Systems steht im Mittelpunkt der Entscheidung Bestimmung als Archiv: Objekte sollen gespeichert und auch nach einem längeren Zeitraum in einem funktionalen Format wiedergefunden werden können. Darstellung der Objekte nimmt nicht unbedingt zentrale Rolle ein. Repositorium als designierter Ort zur Präsentation: OER sollen veröffentlicht und präsentiert werden. Darstellung der Objekte spielt große Rolle. Möglichkeit, Objekte gut zitierbar (z. B. mit DOI versehen) anzubieten, wichtiger. Hier spielen möglicherweise auch Überlegungen zu Qualitätssicherung oder redaktionellen Abläufen eine Rolle (siehe Fokus Qualitätskriterien). Natürlich schließen sich die Funktion von Archiv und Publikationsplattform keinesfalls aus; es lohnt sich dennoch, die gewünschte Schwerpunktsetzung mit allen beteiligten Bereichen zu diskutieren.
Zielgruppe	Bezüglich geplanter Nutzungsszenarien und der grundsätzlichen Zugänglichkeit des Repositoriums kann u. a. eine Ausrichtung gewählt werden, die eher „nach innen“ – also hochschulintern – oder „nach außen“ – also im Sinne einer weltweiten Sharing-Plattform – orientiert ist. Zielgruppe – Lehrende der eigenen Hochschule: Anforderungen bezüglich der Einbindung der Objekte in das interne Learning-Management-System oder die interne Auffindbarkeit (z. B. Suche von Unterlagen mit Semesterkürzeln etc.) ergeben sich. Zielgruppe – breite Öffentlichkeit: mehr Aufmerksamkeit auf Schnittstellen, Metadatenstandards und nicht zuletzt auch eine präsentable Landing Page. Im Kontext Zielgruppe ist weiter zu bedenken, ob etwa die Nutzung der freien Lernmaterialien durch Studierende ein explizit unterstütztes Nutzungsszenario darstellen soll.
Workflows	Die Einbindung des Repositoriums in die lokale Systemlandschaft ist abhängig von gewünschten Nutzungsszenarien und Zielgruppen. So ist es von strategischem Interesse, aus welchen Systemen OER in das Repositorium übergeben werden können (sei es als Volldaten oder in Form einer verlinkten externen Ressource, die im Repositorium nur als Metadatensatz existiert), sowie in welche Systeme Inhalte des Repositoriums eingebunden werden können. Auch die jeweiligen Abläufe für Upload oder Publikation von Objekten in dem Repositorium haben – in enger Verbindung mit dem Faktor „Qualitätssicherung“ (s. u.) – großen Einfluss auf die technische Ausgestaltung des Systems.

Qualitäts-sicherung	Entscheidungen, ob im Repositorium veröffentlichte Objekte vorab einen Qualitätssicherungsprozess (z. B. einen redaktionellen Ablauf oder Peer Review) durchlaufen müssen oder ob die Sicherung der Qualität etwa durch die Einschränkung von Upload-Berechtigungen auf eine bestimmte Nutzergruppe (z. B. nur Nutzer:innen mit OER-Zertifizierung) erfolgt, beeinflussen in hohem Maß, wie das Repositorium technisch umgesetzt wird.
Betrieb	Der Betrieb eines Repositoriums muss daher langfristig gewährleistet sein, und die Institution muss dementsprechend die notwendigen Ressourcen zur Verfügung stellen. Diese langfristige Bindung muss auch bei Entscheidungsprozessen mit berücksichtigt werden.

Werden Entscheidungen auf den genannten Ebenen mit den Anforderungen der einzelnen involvierten Bereiche getroffen, entsteht ein konsistentes und im spezifischen Setting von Workflows, Systemlandschaft und genereller funktionaler Ausrichtung zweckmäßiges System.

Auf technischer Ebene kann, aufbauend auf den Entscheidungen aus den vorangegangenen Betrachtungen, darüber nachgedacht werden, welche Umsetzungsform mit den vorhandenen Möglichkeiten realisiert werden kann. Hier können nun Abwägungen getroffen werden, ob ein OER-spezifisches Repositorium oder ein gesamt-institutionelles Repositorium passender ist, ob ein bereits bestehendes System um die Option, auch OER darin abzulegen, erweitert werden kann oder ob es besser ist, ein neues System aufzusetzen.

Im Folgenden sollen die Implikationen von zwei unterschiedlichen, jedoch gleichwertigen Umsetzungsbeispielen dargelegt werden, wie Lösungen für eine institutionelle OER-Infrastruktur aussehen können. Neben den nachkommenden zwei Beispielen gäbe es ebenso weitere Möglichkeiten, wie beispielsweise Fremdhosting oder die Möglichkeit einer zweiten Instanz der sich bereits im Einsatz befindenden Repositoriensoftware, die nur für OER genutzt werden könnte. Es wird jedoch fokussiert auf die Nutzung eines bestehenden institutionellen Repositoriums für OER und auf den möglichen Aufbau eines auf OER spezialisierten Repositoriums.

4.1. Bestehendes institutionelles Repositorium

Da sich die grundlegenden Anforderungen an ein allgemeines Repositorium und an ein OER-Repositorium wenig unterscheiden, kann selbstverständlich ein bestehendes institutionelles Repositorium auch für OER verwendet werden.

Dies bedeutet, dass eine institutionelle Verankerung, personelle Zuständigkeit und fachliches Know-How sowie die Integration in die bereits vorhandene Systemlandschaft und Abläufe wie Data Lifecycle bereits ausgearbeitet sind und sofort genutzt werden können. So kann die Verwendung von bereits bestehenden institutionellen Repositorien für OER auf Ebene der Organisation Vorteile bringen, da etwa Weiterentwicklungen, Workflows, Policies etc. allen Teilbereichen des Repositoriums zugutekommen und nicht für jeden Kontext separat entwickelt werden müssen. Auch die das Repositorium umgebenden Abläufe wie Workflows zum Einbringen von Objekten, Policies und Verantwortlichkeiten sind bereits grundsätzlich geklärt. Der Aufwand, die bereits vorhandenen Strukturen an den Kontext OER anzupassen, darf allerdings nicht unterschätzt werden.

Dieser Aufwand kann durchaus erheblich sein, wenn ein Repositorium für einen spezifischen Bereich eingeführt wurde und dieses auf den Bereich hin optimiert wurde. Z. B. kann es sein, dass ein Publikationsrepositorium, das an den Workflow von Retrodigitalisierung hin optimiert ist, nur mit sehr großem Aufwand für OER verwendbar ist. In solchen Fällen könnte es effizienter sein, ein System einzuführen, das für OER optimiert ist. Auch zu beachten sind dabei weitere spezifische Anforderungen, die aus dem E-Learning-Bereich kommen, mit dem Hintergedanken der notwendigen Anbindung der Infrastrukturen (wie ein angebundenes Learning-Management System oder ein Videoportal), aus denen die OER entstehen. Die Akzeptanz der Nutzer:innen sollte daher dabei im Vordergrund stehen, da nur Systeme, die genutzt werden, auch langfristig betrieben werden.

Neben der Bedienbarkeit sind technische Voraussetzungen zu beachten. So ist etwa eine wichtige Anforderung der E-Learning-Zentren an OER-Repositorien, dass Lernobjekte in den Metadaten hinreichend gut beschrieben sind. Eine Voraussetzung für die Entscheidung für ein bestehendes Repositorium ist daher, dass ein OER-spezifischer Metadatenstandard verwendet werden kann oder dass eine ausreichend gute Beschreibung von Lernobjekten mit dem vorhandenen Metadatenstandard möglich ist.

Je flexibler ein Repositorium ist und je mehr Möglichkeiten eine Hochschule hat, auf die technischen Beschaffenheit des Repositoriums einzuwirken, desto einfacher ist es, ein bestehendes System für OER zu nützen. Die Flexibilität bedarf jedoch eines höheren Ressourcenaufwands und es muss abgewogen werden, ob es strategisch günstiger ist, ein bestehendes System anzupassen oder ein neues einzuführen.

4.2. Spezialisiertes OER-Repositorium

Auch wenn die Einrichtung und der Betrieb eines eigenen OER-Repositoriums zusätzlich zu einem bestehenden institutionellen einen Mehraufwand bedeutet, ergeben sich einige Möglichkeiten, die Inhalte gezielter zu präsentieren. Durch ein OER-spezifisches Repositorium kann mit einfachen Mitteln (Branding, optimierte Suche auf didaktische Inhalte) die Auffindbarkeit der Objekte optimiert und die Sichtbarkeit von OER in seiner Gesamtheit erhöht werden. Der Einstiegspunkt des Repositoriums sowie die Darstellung der Landing Page der Objekte kann gezielt für den Einsatzzweck der Lehre angepasst werden. Gliederungen und Sammlungen können fachspezifisch erstellt und präsentiert werden.

Ein spezialisiertes OER-Repositorium verfügt meist bereits über Integrationen in gängige Learning-Management-Systeme; für lernressourcenspezifische Datenformate sind eventuell bereits Viewer-Applikationen vorhanden, welche z. B. H5P-Inhalte direkt im Repositorium darstellbar machen. Zudem werden Metadatenstandards vorkonfiguriert, um die OER auch in didaktischer Hinsicht zu beschreiben.

Auch wenn Publikationsworkflows neu definiert werden müssen, bietet sich hier die Möglichkeit, diese auf OER optimiert zu gestalten. Da auch alle Inhalte des Repositoriums Open Access sind, muss bei der Ausgestaltung von Workflows, Policies und Zugriffsbeschränkungen nur ein Fall berücksichtigt werden, sodass Inhalte nicht gefiltert oder separiert werden müssen. Über alle Schnittstellen sind alle Inhalte des Repositoriums via Open Access verfügbar.

5. OER national suchbar machen

Aktuell werden OER dezentral an den Institutionen verwaltet, archiviert und zur Verfügung gestellt. Um eine zentrale Auffindbarkeit für die nationalen OER – in Form des OERhub – zu gestalten, werden die Metadaten an einer Stelle aggregiert. Dabei greifen das Projekt Open Education Austria und dessen Nachfolgeprojekt Open Education Austria Advanced auf Erfahrungen aus dem Bereich Cultural Heritage zurück, im Zuge dessen die Europeana-Plattform[26] als europaweite Infrastruktur zur Aggregation von Metadaten entwickelt wurde und erfolgreich betrieben wird. Der Metadatenaggregatoren-Ansatz wird auch von Kolleg:innen aus dem deutschen Hochschulraum verfolgt, wie beispielsweise OERSI[27].

5.1. Der OERhub als zentrale Meta-Suchmaschine

Der OERhub als zentrales Projektziel von Open Education Austria Advanced orientiert sich an internationalen Standards bezüglich der Handhabung von Forschungsdaten, wie sie u. a. durch die European Open Science Cloud (EOSC) vorgegeben werden.[28] Die FAIR Data-Prinzipien mit dem Ziel der nachhaltigen Nutzung von Forschungsdaten stellen hier eine zentrale Grundlage dar.[29] An ihr orientiert sich auch die Forschungsdateninfrastruktur im Rahmen der (Weiter-)Entwicklung ihrer Services.[30]

---

26 https://www.europeana.eu/en
27 https://oersi.de/resources/
28 Siehe https://eosc-portal.eu/about/eosc
29 Siehe https://www.go-fair.org/fair-principles/
30 Vgl. Wilkinson, M. D.; Dumontier, M. et al (2016)

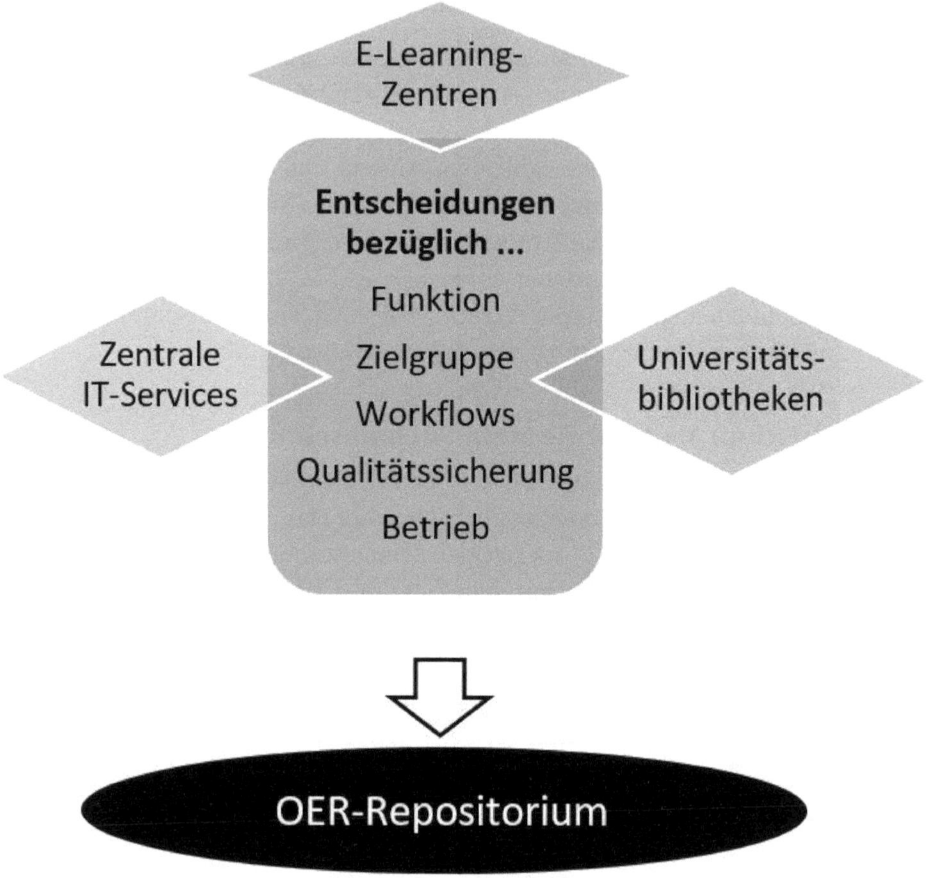

Abbildung 4: Zusammenwirken des OERhub mit institutionellen Repositorien

Als zentrale Meta-Suchmaschine für OER handelt der OERhub ebenso nach diesen Prinzipien mit dem Ziel der optimalen Aufbereitung der auffindbaren OER. Lehrende sollen somit mit dem bestmöglichen Suchergebnis unterstützt werden. OER müssen „findable", „accessible", „interoperable" und „re-usable" sein. Dies bedeutet konkret, dass OER nicht nur von Lehrenden, sondern vor allem auch von Maschinen gefunden werden können, was in einem datengetriebenen Umfeld von Bedeutung ist, damit OER auch automatisiert weitergegeben werden können. Hierbei wird auf Standards bei den Metadaten geachtet, damit die OER nicht nur über den OERhub gefunden werden können (findable). Persistent Identifier bei den OER erleichtern die Zugänglichkeit und sorgen dafür, dass sie nachhaltig verwendet werden können (accessible). Daten, die im OERhub gefunden werden, müssen mit anderen Datensätzen mittels standardisierten Metadaten kombinierbar bleiben, beispielsweise im LOM-Schema (interoperable). Auch die Wiederverwendbarkeit der OER muss durch eine detailreiche Beschreibung in den Metadaten und eine freie Lizenzierung gegeben sein (re-usable).[31]

5.2. Anforderungen für die Anbindung an den OERhub

Die technologische Architektur des OERhub als zentrale Meta-Suchmaschine für den österreichischen Hochschulraum ist stetig erweiterbar und „open for collaboration", wenn entsprechende technische Voraussetzungen gegeben sind.[32]

Die Überlieferung von Metadaten im LOM-Schema ist beispielsweise ein zentrales Erfordernis, um eine einheitliche Darstellung der OER im OERhub zu gewährleisten. „Titel", „Autor:in", „Datum" und Informationen zur Lizenz stellen die Pflichtfelder dar. Zur Auffindbarkeit von OER über die Facettensuche des OERhub trägt ebenso die Information über die Ursprungsdisziplin des Objekts bei – beschrieben durch die ÖFOS[33] – und über die Medientypen, repräsentiert als MIME-Type.[34] Um die Qualität der Suche weiter zu erhöhen, ist es sinnvoll, eine aussagekräftige Beschreibung der didaktischen Einbettung der OER in Form des Learning-Resource Types anzugeben.[35] Eine weitere Voraussetzung ist ein persistenter Link als Verweis auf eine Landing Page. Diese Website stellt alle relevanten Informationen sowie einen Downloadlink der OER zur Verfügung. Auch muss die OER frei veröffentlicht sein, beispielsweise mit einer offenen Creative-Commons-Lizenz.

Die konkrete Anbindung an Quellsysteme (dezentrale Hochschulrepositorien) ist aufgrund der offenen Architektur des OERhub auf unterschiedliche Arten möglich. Es kann hier zwischen der OAI-PMH-Schnittstelle, Application Programming Interfaces (API) des OERhub und weiteren Connectoren frei gewählt werden. Im Rahmen der Qualitätskontrolle der Metadaten-Übertragung bietet der OERhub einen Validator für die übermittelten Metadaten an, mit dem vor der Übertragung an den OERhub geprüft wird, ob die Metadaten die formalen Kriterien erfüllen.

---

31 Vgl. Gröblinger, O.; Ganguly, R. et al. (2021), S. 41.

32 https://www.openeducation.at/suchen/

33 Statistik Austria: Katalog ÖFOS 2012. Siehe https://www.data.gv.at/katalog/dataset/92750ae3-6460-3d51-92a7-b6a5dba70d3d

34 MIME steht für Multipurpose Internet Mail Extension und ist eine standardisierte Art und Weise, das Format eines Dokuments, einer Datei oder einer Auswahl von Bytes anzugeben. MIMEtype-Angaben sind zweiteilig bestehend aus Typ und Subtyp (z. B.: text/csv; text/html oder video/mp4).

35 Vgl. Gröblinger, O.; Ganguly, R. (2021), S. 41.

5.3. Anbindung der jeweiligen OER-Repositorien an den OERhub

Ein Repositorium kann auf unterschiedliche Arten an den OERhub angebunden werden. Es wird hier zwischen zwei Ansätzen unterschieden: Entweder holt sich der OERhub in regelmäßigen Abständen Daten aus dem lokalen Repositorium oder Daten werden aktiv an den OERhub übergeben.

Im Folgenden werden zwei Möglichkeiten der Übergabe von Metadaten an den OERhub dargestellt: bei der Anbindung über OAI-PMH-Schnittstelle werden Metadaten von OERhub abgeholt oder bei der Anbindung via API direkt an den OERhub geliefert.

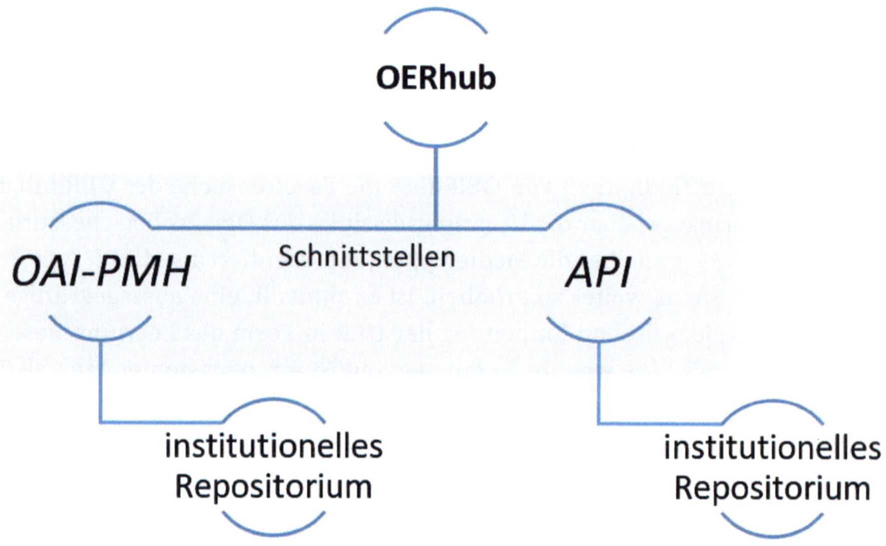

Abbildung 5: Schnittstellen für die Übergabe von Metadaten

5.3.1 Harvesting via OAI-PMH

Fast jedes Repositorium verfügt bereits über eine OAI-PMH Schnittstelle. Die konkrete Funktionalität kann sich jedoch unterscheiden. Beispielsweise kann die Information darüber, welche Datensätze im Repositorium gelöscht wurden, übermittelt werden oder auch nicht. Damit Referenzen auf bereits gelöschte Ressourcen nicht auf dem OERhub verbleiben, wird daher von Seiten des OERhub in definierten Intervallen jeweils der komplette Datensatz abgeholt und ersetzt. Grundvoraussetzung zum Metadaten-Harvest ist dabei, dass alle OER in einem Set als LOM zur Verfügung gestellt werden.

Falls das Datenmodell oder das lokale Applikationsprofil mit den in 5.2. beschriebenen Anforderungen des OERhub inkompatibel sind, ist es notwendig, die via OAI-PMH exponierten Metadaten dahingehend anzupassen. Das kann bedeuten, dass es notwendig ist, Metadaten zu transformieren, anzureichern oder Mappings zwischen verwendeten und erforderlichen Vokabularen oder Taxonomien zu erstellen.

Bei Verwendung eines bereits bestehenden institutionellen Repositoriums kommt hinzu, dass der für OER implementierte Metadatenstandard (z. B. LOM) zusätzlich über die OAI-PMH-Schnittstelle angeboten werden muss. Es entsteht dadurch je nach zugrundeliegender Software ein bestimmter Entwicklungs- und Konfigurationsaufwand. Ein Vorteil dieses Ansatzes ist, dass die Metadaten der Objekte über diese Schnittstelle ohne Zusatzaufwand auch weiteren Institutionen und Metadatenaggregatoren zur Verfügung gestellt werden können. Eine exakte Beschreibung der Metadaten und der verwendeten Taxonomien und Vokabulare als LOM-Applikationsprofil erleichtert den Harvestern die Integration in ihre Systeme.

5.3.2. Push via API

Im Gegensatz zum Harvesting-Ansatz der OAI-PMH-Schnittstelle bietet die API des OERhub die Möglichkeit, Datensätze aktiv einzubringen. Dabei werden Metadaten im JSON-Format[36] übertragen. Wie auch beim OAI-PMH-Harvest wird auf Seiten des OERhub der komplette Datensatz ersetzt. Das bedeutet, dass jeder „push" die Metadaten aller Objekte beinhalten muss.

Diese Art des Metadatentransfers bietet Repositorien, welche über keine OAI-PMH-Schnittstelle verfügen, die Möglichkeit, ihre Objekte über den OERhub auffindbar

36 JSON steht für JavaScript Object Notation und beschreibt einen Standard für die Strukturierung und Darstellung von Daten, um den Datenaustausch zwischen unterschiedlichen Systemen zu ermöglichen. Dieses Datenformat ist unabhängig von einzelnen Programmiersprachen.

zu machen[37]. Es muss hier nicht unbedingt der LOM-Metadatenstandard verwendet werden, wobei die in 5.2 erwähnten Mindestanforderungen erfüllt werden müssen. Somit stellt dies eine flexible Lösung dar, welche aber individuell definiert und implementiert werden muss.

6. Ausblick: Aus der Beratung interessierter Hochschulen bezüglich der Anbindung an den OERhub

Im Zuge der bereichsübergreifenden Zusammenarbeit von E-Learning-Zentren, Zentralen IT-Services und Universitätsbibliotheken bringt die Beratung interessierter Hochschulen zur Teilhabe am OERhub einige Herausforderungen mit sich. Diese erstrecken sich über verschiedene Bereiche, die im Folgenden kurz dargelegt werden sollen.

Äußert eine Hochschule Interesse an der Teilhabe am österreichweiten OERhub, um die an ihrer Institution produzierten OER sichtbar und zugänglich zu machen, so bedarf es einer Beratung mit interdisziplinärer Zielsetzung. Um die bestmögliche Lösung für die Bereitstellung der OER der jeweiligen Hochschule zu finden, müssen Fragen aus unterschiedlichen Bereichen geklärt werden.

Basis bildet der Produktionskontext der OER, der ausschlaggebend dafür ist, auf welche Weise sich unterschiedliche Schritte im OER-Workflow an einer Hochschule zusammensetzen. Es gilt zu klären, in welchem Rahmen OER produziert werden, aber auch, ob es bereits entsprechende Unterstützungsangebote für Lehrende bei der Produktion gibt. Möglicherweise ist ein E-Learning-Zentrum bereits involviert und arbeitet bei der Content-Erstellung mit interessierten Lehrenden zusammen. Im Zuge dessen sollte auch geklärt werden, um welche Art von OER es sich bei dieser Produktion handelt. Ebenso sollten die jeweiligen Datentypen der OER-Arten geklärt werden. Darauf folgend wird der aktuelle Workflow zur Sicherung von OER evaluiert, um einen ersten Einblick in die bestehende Systemlandschaft der Institution zu bekommen. So wird ersichtlich, an welchem digitalen Ort OER aktuell gespeichert werden. Dies könnte von einem bereits genutzten Repositorium, über das Learning-Management-System bis hin zu einem Videoportal oder anderen Quellsystemen reichen, die auf unterschiedliche Weise Metadaten speichern.

Im Fokus dieser Gespräche steht die Verwendung von bereits vorhandenen Systemen, welche die Zentralen IT-Services aber auch Bibliotheken in Betrieb haben, um Synergien aufzuzeigen und zu ihrer Nutzung anzuregen. Oft ist auch das gezielte

37 Vgl. Ladurner,C.; Ortner, C. et al (2021)

Vernetzen der Lehre und Forschung Aufgabe dieser Hochschulberatungen, um im Sinne von Open Education und Open Science zusammenzuarbeiten und querzudenken. Zumeist einander eher unbekannte Stakeholder:innen aus beiden Bereichen werden zusammengebracht, um an Lösungen für die OER-Archivierung an der jeweiligen Hochschule zu arbeiten und die erfolgreiche Zusammenarbeit von E-Learning-Zentren, Zentralen IT-Services und Bibliotheken zu starten.

In diesem Sinne arbeitet das Team von Open Education Austria Advanced, um den Ausbau von universitären Repositorien und Netzwerkstrukturen weiter zu begleiten, nicht nur auf technischer Ebene an der Implementierung weiterer OER-Repositorien (seien es spezifische OER-Repositorien oder auch bereits vorhandene institutionelle Repositorien, die an OER angepasst werden), sondern setzt auch auf die gezielte Nutzung von Synergien aus den Bereichen Open Education und Open Science im Rahmen der Beratung interessierter Hochschulen, um die zentralen Kooperationspartner für die erfolgreiche Umsetzung eines solchen Vorhabens – E-Learning-Zentren, Zentrale IT-Services und Universitätsbibliotheken – zusammenzuführen.

7. Danksagung

Die hier vorgestellte Schnittstellenarbeit wurde durch Fördermittel des Bundesministeriums für Bildung, Wissenschaft und Forschung, Österreich, im Rahmen der Ausschreibung zur digitalen und sozialen Transformation in der Hochschulbildung 2019 für das Vorhaben Open Education Austria Advanced (2020-2024) ko-finanziert; Partner: Universität Wien, TU Graz, Universität Graz, Universität Innsbruck, Forum Neue Medien in der Lehre Austria, ÖIBF.

8. Nachtrag

Gefördert durch das österreichische Bundesministerium für Bildung, Wissenschaft und Forschung. Weitere Informationen unter https://www.bmbwf.gv.at/Ministerium/Presse/Digitale-soziale-Transformation-HS.html (abgerufen am 19.10.2022).

Bibliografie

Breen-Wenninger, Barbara; Louis, Barbara (2020): Orientierung an Studienzielen & Constructive Alignment. Infopool besser lehren. Center for Teaching and Learning, Universität Wien. https://infopool.univie.ac.at/startseite/universitaeres-lehren-lernen/studienzielorientierung-und-constructive-alignment (abgerufen am 19.10.2022)

Clements, Kati; Pawlowski, Jan M.; Manouselis, Nikos (2014): Why Open Educational Resources Repositories Dail. Review of Quality Assurance Approaches. In: EDULEARN14 Proceedings. 6th International Conference on Education and New Learning Technologies. Barcelona, Spain, pp. 929–939. http://library.iated.org/view/CLEMENTS2014WHY (abgerufen am 19.10.2022)

Ebner, Martin; Freisleben-Teutscher, Christian F.; Gröblinger, Ortrun; Kopp, Michael; Rieck, Katharina; Schön, Sandra; Seitz, Peter; Seissl, Maria; Ofner, Sabine; Zwiauer, Charlotte (2016): Empfehlungen für die Integration von Open Educational Resources an Hochschulen in Österreich. Forum Neue Medien in der Lehre Austria. https://www.researchgate.net/publication/303298777_Empfehlungen_fur_die_Integration_von_Open_Educational_Resources_an_Hochschulen_in_Osterreich (abgerufen am 19.10.2022)

European Commission (2021): The EU's Open Science Policy. https://ec.europa.eu/info/research-and-innovation/strategy/strategy-2020-2024/our-digital-future/open-science_en (abgerufen am 19.10.2022)

Gröblinger, Ortrun; Ganguly, Raman; Hackl, Claudia; Kopp, Michael; Ebner, Martin (2021): Dezentral bereitstellen – zentral finden. Zur Umsetzung hochschulübergreifender OER-Angebote. In: Gabellini, Cinzia; Gallner, Sabrina; Imboden, Franziska; Kuurstra, Maaike; Tremp, Peter (Hg.): Lehrentwicklung by Openness – OER im Hochschulkontext. Luzern: Pädagogische Hochschule Luzern, S. 39–44.

Haselwanter, Thomas; Thöricht, Heike (2020): e-Infrastructures Austria Plus. Projektbericht 2017-2019. Innsbruck. https://doi.org/10.25651/1.2020.0006

Kopp, Michael; Neuböck, Kristina; Gröblinger, Ortrun; Schön, Sandra (2021): Strategische Verankerung von OER an Hochschulen. Ein nationales Weiterbildungsangebot für Open Educational Resources. In: Wollersheim, H.-K.; Karapanos, M.; Pengel, N. (Hg.): Bildung in der digitalen Transformation. (Medien in der Wissenschaft 78). Münster, New York: Waxmann, S. 179-183.

Ladurner, Christoph; Ortner, Christian; Lach, Karin; Ebner, Martin; Haas, Maria; Ebner, Markus; Ganguly, Raman; Schön, Sandra (2021): Entwicklung und Implementierung eines Plug-Ins und von APIs für offene Bildungsressourcen (OER). In: Reussner, R.; Koziolek, A.; Heinrich, R. (Hg.): Lecture Notes in Informatics (LNI). Bonn: Gesellschaft für Informatik.

Lingo, Sylvia; Budroni, Paolo; Ganguly, Raman; Zwiauer, Charlotte (2019): Open Education Austria – ein Modell für die Integration von OERs in die österreichischen Hochschulen. In: Zeitschrift für Hochschulentwicklung 14 (2), S. 44. https://doi.org/10.3217/zfhe-14-02/03

Muuß-Merholz, Jöran (2015): Zur Definition von „Open“ in „Open Educational Resources“ – die 5 R-Freiheiten nach David Wiley auf Deutsch als die 5 V-Freiheiten. OERinfo – Informationsstelle OER. https://open-educational-resources.de/5rs-auf-deutsch/ (abgerufen am 08.09.2021)

O'Carroll, Conor; Hyllseth, Berit; van den Berg, Rinskey; Kohl, Ulrike; Kamerlin, Caroline Lynn (2017): Providing Researchers with the Skills and Competencies They Need to Practise Open Science. https://op.europa.eu/en/publication-detail/-/publication/3b4e1847-c9ca-11e7-8e69-01aa75ed71a1/language-en/format-PDF/source-172515559 (abgerufen am 19.10.2022)

Schön, Sandra; Ebner, Martin; Brandhofer, Gerhard; Berger, Elfriede; Gröblinger, Ortrun; Jadin, Tanja; Kopp, Michael; Steinbacher, Hans-Peter (2021): OER-Zertifikate für Lehrende und Hochschulen. Kompetenzen und Aktivitäten sichtbar machen. In: Gabellini, C.; Gallner, S.; Imboden, F.; Kuurstra, M.; Tremp, P. (Hg.): Lehrentwicklung by Openness – Open Educational Resources im Hochschulkontext. Luzern: Pädagogische Hochschule Luzern, S. 29-32. https://doi.org/10.5281/zenodo.5004445

Wiley, David (2014): The Access Compromise and the 5th R – Improving Learning. https://opencontent.org/blog/archives/3221 (abgerufen am 19.10.2022)

Wilkinson, Mark D.; Dumontier, Michel; Aalbersberg, IJsbrand Jan; Appleton, Gabrielle; Axton, Myles; Baak, Arie; Blomberg, Niklas et. al. (2016): The FAIR Guiding Principles for Scientific Data Management and Stewardship. In: Scientific Data 3, 160018 EP. https://doi.org/10.1038/sdata.2016.18

Claudia Hackl berät im Rahmen von „Open Education Austria Advanced“ – einem Digitalisierungsprojekt zur Schaffung attraktiver Lösungen für Open Educational Resources – als Projektmanagerin Hochschulen zur institutionellen Verankerung von Open Educational Resources. Ebenso ist sie Teil des Teams Digitale Lehre des Center for Teaching and Learning der Universität Wien, das mediendidaktische Qualifizierungs- und Unterstützungsangebote für Lehrende bietet.

Christoph Ladurner ist Leiter der Abteilung Digitale Bibliothekssysteme der Universitätsbibliothek der Technischen Universität Graz und dort u.a. für den technischen Betrieb und die Weiterentwicklung des Repositoriums zuständig.

Andreas Parschalk arbeitet seit 2018 an der Abteilung Digitale Medien und Lerntechnologien an der Universität Innsbruck und ist dort u. A. zuständig für das Lernmanagementsystem OpenOlat sowie für Konzeption, Aufbau und Betrieb des OER-Repositoriums. Zuvor war er 12 Jahre an der Universitätsbibliothek im Bereich Digitalisierung und digitale Bibliotheken tätig.

Julia Schindler ist Mitarbeiterin der Abteilung Digitale Medien und Lerntechnologien an der Universität Innsbruck und dort u. a. zuständig für Open Educational

Resources, Educational Design und das Management des Lernmanagementsystems OpenOlat.

Markus Schmid war Mitarbeiter der Abteilung Digitale Medien und Lerntechnologien an der Universität Innsbruck und dort u. a. zuständig für Open Educational Resources und die Systemadministration des Lernmanagementsystems OpenOlat.

Raman Ganguly hat seinen fachlichen Hintergrund in der Softwareentwicklung und Medientechnik. Er leitet die Abteilung IT Support für Research am Zentralen Informatikdienst der Universität Wien und ist für die Entwicklung und den Betrieb von Datenmanagement-Infrastruktur verantwortlich. Seit 2011 beschäftigt er sich mit der Archivierung von digitalen Daten aus der Forschung und Lehre mit dem Schwerpunkt der langfristigen Verfügbarhaltung. Er ist der technische Leiter des an der Universität Wien entwickelten Open-Source-Archivierungssystems PHAIDRA und der technischen Koordination für den internationalen Verbund von PHAIDRA bestehend aus 21 Institutionen. Raman Ganguly berät wissenschaftliche Bibliotheken bei technischen Fragen zum Datenmanagement und ist Vortragender bei den Universitätslehrgängen Data Librarian und Data Steward.

Ortrun Gröblinger ist stellvertretende Leiterin des ZID und Leiterin der Abteilung Digitale Medien und Lerntechnologien an der Universität Innsbruck. Sie studierte „Engineering for computer-based Learning“ und „Hochschul- und Wissensmanagement“. Seit 2010 ist sie Vorstandsmitglied des TIBS und Präsidiumsmitglied im Verein <fnma>. Seit 2016 befasst sie sich intensiv mit dem Thema OER.

Daniel Spichtinger

The Role of Repositories in Horizon 2020 and Horizon Europe Open Access and Data Management Requirements

A Comparative Perspective

Handbuch Repositorienmanagement, Hg. v. Blumesberger et al., 2024, S. 353–367
https://doi.org/10.25364/978390337423219

Daniel Spichtinger | ORCID iD: 0000-0002-9601-8592

Abstract

The European Commission has been a trendsetter in requirements for open access to scientific peer-reviewed publications and for open research data / research data management. This article analyses the provisions and requirements as far as they regard repositories in the EU's Horizon 2020 and the Horizon Europe research funding programmes. Repositories are a cornerstone of the open access and open data / data management requirements in both programmes, with a strengthening of these requirements in Horizon Europe. This will influence researchers and research manager requirements for repositories, even beyond the Horizon programmes. The new requirements have the potential to significantly contribute to the transition towards open science if they are stringently implemented.

Keywords: Horizon 2020; Horizon Europe; data management; open data; repositories

Zusammenfassung

Die Rolle von Repositorien und die Open Access Datenmanagement-Anforderungen in Horizon 2020 und bei Horizon Europe. Eine vergleichende Perspektive

Die Europäische Kommission spielt bei den Anforderungen für den offenen Zugang zu wissenschaftlichen Publikationen und für offene Forschungsdaten bzw. Forschungsdatenmanagement eine Vorreiterrolle. Dieser Artikel analysiert die Bestimmungen und Anforderungen in Bezug auf Repositorien in den EU-Forschungsförderungsprogrammen Horizon 2020 und in Horizon Europe. Repositorien sind ein Eckpfeiler der Anforderungen für den offenen Zugang und die Verwaltung (offener) Daten in beiden Programmen, wobei die Anforderungen in Horizon Europe gestärkt wurden. Dies wird mitbeeinflussen, welche Anforderungen Forscher:innen und Forschungsmanager:innen an Repositorien stellen, auch über die Horizon-Programme hinaus. Die neuen Anforderungen haben das Potenzial, signifikant zum Übergang zur offenen Wissenschaft beizutragen, wenn sie stringent umgesetzt werden.

Schlagwörter: Horizon 2020; Horizon Europe; Datenmanagement; Open Data; Repositorium

1. Introduction

The EU Framework Programmes for Research and Innovation are a series of multi-year funding programmes aimed at promoting research and innovation within the European Union, going back to 1984. The programme from 2014-2022 was called Horizon 2020 and has, since 2021, been replaced by the successor programme Horizon Europe, which will run until 2027. Given its importance as a funding source for research in the EU and beyond (additionally to national funding and other smaller programmes), its legal and technical requirements have the potential to influence research practices and will, consequently, also impact what functionalities researchers and research managers require repositories to deliver.

Open access (OA) to publications and open data and data management have been integrated in both Horizon 2020 and its successor Horizon Europe on a number of levels. In this short article we will specifically look at the provisions and requirements regarding repositories[1] – both for publications and for research data – and compare the previous Horizon 2020 programme[2] and the current Horizon Europe programme in this respect.

The basis for this exercise is a number of EU documents: on the highest level the Horizon 2020 and Horizon Europe regulation constitute the legal base but also tend to be fairly general. On the intermediate level, the Model Grant Agreement (MGA) provides the legal obligations for EU project partners ("beneficiaries"). The Annotated Model Grant Agreement (AGA) further explains these requirements in greater detail. Finally, in Horizon 2020, the Online Manual is strategically placed in the online funding and tender portal (formerly participant portal) and is therefore easily accessible to grant holders and applicants. For Horizon Europe, a new document, the Horizon Europe Programme Guide, lists important information for applicants and thus serves a similar function. The following graphic provides an overview of these documents, which will be quoted as primary sources in the text below.

1 Please note that this article is therefore not an extensive review of the EU's open access and data management mandate but has in its focus those provisions which refer to repositories. Note also that slightly different rules might apply for projects dealing with public health emergencies (e.g. COVID) and for some mono-beneficiary grants.

2 Although Horizon 2020 expired in 2021, its provisions are still relevant, since there are many funded projects which still continue.

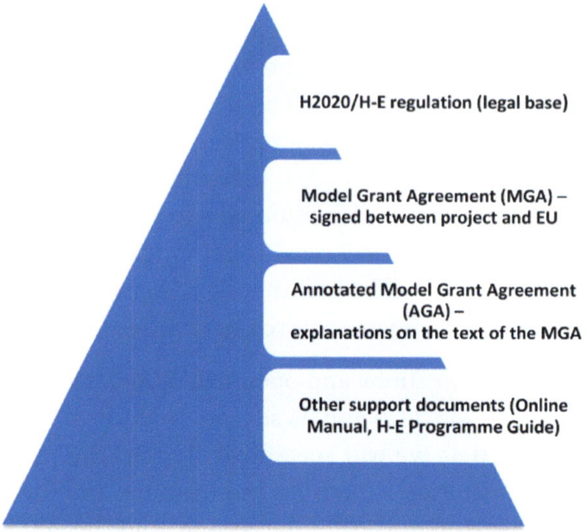

Graphic 1: Sources for EU information on open access and open data requirements in Horizon 2020 and Horizon Europe

2. Open Access to Scientific Publications and Research Data in Horizon 2020 (2014-2020)

On the highest (that is legislative) level, the Horizon 2020 Regulation stipulates that "to increase the circulation and exploitation of knowledge, *open access to scientific publications*[3] should be *ensured*" (own highlight) [4], thus making clear that open access to scientific publications is an obligation for Horizon 2020 grantees. The modes of implementation for this requirement can then be found in the Model Grant Agreement (MGA). As the Horizon 2020 Online Manual explains[5], the OA obligations (in article 29.2. of the MGA) primarily encompass two steps:

3 Understood primarily as scientific articles in Horizon 2020 – although open access to other publications is also strongly encouraged.

4 REGULATION (EU) No 1291/2013 OF THE EUROPEAN PARLIAMENT AND OF THE COUNCIL of 11 December 2013 (2013), p. 107.

5 Horizon 2020 (n.d.)

(a) depositing publications in repositories: beneficiaries must deposit a machine-readable electronic copy of the published version or final peer-reviewed manuscript accepted for publication in a repository for scientific publications. This must be done as soon as possible and at the latest upon publication.

(b) providing open access to them: the manual clarifies that open access can be provided either through a repository of the beneficiary's choice within at most six months (12 months for publications in the social sciences and humanities) or through publication in an open access journal (or in hybrid journals). However, it is interesting to note that in the latter case the article must also be made accessible through a repository upon publication. According to the Horizon 2020 Online Manual this is "to ensure that the article is preserved in the long term"[6].

The manual also provides the following short definition of a repository:

> "Repository" for scientific publications is an online archive. Institutional, subject-based and centralised repositories are all acceptable choices. Repositories that claim rights over deposited publications and preclude access are not.[7]

To help researchers in their choice of repository the manual also refers to The Open Access Infrastructure for Research in Europe (OpenAIRE[8]) as well as the Registry of Open Access Repositories (ROAR[9]) and the Directory of Open Access Repositories (OpenDOAR[10]). Similar information is also provided in the Horizon 2020 AGA on this subject. Slightly different rules apply in public health emergencies, in which case there is a zero-embargo period; furthermore, the relevant guidance from the Commission[11] also refers to preprints in this instance.

For open research data, the Horizon 2020 regulation states that "open access to research data resulting from publicly funded research under Horizon 2020 should be *promoted,* taking into account constraints pertaining to privacy, national security and intellectual property rights".[12] As a result, the Commission launched a flexible pilot for open access to research data (ORD pilot), which was expanded to all thematic areas of the programme as of the Work Programme 2017, but with the option

6 Ibid.
7 Ibid.
8 https://www.openaire.eu/
9 http://roar.eprints.org/
10 https://v2.sherpa.ac.uk/opendoar/
11 European Commission (2020), p. 5.
12 REGULATION (EU) No 1291/2013 OF THE EUROPEAN PARLIAMENT AND OF THE COUNCIL of 11 December 2013 (2013) (Own highlight)

to opt-out under the principle of "as open as possible, as closed as necessary".[13] A key requirement is the creation of a data management plan (DMP), which projects have to submit as an obligatory deliverable by month six of the project and which they should update as needed.

In the Model Grant Agreement, Article 29.3[14], further details are given, namely the requirement for the beneficiary to a) first deposit the data in a research data repository and then to make it possible for "third parties to access, mine, exploit, reproduce and disseminate – free of charge for any user – the following: the data, including associated metadata, needed to validate the results presented in scientific publications as soon as possible"; and then b) to also provide "information – via the repository – about tools and instruments at the disposal of the beneficiaries and necessary for validating the results (and – where possible – provide the tools and instruments themselves)." Over the years, stricter options were added for the health programme, in particular public health emergencies.

Additionally, the Horizon 2020 Annotated Model Grant Agreement (AGA) provides some best practice for research data repositories as follows:

> Useful listings of repositories include the Registry of Research Data Repositories (Re3data) and the Core Trust Seal certified repositories. One key entry point for accessing and depositing related data and tools is Zenodo. For further details on general and discipline-specific repositories visit the EUDAT Collaborative Data Infrastructure.[15]

Through Horizon 2020 there has been a move to see open research data in the larger context of sound data management as an essential part of research practice. In this context, the FAIR principles[16] (that is making data findable, accessible, interoperable, and re-usable) have been prominently integrated into Horizon 2020 data management guidance documents.

---

13 Opt outs are primarily possible for reasons related to personal data protection, IP/commercialisation, or national security.

14 European Commission (2017), p. 69ff.

15 Ibid.

16 Wilkinson, M. et al. (2016)

3. Open Access to Scientific Publications and Research Data in Horizon Europe (2021-2027)

Horizon Europe largely follows the principle of "evolution not revolution", with many provisions from Horizon 2020 being taken as the basis for the new programme, but also extended, updated and modified in line with the experience from the previous programme. Under the umbrella term "open science"[17], which is supposed to be the "modus operandi" in Horizon Europe, the regulation[18] therefore contains a number of updated requirements for open access to publications and research data.

For open access to publications the Horizon Europe regulation (articles 14 and 39) retain the wording of "ensuring" open access. The currently available pre-draft of the Annotated Model Grant Agreement lists open access provisions as part of annex 5, article 17 which deals with "communication, dissemination, open science and visibility". In a nutshell, in Horizon Europe "immediate open access is required i.e. at the same time as the first publication, through a trusted repository using specific open licences".[19] The latest version of the AGA (as of April 1,2023) makes clear that the obligation to ensure open access under the conditions set out in the Grant Agreement is considered a prior obligation, i.e. preceding any subsequent agreement with publishers.[20]

The sentence from the AGA quoted above not only summarises key changes *vis-à-vis* Horizon 2020, most notably the zero-embargo period and the open licencing requirement, but also highlights that the central importance of repositories has been retained and potentially even strengthened in Horizon Europe. The AGA provides an expanded definition of what a repository is but also what does *not* count as a repository:

> A repository is an online archive, where researchers can deposit digital research outputs and provide (open) access to them. Repositories help manage and provide access to scientific outputs and contribute to the long-term preservation of digital assets. They can be institutional, operating with the purpose to collect, disseminate and preserve digital research outputs of individual research organisations (institutional repositories, e.g. the repository of University X) or domain-specific, operating to support specific research communities and

17 Article 2 (5) of the Horizon Europe regulation defines 'open science' as an approach to the scientific process based on open cooperative work, tools and diffusing knowledge.

18 Regulation (EU) 2021/695 of the European Parliament and of the Council of 28 April 2021 (2021)

19 European Commission (2023), p. 281.

20 Ibid., p. 284.

> supported/endorsed by them (e.g. Europe PMC for life sciences including biomedicine and health or arXiv for physics, mathematics, computer science, quantitative biology, quantitative finance and statistics; Phonogrammarchiv for audiovisual recordings the CLARIN-DK-UCPH Repository for digital language data or the European Nucleotide Archive or databases of astronomical observations operated by the European Southern Observatory, among others). There are also general-purpose repositories, such as Zenodo, developed by CERN. Personal websites and databases, publisher websites, as well as cloud storage services (Dropbox, Google drive, etc) are NOT considered repositories. Academia.edu, ResearchGate and similar platforms do not allow open access under the terms required and therefore are also NOT considered repositories.[21]

Of key importance for both open access to publications and research data is the addition of the word "trusted" to repositories. Consequently, the AGA explains that the term trusted repositories can be grouped into three categories which may overlap:

- certified repositories, such as those certified by international organisations or government-authorised certification bodies (e.g. CoreTrustSeal, nestor Seal DIN31644, ISO16363)
- disciplinary or domain repositories commonly used and endorsed by the research communities, and which are recognised internationally
- general-purpose repositories, institutional repositories or any other repositories that present the essential characteristics of trusted repositories, i.e.:
    - display specific characteristics of organisational, technical and procedural quality, such as services, mechanisms and/or provisions that are intended to secure the integrity and authenticity of their contents, thus facilitating their use and re-use in the short- and long-term. Trusted repositories have specific provisions in place and offer explicit information online about their policies, which define their services (e.g. acquisition, access, security of content, long-term sustainability of service including funding, etc.)
    - provide broad, equitable and ideally open access to content free at the point of use, as appropriate, and respect applicable legal and ethical limitations. They assign persistent unique identifiers to con-

21 Ibid., p. 283.

tents (e.g. DOIs, handles, etc.), such that the contents (publications, data and other research outputs) are unequivocally referenced and thus citeable. They ensure that contents are accompanied by metadata sufficiently detailed and of sufficiently high quality to enable discovery, reuse and citation and contain information about provenance and licensing. Their metadata is machine-actionable and standardized (e.g. Dublin Core, Data Cite, etc.) preferably using common non-proprietary formats and following the standards of the respective community the repository serves, where applicable

- facilitate mid- and long-term preservation of the deposited material. They have mechanisms or provisions for expert curation and quality assurance for the accuracy and integrity of datasets and metadata, as well as procedures to liaise with depositors where issues are detected. They meet generally accepted international and national criteria for security to prevent unauthorized access and release of content and have different levels of security, depending on the sensitivity of the data being deposited, to maintain privacy and confidentiality.[22]

Based on a previous draft of these requirements from 2021, an ERC funded study recently found that while 90 % of "trusted" repositories are in line with basic open science requirements, only three repositories fulfilled all the mandatory requirements for metadata, and none met both the mandatory and the recommended metadata requirements set out in the Horizon Europe grant agreements.[23]

Additionally, the AGA also includes three additional requirements, which are mentioned here because they are provided *through* the repository:

1. Licencing requirement: as already mentioned, the Grant Agreement requires that the deposited publications *must* be licensed under the latest version of a Creative Commons Attribution International Public Licence (CC BY) or an equivalent licence. For monographs and other long-text formats the licence may exclude commercial uses and derivative works.

22 Ibid., p. 283f.

23 See https://erc.europa.eu/news-events/news/erc-study-identifies-repositories-allow-researchers-comply-eu-open-science-rules; the full study is available at https://zenodo.org/record/7728016#.ZFEUd3ZByd8

2. Validation requirements: "information must be given via the repository (or via the copy of the publication deposited in the repository) about any research output or any other tools and instruments needed to validate the conclusions of the scientific publication"[24]. Ideally, open access to these should also be provided. This requirement is very similar to Horizon 2020.
3. Metadata requirements: "Metadata should be in line with the FAIR (Findable, Accessible, Interoperable, Reusable) principles, in particular, it should be machine-actionable" and CC-0 licensed. Furthermore, "persistent identifiers (PIDs) must be provided for the Version of Record (VoR) of the publication (such as a Digital Object Identifier (DOI) or a handle), for all author(s) involved in the action (such as ORCIDs or ResearcherIDs) and, if possible, for their organizations".[25]

For open data, article 14 of the Horizon Europe regulation[26] also uses the language of "ensuring" but with the addition of "in accordance with the principle 'as open as possible, as closed as necessary'". It also adds that "the responsible management of research data shall be ensured in line with the principles 'findability', 'accessibility', 'interoperability' and 'reusability' (the 'FAIR principles') and that "[a]ttention shall also be paid to the long-term preservation of data."[27] Article 39 furthermore states that open access to research data

> shall be the general rule under the terms and conditions laid down in the grant agreement, ensuring the possibility of exceptions following the principle 'as open as possible, as closed as necessary', taking into consideration the legitimate interests of the beneficiaries including commercial exploitation and any other constraints, such as data protection rules, privacy, confidentiality, trade secrets, Union competitive interests, security rules or intellectual property rights. Furthermore, [b]eneficiaries shall manage all research data generated in an action under the Programme in line with the FAIR principles and in accordance with the grant agreement and shall establish a Data Management Plan. The work programme may provide, where justified, for additional obligations to use the EOSC for storing and giving access to research data.[28]

24 European Commission (2023), p. 285.
25 Ibid.
26 Regulation (EU) 2021/695 of the European Parliament and of the Council of 28 April 2021 (2021), p. 27.
27 Ibid.
28 Ibid., p. 39.

Already at this level, this provision strengthens the open data requirements and explicitly includes requirements for research data management, most notably a data management plan. The AGA[29] therefore contains a specific section entitled "Open science: research data management" and clarifies that the essence of the requirement is the responsible management of the digital research data generated in the action ('data') in line with the FAIR principles.[30] Beneficiaries should also ensure open access to research data via a trusted repository under the principle 'as open as possible, as closed as necessary'. More specifically, this results in the following requirements for participants:

1. Establishment (and regular updates) of a DMP
2. Deposition in a trusted repository; in some cases, it may be required that the repository takes part in the European Open Science Cloud (EOSC). Data should be kept for a substantial period of at least 5 years and preferably 10 years or longer;
3. Provision of open access "as soon as possible" to the deposited data under CC-BY, CC-0 or an equivalent licence under the "as open as possible, as closed as necessary principle"[31]
4. Provision of information via the repository about any research output or any other tools and instruments needed to re-use or validate the data.

Furthermore, metadata of deposited data must be open under a Creative Common Public Domain Dedication (CC 0) or equivalent (to the extent legitimate interests or constraints are safeguarded), in line with the FAIR principles.

Trusted (as defined above) repositories can be seen as the main go to points in order to comply with these requirements and can therefore be regarded as a central aspect of the Horizon Europe open data and data provision requirements. This impression is reinforced when looking at the Horizon Europe Programme Guide, which states:

> Horizon Europe requires information **via the repository** where publications and data have been deposited on any research output or any other tools and

29 European Commission (2023), p. 285ff.

30 It is also noted that generated data includes re-used data that have been processed or modified in a systematic or methodical way (ibid., p. 285).

31 I.e. unless this is against the beneficiary's legitimate interests, including regarding commercial exploitation; if it is contrary to any other constraints, such as data protection rules, privacy, confidentiality, trade secrets, EU competitive interests, security rules, intellectual property rights or would be against other obligations under the Grant Agreement (ibid, p. 287).

> instruments – data, software, algorithms, protocols, models, workflows, electronic notebooks and others – needed for the re-use or validation of the conclusions of scientific publications and the validation and reuse of research data[32] (own emphasis)

The Guide, furthermore, provides some information on the role of repositories in other open science practices, which Horizon Europe will encourage, most notably preregistration of the research plan in a public repository[33]; on this point the Guide also provides several example preregistration repositories[34], additionally to a more general list of repositories.[35]

4. Conclusions

So far, we have seen that Horizon Europe strengthens the open access, open data and data management provisions already present in Horizon 2020. The following table provides a summary overview of the requirements regarding repositories in Horizon 2020 and Horizon Europe respectively, as described in the main text above.

Table 1: Overview of open access and open data / data management requirements related to repositories

Horizon 2020	Horizon Europe
Basic definition of repositories	Extended definition of repositories (for publications and data) Addition and definition of "trusted" for repositories (for publications and data)
Obligation to deposit and provide open access to scientific publications after 6 to 12 months through a repository (gold OA also possible, if publication is also deposited); Creative Commons licence recommended, ensure open access to bibliographic metadata;	Obligation to deposit and provide open access to the scientific publications immediately (gold OA also possible, if publications is also deposited) as a prior obligation (i.e. surpassing subsequent agreements with publishers); Licencing, validation, and metadata requirements through the repository;

32 European Commission (2023b), p. 41.
33 Ibid, p. 42.
34 Ibid, p. 43.
35 Ibid, p. 50f.

Depositing and providing access to the data and metadata underlying the publication (if no opt out) through a repository, other data optional; Providing information on tools needed to access the data (if possible, the tools themselves).	Manage data according to the FAIR principles and deposit them in a trusted repository; Ensure open access through a CC-BY or CC-0 licence following the principle 'as open as possible as closed as necessary' through a repository; Provide information via the repository about any research output or any other tools and instruments needed to re-use or validate the data (good practice: the tools themselves); Some calls may require EOSC federated repositories.

Several implications of the strengthened mandate in Horizon Europe come to mind. Generally, the new rules succinctly state not only what is expected and required but also what is not accepted (e.g. ResearchGate not counting as an acceptable repository). While this provides more clarity, the stricter rules may, at least in the short term, also lead to a decrease in compliance by researchers until they are fully aware and informed of what is expected of them. For instance, an investigation into the use of creative commons licences Data Management Plans[36] found that only 36 % of DMPs mentioned creative commons in Horizon 2020. It will therefore take time and effort before the more stringent Horizon Europe requirements regarding the use of CC licences are implemented on the ground.

If the strengthened mandate is to have its desired effect (that is contributing to open science as the default), a number of flanking activities are therefore necessary:

- Awareness raising activities to inform researchers and engage them in the discussion: this is already being undertaken by the European Commission itself but also by other organisations, such as OpenAIRE.
- Monitoring: the actual implementation of the mandate needs to be monitored and the relevant data needs to be made publicly available so that it becomes apparent where beneficiaries are struggling (also in order to inform point Support below).
- Compliance/Sanctions: eventually, non-compliance will need to be sanctioned through a range of appropriate measures, which could also include – as the last case scenario – a reduction of the grant.

36 Spichtinger, D. (2022a), p. 1-13.

- Incentives: good data management practices should not only be mandated as an obligation but also be rewarded, e.g. through a dedicated data management prize or through extra money additionally to the EU grant.
- Support: beneficiaries reported lack of support with data management in Horizon 2020[37]; there is therefore a need to provide further assistance to them, for example through a dedicated EU Horizon Europe Data Management helpdesk.

Furthermore, there are also specific repercussions of the strengthened Horizon Europe mandate for repositories and their managers. They need to ensure that they either already conform to the new requirements (e.g. as regards licencing) or that they will upgrade their infrastructure and/or services accordingly. This may be particularly important for small thematic or institutional repositories.[38] Moreover, stakeholders like library services, grant offices and national contact points or similar organisations need to ensure that they are familiar with and can provide advice on the new rules to applicants and grantees.[39] [40] Overall, the strengthened mandate of Horizon Europe has the potential to further accelerate this transition if it is stringently implemented; in this context repositories have a key role to play.

Bibliography

European Commission (2023b) Horizon Europe (HORIZON). Programme Guide. https://ec.europa.eu/info/funding-tenders/opportunities/docs/2021-2027/horizon/guidance/programme-guide_horizon_en.pdf (retrieved 02.05.2023)

European Commission (2023): EU Grants AGA – Annotated Model Grant Agreement EU Funding Programmes 2021-2027. Version 1.0 – DRAFT. 01. April 2023. https://ec.europa.eu/info/funding-tenders/opportunities/docs/2021-2027/common/guidance/aga_en.pdf (retrieved 02.05.2023)

European Commission (2020): Horizon 2020 Projects Working on the 2019 Coronavirus Disease (COVID-19), the Severe Acute Respiratory Syndrome Coronavirus 2 (SARS-CoV-2), and Related Topics. Guidelines for Open Access to Publications, Data and Other Research Outputs. https://ec.europa.eu/research/participants/data/ref/h2020/other/hi/oa-pilot/h2020-guidelines-oa-covid-19_en.pdf (retrieved 05.01.2023)

37 Spichtinger D. (2022b)

38 See also Hahnel, M.; Valen D. (2020), p. 192-198.

39 This is also reinforced by the statement contained in the ERC press release related to the repository study stating that it takes a high level of technical expertise to assess all requirements and corresponding features of repositories.

40 Spichtinger, D. (2023)

European Commission (2017): H2020 Programme Multi-Beneficiary General Model Grant Agreement (H2020 General MGA – Multi) Version 5.0.18 October 2017. https://ec.europa.eu/research/participants/data/ref/h2020/mga/gga/h2020-mga-gga-multi_en.pdf (retrieved 05.01.2023)

European Union (2021): Regulation (EU) 2021/695 of the European Parliament and of the Council of 28 April 2021 Establishing Horizon Europe – The Framework Programme for Research and Innovation, Laying Down Its Rules for Participation and Dissemination, and Repealing Regulations (EU) No 1290/2013 and (EU) No 1291/2013 (Text with EEA Relevance). In: Official Journal of the European Union L 170. https://eur-lex.europa.eu/legal-content/EN/TXT/PDF/?uri=CELEX:32021R0695 (retrieved 05.01.2023)

European Union (2013): Regulation (EU) No 1291/2013 of the European Parliament and of the Council of 11 December 2013 Establishing Horizon 2020 – The Framework Programme for Research and Innovation (2014 2020) and Repealing Decision No 1982/2006/EC (Text with EEA Relevance). In: Official Journal of the European Union L 347. https://eur-lex.europa.eu/legal-content/EN/TXT/PDF/?uri=CELEX:32013R1291 (retrieved 05.01.2023)

Hahnel, Mark; Valen, Dan (2020): How to (Easily) Extend the FAIRness of Existing Repositories. In: Data Intelligence, 2 (1-2), pp. 192-198. https://doi.org/10.1162/dint_a_00041

Horizon 2020 (n.d.): Horizon 2020 Online Manual. https://ec.europa.eu/research/participants/docs/h2020-funding-guide/cross-cutting-issues/open-access-data-management/open-access_en.htm (retrieved 05.01.2023)

Spichtinger, Daniel (2023): Are the RMA Role(s) in Open Science Linked to Funder Requirements, Pre- and Post-award? Lightning Talk Presentation at the 2023 EARMA Conference, Prague https://zenodo.org/record/7895506

Spichtinger, Daniel (2022a): Uncommon Commons? Creative Commons Licencing in Horizon 2020 Data Management Plans. In: International Journal of Digital Curation 17 (1), pp. 1-13. https://doi.org/10.2218/ijdc.v17i1.840

Spichtinger Daniel (2022b): Data Management Plans in Horizon 2020. What Beneficiaries Think and What We Can Learn from Their Experience [version 2; peer review: 2 approved, 1 approved with reservations]. In: Open Res Europe 1 (42). https://doi.org/10.12688/openreseurope.13342.2

Wilkinson, Mark D.; Dumontier, Michel; Aalbersberg, IJsbrand Jan et al. (2016): The FAIR Guiding Principles for Scientific Data Management and Stewardship. In: Scientific Data 3, 160018. https://doi.org/10.1038/sdata.2016.18

Daniel Spichtinger is an independent analyst working on open science topics, including open access and data management policies. From 2012-2018 he was a member of the unit dealing with open science in the European Commission's Directorate-General for Research and Innovation. He also works for the Ludwig Boltzmann Gesellschaft.

Elisabeth Steiner

Zertifizierung von Repositorien

Handbuch Repositorienmanagement, Hg. v. Blumesberger et al., 2024, S. 369–379
https://doi.org/10.25364/978390337423220

Elisabeth Steiner, Universität Graz, ZIM-ACDH, elisabeth.steiner@uni-graz.at | ORCID iD: 0000-0001-9116-0402

Zusammenfassung

In einer sich rasant wandelnden digitalen Welt stehen Repositorien für verlässliche und langzeitverfügbare Informationen und Ressourcen, die Forschungsergebnisse transparent und nachvollziehbar machen und so auch als Grundlage für neue wissenschaftliche Forschung dienen. Schon früh wurde der Bedarf für eine Qualitätskontrolle und eine Bescheinigung dieser Stabilität und „Vertrauenswürdigkeit" erkannt, was sich in unterschiedlichen Zertifizierungsinitiativen niederschlug. Der Beitrag erläutert das Konzept des „Trust" und gibt einen Überblick über Kriterienkataloge und Zertifizierungsrichtlinien, die besonders im geisteswissenschaftlichen und bibliothekarischen Bereich zur Anwendung kommen.

Schlagwörter: Repositorium; Zertifizierung; Vertrauenswürdigkeit

Abstract

Certification of Repositories

In a rapidly changing digital world, repositories stand for reliable and long-term available information and resources that make research results transparent and comprehensible, thus serving as a basis for new scientific research. Early on, the need for quality control and certification of this stability and "trustworthiness" was recognized, which was reflected in various certification initiatives. The contribution outlines the concept of "trust" and gives an overview of criteria and certification guidelines that are especially used in the humanities and the library sectors.

Keywords: Repository; certification; trust

1. Einleitung

Repositorien folgen bei der Erfüllung ihrer Aufgaben Richtlinien und Standards. Die theoretische Grundlage des digitalen Archivs bildet das OAIS-Referenzmodell[1]. Ergänzend dazu stehen zahlreiche andere Empfehlungen oder Best-Practice-Vorgaben zur Verfügung, die sich auf unterschiedliche Teilbereiche oder praktische Anforderungen beziehen. Dazu zählen beispielsweise die FAIR-Prinzipien[2], die COAR-Prinzipien[3] oder die Empfehlungen von Plan S[4].

Die Einhaltung solcher Richtlinien kann durch Akkreditierungsgremien in Form einer Zertifizierung bestätigt werden. Bei der Auswahl von Archivierungspartnern durch Forschende oder Fördergeber stellt die unabhängige Bewertung durch eine externe Begutachtung eine wichtige Entscheidungshilfe dar.

Für Repositorien kommen dabei einerseits Verfahren in Frage, die nicht direkt mit der Aufgabe als Repositorium zusammenhängen, z. B. Zertifikate aus dem Bereich IT-Sicherheit, Datenschutz oder andere Akkreditierungen aus den Normen der International Organization for Standardization (ISO) oder des Deutschen Instituts für Normung (DIN). Andererseits stehen bereits spezielle Verfahren für den Aufgabenbereich von Repositorien und digitalen Archiven zur Verfügung, die der Gegenstand dieses Beitrags sind.

2. Qualitätssicherung für Repositorien

Als exemplarische Möglichkeit zur Qualitätssicherung in Repositorien sei hier das DINI-Zertifikat vorgestellt.

Das DINI-Zertifikat für Open-Access-Publikationsdienste wird von der Deutschen Initiative für Netzwerkinformation e.V. vergeben.[5] Der Kriterienkatalog legt Mindestanforderungen und Empfehlungen fest, was zur Verbesserung der Infrastruktur und der Qualität sowie zu einer Stärkung des Open-Access-Gedankens führen soll. Das Gütesiegel richtet sich in erster Linie an Repositorien, die elektronische Publikationen zur Verfügung stellen, nicht an Forschungsdatenrepositorien oder virtuelle Sammlungen. Weite Verbreitung findet es daher im Bibliotheksbereich.

---

1 The Consultative Committee for Space Data Systems: Reference Model for an Open Archival Information System (OAIS). (2012). Vgl. auch den Beitrag in diesem Band.

2 Wilkinson, M. D. et al. (2016)

3 Confederation of Open Access Repositories: COAR Community Framework for Best Practices in Repositories. (2020)

4 Plan S: Technical Guidance and Requirements, https://www.coalition-s.org/technical-guidance_and_requirements

5 Die Beantragung ist kostenpflichtig und liegt je nachdem, ob die Institution DINI-Mitglied ist oder nicht, bzw. ob sie kommerziell arbeitet oder nicht, zwischen 100 und 500 Euro.

Bisher konnten sich nur deutsche Institutionen zertifizieren lassen, doch mit dem Request for Comments 2022[6] werden die Richtlinien erstmals für österreichische Institutionen angepasst. Die Kriterien beziehen sich teilweise auf allgemeinere Punkte, z. B., dass eine öffentlich zur Verfügung stehende Policy den Dienst beschreiben soll, andererseits auch sehr konkret auf die Implementierung bestimmter Metadatenstandards und technischer Services. Langzeitarchivierung liegt explizit nicht im Fokus des DINI-Zertifikats, allerdings soll die Mindestverfügbarkeit der Publikationen mit Metadaten fünf Jahre nicht unterschreiten.[7] Nach Ausfüllen eines Fragebogens werden die Angaben von zwei externen Gutachter:innen überprüft und bei erfolgreicher Evaluierung darf der Dienst das Zertifikatslogo führen und sich als zertifizierter Open-Access-Publikationsdienst bezeichnen.

Ein anderes Beispiel stellt die Akkreditierung von Forschungsdatenzentren durch den Rat für Sozial- und Wirtschaftsdaten (RatSWD) in Deutschland dar. Zentren stellen einen Akkreditierungsantrag, der vom RatSWD geprüft und bei Einhaltung der Standards und Kriterien positiv bewertet wird.[8]

Auf den Aspekt der Vertrauenswürdigkeit wird zwar im DINI-Zertifikat mehrfach hingewiesen, allerdings zielt die Evaluierung nicht primär auf die Bescheinigung dieser Eigenschaft. Zu diesem Zweck stehen andere Verfahren zur Verfügung, die gemeinsam mit dem grundlegenden Konzept der Vertrauenswürdigkeit von digitalen Archiven im Folgenden vorgestellt werden.

3. Das Konzept der Vertrauenswürdigkeit in Repositorien

Bereits bei der Entwicklung des OAIS-Referenzmodells wurde das Konzept der Vertrauenswürdigkeit (engl. trust/trustworthiness) implizit eingebunden. Besonders hervorzuheben ist hier die Verbindung zur Authentizität des (digitalen) Objektes: „Authentizität: Das Ausmaß, in dem eine Person (oder System) ein Objekt als das ansieht, was es vorgibt zu sein. Authentizität wird auf der Basis von Evidenz beurteilt.“[9]

6 Vgl. Becker, P. et al. (2022)

7 Vgl. DINI AG Elektronisches Publizieren (E-Pub) (2019)

8 Zur Akkreditierung siehe hier https://www.konsortswd.de/datenzentren/akkreditierung

9 nestor: Referenzmodell für ein Offenes Archiv-Informations-System. Deutsche Übersetzung 2.0. 2013. (nestor-materialien 16), S. 9.
Im englischen Original: “Authenticity: The degree to which a person (or system) regards an object as what it is purported to be. Authenticity is judged on the basis of evidence.“ (The Consultative Committee for Space Data Systems: Reference Model for an Open Archival Information System (OAIS). 2012, https://public.ccsds.org/pubs/650x0m2.pdf, S. 1-9).

Ein vertrauenswürdiges Repositorium stellt seiner Zielgruppe nicht nur digitale Objekte zur Verfügung, sondern gleichzeitig auch die Evidenz, um die Qualität und die Provenienz der Information zu beurteilen. Diese Vertrauenswürdigkeit spiegelt sich auf mehreren Ebenen in Repositorien und unter den beteiligten Akteur:innen, besonders auch mit Hinblick darauf, wie Nutzer:innen (digitalen) Ressourcen vertrauen können: "How users trust the documents provided to them by a repository"[10]. Hier sind digitale Anbieter im Vergleich zu etablierten (analogen) Institutionen unter Zugzwang, weil diese bereits Jahrhunderte an ihrer Vertrauenswürdigkeit gearbeitet haben, qualitätssichernde Maßnahmen entwickelt und so das Vertrauen der Zielgruppe erworben haben (z. B. Peer Review). Publizierte Bücher in Bibliotheken haben in der Regel einen bekannten Prozess von der Entstehung bis zur Publikation und Aufnahme in den Bibliotheksbestand durchlaufen, weshalb Nutzer:innen sich bis zu einem gewissen Grad darauf verlassen können, dass hier eine grundlegende Qualitätskontrolle der Inhalte stattgefunden hat.

In der sich schnell wandelnden digitalen Welt geht diese Vertrauenswürdigkeit wie auch die vertrauten Abläufe der Publikation von Daten bzw. Information verloren. Nutzer:innen fällt es oft schwer, den Überfluss an Information zu selektieren und zu bewerten. Deswegen kommt in der virtuellen Welt dem Erhalt der verlässlichen Erreichbarkeit und Zugänglichkeit (im Sinne der wissenschaftlichen Zitierbarkeit) und der Seriosität (im Sinne der wissenschaftlichen Qualität) besondere Bedeutung zu. Vor allem gilt das für Forschungsdaten im engeren Sinne (Messdaten, Rohdaten etc.) im Vergleich zu Publikationen wie Monographien oder Zeitschriftenartikeln, die auch im digitalen Medium einem ähnlichen Muster folgen wie im vertrauten analogen Umfeld.

Die 2020 publizierten TRUST Principles nehmen das Konzept der Vertrauenswürdigkeit erneut auf und fassen die damit verbundenen Empfehlungen für digitale Archive plakativ zusammen[11]:

10 Research Libraries Group (RLG): Trusted Digital Repositories: Attributes and Responsibilities. (2002), S. 9.

11 Lin, D. et al. (2020)

Principle	Guidance for repositories
Transparency	To be transparent about specific repository services and data holdings that are verifiable by publicly accessible evidence.
Responsibility	To be responsible for ensuring the authenticity and integrity of data holdings and for the reliability and persistence of its service.
User Focus	To ensure that the data management norms and expectations of target user communities are met.
Sustainability	To sustain services and preserve data holdings for the long-term.
Technology	To provide infrastructure and capabilities to support secure, persistent, and reliable services.

Transparenz, Verantwortung, Zielgruppenorientierung, Nachhaltigkeit und Technologie bilden demnach die Grundpfeiler von vertrauenswürdiger Repositorienarbeit. Mit der Erwähnung der Authentizität und dem Fokus auf die Nutzungsgruppe finden Konzepte aus dem OAIS-Referenzmodell erneut Verwendung. Doch wie können Repositorien dieses Vertrauen (*trustworthiness*) in ihre Ressourcen und ihre Institution unter Beweis stellen?

3.1. Trusted Digital Repositories

Die Research Libraries Group (RLG) stellte mit ihren Attributes and Responsibilities[12] den ersten Kriterienkatalog für vertrauenswürdige digitale Repositorien vor. Darauf folgten weitere Initiativen, die auch die Formalisierung dieser Richtlinien als Zertifizierungen verfolgten.

Im deutschsprachigen Raum wurde ab 2004 vom Kooperationsverbund nestor ein Kriterienkatalog entwickelt, der in der Entwicklung der DIN-Norm 31644 „Kriterien für vertrauenswürdige digitale Langzeitarchive" resultierte.[13]

Aufbauend auf den Überlegungen von RLG und nestor wurde 2007 vom Online Computer Library Center (OCLC) und vom Center for Research Libraries (CRL) die Trustworthy Repositories Audit & Certification: Criteria and Checklist (TRAC)[14] vorgestellt. Fortgesetzte Arbeit mündete schließlich in die Publikation des ISO-Standards 16363.

12 RLG: Trusted Digital Repositories (Anm. 8).

13 nestor: nestor-Kriterienkatalog vertrauenswürdige digitale Langzeitarchive, Version 2. 2008. (nestor-materialien 8); nestor-Siegel für vertrauenswürdige digitale Langzeitarchive https://www.langzeitarchivierung.de/Webs/nestor/DE/Zertifizierung/nestor_Siegel/siegel.html

14 OCLC and CRL (2007)

Im europäischen Raum etablierte sich mit der Veröffentlichung des Data Seal of Approval in den Niederlanden eine weitere Möglichkeit zum Nachweis der Vertrauenswürdigkeit. 2017 fusionierte das vom Data Archiving and Networked Services (DANS) vergebene Siegel mit der WDS Regular Member Certification (seit 2011 vom World Data System Scientific Committee vergeben) zum CoreTrustSeal.[15]

Im Gegensatz zu den genannten Ansätzen zählt die Methode Digital Repository Audit Method Based on Risk Assessment (DRAMBORA)[16] nicht zu den Kriterienkatalogen, sondern versucht, in einem Risikomanagement-Prozess Gefahrenpotential für Archive und die darin gespeicherte Information aufzufinden und zu beherrschen.

Die meisten Kriterien in den genannten Anforderungskatalogen beziehen sich auf die Organisation, Dokumentation, Arbeitsabläufe und -prozesse und Transparenz im Repositorium und nicht, wie häufig angenommen, auf konkrete technische Umsetzungsfragen.[17] Die Richtlinien unterscheiden sich teilweise in Umfang, Aufbau und Evaluierung, wenn sie auch die gleichen Ziele verfolgen; so evaluiert beispielsweise das CoreTrustSeal 16 Kriterien, das nestor Siegel 34, ISO 16363 über 100.

2010 einigten sich die führenden Anbieter der Repositorienzertifizierung in einem Memorandum of Understanding auf ein gemeinsames Stufenmodell. Das Ergebnis besteht aus drei Zertifizierungsschritten[18]:

- Basic Certification
  CoreTrustSeal (self audit)
- Extended Certification
  Basic + ISO 16363/DIN 31644 (self audit)
- Formal Certification
  Basic + ISO 16363/DIN 31644 (external audit)

Das CoreTrustSeal bietet den Einstieg für die meisten Repositorien, die sich erstmals als vertrauenswürdig zertifizieren lassen. Der Bearbeitungsaufwand für den Zertifizierungsprozess steigt je nach Stufe, mittlerweile werden auch für die Begutachtung in den selbstevaluierenden Verfahren (zwei externe Gutachter:innen pro

---

15 Core Trust Seal http://coretrustseal.org

16 DCC and DPE: Digital Repository Audit Method Based on Risk Assessment (DRAMBORA); Donnelly, M. et al. (2009)

17 Zu solchen Fragen gibt es jedoch ebenfalls Empfehlungen, wie z. B.: Confederation of Open Access Repositories: COAR Community Framework for Best Practices in Repositories (2020), oder die Vision der COAR Next Generation Repositories in Rodrigues, E. et al. (2017).

18 Siehe http://www.trusteddigitalrepository.eu

Antrag) Gebühren erhoben.[19] Eine öffentlich zugängliche (am besten englische) Dokumentation bildet die Grundlage für die durchgeführte Peer Review. Der interne Aufwand umfasst daher nicht nur die direkte Beantwortung der Fragen im Kriterienkatalog, sondern besonders die Herstellung der dafür notwendigen Voraussetzungen; dies reicht von der Erstellung entsprechender Dokumentation, Übersetzung von bestehenden Dokumenten bis hin zu Abstimmungsarbeit innerhalb des Repositoriums wie auch oft mit anderen Abteilungen (Rechtsabteilung, IT-Services, Forschungsmanagement etc.). Eine erfolgreiche Zertifizierung berechtigt zum Führen eines entsprechenden Nachweises auf der eigenen Webpräsenz (Logo), wie auch zur Aufnahme in die Liste des jeweiligen Zertifizierungsgremiums. In Verzeichnissen für Forschungsdatenrepositorien (Registries wie z. B. re3data.org[20] oder OpenDOAR[21]) wird die Zertifizierung ebenso gesondert als Kriterium erfasst. Beispielsweise führt re3data.org mit Stichtag 10.6.2022 41 Repositorien in Österreich, Open DOAR 48; davon verfügen drei über das CoreTrustSeal. Die Zertifizierungen tragen üblicherweise ein Ablaufdatum, so erwartet das CoreTrustSeal eine erneute Zertifizierung nach drei Jahren. Dies spiegelt die sich ständig verändernden Rahmenbedingungen von digitalen Repositorien wider und versteht Qualitätskontrolle und Vertrauenswürdigkeit als iterative Prozesse, die kontinuierliche Aufmerksamkeit benötigen.

Derzeit verlangen die Zertifizierungsrichtlinien die Festlegung auf eine Zielgruppe, d. h. generalisierte Repositorien[22] (z. B. Zenodo, Figshare, OSF etc.) fallen per Definition aus dem Fokus, obwohl einige von ihnen die Kriterien erfüllen könnten. Trotz bisher noch fehlender offizieller Zertifizierung können solche Anbieter eine gute Alternative sein, wenn auch die Unterstützung beim Forschungsdatenmanagement und fachspezifische Harmonisierung und Optimierung definitiv verloren gehen. Dieser Gesichtspunkt wird beim CoreTrustSeal unter dem Stichwort level of curation erfasst: Findet eine Kuratierung der Daten vor dem Abspeichern statt und in welchem Umfang? Je höher die Stufe der Kuratierung, desto höher die Datenqualität[23].

---

19 CoreTrustSeal: EUR 3.000, nestor Siegel: EUR 500.
20 re3data.org, Registry of Research Data Repositories https://www.re3data.org
21 OpenDOAR, Directory of Open Access Repositories https://v2.sherpa.ac.uk/opendoar
22 Für eine Auflistung mit Vergleich der wichtigsten Eigenschaften siehe Stall, S. et al. (2020).
23 Beispielsweise mit Hinblick auf die FAIRness der Daten, vgl. dazu die Beiträge in diesem Band.

4. Vorteile und Herausforderungen für Forschende und Institutionen

Für Forschende sind die oben genannten Verzeichnisse für Repositorien oft die erste Anlaufstelle, wenn sie nach Archivierungspartnern suchen. In der Forschungsförderung wird mittlerweile die Ablage der Daten in einem Repositorium verlangt bzw. in einem zertifizierten Repositorium empfohlen.[24] So wird die nachhaltige Verfügbarkeit der öffentlich geförderten Daten und Ergebnisse sichergestellt und diese stehen Forschenden für aufbauende Studien zur Verfügung.

Die Vorteile der Zertifizierung von Repositorien für Forschende und Fördergeber liegen damit auf der Hand. Doch warum sollten sich Repositorien einer solchen Prozedur unterziehen? Immerhin kostet die Zertifizierung Geld, nicht nur in Form von direkten Gebühren, sondern auch in Form von Personal, das die Zertifizierung durchführt und entsprechende Dokumentation verfasst und Arbeitsabläufe anpasst; so können je nach Ausgangslage durchaus aufwändige Änderungen notwendig sein. Jedoch bietet die Zertifizierung die Möglichkeit, den aktuellen Stand im Repositorium zu evaluieren und Verbesserungspotential zu erkennen. Das wird durch die externe Review erleichtert, da mit Hinblick auf das eigene Repositorium eine gewisse „Betriebsblindheit" auftreten kann. Gerade für die Dokumentation und Standardisierung von Arbeitsprozessen kann diese Perspektive sehr wertvoll sein. Zusätzlich zu diesem (nicht monetär bezifferbaren) Vorteil führt eine erfolgreiche Zertifizierung in der Regel zu einer höheren nationalen und internationalen Sichtbarkeit des Repositoriums, was wiederum zu besserer Finanzierung und erhöhter Projektauslastung führen kann.[25]

5. Fazit

Die Zertifizierung als vertrauenswürdiges digitales Repositorium bringt allen Beteiligten durchwegs Vorteile. Die dadurch hergestellte Transparenz und Nachvollziehbarkeit verbessert die Qualität der Forschungsdaten, ausreichende Dokumentation fördert die Verständlichkeit und Weiterverwendbarkeit (Stichwort FAIR Data, Open Access und Open Science). Repositorien können so optimal ihre Funktion in der Unterstützung von wissenschaftlicher Forschung und Lehre wahrnehmen. Voraussetzung für die Zertifizierung und den Betrieb eines Repositoriums insgesamt bleibt die ausreichende organisatorische und damit auch finanzielle Selbstverpflichtung

24 Siehe z. B. die Open-Access Policy des FWF: https://www.fwf.ac.at/ueber-uns/aufgaben-und-aktivitaeten/open-science/open-access-policy

25 Zu den Vorteilen der Zertifizierung für die Repositorien vgl. weiterführend Donaldson, D. R. et al. (2017), S. 130-151.

der betreibenden Institution. Repositorien sollten sich hier in ein Gesamtkonzept für Forschungsdatenmanagement einfügen, das Forschenden idealerweise über den gesamten Datenlebenszyklus hinweg Unterstützung bietet. Diese Funktion wird mehr und mehr von Data Stewards erfüllt, die das Bindeglied zwischen Forschenden und Forschungsinfrastruktur bilden. Nur nach Ende des Projektes einen Speicherort mit persistenter Identifikation zur Verfügung zu stellen, scheint hier zu kurz gegriffen: eine fachspezifische Datenmanagementbegleitung des gesamten Forschungsprozesses wäre der vielversprechendste Lösungsweg[26].

Bibliografie

Becker, Pascal; Beucke, Daniel; Blumtritt, Ute et al. (2022): DINI-Zertifikat für Open-Access-Publikationsdienste 2022 – Request for Comments. https://doi.org/10.5281/zenodo.6389914

cOAlition S: Plan S Principles and Implementation. Part III: Technical Guidance and Requirements. https://www.coalition-s.org/technical-guidance_and_requirements (abgerufen am 10.06.2022)

Confederation of Open Access Repositories (2022): COAR Community Framework for Best Practices in Repositories. https://doi.org/10.5281/zenodo.4110829

The Consultative Committee for Space Data Systems (2012): Reference Model for an Open Archival Information System (OAIS). https://public.ccsds.org/pubs/650x0m2.pdf (abgerufen am 10.06.2022)

DCC and DPE: Digital Repository Audit Method Based on Risk Assessment (DRAMBORA). https://www.repositoryaudit.eu (abgerufen am 10.06.2022)

DINI AG Elektronisches Publizieren (E-Pub) (2019): DINI-Zertifikat für Open-Access-Publikationsdienste. Version 6.0. 2019. http://dx.doi.org/10.18452/20545

Donaldson, Devan Ray; Dillo, Ingrid; Downs, Robert; Ramdeen, Sarah (2017): The Perceived Value of Acquiring Data Seals of Approval. In: International Journal of Digital Curation 12, pp. 130-151. https://doi.org/10.2218/ijdc.v12i1.481

Donnelly, Martin; Innocenti, Perla; McHugh, Andrew; Ruusalepp, Raivo (2009): DRAMBORA Interactive. User Guide. https://www.dcc.ac.uk/sites/default/files/DRAMBORA_Interactive_Manual%5B1%5D.pdf (abgerufen am 10.06.2022)

Gänsdorfer, Nikos (2020): Gespräche mit Data Stewards. Anforderungen, Kompetenzen, Aufgaben. https://doi.org/10.25365/phaidra.241

Lin, Dawei; Crabtree, Jonathan; Dillo, Ingrid et al. (2020): The TRUST Principles for Digital Repositories. In: Scientific Data 7, p. 144. https://doi.org/10.1038/s41597-020-0486-7

Keitel, Christian; Schoger, Astrid et al. (Hg.) (2013): Vertrauenswürdige digitale Langzeitarchivierung nach DIN 31644. Berlin/Wien/Zürich: Beuth.

26 Diese Feststellung trifft auch Gänsdorfer in seiner Studie zu Data Stewardship in Österreich, vgl. Gänsdorfer, N. (2020)

Nestor (2008): nestor-Kriterienkatalog vertrauenswürdige digitale Langzeitarchive. Version 2. (nestor-materialien 8). http://nbn-resolving.de/urn:nbn:de:0008-2008021802

Nestor (2013): Referenzmodell für ein Offenes Archiv-Informations-System. Deutsche Übersetzung 2.0. (nestor-materialien 16). http://nbn-resolving.de/urn:nbn:de:0008-2013082706

OCLC and CRL (2007): Trustworthy Repositories Audit & Certification. Criteria and Checklist. https://www.crl.edu/sites/default/files/d6/attachments/pages/trac_0.pdf (abgerufen am 10.06.2022)

Research Libraries Group (RLG) (2002): Trusted Digital Repositories: Attributes and Responsibilities. Mountain View, California: RLG. http://www.oclc.org/research/activities/past/rlg/trustedrep/repositories.pdf (abgerufen am 10.06.2022)

Rodrigues, Eloy; Bollini, Andrea; Cabezas, Alberto et al. (2017). Next Generation Repositories. Behaviours and Technical Recommendations of the COAR Next Generation Repositories Working Group. https://doi.org/10.5281/zenodo.1215014

Stall, Shelley; Martone, Maryann E.; Chandramouliswaran, Ishwar et al. (2020): Generalist Repository Comparison Chart. https://doi.org/10.5281/zenodo.3946720

Wilkinson, Mark. D.; Dumontier, Michel; Aalbersberg, IJsbrand Jan et al. (2016): The FAIR Guiding Principles for Scientific Data Management and Stewardship. In: Scientific Data 3, 160018. https://doi.org/10.1038/sdata.2016.18

Elisabeth Steiner studierte Linguistik, Germanistik und Digital Humanities in Graz (AT), Aarhus (DK) und Köln (DE). Seit 2012 verstärkt sie das Team des ZIM-ACDH an der Universität Graz in den Bereichen Metadatenmanagement und Repositorienmanagement. Sie beschäftigt sich dabei praktisch und theoretisch mit der Langzeitarchivierung und -verfügbarkeit von geisteswissenschaftlichen Forschungsdaten und lehrt zu diesen Themengebieten.

Praxisbeispiele

Thomas Haselwanter, Heike Thöricht

Erste Schritte zum Repositorium für Forschungsdaten an der Universität Innsbruck

Handbuch Repositorienmanagement, Hg. v. Blumesberger et al., 2024, S. 383–409
https://doi.org/10.25364/978390337423221

Thomas Haselwanter, Universität Innsbruck, ZID, Thomas.Haselwanter@uibk.ac.at | ORCID iD: 0000-0001-9160-0180
Heike Thöricht, Universität Innsbruck, heike.thoericht@uni-bremen.de | ORCID iD: 0000-0002-1822-7559

Zusammenfassung

Mit der zunehmenden Digitalisierung in der Forschung wird Open Access nun auch im Bereich der Forschungsdaten vermehrt eingefordert. Mit der Veröffentlichung von Forschungsdaten soll ein weiterer Bestandteil des wissenschaftlichen Prozesses über das Internet offen zugänglich, nachvollziehbar und nachnutzbar gemacht werden. Neue Vorgaben der Fördergeber initiierten den Aufbau von organisatorischen und technischen Infrastrukturen an den Forschungsstätten. Schulungen und Beratungen zum Forschungsdatenmanagement und entsprechende Systeme zur Unterstützung werden benötigt. Daher starteten 2020 die Technische Universität Wien, Technische Universität Graz und Universität Innsbruck mit dem Aufbau institutioneller Repositorien für Forschungsdaten. Die folgende Darstellung der ersten Schritte am Beispiel des institutionellen Repositoriums für Forschungsdaten der Universität Innsbruck auf Basis der Open-Source-Software invenio v7.0 dient der Unterstützung beim Aufbau weiterer Repositorien.

Schlagwörter: Open Data; Forschungsdatenrepositorium; Ingestprozess; Nutzungsbedingungen; Ablagerichtlinien; Forschungsdatenmanagement

Abstract

First Steps Towards an Institutional Research Data Repository at the University of Innsbruck

With the increasing digitisation in research, open access is now also increasingly demanded in the field of research data. The publication of research data is intended to make another component of the scientific process openly accessible, traceable and reusable via the internet. New requirements of the funders initiated the development of organizational and technical infrastructures at the research institutions. Training and consulting on research data management and corresponding support systems are needed. Therefore, in 2020, the Vienna University of Technology, the Graz University of Technology and the University of Innsbruck started to establish institutional repositories for research data. The following contribution describes the first steps and is serves to support the establishment of further repositories, using the example of the institutional repository for research data at the University of Innsbruck based on the open-source software invenio v7.0.

Keywords: Open data; research data repository; ingest process; terms of use; data deposition policy; research data management

1. Einleitung

Mit der zunehmenden Digitalisierung der Forschung wird nun parallel zu Open Access bei wissenschaftlichen Publikationen auch der offene Zugang zu Forschungsdaten vermehrt eingefordert. Mit der Veröffentlichung von Forschungsdaten soll ein weiterer Bestandteil des wissenschaftlichen Outputs über das Internet offen zugänglich, nachvollziehbar und nachnutzbar gemacht werden.

Initiativen wie die European Open Science Cloud (EOSC) und GO FAIR sowie neue Vorgaben der Fördergeber initiierten den Aufbau von organisatorischen und technischen Infrastrukturen und Services an den Forschungsstätten. So werden beispielsweise neben Schulungen und Beratungen zum Forschungsdatenmanagement auch geeignete Forschungsdaten-Repositorien benötigt. Die Europäische Union fordert in ihren Horizon-2020-Projekten seit 2017 die Veröffentlichung der Forschungsdaten, die die Ergebnisse validieren. Der österreichische Fonds zur Förderung der wissenschaftlichen Forschung (FWF) folgte mit seiner Open-Access Policy für Forschungsdaten im Januar 2019[1]. Die Österreichische Forschungsförderungsgesellschaft (FFG) hat mit dem Call „IKT der Zukunft – Informations- und Kommunikationstechnologien“[2] am 1. Dezember 2020 und der Ausschreibung der „Stiftungsprofessur BMK“[3] im Mai 2021 nachgezogen.

Was es in dieser Hinsicht allerdings immer zu beachten gilt, ist der Grundsatz „as open as possible and as closed as necessary“, da es Gründe rechtlicher, ethischer oder anderer Natur geben kann, die gegen eine Veröffentlichung sprechen. Falls dies der Fall sein sollte, so sollen die Daten zumindest „accessible“ gemäß den FAIR-Prinzipien[4] sein.[5] Das heißt, sie sollen so abgelegt werden, dass bei berechtigtem Interesse Zugriff auf die Daten gewährt werden kann.

Vorangegangene Initiativen in Richtung Forschungsdatenmanagement und Repositorien für Forschungsdaten wurden durch die vom Bundesministerium für Bildung, Wissenschaft und Forschung geförderten Hochschulraum-Strukturmittel-Projekte e-Infrastructures Austria[6] (2014–2016) unter der Leitung der Universität

1 Siehe https://www.fwf.ac.at/ueber-uns/aufgaben-und-aktivitaeten/open-science/open-access-policy/open-access-policy-fuer-forschungsdaten

2 Siehe https://www.ffg.at/sites/default/files/allgemeine_downloads/thematische%20programme/IKT/AusschreibungsLeitfaden_IKTdZ_2020_Resilienz_Distancing_20201130_1.pdf

3 Siehe https://www.ffg.at/ausschreibungen/stiftungsprofessur-2021

4 Vgl. Wilkinson, M. D.; Dumontier, M.; Aalbersberg, IJ. J. et al. (2016)

5 Siehe hierzu beispielsweise auch: Landi, A.; Thompson, M.; Giannuzzi, V. et al. (2020), S. 47-55 und Eberhard, I. (2019), S. 516-523.

6 Projektwebsite: https://e-infrastructures.univie.ac.at/

Wien und e-Infrastructures Austria Plus[7] (2017–2019) unter der Leitung der Universität Innsbruck umgesetzt. Im aktuellen Projekt FAIR Data Austria[8] (2020–2022) starteten die Technische Universität Wien, Technische Universität Graz und Universität Innsbruck mit der Implementierung institutioneller Repositorien für Forschungsdaten. Die folgende Darstellung der ersten Schritte am Beispiel des institutionellen Forschungsdaten-Repositoriums der Universität Innsbruck auf Basis der Open-Source-Software InvenioRDM[9] dient der Unterstützung beim Aufbau von Repositorien durch andere Forschungsstätten.

Die Implementierung des Repositoriums war Teil eines internen Forschungsdatenmanagement-Projekts (März 2020–März 2022). Die Forschungsdatenmanagement-Projektgruppe bestand aus den Leiter:innen und Mitarbeiter:innen der Universitäts- und Landesbibliothek Tirol, des projekt.service.büros, des Vizerektorats für Forschung und des Zentralen Informatikdienstes.

Zu Beginn wurde ein Projektplan mit den Arbeitspaketen Forschungsdatenmanagement-Services, Forschungsdatenmanagement-Policy und Repositorium erstellt. Das Arbeitspaket Repositorium enthielt sowohl organisatorische als auch technische Themen, wie u. a. den Ingestprozess[10], Schnittstellenkonzepte zu internen und externen Systemen und Compliance[11]. Im Laufe des Projekts gab es einen regelmäßigen Austausch mit der Technischen Universität Wien und der Technischen Universität Graz, die ebenfalls ein Forschungsdaten-Repositorium auf Basis von invenioRDM im Rahmen des Projekts FAIR Data Austria aufbauen. Auch die Kommunikation mit der Universität Wien bezüglich deren Repositorium Phaidra[12], welches bereits seit 2008 die Veröffentlichung von Forschungsdaten ermöglicht, erwies sich als hilfreich. Ebenso wurden Erkenntnisse zum Aufbau und zu den Anforderungen

7 Projektwebsite: https://datamanagement.univie.ac.at/home/aktuelles/details/news/e-infrastructures-austria-plus/?tx_news_pi1%5Bcontroller%5D=News&tx_news_pi1%5Baction%5D=detail&cHash=6cf77981c441e30ab0f47400d2a8a871

8 Projektwebsite: https://forschungsdaten.at/projekte/fda/

9 The InvenioRDM project: https://invenio-software.org/products/rdm/

10 Im Arbeitspaket Ingestprozess wird der Ablauf festgelegt, wie die Forschungsdaten der Wissenschaftler:innen in das Repositorium gelangen.

11 Das Arbeitspaket Compliance umfasst die Erstellung von Nutzungsbedingungen, Ablagerichtlinien und Datenschutzbestimmungen. Auch die Listung bei re3data.org – Registry of Research Data Repositories (https://doi.org/10.17616/R3D) ist Teil des Arbeitspakets.

12 https://phaidra.univie.ac.at/

an das Repositorium durch diverse Recherchearbeiten gewonnen (z. B. Assessment-Informationen von Core Trust Seal[13], Zenodo[14], Harvard Dataverse[15]).

Vor diesem Hintergrund werden diese Themen im Folgenden näher behandelt:

- Wozu ein institutionelles Repositorium für Forschungsdaten?
- Der Plan zur Einrichtung eines Repositoriums
- Der Ingestprozess: Wie kommen die Daten ins Repositorium?
- Das Repositorium als Bestandteil einer FAIRen Forschungsinfrastruktur
- Nutzungsbedingungen, Ablagerichtlinien, Datenschutzbestimmungen

2. Erste Schritte zum Forschungsdaten-Repositorium der Universität Innsbruck

2.1. Wozu ein institutionelles Repositorium für Forschungsdaten?

Die am häufigsten gestellte Frage vor und während des gesamten Prozesses war: Warum braucht eine Universität ein institutionelles Repositorium für Forschungsdaten?

Forschungsdaten in all ihrer Vielfalt sind auch deshalb wertvoll, weil ihre Erhebung, Aufbereitung und Auswertung mit sehr viel Ressourcenaufwand verbunden sind. Sie sind ein wesentliches Fundament der Forschung. Mittlerweile sind Forschungsdaten durch ihr Teilen und ihre Veröffentlichung zu einem essenziellen Baustein geworden, der auch von Dritten im Zuge der Formulierung neuer Fragestellungen verwendet und in neue Kontexte eingebettet werden kann. Ein von der Forschungseinrichtung bereitgestelltes eigenes Repositorium spiegelt die Anerkennung dieser Daten als Forschungsleistung wider. Entsprechend erkennen auch Fördergeber die Bereitstellung dieser Infrastruktur als wichtigen Beitrag der Forschungseinrichtungen an.

Generell bietet ein Forschungsdaten-Repositorium wesentliche Systemeigenschaften:

- langfristige Ablage und Sicherung der Forschungsdaten (mindestens 10 Jahre)
- Möglichkeit zu weltweitem Zugriff und Austausch der Daten

13 Das Core Trust Seal ist eines der möglichen Zertifikate für Forschungsdaten-Repositorien. Einsehbar sind die erfolgreichen Einlangungen zertifzierter Repositorien unter: https://amt.coretrustseal.org/certificates/

14 https://zenodo.org/

15 https://dataverse.harvard.edu/

- Erfüllung der FAIR-Prinzipien[16]
- Auffindbarkeit der Daten durch Durchsuchbarkeit des Repositoriums und durch die Vergabe von Metadaten
- Ermöglichung neuer Kooperationen
- Verbesserung der Zitierfähigkeit durch die Vergabe von persistenten Identifikatoren, u. a. DOIs, ORCID iD
- Regelung der Nachnutzung durch die Vergabe von Lizenzen
- Authentifizierung und Autorisierung von Benutzer:innen

Die erste Wahl zur Ablage der Forschungsdaten sind nach Meinung von Expert:innen von OpenAIRE 21 sogenannte fachspezifische Repositorien[17]. Bei Repositorien wie Pangaea[18], AUSSDA[19], GESIS[20] und ARCHE[21] nehmen Forschende Kontakt zu den jeweiligen Repositorienbetreiber:innen vor der Ablage und der Veröffentlichung der Daten auf und übermitteln die Daten gemeinsam mit Informationen zur Nachnutzung (z. B. einer Dokumentation). Das zuständige Personal begleitet mit seinem Fachwissen durch den Prozess und gibt vor der Veröffentlichung Rückmeldungen, falls in den Daten oder Metadaten Anpassungen notwendig sind. Bei fachspezifischen Repositorien gehen eine höhere Sichtbarkeit und Datenqualität mit einem höheren Abstimmungsprozess mit den Repositoriumsbetreiber:innen und Aufbereitungsaufwand einher. Entsprechende Repositorien sind über die Plattform re3data.org[22] auffindbar. Allerdings gibt es bis dato noch nicht für jeden Fachbereich ein spezifisches Repositorium.

---

16 Siehe https://www.force11.org/group/fairgroup/fairprinciples
17 Rex, J. (2018)
18 https://www.pangaea.de/
19 The Austrian Social Science Data Archive: https://aussda.at/
20 https://www.gesis.org/institut/abteilungen/datenarchiv-fuer-sozialwissenschaften
21 A Resource Centre for the HumanitiEs: https://arche.acdh.oeaw.ac.at/browser/
22 Das Registry of Research Data Repositories ist ein Verzeichnis, welches einen Überblick über existierende Repositorien für Forschungsdaten bietet. Betrieben wird es durch das Karlsruher Institut für Technologie. Siehe https://www.re3data.org/

2.1.1. Warum ein institutionelles Forschungsdaten-Repositorium für die Universität Innsbruck?

In ihrer Open-Access-Policy empfiehlt die Universität Innsbruck die Veröffentlichung von Forschungsdaten seit 2017.[23] Im Gegenzug verpflichtet sie sich zur Bereitstellung entsprechender Infrastruktur für diese Daten. In Anerkennung der Bedeutung von Open Data sieht sie sich in der Verantwortung, ein System für ihre Forschenden bereitzustellen, das der Vielfalt von Methoden, Datenmanagementpraktiken und Datensätzen ihrer 16 Fakultäten und 85 Institute gerecht werden kann.

> Die Universität Innsbruck hat sich zum Ziel gesetzt, allen Mitarbeiter*innen der Universität Innsbruck (...) sowie allen Studierenden, die für ein Doktoratsstudium an der Universität Innsbruck eingeschrieben sind, die Möglichkeit zu bieten, den Output ihrer Leistungen dauerhaft zu sichern, zu dokumentieren und im Internet weltweit verfügbar zu machen.
> Dadurch möchte die Universität die Verfügbarkeit langfristig sichern, das in der Forschung gewonnene Wissen erhalten, den Wissenstransfer in neue Kontexte unterstützen sowie neue Methoden und Ressourcen in die Lehrpläne der Universität integrieren.[24]

Das Repositorium dient zudem auch als langfristig angelegtes Schaufenster der Leistungen, die aus den Projekten und Forschungsvorhaben hervorgegangen sind. Forschende, Projekte und die Universität gewinnen durch das institutionelle Repositorium an Sichtbarkeit. Gleichzeitig handelt es sich um ein System, bei dem die Nutzungsrechte bei den Personen bleiben, die die Daten hochladen (das ist bei der Nutzung der Repositorien von wissenschaftlichen Zeitschriften nicht immer der Fall).

Nach einem längeren Prozess im Laufe der e-Infrastructures Austria-Projekte stand schließlich fest, dass die Universität Innsbruck ihren Forschenden ein institutionelles Repositorium für Forschungsdaten zur Verfügung stellen wird. Gewählt wurde die Software InvenioRDM, ein Open-Source-System, das am CERN entwickelt wurde und das sowohl die Anbindung an existierende Systeme als auch eine Anpassung an die Anforderungen und Wünsche von Forschenden und Fördergebern ermöglicht.[25]

---

23 Universität Innsbruck (Hg.) (2017), S. 360.
24 Universität Innsbruck (Hg.) (2021), S. 1.
25 Die Technische Informationsbibliothek (TIB) Hannover gibt konkrete Empfehlungen für die Gestaltung eines Repositoriums nach den FAIR-Prinzipien: Kraft, A. (2017).

2.1.2. Welche Alternativen gibt es für andere Forschungsstätten?

Eine Möglichkeit für kleinere Forschungsstätten oder eine potentielle Übergangslösung für diejenigen ohne eigenes Repositorium stellt Zenodo[26] dar. Die Nutzung der Plattform Zenodo, die durch die EU bereitgestellt wird, ist derzeit kostenfrei. Zenodo weist aber in den Nutzungsbedingungen darauf hin, dass die Kostenfreiheit denen gewährt wird, die über kein organisiertes Datenzentrum (= Rechenzentrum oder IT-Zentrum) verfügen.[27] Neben Zenodo gibt es weitere generische Forschungsdaten-Repositorien: Harvard Dataverse[28], Dryad[29], figshare[30], Mendeley Data[31], OSF[32] und Vivli[33].[34]

Zudem gibt es auch Software-as-a-Service-Repositorien von Anbietern wie z. B. figshare. Dabei werden die Software und ihr Betrieb von externen Anbieter:innen eingekauft. Die Mitwirkung bei einer möglichen Weiterentwicklung kann eingeschränkt sein.

3. Der Plan zur Einrichtung eines Repositoriums für Forschungsdaten

Neben der technischen Installation des Repositoriums wurden folgende Themen im Forschungsdatenmanagement-Projekt umgesetzt, auf die im Folgenden näher eingegangen wird:

- Der Ingestprozess: Wie kommen die Daten ins Repositorium?
- Das Repositorium als Bestandteil einer FAIRen Forschungsinfrastruktur
- Nutzungsbedingungen, Ablagerichtlinien und Datenschutz

---

26 Zenodo ist ein Online-Speicherdienst, der hauptsächlich für wissenschaftliche Datensätze, aber auch für wissenschaftsbezogene Software, Publikationen, Berichte, Präsentationen, Videos etc. verwendet werden kann. Finanziert wird der Dienst über die Europäische Kommission. Website von Zenodo: www.zenodo.org

27 CERN (ed.) (2021)

28 https://dataverse.harvard.edu/

29 https://datadryad.org/

30 https://figshare.com/

31 https://data.mendeley.com/

32 https://osf.io/

33 https://vivli.org/

34 Stall, S.; Martone, M. E.; Chandramouliswaran, I. et al. (2020)

3.1. Der Ingestprozess: Wie kommen die Daten ins Repositorium?

Einer der ersten Schritte war die Entwicklung eines Konzepts zum Ingestprozess. Ein solches bildet ab, wie die Daten in das Repositorium kommen. An der Universität Innsbruck gibt es eine Vielzahl an Fakultäten, Forschungsmethoden und -daten, inklusive der sogenannten Long-Tail-Disziplinen. In diesen Disziplinen entstehen in der Regel viele Datensätze von jeweils geringem Speichervolumen. Diese unterscheiden sich meist in ihren Erhebungsmethoden und lassen sich daher schwer standardisieren. Das geplante Repositorium soll auch für diese Datensätze ein Ablage- und Veröffentlichungssystem darstellen. Bereits 2018 hat PLAN-E[35], die Plattform der nationalen eScience-Zentren in Europa, die Unterrepräsentation dieser Wissenschaften im Rahmen eines Workshops thematisiert und empfiehlt ausdrücklich die Erweiterung des operativen Anwendungsbereichs der European Open Science Cloud, um den Long Tail der Wissenschaften und Daten explizit anzusprechen.[36]

Im Fall eines Long-Tail-Repositoriums ist es üblich, dass es einen sogenannten Self-Ingestprozess gibt. Das bedeutet, dass die Forschenden ihre Daten selbst in das Repositorium stellen, ohne dabei redaktionell durch das Repositorienpersonal betreut zu werden, sodass die Daten ohne Kontrolle durch die Systembetreiber:innen abgelegt bzw. veröffentlicht werden. Ein solcher Ansatz ist auch für das Long-Tail-Repositorium an der Volluniversität Innsbruck notwendig, da andernfalls das Repositorienpersonal in Besitz umfassender und tiefgehender Fachkenntnisse sein müsste, um die Forschungsdaten zu sichten und zu überprüfen, was mit enormem Ressourcenaufwand verbunden wäre.

Die Forschenden der Universität Innsbruck werden ihre Daten selbst auf die Plattform hochladen, Metadaten dazu eingeben, anschließend die Forschungsresultate langfristig ablegen und veröffentlichen, falls dies rechtlich möglich ist und von ihnen gewünscht wird.

35 https://plan-europe.eu/
36 PLAN-E (ed.) (2018)

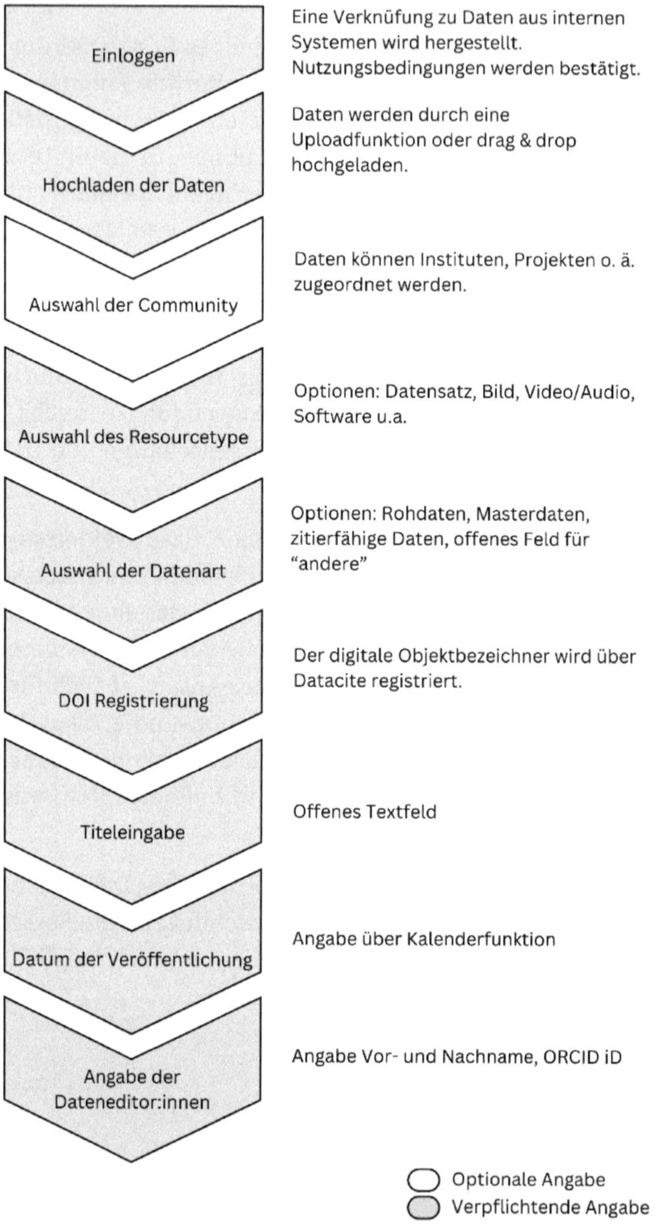

Abbildung 1: Auszug aus dem Self-Ingest-Prozess der Universität Innsbruck, Stand: 27.07.2021

Das entwickelte Konzept zum Ingestprozess bildet ab, was genau und zu welchem Zeitpunkt im Zuge des Ablageprozesses passiert. Ausgangspunkt für die Entwicklung des Ingestprozesses an der Universität Innsbruck war jener von Zenodo, da auch Zenodo auf der Invenio-Software basiert, es bereits seit 2013 nutzt und dort hinsichtlich des Ablage- und Veröffentlichungsprozesses ebenfalls der Self-Ingest-Ansatz verfolgt wird. [37]

Nach der Anmeldung im Repositorium werden die Daten hochgeladen und anschließend mit Metadaten (z. B. Titel der Daten, Kurzbeschreibung der Daten) angereichert. Wesentlich war es, in der Entwicklung des Ablageprozesses festzulegen, welche Angaben verpflichtend (im Beispiel die Felder mit grauem Hintergrund, z. B. Auswahl Uploadtyp) und welche optional (im Beispiel die Felder mit weißem Hintergrund, z. B. Auswahl der Community) sind, um die Daten zu veröffentlichen. Ausschlaggebend war hier insbesondere das DataCite Metadata Schema[38]. Das Schema ist eine Liste von Kernmetadateneigenschaften, die für eine genaue und konsistente Identifizierung einer Ressource für Zitier- und Abrufzwecke ausgewählt wurden. Das Schema differenziert zwischen verpflichtenden, optionalen und empfohlenen Angaben. Die Pflichtangaben sind Daten, die für die Zitierung und Abrufmöglichkeit unumgänglich sind. Dazu zählen z. B. die Angabe der Creators, Titel der Daten sowie das Veröffentlichungsjahr und die Lizenz.[39]

Von besonderer Bedeutung ist beim Ingestprozess auch die Zugriffsregelung seitens der Forschenden (Werden die Daten zur Sicherung abgelegt, mit anderen geteilt oder veröffentlicht? Wann sollen die Daten veröffentlicht werden?) und die Lizenzauswahl (Unter welchen Bedingungen dürfen die Daten durch Fremde nachgenutzt werden?). Bei der Wahl der Lizenz braucht es besondere Aufmerksamkeit. So kann diese z. B. bei Zenodo im Nachhinein seitens der Hochladenden nicht mehr geändert werden. Mit der Veröffentlichung des (Meta)Datensatzes wird schließlich ein DOI vergeben.

3.2. Das Forschungsdaten-Repositorium als Bestandteil einer FAIRen Forschungsinfrastruktur

Das Forschungsdaten-Repositorium soll an der Universität Innsbruck keine Insellösung werden. Das langfristige Ziel ist die Etablierung einer nachhaltigen FAIRen Forschungsinfrastruktur, die auch bestehende Systeme einbindet. Hierzu wurden

37 Für weitere Informationen zum Ablageprozess bei Zenodo siehe Haselwanter, T.; Thöricht, H. (2019).
38 https://schema.datacite.org/
39 Für weitere Angaben und Details siehe DataCite Metadata Working Group (ed.) (2019), S. 7.

als nächster Schritt mögliche Schnittstellen zu internen und externen Systemen in einem Konzept abgebildet. Intern betraf das die selbst entwickelten Forschungsinformationssysteme Forschungsleistungsdatenbank (FLD), die die Leistungen der Forschenden abbildet, und die Projektdatenbank (PDB), die Informationen zu den geförderten Forschungsprojekten der Universität sammelt. In Besprechungen wurde festgelegt, welche Informationen aus diesen Systemen in das Repositorium übernommen werden. Dies soll den Eingabeprozess der Forschenden erleichtern und das Fehlerpotential minimieren. So sollen Forschende z. B. statt der textuellen Eingabe des Projektnamens Vorschläge ihrer Projekte aus der Projektdatenbank mittels Anklicken auswählen können. Andererseits wurde abgestimmt, welche Informationen in die internen Systeme zurückgesandt werden sollen. Das sind z. B. DOIs und die Kurzbeschreibung der Daten in der FLD.

3.2.1. Bestandsaufnahme existierender Forschungsinfrastruktur

Bei der Betrachtung der vorliegenden Daten aus den lokalen Forschungsinformationssystemen (FIS) zeigte sich, dass die Systeme historisch gewachsen sind und vorwiegend dem für sie vorgesehenen Zweck, nämlich meistens als Werkzeuge zum Erstellen von Reports dienen. Zudem wurde sichtbar, dass zwischen dem Großteil der FIS-Daten keinerlei Verbindungen bestehen. Eine Bestandsaufnahme der bestehenden Forschungsinfrastruktur verdeutlichte, dass die Verantwortlichen nicht nur im Zusammenhang mit der Implementierung des Repositoriums, sondern hinsichtlich der gesamten Forschungsinfrastruktur der Universität Innsbruck vor großen Herausforderungen stehen würden.

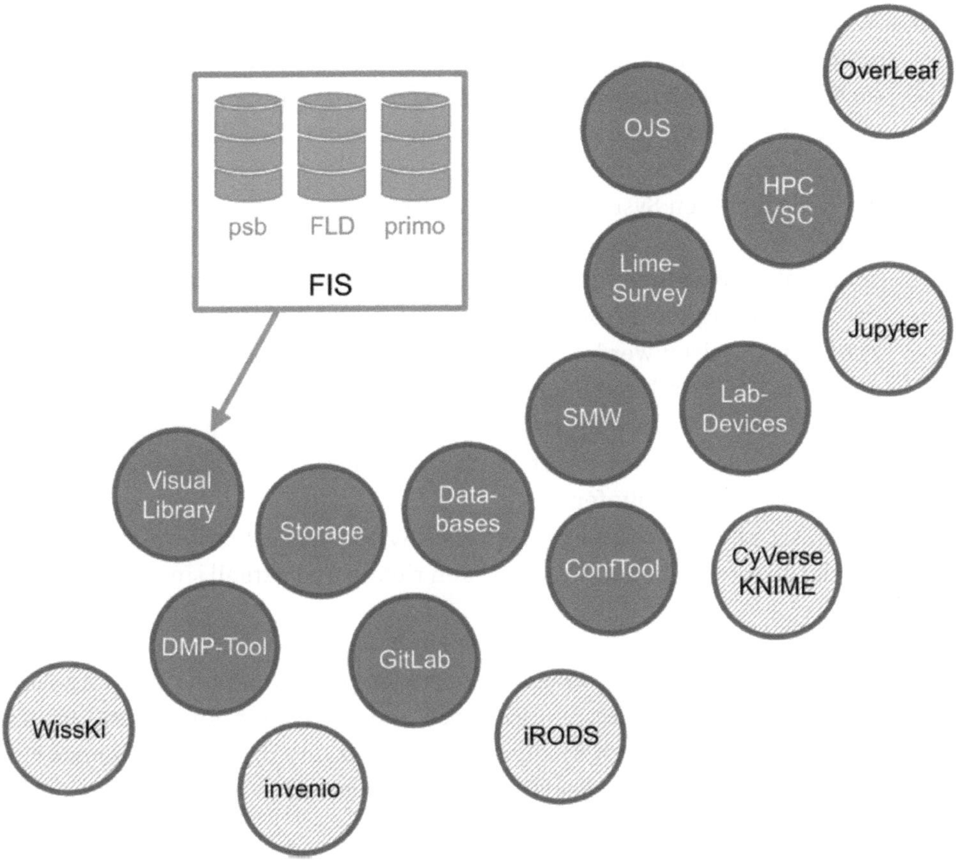

Abbildung 2: Forschungsinfrastruktur der Universität Innsbruck – ein Bündel von Services, ohne Anbindung an Forschungsinformationssysteme, Stand: 10. Dezember 2020

Insbesondere wurden die folgenden notwendigen Handlungsfelder sichtbar:

- Die vorliegenden FIS-Daten enthalten teilweise nur die internen Identifikatoren des jeweiligen Systems, die keine systemübergreifenden Verbindungen möglich machen. Daher sind die vorliegenden Daten mit globalen Identifikatoren (z. B. mit persistenten Projektnummern) anzureichern.

- Als Standard für die FIS-Daten sollten die OpenAIRE Guidelines[40] verwendet werden. In diesen Guidelines sind die Entitäten, Datenfelder und persistenten Identifikatoren definiert, die sicherstellen, dass die entstehenden FIS-Daten genügend Informationen für die Vorgaben der Fördergerber und zukünftiges Research Assessment enthalten.
- Auch die weiteren Systeme der Forschungsinfrastruktur sind bislang unabhängig voneinander gewachsen („Insellösungen") und nicht miteinander verknüpft. Wesentlich für eine nachhaltige Forschungsinfrastruktur ist aber die Einbindung dieser Stand-alone-Systeme in die Überlegungen. Nur so kann gewährleistet werden, dass die Meta-/Forschungsdaten dieser Systeme ebenfalls FAIR sind und auch als Leistungen der Forschenden sichtbar gemacht werden. Hier sind Brücken zwischen den Systemen zu definieren. (Welche Informationen liegen in den Systemen vor? Wie lassen sich diese Informationen verknüpfen?)
- Zukünftig ist auch festzulegen, welches System das datenführende sein soll, das darüber entscheidet, welche Daten richtig und aktuell sind.

Die aktuellen nationalen bzw. internationalen Projekte RIS Synergy (März 2020-März 2024)[41] und Aurora Alliance – Research and Innovation for Societal Impact (2021-2024)[42] verdeutlichen sowohl die neue Relevanz und Urgenz des Themas Forschungsinfrastruktur als auch die dahingehende Dynamik.

3.2.2. Research Graph Meta Model

Alle diese Verbindungen zwischen den Daten – das Anreichern von Metadaten um PIDs und die Transformation von Forschungsdaten zu FAIR Daten – benötigen ein darauf abgestimmtes Datenmodell. Das Research Graph Meta Model[43] ist mittlerweile Basis für einige Research-Graph-Initiativen, die darauf abzielen, Forschende, Forschungsinstitutionen, Fördergeber, Forschungsprojekte, Publikationen, Journale und Forschungsdaten miteinander zu verknüpfen. Damit eignet es sich zusammen mit den schon erwähnten OpenAIRE Guidelines als Basis für das Datenmodell.

---

40 https://guidelines.openaire.eu/en/latest/

41 Projektwebsite von RIS Synergy (Projektleitung: Technische Universität Wien: https://forschungsdaten.at/ris/

42 https://aurora-universities.eu/aurora-alliance-research-and-innovation-for-societal-impact-project-accepted/

43 Aryani, A.; Poblet, M; Unsworth, K. et al. (2018)

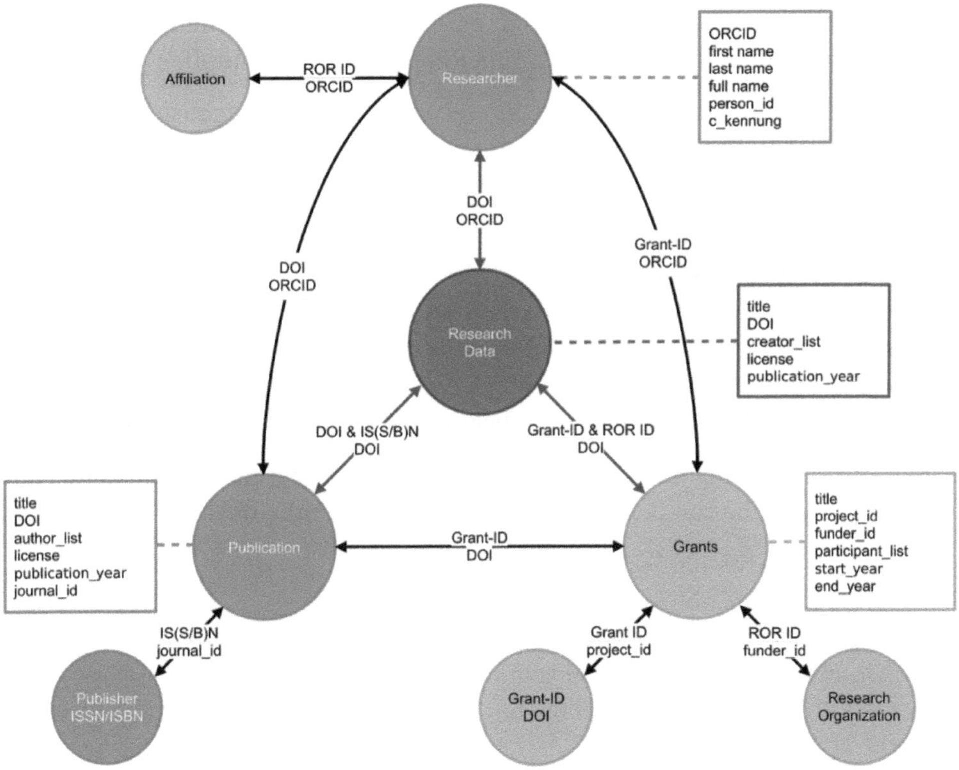

Abbildung 3: Konzept einer nachhaltigen Forschungsinfrastruktur der Universität Innsbruck, Stand: 10. Dezember 2020

Im Research Graph Model wird ersichtlich, welche Entitäten verwaltet werden müssen:

- forschende Person
- Publikation
- Förderung
- Forschungsdaten
- Organisation (Forschungsstätte, Fördergeber, Journale, Verlage)

Die benötigten Datenfelder der Entitäten werden in den OpenAIRE Guidelines definiert. Werden die OpenAIRE Guidelines berücksichtigt, ergeben sich automatisch

Verbindungen zwischen verschiedenen Entitäten: Forschende und Publikationen oder Datensätze sind beispielsweise immer miteinander verknüpft.[44]

Im Research Graph Model ist eine Reihe weiterer Use Cases aufgelistet, die im Graphen ebenfalls als Verknüpfungen umgesetzt werden. Daraus ergeben sich zusätzliche Bedingungen für Datenfelder, die vorhanden sein müssen, damit der Research Graph umgesetzt wird, und die in den OpenAIRE Guidelines definiert, aber nicht verpflichtend sind.

Ein Beispiel ist die Verbindung zwischen Publikationen und Datensätzen. Diese Verbindung ist in den OpenAIRE Guidelines eine optionale Verknüpfung über das sogenannte Datenfeld „Related Identifier". Die Datenfelder werden dadurch in dem erstellten Datenmodell ebenfalls verpflichtend.

Sollen alle Verbindungen im Research Graph Model umgesetzt werden, müssen die Entitäten eine Reihe von persistenten Identifikatoren enthalten:

- ORCID iDs für alle Forschenden
- DOIs für alle Publikationen, Datensätze
- ROR-iDs für Forschungsinstitutionen und Fördergeber
- Grant-iDs für geförderte Forschungsprojekte
- IS(S/B)Ns für Journale und Bücher

Zur Klassifikation von Publikationen und Forschungsdaten wird die österreichische Version (ÖFOS 2012) der Fields of Science and Technology (FOS)[45] verwendet. Eine Reihe von Klassifizierungsschemata ist in verschiedenen Standards für Metadaten in Verwendung. DataCite verwendet z. B. die Field of Science and Technology (FOS) Classification[46] als Standard. Andere Standards verwenden komplexe Klassifikationsschemata wie die Dewey Decimal Classification. In Österreich wird die ÖFOS von Fördergeber und Ministerium verwendet und gefordert, weshalb auch alle Universitäten ÖFOS schon seit langem verwenden. Es macht daher Sinn, in dem Datenmodell ebenfalls das ÖFOS-Schema zur Klassifizierung zu verwenden.

Die Einführung der Entitäten in der dargestellten Form möglichst in allen Systemen ermöglicht die Aggregation vorliegender Daten. Das Forschungsdaten-Repositorium wird der Kernbestandteil des zukünftigen, systemübergreifenden, auf VIVO basierenden FIS-/CRIS-System sein.

44 Vgl. Haak, L.; Meadows, A.; Brown, J. et al. (2018)
45 Organisation for Economic Co-operation and Development (ed.) (2007)
46 Ebd.

3.2.3. Entwicklung einer nachhaltigen Forschungsinfrastruktur

In Abstimmung mit anderen Stakeholdern an der Universität (insbesondere den Verantwortlichen für die technischen Systeme) wurde ein gemeinsames Konzept zur Etablierung einer Forschungsinfrastruktur erstellt, um die Systeme miteinander zu verbinden.

Aus den bestehenden Systemen werden die Daten in VIVO[47], einem Open-Source-CRIS-System[48], übernommen, dort mit weiteren Daten aus externen Quellen aggregiert und für das Repositorium vorbereitet. Dieser Schritt ermöglichte im Projekt die Flexibilität, die Vorbereitung benötigter Metadaten unabhängig von der Veröffentlichung des Source Codes von InvenioRDM zu starten und zu einem späteren Zeitpunkt die Implementierung des Repositoriums zu beschleunigen. Eingriffe in die bereits etablierten Forschungsinformationssysteme wurden durch die Verwendung von VIVO vermieden, und so konnte der Betrieb der existierenden Systeme ohne Störungen fortgesetzt werden.

VIVO, zunächst nur als Hilfssystem geplant, wird zu einem wesentlichen Bestandteil des Gesamtsystems. Es wird die (Meta-)Daten aller lokalen Systeme bündeln und an externe Systeme weitergeben. Ergänzungen und Erweiterungen der lokalen Forschungsinfrastruktur sowie Mappings und andere offene Themen wurden an der Universität Innsbruck im März 2021 angegangen. Zur Schaffung des geplanten Gesamtsystems wurde erworbenes Know-how an entsprechende Systemverantwortliche transferiert, um diese Mitarbeiter:innen einbinden zu können.

---

47 https://vivo.lyrasis.org/

48 "A current research information system (CRIS) is a database or other information system to store, manage and exchange contextual metadata for the research activity funded by a research funder or conducted at a research-performing organisation (or aggregation thereof)." Siehe auch Wikipedia: Current research information system. https://en.wikipedia.org/wiki/Current_research_information_system

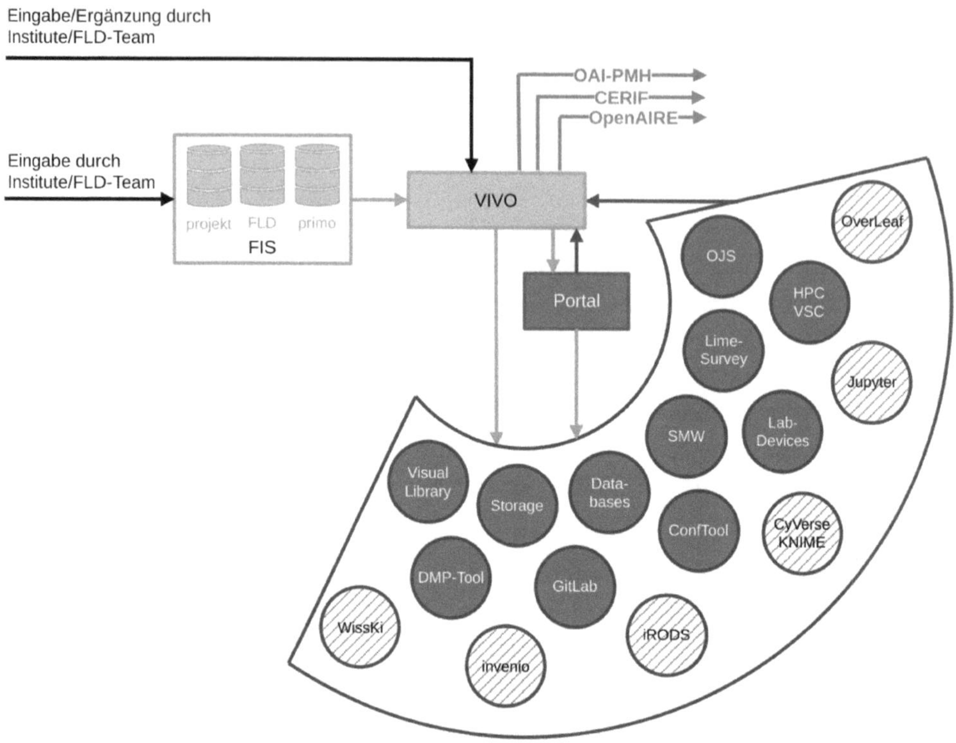

Abbildung 4: Abgestimmtes Konzept für eine nachhaltige Forschungsinfrastruktur der Universität Innsbruck, Stand: 10. Dezember 2020

Die Entitäten und das umfangreiche und flexible Beziehungsmanagement fördern den Aufbau skalierbarer und qualitätsorientierter Forschungsinformationssysteme.

3.2.4. Nutzungsbedingungen, Ablagerichtlinien und rechtliche Aspekte

Neben den technischen Vorbereitungen wurde durch die Erstellung von Nutzungsbedingungen, Ablagerichtlinien und Datenschutzbestimmungen am Thema Compliance gearbeitet. Diese Unterlagen sind für den Betrieb eines Repositoriums unumgänglich. Die Listung bei re3data.org, die der FWF für die Veröffentlichung der

Daten aus den geförderten Projekten einfordert[49], ist seitens re3data.org an die Vorlage von Nutzungsbedingungen geknüpft. Die Nutzungsbedingungen[50] beschreiben den Dienst, regeln den Zugang zur Plattform und die Verantwortlichkeiten der Repositorienbetreiber:innen und User:innen. Ablagerichtlinien[51] geben Informationen zur Datenablage, zum Zugriff und zur Wiederverwendung sowie zur möglichen Entfernung von Daten. Ergänzend könnten auch FAQs auf der Website abgebildet werden[52]. Die Datenschutzbestimmungen[53] informieren zum Umgang mit personenbezogenen Daten.

Mit der Entwicklung eigener Nutzungsbedingungen und Ablagerichtlinien gerieten folgende Fragen immer stärker in den Fokus der Diskussionen: Wer darf das Repositorium nutzen, um die eigenen Daten abzulegen und zu veröffentlichen? Welche Daten dürfen dort abgelegt oder veröffentlicht werden? Wie sieht es mit Urheber- und Verwertungsrechten aus? Wie kann eine Qualitätssicherung seitens der Repositorienbetreiber:in erfolgen?

Einige Fragen wurden in der Forschungsdatenmanagement-Projektgruppe und in der Steuerungsgruppe Forschungsdatenmanagement erörtert. Andere wurden im Austausch mit anderen Forschungsstätten geklärt.

Nutzer:innengruppe

Die Beteiligten am Forschungsdatenmanagement-Projekt diskutierten die Zielgruppe und entschieden sich dafür, dass das Repositorium möglichst vielen Personengruppen der Universität Innsbruck zur Verfügung gestellt wird.

> Berechtigte Nutzende der Plattform (nachfolgend „Nutzer*innen“) sind alle Mitarbeiter*innen der Universität Innsbruck (= das gesamte wissenschaftliche und das gesamte allgemeine Personal mit einem Beschäftigungsverhältnis) sowie alle Studierenden, die für ein Doktoratsstudium an der Universität Innsbruck eingeschrieben sind. Zudem haben externe Personen die Möglichkeit, Forschungsdaten in der Plattform der Universität Innsbruck abzulegen, soweit

49 Siehe https://www.fwf.ac.at/de/forschungsfoerderung/open-access-policy/open-access-fuer-forschungsdaten

50 Universität Innsbruck (Hg.) (2022b)

51 Universität Innsbruck (Hg.) (2021)

52 Beispiel für eine solche FAQ-Seite: die UCL Research Data Repository FAQs des University College London. Siehe https://www.ucl.ac.uk/library/research-support/research-data-management/ucl-research-data-repository-faqs

53 Universität Innsbruck (Hg.) (2022a). Vgl. Privacy policy von Zenodo: https://about.zenodo.org/privacy-policy/

> eine Vereinbarung zur Zusammenarbeit mit der Universität Innsbruck besteht.[54]

Darüber hinaus wird auch Forschenden aus Kooperationsprojekten die Möglichkeit gegeben, das Repositorium zu verwenden. Zur Diskussion steht auch die Datenablage für Abschlussarbeiten von Masterstudierenden. Dazu ist mittelfristig eine Abstimmung des Prozesses mit dem Vizerektorat für Lehre und Studierende vorgesehen.

Forschungsdaten

Sowohl Fördergeber als auch Forschungseinrichtungen fordern die Zugänglichkeit zu Forschungsdaten, um die Replizierbarkeit der Forschungsergebnisse und die Nachnutzung der Daten zu steigern. Das Forschungsdaten-Repositorium ist jenes System, das den Forschenden die Erreichung der Ziele ermöglichen soll.

> Das Repositorium dient der langfristigen Ablage und/oder Veröffentlichung von Daten, die der Replizierbarkeit der Forschungsergebnisse und der Nachnutzung dienen. Vor diesem Hintergrund dürfen Daten aller Forschungsbereiche sowie alle Arten und Status von Daten abgelegt werden. Der Inhalt darf allerdings nicht die Privatsphäre und das Urheber*innenrecht verletzen oder gegen Vertraulichkeits- oder Geheimhaltungsvereinbarungen verstoßen. Nutzer*innen müssen sicherstellen, dass alle sensiblen Informationen entweder anonymisiert, ausgelassen oder verschleiert werden (z. B. personenbezogenen Daten, vertrauliche Daten oder geografische Informationen zu ungeschützten archäologischen Fundstellen oder gefährdeten Tieren). Falls eine Erlaubnis zur Veröffentlichung sensibler Informationen vorliegt, ist diese ebenfalls im Repositorium bereitzustellen.[55]

Mit Ausnahme von Daten mit besonderer Schutzwürdigkeit (z. B. nichtanonymisierte Daten) schränkt die Universität Innsbruck die Forschenden in der Ablage ihrer Daten nicht ein.[56] Die Forschenden als die Expert:innen für die eigenen Forschungsdaten entscheiden, welche Daten im Repositorium abgelegt werden. Die

54 Universität Innsbruck (Hg.) (2022b)

55 Universität Innsbruck (Hg.) (2021), S. 2.

56 Daten mit solcher besonderen Schutzwürdigkeit könnten zukünftig in einem eigenen System gespeichert werden, das besonderen Schutz für diese Daten bietet. Das University College London bietet hier z. B. einen sogenannten Data Safe Haven: https://www.ucl.ac.uk/isd/services/file-storage-sharing/data-safe-haven-dsh. Möglich wäre es für die Universität Innsbruck, ebenfalls ein solches System und einen entsprechenden Prozess einzurichten. User:innen können dann im Forschungsdaten-Repositorium einen reinen Metadateneintrag umsetzen, in dem andere mögliche

Alleinstellungsmerkmale des Repositoriums sind die systematische Ablage mit der Möglichkeit, die Daten zu beschreiben (u. a. Kurzbeschreibung, Verschlagwortung, Angabe der Version) und die Veröffentlichung der Daten mit einem PID. Das Verhältnis vom Aufwand der Datenaufbereitung zur Nachnutzung kann die Entscheidung der Forschenden beeinflussen. Ist dieser in Relation zur Wahrscheinlichkeit, dass die Daten nachgenutzt werden, sehr groß, können sich Forschende auch gegen die Ablage der Daten in einem Repositorium entscheiden. Seitens der Repositorienbetreiber:innen kann die Ablage von Daten im Repositorium besonders empfohlen werden, wenn diese mit großem Ressourcenaufwand generiert wurden, wenn sie nur selten erhoben werden (können) und/oder ihre Nachnutzung erwartungsgemäß groß ist.

In Abgrenzung zu Sync-&-Share-Systemen haben User:innen keine Möglichkeit, die Daten im Repositorium zu bearbeiten, nachdem sie dort hochgeladen wurden. Die dazugehörigen Metadaten können nachträglich angepasst, aber der Datensatz und die Daten selbst können nicht mehr geändert werden. Falls z. B. ein Fehler im hochgeladenen Datensatz gefunden wird, ist es notwendig, eine korrigierte, neue Version des Datensatzes ins Repositorium hochzuladen. Eine Bearbeitung der Daten im Repositorium selbst ist dabei nicht möglich, die Daten müssen lokal oder in einem Sync-&-Share-System bearbeitet und dann erneut hochgeladen werden. Das heißt, für Daten, die noch weiterbearbeitet werden sollen, ist das Repositorium keine geeignete Lösung.

Generell sind Daten in sämtlichen Formaten im Repositorium ablegbar. Jedoch gibt es für die Verwendung von Dateiformaten auf forschungdaten.info Empfehlungen[57], auf die in den Ablagerichtlinien verwiesen wird. Wesentlich sind dabei die Kompatibilität, die Eignung zur Langzeitarchivierung und die mögliche verlustfreie Konvertierung in alternative Formate.

Urheberrechte und Lizenzen

Spätestens vor einer möglichen Veröffentlichung von Forschungsdaten ist die rechtliche Lage der Forschungsdaten zu klären. Die juristische Maxime ist dabei: „Es kommt darauf an."[58] Nicht alle Forschungsdaten genießen urheberrechtlichen Schutz, da hierzu verschiedene Bedingungen erfüllt sein müssen. In Österreich,

---

Nachnutzer:innen mehr über den Zugang zu den Daten und die Bedingungen erfahren. Die Daten selbst lägen aber im besonders geschützten System.

57 Böker, E. (2021): Formate erhalten. https://www.forschungsdaten.info/themen/veroeffentlichen-und-archivieren/formate-erhalten/

58 Losehand, J. (2016)

Deutschland und in der Schweiz ist eine wesentliche Voraussetzung die sogenannte Schöpfungshöhe[59]: Ein Teil der Forschenden und/oder die geistige intellektuelle Höhe müssen in den Daten erkennbar sein. Gerade dies jedoch widerspricht dem wissenschaftlichen Bestreben, dass die Daten möglichst unabhängig von den Forschenden sein sollen.

Die Empfehlung der Expert:innen auf forschungsdaten.info auf die Frage nach dem Umgang mit Urheberrechten ist, mit den Daten so umzugehen, als unterlägen sie dem Urheberrecht, und in der Praxis die Urheber:innen namentlich zu nennen und sie bei Publikationsentscheidungen einzubeziehen.[60]

> Berechtigungen zur Ablage: Die Nutzer*innen dürfen Inhalte speichern, für die sie die entsprechenden Rechte besitzen. Die Einhaltung von Urheber*innen- und Verwertungsrechten Dritter liegt in der Verantwortung der Nutzer*innen der Forschungsdaten.[61]

Ablage und Veröffentlichung der Forschungsdaten im Repositorium haben keinen Einfluss auf die Eigentumsrechte an den Daten. Die Daten bleiben im Eigentum der Datenproduzent:innen.

Handelt es sich um Forschungsdaten, die dem Schutzrecht unterliegen, ist für eine mögliche Nachnutzung durch andere Forschende eine geeignete Lizenz zu wählen. Mit einer Lizenz räumt die hochladende Person anderen die Rechte zur Nutzung von diesen geschützten Inhalten ein.[62] Beim Hochladen der Daten im institutionellen Repositorium können Forschenden aus 160 möglichen Lizenzen wählen, inklusive der verbreiteten Creative-Commons-Lizenzen.[63]

Qualitätssicherung und Compliance-Checks

Wie kann nun eine Qualitätssicherung erfolgen, wenn die Daten von Forschenden ohne vorherige Kontrolle durch den Repositorienbetrieb abgelegt und veröffentlicht werden? Eine Antwort lieferte Barbara Hirschmann in ihrem Vortrag „Three years of publishing data in ETH Zurich's Research Collection“[64] beim Schweizer Research Data Day 2020:

---

59 Vgl. Wikipedia: Schöpfungshöhe. https://de.wikipedia.org/wiki/Sch%C3%B6pfungsh%C3%B6he

60 Siehe https://www.forschungsdaten.info/themen/rechte-und-pflichten/urheberrecht/

61 Universität Innsbruck (Hg.) (2021), S. 2.

62 Kreutzer, T.; Lahmann, H. (2021), S. 49-56.

63 Eine Unterstützung bei der Auswahl einer geeigneten Lizenz kann der Online License Selector sein: https://ufal.github.io/public-license-selector/

64 Hirschmann, B. (2020)

- Die Daten werden auf Viren geprüft.
- Die Lesbarkeit der Daten wird geprüft, indem die Daten mit allgemeinen Tools geöffnet werden. Bei größeren Datensammlungen erfolgt eine Stichprobe.
- Dateiformate werden mittels DROID erkannt.
- Die Kompatibilität von Dateiformaten und gewählten Aufbewahrungsfristen wird geprüft.
- Neue Formate werden in der Dateiformat-Registrierung ergänzt.
- Dateinamen, Ordnernamen und -strukturen werden auf Verständlichkeit geprüft.

Wo automatische Prüfungen möglich sind, wird dies bevorzugt. Wenn bei diesen Checks dem Repositorienpersonal Abweichungen auffallen, werden diese den User:innen mit Empfehlungen mitgeteilt. Die Forschenden entscheiden letztendlich, ob sie etwaige Anpassungen umsetzen. Folglich heißt Qualitätssicherung nicht, dass das Repositorienpersonal Fehler behebt und Daten oder Metadaten korrigiert. Zudem sind User:innen für die Einhaltung von Gesetzen und Policies verantwortlich. Mit der Einreichung ihrer Daten stimmen sie den Nutzungsbedingungen zu und bestätigen so ihre Rechtmäßigkeit und Richtigkeit laut:

- Urheberrechtsgesetz in Österreich[65]
- Datenschutzgesetz in Österreich[66]
- Forschungsorganisationsgesetz in Österreich[67]

65 Bundesgesetz über das Urheberrecht an Werken der Literatur und der Kunst und über verwandte Schutzrechte (Urheberrechtsgesetz). StF: BGBl. Nr. 111/1936 (StR: 39/Gu. BT: 64/Ge S. 19.). https://www.ris.bka.gv.at/GeltendeFassung.wxe?Abfrage=Bundesnormen&Gesetzesnummer=10001848

66 Bundesgesetz zum Schutz natürlicher Personen bei der Verarbeitung personenbezogener Daten (Datenschutzgesetz – DSG). StF: BGBl. I Nr. 165/1999 (NR: GP XX RV 1613 AB 2028 S. 179. BR: 5992 AB 6034 S. 657.) [CELEX-Nr.: 395L0046]. https://www.ris.bka.gv.at/GeltendeFassung.wxe?Abfrage=Bundesnormen&Gesetzesnummer=10001597

67 Bundesgesetz über allgemeine Angelegenheiten gemäß Art. 89 DSGVO und die Forschungsorganisation (Forschungsorganisationsgesetz – FOG)
StF: BGBl. Nr. 341/1981 idF BGBl. Nr. 448/1981 (DFB) (NR: GP XV RV 214 AB 778 S. 81. BR: S. 413.). https://www.ris.bka.gv.at/GeltendeFassung.wxe?Abfrage=Bundesnormen&Gesetzesnummer=10009514

- Vorgaben der jeweiligen Universität (z. B. Open-Access Policy der Universität[68]), Forschungsdatenmanagement-Policy, DOI-Policy der Universität[69], Regeln zur Sicherung guter wissenschaftlicher Praxis der Universität[70]

Zur Minimierung des Risikos und als Unterstützung der Forschenden informiert das Repositorienpersonal diese, falls Verletzungen dieser Vorgaben bei der Qualitätssicherung sichtbar werden.

Darüber hinaus kann eine vorherige Konsultation des Forschungsdatenmanagement-Services (z. B. bereits im Zuge einer Beratung zu Datenmanagementplänen) äußerst hilfreich sein, da es bereits hier um die Wahl von geeigneten Repositorien, Dateiformaten, Lizenzen und Ähnliches geht. Wenn sich Forschende vor oder bei dem Projektstart damit bewusst auseinandersetzen und dazu beraten lassen, wie die Daten am Ende des Projekts aussehen sollten (z. B. Vorgaben von Fördergeber oder Anforderungen von Repositorien), kann dies mögliche Mehrarbeit am Ende des Projekts deutlich reduzieren.

4. Ausblick

Die ersten Schritte in Richtung institutionelles Forschungsdaten-Repositorium der Universität Innsbruck konnten durch die Vorbereitung der Forschungsinfrastruktur und der Compliance-Themen gesetzt werden.

Gegenwärtig befindet sich das Forschungsdaten-Repositorium[71] im Betrieb für Friendly User (Stand: März 2022) und ist auch auf re3data.org gelistet. Eine vollständige Produktivsetzung ist für Herbst 2022 geplant. Mit dem Forschungsdatenmanagement-Projekt wird das Thema Repositorium nicht abgeschlossen sein. Neben einer kontinuierlichen Weiterentwicklung des Systems mit dem Ziel einer Core-Trust-Seal-Zertifizierung wird eine begleitende Bewerbung des institutionellen Repositoriums angestrebt.

In den dargestellten ersten Schritten wurde großer Handlungsbedarf seitens der Forschungseinrichtungen unter Einbindung ihrer verschiedenen Stakeholder:in-

68 Z. B. Open-Access Policy der Universität Innsbruck: Universität Innsbruck (Hg.) (2017)

69 Z. B. DOI-Policy der Universität Innsbruck: Universität Innsbruck (Hg.) (2019). Eine institutionelle Muster-DOI-Policy wurde 2019 im Rahmen des e-Infrastructures Austria Plus erstellt. Siehe Ferus, A.; Gstrein, S.; Hikl, A. L. et al. (2019).

70 Z. B. Universität Innsbruck: Sicherung guter wissenschaftlicher Praxis. https://www.uibk.ac.at/de/forschung/qualitaetssicherung/gwp/

71 https://researchdata.uibk.ac.at/

nen sichtbar. Durch diese Publikation hoffen die Autor:innen, mit den bereitgestellten Informationen und Materialien andere Forschungsstätten und ihre Mitarbeiter:innen in ihren eigenen Prozessen zu unterstützen. Jedenfalls braucht es eine treibende Kraft – in unserem Fall war das das Vizerektorat für Forschung – und das Engagement der Beteiligten in der Forschungsdatenmanagement-Gruppe, die das Thema nach oben und in die Breite getragen haben. Ersichtlich wurde auch der Bedarf an Ressourcen und die Notwendigkeit der Entwicklung einer nachhaltigen Forschungsinfrastruktur, von der das Repositorium für Forschungsdaten einen integralen Bestandteil darstellen sollte. Mindestens ebenso notwendig sind beratende und unterstützende Ressourcen für die Wissenschaftler:innen, um die technische Infrastruktur adäquat nutzen und den Anforderungen der Fördergeber gerecht werden zu können (Stichwort: FAIR-Prinzipien). Diese Forschungsdatenmanagement-Unterstützung reicht von der Beratung zu Datenmanagementplänen (Verantwortlichkeiten, Rechte, Lizenzen, Formate, Repositorien usw.) vor Projektbeginn bis hin zur Unterstützung bei der Veröffentlichung der Daten beim Projektabschluss.

Bibliografie

Aryani, Amir; Poblet, Marta; Unsworth, Kathryn; Wang, Jingbo; Evans, Ben; Devaraju, Anusuriya; Hausstein, Brigitte; Klas, Claus Peter; Zapilko, Benjamin; Kaplun, Samuele (2018): A Research Graph Dataset for Connecting Research Data Repositories Using RD-Switchboard. In: Scientific Data 5, 180099. https://doi.org/10.1038/sdata.2018.99

CERN (ed.) (2021): Zenodo Terms of Use v1.2. https://doi.org/10.5281/zenodo.3896780

DataCite Metadata Working Group (ed.) (2019): DataCite Metadata Schema Documentation for the Publication and Citation of Research Data. Version 4.3. DataCite e.V. https://doi.org/10.14454/7xq3-zf69

Eberhard, Igor (2019): Forschen zwischen Leerstellen und Negativräumen. Schwierigkeiten und Unmöglichkeiten von Open Science bei ethnographischem und sozialwissenschaftlichem Forschen: Ein Erfahrungsbericht. In: Mitteilungen der Vereinigung Österreichischer Bibliothekarinnen und Bibliothekare 72 (2), S. 516–523. https://doi.org/10.31263/voebm.v72i2.3053

Ferus, Andreas; Gstrein, Silvia; Hikl, Anna-Laetitia; Kaier, Christian; Kranewitter, Michael; Marín Arraiza, Paloma; Mayer, Adelheid (2019): Institutionelle Muster-DOI-Policy. Digitale Bibliothek der Universität Innsbruck. https://doi.org/10.25651/1.2019.0001

Haak, Laurel; Meadows, Alice; Brown, Josh (2018): Using ORCID, DOI, and Other Open Identifiers in Research Evaluation. In: Frontiers in Research Metrics and Analytics 3 (28). https://doi.org/10.3389/frma.2018.00028

Haselwanter, Thomas; Thöricht, Heike (2019): Der Ablageprozess von Forschungsdaten und was von Zenodo gelernt werden kann. Universität Innsbruck. https://doi.org/10.25651/1.2019.0006

Hirschmann, Barbara (2020): Three Years of Publishing Data in ETH Zurich's Research Collection. Lessons Learned and New Developments. https://doi.org/10.3929/ethz-b-000446811

Kraft, Angelina (2017): Die FAIR Data Prinzipien für Forschungsdaten. https://blogs.tib.eu/wp/tib/2017/09/12/die-fair-data-prinzipien-fuer-forschungsdaten/

Kreutzer, Till; Lahmann, Henning (2021): Rechtsfragen bei Open Science. Ein Leitfaden. 2. Aufl. Hamburg: University Press. https://dx.doi.org/10.15460/HUP.211

Landi, Annalisa; Thompson, Mark; Giannuzzi, Viviana; Bonifazi, Fedele; Labastida, Ignasi; Bonino da Silva Santos, Luiz Olavo; Roos, Marco (2020): The “A” of FAIR – As Open as Possible, as Closed as Necessary. In: Data Intelligence 2 (1-2). https://doi.org/10.1162/dint_a_00027

Losehand, Joachim (2016): Rechtliche Aspekte beim Umgang mit Forschungsdaten. https://www.ffg.at/sites/default/files/160628_ffg_forschungsdaten_losehand.pdf (abgerufen am 14.04.2023)

Organisation for Economic Co-operation and Development (ed.) (2007): Working Party of National Experts on Science and Technology Indicators. Revised Field of Science and Technology (FOS) Classification in the Frascati Manual. https://www.oecd.org/science/inno/38235147.pdf (abgerufen am 14.04.2023)

PLAN-E (ed.) (2018): The Long Tail of Science and Data. A PLAN-E Workshop in the Context of the EOSC. Workshop Report. https://planeurope.files.wordpress.com/2018/10/report-plan-e-workshop-the-long-tail-of-science-and-data-version-1-0.pdf (abgerufen am 14.04.2023)

Rex, Jessica (2018): As Open as Possible, as Closed as Necessary – Forschungsdaten in Horizon 2020? https://os.helmholtz.de/veranstaltungen/#c107089 (abgerufen am 08.02.2024)

Stall, Shelley; Martone, Maryann E.; Chandramouliswaran, Ishwar; Crosas, Mercè; Federer, Lisa; Gautier, Julian; Hahnel, Mark; Larkin, Jennie; Lowenberg, Daniella; Pfeiffer, Ninnicole; Sim, Ida; Smith, Tim; Van Gulick, Ana E.; Walker, Erin; Wood, Julie; Zaringhalam, Maryam; Zigoni, Alberto (2020): Generalist Repository Comparison Chart. https://doi.org/10.5281/zenodo.3946720

Universität Innsbruck (Hg.) (2017): Mitteilungsblatt der Leopold-Franzens-Universität Innsbruck. https://www.uibk.ac.at/service/c101/mitteilungsblatt/2016-2017/27/mitteil.pdf (abgerufen am 14.04.2023)

Universität Innsbruck (Hg.) (2019): Institutionelle Policy für die Registrierung von Digital Object Identifiers (DOIs) an der Universität Innsbruck. https://www.uibk.ac.at/ulb/services/doi_policy_uni_ibk_final_130220.pdf (abgerufen am 14.04.2023)

Universität Innsbruck (Hg.) (2021): Ablagerichtlinien des Repositoriums für Forschungsdaten der Universität Innsbruck. Universität Innsbruck. https://doi.org/10.48323/9sxsj-z2968

Universität Innsbruck (Hg.) (2022a): Datenschutzbestimmungen des Repositoriums für Forschungsdaten der Universität Innsbruck. Universität Innsbruck. https://doi.org/10.48323/wj9cq-6a619

Universität Innsbruck (Hg.) (2022b): Nutzungsbedingungen des Repositoriums für Forschungsdaten der Universität Innsbruck. https://doi.org/10.48323/9sxsj-z2968

Wilkinson, Mark D.; Dumontier, Michel; Aalbersberg, IJsbrand Jan et al. (2016): The FAIR Guiding Principles for Scientific Data Management and Stewardship. In: Sci Data 3, 160018. https://doi.org/10.1038/sdata.2016.18

Thomas Haselwanter hat Angewandte Physik studiert und ist seit 2010 an der Universität Innsbruck im Zentralen Informatikdienst beschäftigt. Nach der Leitung der Abteilung „Web- und Informationssysteme“ an der Universität Innsbruck führt er seit 2022 die Abteilung „Digitale Forschungsservices“. Von 2017 bis 2019 leitete er das HRSM-Projekt „e-Infrastructures Austria plus“.

Heike Thöricht unterstützte die Leitung des Hochschulraum-Strukturmittel-Projekts „e-Infrastructures Austria plus“ von 2018–2019. Sie entwickelte sich zur Ansprechperson bezüglich Forschungsdatenmanagement an der Universität Innsbruck, bis sie Juli 2022 in ihrer neuen Rolle als Data Steward für Sozial- und Geisteswissenschaften im Data Science Center der Universität Bremen tätig wurde.

Edith Leitner, Lisa Schilhan

Marketingtools für Bibliotheksdienstleistungen am Beispiel von Open-Access-Zeitschriften[1]

Handbuch Repositorienmanagement, Hg. v. Blumesberger et al., 2024, S. 411–435
https://doi.org/10.25364/978390337423222

Edith Leitner, Universität Mozarteum Salzburg, Universitätsbibliothek, edith.leitner@moz.ac.at |
ORCID iD: 0000-0003-3033-2906
Lisa Schilhan, Universität Graz, Universitätsbibliothek, lisa.schilhan@uni-graz.at | ORCID iD: 0000-0002-1425-850X

1 Dieser Beitrag übernimmt großteils das Marketingschema der Masterarbeit von Edith Leitner: Leitner, E. (2017).

Zusammenfassung

Marketing bedeutet im besten Fall nicht mehr nur die Vermarktung von Produkten und Dienstleistungen, wie das bei der Make-and-Sell-Philosophie der Fall ist. Vielmehr ist das Ziel, bereits bei der Entwicklung und Einrichtung von Dienstleistungen analytischer und somit gezielter vorzugehen. Auch in Bibliotheken können neue Dienstleistungen unter Berücksichtigung der Wünsche von definierten Zielgruppen geplant und erstellt werden. Die drei Planungsphasen – Sense, Respond und Sell – tragen zum Gelingen einer neuen Dienstleistung bei. In allen drei Planungsphasen gibt es etablierte Werkzeuge und Vorgehensweisen. Anhand der geplanten Plattform für die Veröffentlichung von institutionellen Open-Access-Zeitschriften an der Universitätsbibliothek Mozarteum werden ausgewählte Analyseschritte und Tools vorgestellt.

Schlagwörter: Bibliothek; Marketing; Dienstleistung; Open Access; Publikation; Zeitschriften

Abstract

Marketing Tools for Library Services, Shown by the Example of Open-Access Journals

In the best-case scenario, marketing no longer just means marketing products and services, as is the case with the make-and-sell philosophy. It is rather the goal to take a more analytical and thus more targeted approach as early as during the development and establishment of services. In libraries, too, new services can be planned and created taking into account the wishes of defined target groups. The three planning phases – sense, respond and sell – contribute to the success of a new service. There are established tools and procedures in all three planning phases. Using the planned platform for the publication of institutional open-access journals at the Mozarteum University Library as an example, selected analysis steps and tools will be presented.

Keywords: Library; marketing; services; open access; publication; journals

1. Einleitung

Die Universitätsbibliothek des Mozarteums plante die Einführung einer Open-Access-Zeitschriften-Plattform entlang des hier vorgestellten Marketingkonzeptes. Dieses Marketingkonzept umfasst die Entwicklung, Errichtung und Vermarktung der Dienstleistung und gliedert sich somit in die drei Planungsphasen: 1.) Sense, 2.) Respond und 3.) Sell.

Für jede Planungsphase werden passende Werkzeuge vorgestellt und Analyseschritte aufgezeigt. So erfolgt in der Sense-Phase die Analyse der internen Situation, die Kund:innen- und Dienstleistungsanalyse sowie die SWOT-Analyse. Inhaltlich erfährt diese Phase die ausführlichste Darstellung in diesem Beitrag.

In der Respond-Phase werden die Ansoff'sche Matrix und die „6 Ps" für die Planung herangezogen und in der Sell-Phase wird der Marketingmix zusammengestellt.

Die Universitätsbibliothek Graz steuert zudem die Sichtweise und jahrelange Erfahrung mit dem Zeitschriftenmodul des Repositoriums von Visual Library bei. Mit dem Hinweis auf den notwendigen Umsetzungsplan und die Evaluierung des Konzeptes endet dieser Entwurf.

Die hier angewendeten Marketingtools können aber auch bei der Planung und Einführung von anderen Dienstleistungen herangezogen werden. Es ist also möglich, dieses Konzept als eine Art Basis-Anleitung für jedes neue Projekt zu verwenden, das man anhand der drei Phasen organisieren möchte. Jede Phase und jedes Tool werden bezüglich Funktion kurz vorgestellt und dann anhand des konkreten Falles veranschaulicht, wobei der Schwerpunkt auf der Sense-Phase liegt.

Da es sich hierbei nur um eine Auswahl handeln kann – schließlich gibt es so viel mehr Marketingwerkzeuge und -strategien[2] – verhilft die eigene weitere Auseinandersetzung mit anderen Tools sicherlich zur Verfeinerung oder zu einer anderen Akzentsetzung.

2 Einen ersten Überblick findet man beispielsweise bei: Mödinger, W.; Schmid, S.; Seitz, J. (2018).

2. Sense-Phase

In der Sense-Phase erfolgt zunächst die Betrachtung der internen Situation, sowie die Kund:innen- und der Dienstleistungsanalyse. In einer anschließenden SWOT-Analyse[3] werden diese gesammelten Informationen unter Einbeziehung äußerer Faktoren für eine Einschätzung bezüglich der internen Schwächen und Stärken sowie der externen Möglichkeiten und Risiken zusammengeführt.

2.1. Sense-Phase – interne Situation

Das vorrangige Ziel der Analyse der internen Situation besteht darin, sich über das Selbstverständnis der Bibliothek und der Trägerorganisation, also der Hochschule zu informieren: Wie präsentiert sich die Bibliothek beispielsweise im Mission-Statement und/oder den Leitlinien und ergeben sich daraus Hinweise, dass die geplante Dienstleistung mit den Zielen und Möglichkeiten der Bibliothek vereinbar ist?[4]

Hinsichtlich der Trägerorganisation sollte untersucht werden, ob für diese neue Dienstleistung eine dauerhafte finanzielle Unterstützung realistisch ist. Dazu werden die Ziele, die sich in der Corporate Mission / den Leitlinien, den Leistungsvereinbarungen der Hochschule mit dem Bundesministerium sowie den Entwicklungsplänen und der Open-Access Policy befinden und welche beispielsweise Open Science, Open Access oder ganz konkret die Publikation von Open-Access-Zeitschriften ansprechen, zusammengetragen und in eine Aufstellung gebracht. Sollte bereits eine institutionelle Roadmap für Open Science vorhanden sein oder gerade entwickelt werden, dann wäre das eine hervorragende Basis. Je stärker die zu entwickelnde Dienstleistung mit den Aufträgen und Zielen der Institution vereinbar ist, umso eher kann mit Unterstützung gerechnet werden. Die Ergebnisse in Form von konkreten Passagen aus den genannten Dokumenten können in einem späteren Schritt bei den Verhandlungen mit dem Rektorat herangezogen werden.

In der Open-Access Policy der Universität Graz wird in drei Abschnitten auf die Herausgabe von Open-Access-Zeitschriften Bezug genommen:

> 4. Die Universität Graz fördert das Engagement ihrer Mitarbeiterinnen und Mitarbeiter als Gutachterinnen für und Herausgeber von Open-Access-Zeitschriften. [...]

---

3 Strength, Weakness, Opportunities, Threats

4 Bei dieser Analyse kann auch das Markensteuerrad von Esch nützlich sein. Siehe beispielsweise den Blogbeitrag Pundy, D. (2021).

> 7. Open-Access-Publikationen (‚Green' und ‚Golden') sowie Mitarbeit (Herausgeberschaft, Editorial Board, Gutachtertätigkeit) bei Open-Access-Zeitschriften werden in der Wissensbilanz der Universität Graz gesondert ausgewiesen.
> 8. Diese Tätigkeiten werden bei der Evaluierung der Forschungsleistungen der Wissenschaftlerinnen und Wissenschaftler, insbesondere auch bei Habilitations- und Berufungsverfahren, durch die Universität gesondert berücksichtigt.[5]

In der Leistungsvereinbarung der Universität Graz 2019-2021 wird unter dem Schwerpunkt „Smart University" die Unterstützung von Open-Access-Zeitschriften erwähnt:

> Der Ausbau der Open Access Journale und Publikationen und der offene Zugang zu Literatur, Forschungsdaten sowie Lehr- und Lernmaterialien stellen weitere unentbehrliche Maßnahmen dar. Begleitet wird dies durch die Zurverfügungstellung einer zeitgemäßen digitalen Infrastruktur und elektronischer Workflows.[6]

Die Universität Mozarteum legte bereits 2018 in der vom Rektorat verabschiedeten Open-Access Policy fest, dass für universitätseigene Zeitschriften ein Zeitschriftenserver eingerichtet wird.[7]

Die Leistungsvereinbarung von 2022-24 sieht die Universitätsbibliothek als „Ausgangs- und Knotenpunkt eines infrastrukturellen Forschungsservices", welches auch weiterentwickelt werden sollte. Genannt werden die Bereiche Open Access, Open Data, Open Science und Open Educational Resources.[8]

Die Digitalisierungsstrategie ist derzeit das aktuellste Papier und hier wird das Bekenntnis zu Open Science samt Rolle der Bibliothek deutlich hervorgehoben:

> Eine zentrale Rolle bei Digitalisierungsvorhaben in diesem Handlungsfeld spielt die Universitätsbibliothek Mozarteum Salzburg. Mit dem Bereich der digitalen Produktion und Publikation wird auf eine zentrale Herausforderung in den Digitalisierungsbemühungen an Universitäten reagiert. Einerseits soll dem gesellschaftlichen Anspruch des Open Access entsprochen, andererseits die digitale Souveränität über die an der Universität entstandenen Produktionen sichergestellt werden.

---

5 Open-Access Policy der Universität Graz: https://ub.uni-graz.at/de/forschen-publizieren/open-access-policy-der-universitaet-graz/

6 Universität Graz; Bundesministerium für Bildung, Wissenschaft und Forschung: Leistungsvereinbarung, S. 7.

7 Universität Mozarteum Salzburg (2018), S. 2.

8 Universität Mozarteum Salzburg (2021a), S. 24, S. 53 u. S. 55.

All diese Ambitionen decken sich mit dem Anspruch einer offenen Universität, in der bestmöglich Partizipation und Transparenz gelebt werden. Damit einher geht ein klares Bekenntnis zu Open Science, das von Open Access über Open Data bis hin zu Citizen Science reicht und komplexe rechtliche Herausforderungen wie etwa Fragen zum Datenschutz oder zum Lizenz- und Urheberrecht inkludiert.[9]

2.2. Sense-Phase – Kundenanalyse

Die Sense-Phase beinhaltet zudem die Kund:innenanalyse, bei der die Zielgruppe definiert wird. Im konkreten Fall betrifft es jene Wissenschaftler:innen, die eine Zeitschrift oder Schriftenreihe Open Access veröffentlichen möchten. Man könnte hier noch differenzieren, ob es sich um die Herausgeber:innenschaft einer neu zu gründenden Zeitschrift oder die Transformation einer bestehenden Subskriptionszeitschrift handelt.

Die definierte Zielgruppe erhält einen Fragebogen, der zunächst über die geplante Dienstleistung und den Zweck des Fragebogens informiert. Hierbei erweist sich, dass bereits ein Fragebogen Marketingaufgaben erfüllt, weil damit die Zielgruppe auf das Thema aufmerksam gemacht wird und sich von Anfang an eingebunden fühlen kann.

Der Fragebogen sollte zum einen klären, wie viele Wissenschaftler:innen sich für die neue Dienstleistung interessieren, also wie hoch der Bedarf einzuschätzen ist. Am besten ist dies kombiniert mit dem zeitlichen Aspekt, womit eine Basis für die Planung des personellen Aufwandes geschaffen wird. Außerdem gilt es herauszufinden, ob es begrüßt wird, dass die Bibliothek diese Dienstleistung anbietet, und welche Leistungen im Speziellen gewünscht sind.

Die Umfrage am Mozarteum enthielt u. a. folgende Fragen:

- Wird bereits eine Zeitschrift herausgegeben oder ist eine Herausgabe in den nächsten zwei Jahren geplant?
- Kann man sich vorstellen, diese zusätzlich Open Access zu veröffentlichen?
    - Wenn nein: Warum nicht?
    - Wenn ja: Würde man es begrüßen, wenn die Veröffentlichung und Archivierung der Zeitschrift von Seiten der Bibliothek erfolgt?
- In welchem Intervall soll die Zeitschrift / sollen einzelne Artikel erscheinen?
- Welche Anforderungen müssten bei der Open-Access-Veröffentlichung der Zeitschrift erfüllt werden? Elemente wie Responsive Design, Dateiformate,

9 Universität Mozarteum Salzburg (2021b)

Indexierung, Statistik, bevorzugter Persistent Identifier und Langzeitarchivierung wurden dabei angeführt und die jeweilige Bedeutung wurde abgefragt.

2.3. Sense-Phase – Dienstleistungsanalyse

In dieser Phase wird die Dienstleistung definiert und ein Blick auf das Anliegen der Bibliothek geworfen: Warum will die Bibliothek diese Dienstleistung anbieten bzw. welches (Marketing-) Ziel soll damit für die Bibliothek erreicht werden.

Anschließend betrachtet man die Publikationsdienstleistung als Kombination der Prozessphasen Potenzialorientierung, Erstellung und Ergebnis. Analog dazu werden die notwendigen Kommunikationsleistungen – extern, intern und interaktiv – beschrieben. Hier geht es darum, einen ersten Überblick über die Anforderungen, die diese Dienstleistung mit sich bringt, zu erhalten.

Letztendlich werden in dieser Planungsphase, der Sense-Phase, die eingeholten Angebote aufgelistet und beschrieben sowie anhand der drei Kriterien Vorteil, Kompatibilität und Komplexität analysiert.

2.3.1. Definition und Marketingziel

In unserem konkreten Fall geht es um eine Publikationsdienstleistung, bei der für die Veröffentlichung von Open-Access-Zeitschriften eine Plattform und personelle Unterstützung angeboten werden.

Die Frage nach dem Marketingziel bei der Entwicklung der neuen Dienstleistung kann pauschal mit der Bindung der Forschenden an die Bibliothek beantwortet werden. Ergänzend zum bisherigen Dienstleistungsangebot präsentiert sich die Bibliothek als zeitgemäße Partnerin bei der digitalen Veröffentlichung von wissenschaftlicher Literatur.

2.3.2. Dienstleistungen als Kombinationsprozess

Dienstleistungen lassen sich als Kombinationsprozess bestehend aus drei Phasen beschreiben. In der ersten Phase, der Potenzialorientierung, gilt es auszuloten, ob und inwiefern der/die Dienstleistungsanbieter:in die Fähigkeit und die Bereitschaft zur Erbringung der Dienstleistung aufbringt. Diese Überlegungen werden dann in der SWOT-Analyse bei den Stärken und Schwächen ersichtlich. In der zweiten Phase, dem Erstellungsprozess, erfolgt die Erbringung der Dienstleistung, bei der der Prozess durch den/die Dienstleistungsnachfrager:in ausgelöst wird. Die dritte

Phase ist die Ergebnisphase, also jene der Wirkung des Dienstleistungsergebnisses.[10]

Hier kommen drei Marketingbereiche zum Einsatz, nämlich das externe, interne und interaktive Marketing. Beim externen Marketing richtet sich die Bibliothek allgemein an die Leitung der Trägerorganisation und an die Herausgeber:innen, beispielsweise in Form von Information über die Dienstleistung.

Das interne Marketing findet zwischen der Bibliotheks- bzw. Projektleitung und den Mitarbeitenden statt und umfasst die Investition in das Training, die Motivation, adäquate Information und Teamarbeit.

Beim interaktiven Marketing geht es darum, die Herausgeber:innen zu überzeugen, dass mit Inanspruchnahme der Dienstleistung das Richtige getan wird. Neben den technischen Faktoren sollten daher auch die funktionalen und emotionalen Kriterien passen. Dazu gehört beispielsweise das Gefühl, dass sich der/die Bibliothekar:in ausreichend Zeit für die Betreuung nimmt.[11]

Die Bedeutung einer guten Interaktion zwischen Bibliothekar:in und Herausgeber:in kann nicht hoch genug eingeschätzt werden. Schließlich ist der/die Herausgeber:in selbst und in unserem Fall außerdem ihr/sein Gut in Form einer Publikation in den Prozess der Dienstleistung integriert. Das bedeutet, dass die inhaltliche Ebene und ein Teil der operativen Ebene von Seiten der Herausgeber:innen abgedeckt werden und somit diese selbst entscheidend zu Erfolg und Misserfolg beitragen. Daher liegt der Fokus von Seiten der Bibliothek zum einen auf dem Übertragungsmedium (Plattform) und zum anderen auf der Interaktion (Einschulung und Unterstützung).[12]

Hinsichtlich Interaktion ist es wichtig, Voraussetzungen für ein optimales Zusammentreffen und Zusammenwirken von Bibliothekar:in und Herausgeber:in zu schaffen und beispielsweise durch adäquate Schulungen der zuständigen Bibliothekar:innen Schwankungen in der Dienstleistungsqualität zu vermindern.

Auch wenn die Kommunikation vorbildlich funktioniert, wird sich eine Dienstleistung trotzdem nicht durchsetzen, wenn das Produkt an sich nicht überzeugt. Daher ist die Auseinandersetzung mit den unterschiedlichen, bereits am Markt befindlichen Produkten wichtig, und diese sollten so umfassend wie möglich beschrieben werden. Dabei empfiehlt es sich, ein besonderes Augenmerk auf die fol-

---

10 Hilke, W. (1984), S. 17ff.

11 Kotler, P.; Armstrong, G.; Wong, V. et al. (2010), S. 701f.

12 Kotler, P.; Armstrong, G.; Wong, V. et al. (2010), S. 694f.

genden drei Faktoren zu legen: Vorteil, Kompatibilität und Komplexität der Dienstleistung.[13] Zunächst werden daher die herangezogenen Angebote vorgestellt und anschließend anhand der drei Kriterien analysiert.

2.3.3. Vorstellung der Plattformen

Für die Universität Mozarteum kamen drei Plattformen in die engere Auswahl. Zum einen war dies das Zeitschriften-Modul von Visual Library, gehostet von der OBVSG. Dazu kamen die beiden Open-Source-Lösungen Open Journal Systems (OJS) und Janeway, die ebenso die Option eines externen Hostings anbieten. Über die beiden Open-Source-Plattformen kann der gesamte Redaktionsprozess koordiniert werden. Es handelt sich dabei um ein strukturiertes Konzept folgender praxisorientierter Nutzer:innenrollen[14], die in unterschiedlichen freigeschalteten Funktionen miteinander arbeiten: Systemadministrator:in, Website-Administrator:in, Journal-Manager:in und Redakteur:in, Autor:in, Gutachter:in, Leser:in.

Zahlreiche Informationsmaterialien und Anleitungsvideos stehen vor allem bezüglich Open Journal Systems zur Verfügung.[15]

Im Gegensatz zu den beiden Open-Source-Modellen beschränkt sich das Visual-Library-Zeitschriftenmodul auf die Präsentation der Zeitschrift und Veröffentlichung der fertigen Beiträge im PDF-Format. Da das Hochladen der Artikel von Seiten der Bibliothek erfolgt, sind hier keine aufwendigen Schulungen für die Herausgeber:innen notwendig.

2.3.4. Vorteils-, Kompatibilitäts- und Komplexitätsanalyse

Diese Dienstleistung punktet vor allem, wenn die Herausgeber:innen die Vorteile erkennen, eine Kompatibilität mit den eigenen Abläufen gegeben ist und sich die Anwendung durch geringe Komplexität, also hohe Benutzungsfreundlichkeit, auszeichnet. Diese Kriterien werden nun herangezogen, um zum einen allgemein die Herausgabe einer Open-Access-Zeitschrift und zum anderen jeweils die drei oben genannten Plattformen zu analysieren.

---

13 Kotler, P.; Armstrong, G.; Wong, V. et al. (2010), S. 309.

14 Schubert, Bernhard; Blechl, Guido (2020): Vortrag: Open Journal Systems (OJS3). Softwaregestützter Workflow für das Zeitschriftenmanagement. Universitätsbibliothek Wien. Und: Schubert, Bernhard; Blechl, Guido (2020): Handout: Walk Through – Ein typischer Workflow in einer OJS-Zeitschrift in OJS 3.2.1.2. Universitätsbibliothek Wien.

15 OJS FAQs: https://openjournalsystems.com/faq/

Vorteilsanalyse

- Als Vorteil von Open-Access-Zeitschriften kann vor allem der größere potenzielle Nutzer:innenkreis durch eine erhöhte Reichweite angeführt werden.
- Die Frage der längerfristigen Archivierung ist ebenso besser gelöst, da die Daten bei nachhaltigen Institutionen wie Universitäten abgelegt werden, die, im Gegensatz zu Verlagen, nicht profitorientiert agieren müssen.
- Die Souveränität bezüglich der eigenen Daten stellt einen weiteren bedeutenden Vorteil dar.
- Wenn die Zeitschrift bisher nur in Printform erschienen ist und nun zu einer reinen Open-Access-Zeitschrift wird, entfallen außerdem Arbeitsschritte und Kosten, wie beispielsweise Druck, Versand, Subskriptions- und Einnahmenverwaltung.
- Die bei beiden Open-Source-Lösungen angebotene Möglichkeit zur Abwicklung des gesamten Redaktionssystems schafft eine Arbeitserleichterung, da die Übersichtlichkeit und Nachvollziehbarkeit der Arbeitsschritte gegeben ist. Die einmal eingerichteten, automatisierten Mails beschleunigen den Prozess.
- Das Visual-Library-Zeitschriftenmodul bietet den Vorteil der automatischen Schnittstelle zum Bibliothekskatalog. Damit einhergehend werden die Werke über eine Browsersuche (z. B. Google) auffindbar.
- Probleme, die mit Raubverlagen entstehen könnten, entfallen bei der Herausgabe an der eigenen Institution.
- Gegenüber Verlagszeitschriften erfolgt eine Kostenersparnis hinsichtlich Druckkostenzuschuss oder APCs (Article Processing Charges). Verlagszeitschriften können zudem kaum mit Zeitersparnis punkten, wenn die Vorarbeiten wie beispielsweise der Redaktions- oder Reviewprozess und das Lektorat dennoch von Seiten der Herausgeber:innen zu leisten sind.
- Ein Nachteil ist der hohe Personaleinsatz, um die Professionalität des Zeitschriftenauftritts von Verlagen zu erreichen.

Kompatibilitätsanalyse

Im Sinne der Kompatibilität soll eine Strategie gefunden werden, damit Herausgeber:innen die neue Dienstleistung effektiv in ihren Arbeitsalltag integrieren können.

Bei bestehenden Zeitschriften kann ein/e Herausgeber:in bei der Verwendung des Visual-Library-Zeitschriftenmoduls den bisherigen Redaktions- und Produktionsprozess beibehalten. Das gesamte Heft und/oder die einzelnen Artikel können entweder über Mail oder bei größeren Dokumenten über das österreichische Hochleistungsdatennetz Aconet an die Bibliothek gesendet werden. Dieser Vorgang ist nicht aufwendig und hatte bei der Weitergabe für den Druck ebenfalls zu erfolgen. Der Redaktionsprozess erfährt hier somit keine nennenswerten Änderungen.

Unabhängig von der gewählten Plattform müssen jedoch sowohl bei neuen als auch bei zu transformierenden Zeitschriften das Layout, der Satz, die Struktur der Artikel für den Internetauftritt eingerichtet und für die Auffindbarkeit angepasst werden. Die Rechte und Lizenzen sind festzulegen und für Persistent Identifier ist zu sorgen.

Die Open-Source-Systeme erfordern die Aneignung von Anwender:innenkenntnissen. Entscheiden sich die Herausgeber:innen für die Verwendung des automatisierten Redaktionsprozesses, müssen alle Autor:innen, Gutachter:innen und Lektor:innen Zugriff erhalten und die notwendigen Fertigkeiten erlernen. Anleitungen/Einschulungen und Unterstützungsleistungen sollten daher von der Bibliothek oder den Anbieter:innen angeboten werden. Wenn diese Hürde genommen ist, bieten die umfassenden Verwaltungstools dieser Systeme eine gute Übersicht über die Projekte. Diese Systeme sind nach einer Einarbeitungsphase sehr funktional und erhöhen die Transparenz des Redaktionsprozesses.

Komplexitätsanalyse

Da sich bei Visual Library (VL) die Aufgabe der Herausgeber:innen darauf beschränkt, die Artikel über einen Mailaccount oder über Aconet abzuliefern, liegt hier keine komplexe Vorgehensweise vor. Jedoch wird mittels VL auch nur die Veröffentlichung und nicht der gesamte Redaktionsprozess einer Open-Access-Zeitschrift abgedeckt.

Bei den hier besprochenen Open-Source-Systemen ist der Komplexitätsgrad hingegen höher. Vor allem die Herausgeber:innen müssen sich Kenntnisse zur Anwendung der Software aneignen und – sofern nicht extern gehostet – nach jedem größeren Update die Funktionalitäten testen. Je nach Umfang des Schulungs- und Unterstützungsangebotes kann die Komplexität jedoch abgemildert werden.

2.4. Sense-Phase – SWOT-Analyse

In einer SWOT-Analyse werden die bisher gesammelten Informationen sowie die äußeren Faktoren für eine Einschätzung bezüglich der internen Schwächen und Stärken sowie der externen Möglichkeiten und Risiken zusammengeführt. Ziel ist es, durch diese Bündelung ein Bewusstsein für die Gesamtsituation zu erhalten.

Zu beachten ist, dass mit internen Faktoren tatsächlich nur bibliotheksinterne Stärken und Schwächen gemeint sind. Die Einstellung der Hochschule und das Verhalten der Herausgeber:innen zählen zu den externen Chancen und Risiken. Die Aufstellung von Wiesner und Sponholz[16] bietet Anhaltspunkte, welche Faktoren dafür herangezogen werden können. Dabei kann jeder Faktor, je nach Einordnung in zutreffend oder nicht zutreffend, die Seite wechseln: Nicht vorhandene Stärken werden zu Schwächen und umgekehrt.

Stärken	Schwächen
▪ Spezialkenntnisse, -wissen ▪ Besondere Erfahrungen ▪ Kernkompetenzen ▪ Beziehungen ▪ Innovationsfähigkeit ▪ Markenimage, Bekanntheit	▪ Schlechtes Image ▪ Zu teuer ▪ Kapitalmangel ▪ Zu langsam ▪ Schlechte Mitarbeiter:innen ▪ Standortnachteile
Chancen	**Risiken**
▪ Neue Technologien ▪ Neue Trends ▪ Veränderte Kund:innenwünsche ▪ Neue Märkte ▪ Neue Herausforderungen ▪ Boomende Branchen	▪ Neue Technologien ▪ Rohstoffknappheit (z. B. Öl) ▪ Neue Wettbewerber ▪ Gesetzliche Änderungen ▪ Gesellschaftliche Änderungen ▪ Politikwechsel

Im konkreten Fall sieht die SWOT-Analyse für das Mozarteum folgendermaßen aus:

Interne Stärken der Bibliothek:

- sehr motiviert, gesellschaftliche Verantwortung wahrzunehmen und an der Open-Access-Veröffentlichung von Forschungsergebnissen mitzuwirken;

16 Wiesner, K. A.; Sponholz, U. (2007), S. 54.

- starkes Bewusstsein, dass institutionelles Ownership von Daten und Publikationen sowie deren längerfristige Archivierung notwendig sind;
- traditionelles Wissen bezüglich professioneller und standardisierter Aufbereitung der dafür notwendigen Metadaten;
- Nähe zu Forschenden und Publizierenden, da die Bibliothek in anderen Bereichen bereits als kompetenter Kontakt und vertrauenswürdige Institution anerkannt ist;
- vorhandene Kompetenz/Spezialkenntnisse bezüglich Open Access / Open Science (Creative-Commons-Lizenzen, DOIs, ORCID-iD);
- Offenheit für neue Technologien;
- Dienstleistungs-, Schulungs- und Informationskompetenz aufgrund verwandter Dienstleistungen;
- starke Vernetzung mit kompetenten Kolleg:innen anderer Bibliotheken; dieser Erfahrungsaustausch ermöglicht die raschere Professionalisierung in diesem neuen Bereich.

Interne Schwächen der Bibliothek:

- keine Erfahrung bezüglich Publizieren und Vertrieb;
- in manchen Wissenschaftsgebieten geringes Fachwissen;
- die Professionalität von guten Verlagen bezüglich Auftritt, Layout, Vertrieb, Indexierung kann wahrscheinlich nicht oder nur sehr langsam auf demselben Niveau erreicht werden;
- keine ausreichenden IT-Kenntnisse (dies kann jedoch durch externes Hosting kompensiert werden).

Externe Chancen:

- politische Unterstützung für Open-Access-Dienste, Bewusstsein dafür, dass ein Doubledipping[17] der Verlage viel Steuergeld kostet;
- die Universität unterstützt diese Dienstleistung im Zuge des Digitalisierungsprojektes und in der Open-Access Policy;
- erhöhter Bedarf an frei zugänglichen Online-Texten wurde mit der Corona-Pandemie sichtbar; damit stieg die Bereitschaft, auch selbst Open Access zu publizieren;

---

17 Doubledipping bedeutet in diesem Kontext, dass Verlage bei Hybrid-Zeitschriften doppelt verdienen: Zusätzlich zu den Subskriptionsgebühren werden einzelne Artikel durch Article Processing Charges finanziert. Siehe: https://open-access.network/informieren/glossar#c6207

- Herausgeber:innen besitzen immer mehr digitale Kompetenz; mehr Vielfalt bei der Herausgabe von Texten durch Unabhängigkeit von Verlagsvorgaben ist möglich;
- Einsparung von Druckkostenzuschüssen oder APCs;
- kein Problem mit Raubverlagen;
- die Artikel erreichen bei Open-Access-Veröffentlichung potenziell mehr Leser:innen, deren Leseverhalten zudem generell verstärkt digital stattfindet.

Externe Risiken:

- Aufwand für die Herausgeber:innen ist vor allem bei einer lokal gehosteten Open-Source-Plattform größer;
- Verlage sind traditionelle und verlässliche Partner für wissenschaftliche Veröffentlichungen, und Herausgeber:innen weisen oftmals eine starke Bindung zu ihnen auf;
- das Prestige traditioneller Verlage kann für eine wissenschaftliche Karriere wichtig sein; neue Zeitschriften ohne vererbtes Verlagsprestige können für Nachwuchs-Wissenschaftler:innen ein Risiko darstellen;
- hohe Professionalität von Verlagen bezüglich Verbreitung und Vermarktung.

Fazit

Die größte Herausforderung für eine Bibliothek besteht darin, sich gegenüber Verlagsveröffentlichungen zu beweisen, vor allem, weil das Niveau an Professionalität bezüglich Layout, Werbung und Prestige von einer institutionellen Open-Access-Zeitschriftenplattform erst erarbeitet werden muss. Es besteht für die Herausgeber:innen zudem ein zeitlicher Mehraufwand, wenn nicht auf die Ressourcen des Verlages zurückgegriffen werden kann.

Der Vorteil des Open-Access-Publizierens spricht zwar grundsätzlich für die universitäre Plattform, wobei die Datensouveränität und das Kostenargument stark im Vordergrund stehen. Verlage haben jedoch die Open-Access-Veröffentlichung ebenso als entscheidend für den weiteren Fortbestand erkannt und dafür mehrere lukrative Geschäftszweige entwickelt. Umso wichtiger ist es, eine kostengünstige Alternative anzubieten, damit der gesellschaftliche Auftrag, Wissen der Allgemeinheit zur Verfügung zu stellen, weiterhin erfüllt werden kann.

3. Respond-Phase – „6 Ps"

Aufbauend auf den Ergebnissen der Analysen der Sense-Phase (strategisches Marketing), kann mit der Planung und Konzeption der Dienstleistung begonnen werden. Diese Respond-Phase und die spätere Vermarktung (Sell-Phase) fallen unter das operative Marketing.

Da es sich bei der Plattform für Open-Access-Zeitschriften um die Entwicklung einer neuen Dienstleistung für einen bereits bestehenden Markt (Universitäts-/Hochschulangehörige, die als Herausgeber:innen fungieren wollen) handelt, lautet die Strategie nach der Matrix von Ansoff[18]: Dienstleistungsentwicklung. Für diese Marketingstrategie wird generell empfohlen, im Marketingmix den Fokus auf den Submix Kommunikation zu legen. Der Marketingmix kommt vor allem in der Sell-Phase zum Tragen. Davor ist jedoch, gemäß der Strategie, noch die Dienstleistung zu entwickeln.

Die Konzeption der Dienstleistung orientiert sich an den „6 Ps", also den Marketinginstrumenten Produkt (Dienstleistung), Preis, Platzierung, Promotion (Kommunikation), Personal und Prozess. Denn, so Claudia Jung:

> Jedes Produkt hat einen Preis, benötigt Kommunikation um bekannt zu werden und einen Platz, wo es genutzt wird. Dienstleistungen sind zudem auf qualifiziertes Personal angewiesen. Gut koordinierte Prozesse steigern den Workflow und das Image der Bibliothek als schneller Informationslieferant.[19]

Die Marketinginstrumente sollen zunächst helfen, das vorhandene, notwendige Wissen rund um die Dienstleistung – wie beispielsweise Funktion, Workflows, Anforderungen und Leistungen – mithilfe unterschiedlicher Elemente[20] zu strukturieren und zu bündeln. Bei manchen Elementen, die ursprünglich für Produkte entwickelt wurden, kann die Anwendung auf eine Dienstleistung etwas forciert wirken. Dennoch lohnt der Versuch, sich innerhalb dieser Struktur mit der geplanten Dienstleistung auseinanderzusetzen. Idealerweise sollte es anschließend möglich sein, auf Basis dieses Überblicks die Gestaltung der Dienstleistung und Kommunikation so zu planen, dass ein möglichst großer Anwender:innenkreis angesprochen wird.

---

18 Ansoff, H. I. (1966), S. 132.
19 Jung, C. (2003), S. 26.
20 Diese Elemente sind in der Folge unter Anführungszeichen dargestellt.

3.1. Produkt/Dienstleistung[21]

Das „Kernprodukt“ setzt sich bei einer Open-Access-Zeitschriftenplattform aus den folgenden Funktionen zusammen:

- digitale Administration des Workflows: von der Einreichung über Review und Annahme des Artikels zum Lektorat und Layout (diese Funktion gilt nicht für das Visual-Library-Modul);
- digitale Publikation;
- digitaler Auftritt mit Suchfunktion;
- Archivierung.

Als „Varianten“ können entweder die Unterscheidung in Zeitschriften oder die Schriftenreihe gesehen werden, ebenso die Abstufung bezüglich des Ausmaßes an Unterstützungsleistung von Seiten der Bibliothek. Führen die Herausgebenden die Verwaltung selbstständig durch, dann beschränkt sich die Unterstützung auf den Support beim Aufsetzen des Zeitschriftenauftritts. Zudem können noch Supportleistungen bei Updates benötigt werden. Sollte die Plattform nicht für den Redaktionsworkflow verwendet werden, kann die Bibliothek das Hochladen der Artikel übernehmen.

Die unterschiedlichen gewünschten Dateiformate wie PDF, HTML und/oder EPUB fallen unter „Verpackung“.

Zum „Styling“ zählen die weitreichenden Applikationsmöglichkeiten, die über ein Responsive Design verwirklicht werden, sowie die Usability der Plattform, die möglichst intuitiv sein und ausreichende Informationen zur Verfügung stellen soll. Zum „Styling“ gehören auch die Möglichkeit zur ansprechenden Gestaltung des Auftritts der Zeitschrift, einheitliche Layoutvorlagen für die Artikel, die Qualität der Metadaten und des langfristigen Zugriffs auf die Artikel samt klarer Anleitung für die Nachnutzung über Lizenzen und die Zitierfähigkeit aufgrund von Persistent Identifiers wie beispielsweise DOIs. Maschinenlesbarkeit und Barrierefreiheit fallen ebenso in diesen Bereich.

Überlegt werden sollen zudem die für die Dienstleistung notwendigen Vor-, Konzeptions-, Ereignis- und Ergebnisleistungen.

---

21 Wiesner, K. A.; Sponholz, U. (2007), S. 81.

Unter die „Vorleistung" fallen:

- die Gespräche mit der Universitäts-/Hochschulleitung, bei denen das Unterstützungsniveau für die geplante Dienstleistung eruiert und festgelegt wird;
- die Kalkulation der Finanz- und Personalmittel (siehe auch die Marketinginstrumente Preis und Personal) und die Organisation der Bereitstellung;
- das Einholen verschiedener (Hostings-)Angebote;
- die Festlegung der Zielgruppe;
- die Bedarfserhebung mittels Umfrage.

Zur „Konzeptionsleistung" zählen:

- die Darstellung des Installations- und Updateprozesses für alle drei Modelle;
- die Entscheidung bezüglich Plattform;
- die Schaffung der technischen Voraussetzungen – Programmierung/ Installation;
- die Festlegung der Zuständigkeiten und Workflows;
- das Aneignen der Kenntnisse zur Plattform und den Artikelvorlagen;
- die Konzeption des Auftrittes der Plattform;
- das Zusammenstellen/Konzipieren von Informationsmaterialien und Schulungsangeboten.

Für die Entscheidungsfindung spielen notwendige IT-Kenntnisse eine zentrale Rolle. Open-Source-Software ist grundsätzlich sehr arbeitsaufwendig und erfordert IT-Kenntnisse, die in einer Bibliothek nicht zwingend vorhanden sind. Verfolgt die Institution die Strategie, vermehrt Open-Source-Produkte einzusetzen, möchte jedoch nicht in zusätzliches Personal investieren, gibt es die Möglichkeit des externen Hostings für Open Journal Systems und Janeway.

Zur „Ereignisleistung" gehören alle Unterstützungsleistungen (siehe Kommunikation). Die „Ergebnisleistung" befasst sich mit der Qualitätskontrolle in Form von Feedback und Evaluierung.

3.2. Preis

Im Marketinginstrument Preis werden alle für die Dienstleistung anfallenden Produkt-, Personal- und Kommunikationskosten sowie jene Maßnahmen (Auffindbarkeit, Usability, Geschwindigkeit und Informationsqualität), die den Zeitaufwand für Anwender:innen minimieren, in einer Tabelle gegenübergestellt.[22]

3.3. Platzierung

Bei der Platzierung geht es um das Einbinden der Dienstleistung. Entscheidend ist neben dem Wie (online/digital und 24/7) und dem Wo (Webseite der Bibliothek) auch die dadurch erreichbare Verbreitung, z. B. die direkte Integration der Artikel in den Bibliothekskatalog.[23] Dies ist beim Visual-Library-Zeitschriftenmodul durch die direkte Anbindung der Plattform an den Bibliothekskatalog Primo gegeben. Bezüglich Open Journal Systems und Janeway ist das zusätzliche Programmieren einer Schnittstelle erforderlich oder kann indirekt über die Einbindung von DOAJ (Directory of Open Access Journals) in den Bibliothekskatalog erfolgen. Der Kontakt zwischen Support und Herausgeber:in kann planmäßig – sowohl persönlich als auch automatisiert – stattfinden.

3.4. Kommunikation

Hinsichtlich Kommunikation sollten bei Dienstleistungen, wie bereits erwähnt, neben der externen auch die bibliotheksinterne sowie die interaktive Kommunikation zwischen Herausgeber:in und Bibliothekar:in bei der Anwendung berücksichtigt werden.[24]

Zur „externen Kommunikation" mit der Trägerorganisation zählen Budgetgespräche, Personalplanung, Produktpräsentationen, Festlegung von Kriterien und die Vertragsunterzeichnung der Universitätsleitung. Die Koordinierungsgespräche bezüglich Hard- und Software sowie der Schnittstellen finden mit der IT-Abteilung statt. Die Rechts- und Prüfungsabteilung sollte u. a. hinsichtlich der Verträge, Datenschutzvereinbarungen und möglichen Auftragsverwertungsverträgen eingebunden werden.

Bei der externen Kommunikation mit den Anwender:innen ist es hilfreich, eine Unterscheidung zwischen Informations- und Werbemaßnahmen zu treffen. Im Bereich der Information plant das Mozarteum Informationsveranstaltungen und

22 Weingand, D. E. (1998), S. 96.

23 Kotler, P. (1982), S. 321. Und: Jung, C. (2003), S. 21.

24 Dienstleistungsmarketing, Gabler Wirtschaftslexikon: https://wirtschaftslexikon.gabler.de/definition/dienstleistungsmarketing-27309

Schulungen. Hinsichtlich Werbung kommen einige Bereiche der klassischen Werbung zum Einsatz: Broschüren/Flyer, Plakate, das Direkt-/Dialogmarketing (Gespräche, Mails) und die Corporate Identity.

Die Grazer Universitätsbibliothek präsentiert beispielsweise im Eventkalender der Universität die geplanten Workshops. Das Semesterprogramm wird über Mails an die zuständigen Stellen und Interessent:innen gesendet. Das gesamte Programm wird zudem über Folder und Plakate sichtbar gemacht. Die Einzelveranstaltungen werden im Uni-Newsletter, mittels Intranet-Newsmeldungen und Veranstaltungshinweisen am Display der Bibliothekshalle angekündigt.

Die „interaktive Kommunikation" während der Dienstleistung basiert auf der Vorbereitung und Information der Herausgeber:innen, schließlich wirken sie an der Erstellung der Dienstleistung ganz entscheidend mit. Checklisten, Schritt-für-Schritt-Anleitungen und Videos können diesen persönlichen Kontakt begleiten oder teilweise ersetzen. Für die persönliche Interaktion ist die Qualität des Kontaktes, die durch sachliche und Gesprächskompetenz sowie ausreichend Zeit geprägt wird, ausschlaggebend. Zudem sollte die Kommunikation den Maßstäben wie Freundlichkeit, Höflichkeit und Respekt entsprechen.

Die innerbetriebliche Information bezieht sich zunächst auf die Einschulung der zuständigen Mitarbeiter:innen und dann in weiterer Folge darauf, die Kolleg:innen generell über diese neue Dienstleistung zu informieren: Wie präsentieren sich Treffer im Bibliothekskatalog und an welche Kontaktpersonen kann bei Anfragen verwiesen werden?

An der Universität Graz kommt bereits seit 2013 das Visual-Library-Zeitschriftenmodul zur Anwendung, wobei für Herausgeber:innen von Open-Access-Zeitschriften unterschiedliche Unterstützungsmöglichkeiten von Seiten der Bibliothek angeboten werden. In der Regel beginnt der Kontakt mit einem persönlichen Informationsgespräch, in welchem die technischen und inhaltlichen Voraussetzungen der Plattform, Grundlagen des Workflows und Informationen zu best practices vermittelt werden. Die Herausgeber:innen skizzieren dabei das Zeitschriftenprojekt, und Fragen zu Layout, Paginierung, DOI, ISSN-Vergabe und Indexierung in Literaturdatenbanken werden besprochen. Soweit es sinnvoll ist, werden Schulungen für alle Zeitschriftenherausgeber:innen angeboten (z. B. Academic Search Engine Optimization). Im laufenden Betrieb ist eine ständige Kommunikation mit den Redaktionen durch den Upload der Ausgaben sowie Änderungen in Workflows und Updates gegeben.

Ein bewährtes Mittel, um die Kommunikation unter den Herausgeber:innen zu unterstützen, ist ein jährliches Treffen aller Herausgeber:innen der eigenen Institution. Diese gemeinsamen Netzwerktreffen sind für die zuständigen Bibliothekar:innen äußerst informativ. Gemeinsame Initiativen, Fördermöglichkeiten oder Ressourcenfragen können dabei erörtert werden.

3.5. Personal

Das Marketinginstrument Personal befasst sich mit den Aspekten der Personalplanung und -auswahl, ebenso mit der Einschulung, Fortbildung und Motivation.[25] Wenn die Dienstleistung von denselben Personen geplant und umgesetzt wird, die diese Dienstleistung später administrieren, besteht zumeist eine ideale, sehr motivierende Ausgangslage, da man von Beginn an dabei ist und mitentscheiden kann. Die Zeitplanung bezüglich Einführung der Dienstleistung und Einschulung soll bei allen Fällen gut aufeinander abgestimmt werden.

3.6. Prozess

Das Marketinginstrument Prozess setzt sich mit den Abläufen auseinander, zum einen aus der Sicht der Anwender:innen hinsichtlich Herausgabe, Publikation und Rezeption, zum anderen aus der Sicht der Bibliothek hinsichtlich Interaktionsprozess und -technik sowie des Erstellungsprozesses.[26] Die Darstellung der Prozesse erfolgt am besten in Form von Workflows, bei denen Zuständigkeiten genau zugeschrieben werden. Das Durchspielen in Testsystemen erweist sich ebenfalls als sehr hilfreich.

Der Interaktionsprozess sollte, wie bereits angesprochen, die Kriterien der Usability, Convenience, Erkennbarkeit, Geschwindigkeit, Bearbeitungsqualität und leichten Response erfüllen. Letzteres bedeutet, dass der/die Anwender:in unkompliziert mit dem Support in Kontakt treten kann und eine rasche Rückmeldung erhält.

Es werden sowohl automatisierte als auch persönliche Interaktionstechniken angeboten. So sollten alle wichtigen Hinweise und Informationen in Form von Checklisten, Anleitungen und Videos online abrufbar sein. Die Schulungen und Informationsveranstaltungen hingegen erfolgen persönlich und, wo sinnvoll, kollektiv. Individuelle Anfragen können zudem sowohl telefonisch als auch schriftlich oder vor Ort in der Bibliothek erfolgen.

---

25 Wiesner, K. A.; Sponholz, U. (2007), S. 96, S. 132. Und: Umlauf, K. (2014), S. 10.
26 Wiesner, K. A.; Sponholz, U. (2007), S. 95.

Während der Herausgabe- und Publikationsprozess bei Open Journal Systems und Janeway grundsätzlich individuell von Seiten der Herausgeber:innen erfolgt, liegt der Upload-Prozess bei Visual Library in den Händen der Bibliothek. Das Mozarteum plant, dieses Service auch bei einer Open-Source-Plattform anzubieten, sofern kein gesamter Redaktionsprozess über die Plattform erfolgen soll und die Personalressourcen dies ermöglichen.

4. Sell-Phase – Marketingmix

Die Marketinginstrumente zeichnen das Gesamtbild der Dienstleistung und liefern die Basis für ein Pflichtenheft und die Umsetzung. Aus der Gesamtheit sollen jedoch auch jene ausgewählt und zu einem Marketingmix kombiniert werden, die als besonders wichtig gesehen werden, um die Dienstleistung zu starten und eine starke Nutzung der Dienstleistung zu erreichen. Es gilt, die bestmögliche Kombination für einen bestimmten Zeitraum zu finden und die Intensität des jeweiligen Einsatzes festzulegen.[27] Ziel ist, dass eine harmonische Mischung entsteht, bei der sich die Wirkung verschiedener Instrumente durch deren Kombination positiv verstärkt und vor allem Widersprüchlichkeiten vermieden werden. Gelingen kann dies nur über eine einheitliche Idee/Leitlinie, die in der Analysephase mitentwickelt wird.[28] Diese lautet hier: Eine nutzungsfreundliche Plattform zur Herausgabe von Open-Access-Zeitschriften soll eingerichtet werden.

Das Dominanz-Standard-Modell von Richard Kühn[29] hilft bei der Filterung dieser Marketinginstrumente. Er bestimmt die Wichtigkeit anhand von zwei Faktoren: erstens über die Bedeutung für die Nutzungsintensität und zweitens über den Freiheitsgrad bei der Realisierung. Daraus ergeben sich folgende vier Kategorien: 1.) dominierende Instrumente, 2.) Standard-Instrumente, 3.) komplementäre Instrumente und 4.) marginale Instrumente. Die dominierenden Instrumente sowie die Standard-Instrumente erweisen sich als ausschlaggebend für den Erfolg oder Misserfolg der Dienstleistung. Dennoch werden die Standard-Instrumente in der Sell-Phase nicht mehr berücksichtigt, da deren Ausgestaltung, etwa durch technische Normierung oder andere Standards, bereits festgelegt ist. Hier kann man zu diesem Zeitpunkt kaum mehr entscheidende Verbesserungen erreichen, die zur Steigerung der Nutzung beitragen.[30]

27 Kuß, A.; Kleinaltenkamp, M. (2009), S. 28, S. 287f.
28 Kühn, R; Vifian, P. (2004), S. 15.
29 Marketing-Know-how: Dominanz-Standard-Modell nach Kühn, Marketingingenieur: http://www.marketingenieur.ch/2017/02/marketing-know-how-dominanz-standard.html
30 Kühn, R; Vifian, P. (2004), S. 46.

Flankierend zu den dominierenden Instrumenten werden die komplementären Instrumente eingesetzt. Sie sind zwar nur sekundär, aber in ihrer Rolle der Vervollständigung des Maßnahmenpaketes doch bedeutend genug, wohingegen den marginalen Instrumenten faktisch keine Erfolgsbedeutung hinsichtlich Steigerung der Nutzung zugesprochen wird.[31] Diese wurden zumeist einmal festgelegt wie die Produkt- und Personalkosten oder erfolgen einmalig, wie beispielsweise die Gespräche mit der Trägerorganisation.

Die einzelnen Marketinginstrumente werden einer dieser Kategorien zugeordnet und im Koordinatensystem verortet. Da die Übergänge zwischen den Faktoren fließend sind, operiert das Dominanz-Standard-Modell mit Skalen. Dadurch ist eine zusätzliche Gewichtung möglich, je nachdem, wo man das einzelne Marketinginstrument im Feld ansiedelt. Je weiter oben es angesiedelt ist umso bedeutender, und je weiter rechts im jeweiligen Feld umso mehr Gestaltungsspielraum weist das jeweilige Instrument auf. Die wichtigsten Instrumente werden sich somit oben rechts befinden.

Für die Open-Access-Zeitschriftenplattform im speziellen und generell für Publikationsdienstleistungen ergibt sich folgender Marketingmix: Die externe sowie interaktive Kommunikation zwischen der Universitätsbibliothek und den Anwender:innen zählt ebenso zu den dominierenden Instrumenten wie die Prozesse. Das bedeutet, dass Information und Werbung gemeinsam mit den Interaktionsprozessen erwartungsgemäß zu den wichtigsten Elementen des Marketingmix gehören.

Konkret sind damit neben möglichen Werbemaßnahmen Infoveranstaltungen, Schulungen, die Homepage, Broschüren, Plakate und Mails gemeint, die ein höchstmögliches Niveau an Qualität/Professionalität und Kompetenz aufweisen sollten. Sehr bedeutend und gleichzeitig mit großem Gestaltungsspielraum wird auch die interaktive Umgangsform bei den Schulungen und Unterstützungsleistungen eingestuft. Diese sollten mit viel Gespür für die Anwender:innen erfolgen. Zudem sollten unterschiedliche Kommunikationskanäle zur Verfügung stehen und Rückmeldungen respektvoll entgegengenommen werden. Schließlich trägt die interaktive Kommunikation stark zur Bewertung der gesamten Dienstleistung bei. Im Vergleich zur Werbung, wo der Gestaltungsspielraum sehr groß ist, sind die Möglichkeiten bei Informationsveranstaltungen, Schulungen und Infoblättern geringer.

31 Kühn, R; Vifian, P. (2004), S. 46.

Auch wenn die Konzeption der Plattform eigentlich eine Vorleistung ist, gehört sie beim Marketingmix in den Bereich der dominierenden Instrumente, da bei Evaluierungen die Usability immer wieder hinterfragt und, der Zielgruppe entsprechend, optimiert werden muss. Neben der Usability geht es jedoch auch um die leichte und schnelle Auffindbarkeit der Dienstleistung/des Accounts, um den Zeitaufwand bei den Anwender:innen möglichst gering zu halten.

Als komplementäre Instrumente zur externen und interaktiven Kommunikation erweisen sich Personal und interne Kommunikation von Bedeutung. Schließlich kann eine gute Informations- und Unterstützungsleistung nur erfolgen, wenn motiviertes und geschultes Personal vorhanden ist.

5. Umsetzungsplanung

Den Abschluss des Marketingkonzeptes bildet die Umsetzungsplanung, die sich von der ersten Information bis zur Evaluierung der Dienstleistung erstreckt. Dabei werden die einzelnen Schritte samt Zuständigkeiten und Zeitpunkt aufgelistet. Zunächst wird das Datum der Markteinführung festgelegt und davon ausgehend werden die Schritte und notwendigen Zeiträume zur Erreichung des Ziels eruiert. In die Zeitdauer der Tätigkeiten sollten Puffer einkalkuliert werden. Verzögerungen und Probleme bei der Entwicklung erfordern höchstwahrscheinlich eine oftmalige Überarbeitung des Planes. Dennoch ist eine detaillierte Planung von Vorteil, um das Ziel nicht aus den Augen zu verlieren. Die Umsetzungsplanung kann anhand eines professionellen GANTT-Diagramms[32] erfolgen oder einfach mittels einer chronologischen Tabelle samt Zuständigkeiten (Zuständigkeit – Aufgabe – Datum/Zeitraum).

6. Schluss

Wie in jedem Managementprozess steht man mit der Festlegung des Marketingkonzeptes erst vor dem allerletzten Schritt, nämlich der Evaluierung. Sofern das Gesamtkonzept einmal erstellt wurde, sollten die einzelnen Phasen – Analyse, Konzeption und Start der Dienstleistung – noch einmal durchdacht und überarbeitet werden. Dementsprechend stellt auch das hier auszugsweise vorgestellte Konzept bezüglich Plattform für Open-Access-Zeitschriften nur einen ersten provisorischen Entwurf dar.

32 Gantt Diagramm: https://www.gantt.com/ge/

Das Mozarteum hat sich letztendlich für die Plattform von Open Journal Systems entschieden, welche von der SLUB Dresden/FID musiconn[33] betreut wird. Ausschlaggebend war neben den Kostengründen auch die Möglichkeit, den gesamten Redaktionsprozess betreuen zu können. Dennoch schließt die UB Mozarteum nicht aus, dass zu einem späteren Zeitpunkt, bei großer Nachfrage, das Visual-Library-Zeitschriftenmodul ebenso angeboten wird. Janeway kam nur deshalb nicht in Frage, weil Open Journals Systems das kostengünstigere und unkompliziertere Hosting anbietet. Abgesehen davon präsentiert sich Janeway sehr überzeugend, vor allem bezüglich Bedienungsfreundlichkeit und aufgrund des flexibleren, redaktionellen Workflows.

Bibliografie

Ansoff, Harry Igor (1966): Management Strategie. München: Verlag Moderne Industrie.

Hilke, Wolfgang (1984): Dienstleistungsmarketing aus Sicht der Wissenschaft, Diskussionsbeiträge des Betriebswirtschaftlichen Seminars der Universität Freiburg. Freiburg. Zitiert nach: Meffert, Heribert; Bruhn, Manfred (1995): Dienstleistungsmarketing. Grundlagen, Konzepte, Methoden. Wiesbaden: Gabler.

Jung, Claudia (2003): Marketing Strategies for Academic Libraries. Hochschule Hannover: Hannover.

Kotler, Philip (1982): Marketing for Nonprofit Organizations. 2. Aufl. Englewood Cliffs (New Jersey): Prentice-Hall.

Kotler, Philip; Armstrong, Gary; Wong, Veronica; Saunders, Wong (2010): Grundlagen des Marketing. 5. erw. Aufl. München: Pearson.

Kühn, Richard; Vifian, Patric (2004): Marketing. Analyse und Strategie. 10. Aufl. Zürich: Werd Verlag.

Kuß, Alfred; Kleinaltenkamp, Michael (2009): Marketing-Einführung. Grundlagen, Überblick, Beispiele. 4. Aufl. Wiesbaden: Gabler.

Leitner, Edith (2017): Marketingkonzept für ein Repositorium am Beispiel der Universität Mozarteum Salzburg. https://edoc.hu-berlin.de/handle/18452/2807

Mödinger, Wilfried; Schmid, Sybille; Seitz, Jürgen (2018): Marketing heute. Grundlagen, Perspektiven, Praxisbeispiele. Haan-Gruiten: Verlag Europa-Lehrmittel Nourney.

Pundy, Doris (2021): Markensteuerrad nach Esch. Analyse der Markenidentität. https://www.sortlist.de/blog/markensteuerrad/ (abgerufen am 04.01.2022)

Umlauf, Konrad (2014): Bibliotheksmarketing. Grundsätze, Defizite und Grenzen. Vortrag gehalten auf dem Bayerischen Bibliothekstag am 20.11.2014 in Rosenheim. (Berliner Handreichungen. 379.) Berlin: Institut für Bibliotheks-und Informationswissenschaft der Humboldt-Universität.

---

33 Fachinformationsdienst Musikwissenschaft an der Sächsischen Landesbibliothek Staats- und Universitätsbibliothek Dresden.

Universität Graz; Bundesministerium für Bildung, Wissenschaft und Forschung (Hg.): Leistungsvereinbarung 2019-2021. https://static.uni-graz.at/fileadmin/Lqm/Dokumente/Leistungsvereinbarung_2019-2021.pdf (abgerufen am 15.08.2021)

Universität Mozarteum Salzburg (2018): Open Access Policy der Universität Mozarteum Salzburg. Mitteilungsblatt der Universität Mozarteum Salzburg, 01. Stück, ausgegeben am 17.10.2018. https://apps.moz.ac.at/apps/fe/mbl/ (abgerufen am 15.01.2024)

Universität Mozarteum Salzburg (2021a): Kundmachung der Leistungsvereinbarung 2022-2024 zwischen der Universität Mozarteum Salzburg und dem Bundesministerium für Bildung, Wissenschaft und Forschung. Mitteilungsblatt der Universität Mozarteum Salzburg, 11. Stück, ausgegeben am 16.12.2021. https://apps.moz.ac.at/apps/fe/mbl/ (abgerufen am 15.01.2024)

Universität Mozarteum Salzburg (2021b): Strategiepapier Digitalität der Universität Mozarteum Salzburg. Mitteilungsblatt der Universität Mozarteum Salzburg, 13. Stück, ausgegeben am 21.12.2021. https://apps.moz.ac.at/apps/fe/mbl/ (abgerufen am 15.01.2024)

Weingand, Darlene E. (1998): Future-Driven Library Marketing. Chicago: American Library Association.

Wiesner, Knut A.; Sponholz, Uwe (2007): Dienstleistungsmarketing. Wien: Oldenbourg Verlag.

Edith Leitner studierte Politikwissenschaft in Salzburg und Bordeaux sowie Bibliotheks- und Informationswissenschaften in Berlin und ist an der Universitätsbibliothek Mozarteum Salzburg seit 2014 für das Repositorium und den Bereich Open Science zuständig sowie seit 2022 stellvertretende Bibliotheksleiterin.

Lisa Schilhan promovierte in Kunstgeschichte an der Universität Graz und baute als Open-Access-Beauftragte der Universität Graz das institutionelle Repositorium unipub auf. Sie betreut die an der Universität herausgegebenen Gold-Open-Access-Zeitschriften, die auf dem Repositorium publiziert werden, und leitet seit März 2019 die Publikationsservices der Universität Graz.

Georg Mayr-Duffner

Erste Schritte in Goobi workflow mit Goobi-to-go

Handbuch Repositorienmanagement, Hg. v. Blumesberger et al., 2024, S. 437–453
https://doi.org/10.25364/978390337423223

Georg Mayr-Duffner, Wirtschaftsuniversität Wien, Bibliothek, georg.mayr-duffner@wu.ac.at |
ORCID iD: 0000-0002-8935-175X

Zusammenfassung

Viele Institutionen, die in größerem Ausmaß Digitalisierungsprojekte durchführen, verwenden mittlerweile das Open-Source-Tool Goobi workflow. Kernstück dieser Software ist das Workflow-Management, anhand dessen das digitale Objekt auf seinem Weg durch das System geführt wird – vom ersten Schritt, wie dem Anlegen eines Metadatensatzes, bis zum letzten, beispielsweise der Ablage in einem externen LZA-System. Auf der flexiblen Gestaltung dieses Workflow-Managements beruht wohl der Erfolg der Software, die mittlerweile von Bibliotheken, Archiven, Museen und anderen Einrichtungen unterschiedlichster Größe aus vielen Ländern in Europa, Afrika, Amerika und Asien angewendet wird: Zum einen skaliert sie sehr gut mit der Größe der Einrichtungen, zum anderen lassen sich damit gleichzeitig völlig unterschiedliche Projekte realisieren. Für die Präsentation der Daten aus Goobi workflow bietet sich Goobi viewer an, ebenfalls eine Open-Source-Software. Beide Tools sind voneinander unabhängig und können jeweils auch mit anderen Anwendungen kombiniert werden. Um Goobi einfach auszuprobieren, wird von der Firma Intranda GmbH, die die Software entwickelt, Goobi-to-go zur Verfügung gestellt. Dabei handelt es sich um ein Bündel aus Goobi workflow und Goobi viewer, das in wenigen Schritten auf einem herkömmlichen Arbeitsplatzrechner installiert wird. Dieser Beitrag erklärt anhand dieses Pakets die grundlegenden Funktionen und Konfigurationen von Goobi workflow.

Schlagwörter: Goobi; Digitalisierungssoftware; Workflow-Management

Abstract

First Steps with Goobi Workflow Using Goobi-to-go

Many institutions that carry out digitisation projects on a larger scale now use the open source tool Goobi workflow. At the heart of this software is the workflow management, which guides the digital object on its way through the system, from the first step, such as the creation of a metadata record, to the last step, such as filing in an external long-term preservation system. Libraries, archives, museums and other institutions of all sizes from many countries in Europe, Africa, America, and Asia are using the software. Its success is based on the flexible design of the workflow management: Firstly, it scales very well with the size of the facilities; on the other hand, completely different projects can be realized at the same time. Goobi viewer, also an open-source software, is ideal for presenting the data from Goobi workflow. Both tools are independent of each other and each of them works well in combination with third party software. Intranda GmbH, the company that has developed the Goobi software, provides Goobi-to-go for the purpose of trying out

Goobi. Goobi-to-go bundles Goobi workflow and Goobi viewer in a single installable package for use on a conventional workstation computer in just a few steps. This package is used in this contribution in order to explain the basic functions and configurations of Goobi workflow.

Keywords: Goobi; digitisation software; workflow management

1. Überblick

Der Name Goobi steht für ein Software-Ökosystem aus dem Bereich der Digitalisierung. Im Mittelpunkt stehen dabei die beiden Applikationen Goobi workflow und Goobi viewer. Hinter diesen Produkten steht das Göttinger Unternehmen Intranda, das die Software pflegt und weiterentwickelt. Goobi wird als Open-Source-Software entwickelt und nur wenige, besonders aufwändige Erweiterungen vertreibt Intranda unter einer kommerziellen Lizenz. Goobi workflow und Goobi viewer, sowie die Plugins, deren Entwicklung bereits bezahlt ist, stehen unter der GNU General Public License, version 2.0[1]. So können die täglichen Entwicklungsschritte im Quelltext auf Github[2] nachvollzogen werden und die Community kann Korrekturen und Verbesserungen direkt als Code einbringen.

1.1. Dokumentation

Open Source bedeutet aber im Idealfall nicht nur, dass der Code frei verfügbar ist, sondern auch, dass die Dokumentation, also Handbücher, Anleitungen und Schulungsunterlagen offen verfügbar sind. Intranda geht auch hier den Open-Source-Weg konsequent und pflegt diese Unterlagen wie den Code auf Github und stellt sie ohne Hürden auf https://docs.goobi.io zur Verfügung. Diese Dokumente stehen unter einer CC-BY-NC-ND-Lizenz[3,4]. Die Handbücher richten sich in eigenen Unterbereichen an die verschiedenen Zielgruppen und bemühen sich, eine der jeweiligen Zielgruppe entsprechend niederschwellige Darstellungsweise zu wählen. So bietet der Anwenderbereich von Goobi workflow eine einfache bebilderte Schritt-für-Schritt-Erklärung der Anwendungsoberfläche, während im Bereich Management

1 https://www.gnu.org/licenses/old-licenses/gpl-2.0.en.html
2 https://github.com/intranda
3 Siehe „Urheberrechte“ unter https://docs.goobi.io/goobi-workflow-de/ und unter https://docs.goobi.io/goobi-viewer-de/
4 http://creativecommons.org/licenses/by-nc-nd/4.0/

davon ausgegangen wird, dass gewisse Kompetenzen, wie das Zurechtfinden in einem Dateisystem, vorhanden sind.

1.2. Goobi workflow

Steffen Hankiewicz, Geschäftsführer der Intranda GmbH und als Entwickler maßgeblich für Goobi workflow verantwortlich, bezeichnet Goobi workflow als „Workflow Tracking Tool", welches seit 2004 entwickelt wird.[5] In dieser Webanwendung werden Regeln festgelegt, nach denen die Abläufe in einem Digitalisierungs(teil)projekt stattfinden. Dafür wird der Weg eines Objekts von der Registrierung im System bis zum Abschluss des Digitalisierungsworkflows in kleine Schritte zerlegt, die einzelnen Aufgaben entsprechen, die einer Rolle zugeordnet werden können. Bei den Rollen kann es sich um Benutzerrollen, die mit bestimmten Berechtigungen verknüpft sind, handeln, aber auch um ein (externes) Script oder Computerprogramm im Fall eines automatisierten Schrittes. Im Durchlauf eines Objekts durch die Digitalisierungsroutine wird dann Schritt für Schritt der Workflow durchlaufen. Die/der Benutzer:in sieht dabei nur jeweils jene Aufgaben, die auch ihrer/seiner Rolle entsprechen. Die flexible Gestaltung mit Plugins erlaubt es, für die unterschiedlichsten Anforderungen passende Funktionalitäten innerhalb der Software bereitzustellen, beginnend beim Datenimport, über Seitenlayouterkennung und Qualitätskontrolle bis hin zum Export in ein Langzeitarchivierungssystem. Ebenso können die eingebauten Statistikfunktionen, die die Überwachung der Projektfortschritte erlauben, mittels Plugins erweitert werden.

1.3. Goobi viewer

Mit dem Goobi viewer entwickelt Intranda eine flexible Präsentationsplattform für digitale Objekte und Sammlungen. Viewer und workflow passen sehr gut zusammen, weil sie im selben Unternehmen aufeinander abgestimmt entwickelt werden, können aber jeweils auch mit anderen Softwarekomponenten von Drittanbietern kombiniert werden. Metadaten und Volltexte von Objekten, die an den Goobi viewer übergeben werden, werden von einem Apache Solr-Indexer indexiert und somit durchsuchbar gemacht. Um den Auftritt der digitalen Sammlungen mit verschiedenen Seitentypen systematisch gestalten zu können, enthält der Goobi viewer auch ein Content-Management-System. Neben diversen Exportoptionen bietet der viewer auch eine REST-Schnittstelle und eine IIIF-Presentation-API. Weitere besondere Features sind für den Bereich Crowdsourcing zu finden. Zum einen

5 Hankiewicz, S. (2018), S. 77.

sind sogenannte „Kampagnen“ eingebaut, mit denen der Öffentlichkeit die Möglichkeit gegeben wird, an einer bestimmten Aufgabe für einen begrenzten Zeitraum mitzuarbeiten. Zum anderen gibt es ein dezidiertes Crowdsourcing-Modul (kostenpflichtig unter einer kommerziellen Lizenz), über welches die Öffentlichkeit an der Transkription und an der inhaltlichen Erschließung der Digitalisate mitwirken kann.

1.4. Anwendungsbeispiele

Die oben beschriebene Flexibilität erlaubt es, die beiden Softwarekomponenten in unterschiedlichen Umgebungen einzusetzen. Goobi viewer bietet keine Benutzerschnittstelle für die Aufnahme neuer Objekte. Stattdessen erwartet es, von einem zweiten System mit Objekten und Metadaten versorgt zu werden, was aufgrund der Verwendung standardisierter Formate verschiedenste Kombinationen erlaubt. Denkbar wäre beispielsweise, Goobi viewer an ein Archivinformationssystem anzuhängen, um digitales Archivgut verfügbar zu machen. Goobi workflow andererseits wird gerne verwendet, um komplexe Ingestvorgänge – häufig im Zusammenhang mit Digitalisierungsaufgaben – zu organisieren und die Endprodukte an ein Repositorium zu übergeben[6]. Viele Institutionen entscheiden sich aber dafür, beide Komponenten gemeinsam einzusetzen. Je nach Konfiguration entsteht so eine Digitale Bibliothek, wie beispielsweise bei der digitalen Landesbibliothek Oberösterreich[7] und den Digitalen Sammlungen der Herzogin Anna Amalia Bibliothek[8] oder ein Repositorium wie im Fall der E-Medien der Arbeiterkammern und des ÖGB-Verlags[9]. In allen drei Fällen finden die Verwaltung von Metadaten und die Sammlungsorganisation in Goobi workflow statt, während der viewer für die Darstellung und den öffentlichen Zugang zuständig ist. Letzteres inkludiert auch Schnittstellen für den automatisierten Zugriff wie OAI-PMH.

6 Vgl. Frost, H. et al. (2019)
7 https://digi.landesbibliothek.at/
8 https://haab-digital.klassik-stiftung.de
9 https://emedien.arbeiterkammer.at/

2. Goobi-to-go

2.1. Was ist Goobi-to-go?

Üblicherweise werden Goobi workflow und Goobi viewer auf zwei getrennten Servern installiert. Diese Aufstellung ist auch sinnvoll, um die workflow-Applikation, die häufig nur innerhalb der Institution zugänglich sein soll, von der allgemein zugänglichen Präsentationssoftware zu trennen. Mit Goobi-to-go[10] bietet Intranda eine sehr einfach zugängliche Möglichkeit, Goobi workflow und Goobi viewer zusammen zu testen.

Setup und Wartung eigener Server für das Testen bedeuten einen großen Aufwand, der mitunter in keinem Verhältnis zum Aufwand der Tests steht. Dieses Dilemma löst Goobi-to-go, indem es eine vollständige lauffähige Anwendungsumgebung mitbringt. Es enthält Goobi viewer und Goobi workflow sowie alle für den Betrieb notwendigen Programme in der jeweils erforderlichen Version, insbesondere eine Java-Laufzeitumgebung, ein H2-Datenbankmanagementsystem und einen Apache Tomcat-Server. Das Softwarepaket ist damit unabhängig von eventuell am Rechner installierter Software und kann nach dem Download und Entpacken direkt gestartet werden. Auf dem Rechner wird nichts geändert, außer dass Speicherplatz belegt wird. Wird es nicht mehr benötigt, wird der Goobi-to-go-Ordner einfach gelöscht, ohne dass Spuren davon zurückbleiben. Da eine Goobi-to-go-Anwendung keine Einstellungen und Abhängigkeiten außerhalb des eigenen Ordners kennt, können auf einem Rechner auch mehrere „Goobi-to-gos" mit unterschiedlichen Konfigurationen oder in unterschiedlichen Versionen liegen, was das Testen unterschiedlicher Szenarien erheblich vereinfacht.

2.2. Goobi-to-go starten

Um Goobi-to-go zu starten, muss das Softwarepaket von der Seite https://goobi.io/goobi-to-go/ heruntergeladen werden. Aktuell werden Pakete für Windows, macOS und Linux angeboten[11]. Es handelt sich dabei um eine Zip-Datei im Umfang von gut 1,1 GB. Nach dem Download wird die Datei entzippt. Der dabei extrahierte Ordner g2g muss jedenfalls an einem Ort abgelegt werden, von dem aus der/die User:in berechtigt ist, Programme auszuführen. In diesem Ordner befindet sich ein Starter, der auf Linux GoobiToGo, auf Windows GoobiToGo.exe und auf

10 https://goobi.io/goobi-to-go

11 Dieser Beitrag basiert auf dem Goobi-to-go Snapshot 20211220. Der darin enthaltene Goobi workflow trägt die Versionsnummer 21.11.5, der Goobi viewer trägt die Versionsnummer 21.12.

macOS GoobiToGo.command heißt. Nach einem Doppelklick auf den Starter[12] wird die Anwendung gestartet. Dies bedeutet, dass ein Server[13] auf dem Rechner gestartet wird, der die Webapplikationen viewer und workflow bereitstellt und diese beiden mit einer Datenbank versorgt. Sobald der Startvorgang abgeschlossen ist, wird das Startfenster geschlossen, dafür erscheint ein Goobi-Symbol in der Task- bzw. Menüleiste. Über dieses Symbol lassen sich viewer und workflow öffnen, sowie der Server herunterfahren. Seit Ende September 2021 gibt es hier zudem Zugriff auf Hilfe- und Infoseiten, die ebenfalls im heruntergeladenen Paket integriert sind.

2.3. Goobi workflow erkunden

Wenn der Goobi-to-go-Server gestartet ist, kann Goobi workflow mit Klick auf den entsprechenden Menüeintrag im Goobi-to-go-Menü geöffnet werden. Alternativ kann im Webbrowser auch die Adresse der Anwendung direkt eingegeben werden. Diese ist vorkonfiguriert als https://localhost:8888/goobi.[14] Im Browser öffnet sich die Anmeldeseite von Goobi workflow. Hier kann man sich mit einem der vorgefertigten Benutzerkonten anmelden, die auf der Seite https://goobi.io/goobi-to-go dokumentiert sind. Diese Benutzerkonten unterscheiden sich in ihren Rollen und Berechtigungen.

Loggt man sich mit dem Adminstrator:innenaccount „goobi" ein, landet man auf einer Dashboardseite, die einen Überblick über die laufenden Projekte und Schnellzugriff auf wichtige Funktionen wie Vorgangssuche und Produktionsvorlagen bietet. Zudem wird der Newsfeed von Intranda eingeblendet. In der permanenten Menüleiste finden sich Zugriffsmöglichkeiten auf die einzelnen Funktionalitäten der Anwendung, für die der Account berechtigt ist:

12 Die Anwendung kann auch von der Kommandozeile aus gestartet werden. Dies ist auf https://goobi.io/goobi-to-go/ für die unterschiedlichen Betriebssysteme dokumentiert.

13 Ein Server bezeichnet in diesem Fall ein Programm, das anderen Programmen Dienste zur Verfügung stellt. Dieser Server stellt einerseits den Webapplikationen ein Datenbanksystem zur Verfügung, andererseits den Browsern auf dem Rechner die Applikationen Goobi workflow und Goobi viewer selbst.
Obwohl es sich um einen Webserver handelt, bedeutet das nicht automatisch, dass von fremden Rechnern aus auf die Goobi-to-go-Anwendungen zugegriffen werden kann. Damit das möglich ist, müssen bewusst die entsprechenden Ports in der Firewall, die jedes moderne Betriebssystem von Haus aus mitbringt, geöffnet werden. Standardmäßig sind diese zu.

14 Die Portadressen der einzelnen Komponenten können in der Konfigurationsdatei g2g/config/g2g_config.xml angepasst werden, dies kann nötig sein, wenn es einen Konflikt mit anderen Anwendungen auf dem Rechner gibt, die dieselben Ports verwenden. Nach der Portänderung muss Goobi-to-go neu gestartet werden.

- „Meine Aufgaben“ öffnet die Aufgabenliste mit allen Aufgaben, die den Benutzerrollen des/der eingeloggten User:in zugewiesen sind und entweder offen sind (also noch nicht von einem/einer Benutzer:in übernommen wurden) oder bereits von der/dem gerade eingeloggten Benutzer:in übernommen aber noch nicht abgeschlossen wurden.[15]
- „Workflow“ öffnet ein Dropdown-Menü, das Zugriff auf alle Funktionen rund um die Vorgänge der einzelnen Objekte erlaubt. Insbesondere lassen sich hier die Vorgänge auflisten oder suchen, zum anderen werden unter „Produktionsvorlagen“ die Workflows konfiguriert und neue Vorgänge anhand einer Produktionsvorlage angelegt.
- Unter „Administration“ finden sich alle Konfigurationsmöglichkeiten für Goobi workflow, sofern es dafür ein grafisches Interface gibt.
- „Controlling“ erlaubt Zugriff auf die Statistiken.
- Das Goobi-Logo und der Menüpunkt „Dashboard“ führen beide zum Dashboard zurück.

2.4. Das zentrale Objekt – der „Vorgang”

Das Tracking der Digitalisierung eines Objekts in Goobi workflow findet in Form eines „Vorgangs“ statt. Dies ist das zentrale Objekt, das unter einem eindeutigen Vorgangstitel und einer ID alle zugehörigen Daten, wie Metadaten, Masterdateien und Derivate speichert. In Goobi wird der Vorgang üblicherweise mit dem Vorgangstitel identifiziert, der meist automatisch aus Teilen der Autor:innennamen, des Titels und einem Identifier aus den Metadaten gebildet wird[16]. Dadurch erhält es einen sprechenden Teil, der die Identifizierung durch Bearbeiter:innen erleichtert. Will man sich den angelegten Vorgang im lokalen Speicher des PCs ansehen, benötigt man die Vorgangs-ID, die beim Anlegen des Vorgangs von Goobi workflow hochgezählt wird. Um sie sichtbar zu machen, kann in der Liste der Vorgänge die entsprechende Spalte angewählt werden. Im Speicher sind die Vorgänge unter g2g/workspace/workflow/metadata/ zu finden. Der Vorgangsordner ist mit der Vorgangs-ID benannt und enthält eine METS-Datei meta.xml mit den Metadaten des Vorgangs. Daneben gibt es je nach Bedarf Ordner für diverse Objekte wie bspw. Bilder (images) oder OCR-Daten (ocr). Verweist der Vorgang auf eine andere Hierarchiestufe, beispielsweise einen Zeitschriftenband, wenn im Vorgang ein Zeitschriftenheft digitalisiert wird, wird für dieses sogenannte „Anker-Objekt“ eine eigene METS-Datei meta_anchor.xml abgelegt.

15 In Goobi-to-go haben die beiden Administratorkonten in den Voreinstellungen keine Aufgabenbereiche zugeordnet, weshalb die Listen hier leer sind.

16 In Goobi-to-go sind bereits drei Mustervorgänge in zwei Projekten angelegt.

2.5. Einen Vorgang durchspielen

In Goobi-to-go sind bereits zwei Muster-Produktionsvorlagen angelegt, anhand derer die Workflows direkt ausprobiert werden können. Im Menü unter „Workflow > Produktionsvorlagen“ werden der „Manuscript_Workflow“ für das „Manuscript_Project“ und der „Sample_Workflow“ für das „Archive_Project“ aufgelistet. Mit Klick auf das Stiftsymbol gelangt man in die Bearbeitungsansicht der Vorlage und sieht im Block „Abfolge der Aufgaben“, welche Schritte vorgesehen sind. Bereits in dieser Übersicht lässt sich erkennen, ob ein Schritt durch eine:n Bearbeitenden auszuführen ist oder automatisch abgearbeitet wird. In diesem Beispiel ist Schritt 5 „Image processing“ ein automatischer Schritt, was durch das Zahnradsymbol gekennzeichnet wird. Zudem kommt ein Plugin zum Einsatz, ersichtlich aus dem Puzzleteil-Symbol in der Spalte „Aktionen“.

Weitere Details zu dem jeweiligen Schritt werden sichtbar durch Klick auf den Pfeil in der Spalte „Titel“. Hier interessiert uns nun besonders die Zeile „Zugewiesene Rechte“: Dabei handelt es sich um die Benutzergruppe, die nötig ist, um den Schritt durchführen zu dürfen. Wollen wir einen Vorgang durchspielen, haben wir zwei Möglichkeiten: Wir können ein Benutzerkonto allen benötigten Benutzergruppen zuweisen oder wir wechseln für jeden Schritt das Konto. In letzterem Fall ist es möglicherweise sinnvoll, mit zwei Browsern oder einem normalen und einem Inkognitofenster desselben Browsers parallel zu arbeiten. So kann man in einem Fenster ständig mit dem Admin-Account eingeloggt sein und beobachten, was passiert, während man im anderen mit den jeweils benötigten Funktionskonten die Schritte abarbeitet. Welches Konto welchen Gruppen zugewiesen ist, kann in der Liste unter dem Menüpunkt „Administration > Benutzer“ kontrolliert werden.

Über den aktuellen Zustand eines Schritts informiert der Status. Dieser wird in einer Art Fortschrittsbalken farblich gekennzeichnet:

- Gesperrt (rot): Der Schritt kann noch nicht ausgeführt werden, da der vorhergehende noch nicht abgeschlossen wurde.
- Offen (orange): Dieser Schritt ist zur Bearbeitung offen und befindet sich in der Aufgabenliste aller berechtigten Nutzer:innen.
- In Bearbeitung (gelb): diese Aufgabe wurde von einem/einer Benutzer:in übernommen oder wird gerade von einem Skript automatisch abgearbeitet.
- Abgeschlossen (grün): Diese Aufgabe wurde abgeschlossen.
- Fehler (rot schraffiert): Bei der Bearbeitung der Aufgabe ist ein Fehler aufgetreten. Bis zur Behebung des Fehlers ist der Vorgang angehalten. Eine Möglichkeit, die Goobi dazu bietet, ist, eine Korrekturmeldung an jene Benutzer:innengruppe zu senden, die den Fehler beheben kann (beispielsweise

durch erneutes Scannen). Für die Fehleranalyse hilfreich sind die Einträge im Vorgangslog, das bei den einzelnen Aufgaben und auf der Übersichtsseite des Vorgangs angezeigt wird.

Die Schritte und die benötigte Benutzergruppe für den „Manuscript_Workflow" sind:

Nr.	Titel	Benutzer:innengruppe	Konto
1	Data Import	Project Management	testprojectmanagement
2	Get manuscript from book depot	Book managing officers	testbookmanager
3	Scanning	Scanning officers	testscanning
4	Quality Control	Quality control officers	testqc
5	Image processing	(automatischer Schritt)	–
6	Metadata enrichment	Metadata officers	testmetadata
7	Export to viewer	(automatischer Schritt)	–
8	Bring manuscript back to book depot	Book managing officers	testbookmanager

Die zweite Produktionsvorlage „Sample_Workflow" unterscheidet sich hier nur dadurch, dass die Tätigkeit des Book managing officers (Werk ausheben bzw. zurückstellen) ausgelassen werden[17].

Schritt 1 – Data Import

Die vorliegende Konfiguration geht davon aus, dass ein Werk digitalisiert wird, das in einem Bibliothekskatalog verzeichnet ist. Vorkonfiguriert sind der Katalog der Library of Congress und der K10Plus-Verbundkatalog. Mit einem Konto, das der Benutzer:innengruppe „Project Management" zugeordnet ist, oder auch mit einem der Admin-Konten kann ein neuer Vorgang angelegt werden, indem am Dashboard im Produktionsvorlagen-Widget bei der gewünschten Produktionsvorlage auf den blauen Button mit dem Dokumentensymbol (Titel: „Einen Vorgang auf Basis dieser Produktionsvorlage anlegen") geklickt wird (nicht auf den weißen Pfeil!).

Daraufhin öffnet sich ein Formular, das eine „Suche im Opac" anhand einer ID oder eines Barcodes erlaubt. Für diese Demonstration wird die ID 150899661 aus dem K10Plus-Katalog in das entsprechende Feld eingegeben und mit „Übernehmen" bestätigt. Goobi holt sich die Daten über die SRU-Schnittstelle und befüllt damit das

17 Hier wäre es wünschenswert, mehr bzw. vor allem unterschiedlichere Workflows vorinstalliert mitzubekommen, mit denen eine größere Bandbreite der Funktionalitäten demonstriert werden kann.

Formular. Händisch zu befüllen ist das Feld „Autoren“[18], damit auch der Vorgangstitel diese Komponente enthält. Grundsätzlich müssen alle mit * gekennzeichneten Felder befüllt werden, insbesondere muss eine Digitale Sammlung ausgewählt werden, allerdings wird der Vorgangstitel, wenn er freigelassen wird, automatisch aus den Feldern „ATS“ und „Identifier digital“ erzeugt, wobei „ATS“ wiederum aus den Inhalten der Felder „Autoren“ und „Titel“ erzeugt wird (ATS = Autor-Titel-Schlüssel). Die Angabe der geschätzten Seitenzahl wird für die Berechnung des Projektfortschritts in den Statistiken benötigt. Beim Abspeichern werden allenfalls die Felder ATS und Vorgangstitel erzeugt und der Vorgang im Speicher abgelegt. Zum Abschluss des Schritts kann noch ein Laufzettel im PDF-Format erzeugt werden.

Schritt 2 – Get manuscript from book depot

Dieser Schritt ist dazu gedacht, dass ein/e Bearbeiter:in ein Werk aushebt. Der Account testbookmanager zeigt nur zwei Menüpunkte an – neben dem Dashboard „Meine Aufgaben“. Dort ist der neu erstellte Vorgang mit der Aufgabe „Get manuscript from book depot“ zu finden. Die Aufgabe wird mit einem Klick auf den blauen Button mit dem Häkchensymbol (Titel „Die Bearbeitung dieser Aufgabe übernehmen“) übernommen. Im nächsten Fenster werden die Aufgabendetails angezeigt. Hier können im Widget „Vorgangslog“ allgemeine Kommentare und Meldungen verfasst werden. Im Widget „Mögliche Aktionen“ kann die erfolgreiche Erledigung mit „Die Bearbeitung der Aufgabe abschließen“ quittiert werden, insbesondere kann an dieser Stelle aber auch eine Fehlermeldung an einen der vorhergehenden Schritte abgesetzt werden. Die Aufgabe scheint dann in der Aufgabenliste jener Personen auf, die der Benutzer:innengruppe des gewählten Schritts angehören, oder die Bearbeitung der Aufgabe kann abgebrochen werden, wodurch sie wieder in der Aufgabenliste der für diesen Schritt zuständigen Bearbeiter:innen aufscheint.

Die hier beschriebenen Funktionen gelten bei jeder Übernahme einer Aufgabe. Im Folgenden wird nicht mehr darauf eingegangen.

18 Warum an dieser Stelle keine Automatisierung stattfindet, ist schleierhaft und seitens Intranda vielleicht zu überdenken. Unter Zuhilfenahme des Opac SRU Plugins (https://github.com/intranda/goobi-plugin-opac-sru) ist es jedenfalls möglich, die Übersetzung der OPAC-Daten granular zu steuern und auch hier die Daten automatisch zu übernehmen.

Schritt 3 – Scanning

In diesem Schritt werden die gescannten Bilddateien hochgeladen. Im Widget „Dateien“ wird mit Klick auf „Dateien auswählen“ ein Dateibrowser geöffnet. Hier können nun die zu übertragenden Bilder ausgewählt werden[19], im Reiter „Übersicht“ kann das Ergebnis der Übertragung kontrolliert werden. Das Widget „Eigenschaften“ erlaubt die Angabe von Details zum Scanvorgang – voreingestellt ist die Frage nach dem Öffnungswinkel des zu scannenden Objekts und nach der Schreibrichtung (RTL = right to left, wie beispielsweise Hebräisch oder Arabisch).

Schritt 4 – Quality Control

In diesem Schritt soll geprüft werden, ob die gescannten und hochgeladenen Bilder den Qualitätskriterien entsprechen. In diesem Schritt kommt das Plugin „Bildkontrolle“ zum Einsatz. Bei der Übernahme der Aufgabe sieht der/die Bearbeiter:in daher im Widget „Mögliche Aktionen“ einen zusätzlichen Button mit Puzzlesteinsymbol mit der Beschriftung „Plugin: Bildkontrolle“. Das Plugin zeigt eine Galerie der gescannten Bilder an und bietet grundlegende Bildkontrollfunktionen (Zoom und Rotation). Mit „Ergebnisse speichern und abschließen“ wird die Aufgabe abgeschlossen. Sie kann hier auch wieder abgebrochen werden und, wie bei Schritt 2 beschrieben, dem Scanning mit einer Korrekturmeldung zurückgegeben werden.

Schritt 5 – Image Processing

In diesem automatischen Schritt werden von den Masterdateien die Derivate für die weitere Verwendung erstellt, beispielsweise werden hier aus TIFF-Dateien JPG-Dateien generiert.

Schritt 6 – Metadata enrichment

In diesem Schritt werden die Metadaten im METS-Editor eingegeben. Bei der Übernahme der Aufgabe gibt es unter „Mögliche Aktionen“ den Button „Metadaten bearbeiten“, mit dem der Editor geöffnet wird. Das Editorfenster ist dreigeteilt: links wird der Strukturbaum dargestellt, wo das aktuell zu bearbeitende Strukturelement ausgewählt wird. Rechts werden die Digitalisate angezeigt. In der Mitte befindet sich der eigentliche Editor, wo verschiedene Arten von Metadaten bearbeitet werden können. Vier Bearbeitungsmodi kennt der viewer, die über Reiter zugänglich sind:

19 In Goobi-Installationen ist es sinnvoll, dass Scan-Mitarbeiter:innen ihr Arbeitsverzeichnis am Server auf ihrem Arbeitsplatzrechner als Netzlaufwerk einbinden, um größere Datenmengen leichter zu übertragen.

Im ersten Reiter wird die Paginierung des Digitalisats festgelegt. Die Nummerierung kann Seite für Seite festgelegt oder automatisch durchgezählt werden, wobei auch ungezählte Seiten, fingierte Paginierung und Doppelseiten berücksichtigt werden können.

Im zweiten Reiter, „Strukturdaten", können Strukturen innerhalb des Werks identifiziert werden. Dabei kann es sich um physische Strukturen wie Buchdeckel oder Farbkeil handeln, aber auch um inhaltliche wie Kapitel, Verzeichnisse oder Abbildungen. Die Lokalisierung ist dabei nicht auf die Seitenangabe beschränkt, sondern es kann der genaue Bildausschnitt im Digitalisat identifiziert werden. Zusätzlich kann jedem Strukturelement auch ein Satz Metadaten mitgegeben werden. In welchem Umfang, hängt davon ab, welche Metadaten für das jeweilige Element im Regelsatz (s. Abschnitt Konfiguration/Der Regelsatz, $$$S. 11$$$) definiert sind.

Der dritte Reiter, „Metadaten", dient zur Eingabe der bibliographischen Metadaten. Dieser ist im Prinzip vorausgefüllt mit den Daten aus dem Katalog, allerdings wird hier der Name nicht mit übernommen und muss gesondert eingegeben werden. Welche Metadaten eingegeben werden können, wird durch den Regelsatz für den Dokumententyp wie auch für jedes Strukturelement bestimmt. Eine Verknüpfung mit Normdaten ist vorgesehen, implementiert sind in Goobi-to-go die GND, VIAF, KulturNav und Geonames. Wie ein Feld dargestellt wird, ob als Freitextfeld oder mit kontrolliertem Vokabular, wird über die Datei g2g/workspace/workflow/config/goobi_metadataDisplayRules.xml kontrolliert.

Der vierte Reiter bietet die Möglichkeit, ein Bild von einer beliebigen Stelle durch ein neues auszutauschen, beispielsweise, um es durch einen Scan mit einer besseren Qualität zu ersetzen.

Der Metadateneditor bietet ein eigenes Einstellungsmenü, mit dem die Ansicht nach Bedarf geändert werden kann. Außerdem können die eingegebenen Daten vor dem Speichern validiert werden. In diesem Fall wird Feld für Feld die Eingabe mit einem allenfalls im Regelsatz vorhandenen Validierungscode abgeglichen.

Mit Klick auf das Haussymbol ganz rechts oben und „Speichern und zurück" kehrt man zur Aufgabenübersicht zurück, wo man die Bearbeitung wie gewohnt abschließen kann.

Schritt 7 – Export in viewer

Wieder ein automatischer Schritt – die Daten werden an den viewer übergeben, wo sie indexiert werden und danach sofort angezeigt werden können.

Schritt 8 – Bring manuscript back to book depot

Mit dieser Aufgabe wird im Vorgang dokumentiert, dass das Werk wieder zurückgestellt wird.

2.6. Konfiguration

Hier werden wichtige Konfigurationen und Konfigurationsdateien kurz beschrieben. Die Konfigurationsdateien sind durchgängig XML-Dateien, die relativ einfach angepasst werden können. Die bereits erwähnte Flexibilität bedingt allerdings auch eine gewisse Komplexität. Mit der in Goobi-to-go bereits vorliegenden Konfiguration können Standardfälle sicher weitestgehend, allenfalls mit wenigen Änderungen, bearbeitet werden. Im Echtbetrieb finden sich dann aber fast immer Gegebenheiten, die eine tiefergehende Beschäftigung mit der Konfiguration verlangen. Hinzu kommt die Vielzahl an Plugins, die den Funktionsumfang stark erweitern, aber ebenfalls korrekt konfiguriert werden müssen. In Einzelfällen sind dazu auch Kenntnisse in XSLT nötig.

2.6.1. Der Regelsatz

Die zentrale Konfiguration für die Metadaten, die in einem Vorgang zur Verfügung stehen, findet im Regelsatz statt. Hier wird festgelegt:

- welche Metadatentypen (Titel, Körperschaft, etc.) existieren, sowie ihre Übersetzung in die gewünschten Anzeigesprachen. Darüber hinaus können hier für jeden Typ Validierungsregeln in Form von regulären Ausdrücken definiert werden.
- Metadatengruppen, die verwendet werden sollen – beispielsweise für ein strukturiertes Titelelement.
- die Strukturtypen, die verwendet werden können. Dabei handelt es sich sowohl um Dokumenttypen (Buch, Artikel,) als auch um Strukturtypen, die einen Teil eines Werks beschreiben (Buchdeckel vorne, Deckblatt, Abbildung). Wie bei den Metadatengruppen wird hier definiert, welche der Metadatentypen im jeweiligen Strukturtyp zulässig sind, ob sie obligatorisch oder optional und ob sie wiederholbar sind.
- Formatierungsregeln für die Umsetzung der zuvor festgelegten Regeln in einem Metadatenformat. Der vordefinierte Regelsatz in Goobi-to-go enthält Formatierungsregeln für die Umsetzung in PicaPlus, MARC, LIDO und METS/MODS.

Die Regelsätze werden in g2g/workspace/workflow/rulesets abgelegt[20]. Ein neuer Regelsatz muss Goobi unter „Administration > Regelsätze" bekanntgegeben werden. Hier wird dann auch festgelegt, ob die Anzeigenreihenfolge der Metadatenfelder der Reihenfolge im Regelsatz folgen soll – ansonsten ist sie alphabetisch. In der hier beschriebenen Version ist kein Editor für die Regelsätze eingebaut. Dementsprechend erfolgt die Bearbeitung in einem einfachen Texteditor außerhalb von Goobi[21].

2.6.2. Projekte

Unter „Administration > Projekte" werden Digitalisierungsprojekte definiert. Hier werden zum einen organisatorische Details angegeben (Anzahl der Vorgänge, Anzahl der Seiten usw.), um den Status bzw. die Zielerreichung von Digitalisierungsprojekten statistisch analysieren zu können, aber auch technische Details festgelegt (Speicher- und Exportformat, Verzeichnispfade) und Parameter für die METS-Metadaten.

2.6.3. Produktionsvorlage

Unter „Workflow > Produktionsvorlagen" können neue Produktionsvorlagen angelegt werden. Hier wird in einem ersten Schritt festgelegt, welchen Laufzettel und welchen Regelsatz ein Vorgang verwenden soll, sowie zu welchem Projekt die Vorgänge gehören. Im zweiten Schritt werden die Aufgaben angelegt und einzeln konfiguriert.

2.6.4. Digitale Sammlungen

Vorgänge werden einer oder mehreren Sammlungen zugeordnet. Dies geschieht bereits beim Anlegen des Vorgangs und kann später im Metadateneditor auch nachträglich adaptiert werden. Die Sammlungen werden in der Datei g2g/workspace/workflow/config/goobi_digitalCollections definiert. Dort kann auch die Zuordnung einer oder mehrere Sammlungen zu einem Projekt vorgenommen werden.

20 Die Dokumentation der Regelsätze ist zu finden unter https://docs.goobi.io/ugh-de/3

21 Ein Editor für Regelsätze und Konfigurationsdateien kann mittlerweile mit Plugins in Goobi workflow installiert werden (https://docs.goobi.io/goobi-workflow-plugins-de/administration/intranda_administration_config_file_editor und https://docs.goobi.io/goobi-workflow-plugins-de/administration/intranda_administration_ruleset_editor).

2.6.5. Metadatenanzeige

In der Datei g2g/workspace/workflow/config/goobi_metadataDisplayRules.xml kann projektabhängig definiert werden, wie die Metadaten im Metadateneditor dargestellt werden sollen, wie beispielsweise Auswahlbox (Dropdown) oder Mehrfachauswahl aus einer festgelegten Anzahl an Werten oder auch die Verknüpfung mit einer Liste aus dem Vokabularmanager. Der Vokabularmanager ist in „Administration > Vokabularverwaltung" zu finden.

2.6.6. OPAC-Anbindung

Der Metadatenimport aus Bibliothekskatalogen wird über die Datei g2g/workspace/workflow/config/goobi_opac.xml gesteuert. Es werden die Dokumenttypen festgelegt, die aus den Katalogen abgerufen werden können, und für jeden Katalog die Verbindungsdetails und die Suchfelder, in denen ein Datensatz per ID oder Barcode gesucht werden kann.

2.6.7. Anlegemaske

Das Aussehen und Verhalten der Anlegemaske für die Vorgänge wird über die Datei g2g/workspace/workflow/config/goobi_projects.xml gesteuert. Das betrifft sowohl die Auswahl der verfügbaren Metadatenfelder, als auch automatische Abläufe wie die Generierung des Vorgangstitels. Außerdem können der abzurufende Katalog hier definiert und die für die Generierung der Tiff-Header benötigten Felder aus den Metadaten vorbefüllt werden.

3. Schlussbemerkung

Dieser Artikel bietet nur einen Überblick über die grundlegenden Funktionalitäten von Goobi workflow und die wichtigsten Konfigurationen. Für eine tiefere Beschäftigung ist der Blick in die Dokumentation zu empfehlen. Außerdem gibt es eine sehr aktive User-Community, die auf https://community.goobi.io erreicht werden kann. Dort bekommt man nicht nur hilfreiche Tipps, sondern trifft mitunter auch auf Denkanstöße für ganz neue Verwendungsmöglichkeiten dieser wandlungsfähigen Software.

Schließlich sei angemerkt, dass Goobi-to-go sich nicht nur dafür eignet, die Programme kennenzulernen. Da es sich um die vollständigen Goobi-Programme handelt, können auch komplexe Szenarien getestet werden. Es ist damit leicht, für unterschiedliche Testzwecke neue Goobi-Instanzen einzurichten. Diese Möglichkeit einer einfach verfügbaren Testinfrastruktur wird nicht zuletzt durch ein Plugin[22] unterstützt, mit dem Konfiguration und Datenbank von einem existierenden Goobi workflow in ein neues exportiert werden können. Somit kann in einigen wenigen Schritten das eigene Produktionssystem in einer Goobi-to-go-Instanz repliziert werden. Die Tests finden dann mit den aktuellen Einstellungen und den eigenen Vorgängen und Daten statt.

Bibliografie

Frost, H.; Mangiafico, P. (2019): Integrating Digitization Workflow with the Stanford Digital Repository. Stanford University Libraries. https://repo.samvera.org/concern/parent/cdbeada1-0946-462c-a288-6c7647315bfd/file_sets/22df08d1-97bb-4908-911c-6a5f5f01ffb4 (abgerufen am 28.03.2022).

Hankiewicz, S. (2018): Goobi entwickeln. Eine Open-Source Software zur Verwaltung von Workflows in Digitalisierungsprojekten. In: Neuböck, Gregor (Hg.): Digitalisierung in Bibliotheken. Viel mehr als nur Bücher scannen. Berlin: De Gruyter Saur. (Bibliotheks- und Informationspraxis 63), S. 77–87.

Georg Mayr-Duffner ist seit 2014 Systembibliothekar an der Wirtschaftsuniversität Wien. Seit 2016 arbeitet er an der technischen Umsetzung der Digitalen Sammlungen der WU-Bibliothek mit Goobi workflow und Goobi viewer.

22 https://docs.goobi.io/goobi-workflow-plugins-de/administration/intranda_administration_goobi2goobi

János Békési

UNIDAM. Ein Bildrepositorium für Forschung und Lehre

Erfahrungsbericht und Schlüsse aus der Praxis

Handbuch Repositorienmanagement, Hg. v. Blumesberger et al., 2024, S. 455–465
https://doi.org/10.25364/978390337423224

János Békési, Universität Wien, Zentraler Informatikdienst, janos.bekesi@univie.ac.at |
ORCID iD: 0000-0001-6270-1193

Zusammenfassung

Nach einer kurzen Skizze der (Vor-)Geschichte des Digital Asset Management Systems der Universität Wien (UNIDAM), das Forschung und Lehre umfangreiches Bildmaterial zur Verfügung stellt, werden die technischen und organisatorischen Erwägungen beschrieben, die zur Auswahl des derzeitigen Systems geführt haben. Die (auch historischen) Besonderheiten des Repositoriums werden ebenso thematisiert wie die Schwierigkeiten der Migrationsphase, die den notwendigen Versionssprung begleitet haben. Eine Einschätzung des laufenden Betriebs im Kontext der universitären Datenmanagement-Infrastruktur wird aus technischer Perspektive vermittelt, aus der Sicht der Institution als Betreiberin und auch aus der Sicht der Benutzer:innen. Auch die "Lessons Learned" werden angesprochen, die sich über die Jahre oft aus unerwarteten Richtungen ergeben haben. Als Beispiel darf die Einsicht gelten, dass ein wissenschaftlicher, nicht zu spezialisierter Hintergrund äußerst hilfreich ist, um die Wünsche und Bedürfnisse der Benutzer:innen aus durchaus disparaten Fächern nachvollziehen und in eine technische Anforderung umsetzen zu können; für Letzteres erweist sich naturgemäß eine gewisse technische Affinität als unabdingbar. In einem Ausblick kommen die mittelfristigen Ausbau- und Planungsstrategien zur Sprache, für die UNIDAM und ähnliche Services in den nächsten Jahren ein wichtiger Bestandteil sind, sowie rund um UNIDAM entstandene Initiativen.

Schlagwörter: DAMS; Repositorium; Urheberrecht; Forschung; Organisatorische Perspektiven; Lehrinfrastruktur; Bewährte Verfahren; Software-Migration; Software-Version; Institutionelle Unterstützung

Abstract

UNIDAM. An Image Repository for Research and Teaching. A Field Report and Conclusions from Practical Experience

A short depiction of the history of UNIDAM, the University of Vienna's Digital Asset Management System, is followed by technological and organisational considerations that lead to the choice of the present system. The particularities of the repository will be described as well as the difficult phase of migration from the former software version to the current one. An evaluation of current operations is given from a technical, an institutional and a user-centred view. Also, lessons learned over the years will be addressed, e.g. the confirmation that a scientific albeit not too specialised background might be helpful to understand wishes and needs from quite different domains, and to translate those into technical requirements. A short prospect depicts mid-term planning strategies which contain UNIDAM and its surrounding services as important components for the research and teaching infrastructure of the University of Vienna.

Keywords: DAMS; digital assets repository; copyright; research; organisational perspectives; teaching infrastructure; best practice; software migration; software version; institutional support

1. Einleitung

UNIDAM, das UNIversity Digital Asset Management System der Universität Wien, ist eine mächtige integrierte und programmierbare Datenbank zur Verwaltung, Suche und Präsentation digitaler Daten, wobei hauptsächlich Bild- und kaum Ton- oder Videomaterial vorgehalten wird. Die zugrundeliegende easydb in der Version 5 wird im Museumskontext ebenso eingesetzt wie im Universitätsbereich oder für Objektsammlungen aus kulturellen Kontexten; ihre Programmierbarkeit erlaubt den Einsatz auch in speziellen Fachdomänen, z. B. bei der Sammlung von 3D- bzw. Virtual-Reality-Daten. Die Benutzung und Administration erfolgen über ein zeitgemäßes Webbrowser-Interface.[1]

1 In der Version 5 (im Jänner 2024 Version 5.126.0) besteht die easydb aus einem Ensemble von Docker-Containern, die jeweils spezifische Funktionsgruppen einkapseln (Datenbank, Suchindex, Assetverwaltung, allgemeiner Server und Frontend für das Web). Durch diese Architektur sind Updates sehr leicht durchzuführen, indem die neuen Versionen vom Docker-Repository heruntergeladen und die Container neu erstellt und gestartet werden. Eine unabsichtliche Beschädigung der relevanten Programmteile kann dadurch ebenso vermieden werden.

2. Historischer Überblick

Das Bildrepositorium UNIDAM nahm 2006 mit 160.000 Assets bzw. Bildobjekten seinen Betrieb auf.[2] Der Zweck der umfangreichen Sammlung war und ist die Bereitstellung von digitalisiertem Material für Lehre und Forschung, wobei ein Hauptkriterium die mit Passwort geregelte Zugänglichkeit darstellt, um den Urheber- und Bildrechtseinschränkungen im Bereich von Lehre und Forschung zu entsprechen (im Gegensatz zum Langzeitarchivierungssystem PHAIDRA, das öffentlichen Zugang ermöglicht).

Diese Assets entstammen unterschiedlichen Quellen aus vorwiegend geisteswissenschaftlichen Disziplinen; der Hauptanteil besteht aus Bildern der Kunstgeschichte, wo der unmittelbare Bedarf bestand, die Diamagazine in Überblicksvorlesungen durch PowerPoint-Präsentationen auf USB-Sticks, CDs oder direkt von der Website zu ersetzen. Bis 2014 wuchs der Bestand jährlich um ungefähr ein Fünftel an, wobei die Kunstgeschichte stets den größten Anteil stellte. Zu diesem Zeitpunkt kam die Betreuung des Servers, die durch einen IT-Beauftragten eines Instituts der Universität nebenher erfolgte, aus verschiedenen organisatorischen Gründen zum Erliegen, sodass für drei Jahre nur eine rudimentäre Begleitung durch den ZID, den Zentralen Informatikdienst der Universität Wien, möglich war, die im Wesentlichen nur den ununterbrochenen Betrieb gewährleisten konnte. Abgesehen von der Betreuungsproblematik hatte sich die Repositoriumssoftware gut bewährt, weshalb auch im Jahr 2017 die Entscheidung zugunsten der neuen Version 5 der easydb gefällt wurde, und zugleich Mittel zur Verfügung standen, um die dadurch notwendig gewordene Migration der Daten durch eine Vollzeitstelle abzusichern.

---

2 UNIDAM wurde nach erfolgter Bedarfserhebung und Ausschreibung im Jahr 2005 im März 2006 durch die easydb 3 der Berliner Programmfabrik realisiert, wobei die einmalig zu begleichenden Lizenzkosten, der Support nach Stundenaufwand und die hohe Flexibilität der Anpassung den Ausschlag gegenüber anderen Anboten gaben. Auch konnte die easydb 3 auf zufriedene Kunden in der Schweiz und in Deutschland verweisen, etwa auf die Freie Universität Berlin oder die Universitätsbibliothek Heidelberg, und nicht zuletzt war die weite Verbreitung der verwendeten Programmiersprache PHP ein weiteres Motiv, sodass im Bedarfsfall leicht Programmierer:innen für kleinere Anpassungen zu finden waren. Eine von der Universitätsbibliothek Wien beauftragte Evaluierung des Systems im Jahr 2012 bescheinigte dem System geringe Kosten für Anschaffung und Support, was der Grund dafür gewesen sein dürfte, sich nicht auf alternative, entwicklungsintensive Open-Source-Lösungen einzulassen. In diesem Jahr wurde erwogen, die Langzeitarchivierungssoftware PHAIDRA und UNIDAM zusammenzulegen, um Synergien zu nutzen. Dieses Vorhaben wurde nach einigen Monaten wegen zu großer Komplexität aufgegeben, und nach einer aus Kostengründen betreuungsfreien Zeit von weiteren zwei Jahren wurde UNIDAM ab 2017 durch eine Vollzeitstelle auf die Version 5 der easydb migriert und die Serverhardware durch Integration in die virtuelle Infrastruktur des ZID ersetzt. Bei dem ursprünglichen System der Version 3 handelte es sich um ein Framework aus PHP-, Python- und C-Komponenten sowie einer Postgresql-Datenbank, deren Inhalte über einen Apache-Server ausgeliefert wurden.

In weiterer Folge konnte der Blick vom bloßen Erhalt des Datenbestands auf Perspektiven zukünftiger Entwicklung gerichtet werden, von denen weiter unten die Rede sein wird.

3. Daten

An der Universität Wien (und auch an anderen Universitäten, die die easydb verwenden) sind jene Fachrichtungen in UNIDAM repräsentiert, die mit Bild- oder Videomaterial als Endpunkt der Forschung arbeiten oder zur Illustration in der Lehre gebrauchen und nicht mehr weiterverarbeiten, wie das etwa bei tomografischen Bildern oder ähnlichen Ergebnissen bildgebender Verfahren der Fall ist. Kunstgeschichte und Klassische Archäologie sind hier herausragende Beispiele, da sie beide sehr viel Bildmaterial in der Lehre einsetzen (allein die Überblicksvorlesung der Kunstgeschichte, der „Zyklus“, präsentiert pro Semester bis zu tausend Bilder). Zur Präsentation von Inhalten für eine allgemeine Öffentlichkeit wird UNIDAM bislang nicht genutzt – Urheber- und Bildrechte sind in den wenigsten Fällen im Besitz der Universität, sodass in der großen Mehrzahl der Fälle die Bilder nur im Kontext von Forschung und Lehre gezeigt werden können. Allerdings werden bereits Überlegungen angestellt, einzelne Exponate der Fotosammlung des Instituts für Kunstgeschichte öffentlich zu machen, wozu sich UNIDAM ebenso eignen würde.

Welcher Art waren und sind die Daten in UNIDAM? In der Hauptsache belieferten die Geisteswissenschaften bzw. Humanities die Datenbank, MINT-Fächer blieben unberücksichtigt (mit Ausnahme historischer Diabestände der Astronomie), d. h. von Ägyptologie über Numismatik bis hin zur Ur- und Frühgeschichte sind beinahe alle geisteswissenschaftlichen Disziplinen vertreten. Die Systematik der Einordnung in sogenannte Pools in UNIDAM (vergleichbar mit thematischen Ordnern) ist selbst ein Zeugnis des jeweiligen Fachverständnisses in der Entstehungs- bzw. Einrichtungszeit und spiegelt die Bedürfnisse der beteiligten Einzelwissenschaften zu einem bestimmten Zeitpunkt. Vor allem Bild-, aber auch etwas Videomaterial für die Lehre ist im Repositorium zu finden, wobei die Grenzen zu forschungsrelevantem Material oft fließend sind; die Bilder werden natürlich auch für den Erkenntnisprozess in der Forschung herangezogen. Manche Bildsammlungen sind ausschließlich für diesen Zweck erstellt worden, z. B. die Fotosammlung des Instituts für Evolutionäre Anthropologie.

Über die lange Zeit der Bestehens von UNIDAM haben sich die Verwendungsmuster immer wieder geändert, an unterschiedliche Vorgaben und technologische Einflüsse angepasst und in einem breiten Spektrum modifiziert: Das reicht von Vernachlässigung über semester- und lehrkraftspezifischen Anstieg der Verwendung bis hin zu vertieftem und intensiviertem Gebrauch in Teilbereichen. Das Auf und Ab dieser Nutzungen hängt selbstverständlich auch immer von der technologischen Affinität und Bereitschaft der beteiligten Lehrkräfte und Studierenden ab, sowie von einem gewissen Maß an Werbung für den Service an sich, die dem Engagement der beteiligten Personen in den Instituten entspricht.

4. Vernetzung

Ein wichtiges Alleinstellungsmerkmal des UNIDAM-Systems ist die Verbindung mit Partneruniversitäten und -institutionen, die ebenfalls die easydb einsetzen und Teile ihres Datenbestands für andere zugänglich machen, so etwa die Universität Basel oder das Kunstgeschichtliche Institut der Freien Universität Berlin. Umgekehrt stellt die Universität Wien über den sogenannten Connector dem Verbund der easydbs ca. 370.000 Bildobjekte, also fast zwei Drittel des Bestands, zur Verfügung, die dann über Suchanfragen leicht gefunden und (mit Einschränkungen hinsichtlich der Bildqualität) in eigenen Zusammenhängen verwendet werden können. Dadurch ergibt sich ein virtueller Verbund von Bilddaten, der wie ein einziger großer Bestand durchsuchbar ist und dessen Inhalte in eigenen sogenannten „Mappen" für den die weitere Verarbeitung gespeichert werden können.

Wie bereits erwähnt, konnte der anspruchsvolle Versionssprung der easydb von Version 4 auf die mit geänderter Technologie und vor allem zeitgemäßem User:inneninterface ausgestattete Version 5 durch die Widmung einer Vollzeitstelle am Zentralen Informatikdienst der Universität Wien realisiert werden. Da diese Aktualisierung auch eine des Betriebssystems sowie die Übersiedelung auf einen virtuellen Server nach sich zog, betrug die endgültige Zeitdauer für diese Maßnahmen 16 Monate, was angesichts der Anforderungen (Migration von 6-7 Terabytes Datenmaterial, Migration der Datenstruktur mithilfe spezieller Skripte, Testing, Qualitätssicherung usw.) nicht zu knapp bemessen war. Für manche Arbeitsschritte eignete sich nur die vorlesungsfreie Zeit, um den laufenden Betrieb nicht zu beeinträchtigen. Insbesondere die umfangreiche Rechteverwaltung (3.500 Benutzer:innen, 110 Gruppen für Benutzer:innen und 300 sogenannte Pools mit je eigenen Zugriffsrechten) machte es zu einer heiklen Aufgabe, dies von der Version 4 in die Version 5 überzuführen. Die Wiener UNIDAM-Instanz ist übrigens von allen installierten easydbs diejenige mit dem komplexesten Rechtemanagement.

5. Technische Merkmale

Im Folgenden sollen einige technische Charakteristika von UNIDAM aufgezeigt werden: Zum Zeitpunkt der Abfassung Drucklegung (Anfang 2024) enthält UNIDAM ungefähr 610.000 Objekte, davon 3.200 Video-, 4.500 Audio- und 460.000 Bildobjekte; pro Monat finden 25.000 Logins statt und 13.000 Suchanfragen. Die easydb enthält ca. 60 Objekttypen, in der Hauptsache Hilfsobjekte, die Metadaten für die Hauptbildobjekte enthalten. Der virtualisierte Server ist mit 12 CPUs und 32 Gigabyte RAM ausgestattet, das Datenmaterial nimmt 7,8 Terabyte ein.

Aus technischer Perspektive ist es wichtig, schnell reagieren zu können, insbesondere bei Fehlbedienungen und allfälligen betrieblichen Schwierigkeiten. Daher erweist sich die Beherrschung der eingesetzten Programmiersprachen als notwendig. Für die easydb und die sie umgebenden Services konnten mit Python alle auftretenden Fehler innerhalb kürzester Zeit über das easydb-API via Skript behoben werden, ohne den Hersteller Programmfabrik einbinden zu müssen. Dies ist auch deshalb von Vorteil, weil in einem solchen Fall immer mit gewissen Verzögerungen zu rechnen ist, während derer der Betrieb eventuell stark eingeschränkt werden müsste. Da die Teams des Langzeitarchivierungssystems PHAIDRA und UNIDAM derselben Abteilung des ZID angehören („IT Support for Research: Data Management"), kommt es immer wieder zu gewünschten Synergieeffekten und kurzfristiger Zusammenarbeit, etwa im Bereich der Systemadministration, bzw. von DevOps (Einrichtung von Backups, Erweiterung von Festplatten oder Hauptspeicher etc.). Kleinere Erweiterungen des Funktionsumfangs der Datenbank waren mit JavaScript bzw. CoffeeScript in Gestalt von Plug-ins ebenfalls gut realisierbar.

Der laufende Betrieb seit der Umstellung von easydb 4 auf easydb 5 im Herbst 2018 gestaltete sich problemlos, abgesehen von wenigen Zwischenfällen, die entweder fehlerhafte Updates oder Bedienfehler zur Ursache hatten und rasch behoben werden konnten. In dieser Hinsicht bietet die enge Zusammenarbeit mit dem Hersteller eindeutige Vorteile für beide Seiten, da die Wiener Installation, wie bereits erwähnt, aufgrund der umfangreichen Rechteverwaltung einzigartig ist (sodass sie dem Hersteller wegen der zahlreichen Benutzeraccounts immer wieder als Kopiervorlage für interne Tests dient), und gelegentlich von Seite des ZID eingemeldete Fehler in der Regel beim nächsten Update, das alle zwei bis drei Wochen erfolgt, behoben werden. Durch die Auslegung der easydb als zusammengehörige Docker-Container verläuft das Update ohne nennenswerte Downtime, was die Betreuung sehr erleichtert.

6. Institutionelle und benutzer:innenorientierte Perspektive

Aus institutioneller Perspektive war die Entscheidung richtig, den Betrieb des Repositoriums UNIDAM an der Schnittstelle zwischen Universitätsbibliothek und Zentralem Informatikdienst anzusiedeln, wobei der organisatorische Teil von der UB, der technische vom ZID bestritten wird. Dass die personelle Zusammenarbeit sich sehr gut bewährt, ist ein zusätzlicher Glücksfall, der einige neue Projekte und Initiativen rund um das Datenmanagement hervorgebracht hat. Die Möglichkeit, die Verwaltung für größere Gruppen von Benutzer:innen (Kunstgeschichte, Klassische Archäologie, Alte Geschichte) über die UNIDAM-Rechteverwaltung in die Hände der jeweiligen IT-Verantwortlichen zu legen, hat die Identifikation mit den Zielen und dem Einsatz von UNIDAM in diesen Bereichen gefördert.

Was die Zustimmung seitens der Benutzer:innen betrifft, so wird die neue, modernisierte Benutzer:innenoberfläche inzwischen gut angenommen, wobei unmittelbar nach dem Umstieg auf die Version 5 manchmal Unmut geäußert wurde, der auf Nachfrage meist der Anforderung entsprang, eingeschliffene Verwendungsmuster und Erwartungen ändern zu müssen. In wenigen Fällen wurde das Feedback unzufriedener Nutzer:innen auch als Anlass für Änderungen seitens des Herstellers genommen. Ein Beispiel hierfür war die mangelnde Eindeutigkeit bei der Zuordnung von Pools aus Partneruniversitäten, die über die Connector-Verbindung in UNIDAM angezeigt wurden. Ein innerhalb weniger Wochen geliefertes Systemupdate sorgte dafür, dass jeder angezeigte Pool seine Ursprungs-easydb erkennen lässt. Mittlerweile werden die neuen Features der Version 5 gerne benutzt, und Beschwerden sind fast völlig verschwunden, was das UNIDAM-Team als Zeichen dafür deutet, dass das Repositorium seine Aufgabe tadellos erfüllt. Bewährt hat sich in dieser Hinsicht auch eine regelmäßige, ungefähr halbjährliche Kommunikation mit „Power-Usern“, d. h. Benutzer:innen, die über mehr Rechte und mehr Investment in UNIDAM verfügen als Normalbenutzer:innen, oft als Anlaufstelle für deren Kümmernisse fungieren und dadurch allgemeineres Feedback erhalten als das UNIDAM-Team selbst. Sie nehmen auch immer wieder Verbesserungsvorschläge bzw. Wünsche nach Funktionserweiterungen entgegen, die nach Maßgabe von Zeit und Notwendigkeit vom Hersteller bei regelmäßigen Updates berücksichtigt werden.

7. Lessons Learned

Im Verlauf der letzten vier Jahre, also seit dem Umstieg auf die neue Version der easydb, haben sich einige Punkte herauskristallisiert, die man als Lessons Learned bezeichnen könnte, als Bereiche und Problemfelder, in denen etwas sehr gut oder auch weniger gut funktioniert hat.

- Die enge Verzahnung und das gute Einvernehmen innerhalb der betroffenen technischen und organisatorischen Parteien der Institution (Universitätsbibliothek und am ZID die Abteilung IT Support for Research: Data Management) hat sich als unschätzbarer Vorteil erwiesen, um eine Kultur der kurzen Wege zu pflegen.
- Die sorgfältige Planung von Änderungsschritten hat sich genauso bewährt: Dass eine geplante längere Wartezeit allemal besser ist als eine noch so kurze ungeplante Ausfallzeit des Services, scheint trivial, erhöht aber das Vertrauen der Benutzer:innen in seine Verfügbarkeit.
- Die mehrschichtige Funktionsweise der organisatorischen Einheiten rund um UNIDAM trägt viel zur Betriebssicherheit und Stabilität bei, wobei die Schichten durch Personen unterschiedlicher Abteilungen bzw. Teams repräsentiert sind.
- Ein wissenschaftlicher, nicht allzu spezialisierter Hintergrund ist mitunter hilfreich, um die Wünsche und Schwierigkeiten der Benutzer aus disparaten Fächern nachvollziehen und in eine technische Anforderung übersetzen zu können; für Letzteres erweist sich naturgemäß eine gewisse technische Affinität als unabdingbar.
- Die gute Zusammenarbeit mit dem Hersteller des easydb-Systems und die Teilnahme an dessen thematischen Workshops ermöglichen den Blick über den Tellerrand auf andere Implementationen und Anwendungsfälle des Systems (was ist möglich, welche Features werden anderswo genutzt, wie gehen andere Institutionen mit denselben Problemen um etc.).
- Manche aussichtsreiche oder spannende Ergänzungen zu UNIDAM wurden nach kurzer Probezeit wieder verworfen, da von Seiten der Benutzer:innen kein Bedarf bestand bzw. der nichtöffentliche Charakter des Repositoriums gewisse Funktionalitäten nicht zulässt. So wird z. B. eine Realisierung von Konnektivität im Sinne von Linked Open Data allenfalls einseitig bleiben, weil standardisierte und Normdaten nur ins System eingespielt werden, jedoch keine Daten wieder hinausgelangen, wie es dafür erforderlich wäre.
- Ein Mangel sollte zu guter Letzt noch angeführt werden, nämlich die Tatsache, dass das Erfahrungswissen, das sich aus dem täglichen Umgang mit UN-

IDAM ergibt, auf eine einzige Person beschränkt bleibt und durch kontinuierlich erfolgende Dokumentation nur teilweise substituiert werden kann. Hier gibt es institutionellen bzw. organisatorischen Verbesserungsbedarf.

8. Ausblick

Am Ende seien noch einige mittelfristige Planungen in Hinblick auf UNIDAM angesprochen, die im Team erwogen werden, ebenso wie Initiativen zum Data Management, die im Umkreis der easydb entstanden sind. Die Anbindung externer Services an UNIDAM wird in Zukunft wichtiger, und daher gehen die Anstrengungen für eine Erweiterung mittels Plug-in in Richtung Moodle-Konnektivität, sodass z. B. in Moodle angebotene Lehrveranstaltungen integrierte Verweise auf die entsprechenden Bildsammlungen in UNIDAM enthalten können. Eine in Erprobung befindliche Ergänzung (ebenfalls mittels Plug-in) soll die Metadaten der Bilder der Kunstgeschichte durch standardisierte ikonographische Einträge bereichern, wofür das Normvokabular Iconclass verwendet wird. Das UNIDAM-Team plant auch die Verknüpfung von Handschriftenscans, die als Bilder in die Datenbank eingespielt wurden, mit der Handschriftenerkennung Transkribus, um einen Workflow für Forschende optimal gestalten zu können, d. h. die Anreicherung von Scans mit aus OCR und HCR gewonnenen Transkriptionen, die als Text wieder von der easydb durchsuchbar sind. In den nächsten ein bis zwei Jahren wird außerdem eine weitere, nunmehr dritte Migration (von Version 5 auf Version 6 bzw. „Fylr") notwendig werden, die vor allem Erleichterungen beim Erstellen von Plug-ins, ein aufgeräumteres Administrationsinterface sowie deutliche Performancegewinne durch Neuprogrammierung zentraler Softwarekomponenten verspricht.

Ausserhalb des Kontexts von UNIDAM wurde die easydb mittlerweile in mehreren Projekten eingesetzt, da die schnelle Anpassung des Datenmodells, die bewährte Benutzer:innenführung und das inzwischen angesammelte Know-How eine gute Basis für Datenbanken in der Forschung, z. B. der Historischen Sammlung des Zoologischen Instituts, darstellen. Daher sind die beteiligten Forscher:innen äußerst zufrieden mit den vom UNIDAM-Team eingerichteten und maßgeschneiderten Lösungen. Diese Initiative, die easydb als schnell zu modellierende und gut zu bedienende mächtige Forschungsdatenbank zu empfehlen, hat dazu geführt, dass bereits bei einigen Projekten der Universität dieses Setup ausprobiert wurde. Weiters gehen die Bestrebungen dahin, die easydb nachdrücklicher als ein Workflowtool einzusetzen und zu positionieren, das Forschungsdaten bearbeiten, ordnen und selektieren kann, bevor sie als Resultate der Langzeitarchivierung (PHAIDRA) überantwortet werden.

Die Aussichten auf eine weitergehende Integration von UNIDAM und im Umfeld gruppierten Services lassen in Zukunft eine robuste Infrastruktur für Bildmaterial in Lehre und Forschung erwarten.

Quellenverzeichnis

Easydb Documentation. https://docs.easydb.de/en

Flexible Daten- und Medien-Verwaltung mit easydb. https://www.programmfabrik.de

Ganguly, Raman: persönliche Mitteilung, Mai 2022.

Pausz, Ralf: persönliche Mitteilung, Juni 2022.

Programmfabrik. Home of fylr.io & easydb.de. https://github.com/programmfabrik

János Békési studierte Philosophie und Kunstgeschichte in Wien und Berlin, Lehrtätigkeit an der Universität Wien und Mitarbeit am Institut Wiener Kreis, Geschäftsführer und technischer Leiter der Webagentur Meta-Ware, seit 2017 im Team der Abteilung „IT Support for Research: Data Management“ am Zentralen Informatikdienst der Universität Wien.

Gregor Neuböck

Zeitgemäße visuelle Darstellung von Digitalisaten in einem Repository – am Beispiel der DLOÖ – kann nur gelingen, wenn Daten geeignet in Format gebracht werden

Handbuch Repositorienmanagement, Hg. v. Blumesberger et al., 2024, S. 467–487
https://doi.org/10.25364/978390337423225

Gregor Neuböck, Wienbibliothek im Rathaus, gregor.neuboeck@wienbibliothek.at | ORCID iD: 0000-0002-2979-4356

Zusammenfassung

Auf Basis der rasanten Entwicklungen im Bereich der Informationstechnologien konnten die Mittel zur Darstellung von Büchern in digitaler Form einen unglaublichen Qualitätssprung machen. Grundlage dafür ist die Qualität der Datensätze und Scans, wobei letztere sehr stark von der Qualität der Scanner, den Einstellungen und den Arbeitsabläufen abhängt. Die Qualität der Datensätze wiederum hängt von verschiedenen weiteren Faktoren ab. Die Orientierung an internationalen Standards kann dabei sicherlich zu den wichtigsten Kriterien gezählt werden, aber auch die Granularität der erfassten Daten stellt eine essentielle Grundlage für eine optimierte Visualisierung dar. Im Anschluss erläutere ich die derzeitigen Möglichkeiten der Visualisierung anhand der Digitalen Landesbibliothek Oberösterreich DLOÖ. Der hier vorliegende Beitrag behandelt genau diese Faktoren möglichst umfassend, sowie im Kernpunkt die darauf aufbauenden visuellen Darstellungsmöglichkeiten, ohne den Rahmen dieses Beitrags zu sprengen.

Schlagwörter: Visualisierung; Digitalisierung; Repositorium; Goobi; Retrodigitalisierung

Abstract

The Contemporary Visual Representation of Digital Copies in a Repository – Using the DLOÖ as an Example – Can Only Succeed if the Data Are Formatted Appropriately

The developments in the field of information technologies in the recent years have been so rapid that today the means of presenting books in digital form have improved in an incredible way, thus ensuring advancements in the quality of the digitisation. The prerequisite for this is the quality of the data sets and the scans, the latter depending very much on the quality of the scanners, their settings and the workflows in scanning mode. Besides, the quality of the records depends on several other factors. The orientation to international standards can certainly be counted among the most important criteria, but the granularity of the collected data is also an important basis for optimised visualizations. In the following, I will explain the current possibilities of visualisation by reference to the Digital State Library of Upper Austria DLOÖ. This contribution deals with precisely the above-mentioned factors as comprehensively as possible as well as with the resulting visual display options, without going beyond the scope of the publication.

Keywords: Visualisation; digitisation; repository; Goobi; retro-digitisation

1. Einleitung

Die Digital Humanities treiben die Entwicklungen zur Visualisierung von Daten seit vielen Jahren mit zunehmendem Tempo voran.

Visualisierung kann dabei helfen, Daten möglichst umfassend, aber gleichzeitig klar und übersichtlich darzustellen, ohne dabei wichtige Details zu verbergen oder gar zu verändern. Das Gesehene in einem Repository ist niemals mit einer wirklichkeitsgetreuen Abbildung gleichzusetzen, sondern ist immer eine Folge der Verarbeitung des einzelnen Individuums auf Basis dessen Vorwissens bzw. Wissensstands[1]. In diesem Sinne ist bei der Gestaltung von Visualisierungen darauf zu achten, dass diese möglichst selbsterklärend sind und im besten Fall eine Art lernende Oberfläche[2] bilden. Im Idealfall werden die Benutzer:innen einerseits bei ihrem individuellen Wissensstand abgeholt und andererseits sorgen die Visualisierungen für eine optimale Wissensorganisation. Die Digitalisierung bzw. die Entwicklung des Semantic Web hat dazu geführt, dass nicht nur die Objekte selber (Scans der einzelnen Seiten) sondern auch ihre Beschreibungen digital verfügbar sind. Es gibt also einen rasant wachsenden Bereich an Struktur- und Metadaten. Damit in diesem riesigen Datenmeer der Überblick gewahrt bleiben kann, Suchanfragen also erfolgreich und zielgerichtet, aber niemals unwissentlich ausschließend sind, ist es zielführend, die Wissensorganisation über Modellansätze zu realisieren. Dazu zählen z. B. die Taxonomie, die in abgewandelter Form heute auch in Form des Tagging angewendet werden kann, Thesauri im Sinne einer Vernetzung verwandter Begriffe (siehe z. B. Named Entity Recognition, NER) in einem semantischen Netz sowie Ontologien, die man als[3] „[...] logisch einwandfrei definierte, maschinell interpretierbare Beschreibungen des Weltwissens [...]"[4] bezeichnen kann. NER bezieht sich auf die automatisierte Erkennung von Eigennamen durch Algorithmen, was wesentlich schwieriger ist, als es auf den ersten Blick erscheint. Denn Entitäten sind nicht immer sofort ganz klar und eindeutig zu erkennen. Orts-, Personen-, Organisations- und Produktnamen werden ganz eindeutig als Entitäten bezeichnet.[5]

1 Pamperl, B. (2017), S. 90f.
2 Im Sinne einer *Lernenden Organisation* sollte sich auch eine Lernende Oberfläche den Benutzer:innen anpassen, indem z. B. Inhalte, in Abhängigkeit der Nutzung, einem Ranking unterzogen werden sollten.
3 Keller, S. et. al. (2014), S. 11–14.
4 Keller, S. et. al. (2014), S. 13.
5 Roth, J. (2002), S. 5f.

Paik et al.[6] unterscheiden neun Hauptkategorien. Eine Kategorie wird als Misc.[7] bezeichnet. Alle Hauptkategorien besitzen zudem Unterkategorien, wodurch sich schlussendlich 30 Kategorien ergeben.

In der Retrodigitalisierung steht verstärkt das Bild im Zentrum und wird, so wie Pamperl es beschreibt, zum Wissenschaftsbild[8]. Windhager spricht in der Biographieforschung von einer „Weiterentwicklung von Bildern zu genuinen Funktionsträgern eines dynamischen und kritischen geschichtswissenschaftlichen Diskurses"[9].

Die reale Umsetzung von Digitalisierungsprojekten erweist sich immer als hochkomplexer, extrem herausfordernder und permanenter Erneuerungsprozess.

Allen Beteiligten sollte von Anfang an klar sein, dass Digitalisierungsprojekte einen langen Atem sowie personelle und monetäre Ressourcen erfordern, die budgetiert und bereitgestellt werden müssen. Im Vorfeld sollte also schon abgeklärt werden, ob diese von den jeweiligen Institutionen dauerhaft aufgebracht werden können.

Neben den Bibliothekar:innen und Programmierer:innen kann man nur dazu raten, pädagogisch geschultes Personal und Anwender:innen in Entwicklungsprozesse einzubinden, damit nicht an den Benutzer:innen vorbeientwickelt wird.

Der hier vorliegende Beitrag beschäftigt sich mit zentralen Komponenten von Repositorien, welche die Visualisierung von Daten und die damit verbundene Qualität der Darstellung für die Benutzer:innen erheblich beeinflussen. Da auch an der Oberösterreichischen Landesbibliothek die Anzahl der digitalisierten Werke[10] und in einem noch wesentlich höheren Ausmaß, die mit diesen Werken verbundenen Struktur- und Metadaten eine nicht mehr überblickbare Menge erreicht haben, sind auch wir auf verschiedene Werkzeuge der Digital Humanities zur Informationsvisualisierung angewiesen. Etwa, wie man z. B. Suchanfragen oder vorhandene Geodaten geeignet darstellt.[11] Auf Basis dieser Daten werden die derzeit verwendeten Werkzeuge und deren Visualisierung innerhalb der Digitalen Landesbibliothek Oberösterreich (DLOÖ) vorgestellt.

---

6 Paik, L. et al. (1993), S. 156.

7 Unter dieser Kategorie werden alle Entitäten angeführt, die keiner der anderen Kategorien zugeordnet werden können.

8 Pamperl, B. (2017), S. 92.

9 Windhager, F. (2017), S. 71.

10 Mit Stand vom 01.10.2021 sind innerhalb der Digitalen Landesbibliothek Oberösterreich (DLOÖ https://digi.landesbibliothek.at) beinahe 6.500 Werke digitalisiert, was ca. 600.000 Seiten entspricht.

11 Pamperl, B. (2017), S. 93f.

Es besteht weder der Anspruch auf Vollständigkeit aller einflussnehmenden Faktoren, noch auf detaillierte Ausarbeitung dieser. Vielmehr geht es darum, einen praxisnahen Blick auf diese zu werfen und Anregungen für die eigene Arbeit zum Thema Visualisierung in der Digitalisierung zu finden.

2. Qualität der Datensätze

2.1. Standards

Wie eingangs erwähnt, hängt die Qualität der Datensätze sehr stark von der Orientierung an internationalen Standards ab[12]. Bei der Datenvisualisierung[13] sollte man sich immer bewusst machen, dass diese schon eine Form der Interpretation von Rohdaten darstellt. In diesem Sinne sollte das Ergebnis immer kritisch hinterfragt werden.[14]

Auch kann es im Laufe der Zeit passieren, dass sich die Datenfelder vielmehr an den Wünschen der einzelnen Protagonist:innen[15] als an internationalen Standards orientieren. Verlockend erscheinen die grenzenlosen Möglichkeiten, den Aufbau von Datenfeldern abseits von Normierungen ausschließlich an den Wünschen der Beteiligten zu orientieren.

Man sollte sich dessen bewusst sein, dass das Erstellen von Datenfeldern, ohne sich über deren Normierung Gedanken zu machen, zu datenbanktechnischen Problemen mit langfristigen Auswirkungen führen kann. Repositorien erfordern zwingend laufend Verbesserungen und müssen an aktuelle technische Standards angepasst werden[16]. Werden bei diesen Erneuerungs- und Entwicklungsprozessen Standards nicht eingehalten, ist mittel- und langfristig ein erheblicher Mehraufwand für die Erhaltung und Pflege der Daten zu erwarten. Im schlechtesten Fall kann dies sogar zu Datenverlust führen, weil keine maschinelle Verarbeitung mehr möglich ist.

Zudem gewinnt die Normierung von Datenfeldern noch rascher an Bedeutung, wenn das eigene Repository an internationale Plattformen (Europeana[17], Verzeichnis digitalisierter Drucke[18],....) angedockt werden soll. Dann wird es nötig, eine

---

12 http://www.loc.gov/standards/mets/

13 z. B. Suchanfragen, Timelines, Kalendersuche etc.

14 Pamperl, B. (2017), S. 95.

15 Wissenschaftler:innen, Bibliothekar:innen, Sammlungsleiter:innen und dgl.

16 https://forschungsdaten.info/themen/beschreiben-und-dokumentieren/metadaten-und-metadatenstandards/

17 https://www.europeana.eu/de

18 https://www.zvdd.de/startseite/

Nachnutzung über APIs, Schnittstellen (z. B. IIIF[19], REST, OAI-PMH[20], SRU) und anerkannte Datenstandards wie z. B. JSON zu ermöglichen. In der DLOÖ werden viele verschiedene maschinell lesbare und international anerkannte Datenformate via OAI-PMH angeboten.

Der Wissenschaftsbetrieb ist bestrebt, internationale Datenstandards einzuhalten, damit ein möglichst reibungsloser und barrierefreier Datenaustausch ermöglicht wird. Dieser kann zusätzlich noch verbessert werden, indem auf Titeläquivalenz[21] geachtet wird, Farbe und Kontrast parallel eingesetzt werden, Optionen zur Tastaturnavigation angeboten werden, strukturierte Inhalte vorhanden sind, die Verständlichkeit[22] gegeben ist und eine Geräteunabhängigkeit[23] garantiert werden kann.[24]

2.2. Scans

Die Qualität der Scans ist ein maßgebender Faktor bei der Visualisierung von Daten. Auch im Sinne eines bestandsschonenden Umgangs sollte auf eine nachhaltige Scanstrategie geachtet werden, um nicht alle paar Jahre in die Verlegenheit zu geraten, Scans neu anlegen zu müssen. Es liegt auf der Hand, dass jede noch so schonende Prozedur Bücher belastet, was angesichts des Mehrwerts, Materialien unabhängig von Ort und Zeit für Wissenschaft und Allgemeinheit verfügbar zu machen, in Kauf genommen wird.

Beim Neukauf eines Scanners sollte man sich zu Beginn einen Überblick über geeignete Scangeräte hinsichtlich Scangröße, Scanauflösung und Farbtiefe verschaffen. Die Scanauflösung Dots per Inch (DPI) ist eine drucktechnische Angabe und nutzt das Farbmodell CMYK. Pixel per Inch (PPI) ist eine digitale Angabe und verwendet das additive Farbmodell RGB. Die Farbtiefe ist ein entscheidender Wert, um eine wirklichkeitsgetreue Abbildung von Farben zu ermöglichen. Lange Zeit galt eine Farbtiefe von 24 Bit (True Color) als der beste Standard, mittlerweile werden auch Systeme mit bis zu 30 Bit (Deep Color) bei Scannern angeboten.

Neben diesen grundlegenden Parametern sollte man sich auch überlegen, ob man einen Zeilenscanner oder einen Scanner mit einem Flächenchip (vergleichbar mit

19 https://docs.goobi.io/goobi-viewer-de/conf/1/33/2
20 https://digi.landesbibliothek.at/viewer/oai
21 Jede Grafik benötigt eine Textbeschreibung.
22 Richtige Sprachauszeichnung, Verständlichkeit der Navigation, angebotene Orientierungshilfen.
23 Verschiedene Betriebssysteme, Unterstützung verschiedener Versionierungen von Softwareprodukten.
24 Kogler, G. (2014), S. 5–8.

einer Digitalkamera) einsetzen möchte. Zeilenscanner bieten die besseren Auflösungen über große Flächen und arbeiten mit einem Zeilensensor (Abtastrate beachten!), der Zeile für Zeile das darunterliegende Objekt ausliest und gleichzeitig für jedes Pixel alle RGB-Farben aufnimmt. Kamerasysteme sind ungleich flexibler und weisen eine wesentlich höhere Scangeschwindigkeit auf. Allerdings müssen durch ihren spezifischen Bildsensor, Bildpunkte im Blau- und Rotbereich stark interpoliert (digital ergänzt) werden.

Digitalisierung ist immer im Dilemma zwischen den Ansprüchen, möglichst nahe am Original zu sein und gleichzeitig einen optimierten Digitalisierungsworkflow zu etablieren. Um die Auflösung eines Scanners beurteilen zu können, ist es wichtig, zwischen absoluter[25] und relativer[26] Auflösung zu unterscheiden. So wird vielleicht auch klar, dass eine hohe relative Auflösung per se noch kein scharfes Bild garantiert. Wenn z. B. in das Bild stark reingezoomt wird, sinkt im Bildausschnitt die relative Auflösung, bis das Bild irgendwann unscharf wirkt. Beim Scanner-Ankauf ist daher darauf zu achten, über welche Fläche eine optische Auflösung garantiert wird, um beim Zoomen auch noch scharfe Bilder zu ermöglichen. An der Oberösterreichischen Landesbibliothek wird jedes Objekt seit über zehn Jahren mit einer relativen Auflösung von 600 PPI gescannt. Nur ganz selten verringern wir bei sehr großen Karten oder Leporellos die Auflösung, um nicht allzu große Bilddateien zu erhalten.

Hat nun eine engere Auswahl an geeigneten Geräten stattgefunden, sollten alle in Betracht kommenden Scanner mit eigenen Materialien[27] eingehend getestet werden. Neben Problemen bei den mechanischen Abläufen[28] kann es auch vorkommen, dass Scanner die Farben nicht wirklichkeitsgetreu abbilden oder die angegebene Auflösung[29] gar nicht erreichen bzw. mit interpolierten Auflösungen[30] arbeiten. Auch die Scangeschwindigkeit sollte in einem eigenen Test über verschiedene Flächen mit unterschiedlichen Auflösungen überprüft und mit den Herstellerangaben verglichen werden. Die Ausführung und Qualität der Linsen beeinflussen alle

---

25 Entspricht der maximalen Scanfläche von z. B. 1250x3200 Pixel.

26 Entspricht der Anzahl an Pixel/Dots per Inch, also einer Dichteangabe.

27 Man sollte eine heterogene Auswahl aller in der Bibliothek vorkommenden Dokumententypen testen.

28 Wie öffnet die Glasplatte? Gibt es eine Buchstütze? Wie wird das Buch eingelegt? Kann ich auch ohne Glasplatte scannen?...

29 Sollte immer mit dem Zusatz „optisch“ angegeben sein, z. B. 600PPI optisch.

30 Diese werden durch Algorithmen errechnet und sollten unbedingt vermieden werden.

Qualitätskriterien eines Bildes und sollten mit eigenen Materialien eingehend geprüft werden[31]. Testcharts für Auflösung[32] und Kalibrierung[33] helfen dabei, die technischen Angaben normiert zu überprüfen und die Daten der Hersteller zu verifizieren. Regelmäßig sollte die Kalibrierung eines Scanners im Alltagsbetrieb vorgenommen werden, um abhängig von den jeweiligen Herstellerangaben optimale Ergebnisse und eine gleichbleibende Qualität zu halten.

3. Software

Welche Software man als Repository einsetzt, hängt stark von den benötigten Funktionalitäten und Anforderungen ab.

An der Oberösterreichischen Landesbibliothek kommt eine international verwendete Open-Source Software zum Einsatz, die von vielen verschiedenen Protagonisten entwickelt wird.

Noch vor wenigen Jahren stand man Open Source sehr kritisch gegenüber, da man der Ansicht war, dass die Weiterentwicklung dadurch nicht gewährleistet sei, ganz im Gegensatz zu proprietärer Software, der man genau diese Eigenschaft zusprach. Mittlerweile hat sich dieses Bild stark gewandelt, denn es hängt nicht von der Lizenz einer Software, sondern von der Bedeutung der Community ab, welche eine Software einsetzt. Gibt es wesentliche Stakeholder, kann davon ausgegangen werden, dass die Software langfristig weiterentwickelt wird und die Community über das entsprechende Entwicklungspotential verfügt. Einerseits ist dies wichtig, um Features zu entwickeln, die die aktuell vorhandenen technischen Möglichkeiten ausreizen, andererseits um einen möglichst barrierefreien Zugang auf allen möglichen Endgeräten mit verschiedensten Betriebssystemen auf unterschiedlichen Browsern[34] zu garantieren.

Ein weiteres Kennzeichen von Open Source ist der permanente Entwicklungsprozess, was nichts mit dem in der Softwareentwicklung verwendeten Begriff der Betaversion[35] zu tun hat, sondern auf einen andauernden Entwicklungsprozess hinweist, der wiederum der Garant für Innovation, Stabilität und Aktualität ist. Die Schlussfolgerung daraus muss sein, dass man als Projektmanager:in Softwareentwicklung als einen permanenten Verbesserungsprozess sieht. Nichts ist weniger

31 Gold kann einen grünlichen Anteil bekommen oder es kommt im Randbereich von Bildern wegen größerer Linsenfehler zu Verzerrungen.

32 USAF Resolution Test Chart

33 ISO-Standards 12641-2

34 Auch alle aktuellen Versionierungen eines Browsers sollten fehlerfrei funktionieren.

35 Software, die noch nicht für den Produktionsbereich geeignet ist, weil noch zu viele Bugs vorhanden sind.

nachhaltig, als isolierte Digitalisierungsprojekte, die ein Budget und einen zeitlich begrenzten Ablauf haben, ohne dass in irgendeiner Form darüber nachgedacht wurde, wie eine dauerhafte Weiterführung oder Einbindung in vorhandene Digitalisierungsprojekte gewährleistet werden könnte. Die Gefahr, dass finanzielle und personelle Ressourcen nicht nachhaltig eingesetzt werden, ist hierbei groß.

In jedem Fall darf nochmals explizit darauf hingewiesen werden, sich an internationale Datenstandards zu halten, insbesondere auch darauf, dass die verwendete Software die Einhaltung dieser ermöglicht, denn nur sie garantieren am ehesten einen problemlosen Umstieg auf ein anderes Softwareprodukt, sollte dies einmal erforderlich sein.

Ein weiterer Punkt ist die Plattformunabhängigkeit der Software, sodass kein eigener Client für den Zugriff auf die Produktionssoftware erforderlich ist. Für den Zugriff sollten nur ein herkömmlicher Browser und eine Internetverbindung erforderlich sein. Serverbasierte Software kann also unabhängig von Ort, Zeit und Gerätekonfiguration verwendet werden. Nebenbei fallen bei Open Source auch keine Lizenzgebühren an und es können nach Bedarf neue Benutzer:innen angelegt werden. So ergibt sich kein großer Aufwand, externe Dienstleister, aber auch Mitarbeiter:innen im Homeoffice in den Arbeitsprozess einzubinden. Heute sind derartige Systeme in aller Munde und werden gemeinhin unter dem Sammelbegriff Cloud-Computing geführt.

4. Visualisierungen

Im Kapitel Visualisierungen werden verschiedene Anwendungsbereiche innerhalb der DLOÖ behandelt. Neben der Bildanzeige zählen dazu aber auch die Darstellungen der Struktur- und Metadaten, bzw. welche Anwendungsmöglichkeiten sich aus diesen Daten für die visuelle Darstellung in einem Repository allgemein ergeben.

Auch wenn im Zentrum dieses Beitrags die bildliche Darstellung der Digitalisate steht, bedarf dieses Thema doch einer viel umfassenderen Behandlung, weswegen auch auf die Performanz eingegangen wird, da diese als sehr entscheidend für hohe Kund:innenzufriedenheit angesehen werden muss. Die Konfiguration hat auf die Performanz einen großen Einfluss, daher wird auch diese in einem Unterkapitel angesprochen. Die meisten Projektmanager:innen an Bibliotheken werden wenig bis gar nichts an der Konfiguration verändern, nichtsdestotrotz ist es doch unumgänglich, dass man sich dieser von mir angesprochenen Parameter bewusst wird, damit man darauf Einfluss nehmen kann.

4.1. Einstellungen der Bildanzeige

4.1.1. Performanz

Da sich die ursprünglich gescannten Bildformate nicht für performante Darstellungen eignen[36], müssen diese komprimiert werden. An der Oberösterreichischen Landesbibliothek verwenden wir als Bildformat TIFF.[37] Diese Bilder dienen in erster Linie der Archivierung.

Zum Einsatz kommen verschiedene Kompressionsverfahren, wobei die JPEG-Komprimierung sicherlich eine der häufigsten Formen ist. Die eingesetzte Auflösung und das Format der Bilder hängen stark mit den jeweiligen Anforderungen im Repository zusammen. Eine von der Gerätekonfiguration bestimmte (Barrierefreiheit, Software-Ergonomie beachten!) Auslieferung der Bildformate in Abhängigkeit von Bildschirmgröße, Auflösung und Browser sollte im Idealfall automatisch ablaufen (Responsives Webdesign).

Die Einstellungen der Zoomfunktion können die Performanz erheblich beeinflussen. Möglichst hohe Zoomstufen sind aus Benutzer:innensicht sicherlich positiv zu bewerten, es sollte allerdings bedacht werden, dass die Bildgröße den Arbeitsspeicher erheblich belasten kann und als Folge davon die Performanz darunter leidet. Geeignete technische Lösungen (z. B. Kompressionsformate, Kacheln...) helfen, einen guten Kompromiss zwischen Qualität und Performanz zu finden, und tragen dazu bei, dass auch Zugriffe von leistungsschwächeren Geräten performant ablaufen können.

Eine weitere Möglichkeit wäre das Anbieten verschiedener Bildformate, damit man in Abhängigkeit von Internetverbindung und Arbeitsspeicher ein stets performantes System etabliert.

Eine begrenzte Anzahl der mit einem bestimmten Lademechanismus geladenen Bilder kann Speicherüberläufe bei sehr großformatigen Werken verhindern. Clientseitiges Proxy-Caching kann im Fall unerwünschter Effekte auf die Performanz unterbunden werden. Und schlussendlich darf ich noch auf den Unterschied zwischen server- und clientseitiger Rechenleistung hinweisen. Über die Softwarekonfiguration kann darauf Einfluss genommen werden.

---

36 Bei den Scans handelt es sich um hochauflösende Bilder, die daher mit hohen Dateigrößen aufwarten.

37 TIFF bietet eine verlustfreie Speicherung der Daten.

4.1.2. Konfiguration der Bildanzeige

Gibt es Probleme in der Bildanzeige, die auf lange Ladezeiten oder auf ein bestimmtes Softwareprodukt zurückzuführen sind, können diese bei Benutzer:innen zu großem Unmut führen. Im schlimmsten Fall führt es sogar dazu, dass diese als Kund:innen verloren gehen. Ein niedrigschwelliger Zugang zu einem Feedbacksystem ist eine Möglichkeit, diesem Unmut zu begegnen.

Ebenso sollte an allen nur möglichen Schrauben der Konfiguration gedreht werden, um ein schlankes und performantes System zu etablieren.

Das Kacheln[38] und die damit verbundene Bildgröße der in den verschiedenen Zoomstufen verwendeten Bilder stellt eine zentrale Möglichkeit zur Verbesserung der Performanz dar. Mit der Skalierung, den sogenannten ScaleFactors[39], werden die Kachelgrößen definiert, um so die verschiedenen Zoomstufen anzeigen zu können. Dies ist grundsätzlich sehr positiv zu sehen, weil dadurch Bilder wunschgemäß skaliert werden können, allerdings kann das bei sehr groß skalierten Bildern zu einer Überlastung des Arbeitsspeichers führen.

In Goobi wird zur Bildanzeige der webbasierte Viewer OpenSeadragon[40], basierend auf einer IIIF-API[41], verwendet. Dieser lässt sich auf vielfache Weise bezüglich der zuvor genannten Parameter konfigurieren. Innerhalb der IIIF-API unterscheidet man Image API, Presentation API, Authentication API, Content Search API, Change Discovery API und Content State API.[42] Diese Schnittstellen ermöglichen die Darstellung digitalisierter Inhalte auf unterschiedlichsten Systemumgebungen. Hinter dieser Initiative stehen viele Bibliotheken und Universitäten, aber auch Anbieter digitaler Inhalte.[43]

4.2. Visualisierungen in Goobi

In Goobi[44] gibt es eine Fülle an verschiedenen Visualisierungen. Innerhalb der DLOÖ werden nicht alle Möglichkeiten, die Goobi zur Visualisierung anbietet, aus-

38 Darunter versteht man das mosaikartige Zusammenbauen eines Bildes. Gleichzeitig wird durch diesen Mechanismus beim Aufbau eines großen Bildes wesentlich weniger Arbeitsspeicher benötigt.
39 Goobi viewer Handbuch. Konfiguration der Bildanzeige https://docs.goobi.io/goobi-viewer-de/conf/1/11/3
40 OpenSeadragon. 2021 https://openseadragon.github.io/
41 https://docs.goobi.io/goobi-viewer-de/conf/1/33/2
42 https://iiif.io/
43 https://iiif.io/community/consortium/members/
44 Softwarepaket für Digitalisierungsprojekte, bestehend aus Präsentations- und Produktionssoftware.

geschöpft. Auf den folgenden Seiten stelle ich die bei uns verwendeten Visualisierungen vor. Grundsätzlich sollte darauf geachtet werden, dass alle Elemente in einem Repository barrierefrei sind und auf unterschiedlichsten Geräten und Konfigurationen laufen. Um dies bestmöglich zu erreichen, ist eine Orientierung an den Richtlinien des W3-Consortiums[45] unumgänglich.

4.2.1. Bildanzeige

Die Bildnavigation sollte verschiedene Optionen enthalten, um den Benutzer:innen eine möglichst vielfältige, zugleich intuitive und einfache Bedienung zu ermöglichen. Neben einer Dropdown-Schaltfläche, um auf individuelle Buchseiten wechseln zu können, sowie den Blätterfunktionen „Vor", „Zurück", „erstes Bild" und „letztes Bild", ist eine Doppelseitenansicht und das Rotieren des Bildes in 90°-Schritten als obligatorisch anzusehen. Besonders möchte ich auf die Korrekturmöglichkeit (zugehörige Schaltfläche erscheint erst in der Doppelseitenansicht) der Doppelseitenansicht hinweisen, die immer dann erforderlich ist, wenn man sich beim Wechsel in die Doppelseitenansicht gerade auf einer Recto-Seite befunden hat, weil dann rechte und linke Seite des Buches genau vertauscht sind. Das Zoom kann entweder mit einem Schieberegler oder per Scrollrad der Maus stufenlos verändert werden.

Die Seitenvorschau dient dazu, Buchseiten mit Abbildungen oder anderweitigen Besonderheiten rasch identifizieren zu können. Da sie aber eine völlig andere Navigation als die der Einzelbilder benötigt, wird diese als eigener Menüpunkt links der Bildanzeige angezeigt[46]. Größe und Auflösung der Vorschaubilder sind dabei so gewählt, dass vorhandene Abbildungen und dergleichen rasch erkannt werden können, ohne allerdings lange Ladezeiten zu verursachen.

Die Vollbildanzeige[47] ergänzt die normale Bildanzeige. Neben der Darstellung hoher Zoomstufen ist diese auch bei kleinen Bildschirmgrößen (Handy, Tablet) ein wichtiges Hilfsinstrument. In der Vollbildanzeige können mithilfe des Zooms Details von Büchern im Format Großfolio dargestellt werden, die beim Original ein gutes Vergrößerungsglas erfordern würden. Neben der Bildanzeige lassen sich bibliografische Daten, Werkzeuge zur Bildmanipulation oder der Volltext einer eventuell vorhandenen Transkription einblenden.

---

45 https://www.w3.org/

46 https://digi.landesbibliothek.at/viewer/!thumbs/AC00969620/1/

47 https://digi.landesbibliothek.at/viewer/fullscreen/AC05371191/265/

Ein Dropdown-Feld zur Auswahl von Volltextseiten[48] sollte ebenfalls zur Verfügung gestellt werden. So können bei nur teilweise transkribierten Werken rasch die Seiten mit Volltext[49] herausgefiltert werden. Volltexte werden bei uns automatisiert für Antiqua- und Frakturschriften erstellt. Nicht jede Frakturschrift wird gut erkannt, insbesondere bei stark ausgeschmückten Frakturschriften und bei Versalien treten verstärkt Probleme auf, und bei den in Inkunabeln bevorzugt verwendeten Schriften wie z. B. Textura, Rotunda oder Breidenbach treten noch wesentlich größere Probleme in der Texterkennung auf. Das derzeit bei uns eingesetzte Produkt zur Texterkennung ist Tesseract, eine von Google entwickelte freie Software.

Nichtsdestotrotz bietet der Volltext Möglichkeiten, mit digitalisierten Büchern zu arbeiten, wie dies beim gedruckten Buch bisher nicht möglich war, und alternativ können fehlerhafte Volltexte mit einem Crowdsourcingmodul (siehe Kapitel 4.2.6.) verbessert werden.

Die Software Transkribus[50], welche schon von der UB Greifswald[51] eingesetzt wird, stellt für alte Drucke und Handschriften eine wertvolle Ergänzung in der Texterkennung dar. Es handelt sich dabei um ein lernendes System zur automatisationsunterstützten Texterkennung. Das bedeutet, dass man die Software zu Beginn für eine bestimmte Schrift (gleich ob Druck- oder Handschrift) manuell trainieren muss. Mit jeder weiteren Trainingsseite werden stetig mehr Wörter eines Textes automatisch erkannt. Die Erkennungsraten können in der Folge auf deutlich über 95% steigen. Der Text kann anschließend in den Formaten PDF, Excel, DOCX, TXT und TEI exportiert und so in Goobi als Volltext eingespielt werden. Zurzeit gibt es schon unzählige gut trainierte Vorlagen für Druck- und Handschriften. Aktuell gibt es auch an der Oberösterreichischen Landesbibliothek Planungen, die Software als alternative OCR-Lösung in den Goobi-Workflow einzubauen.

4.2.2. Inhaltsverzeichnis

Den Menüpunkt Inhaltsverzeichnis[52] möchte ich als Spezifikum unserer Bibliothek vorstellen. An der Oberösterreichischen Landesbibliothek wird jedes digitalisierte Buch mit einer möglichst hohen Dichte an Meta- und Strukturdaten versehen. Das bedeutet, wir erfassen alle Abbildungen, Kapitel, Vorwörter, Einleitungen, Regi-

48 Dazu muss im Menü links der Bildanzeige zuerst von „Bildanzeige“ zu „Volltext“ gewechselt werden.
49 https://digi.landesbibliothek.at/viewer/fulltext/177/159/
50 Transkribus. READ-COOP SCE, 2021 https://readcoop.eu/de/transkribus/
51 https://www.digitale-bibliothek-mv.de/viewer/fulltext/PPNUAG-HGW_obj_5442087/1/
52 https://digi.landesbibliothek.at/viewer/!toc/AC02003800/1/LOG_0003/

ster, Tabellen usw. in Handarbeit. Große Player wie Google setzen zur automatisierten Verarbeitung von Meta- und Strukturdaten neuronale Netzwerke ein. Für kleinere Institutionen wie Bibliotheken und Archive sind derartige Anwendungen derzeit weder verfügbar noch leistbar.

In jedem Fall ist diese hohe Dichte an Meta- und Strukturdaten die Basis für vielseitige Visualisierungen bei Suchanfragen. Insgesamt spielen Visualisierungen bei komplexen Suchanfragen, spezifischen Sammlungen (Digitale Kollektionen[53]), der Kalendersuche[54], der Zeitleiste[55] und der Darstellung von Geodaten innerhalb der DLOÖ eine tragende Rolle.

Die hohe Dichte an Meta- und Strukturdaten hat aber auch noch eine andere, sehr wesentliche Bedeutung für Bibliotheken. Google bewertet bei Suchanfragen die in Struktur- und Metadaten erfassten Einträge wesentlich höher als reinen Volltext und setzt diese dementsprechend im Ranking weiter nach vorne. Als Folge davon ergibt sich eine wesentlich verbesserte Außenwirkung der eigenen Institution, insbesondere was identitätsstiftende Bestände (Obderennsia) angeht.

4.2.3. Bibliografische Daten

Die bibliografischen Grunddaten eines Werkes[56] reichern wir mit vielen weiteren Daten an. Neben persistenten Verknüpfungen mit wichtigen Datenbanken, wie z. B. Hill Museum und Manuscripta speziell für Handschriften[57] und ISTC[58], GW[59] oder Hain[60] für Inkunabeln[61], finden sich dort auch Lizenzangaben oder GND-Einträge, die zudem vollständig indexiert werden. So kann z. B. nach unterschiedlichen Schreibweisen eines Autors oder einer Autorin gesucht werden. Mit Göthe, Johann W. êvonë findet man in der Erweiterten Suche (nach Autor und Sammlung Handschriften) exakt einen Brief von ihm, der sich in unserem Besitz befindet.

---

53 https://digi.landesbibliothek.at/viewer/browse/

54 https://digi.landesbibliothek.at/viewer/searchcalendar/

55 https://digi.landesbibliothek.at/viewer/timematrix/

56 Sie werden bei uns meist aus dem Katalog importiert und können im Viewer über den Menüpunkt „Bibliografische Daten" aufgerufen werden.

57 https://digi.landesbibliothek.at/viewer/!metadata/490/1/-/

58 Incunabula Short Title Catalogue. Consortium of European Research Libraries, 2021 https://data.cerl.org/istc/_search

59 Gesamtkatalog der Wiegendrucke. Staatsbibliothek zu Berlin – Preußischer Kulturbesitz, 11.08.2021 https://www.gesamtkatalogderwiegendrucke.de/

60 Ludwig Hain: Repertorium bibliographicum. 1826-1838 https://digi.landesbibliothek.at/viewer/toc/AC02291478/1/

61 https://digi.landesbibliothek.at/viewer/!metadata/Ink-46/1/LOG_0000/

4.2.4. Werkzeuge

In diesem Kapitel werden verschiedene Werkzeuge vorgestellt, die dabei helfen, Digitalisate mit zusätzlichen Daten anzureichern, oder erweiterte Funktionen (z. B. Funktion „Bildausschnitt teilen") bieten.

4.2.4.1. Bildmanipulation

Die Bildmanipulation kann etwa bei schwer lesbaren Textstellen oder anderen schlecht erkennbaren Darstellungen in alten Drucken und Handschriften eingesetzt werden. Invertieren von Farben, Graustufen, Schärfen, Sättigung, Kontrast, Helligkeit und Färbung kann dabei hilfreich sein, Details (besser) zu erkennen bzw. zuvor vielleicht sogar Verborgenes plötzlich zu entdecken.

4.2.4.2. Bildausschnitt teilen

Um einen Bildausschnitt zu teilen, bieten wir entweder eine Hinweisbox[62] innerhalb eines Bildes oder den Link eines IIIF-Bildfragments an, welches eher im wissenschaftlichen Bereich zum Einsatz kommen wird[63] und in geeigneten Viewern für Vergleichsansichten eingesetzt werden kann.

4.2.5. Merklisten

Merklisten können nur dann benutzt werden, wenn man sich zuvor einmalig registriert hat und angemeldet ist.

Merklisten sind ein Instrument zur Organisation von Werken bzw. auch einzelner Seiten. Diese können über die zugewiesene Merkliste jederzeit rasch aufgerufen werden. Gleichzeitig können diese aber auch von Wissenschaftler:innen zur Darstellung IIIF-fähiger Vergleichsansichten eingesetzt werden.

4.2.6. Mitarbeit

Der Begriff Mitarbeit subsumiert in Goobi den allgemein bekannten Begriff Crowdsourcing. Die momentan eingesetzte Version wurde seit ihrer Erstentwicklung schon mehrmals überarbeitet und visuell an technische Vorgaben und Wünsche der Kund:innen angepasst. Crowdsourcing hat innerhalb der DLOÖ eine große Bedeutung, wurden bisher doch beinahe 70.000 Seiten von externen Benutzer:innen

62 Bildausschnitt Pegasus aus Astronomicum Caesareum VD16 A 3074 https://digi.landesbibliothek.at/viewer/!image/AC01107590/17/LOG_0024/#xywh=2500,4873,1253,1237

63 IIIF-Bildfragment Hercules aus Astronomicum Caesareum VD16 A 3074 https://digi.landesbibliothek.at/viewer/api/v1/records/AC01107590/files/images/00000017.tif/3792,5951,1189,1118/max/0/default.jpg

bearbeitet. Der Großteil davon wird im Modus „Volltexte bearbeiten" geleistet. Sollten bei einem Werk auf einer Seite noch keine Volltexte vorhanden sein, dann wird auch der Modus Transkribieren angeboten, bei dem keine Wortkoordinaten[64] erfasst werden. Zusätzlich stehen noch die Optionen „Inhalte erfassen" und Kommentare zur Auswahl[65].

Die neueste Entwicklung im Bereich Crowdsourcing nennt sich Kampagnen. Diese sind im Gegensatz zum herkömmlichen Crowdsourcing vielfältig steuerbar. Mit ihnen lässt sich eine Auswahl bestimmter Werke festlegen und es kann eine zeitliche Befristung eingestellt werden. Für Beiträge kann ein zwingender Review und eine Zugriffslizenz festgelegt werden. Über einen Log können Nachrichten innerhalb einer Kampagne gespeichert und optional allen Teilnehmer:innen zur Verfügung gestellt werden. Eine Statistik gibt einen Überblick darüber, welcher Prozentanteil der Kampagne schon abgearbeitet wurde.

Grundsätzlich kann zum Thema Mitarbeit angemerkt werden, dass unsere bisherigen Erfahrungen äußerst positiv sind. Mitarbeiter:innen sind durchgehend hoch motiviert, eine qualitativ einwandfreie Arbeit abzuliefern, und weit davon entfernt, Arbeit minderer Qualität zu leisten oder vielleicht sogar bewusst falsche Angaben einzuarbeiten. In Zukunft wird sich unser Crowdsourcing verstärkt in Richtung Kampagnen weiterentwickeln, weil diese Form wesentlich granularer justierbar ist.

4.2.7. Kartendarstellungen

Goobi verfügt über ein Karten-Widget, welches OpenStreetMap nutzt und bei Vorhandensein von Geodaten in einem Werk automatisch links der Bildanzeige eingeblendet wird. Geodaten können auf viele verschiedene Arten innerhalb von Goobi erfasst werden.

4.2.7.1. Koordinatenrechteck

Mit Hilfe der Boundingbox[66] können in Goobi über die Bibliografische Aufnahme Koordinaten aus dem Katalogfeld 034 übernommen werden. Da bei unseren Beständen die meisten Karten als Strukturelemente erfasst werden, hat diese Form der Datenübernahme eher untergeordnete Bedeutung für uns. Die Daten lassen

64 Diese bilden die Basis des Highlightings bei Suchanfragen.
65 Diese werden unterhalb eines Bildes erfasst und angezeigt https://digi.landesbibliothek.at/viewer/image/171/1/
66 https://boundingbox.klokantech.com/

sich aber auch per Copy and Paste in die betreffenden Koordinatenfelder des Strukturdatums Karte eintragen. Dazu wird zuerst ein Rechteck um das gewünschte Gebiet in der Boundingbox aufgezogen. Die Boundingbox liefert nun die erforderlichen W-O-N-S-Koordinaten.

Die Kartenausschnitte werden, wie in folgenden beiden Beispielen[67], in einem Widget dargestellt.

4.2.7.2. Verortungen

Für Orte und Plätze können ebenso Geodaten erfasst werden. Orte werden mit einem eigenen Symbol angezeigt. Beide Typen (Orte und Kartenausschnitte) können nebeneinander im Kartenwidget dargestellt werden.

Die Geodaten können über das Feld Geographisches Schlagwort und das Auswahlfeld Geonames[68] verknüpft werden. Dazu wird der persistente Identifier für einen Ort in das Feld Geonames in Goobi eingefügt[69]. Wird anstatt Geonames im Auswahlfeld GND ausgewählt, so werden die GND-Daten automatisch mit dem Widget verknüpft.

Optional kann auch das Feld Koordinaten verwendet werden. Dieses ist sehr flexibel und benötigt bloß Latitude (Breite) und Longitude (Länge) in folgender Form: Latitude / Longitude. Die Koordinaten kann man sich mit unterschiedlichsten Tools wie z. B. Geonames, GoogleMaps[70] oder Geoplaner[71] beschaffen.

4.2.8. Bildbereiche

Bildbereiche ist ein neues Feature in Goobi-Production, mit dessen Hilfe man auf einer Seite viele einzelne Strukturen erstellen kann. So lassen sich auf einer Seite mit mehreren Strukturelementen mehrere Abbildungen und Karten als eigene Elemente erfassen. Im Viewer wird dann beim Anklicken eines bestimmten Bildbereiches der Rest des Bildes abgedunkelt. Dadurch wird der Zusammenhang zwischen Text und Bildbereich den Nutzer:innen kenntlich gemacht.

---

67 https://digi.landesbibliothek.at/viewer/image/AC04601669/34/LOG_0012/ ; https://digi.landesbibliothek.at/viewer/image/AC05371191/105/LOG_0083/
68 https://www.geonames.org/
69 Z. B. Gmunden https://www.geonames.org/2778436
70 https://www.google.com/maps
71 https://www.geoplaner.de/

Folgendes Beispiel[72] zeigt als Hauptstrukturelement eine Karte, auf deren Seite sich mehrere Abbildungen befinden. Diese wurden zuvor in Goobi als Unterstrukturelemente der Karte erfasst. Erkennbar sind diese an dünnen farbigen Umrandungen, sobald man sich auf der Karte befindet. Um nun im Viewer eines dieser Unterstrukturelemente gezielt aufzurufen, kann man entweder direkt im Bild auf einen der farbigen Rahmen oder links unter Inhalt auf die gewünschte Abbildung ([Abb.]: Royan) klicken.

4.2.9. Suche

Suchtreffer werden immer im Kontext des jeweiligen Werkes dargestellt und unterhalb des Werktitels aufgelistet. Die Treffer werden in Metadaten- und Volltexttreffer unterteilt und durch Highlighting im Werk hervorgehoben. Durch diese Form der Organisation können mehrere Suchtreffer innerhalb eines Werkes übersichtlich dargestellt werden.

Die Erweiterte Suche kann aber noch viel mehr. Es können hochkomplexe Suchanfragen mit mehreren Suchgruppen erstellt werden, die ihrerseits wiederum mit Booleschen Operatoren verknüpft werden. Kommt es bei einer Suchanfrage zu einer zu großen Treffermenge, kann diese über unterschiedliche Facettierungen[73] eingegrenzt werden.

4.2.10. Kalendersuche

Die Kalendersuche[74] nutzt das Datumsfeld in Goobi. Das Datumsfeld kann optional bis auf den Tag genau ausgefüllt werden[75]. Sehr häufig wird diese Form der Suche bei unseren Verlustlisten Österreich-Ungarns eingesetzt, wenn die Volltextsuche zu keinem Ergebnis geführt hat, der Zeitraum des Todes aber ungefähr bekannt ist. Im ersten Schritt wird ein Kalenderjahr ausgewählt. Im zweiten Schritt wird ein Jahreskalender angezeigt, bei dem alle Tage mit veröffentlichten Werken direkt zum betreffenden Werk verlinkt sind. So lässt sich rasch eine Verlustliste eines bestimmten Tages aufrufen. Und weil wir jedes Kapitel (Mannschaft, Offiziere, ...) inklusive aller Unterkapitel (nach Alphabet des Familiennamens) erfasst haben, kann man rasch zu einem bestimmten Namen wechseln.

---

72 https://digi.landesbibliothek.at/viewer/image/AC10154567/91/LOG_0043/

73 Zeitraum, Sammlung, Dokumenttyp, Person, Erscheinungsjahr, ...

74 https://digi.landesbibliothek.at/viewer/searchcalendar/

75 Verlustlisten Österreich-Ungarns https://digi.landesbibliothek.at/viewer/search/-/- /1/CURRENTNOSORT/DC%3Aperiodika.verlustliste/

4.2.11. Zeitleiste

Die Zeitleiste[76] ermöglicht das Browsen durch die Jahrhunderte. Via Schieberegler kann eine Jahresauswahl getroffen werden. Die einzelnen Werke werden durch Anklicken aufgerufen. In der derzeitigen Konfiguration werden maximal 36 Treffer dargestellt.

4.2.12. TagClouds

Sie spiegeln durch ihre Größe die Dichte der jeweils in den Werken vorkommenden Daten wider. Diese werden nach Titel, Orte und Jahre sortiert. Ein Klick auf einen bestimmten Tag öffnet die dargestellte Treffermenge[77].

4.2.13. Wissenschaftliche Beschreibungen

Für Wissenschaftler:innen bieten wir ein Werkzeug zur Beschreibung einzelner Werke an. Dazu kann ein PDF in den Workflow mithilfe eines vorgefertigten Templates eingespielt werden. Das PDF wird nach dem Hochladen innerhalb der Website in HTML dargestellt. Die Formatierungen des PDFs werden bei diesem Prozess vollständig übernommen, sodass das Layout des PDFs erhalten bleibt. Neben der URN des Werkes wird auch eine PURL[78] für die Seite angegeben. Sie dient dazu, auf die Seite referenzieren zu können, was für die Zitierbarkeit und wissenschaftliches Arbeiten von Bedeutung ist.[79]

---

76 https://digi.landesbibliothek.at/viewer/timematrix/

77 https://digi.landesbibliothek.at/viewer/tags/

78 Das ist eine Möglichkeit, um – wie bei URNs – konstante bzw. persistente Inhalte von Webseiten bereitzustellen.

79 https://digi.landesbibliothek.at/viewer/overview/422/1/,
https://digi.landesbibliothek.at/viewer/overview/438/1/,
https://digi.landesbibliothek.at/viewer/overview/20/1/

5. Fazit

Ein Repositorium und die darin enthaltenen Visualisierungen sind immer genau so gut, wie sie betreut, gewartet und weiterentwickelt werden. Um dies zu gewährleisten, sind einerseits personelle und andererseits finanzielle Mittel erforderlich. Repositorienmanager:innen sind dazu aufgerufen, sich intensiv mit der Materie und ihrem System zu beschäftigen. Es genügt nicht, Abteilungsleiter:in zu sein.

Es ist weder notwendig noch zwingend erforderlich, über Programmierkenntnisse zu verfügen oder einen Informatikabschluss zu besitzen, aber es ist unabdingbar, sich mit seinem Repositorium und dessen Möglichkeiten eingehend auseinanderzusetzen. Diejenigen, die ihre Digitalisierungssoftware genau kennen, werden imstande sein, die richtigen Fragen an Fachexpert:innen zu stellen. Nur so wird man erforderliche Entwicklungen erkennen und die richtigen Entscheidungen für die Zukunft treffen.

Bibliografie

Ciula, Arianna; Eide, Øyvind; Marras Christina; Sahle, Patrick (2018): Models and Modelling between Digital and Humanities. Remarks from a Multidisciplinary Perspective. In: Historical Social Research 43 (4), pp. 343-361.

Keller, Stefan Andreas; Schneider, René; Volk, Benno (2014): Die Digitalisierung des philosophischen Zettelkastens. In: Keller, Stefan Andreas; Schneider, René; Volk, Benno (Hg.): Wissensorganisation und -repräsentation mit digitalen Technologien. Berlin: de Gruyter Saur, S. 1-17.

Kogler, Gerald (2014): Barrierefreier Zugang zu offenen Geodaten unter besonderer Berücksichtigung sehbeeinträchtigter Personen. Bachelorarbeit aus Wirtschaftsinformatik. Johannes Kepler Universität Linz. https://www.academia.edu/18954553/Barrierefreier_Zugang_zu_offenen_Geodaten_unter_besonderer_Ber%C3%BCcksichtigung_sehbeeintr%C3%A4chtigter_Personen (abgerufen am 10.08.2021)

Paik, Woojin; Liddy, Elizabeth D.; Yu, Edmund; McKenna, Mary (1993): Categorizing and Standardizing Proper Nouns for Efficient Information Retrieval. In: Boguraev, Branimir; Pustejovsky, James (eds.): Acquisition of Lexical Knowledge from Text. Ohio: State University, pp. 154-160. https://aclanthology.org/W93-0114.pdf (abgerufen am 03.02.2023)

Pamperl, Beate (2017): Visualisierungen in den Digital Humanities – Ein Überblick. In: Maske und Kothurn 63 (1), S. 90-98. https://dx.doi.org/10.7767/muk-2017-630114

Roth, Jeannette (2002): Der Stand der Kunst in der Eigennamen-Erkennung. Mit einem Fokus auf Produktenamen-Erkennung. Lizentiatsarbeit. Universität Zürich, Philosophische Fakultät. https://www.cl.uzh.ch/dam/jcr:00000000-6a77-a254-0000-00006a27b71e/lizjeannetteroth.pdf (abgerufen am 16.04.2023)

Windhager, Florian (2017): Choreographien der Existenz. Zur multimodalen Erweiterung biographischer Forschung und Lehre durch Verfahren der visuellen Analyse und Synthese. In: BIOS – Zeitschrift für Biographieforschung, Oral History und Lebensverlaufsanalysen 30 (1-2), S. 60-75. https://doi.org/10.3224/bios.v30i1-2.06

Gregor Neuböck leitete die Digitalen Services an der Oberösterreichischen Landesbibliothek bis Oktober 2023. Seit November 2023 leitet er die Stabsstelle Digitales Sammlungsmanagement der Wienbibliothek im Rathaus. Er veröffentlichte unzählige Fachartikel zum Thema Digitalisierung. Zuletzt erschien von ihm in den VÖB-Mitteilungen: 2019 Crowdsourcing an der Oberösterreichischen Landesbibliothek und 2018 sein Buch bei Walter de Gruyter: Digitalisierung in Bibliotheken: viel mehr als nur Bücher scannen.

Harald Eberle

Inhaltsbasierte Bilderschließung durch Crowd und Cloud

Handbuch Repositorienmanagement, Hg. v. Blumesberger et al., 2024, S. 489–502
https://doi.org/10.25364/978390337423226

Harald Eberle, Vorarlberger Landesbibliothek, harald.eberle@vorarlberg.at | ORCID iD: 0000-0001-9251-2924

Zusammenfassung

Die Vorarlberger Landesbibliothek ist bestrebt, ihre Bildsammlungen durch Retrodigitalisierung zu sichern und über ihr Repositorium volare benutzungsfreundlich bereitzustellen. Allerdings können die durch Massendigitalisierung entstandenen Datenmengen mit den vorhandenen personellen Ressourcen nicht in der gewünschten Qualität abgearbeitet werden. Deshalb wird mit neuartigen Methoden versucht, eine möglichst effiziente Bilderschließung zu bewerkstelligen. Über die Crowdsourcing-Plattform sMapshot lassen sich Landschaftsbilder nicht nur verorten, sondern exakt in einem digitalen 3D-Globus platzieren. Die auf diese Weise produzierten Geoinformationen ermöglichen es, Namen der abgebildeten Orte, beispielsweise von Städten, Ortsteilen oder Bergen, zu berechnen. Zudem wird mit maschinellem Sehen[1] experimentiert, um historische Aufnahmen automatisiert zu beschreiben.

Schlagwörter: Crowdsourcing; Georeferenzierung; Bildbeschreibung; Maschinelles Sehen; Künstliche Intelligenz; Metadatenanreicherung

Abstract

Content-Based Image Description Through Crowd and Cloud

The Vorarlberg State Library uses retro digitisation to facilitate long-term and user-friendly access to its image collections trough the institutional repository volare. As traditional resources and means are limited when it comes to processing large data volumes, new and innovative methods are being explored to generate high-quality descriptions and metadata in a more efficient way. The crowdsourcing platform sMapshot not only allows the georeferencing of digital image files to a geographical location but also the positioning of landscape images on a virtual 3D globe. This geoinformation enables the calculation of place names such as cities, districts or mountains. In the context of machine-based descriptions for historic photographs, the Vorarlberg State Library is also experimenting with machine vision.

Keywords: Crowdsourcing; georeferencing; image description; machine vision; artificial intelligence; metadata enrichment

1 Das maschinelle Sehen als Teilgebiet der Informatik beschäftigt sich mit der Erfassung visueller Informationen eines Computers in seiner Umwelt. Dabei geht es in erster Linie um das einfache Erfassen von Gegenständen und Personen, und nicht um die Interpretation und das Verständnis eines tieferen Sinnes.

1. Einleitung

Zu den Aufgaben von Gedächtnisinstitutionen gehört es, das kulturelle Erbe in all seinen medialen Ausprägungen zu sammeln, zu dokumentieren und zu vermitteln. Seit der Jahrtausendwende werden in vielen Institutionen immer größere Retrodigitalisierungsprojekte in Angriff genommen, um analoge Vorlagen digital zu sichern. Dadurch können die Originalvorlagen geschont und eine bessere Zugänglichkeit ermöglicht werden. Waren diese Projekte in der Vergangenheit oft auf Textdokumente beschränkt, erweitert sich der Fokus nun auch auf Lichtbildwerke.[2] Aufgrund des Umfangs der Projekte stellt die manuelle Erschließung der Bilddaten die einzelnen Institutionen vor große finanzielle und personelle Herausforderungen. „Der klassische Ansatz – die manuelle Annotation des Bildinhaltes mittels alphanumerischer Texte – hat sich in der Vergangenheit als zu fehleranfällig und zu kostenintensiv erwiesen".[3] Die ständig wachsende Menge an digitalisierten und digital entstandenen Bilddaten erfordert neuartige Methoden, um eine regelwerkskonforme Erfassung und eine verbesserte Auffindbarkeit in den Repositorien zu ermöglichen. Die Vorarlberger Landesbibliothek verfolgt zwei Ansätze, um die anfallenden Bilddaten effizient und qualitativ hochwertig zu erschließen und so einen erheblichen Mehrwert für die Forschung zu generieren. Der erste Ansatz bezieht sich auf die dreidimensionale Georeferenzierung historischer Landschaftsbilder durch Crowdsourcing über die Plattform sMapshot. Die Webanwendung ermöglicht es, einen virtuellen Globus der Vergangenheit aufzubauen und die genauen Ortsnamen zu berechnen, die im Bild sichtbar sind.[4] Der zweite Ansatz nutzt maschinelles Lernen, ein Teilgebiet der künstlichen Intelligenz, um Bildklassifizierung durch Objekterkennung und Personenidentifizierung durch Gesichtserkennung zu ermöglichen. Dabei wird versucht, die abgebildeten Objekte und Personen automatisiert und mit entsprechenden Normdaten zu beschreiben. Um die Möglichkeiten der oben beschriebenen Ansätze sinnvoll einschätzen zu können, wird in diesem Beitrag auf die Technik und Workflows sowie deren Vor- und Nachteile eingegangen. Ziel ist es, einen Überblick über die Möglichkeiten und Anwendungsszenarien des Repositorienmanagements zu geben. Einige Abschnitte dieses Aufsatzes wurden bereits veröffentlicht.[5]

---

2 Helm, W. (2019), S. 127–134.
3 Volmer, S. (2012), S. 3.
4 Produit, T.; Ingensand, J. (2019), S. 273f.
5 Eberle, H. (2020)

2. Georeferenzierung historischer Landschaftsbilder durch Crowdsourcing

Historische Landschaftsbilder liefern Informationen über die Veränderung der Landschaft und sind eine wertvolle Informationsquelle, beispielsweise im Bereich der Raum- und Stadtplanung, aber auch in der Regional- und der Kulturgeschichtsforschung. Um historische Aufnahmen der Öffentlichkeit zugänglich machen zu können, sind die in den Gedächtnisinstitutionen meist nur rudimentär vorhandenen Bildbeschreibungen oft nicht ausreichend. Das von der westschweizer Fachhochschule für Management und Ingenieurwesen Waadt (HEIG-VD) entwickelte Projekt sMapshot hat sich zum Ziel gesetzt, eine dreidimensionale Georeferenzierung historischer Bilder mit Hilfe des geografischen Wissens von Freiwilligen zu realisieren. Diese Geoinformationen können verwendet werden, um einen „virtuellen Globus der Vergangenheit aufzubauen und um die genauen Ortsnamen zu berechnen, die im Bild sichtbar sind".[6] Damit entsteht die Möglichkeit, historische Aufnahmen exakt zu lokalisieren, mit Geoinformationen anzureichern und so die Bildrecherche zu erleichtern.

2.1. Methoden zur Georeferenzierung von Bildern

In der Literatur werden drei Methoden zur Georeferenzierung von Einzelbildern beschrieben.[7] Die erste und einfachste Methode ist die Verortung durch eine Punktkoordinate. Dabei kann der Punkt des Aufnahmestandorts oder die exakte Position des Objektes erfasst werden. Die Referenzierung des Aufnahmepunktes beherrschen bereits viele GPS-Kameras automatisiert. Zudem ermitteln einige Geräte die Blickrichtung mit Hilfe eines digitalen Kompasses. Die Punktverortung ermöglicht zwar eine Beschreibung des Standortes, nicht aber die genaue Definition des sichtbaren Bildbereichs. Für die Nachnutzung hilfreicher ist die Erfassung des Objektmittelpunktes auf der Erdoberfläche. Für die Verortung von senkrecht aufgenommenen Bildern wird meist die zweite Methode, die Georeferenzierung einer Fläche durch mindestens vier Randkoordinaten, angewendet. Die Flächenverortung eignet sich hervorragend für senkrecht aufgenommene Luftbilder, sogenannte Orthofotos. Bei Bildern, die schräg aus der Luft, beispielsweise aus Flugzeugen, Hubschraubern oder Heißluftballons aufgenommen werden, eignet sich diese Methode nicht. Bei solchen Aufnahmen werden nämlich nicht rechteckige Flächen, sondern komplexe Polygone im Raum abgebildet. Für diese Art der Bilder ist die dritte Me-

6 Produit, T.; Ingensand, J. (2019), Anm. 3, S. 273.
7 Vgl. Produit, T.; Ingensand, J. (2016)

thode, das Monoplotting, geeignet. Es basiert auf dem Konzept, mehrere Referenzpunkte, sogenannte Ground Control Points, im Bild und im virtuellen Globus zu identifizieren und deren genaue Position zu berechnen. Neben dem Bildaufnahmepunkt lassen sich so zusätzlich die drei Bildorientierungswinkel Omega, Phi und Kappa ermitteln.[8] Diese Informationen dienen einer genauen Positionierung des Rasterbildes über dem dreidimensionalen virtuellen Globus und ermöglichen so die Berechnung des im Bild sichtbaren Bereiches.

2.1.2. sMapshot

Das Konzept zur Verortung einzelner Aufnahmen in dreidimensionalen Landschaftsmodellen wurde bereits im Jahr 2015 vorgestellt.[9] Seit 2016 entwickelt die HEIG-VD die Plattform sMapshot, die es freiwilligen Teilnehmenden ermöglicht, historische Bilder mittels Monoplotting zu georeferenzieren. Als erste Institution stellte die Bibliothek der ETH Zürich im Jänner 2018 mit ihrer Kampagne Schweizer Luftbilder von Walter Mittelholzer auf sMapshot zur Verfügung.[10] Die Nutzung von sMapshot außerhalb der Schweiz war vorerst nicht vorgesehen, da lediglich das 3D-Modell und die Luftbilder der swisstopo (Bundesamt für Schweizer Landestopografie) als hochauflösende Basisdaten zur Verfügung standen, nicht aber die Daten anderer Länder. Aus diesem Grund beauftragten die Vorarlberger Landesbibliothek und das Landesamt für Vermessung und Geoinformation die Erweiterung von sMapshot zur Georeferenzierung von Bildern auf dem gesamten Globus. Zudem sollten die bereits vorhandenen und qualitativ hochwertigen Geobasisdaten aus Vorarlberg bzw. Österreich eingebunden werden. Mit der Sammlung *Historische Schrägluftbilder der Alpine Luftbild GmbH* lancierte die Vorarlberger Landesbibliothek im Sommer 2020 ihre erste Kampagne auf Basis der österreichischen Verwaltungsgrundkarten (basemap.at) auf sMapshot.[11]

Die Bearbeitung historischer Landschaftsbilder auf sMapshot nutzt spielerische Elemente und verläuft in mehreren Schritten. Bilder können sowohl anonym als auch unter einem Namen bzw. einem Pseudonym referenziert werden. Die Registrierung bietet den Vorteil, dass die Arbeit der jeweiligen Person sichtbar wird. Die teilnehmende Person wählt zunächst auf einer Landkarte ein Bild aus, welches georeferenziert werden soll. Im ersten Schritt wird der ungefähre Aufnahmestandort bestimmt. Im zweiten Schritt muss die ungefähre Blickrichtung festgelegt wer-

8 Produit, T.; Ingensand, J. (2016), Anm. 3, S. 273.
9 Produit, T.; Ingensand, J. (2018), S. 113–126.
10 Graf, N. (2018)
11 Huonder, F. (2020)

den. Anschließend platziert sMapshot das Bild neben dem bereits provisorisch ausgerichteten Kartenausschnitt. Nun beginnt die eigentliche Georeferenzierung, bei der mindestens sechs übereinstimmende Punkte zwischen Bild und virtuellem 3D-Globus gefunden werden müssen.

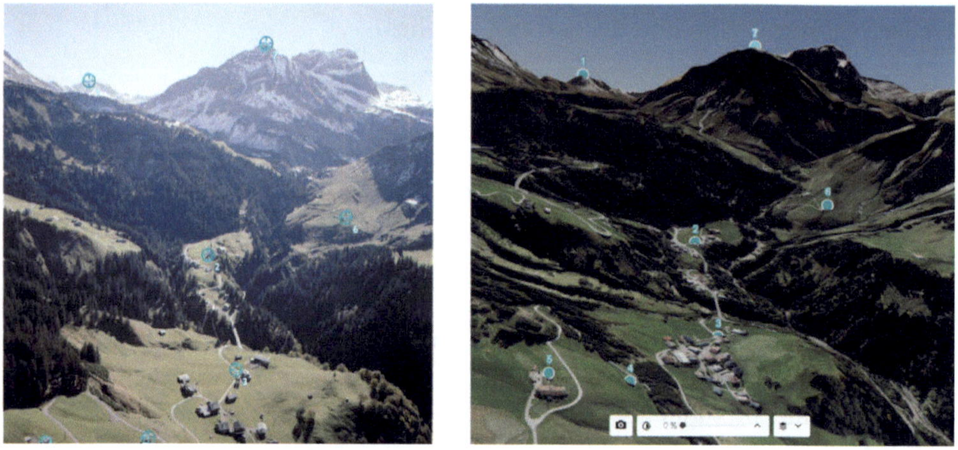

Abb. 1: Zur Georeferenzierung müssen mindestens sechs übereinstimmende Punkte sowohl im Bild als auch im virtuellen Globus angegeben werden.

Als Punkte eignen sich besonders geografisch markante Bergspitzen, Straßenkreuzungen oder Gebäudeecken. Die Verwendung von Gebäudedachflächen eignet sich hingegen nicht, da die Gebäudehöhen aus dem Geländemodell herausgerechnet wurden. Idealerweise sollten die Punkte gleichmäßig über das Bild verteilt sein, damit eine möglichst große Abdeckung gewährleistet ist. Wird der Vorgang abgeschlossen, so muss die Referenzierung noch systemseitig validiert werden. Mitarbeitende der Vorarlberger Landesbibliothek prüfen dann die Qualität der Verortung und haben die Möglichkeit, entsprechende Verbesserungen vorzunehmen. Bei einer mangelhaften Verortung besteht zudem die Option, diese abzulehnen und den Freiwilligen erneut zur Referenzierung bereitzustellen. Insgesamt zeigt sich, dass die bereitgestellten Kampagnen von der Crowd sehr gut angenommen und rasch abgearbeitet werden. Zudem ist die Qualität der erstellen Daten in der Regel so gut, dass lediglich in Ausnahmefällen Verbesserungen vorgenommen werden müssen.

2.2. Metadatenanreicherung

Nach Abschluss einer Kampagne können für alle Bilder der Aufnahmestandort, die Aufnahmehöhe und der Footprint aus sMapshot exportiert werden. Beim Footprint handelt es sich um die Koordinaten des Polygons der auf der Aufnahme abgebildeten Fläche. Diese Polygone lassen sich mittels Geoverarbeitungswerkzeugen mit beliebigen Geodatensätzen verschneiden, um so weitere Stichwörter zum abgebildeten Bildausschnitt zu schaffen. Besonders gut eignen sich dazu Geodaten von Katastralgemeinden, Bergspitzen, Fließgewässer, Parzellen oder Flurnamen. Weitreichende Bildausschnitte generieren eine Fülle an neuen Metadaten, umso mehr sollte bei den jeweiligen Stichwörtern auf Relevanz geachtet werden. Zudem können auch der exakt erfasste Ausschnitt, der Aufnahmepunkt, die Flughöhe sowie die Blickrichtung einen Mehrwert für künftige Nutzungsszenarien und Forschungen generieren.

2.3. Aktueller Stand

Mit Sommer 2021 hat die Vorarlberger Landesbibliothek drei Kampagnen mit rund 13.000 Einzelbildern zur Georeferenzierung bereitgestellt.[12] Pro Tag werden von der Crowd durchschnittlich 100 Bilder abgearbeitet und von den Mitarbeitenden der Vorarlberger Landesbibliothek validiert. Um Aufmerksamkeit für das Projekt im eigenen Bundesland zu erregen, strahlte das ORF-Landesstudio Vorarlberg am 2. August 2021 einen Beitrag im Rahmen der Nachrichtensendung Vorarlberg Heute aus.[13] Nach Ausstrahlung dieses Beitrags wurden rund 15 neue Personen, die sich an der Verortung beteiligten, verzeichnet. Insgesamt ist allerdings festzustellen, dass sich besonders die bereits bestehenden Mitglieder der Schweizer sMapshot-Community am intensivsten an dem Projekt beteiligen. Die beiden aktivsten Personen verorteten bereits jeweils über 20.000 Bilder in allen von sMapshot-Partnern zur Verfügung gestellten Kampagnen.[14] Die Logfiles zeigen eine durchschnittliche Bearbeitungsdauer von 5,3 Minuten pro Bild. Bei diesen beiden gerade erwähnten Personen ergibt das eine erbrachte Leistung von jeweils über 1.700 Stunden, also mehr als das jährliche Arbeitszeitausmaß einer vollzeitbeschäftigten Arbeitskraft. Insgesamt wurden über die Plattform sMapshot bereits über 187.000 Bilder aus den diversen Institutionen verortet, das entspricht einer erbrachten Leistung der Crowd von rund 16.500 Stunden.

---

12 https://smapshot.heig-vd.ch/owner/vlb

13 sMapshot. Die partizipative Zeitmaschine. vorarlberg.ORF.at, 02.08.2021: https://vorarlberg.orf.at/stories/3115329/

14 https://smapshot.heig-vd.ch/#Teilnehmer

2.3.1. Inhaltsbasierte Bilderschließung mittels visueller Merkmale durch Maschinelles Sehen

Das Thema Objekterkennung in digitalen Bildern durch künstliche Intelligenz ist derzeit in aller Munde. Ob in industriellen Herstellungsprozessen, beim autonomen Fahren oder bei Videoüberwachungssystemen – die Auswertung des visuellen Materials spielt eine immer größere Rolle. Viele wissenschaftliche Disziplinen setzen Objekterkennung auf Basis von maschinellem Lernen bereits erfolgreich ein. In Gedächtnisinstitutionen hingegen haben Technologien für die maschinelle inhaltsbasierte Bilderschließung noch kaum Einzug gehalten. Im Rahmen einer Masterthesis[15] wurde für die Vorarlberger Landesbibliothek ein Prototyp entwickelt, mit dem historische Lichtbildwerke unter Einsatz von künstlicher Intelligenz maschinengestützt erschlossen und in weiterer Folge an Metadatenverwaltungssysteme zur Archivierung und Recherche übergeben werden können. Ein besonderes Augenmerk wurde dabei auf die Bildklassifizierung durch Objekterkennung, die Personenidentifizierung durch Gesichtserkennung sowie die optische Zeichenerkennung gelegt. Zudem wurde geprüft, inwieweit das Modell auch trainiert werden kann, um markante landeskundliche Elemente wie beispielsweise Gebäude, Berge oder Landschaften erkennen zu können.

2.3.2. Identifizierung von landeskundlich relevanten Personen durch Gesichtserkennung

Die Identifizierung von landeskundlich relevanten Personen auf historischen Bildern stellt für die Nachnutzbarkeit und Auffindbarkeit einen enormen Mehrwert dar. Allerdings müssen bei Personenbildern die rechtlichen Rahmenbedingungen genau geprüft werden. So ist jedenfalls der Bildnisschutz gemäß § 78 UrhG der abgebildeten Person zu beachten. Sind Personen abgebildet, so sind die berechtigten Interessen der abgebildeten Person (bei bereits verstorbenen abgebildeten Personen die naher Angehöriger) sowie die berechtigten Interessen der beteiligten Institution gegeneinander abzuwägen. Grundsätzlich bedarf es bei der Veröffentlichung eines Personenbildnisses der Zustimmung der abgebildeten Person bzw. nach deren Tod der Zustimmung der Angehörigen. Unabhängig davon stehen einer Veröffentlichung von Bildnissen von Personen der Öffentlichkeit, etwa Politikern, Schauspielern und Menschen von zeitgeschichtlicher Bedeutung, grundsätzlich keine berechtigten Interessen der Abgebildeten beziehungsweise deren Angehörigen entgegen, sofern die Abbildung nicht im Einzelfall geeignet ist, das Privatleben der Person preiszugeben, sie zu entwürdigen, herabzusetzen oder bloßzustellen.[16]

15 Eberle, H. (2020)
16 Vgl. § 23 KunstUrhG Abs. 1f.

Ebenfalls stellen Personenbildnisse auch personenbezogene Daten gemäß der Datenschutzgrundverordnung dar. In Bezug auf Abbildungen lebender Personen bedarf es einer Rechtsgrundlage zur Verarbeitung dieser Daten. Als solche kommt grundsätzlich die Einwilligung des Betroffenen in Betracht.[17] Erwägungsgrund Nr. 27 der DSGVO stellt allerdings klar, dass die DSGVO keine Anwendung auf personenbezogene Daten Verstorbener findet. Aufgrund dieser rechtlichen Rahmenbedingungen wurden sowohl die Trainingsdaten als auch die Testdaten sehr sorgsam gewählt. Für die Entwicklung des Prototyps wurde auf die Face-Recognition-Plattform der Microsoft Cognitive Services zurückgegriffen, da sich diese im Besonderen bei der Qualität der Gesichtserkennung von anderen Dienstleistern abhebt.[18] Jede im Erkennungsmodell individualisierte Person kann bis zu 248 Trainingsbilder besitzen. Microsoft empfiehlt zudem, die Gesichter aus den Bildern freizustellen, damit pro hochgeladenem Bild nur ein Gesicht abgebildet ist.[19] Um ein möglichst optimales Erkennungsergebnis zu erreichen, verfügen Trainingsdaten nach Möglichkeit über unterschiedliche Blickwinkel und verschiedene Belichtungen. Zudem sollten die Bilder zumindest eine Auflösung von 200 x 200 Pixel haben. Der Abstand zwischen den Augen sollte mindestens 100 Pixel betragen.[20] Probleme in der Gesichtsdetektion bereiten beispielsweise Aufnahmen mit extremer Über- oder Unterbelichtung, Verdeckungen von zumindest einem Auge, extreme Gesichtsausdrücke oder markante Kopf- oder Gesichtsbehaarung.[21] Um in weiterer Folge eine regelwerkskonforme Personenbeschreibung zu ermöglichen, wird im Modell nicht nur der Name der Person, sondern auch der eindeutige Identifier aus der Gemeinsamen Normdatei (GND) hinterlegt. Ist das Modell trainiert, so kann es validiert und verwendet werden. Im Rahmen erster Tests funktionierte die Erkennung einer landeskundlich relevanten Person immer korrekt und die Erkennungssicherheit schwankte zwischen 60 und 79 Prozent.[22]

2.3.3. Bilddatierung mittels Age Prediction

Der internationale Katalogisierungsstandard Ressource Description and Access (RDA) sieht für jede Ressource die Erfassung einer Veröffentlichungsangabe vor. Diese beinhaltet unter anderem das Erscheinungsdatum. Ist für eine Ressource kein Erscheinungsdatum angegeben, wird versucht, das wahrscheinliche Jahr zu

17 Vgl. DSGVO Art. 6, Abs. 1, lit. a.
18 Singh, J. (2019)
19 https://docs.microsoft.com/en-us/azure/cognitive-services/face/concepts/face-recognition
20 https://docs.microsoft.com/en-us/rest/api/cognitiveservices/
21 https://docs.microsoft.com/en-us/azure/cognitive-services/face/concepts/face-recognition
22 Eberle, H. (2020), Anm. 14, S. 52.

ermitteln.[23] Bei historischen Lichtbildwerken erweist sich eine genaue Datierung oft als schwierig, da sie in den meisten Fällen nicht überliefert ist. Im Rahmen des Prototyps wurde ein Algorithmus entwickelt, um eine automatisierte Schätzung der Datierung zu ermöglichen: ist eine abgebildete Person über einen Normdatensatz wie beispielsweise die GND individualisiert, so ist in vielen Fällen das Geburts- und Sterbedatum bekannt. Diese Daten lassen sich über eine Schnittstelle maschinengestützt abgreifen und verarbeiten. Die Microsoft Cognitive Services bieten neben der Gesichtsdetektion und der Gesichtserkennung auch Methoden, um Attribute wie beispielsweise das Geschlecht, die Emotion oder das Alter zu bestimmen. Durch die Berechnung der Differenz des durch die künstliche Intelligenz berechneten Alters und des Geburtsjahrganges kann das ungefähre Aufnahmejahr des jeweiligen Lichtbildwerkes bestimmt werden. Werden mehrere via GND individualisierte Personen mit vorhandenen Lebensdaten erkannt, so wird für jede Person ein potentielles Aufnahmejahr ermittelt, ein Mittelwert berechnet und als geschätztes Aufnahmejahr ausgegeben.

Abb. 2: Bilddatierung mittels Age Prediction anhand des Bildes https://pid.volare.vorarlberg.at/o:87126

23 Wiesenmüller, H.; Horny, S. (2015), S. 48f.

2.3.4. Erkennung von visuellen Merkmalen anhand von maschinellem Sehen

Das Erkennungsmodell von Microsoft für maschinelles Sehen, welches mit umfangreichen Datensätzen trainiert und laufend weiterentwickelt wird, basiert auf tausenden Objekten, Landschaften und Lebewesen.[24] Auf Basis dieses Modells werden erweiterte Algorithmen angeboten, welche Daten verarbeiten und daraus generierte Informationen zurückgeben können. Für die verbale Beschreibung von Bildern sind die sogenannten freien Schlagworte von Interesse. Dabei sind diese weder innerhalb von Normdaten organisiert, noch in hierarchische Strukturen eingeordnet. Dennoch kann eine solche Auflistung von Schlagworten die Grundlage für eine verbale Bildbeschreibung bilden und ist deshalb wertvoll für die Erschließung von Bildmaterial.[25]

Abb. 3: Vergabe freier Schlagwörter am Beispiel des Objektes https://pid.volare.vorarlberg.at/o:113467. Foto: Vorarlberger Landesbibliothek, Oliver Benvenuti

24 Salvaris, M. (2019), S. 109f.
25 https://docs.microsoft.com/de-de/azure/cognitive-services/computer-vision/concept-tagging-images

Einschränkend muss erwähnt werden, dass das zugrundeliegende Modell von Microsoft anhand von aktuellen Bildern trainiert wird. Aus diesem Grund liefert diese Methode besonders bei der Erkennung von historischen Objekten wie beispielsweise historischen Fahrzeugen oder historischen Gebrauchsgegenständen nur bedingt korrekte oder gar keine Ergebnisse.

2.3.5. Erkennung und Beschreibung markanter landeskundlicher Objekte

Im Rahmen der Erstellung des Prototyps für die Vorarlberger Landesbibliothek wurde ebenfalls mit der Erstellung eines domänenspezifischen Modells experimentiert, um markante landeskundliche Elemente wie Gebäude, Berge oder sonstige relevante Orte zu erkennen. Microsoft empfiehlt, solche Modelle mit mindestens 250 Bildern pro Objekt zu trainieren.[26] Im historischen Kontext stellt dies ein großes Problem dar, da nur in den wenigsten Fällen so viele Aufnahmen in ausreichender Qualität überliefert wurden. Zudem werden neben den Trainingsdaten auch Daten zur Validierung benötigt. So wurde das Modell im Experiment lediglich mit sechs landeskundlichen Objekten trainiert. Die im Rahmen der Validierung durchgeführten Tests lieferten eine Erkennungsgenauigkeit zwischen 53 und 99 Prozent.[27] Aufgrund des unausgewogenen Datenbestandes kam es in vielen Fällen zu einer sogenannten Überanpassung. Das führte dazu, dass für Objekte, die im Modell nicht trainiert worden sind, das ähnlichste Objekt als wahrscheinlichste Klassifizierung ermittelt wurde. Aus diesen Gründen und weil der Aufwand in keinem Verhältnis zum erwarteten Nutzen steht, wurde die Idee eines domänenspezifischen Erkennungsmodells zur Erschließung landeskundlicher Elemente wieder verworfen.

26 https://docs.microsoft.com/de-de/azure/cognitive-services/Custom-Vision-Service/overview
27 Eberle, H. (2020), S. 65.

3. Fazit

Seit vielen Jahren werden in Gedächtnisinsitutionen immer mehr Retrodigitalisierungsprojekte in Angriff genommen, um analoge Fotos digital zu sichern und nutzerfreundlich vermitteln zu können. Mit den wachsenden Datenmengen steigen aber auch die Anforderungen durch die Standardisierung und Normierung in der deskriptiven Bildbeschreibung. Gleichzeitig fehlt es oft an personellen und finanziellen Ressourcen, um diesen Anforderungen in Qualität und Quantität gerecht werden zu können. So erfolgt die Generierung von Metadaten in vielen Institutionen nach wie vor manuell durch eine verbale Beschreibung des Bildinhaltes. Für die Optimierung dieser Arbeitsabläufe bieten sich neue Methoden an, um das vorhandene Fachpersonal effizient einsetzen zu können. Sowohl die Georeferenzierung über die Plattform sMapshot als auch die Bildbeschreibung durch eine Künstliche Intelligenz könnten Institutionen bei der Erfüllung ihres Sammelauftrages unterstützen und einen Mehrwert bieten, da viele dieser maschinell generierten Informationen bei einer manuellen verbalen Beschreibung gar nicht erfasst werden würden. Dennoch können all diese Methoden nicht die Expertise und das Engagement der einzelnen Mitarbeitenden ersetzen, die für die Umsetzung eines erfolgreichen Erschließungsprojektes sowie das laufende Motivieren der Crowd essentiell sind. Da es zum aktuellen Zeitpunkt noch keine anderen Möglichkeiten gibt, müssen zudem alle Beiträge manuell kontrolliert und validiert werden. Die Nutzung künstlicher Intelligenz zur Bildbeschreibung kann das Personal entlasten, aber nicht vollständig ersetzen. Auch Erkennungsmodelle müssen trainiert, validiert und kontrolliert werden. Die Einordnung eines jeden Bildes in den historischen Kontext benötigt nach wie vor das Spezialwissen im jeweiligen Fachgebiet. Letztlich sind bei allen automatisierten Bildbeschreibungsmethoden nur begrenzte Erfolge zu erwarten, da die Interpretation eines Bildes häufig einen großen Spielraum zulässt.

Bibliografie

Eberle, Harald (2020): Inhaltsbasierte Bilderschließung mittels visueller Merkmale durch Maschinelles Sehen. Am Beispiel der Microsoft Azure Cognitive Services und den Daten des Vorarlberger Landesrepositoriums. Masterarbeit, FHWien der WKW.

Graf, Nicole (2018): sMapshot. Die Crowd lokalisiert Bilder im virtuellen Globus. In: Emenlauer-Blömers, Eva et. al. (Hg.): Konferenzband EVA Berlin 2018. Elektronische Medien & Kunst, Kultur und Historie: 25. Berliner Veranstaltung der internationalen EVA-Serie Electronic Media and Visual Arts. Berlin: Staatliche Museen.

Graf, Nicole (2018): sMapshot ist lanciert. blogs.ethz.ch, 07.02.2018. https://doi.org/10.35016/ethz-cs-4995-de

Helm, Wiebke; Mandl, Thomas; Putjenter, Sigrun; Schmideler, Sebastian; Zellhöfer, David (2019): Distant Viewing-Forschung mit digitalisierten Kinderbüchern. Voraussetzungen, Herausforderungen und Ansätze. In: b.i.t. online 22.

Huonder, Flurina (2020): sMapshot Anpassungen für Vorarlberg. blogs.ethz.ch, 22.06.2020. https://doi.org/10.35016/ethz-cs-12203-de

Produit, Timothée; Ingensand, Jens (2016): A 3D Georeferencer and Viewer to Relate Landscape Pictures with VGI. In: Ali Mansourian, Ali et al. (eds.): AGILE International Conference on Geographic Information, LINK-VGI Workshop.

Produit, Timothée; Ingensand, Jens (2018): 3D Georeferencing of Historical Photos by Volunteers. In: Geospatial Technologies for All. Selected Papers of the 21st AGILE Conference on Geographic Information Science. Cham: Springer.

Produit, Timothée; Ingensand, Jens (2019): smapshot. Georeferenzierung historischer Landschaftsbilder durch Crowdsourcing. In: Geomatik Schweiz 117 (9).

Salvaris, Mathew (2019): Deep Learning mit Microsoft Azure. Bonn: Rheinwerk Verlag.

Singh, Jake (2019): A Comparison of Public Cloud Computer Vision Service. Santa Clara University, 12.09.2019. https://osf.io/9t5qf/ (abgerufen am 25.08.2021)

sMapshot. Die partizipative Zeitmaschine. vorarlberg.orf.at. https://vorarlberg.orf.at/stories/3115329/ (abgerufen am 17.08.2021)

Volmer, Stephan (2012): Inhaltsbasierte Bildsuche mittels visueller Merkmale. Eine Alternative zur Erschließung digitaler Bildinformation. 2. Aufl. Saarbrücken: AV Akademikerverlag.

Wiesenmüller Heidrun; Horny, Silke (2015): Basiswissen RDA. Eine Einführung für deutschsprachige Anwender. Berlin: De Gruyter Saur.

Harald Eberle ist stellvertretender Leiter der Abteilung „EDV und Katalog“ an der Vorarlberger Landesbibliothek. Seit 2014 leitet er das Projekt „volare – Vorarlberger Landesrepositorium“ und ist in der Vorarlberger Landesbibliothek als technischer Experte für die Digitalisierung und die Bereitstellung digitaler Sammlungen verantwortlich.

Christopher Pollin

Datenvisualisierung

Handbuch Repositorienmanagement, Hg. v. Blumesberger et al., 2024, S. 503–520
https://doi.org/10.25364/978390337423227

Christopher Pollin, Universität Graz, Zentrum für Informationsmodellierung, christopher.pollin@uni-graz.at |
ORCID iD: 0000-0002-4879-129X

Zusammenfassung

Daten- bzw. Informationsvisualisierung verfolgt den Zweck, visuelle Darstellungen von Datensätzen zu generieren, die dabei helfen sollen, Aufgaben effizienter zu erledigen. Dieser Artikel gibt einen grundlegenden Überblick über dieses Themenfeld. Dies beinhaltet das Referenzmodell der Informationsvisualisierung nach Card et al., die unterschiedlichen Funktionen und Klassifikationen von Visualisierungen, sowie praxisnahe Beispiele und Werkzeuge, die Potenziale und Herausforderungen des Themengebietes veranschaulichen. Eines dieser Beispiele ist das Visualisierungsprojekt *Poppy Field* von Valentina D'Efilippo. Abschließend wird das Thema im Kontext von Repositorien eingeordnet.

Schlagwörter: Datenvisualisierung; Informationsvisualisierung

Abstract

Data Visualization

The purpose of data or information visualization is to create visual representations of data sets to help to carry out tasks more effectively. This contribution gives a basic overview of this topic. It includes the reference model of information visualization according to Card et al., the different features and classifications of visualizations, as well as practical examples and tools that illustrate the potentials and challenges of the domain. One of these examples is the visualization project *Poppy Field* by Valentina D'Efilippo. Finally, the topic is put into the context of repositories.

Keywords: Data visualization; information visualization

1. Einleitung

Datenrepositorien speichern große Datenmengen und stellen sie den Fachgemeinschaften zur Verfügung. Zu viele und zu dichte Informationsmengen führen zu einem *Cognitive* Overload, also einer kognitiven Überlastung von Benutzer:innen. Eine Möglichkeit, sich in größeren Datenmengen dennoch zurecht zu finden, ist die Daten- bzw. Informationsvisualisierung.

Eine Metauntersuchung von Alejandro Benito und Roberto Therón[1] liefert einen empirischen Überblick über die Schnittmenge in der Forschung rund um Informationsvisualisierung und digitale Geisteswissenschaften. Es zeigt die vielfältigen Anwendungsgebiete von Visualisierung für dieses Fach, die sich von Mensch-Maschinen-Interaktion, Text-, Bild- und Netzwerkanalyse bis hin zu Semantic Web und Datenbanken, sowie dem Management von Forschung erstrecken. Natürlich lassen sich vergleichbare Überschneidungen zwischen der Disziplin der Informationsvisualisierung mit anderen Disziplinen aus den Natur-, Rechts und Wirtschaftswissenschaften festmachen. Überall dort, wo Daten im größeren Ausmaß generiert werden und es den Bedarf gibt, damit arbeiten zu wollen, entsteht fast eine Notwendigkeit visueller Darstellungsformen dieser Daten, um die Kognition von Benutzer:innen zu unterstützen. Da Datenrepositorien einen Mittler zwischen Forschungsdaten und Forschung darstellen, ist es nicht unerheblich, Datenvisualisierung im Zusammenhang mit Datenrepositorien zu diskutieren.

Tamara Munzner definiert Visualisierung im Kontext von Informationssystemen, wie etwa Datenrepositorien, als "visual representations of datasets designed to help people carry out tasks more effectively."[2] Ausgehend von dieser Definition stellt sie drei zentrale Fragen bei der Umsetzung von Visualisierungen:

- Warum wird eine Visualisierung benötigt („Why")?
- Welche Daten werden dargestellt („What")?
- Und wie werden sie dargestellt („How")?

Der vorliegende Text bietet einen praxisorientierten Einstieg in das Thema der Datenvisualisierung und beginnt mit der Darstellung eines Beispiels, das sehr gut geeignet ist, um Grundbegriffe und Best Practices der Datenvisualisierung zu erörtern.[3] Am Beispiel der *Poppy Field – Visualising War Fatalities*, einer interaktiven Datenvisualisierung, werden die grundlegenden theoretischen Rahmenbedingungen, sowie die Begrifflichkeiten des Themenkomplexes erörtert und definiert.

1 Benito, A.; Therón, R. (2020), S. 45-57.
2 Munzner, T. (2014), S. 1.
3 Reiterer, H.; Jetter, H.-C. (2013), S. 295-306.

2. *Poppy Field – Visualising War Fatalities*: Ein Beispiel

Im Projekt "Poppy Field - Visualising War Fatalities"[4] werden Daten des Polynational War Memorial visualisiert. Diese umfassen die Dauer, Anzahl von Opfern, beteiligte Kontinente und Nationen militärischer Konflikte im Zeitraum von 1900 bis 2010. Die Notwendigkeit dieser Visualisierung entsteht nicht nur, weil die visuelle Repräsentation der Daten die Arbeit damit erleichtert, also die Datenexploration ermöglicht, sondern auch, weil damit Geschichten erzählt werden können. Unter "Data Storytelling" wird ein strukturierter Ansatz zur Vermittlung von Erkenntnissen aus Daten verstanden, der aus der Kombination dreier Schlüsselelemente besteht: Daten („What"), visuelle Darstellungen („How") und Erzählungen („Why").[5] Für Valentina D'Efilippo[6] ist im Projekt "Poppy Field" eben ein Zweck der Datenvisualisierung, neben der Exploration der Daten, das Erzählen einer Geschichte. Das Ergebnis des Projektes ist in Abbildung 1 ersichtlich. Mohnblumen, seit dem Ersten Weltkrieg ein Symbol des Gedenkens, repräsentieren jeweils einen militärischen Konflikt. Je größer eine Mohnblume, desto höher ist die Zahl der Opfer, wobei die unterschiedlichen Blütenfarben die Beteiligung der Kontinente aufzeigen. Aus dem Startpunkt auf der Zeitleiste und dem Endpunkt, definiert jeweils als Punkt auf einem Feld aus Datum (x-Achse) und Kriegsdauer (y-Achse), ergibt sich ein gebogener Stängel. Das Ergebnis ist ein Informationsraum in Form eines schematischen Mohnblumenfelds, der eine Vielzahl an Datenpunkten unterschiedlichen Typs kodiert und miteinander in Verbindung setzt. Etwas, das mit einer reinen Auflistung der Daten in einer Liste oder Tabelle die kognitiven Fähigkeiten des Menschen überfordern würde.

---

[4] D'Efilippo, V.; Pigelet, N. (2018)
[5] Weber, W. (2020), S. 295-311.
[6] D'Efilippo, V.; Ball, J. (2013), S. 100f.

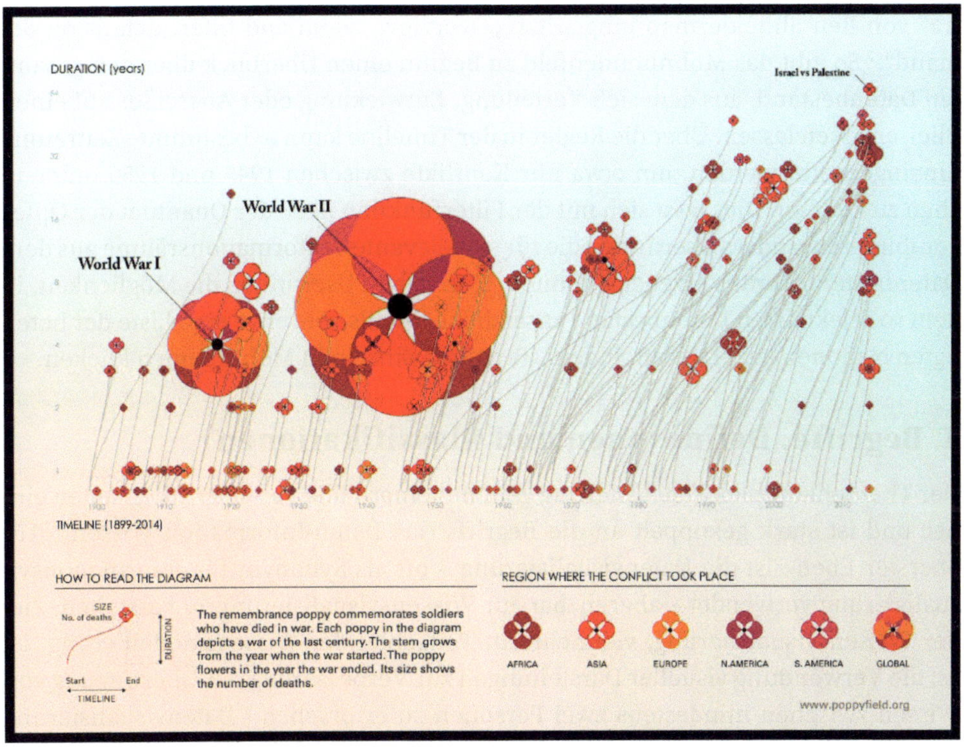

Abbildung 1: Valentina D'Efilippo, Nicolas Pigelet: *Poppy Field – Visualising War Fatalities*, URL: https://www.poppyfield.org/fig00/PoppyField.jpg.

Beim Betrachten der Abbildung sind zwei Dinge sofort erkennbar: zwei dominierende Mohnblumen in der ersten Hälfte – die beiden Weltkriege – und eine Häufung von langstängeligen, kleineren Blumen in der zweiten Hälfte, die eine Vielzahl langandauernder, aber eben kleinerer Konflikte zeigt, wie etwa den israelisch-palästinensischen Konflikt rechts oben. Sowohl die Datenexploration als auch eine ästhetische und dem Thema angemessene Vermittlung, die besonders dem "Data Storytelling" geschuldet ist, sind so gegeben. Auch eine weitere wichtige Dimension der Datenvisualisierung kann damit gezeigt werden: die Interaktion. Erst durch die interaktiven Möglichkeiten einer Webanwendung kann eine Überflutung an Information, die beispielsweise durch Beschriftung jedes einzelnen Konfliktes anfallen würde, vermieden werden. Vorbildlich wird das "Information Visualisation Mantra" von Ben Shneiderman umgesetzt: „Overview, zoom and filter, details on demand".[7] So gibt das Mohnblumenfeld zu Beginn einen Überblick über den gesamten Datenbestand, aus dem sich Verteilung, Entwicklung oder Ausreißer auf einen Blick erfassen lassen. Über die Regler in der Timeline kann in bestimmte Zeiträume hineingezoomt werden, um etwa nur Konflikte zwischen 1945 und 1950 untersuchen zu können. Dies lässt sich mit der Filterfunktion nach der Quantität der Opfer kombinieren, sodass User:innen die für sie relevanten Informationsräume aus dem Datenbestand heraus erzeugen können. Nun haben User:innen die Möglichkeit, in dem so selektierten Datenbestand zusätzliche Details, wie etwa eine Liste der beteiligten Nationen, zu erhalten, indem sie auf die einzelnen Mohnblumen klicken.

3. Begriffe, Definitionen und Klassifikationen

Der Themenkomplex Visualisierung geht mit einer Fülle von Begrifflichkeiten einher und ist stark gekoppelt an die Begriffstrias Daten-Information-Wissen.[8] Auf oberster Ebene ist die Datenvisualisierung – oft als Synonym für Informationsvisualisierung verwendet – abgrenzbar zur Wissensvisualisierung zu verstehen. Ziel der Wissensvisualisierung, vielmehr ein Teilgebiet der Wissensmodellierung, ist es, die Verwendung visueller Darstellungen zur Verbesserung der Übertragung von Wissen zwischen mindestens zwei Personen zu erforschen.[9] Datenvisualisierung aber umfasst die Anwendung computerbasierter, interaktiver, visueller, externer Repräsentationen von abstrakten Daten mit dem Ziel, menschliche Kognition zu erweitern. Die Datenvisualisierung eröffnet einen Kommunikationsweg für abstrakte Daten, wohingegen die Wissensvisualisierung die Übertragung von Wissen fokussiert.

Die Datenvisualisierung kann nun weiter aufgeteilt werden in Scientific Visualization" (SciVis) und Information Visualization (InfoVis)[10] und teilweise auch in eine eigene dritte Kategorie der Geographic Visualization (GeoVis).[11] Diese drei Kategorien unterscheiden sich in der Wahl der räumlichen Repräsentation der Daten – der Projektion. Für eine SciVis ist die räumliche Position mit dem Datensatz gegeben. Das heißt beispielsweise, dass ein menschliches Gehirn den Raum darstellt, auf dem bestimmte Gehirnareale eingefärbt werden, um gemessene Gehirnaktivitäten – also Daten – abzubilden. In der InfoVis bzw. in der GeoVis wird der Raum zur

7 Shneiderman, B. (1996), S. 336-343.
8 Eine ausführliche Diskussion dieser Begriffe im Kontext der Informationswissenschaft findet sich bei Favre-Bulle, B. (2001) und bei Rowley, J. E. (2007), S. 163-180.
9 Meyer, R. (2010), S. 23.
10 Nazemi, K. et al. (2021), S. 477f.
11 Andrews, K. (2020)

Datenrepräsentation erst geschaffen. Hier muss erst ein geeigneter Raum generiert werden, um anhand von Daten eine bestimmte Aufgabe effektiv darstellen und bearbeiten zu können. Für InfoVis heißt das, dass diagrammatische Darstellungen gewählt und Daten etwa in einem Liniendiagramm dargestellt werden. Ein Beispiel hierfür ist auch das Projekt *Poppy Field*, da es sich einer Komposition von visuellen Strukturen bedient. Für GeoVis ist das ähnlich, wobei der Raum durch geografische Karten, wie etwa Datensätze auf einer Weltkugel oder Landkarte, gegeben ist.

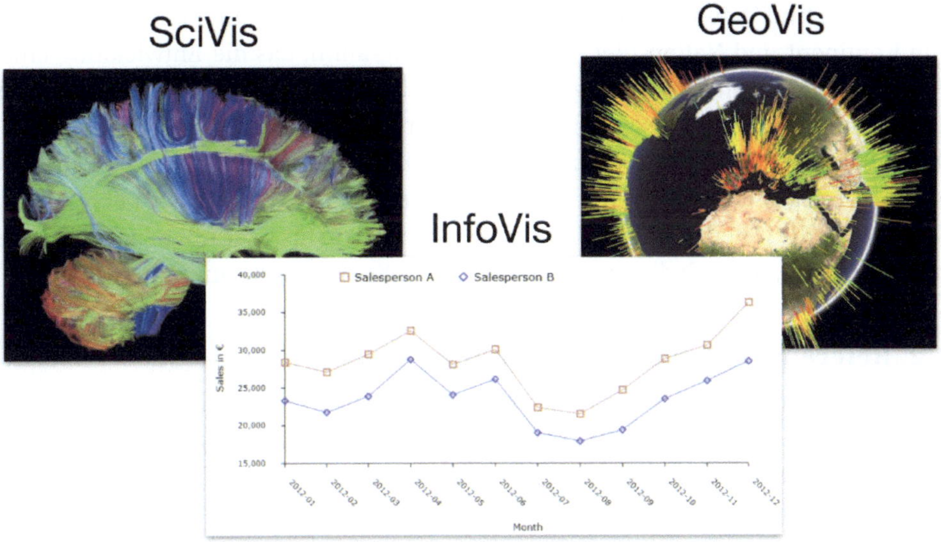

Abbildung 2: Eigene Darstellung: SciVis, InfoVis, GeoVis

3.1. Klassifikation von Datenvisualisierungen

Klassifiziert werden Datenvisualisierungen nach ihrer Lesart und ihrer Komplexität. Die Lesart einer Visualisierung kann author-driven oder reader-driven sein. Als author-driven werden Visualisierungen bezeichnet, die einen angeleiteten, das heißt einen erklärenden Charakter, haben. Ziel ist es, eine Aussage sichtbar und nachvollziehbar für Leser:innen zu machen. Das Data Storytelling hat genau diese Funktion und wird auch als "Explanatory-Data Visualisation" oder auch "Narrative-Information Visualisation" bezeichnet. Dem gegenüber steht die Gruppe der „Exploratory-Data Visualisation", also der Visualisierungen, die reader-driven sind. Diese Klasse an Visualisierungen ist nicht angeleitet und folgt einem explorativen Paradigma, in dem Leser:innen über Funktionalitäten unterschiedliche Views - also Perspektiven auf Daten - selbstständig erzeugen können. Indem über die Filterfunktionen im

Poppy Field Project der Informationsraum angepasst werden kann, werden von User:innen neue Views generiert und der Datenbestand exploriert. Das *Poppy Field Project* kann aber durchaus auch als hybride Lösung mit explorativen, aber auch erklärenden Elementen verstanden werden.[12]

Komplexität als *Klassifikationskriterium* bezieht sich auf die Anzahl der Datendimensionen. Darunter versteht man die Anzahl der diskreten Informationsarten, die in einem Diagramm visuell kodiert sind. Im anfangs angeführten Beispiel der Mohnblumen gibt es fünf Datendimensionen: die Zahl der Opfer, Start- und Endzeitpunkt, sowie Kontinent und Nation. Bei einem Liniendiagramm, das die Entwicklung eines Preises über die Zeit hinweg zeigt, reichen zwei Dimensionen für Preis und Datum. Die Komplexität nimmt also mit der Anzahl der Dimensionen zu, nicht aber mit der Anzahl der Datensätze. Eine Visualisierung wird also nicht komplexer, wenn statt 100 Konflikten 1.000 dargestellt werden. Mit höherer Komplexität wird es auch herausfordernder, die Daten und ihre Abhängigkeiten effizient für User:innen nachvollziehbar zu machen, da auch die Anzahl der visuellen Kodierungen zunimmt.[13]

3.2. Referenzmodell der Informationsvisualisierung

Zentrale Elemente der Informationsvisualisierung sind Daten, die Wahl der visuellen Kodierung bzw. visuellen Strukturen und der Views. Diese Begriffe, die zum Teil schon erwähnt wurden, lassen sich gut anhand des *Referenzmodells der Informationsvisualisierung* nach Card et al.[14] definieren.

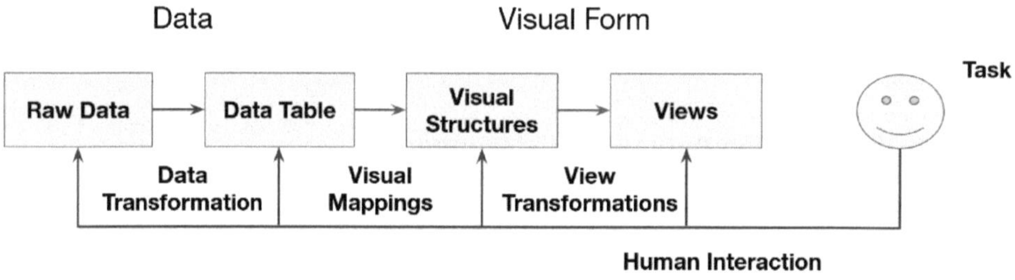

Abbildung 3: Eigene Darstellung: Referenzmodell der Informationsvisualisierung nach Card et al.

Den Ausgangspunkt bilden rohe Daten. Im Prozess der Data Transformation werden rohe Daten in strukturierte Daten, die Data Tables, überführt. Das heißt, dass

[12] Weber, W. (2020), S. 299-301.
[13] Iliinsky N.; Steele, J. (2011)
[14] Card, S. et al. (1999), S. 12-25.

Zahlenwerte und Text ihre Bedeutung durch ein Modell bzw. ein Schema erhalten. Die auf rein syntaktischer Ebene befindlichen Daten werden kontextualisiert und so zu Information. Die Zahl „1945“ ist nicht mehr eine Zeichenkette, sondern das Enddatum eines Konfliktes. Auf dem Weg hin zur Visualisierung müssen die strukturierten Daten nun auf visuelle Strukturen gemappt werden. Die Aufgabe des *Visual* Mappings ist es, die Daten, die in Data Tables strukturiert sind, den verschiedenen visuellen Ausprägungen der verfügbaren Visual Structures zuzuordnen. Diese visuellen Strukturen sind die Archetypen der eigentlichen Visualisierungen und definieren die grundsätzliche Art der Informationsdarstellung: Balkendiagramme, Netzwerke oder Treemaps. Das Visual Mapping bestimmt, welche Datenwerte welchen visuellen Variablen der visuellen Strukturen zugeordnet werden. Visuelle Variablen sind beispielsweise Position, Höhe, Breite, Farbe oder Form. Im Beispiel aus Abbildung 1 wird der quantitative Wert der Opferzahl in Form des Durchmessers der Mohnblume kodiert. Die Dauer des Konflikts wird als geschwungene Linie zwischen zwei Punkten in einem Koordinatensystem kodiert und Farben repräsentieren die unterschiedlichen Kontinente. Die Visual Structure entspricht so einem Punktdiagramm, das den Anforderungen der Daten entsprechend adaptiert wurde.

Wie bereits erwähnt, entstehen die Views durch die Interaktivität der User:innen, die in der Lage sind, den Informationsraum ihren Anforderungen entsprechend anzupassen. Das Hineinzoomen in die Jahre 1945 bis 1960 ist ein solcher View, wie auch das gefilterte Ergebnis nach allen Konflikten, die am asiatischen und afrikanischen Kontinent stattfanden. Genau diese Anforderungen sind wichtig und auch im Referenzmodell mit der Human Interaction und der Task der User:innen abgebildet. An sämtlichen Prozessen, angefangen vom Informationsbedürfnis, über die Datenerzeugung und -modellierung, bis zum Design und der Implementierung sind Akteure beteiligt. Tamara Munzner fasst dies als “Human in the Loop”[15] zusammen. Viele Probleme und Möglichkeiten werden erst klar, wenn der Mensch sich in iterativen Abläufen damit beschäftigt. Das ist notwendig, um in der großen Menge an möglichen Visualisierungen, die aus einem Datenbestand heraus erzeugt werden können, auch die zu finden, die für die Anwender:innen einen Mehrwert generieren.

15 Munzner, T. (2014), S. 2-4.

3.3. Beschränkungen

Hier gilt es, drei Beschränkungen in der Entwicklung von Visualisierungen zu berücksichtigen: die menschliche Wahrnehmung und Kognition, das Medium zur Darstellung und die algorithmische Verarbeitung durch Computer.

Der Mensch ist gut darin, Muster zu erkennen. Innerhalb einer Menge von gleichen Objekten erkennen Menschen sofort Ausreißer, wenn sie eine andere Farbe, Form, Position oder Größe haben. Im Gegensatz dazu ist es schwieriger, sich wahrgenommene Bilder zu merken und aus der Erinnerung mit anderen zu vergleichen. Ebenso stellt die potenzielle kognitive Überladung ein Problem dar. Diese ist dann gegeben, wenn zu viel Information gleichzeitig auf die User:innen einwirkt, also die Informationsdichte zu hoch ist.

Ein zu viel an Information entsteht ab einem gewissen Punkt, da auch der verfügbare Raum auf einem Bildschirm oder Blatt Papier, also dem Medium der Visualisierung, begrenzt ist. Es können nicht alle Perspektiven auf einen Datensatz gleichzeitig abgebildet werden. Durch Interaktivität, beispielsweise durch eine Weboberfläche, kann das Prinzip der Multiperspektivität umgesetzt werden. Es gilt die Faustregel, pro Visualisierung nur eine Aussage zu kommunizieren, es können aber im Sinne der Multiple Views[16] durch Interaktivität unterschiedliche Visualisierungstypen genutzt werden, um andere Perspektiven auf Daten zu erzeugen.

Die dritte Beschränkung ist schlichtweg dadurch gegeben, dass aus Daten Visualisierungen berechnet werden müssen. Je komplexer die Berechnungen sind, um eine Visualisierung aus einem Datenbestand zu erzeugen, desto länger kann sie dauern oder gar nicht in sinnvoller Zeit generiert werden.[17]

4. Data und Data Tables

Deskriptive Statistik und Datenvisualisierung sind eng miteinander verknüpft. Wo die deskriptive Statistik versucht, empirische Daten quantitativ zu beschreiben, ist es die Datenvisualisierung, die diese Ergebnisse darstellt.[18] Grundlage sind aber stets, wie aus dem Referenzmodell von Card et. al hervorgeht, strukturierte Daten. Abbildung 4 zeigt exemplarische Datensätze, sowie alle Dimensionen (Spalten) aus dem “Poppy Field Project”.[19]

---

16 Windhager, F. (2019), S. 4-6.

17 Munzner, T. (2014), S. 9-16.

18 Shardt, Y.; Weiß, H. (2021), S. 4-30.

19 Die verwendeten Daten für die Webanwendung des “Poppy Field Project” im CSV-Format: https://www.poppyfield.org/data/PoppyDataCSV.csv

wars	from	to	duration	notes	participation	number_	who	where	fatalities	source
War in Eastern	2014	2014	0	This armed con	Ukraine	2	Europe, Asia	Europe	4035	War in Donbas:
Sectarian Confl	2012	2014	2	End year and fa	Central African	1	Africa	Africa	2099	Sectarian Confl
South Sudan C	2011	2014	3	End year and fa	South Sudan	1	Africa	Africa	15000	South Sudan C
Syrian Civil Wa	2011	2014	3	End year and fa	Syria	1	Asia	Asia	260215	Syrian civil war
Yemen vs Al-Qu	2009	2014	5	This conflict is c	Yemen, United	2	Asia, North Am	Asia	4270	Yemen vs Al-Q
Nigerian Govt v	2009	2014	5	This conflict is c	Nigeria	1	Africa	Africa	4627	Nigerian Govt v
Waziristan conf	2007	2014	7	This conflict is c	Pakistan, Afgha	2	Asia	Asia	23494	Waziristan conf
Kivu Conflict	2006	2013	7		Democratic Rep	2	Africa	Africa	10105	Kivu Conflict
Iraqi Insurgency	2003	2014	11	Start year, end	Iraq, United Sta	5	Asia, North Am	Asia	184512	Iraqi Insurgenc

Abbildung 4: Eigene Darstellung: Einträge des Datensatzes aus dem *Poppy Field Project*

Diese „Attribute", wie sie auch genannt werden, können unterschiedlich konfiguriert sein. Die Dimensionen „wars", „notes", „participation", „who", „where" und „source" sind Text, wohingegen „from", „to", „duration", „number_participants" und „fatalities" Zahlen beinhalten. Diese vorerst banale Erkenntnis führt aber dazu, dass nicht jeder Wert für eine Datenvisualisierung gleich verwendet werden kann. Während die Zahlen aus den "fatalities" sinnvollerweise aufaddiert werden können, bleibt dies bei „from" und „to „– zwei Datumsangaben – sinnbefreit. Auch bei den textuellen Dimensionen erkennt man sofort, dass sich „where" von „wars" unterscheidet. Ersteres gibt jedem Konflikt seinen eindeutigen Namen, zweiteres beinhaltet dieselben Begriffe mehrmals. Folglich gibt es unterschiedliche Typen von Attributen. Im Allgemeinen werden nominale bzw. kategoriale, ordinale und quantitative Attribute unterschieden.[20] Ein Beispiel eines quantitativen Attributs ist „fatalities", eines nominalen bzw. kategorialen ist „where" und die Datumsangaben können als ordinale Attribute verstanden werden. Sie sind durch folgende Charakteristika unterscheidbar: mit quantitativen Attributen können arithmetische und statistische Operationen durchgeführt werden. Ordinale und kategoriale bzw. nominale Attribute haben einen einordnenden bzw. gruppierenden Charakter. Erstere lassen sich nach dem Prinzip „etwas ist größer als etwas anderes" sortieren: Das Jahr 1945 ist vor dem Jahr 1950. Mit Zweiteren kann zwar sinnvoll gruppiert werden, aber ohne, dass es eine Struktur oder Ordnung impliziert. Eine Ordnung im Sinne von „Afrika ist höherwertiger als Europa" ist nicht möglich.[21]

20 Munzner, T. (2014), S. 31-33; Ware, C. (2019)
21 Nazemi, K. et al. (2021), S. 480-482.

5. Visual Mapping

Der Prozess des Visual Mappings regelt ausgehend von strukturierten Daten, welche Attribute an welcher Stelle positioniert werden sollen, um eine Visualisierung zur Bearbeitung einer Frage zu erzielen.[22] Eine kommerzielle Softwarelösung zur Generierung von Datenvisualisierungen, die sehr gut diesen Mappingprozess in einem User Interface darstellt, ist Tableau.[23] Ein weiteres und einfacheres, aber freies Tool ist RAWGraphs.[24] In beiden Softwarelösungen kann die Tabelle aus den Poppy Fields als CSV oder Excel geladen und Datendimensionen können auf bestimmte visuelle Strukturen der unterschiedlichen Diagrammtypen (Charts) gemappt werden. Aus der Fülle von unterschiedlichen Visualisierungen – der *The Data Visualisation Catalogue*[25] oder das *Data Viz Project*[26] geben einen guten Überblick – werden ein Säulendiagramm (Bar Chart), eine Kastengrafik (Box Plot) und ein Streudiagramm (Scatter Plot) kurz vorgestellt. Eine weitere Möglichkeit, aus Daten Visualisierungen zu erzeugen, sind Programmiersprachen. Sehr häufig werden Python[27] und R[28] verwendet, um Daten auszuwerten und zu visualisieren, oder Bibliotheken wie D3.js[29], um interaktive Visualisierungen im Web zu implementieren. Letzteres fand auch Verwendung im *Poppy Field Project*.

Zur Erzeugung eines Bar Chart reicht es, zwei Attribute miteinander zu verknüpfen, die auf der x- und y-Achse projiziert werden. Die Zeilen werden nach einem kategorialen Attribut gruppiert, wie etwa „where“, und die Summe der „fatalities“ jeder Gruppe wird ermittelt. Die Kategorien aus der Dimension „where“ kommen auf die x-Achse und die Summen der „fatalities“ auf die y-Achse. Das Bar Chart ist gut geeignet, um einen Überblick über oder einen Vergleich von Daten zu ermöglichen, und es gilt als eine der einfachsten Visualisierungsformen.

22 Nazemi, K. et al. (2021), S. 484-487.
23 Tableau https://www.tableau.com. Für den akademischen Bereich gibt es eine einjährige Testversion.
24 RAWGraphs https://rawgraphs.io
25 The Data Visualisation Catalogue https://datavizcatalogue.com
26 Data Viz Project https://datavizproject.com
27 Zu Libraries in diesem Zusammenhang: Siehe Tanner, G. (2019).
28 Kabacoff, R. (2020): Data Visualization with R https://rkabacoff.github.io/datavis
29 Bostock, M. (n. d.): Data-Driven Documents https://d3js.org

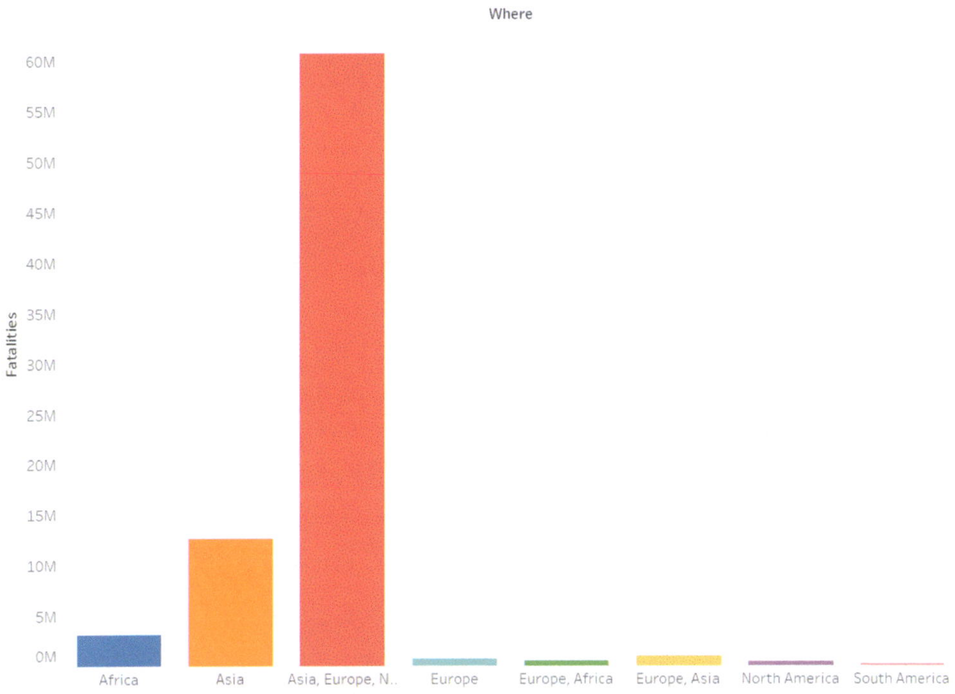

Abbildung 5: Eigene Darstellung. Bar Chart der *Poppy Field*-Daten umgesetzt mit Tableau

Ein Box Plot veranschaulicht aggregierte statistische Werte eines quantitativen Attributes, wie etwa Median, Quartil oder Ausreißer[30] und ist gut geeignet, um die Verteilung von Daten darzustellen. In Abbildung 5 wird die Dauer der Konflikte auf die y-Achse gelegt und die x-Achse beschreibt das Attribut „where". Weiters werden die vorher genannten statistischen Mittel auch sichtbar gemacht. Jeder Punkt repräsentiert einen Konflikt und desto höher der Wert auf der y-Achse ist, desto länger ist die Dauer des Konflikts. Gleichzeitig erkennen wir, dass es in Afrika eine Häufung von Konflikten gibt, die zwischen 1 und 14 Jahren dauern, sowie einige Ausreißer nach oben hin, d. h. deren Dauer länger ist.

---

30 Munzner, T. (2014), S. 308-310.

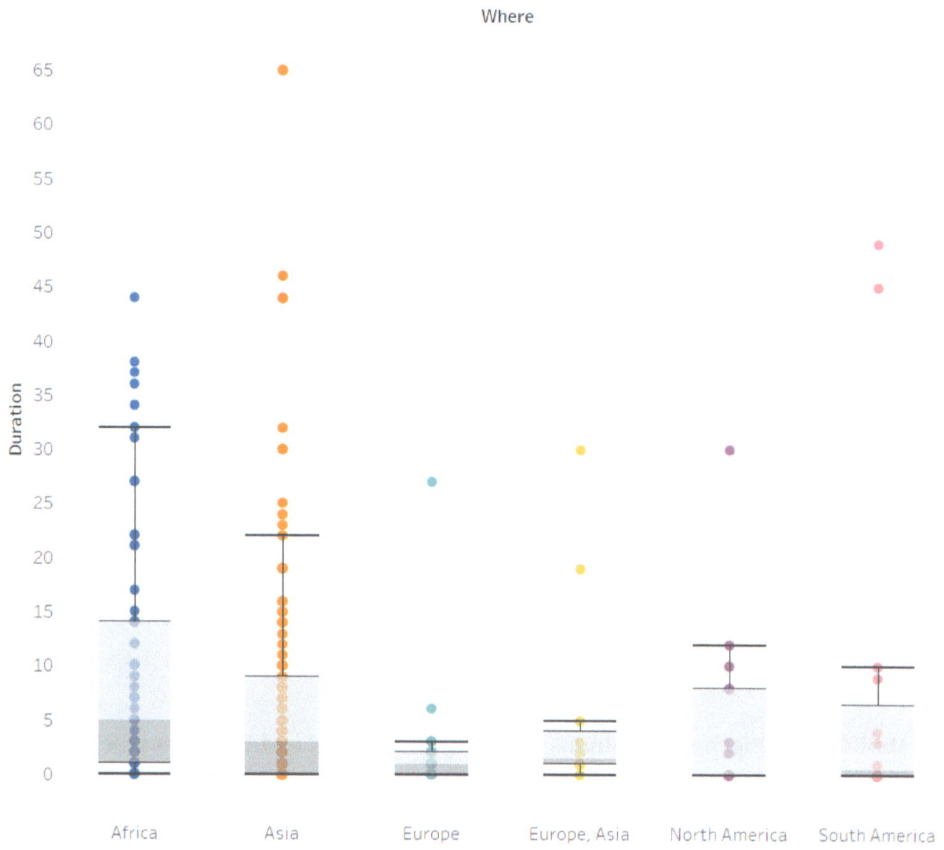

Abbildung 6: Eigene Darstellung. Box Plot der *Poppy Field*-Daten umgesetzt mit Tableau

Ein Scatter Plot ähnelt am stärksten dem *Poppy Field*. Das Koordinatensystem wird durch das Beginndatum und die Dauer des Konfliktes gebildet. Jeder Punkt repräsentiert einen Konflikt, wobei die Größe der Kreise die Anzahl der Opfer wiedergibt und die farbliche Kodierung die regionale Verortung. Was aber auch ersichtlich wird, sind die Grenzen der Darstellung auf nur einer Seite. Sowohl die Anzahl der Opfer, als auch die Dauer der Konflikte liefert eine recht große Bandbreite und sorgt dafür, dass Konflikte nur als kleine Punkte im Vergleich der beiden Weltkriege dargestellt werden können. Selbiges gilt auch für die, die das Koordinatensystem nach oben hinstreckt. Eine Möglichkeit ist, statt einer linearen eine logarithmische Darstellung zu wählen, um so die y-Achse zu stauchen, aber dennoch die Verhältnismäßigkeit beizubehalten.

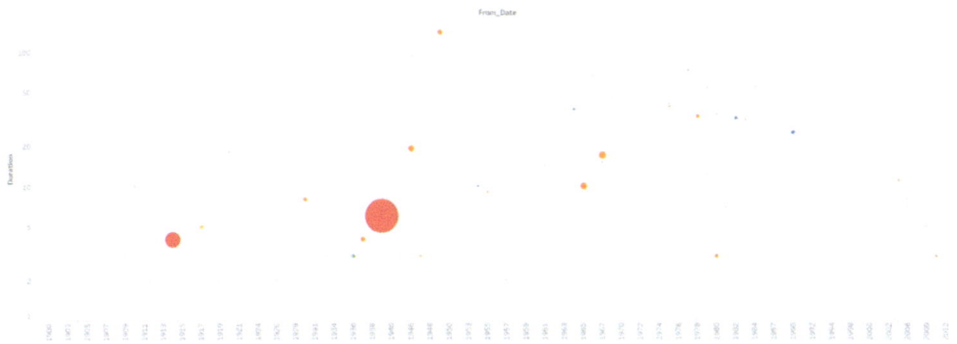

Abbildung 7: Eigene Darstellung. Scatter Plot der *Poppy Field*-Daten umgesetzt mit Tableau

6. Zusammenfassung

Clifford Wulfman fasst entsprechend zusammen: “It is important for creators and readers of these depictions to remember that they are not ‘data’ but readings, interpretations of data meditated by programmed algorithms and hermeneutic desires.”[31]

Wo Datenbestände in ihrer Zusammenschau die kognitiven Fähigkeiten des Menschen überfordern, dort gibt es Potenzial für Datenvisualisierungen. Diese Verfahren der visuellen Analyse und der visuellen Kommunikation erlauben neue Wege zur Analyse und Exploration von Daten- und Quellenmaterial sowie deren Nutzung, um Erkenntnisse weiterzuvermitteln.[32] Datenvisualisierungen sind, so Clifford Wulfman im Zitat zu Beginn der Zusammenfassung, nicht ein fertiges Produkt, sondern eine computerbasierte Form der Kommunikation, die es erst zu interpretieren gilt. Gerade in der geisteswissenschaftlichen Forschung ist multiperspektivischer Diskurs zu einem Forschungsfeld die Norm. Nicht eine Visualisierung ist die einzig korrekte, sondern unterschiedliche Visualisierungsformen können für die Arbeit der Geisteswissenschaftler:innen sinnstiftend sein. Die Visualisierung an sich ist kein Erkenntnisgewinn, sondern erst die Arbeit damit und die Kritik daran. Genauso wichtig in diesem Zusammenhang ist auch, die nicht unmittelbar sichtbaren

31 Wulfman, C. E. (2014), S. 94-109.
32 Windhager, F. (2019), S. 1-2.

Ebenen solcher Diskurse zu berücksichtigen[33]: Wie können beispielsweise Unschärfe, Fragmentierung und Unsicherheiten historischer Information in Visualisierungen berücksichtigt werden? Florian Windhager veranschaulicht dies im Kontext biographischer und historischer Daten. Er sieht einen besonderen Mehrwert in der Darstellung räumlich-zeitlicher und kontextsensitiver Information in einem PolyCube, um die Bewegung von historischen Akteur:innen in Raum und Zeit darzustellen.[34] Weitere Projekte, die neue Darstellungsformen erproben, werden von der interdisziplinären Forschungsgruppe Urban Complexity Lab (UCLAB) der Fachhochschule Potsdam umgesetzt.[35] So wird im Projekt *Reading Traces Visualizing Fontane's Reference Library* erforscht, welche explorativen Wege der Wissensdarstellung im Digitalen für einen Bibliotheksbestand möglich sind.[36]

Visualisierungen sind kein Selbstzweck, sondern haben funktionalen Charakter. Die Darstellungen werden nicht (nur) der schönen Bilder wegen gemacht, wie auch die Generierung davon kein triviales Unterfangen ist. Herausforderungen erstrekken sich ausgehend von den Daten und den Modellen („What"), den Anforderungen, warum man sie benötigt („Why"), und der Frage, wie Daten auf visuelle Strukturen gemappt werden können („How)". Das „How" beinhaltet auch die Paradigmen der Multiple Views und Interaktivität, aus denen heraus unterschiedliche Views von User:innen erzeugt werden.

Die FAIR Kriterien werden zu Recht im Kontext von Datenrepositorien hochgehalten. Daten müssen gefunden werden können und zugänglich, interoperabel und wiederverwendbar sein. Datenvisualisierungen können bei den ersten zwei Kriterien helfen. Nämlich dann, wenn das Finden von gesuchten Objekten aufgrund der schieren Masse nicht mehr möglich ist. Ein gutes Beispiel dafür ist der Wikidata Query Service, der es erlaubt, mittels SPARQL den gesamten Wikidata-Datenbestand abzufragen. Neben einer tabellarischen Darstellung der Suchtreffer können, wenn es die gefundenen Attribute erlauben, unterschiedliche Visualisierungen, wie Bar Chart oder Treemap selektiert werden, um Datenbankabfragen zu visualisieren. Datenvisualisierungen helfen also, Trends, Ausreißer, Beziehungen oder Muster in Daten sichtbar zu machen. Sie helfen dort, wo die kognitiven Fähigkeiten der Anwender:innen überfordert sind. Sie sind keine Erkenntnis per se, sondern helfen dabei, neue Erkenntnisse zu gewinnen, neue Perspektiven einzunehmen, oder eben auch neue Geschichten zu erzählen.

---

33 Graham, E. (2017), S. 449f.

34 Windhager, F. (2019), S. 1-2.

35 Projekte des Urban Complexity Lab (UCLAB) https://uclab.fh-potsdam.de/projects

36 Bludau, M.-J. et al. (2020), S. 77-87 und Reading traces Visualizing Fontane's reference library https://uclab.fh-potsdam.de/projects/reading-traces

Bibliografie

Andrews, Keith (2020): Information Visualisation. Course Notes. Graz: University of Technology Graz. https://courses.isds.tugraz.at/ivis/ivis.pdf (abgerufen am 16.08.2021)

Benito, Alejandro; Therón, Roberto (2020): A Data-Driven Introduction to Authors, Readings, and Techniques in Visualization for the Digital Humanities. In: IEEE Computer Graphics and Applications 40, pp. 45-57. https://doi.org/10.1109/MCG.2020.2973945

Bludau, Mark-Jan et al. (2020): Reading Traces. Scalable Exploration in Elastic Visualizations of Cultural Heritage Data. In: Computer Graphics Forum 39 (3), pp. 77-87.

Card, Stuard; Mackinlay, Jock; Shneiderman, Ben (1999): Readings in Information Visualization. Using Vision to Think. San Francisco: Morgan Kaufmann.

D'Efilippo, Valentina; Ball, James (2013): The Infographic History of the World. Richmond Hill: Firefly Books.

D'Efilippo, Valentina; Pigelet, Nicolas (2018): Poppy Field – Visualising War Fatalities. https://www.poppyfield.org (abgerufen am 24.09.2021)

Drucker, Johanna (2020): Visualization and Interpretation. Humanistic Approaches to Display. Cambridge: Massachusetts Institute of Technology.

Engebretsen, Martin; Kennedy, Helen (eds.) (2020): Data Visualization in Society. Amsterdam: University Press Amsterdam. https://doi.org/10.1515/9789048543137

Favre-Bulle, Bernard (2001): Information und Zusammenhang. Informationsfluß in Prozessen der Wahrnehmung, des Denkens und der Kommunikation. Wien; New York: Springer.

Graham, Elyse (2017): Introduction: Data Visualisation and the Humanities. In: English Studies 98 (5), pp. 449-458. https://doi.org/10.1080/0013838X.2017.1332021

Iliinsky, Noah; Steele, Julie (2011): Designing Data Visualizations. Representing Informational Relationships. Sebastopol: O'Reilly Media. https://www.oreilly.com/library/view/designing-data-visualizations/9781449314774/ch01.html (abgerufen am 24.09.2021)

Meyer, Robert (2010): Knowledge Visualization. In: Baur, Dominikus et. al. (eds.): Trends in Information Visualization. Hauptseminar Medieninformatik WS 2008/2009. An Overview of Current Trends, Development and Research in Information Visualization. Technical Report. München: LMU Munich. Department of Computer Science. Media Informatics Group, pp. 23-30.

Munzner, Tamara (2014): Visualization Analysis and Design. New York: A K Peters/CRC Press.

Nazemi, Kawa; Kaupp, Lukas; Burkhardt, Dirk; Below, Nicola (2021): 5.4 Datenvisualisierung. In: Putnings, Markus; Neuroth, Heike; Neumann, Janna (Hg.): Praxishandbuch Forschungsdatenmanagement. Berlin, Boston: De Gruyter Saur, S. 477-502. https://doi.org/10.1515/9783110657807-026

Rehbein, Malte (2017): Informationsvisualisierung. In: Jannidis, Fotis; Kohle, Hubertus; Rehbein, Malte (Hg.): Digital Humanities. Stuttgart: J. B. Metzler, S. 328-342. https://doi.org/10.1007/978-3-476-05446-3_23

Reiterer, Harald; Jetter, Hans-Christian (2013): Informationsvisualisierung. In: Kuhlen, Rainer; Semar, Wolfgang; Strauch, Dietmar (Hg.): Grundlagen der praktischen Information und Dokumentation. Berlin et al.: De Gruyter Saur, S. 192-206. https://doi.org/10.1515/9783110258264.192

Rowley, Jennifer E. (2007): The Wisdom Hierarchy. Representations of the DIKW Hierarchy. In: Journal of Information Science 33 (2), pp.163-180.

Shardt, Yuri; Weiß, Heiko (2021): Methoden der Statistik und Prozessanalyse. Eine anwendungsorientierte Einführung. Berlin, Heidelberg: Springer Vieweg. https://doi.org/10.1007/978-3-662-61626-0

Shneiderman, Ben (1996): The Eyes Have It. A Task by Data Type Taxonomy for Information Visualizations. In: Proceedings of the IEEE Symposium on Visual Languages. Washington: IEEE Computer Society Press, pp. 336-343.

Tanner, G. (2019): Introduction to Data Visualization in Python. How to Make Graphs Using Matplotlib, Pandas and Seaborn. In: Towards Data Science 23.01.2019. https://towardsdatascience.com/introduction-to-data-visualization-in-python-89a54c97fbed (abgerufen am 24.09.2021)

Ware, Colin (2020): Information Visualization. Perception for Design. 4th edition. Burlington: Morgan Kaufmann.

Weber, Wiebke (2020): Exploring Narrativity in Data Visualization in Journalism. In: Engebretsen, Martin; Kennedy, Helen (eds.): Data Visualization in Society. Amsterdam: Amsterdam University Press, pp. 299-301. https://doi.org/10.1515/9789048543137-022

Windhager, Florian (2019): Choreographien der Existenz. Zur multimodalen Erweiterung biographischer Forschung und Lehre durch Verfahren der visuellen Analyse und Synthese. In: BIOS – Zeitschrift für Biographieforschung, Oral History und Lebensverlaufsanalysen 30 (1-2), S. 60-75.

Wulfman, Clifford E. (2014): The Plot of the Plot. Graphs and Visualizations. In: Journal of Modern Periodical Studies 5 (1) (Special Issue Visualizing Periodical Networks), pp. 94-109. http://www.jstor.org/stable/10.5325/jmodeperistud.5.1.0094

Christopher Pollin ist wissenschaftlicher Mitarbeiter am Institut Zentrum für Informationsmodellierung der Universität Graz. Er promoviert in Digital Humanities und beschäftigt sich mit semantischen Webtechnologien, digitalen Editionen und Informationsvisualisierung. 2022 gründete er das DH/IT-Unternehmen Digital Humanities Craft.

Friedrich Summann

Sichtbarkeit und Qualität von Repositorien – aus Sicht eines Service-Providers am Beispiel BASE

Handbuch Repositorienmanagement, Hg. v. Blumesberger et al., 2024, S. 521–547
https://doi.org/10.25364/978390337423228

Friedrich Summann, Universitätsbibliothek Bielefeld, friedrich.summann@uni-bielefeld.de |
ORCID iD: 0000-0002-6297-3348

Zusammenfassung

BASE (Bielefeld Academic Search Engine) ist eine global agierende wissenschaftliche Suchmaschine mit Fokus auf institutionelle Repositorien und verwandte Datenquellen im akademischen Kontext. Für OAI-PMH Data Provider ist eine Erfassung via BASE ein Mosaikstein zur globalen Sichtbarkeit der Repositorien-Inhalte und der Quelle selbst. Auf der anderen Seite ist BASE als OAI-Service Provider auf die Qualität der bereitgestellten Schnittstellen (speziell OAI-PMH) angewiesen. Das gilt für die technische Erreichbarkeit und Stabilität, aber auch insbesondere für die gelieferten Metadaten, da diese die Grundlage für die qualitative Bearbeitung der Suchanfragen und der Ergebnisanzeige bilden. In dieser Hinsicht kann BASE als Spiegel der globalen Publikationslandschaft dienen und bietet daher mit Tools wie Quellenliste, OAI-PMH Validator und („Goldene Regeln" / „Golden Rules") Empfehlungen, Angebote und Informationen zur Analyse und Optimierung der Repositorien-Infrastruktur. Die Suchmaschine BASE ist seit 2004 produktiv und indexiert zur Zeit mehr als 11.400 Datenquellen auf globaler Basis. Erfasst werden aktuell (Januar 2024) 352 Millionen Publikationen und davon werden ca. zwei Drittel via OAI-PMH Harvesting von Repositorien abgeholt. Daher hat in diesem Kontext BASE mit seinen in der Praxis seit 2004 erworbenen umfassenden Erfahrungen eine gewichtige Rolle in der Repositorien-Community gespielt und hat darauf basierend bei der Abfassung von Guidelines (DRIVER Guidelines, OpenAire Guidelines, DINI-Zertifikat) und Vokabular-Vorbereitungen (COAR Vocabularies) mitgearbeitet. Ganz konkret ist diese Expertise eingeflossen in die sogenannten „Goldenen Regeln" bei BASE, die grundlegende Empfehlungen eingängig und pragmatisch zusammenfassen und damit in effizienter Weise die Maßnahmen zur qualitativen Sichtbarkeit formulieren und unterstützen. Zahlreiche Kommunikationskanäle mit Repositorien-Manager:innen und -Communities (z. B. DSpace, Eprints, Opus, Goobi, MyCoRe, Invenio) haben zudem zur Optimierung von Schnittstellen beigetragen. Solche Bemühungen sind immer von gegenseitigem Nutzen: BASE ist nicht der einzige Service, der diese Schnittstelle nutzt. Daher kommt die Qualität der Quellen allen Mitgliedern der Repositorien-Landschaft zugute, während der Suchservice bei BASE selbst optimiert wird. Abschließend werden diese grundlegenden Punkte der im BASE-Rahmen entwickelten Qualitätsmerkmale an konkreten Beispielen vorgestellt und erläutert.

Schlagwörter: Repositorium; Zertifikat; BASE; Suchmaschine

Abstract

Visibility and Quality of Repositories – From the Perspective of a Service Provider, Using the Example of BASE

BASE (Bielefeld Academic Search Engine) is a global scientific search engine focusing on institutional repositories and related data sources in the academic context. For OAI-PMH Data Providers, the acquisition via BASE is a mosaic piece that contributes to the global visibility of the repository content and the source itself. At the same time, BASE as an OAI service provider is dependent on the quality of the interfaces provided (especially OAI-PMH). This applies to the technical accessibility and stability and is particularly true for the metadata provided, which form the basis for the qualitative processing of search queries and the display of results. In this respect, BASE can serve as a mirror of the global publication landscape and therefore offers recommendations and information for analysing and optimising the repository infrastructure with tools such as the source list, OAI-PMH Validator and the "Golden Rules" ("Goldene Regeln"). The BASE search engine has been productive since 2004 and currently indexes more than 11.400 data sources on a global basis. It currently (January 2024) covers 352 million publications, about two thirds of which are retrieved from repositories via OAI-PMH harvesting. BASE plays an important role in the repository community with its extensive experience and has contributed to the drafting of guidelines (DRIVER Guidelines, OpenAire Guidelines, DINI Certificate) and vocabulary preparations (COAR Vocabularies). This expertise has been incorporated into the so-called "Golden Rules" at BASE, which summarise basic recommendations in a catchy and pragmatic way and thus efficiently formulate and support the measures for qualitative visibility. Numerous communication channels with repository managers and communities (e.g. DSpace, Eprints, Opus, Goobi, MyCoRe, Invenio) have also contributed to the optimisation of interfaces. Such efforts are always of mutual benefit: BASE is not the only service using this interface. Thus, the quality of the sources benefits all members of the repository landscape, and the search service of BASE itself is optimised. At the end of the contribution, the above-mentioned quality features developed within the BASE framework will be presented and explained using specific examples.

Keywords: Repository; certificate; BASE; search engine

1. Einführung

BASE[1] ist eine global agierende wissenschaftliche Suchmaschine mit Fokus auf institutionelle Repositorien und verwandte Datenquellen im akademischen Kontext. Entstanden im Umfeld der OAI-Bewegung galt zudem dem Kontext von Open Access immer ein besonderes Augenmerk bei der Entwicklung.

BASE operiert überwiegend an der Schnittstelle von OAI-Service Providern und OAI-Data Providern. Dementsprechend sind die Randbedingungen dieser Kommunikation von besonderer Bedeutung für BASE und die darin erfassten Quellen. Für OAI-PMH Data Providern ist eine Erfassung via BASE ein relevanter Mosaikstein zur globalen Sichtbarkeit der Repositorien-Inhalte, aber auch des Repositoriums und der Institution, die es betreibt. Weitere Nachnutzungsdienste mit ähnlicher Ausrichtung im Hinblick auf Sichtbarkeit sind einerseits Verzeichnisse (Registries) auf regionaler, nationaler oder internationaler Ebene wie OpenDOAR[2] oder der Open Archives Initiative OAI[3] und andererseits Aggregatoren und mit BASE vergleichbare Suchinstrumente wie OpenAIRE[4] und CORE[5].

Von der Seite des OAI Service Providers betrachtet ist BASE auf die Auffindbarkeit und, wenn diese erfolgt ist, auf die Qualität der bereitgestellten Schnittstellen (speziell OAI-PMH[6]) und der damit transportierten Inhalte in besonderer Weise angewiesen. Das gilt vordergründig für die technische Erreichbarkeit und Stabilität dieser Schnittstellen, weil damit zunächst die Grundlage für die Datenabholung geschaffen wird. Ein besonderer Fokus liegt auf Umfang und Qualität der gelieferten Metadaten, da diese die Basis für die Indexierung und damit für die spätere qualitative Bearbeitung der Suchanfragen und der Ergebnisanzeige bilden.

An dieser Stelle sollte erwähnt werden, dass vor dem Indexieren – und dieses Vorgehen gilt für alle Suchmaschinen – eine breite Palette von Aktivitäten zum Reparieren, Anpassen, Erweitern und Normalisieren der Metadaten stattfindet. Das beinhaltet bei BASE Fehlerbehebungen wie das Entfernen einzelner problematischer Datensätze, Zeichensatzkorrekturen und die Entfernung von Dateiformatfehlern. Die Umsetzung des jeweiligen Metadatenformats (insbesondere beim „unscharfen" Dublin Core-Format) bedeutet potentiell immer die Behandlung proprietärer Festlegungen (nicht immer findet sich z. B. die URL zum Dokument im <dc:identifier>-

---

1 Bielefeld Academic Search Engine: https://www.base-search.net/
2 Directory of Open Access Repositories: https://v2.sherpa.ac.uk/opendoar/
3 https://www.openarchives.org/
4 https://www.openaire.eu/
5 https://core.ac.uk/
6 Open Archives Initiative Protocol for Metadata Harvesting: http://www.openarchives.org/pmh/

Feld), die gegebenenfalls in diesem Schritt korrigiert werden. Bei der Normalisierung werden verschiedene Vokabulare (Standarddefinitionen, aber auch durch eigene Auswertungen abgeleitete Mapping-Tabellen) in festgelegte interne Datenschemata überführt. Mit Text-Mining-Methoden werden dafür geeignete Informationen identifiziert und separat abgelegt wie DOIs, ORCID-iDs und andere Identifier. In einem dreistufigen Verfahren wird der Open-Access-Status aus Angaben zum Repositorium, gegebenenfalls aus Set-Informationen, einem Open-Access-Status-Vokabular oder einer Lizenzangabe abgeleitet und in einem eigenen Feld abgelegt. Die breite Vielfalt der unterschiedlichen Festlegungen führt dazu, dass in BASE für jede Datenquelle ein individueller Pre-Processing-Schritt vorgenommen wird. Ergänzt werden dann bei jedem Satz Informationen, die aus den gesammelten Meta-Informationen zur Datenquelle erhoben werden. Dazu gehören Attribute wie Land und Kontinent und der interne Bezeichner der Quelle, so dass diese Aspekte auch im Zusammenhang mit dem Dokument abfragbar sind. Gleichzeitig können Herkunft und Kontext des Dokuments in den Ergebnislisten über die Information zur Datenquelle näher beschrieben werden. Ein beträchtlicher Teil dieser Vorarbeiten lässt sich in den Möglichkeiten der erweiterten Suchmaske, den angebotenen Facetten zur Suchverfeinerung und letztlich auch in der Ergebnisanzeige wiederfinden. So zeigt die nächste Abbildung die zur jeweiligen Datenquelle in der Trefferliste abrufbare Metainformation.

Datenlieferant: GAMS - Geisteswissenschaftliches Asset Management System (Zentrum für Informationsmodellierung, Universität Graz)
GAMS - Humanities' Asset Management System (Austrian Centre for Digital Humanities, University of Graz)

- URL: http://gams.uni-graz.at/
- Kontinent: Europa
- Land: at
- Breiten- und Längengrad: 47.077787 / 15.449913 (Google Maps | OpenStreetMap)
- Anzahl der Dokumente: 34.896
- Open Access: 34.896 (100%)
- Typ: Digitale Sammlung
- System: Fedora
- Datenlieferant in BASE seit: 2015-05-06
- BASE URL: https://www.base-search.net/Search/Results?q=coll:ftunivgrazgams

Abb. 1: BASE-Zusatzinformation zur Datenquelle in der Ergebnisliste

Mit der Gesamtheit der erfassten Datenquellen als Grundlage kann BASE als ein Spiegel der globalen Publikationslandschaft dienen und bietet mit Tools wie Quellenliste, OAI-PMH-Validator und den sogenannten „Goldene Regeln"-Empfehlungen[7] („Golden Rules") Service-Angebote und Informationen zur detaillierten Analyse der potentiellen sowie der bereits erfassten Datenquellen. Damit wird auch eine Grundlage zur Optimierung der Repositorien-Infrastruktur geliefert, die sowohl in der Startphase bei den vorbereitenden Aktivitäten als auch nach der Bereitstellung zum nachträglichen Feintuning Verwendung finden kann.

Um den Entwicklungen im Bereich der Repositorien Rechnung zu tragen und das Serviceangebot aktuell zu halten, ist BASE darauf angewiesen, neue Entwicklungen zu berücksichtigen. Zuletzt waren das Features wie das Open-Access Boosting (Open-Access-Publikationen werden in den Suchergebnissen höher gerankt) und die gesonderte Behandlung und Bereitstellung für die Suchanfragen von DOI, OA-Status, Lizenzangaben und auch ORCID-Identifier. Die umfangreiche Ausweitung auf Crossref-Quellen[8] für akademische Inhalte und die Anreicherung von Open-Access-Links via unpaywall[9] zeigt auch, dass neue Schnittstellen genutzt werden, wenn diese wertvolle Zusatzinformationen liefern können.

2. BASE, Suchindex und globales Discovery-System

Die Suchmaschine BASE ist seit 2004 produktiv und indexiert 2024 mehr als 11.400 Datenquellen auf globaler Basis. Erfasst werden aktuell (Januar 2024) 352 Millionen Publikationen und davon werden ca. zwei Drittel via OAI-PMH-Harvesting von Repositorien abgeholt. BASE spielt mit seinen umfassenden Praxiserfahrungen[10] eine gewichtige Rolle in der Repositorien-Community und hat auf dieser Grundlage auch bei der Abfassung von Guidelines (DRIVER Guidelines[11], OpenAIRE Guidelines[12], DINI-Zertifikat[13]) und Vokabular-Vorbereitungen (COAR Vocabularies[14]) mitgearbeitet. Ganz konkret bezogen auf die BASE-Anforderungen ist diese Expertise in die „Goldenen Regeln" eingeflossen, die grundlegende Empfehlungen eingängig und praxisorientiert zusammenfassen und damit in effizienter und pragmatischer Weise die konkreten Maßnahmen zur qualitativen Sichtbarkeit formulieren und

7 https://www.base-search.net/about/de/faq_oai.php
8 https://www.crossref.org/
9 https://unpaywall.org/
10 Pieper, D.; Summann, F. (2015)
11 Vanderfeesten, M.; Summann, F.; Slabbertje, M. (2008)
12 https://guidelines.openaire.eu/en/latest/
13 Müller, U.; Scholze, F.; Vierkant, P. et al. (2019)
14 Controlled Vocabularies for Repositories: https://vocabularies.coar-repositories.org/

unterstützen. Zahlreiche Kommunikationskanäle mit einzelnen Repositorien-Manager:innen und auch -Communities (z. B. DSpace, EPrints, Opus, Goobi, MyCoRe, Invenio) haben zudem zur Optimierung der Schnittstellen dieser technischen Systeme beigetragen.

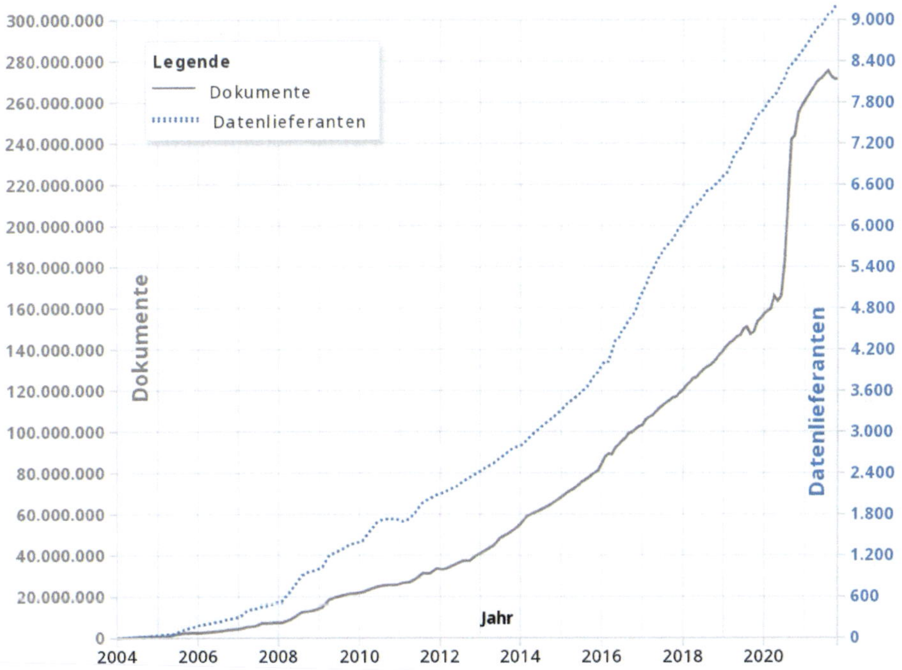

Abb. 2: Die Entwicklung der BASE-Suchmaschine seit 2004

3. Die Goldenen Regeln – aus Praxiserfahrungen kondensierte Empfehlungen

BASE indexiert grundsätzlich alle Quellen mit wissenschaftlichen Inhalten (Zeitschriften, Repositorien, Digitale Sammlungen, Forschungsdatenrepositorien etc.), die über eine OAI-Schnittstelle verfügen und die Metadaten über OAI-PMH liefern. Entsprechend ist die Ausgestaltung dieser Schnittstelle entscheidend, ob und wie die auf diesem Wege erfassten Dokumente optimal und vollständig in BASE präsentiert werden.

OAI-PMH (OAI Protocol for Metadata Harvesting) hat inzwischen eine mehr als 20-jährige Geschichte hinter sich, und natürlicherweise haben sich Probleme[15] mit dem Protokoll herausgestellt und in mancher Hinsicht auch verstärkt. Ein Grundaspekt ist, dass das OAI-PMH-Protokoll nicht web-nativ ist. Das führt dazu, dass es von der technischen Web-Entwicklung entkoppelt ist und – noch ungünstiger – weniger Beachtung bei der Nutzung findet. So fällt es weit weniger auf, wenn es Probleme mit der Schnittstelle gibt. Dies könnte auch der wesentliche Grund sein, warum Google Scholar nach anfänglichen Experimenten mit OAI-PMH auf das Google-übliche Web-Crawling setzte. Der zweite große Problembereich ist die Anfälligkeit für Unterbrechungen und Ausfälle. Zwar erlaubt das Protokoll ein Wiederaufsetzen, was in der Praxis allerdings in den meisten Fällen wirkungslos ist und nur bei externen Verbindungsproblemen hilft. Oftmals hingegen sind die Ursachen interne Probleme (OAI-Meldung „Internal Error") wie Zeichensatzprobleme einzelner Datensätze, was zur nicht überbrückbaren Wiederholung der Fehlersituation führt. Zur Verarbeitung größerer Datenmengen werden die Schnittstellenaufrufe aufgeteilt und sequentiell durchgeführt. Der Datenprovider liefert einen Resumption Token in seiner Antwort, der beim nächsten Aufruf als Parameter mitgeliefert wird und somit als Kontrollelement zur korrekten Abwicklung verwendet wird. Diese Technik zur Weiterschaltung erweist sich als unzuverlässig und vor allem im Fehlerfall als nicht umgehbar. Das hat zur Folge, dass ein immer wiederkehrender Absturz nur in Ausnahmefällen (z. B. durch Editierung des Resumption Tokens, was in manchen Fällen möglich ist) überwunden werden kann. Immerhin kommt eine andere Fehlerquelle recht selten vor – nämlich die Endlosschleife, bei der meist immer die gleiche Antwortdatei ohne ein reguläres Ende ausgegeben wird. Diese Situation ist immer mit der Gefahr verbunden, dass die Festplattenkapazitäten des Datenabrufers zur Neige gehen. Die Probleme haben sich durch die immer größer werdenden Repositorien und die damit verbundenen längeren Laufzeiten des Harvesting-Vorgangs deutlich verstärkt.

15 Tennant, R. (2004), S. 32.

Trotz der offensichtlichen Schwachpunkte des Protokolls haben sich die Weiterentwicklungen wie OAI-ORE[16] und ResourceSync[17] bisher nicht durchsetzen können. Aus dieser rückblickenden Sicht scheint es doch voreilig gewesen zu sein, die Option einer weiteren Protokollversion 3.0 aufzugeben. Da das Protokoll mit seiner Einfachheit durchaus in mancher Hinsicht besser ist als sein Ruf, hätte dieser Schritt ein pragmatischer Ansatz zur Behebung der gravierendsten Fehler sein können. Neben den technischen Problemen wäre die Festlegung eines alternativen Pflichtmetadatenformats mit weniger „Unschärfe" als Dublin Core sicherlich eine weitere Option für eine wesentliche Verbesserung gewesen.

Unabhängig davon hat es sich für BASE als notwendig erwiesen, unablässig auf Entwicklungen im Bereich Repositorien zu reagieren und diese zu integrieren. Dazu gehörten die Erweiterung zusätzlicher Publikationsservertypen wie Digitale Sammlungen oder CRIS-Systeme, aufkommende neue Metadatenformate wie OAI DataCite (oai_datacite) und auch alternative Metadatenschnittstellen wie Crossref.

Vor diesem Hintergrund lassen sich Empfehlungen zu Einstellungsoptionen und Probleme mit OAI-Schnittstellen auf drei unterschiedliche Bereiche aufteilen:

- Protokollfehler und technische Kommunikationsprobleme
- Metadaten-Festlegungen und deren Defizite und Unschärfen
- Allgemeine Kommunikationsregeln

Im Folgenden sollen diese Punkte näher betrachtet werden. Die Betrachtung folgt im Wesentlichen den Goldenen Regeln, ausführliche Details sind dort zu finden.

3.1. OAI-Schnittstelle allgemein

Die OAI-Schnittstelle eines Repositoriums sollte frei zugänglich und stabil sein und konstant antworten. Die Anfrage nach ListRecords im Pflichtformat oai_dc liefert Ergebnisse, ohne dass es dabei zu einem Absturz oder einem Ausgabefehler kommt. In regelmäßigen Abständen sollte die Funktionsfähigkeit der OAI-Schnittstelle, z. B. per Browser, geprüft werden.

16 Open Archives Initiative Object Exchange and Reuse: https://www.openarchives.org/ore/
17 ResourceSync Framework Specification (ANSI/NISO Z39.99-2017): http://www.openarchives.org/rs/1.1/resourcesync

Laut Protokoll ist das Format oai_dc zwingend notwendig, was aus Effizienzgründen – alle optionalen Metadatenformate sind nur in eingeschränktem Umfang vertreten – zur Folge hat, dass meist oai_dc, also Dublin Core, für die Weiterverarbeitung benutzt wird.

Ein recht häufiger Fehler entsteht, wenn das gelieferte XML-Format der Datei formal nicht korrekt ist und dadurch die gesamte Datei nicht weiterverarbeitet werden kann. In diesem Fall kann die Datenstruktur nicht via Standard-Parser-Verfahren analysiert werden. Oftmals ist dieser Fehler verbunden mit falscher Zeichencodierung des Dokuments. Auch diese Eigenschaft kann durch Überprüfung der Schnittstelle im Browser betrachtet werden.

Mit Hilfe des sogenannten inkrementellen Harvestings, wie es im Protokoll über den Parameter ‚from' unterstützt wird, rufen Service Provider nur die Ergänzungen und Veränderungen der Metadaten ab einem durch den Parameter festgelegten Zeitpunkt auf Datensatzbasis ab. Bei der inzwischen sehr großen Zahl von Repositorien mit ihren teilweise hohen Satzzahlen ist es für OAI-Service Provider üblicherweise unverzichtbar, diese Technik zu verwenden, um das aufwändige periodische Komplett-Harvesting zu vermeiden. Dabei müssen die gelöschten Datensätze per Deleting Strategy ‚transient' oder ‚persistent' ausgeliefert werden. Immer wieder kommt es allerdings zu mehr oder weniger umfangreichen Abweichungen, was dazu führt, dass bei BASE periodisch ein sogenannter Refresh vorgenommen wird. Damit wird vermieden, dass neue Datensätze, Korrekturen oder Löschungen fehlen.

3.2. Allgemeine Konfigurationseinstellungen

Bei jeder ListRecords-Antwort einer OAI-Schnittstelle sollten im Idealfall 50 – 1.000 Datensätze ausgegeben werden. Der sogenannte Resumption Token am Ende einer OAI-PMH-Antwortdatei sollte funktionieren und die nächsten Datensätze ausliefern. Werden weniger als 50 Datensätze pro Seite ausgeliefert, führt dies zu entsprechend zahlreichen einzelnen Aufrufen mit entsprechend erhöhtem Kommunikationsaufwand. Mehr als 1.000 Datensätze pro Seite machen dagegen die gelieferten Dateien verhältnismäßig groß und erhöhen damit oftmals das Risiko von Abbrüchen beim Harvesten der Datensätze. Funktioniert der Resumption Token-Mechanismus nicht, ist eine vollständige Indexierung aller Datensätze des Repositoriums nicht möglich.

3.3. Inhalte und Metadatenqualität

Von besonderer Bedeutung für die Qualität der Suche und der Informationsbeschreibung der nachnutzenden Dienste ist die Qualität der gelieferten Metadaten. Insbesondere wird mit der Anwendung von bibliographischer Expertise und Datenpflege (data curation) die Grundlage geschaffen, die die Sichtbarkeit des Repositoriums und seiner Inhalte von automatischen Crawling-Techniken und der Extraktion differenzierter Felder von Webseiten qualitativ unterscheiden lässt. Das gilt insbesondere für die inhaltliche Zuordnung der Felder, aber auch für Umfang und Qualität der jeweiligen Feldinhalte.

3.4. Zeichenkodierung

Probleme gibt es immer wieder mit der Zeichenkodierung, sowohl im internen Datenfluss (was verschiedentlich zu systeminternen Abbrüchen bei der Datenbereitstellung via OAI-PMH führt) als auch beim ausgelieferten XML-Format, was zu Parser-Problemen führen kann. Daher sollten alle Inhalte in der OAI-Schnittstelle (insbesondere die textbasierten Felder Titel, Autor:innennamen, Abstracts) korrekt in UTF-8 kodiert sein. Andere Kodierungen oder doppelte UTF8-Kodierungen erzeugen Fehler in der Indexierung und als Folge auch Fehler bei der Darstellung von Suchergebnissen.

3.5. Vollständigkeit und Qualität der Metadaten

Protokoll bedingt wird von Service Providern überwiegend das Standard- und OAI-PMH-Pflichtformat oai_dc (Dublin Core) verwendet, da jeder Data Provider es anbieten muss und es daher aus Effizienzgründen für alle Datenanbieter Verwendung finden kann. Als allgemeine Anforderung kann festgehalten werden, dass jeder Datensatz einer OAI-Schnittstelle möglichst vollständige Metadaten zu einem Dokument liefern und dabei nach Möglichkeit standardisierte Vokabulare verwenden sollte. Ganz wesentlich – und in gewisser Hinsicht ein K.o.-Kriterium – ist die Angabe einer funktionierenden URL, die auf das Dokument weist, üblicherweise in <dc:identifier>. Nur dann ist möglich, aus den Suchergebnissen einen Link zum Repositorium und dem darin enthaltenen Dokument bereitzustellen.

Allgemein gilt: Je vollständiger die Metadaten sind, umso besser werden die zugehörigen Dokumente aus dem Repositorium in den Suchumgebungen der jeweiligen Service Provider auffindbar sein. Von besonderer Bedeutung ist die Verwendung von standardisierten Vokabularen, um Dokumente sprachübergreifend z. B. einem eindeutigen und korrekten Dokumenttyp oder Nachnutzungsrecht zuzuordnen.

Dublin Core ist das OAI-PMH-Pflichtdatenformat, was gewisse Vorteile für die universelle und effiziente Bereitstellung und Nutzung mit sich bringt. Erkauft wird das allerdings mit einer großen Unschärfe in der Verwendung der Felder und der Präsentation der Feldinhalte.

3.6. Hinweise zu einzelnen Metadaten-Feldern (Dublin Core)

Die folgende Auflistung zeigt eine Liste der Dublin-Core-Felder[18] nach Relevanz (Werte sind Muss, Soll und Kann) aus Sicht der BASE-Suchmaschine:

Information	Element in oai_dc	Angabe
URL der Publikation	<dc:identifier>	Muss
Titel	<dc:title>	Soll
Autor	<dc:creator>	Soll
Publikationstyp	<dc:type>	Soll
Erscheinungsdatum	<dc:date>	Soll
Sprache des Dokuments	<dc:language>	Soll
Zugriffs- und Nachnutzungsrechte	<dc:rights>	Soll
Quellenangabe/Zitation	<dc:source>	Soll
Sonstige an der Publikation Beteiligte	<dc:contributor>	Kann
Dateiformat	<dc:format>	Kann
Inhaltsbeschreibung	<dc:description>	Kann
Schlagwörter	<dc:subject>	Kann
Verlag	<dc:publisher>	Kann
Verwandte Dokumente	<dc:relation>	Kann
Inhaltliche Abgrenzung	<dc:coverage>	Kann

Konkret lässt sich im Hinblick auf die Dublin-Core-Felder festhalten:

Bereits weiter oben ist auf die elementare Notwendigkeit einer URL als Link zum Dokument hingewiesen worden. Es kommt durchaus vor, dass gar kein Link zum Dokument oder zur Landing Page angeliefert wird oder nur ein (lokaler) Identifier, mit dem sich in den meisten Fällen und mit einem gewissen Aufwand ein Link konstruieren ließe. Effizient sind solche individuellen Lösungen aber nicht. Ein weiteres, häufiger vorkommendes Problem ist es, dass im Feld <dc:identifier> Links zum Dokument zu finden sind, die nicht funktionieren – oftmals verursacht durch eine Fehlkonfiguration im zugrundeliegenden Publikationssystem.

Mit Blick auf wissenschaftliche Publikationen und ihre Einordnung und Bewertung sind Informationen in den Feldern Titel <dc:title>, Autor:in (<dc:creator>, <dc:contributor>), Erscheinungsdatum (<dc:date>) und, wenn vorhanden, zur Zitatangabe insbesondere bei Zeitschriftentiteln (<dc:source>) von besonderer Relevanz und

18 Siehe https://www.base-search.net/about/de/faq_oai.php

begründen die Qualität der Metadaten und damit auch die Sichtbarkeit des einzelnen wissenschaftlichen Dokuments.

Persistente Identifier (z. B. DOI, ISBN, ISSN etc.) sollten in <dc:identifier> ausgegeben werden und sind für die Verlinkung von formal oder inhaltlich verbundenen Objekten und das Data Enrichment (in dem aus externen Quellen zusätzliche Daten zu dem über den Identifier zugeordneten Datenobjekt eingespielt werden) von besonderer Wichtigkeit.

Es sei darauf hingewiesen, dass Dublin Core-Felder grundsätzlich wiederholbar sind und daher keine Aufführung mehrerer Attribute (Autoren, Klassifikationscodes) in einem einzigen DC-Feld notwendig ist. Auf der anderen Seite kann bei Datenverbund-Strukturen (Attribute wie E-Mail-Adresse, ORCID-iD oder Affiliationsangaben bei Autor:innen) die Verwendung eines Separatorzeichens, meist ein Semikolon, zur Trennung der jeweiligen Abschnitte sinnvoll sein.

Vokabular-gestützte Felder erlauben eine inhaltsscharfe, generische und einheitliche Verwendung der auftretenden Terme in der Suche, z.B. durch trennscharfe Auswahlboxen und eine präzise Facettierung der Suchergebnisse. Erfahrungsgemäß enthalten solche Felder in der Praxis eine Vielzahl unterschiedlicher Terme, teilweise aus proprietären, oft lokal definierten Vokabularen, teilweise frei wählbar und häufig in verschiedenen Sprachen.

Das gilt ganz besonders für die Felder <dc:date> (Erscheinungsjahr), <dc:language> (Sprache), <dc:type> (Publikationstyp), <dc:rights> für die Lizenzangaben und den Open Access-Status.

Das Feld <dc:date> sollte nur einmal belegt sein. Wenn kein konkretes Erscheinungsdatum vorliegt, sollte geschätzt werden.

Sprache des Dokuments <dc:language>

Angaben zur Sprache eines Dokuments nach ISO 639[19] (2- oder 3-Letter-Code) sollten im Feld <dc:language> zur Verfügung gestellt werden. Angaben zur Sprache werden in BASE für Dokumente ansonsten nicht oder fehlerhaft ausgegeben und die Einschränkung auf eine Sprache funktioniert für die Quelle nicht korrekt.

---

19 ISO 639 Code Tables: https://iso639-3.sil.org/code_tables/639/data

Zugriffs- und Nachnutzungsrechte <dc:rights>

Zugriffsrechte (Access-Status)

Im Feld <dc:rights> sollten Zugangsinformationen zum Volltext nach dem info-eu-repo-Access-Rights-Vokabular oder dem COAR-Access-Rights-Vokabular enthalten sein. Für die Endnutzer:innen ist die Information über den Zugang zu einem Dokument in der Trefferliste von besonderer Bedeutung. Stehen diese Angaben nicht oder nur unzureichend zur Verfügung, werden Informationen zum Zugang von Dokumenten unvollständig, gar nicht oder fehlerhaft ausgegeben und die Einschränkung auf bestimmte Zugangsarten funktioniert für die Quelle nicht richtig.

Nachnutzungsrechte (Lizenzen)

Den Autor:innen sollte die Möglichkeit angeboten werden, Dokumente unter eine Lizenz zu stellen. Dabei sollten möglichst weit verbreitete Lizenzen wie die Creative-Commons-Lizenzen zur Auswahl angeboten werden. Die entsprechende Lizenz sollte in der OAI-Schnittstelle in einem weiteren <dc:rights>-Feld angeliefert werden.

Stehen diese Angaben nicht oder nur unzureichend zur Verfügung, werden Informationen zur Nachnutzung von Dokumenten unvollständig, gar nicht oder fehlerhaft ausgegeben und die Einschränkung auf Nachnutzungsmöglichkeiten funktioniert für die jeweilige Quelle nicht korrekt.

Quellenangabe / Zitation <dc:source>

Angaben zur Quelle oder zur Zitation (insbesondere bei Artikeln, Titel, Band und Heft der Zeitschrift) stehen bevorzugt in <dc:source>. Dabei sollte insbesondere darauf geachtet werden, die ISSN der enthaltenden Zeitschrift anzugeben.

Diese Angaben ermöglichen es Nutzer:innen, die Dokumente besser zu finden und damit auch besser zitieren zu können.

3.7. Über BASE und OAI hinaus: Organisatorische Vorbereitungen

Kontaktpersonen

In den Identify-Angaben der OAI-Schnittstelle ist im Feld adminEmail eine E-Mail-Adresse anzugeben, über die eine Kontaktaufnahme zum technischen Betreiber der OAI-Schnittstelle möglich ist. Zudem ist es empfehlenswert, auf der Homepage des Repositoriums eine (funktionierende) E-Mail-Adresse zur Verfügung zu stellen, über die die direkte Kontaktaufnahme zum Betreiber gewährleistet ist. Nur wenn die E-Mail-Adressen funktionieren und E-Mails gelesen und beantwortet werden, kann bei Problemen oder Fragen Kontakt mit dem/der Repositorium-Verantwortlichen aufgenommen werden.

Kontakt-Bereich mit aktiver E-Mail-Adresse

Die Adress-Information im Identify-Response ist auf die technischen Details der OAI-Schnittstelle ausgerichtet. Für allgemeine Fragen und für Endnutzer:innenanfragen sollte von der Startseite ein Kontakt-Bereich verlinkt werden (Kontakt/Contact). Dort ist die funktionierende E-Mail-Adresse des/der inhaltlichen und/oder technischen Verantwortlichen anzugeben. E-Mails, die an diese Adressen geschickt werden, sollten von den Verantwortlichen regelmäßig gelesen und beantwortet werden. Fehlt ein Kontakt-Bereich oder werden E-Mails nicht gelesen, ist eine Kontaktaufnahme kaum möglich, wenn es bei der Indexierung des Datenlieferanten zu Problemen kommt oder sich Rückfragen ergeben. Dies kann dazu führen, dass die betreffende Quelle nicht indexiert werden kann.

Web-Adresse des Repositoriums

Erfahrungsgemäß sollte die Startseite möglichst unter einer eigenen Subdomain (ohne Port und Unterverzeichnis) angeboten werden. Jede Änderung am Port oder einem Unterverzeichnis führt dazu, dass die Links zu dieser Quelle nicht mehr funktionieren, oft auch die damit verbundene sogenannte OAI base URL. Vermieden werden sollten auch Versionsnummern in der Subdomain oder Verzeichnisnamen (z.B. ojs3.domain.de oder ojs.domain.de/ojs-3/). Wie zuvor erwähnt, führt jede derartige Änderung an der URL dazu, dass Links auf die Quelle nicht mehr erreichbar sind.

Ändert sich etwas an der Internet-Adresse des Datenlieferanten (und sei es nur ein Zeichen), sollte möglichst von der alten Adresse eine Weiterleitung auf die neue gesetzt werden. Es sollte auch darauf geachtet werden, dass die OAI-Schnittstelle durch Setzen einer Weiterleitung weiterhin erreichbar ist.

Üblicherweise führen Fehler in der Erreichbarkeit dazu, dass diese Quellen von den Service Providern gelöscht werden.

Der Name des Repositoriums oder der Titel einer Zeitschrift sollte immer im Quelltext der Webseite an einer Stelle im Klartext zu finden sein, entweder im <title>, der Überschrift (<h1>) oder als Alternativtext eines Logos. Damit ist das Branding des Datenanbieters gewährleistet und zugleich wird mit dieser Information der wissenschaftliche Kontext transparenter.

Startseite auch in Englisch

Für das Repositorium sollte zumindest die Startseite auch in englischer Sprache angeboten werden. Die Repositorien-Community ist global ausgerichtet und durch einen Internetauftritt in englischer Sprache wird einem internationalen Publikum ein unkomplizierter Zugriff auf die Inhalte ermöglicht. Eine englischsprachige Startseite führt auch zu einer besseren Auffindbarkeit der Quelle und ihrer Inhalte in allen damit indexierenden Suchdiensten.

Informationen über grundlegende Änderungen beim Repositorium

Sollten sich der Name des Datenlieferanten oder die URL der OAI-Schnittstelle ändern (z. B. durch den Umzug auf ein anderes technisches System), sollte dieses in den einschlägigen Verzeichnissen mitgeteilt werden, im Falle von BASE über das zugehörige Kontaktformular.

Sichtbarkeit der Quellen und Indexierung in Suchmaschinen

Die Quelle sollte in den OAI- und Repositorien-Verzeichnissen angemeldet sein (z. B. OpenDOAR, ROAR[20], re3data[21], openarchives.org, BASE, aber auch nationale und community-bezogene Auflistungen) und es sollte auf die Aktualisierung bei Änderungen der Angaben geachtet werden.

Auf diese Weise sind die Quelle und damit auch die Schnittstelle weltweit sichtbar und es ermöglicht gegebenenfalls allen interessierten Suchmaschinen die Indexierung von Dokumenten des Repositoriums.

Im Rahmen des Quellen-Discovery werden diese Verzeichnisse z. B. von BASE automatisch (via API oder durch Text Mining) in regelmäßigen Abständen gescannt und neue Einträge gefunden.

Die gute Auffindbarkeit einer Quelle in allgemeinen und wissenschaftlichen Suchmaschinen führt dazu, dass Dokumente aus der Quelle leichter zu finden sind und häufiger abgerufen und genutzt werden.

---

20 Registry of Open Access Repositories: http://roar.eprints.org/
21 Registry of Research Data Repositories: https://www.re3data.org/

4. Die globale Repositorienlandschaft – Analysen aus BASE-Sicht

Im Falle der Suchmaschine BASE liegen die Metadaten in der Rohfassung (nach dem Harvesting-Vorgang) im Datenspeicher, zugleich aber auch in normalisierter Form vor. So werden im Zuge der Normalisierung Datumsformate, Sprachangaben und Publikationstypen angepasst und Inhalte wie DOIs und ORCID-iDs extrahiert. Zudem werden Informationen aus internen und externen Datenquellen ergänzt. Dazu gehören Metainformationen zum Datenanbieter (insbesondere Ländercode, Bezeichnung und ROR-id) und von besonderer Relevanz die Open-Access-Status- und Linkinformationen von unpaywall. Diese Angaben werden vor dem Indexieren in einem speziellen Indexformat abgelegt und sind daher nach der Indexierung in transformierter Form im Index vorhanden und damit in komplexer Weise abfragbar. Dadurch sind direkte Analysen in den Daten möglich, die durch die umfassenden Suchmöglichkeiten im Index ergänzt und unterstützt werden können. Zusätzlich werden Metadaten zu den Repositorien selbst erfasst, um Hinweise zum wissenschaftlichen Kontext (Herkunft, publizierende Institution) insbesondere für die Endnutzer:innen, aber auch für Auswertungszwecke liefern zu können. Insgesamt können dadurch über Analysen umfangreiche Indikatoren[22] für die Repositorienlandschaft auf Länderebene, aber auch zum einzelnen Repositorium selbst geliefert werden.

Da viele der Informationen zu definierten Zeitpunkten abgespeichert werden, können derartige deskriptive Darstellungen über längere Zeiträume vorgenommen werden und es ist damit möglich, Entwicklungen über Timeline-Analysen aufzuzeigen. Im Folgenden sollen einige Auswertungen vorgestellt werden, die Aufschlüsse über die globale und nationale Repositorienlandschaft mit besonderem Fokus auf Österreich erlauben und auf diese Weise auch vergleichende Analysen ermöglichen. Die Auswertungen basieren sämtlich auf den Indexdaten der BASE-Suchmaschine in Kombination mit den im BASE-Kontext erfassten Metadaten der BASE-Datenquellen.

BASE operiert global und von daher kann die Suchmaschine auch Zahlen und Übersichten in Form von Weltkarten ausgeben. So zeigt die nächste Abbildung die Anzahl der Dokumente der Publikationsserver für alle Länder der Erde mit einem Wertebereich und zugeordneter Farbskala von blau (0 = niedrig) bis rot (1.000.000

22 Summann, F.; Czerniak, A.; Schirrwagen, J.; Pieper, D. (2020). S. 35.

und mehr = hoch). Deutlich erkennbar sind die Schwerpunkte in Europa, Nordamerika und Ozeanien, aber auch die starke Rolle der Staaten in Südamerika, China, Indien und Indonesien.

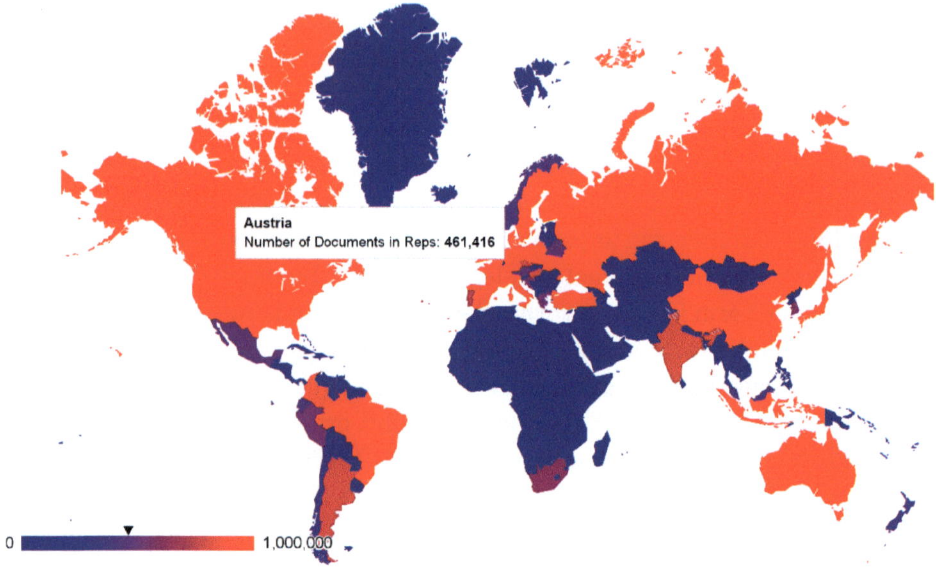

Abb. 3: Heatmap Anzahl Dokumente in Repositorien pro Land (Stand 1.10.2021)

Die folgende Zeitleistendarstellung zeigt die Anzahl neu indexierter Datenquellen pro Jahr seit 2004 für Europa, wobei man einige klare Tendenzen erkennen kann. Nach der ersten Ausbauphase bis 2008 folgt eine eher gleichmäßige Entwicklung, bis ab 2014 wieder eine Zunahme einsetzt. Das ist erklärbar einerseits durch die Ausweitung von Repositorien-Formen durch Digitale Sammlungen und Forschungsinformationssysteme und andererseits durch die zunehmende Integration von reinen bibliographischen Publikationsnachweisen ohne Volltextbereitstellung, wie es bei Publikationssystemen üblich ist.

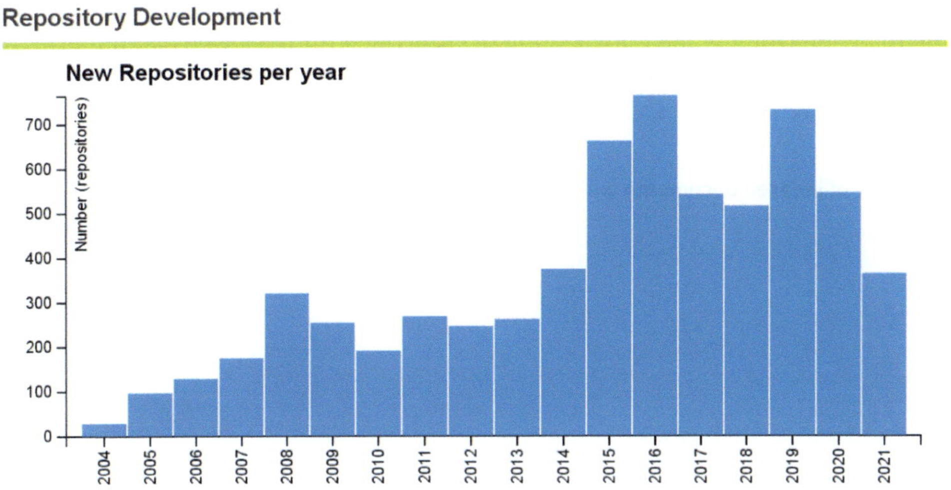

Abb. 4: Neu indexierte Datenquellen in BASE pro Jahr in Europa 2004 – 2021

Für Österreich zeigt sich im Vergleich eine zeitlich etwas andere Verteilung mit einigen Lücken in den betrachteten Jahren und einer zeitlichen Verschiebung der Anstiege.

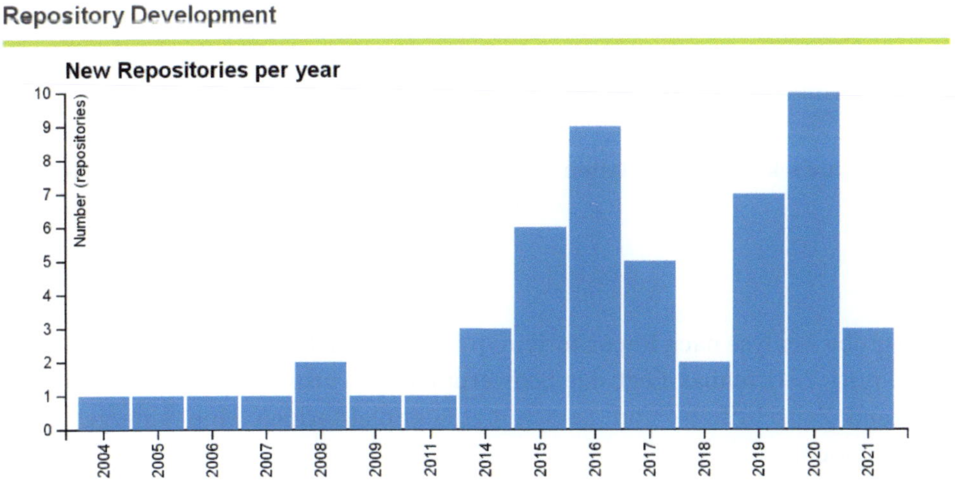

Abb. 5: Neu indexierte Datenquellen aus Österreich in BASE pro Jahr 2004 – 2021

Detaillierter in Bezug auf Anzahl der Repositorien und Anzahl der Dokumente zeigt die folgende Graphik die Entwicklung in Österreich für die jeweils kumulierte Anzahl der Repositorien und der darüber angebotenen Dokumente.

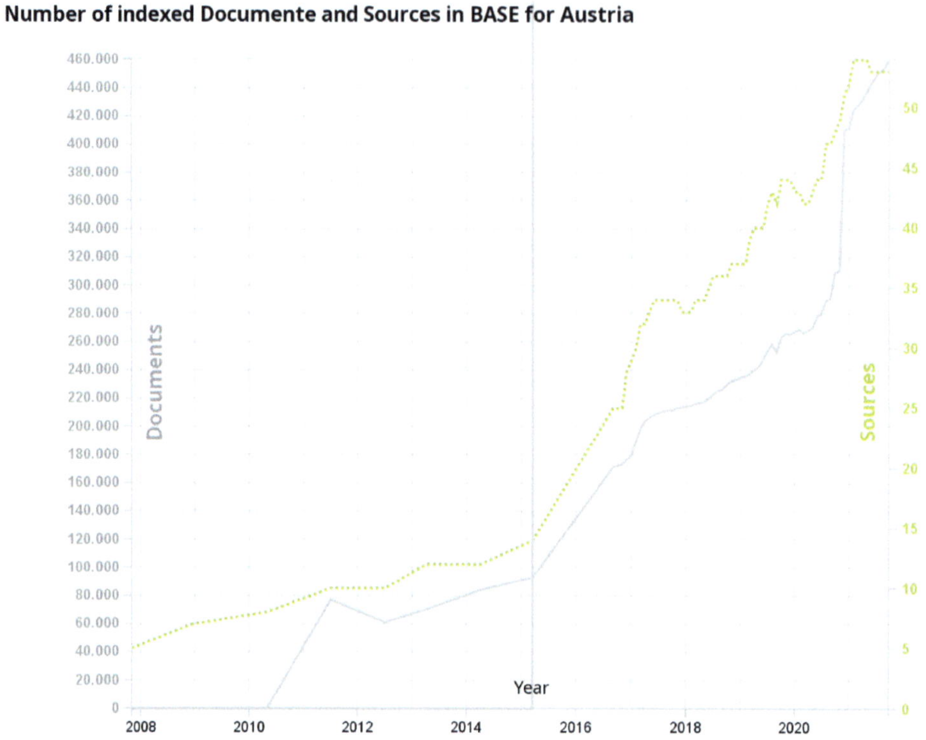

Abb. 6: Entwicklung Anzahl Datenquellen und Anzahl Dokumente im BASE Index aus Österreich

Eine grobe Analyse nach Repositorientyp für Österreich (Stand Oktober 2021) zeigt Abbildung 7. Offenbar liegt der Schwerpunkt auf institutionellen Repositorien, während Zeitschriften- und Forschungsdatenplattformen eine untergeordnete Rolle spielen.

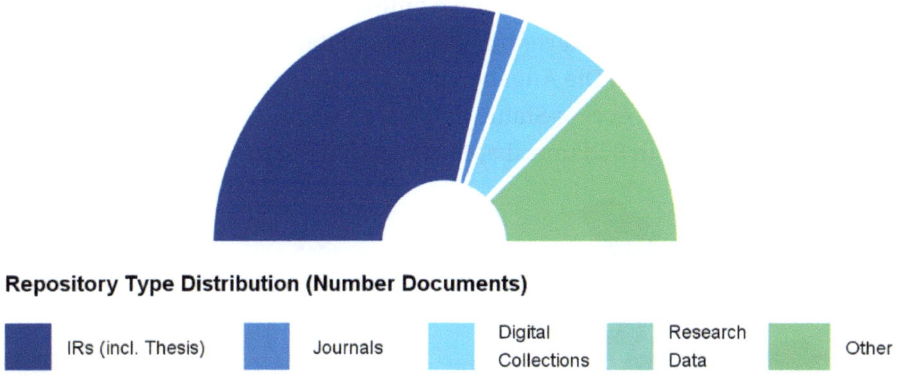

Abb. 7: Verteilung Anzahl Dokumente nach Repositorientyp in Österreich (Stand 01.10.2021)

In Deutschland sieht die Verteilung gleichmäßiger aus. Neben einem höheren Anteil von Zeitschriftenservern fällt auch die vergleichsweise hohe Anzahl von Forschungsdatenservern auf.

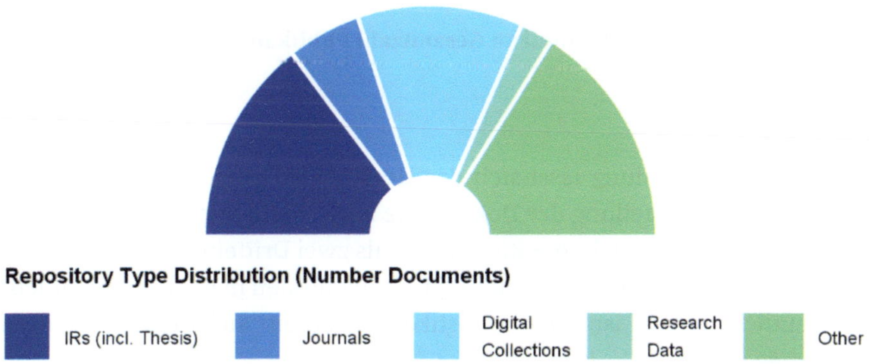

Abb. 8: Verteilung Anzahl Dokumente nach Repositorientyp in Deutschland (Stand 01.10.2021)

BASE versteht sich als Suchmaschine im Kontext der Open-Access-Bewegung. Die nächste Karte zeigt eine Weltkarte mit dem Prozentanteil von Open-Access-Publikationen in BASE pro Land. Die Angaben beruhen auf den normalisierten Angaben in <dc:rights> zum Open-Access-Status und zeigen deutlich den Einfluss von Open-Access-Strategien etwa in Südamerika, Portugal und Spanien.

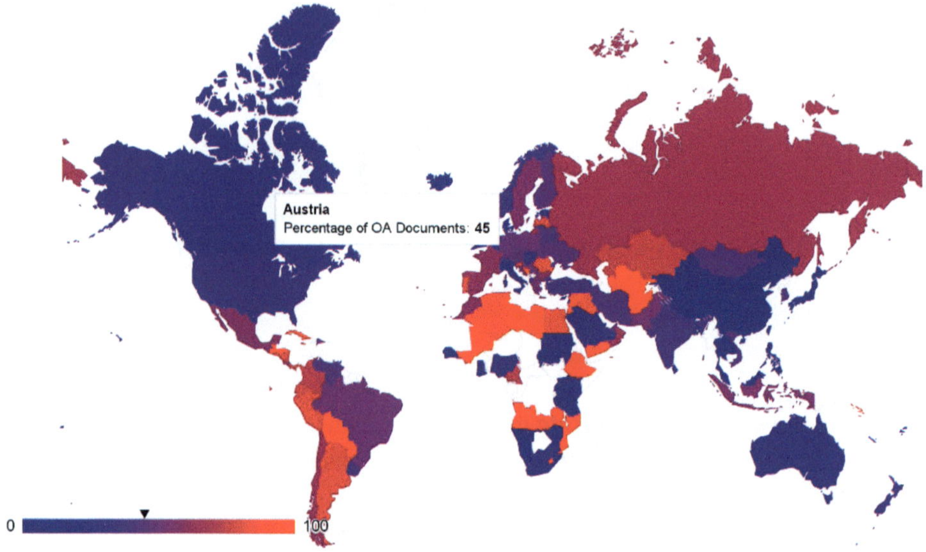

Abb. 9: Prozentualer OA-Anteil an Gesamtzahl Publikationen in BASE pro Land

In der nächsten Abbildung lässt sich der Unterschied zwischen der Schweiz und Österreich bei der Verteilung der Dokumente nach Publikationssprache erkennen. In Österreich liegen die Dokumente zu mehr als zwei Dritteln in deutscher Sprache vor, während in der Schweiz der Anteil für Publikationen in englischer Sprache mit 78 % deutlich höher ist. Die Statistiken basieren auf dem normalisierten <dc:language>-Feld.

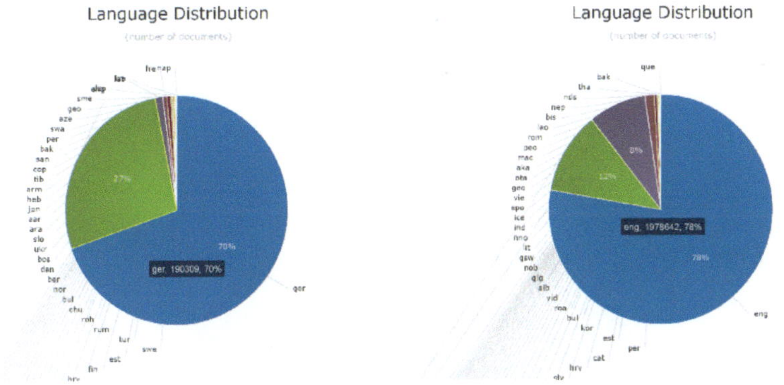

Abb. 10: Verteilung der Dokumente nach Sprache der Publikation (links Österreich, rechts Schweiz, Stand 01.10.2021)

Das nächste Diagramm zeigt die Verteilung der Publikationstypen in den Dokumenten der österreichischen Repositorien. Das dabei verwendete Vokabular ist in BASE aus einer statistischen Auswertung der vorkommenden Terme und ihrer Häufigkeit abgeleitet worden und findet sich auch in der erweiterten Suchmaske als Auswahl für den Suchaspekt „Dokumentart“ wieder.

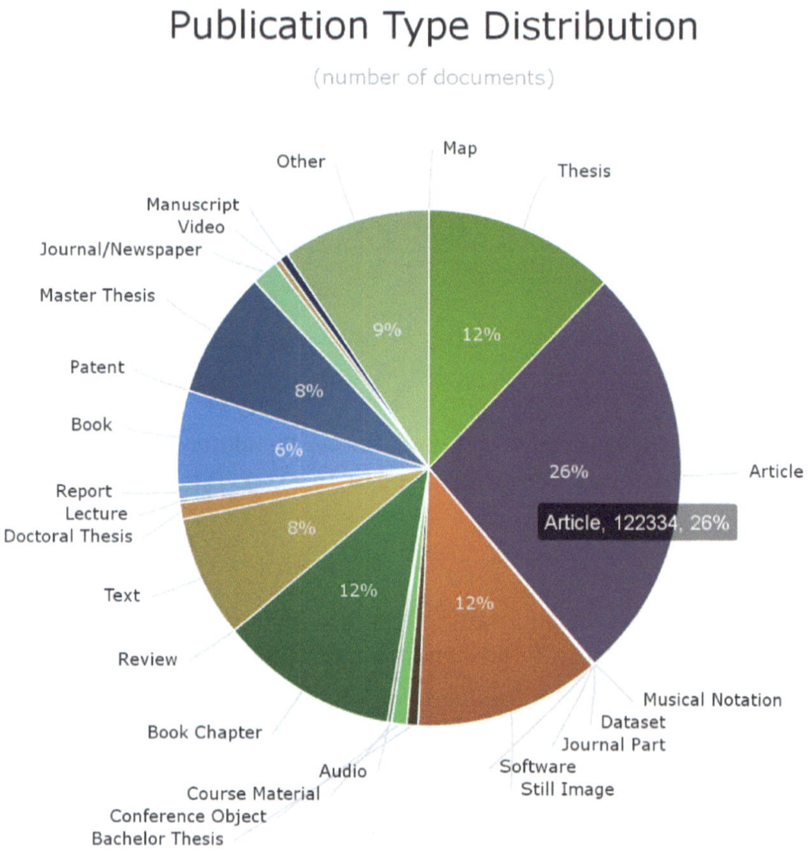

Abb. 11: Verteilung Dokumente nach Publikationstyp für Österreich (Stand 01.10.2021)

Zur Information über Nachnutzungsmöglichkeiten der Dokumente sind die Lizenzbedingungen relevant, die üblicherweise in <dc:rights> ausgegeben werden. Bei diesen Informationen ist der Umfang der verwandten Terme vergleichsweise stark normiert und daher relativ umfassend umzusetzen. Die nächste Graphik zeigt die Verteilung der verschiedenen Lizenzbedingungen und den Anteil solcher Metadatensätze an der Gesamtheit der Publikationen für Österreich im Oktober 2021.

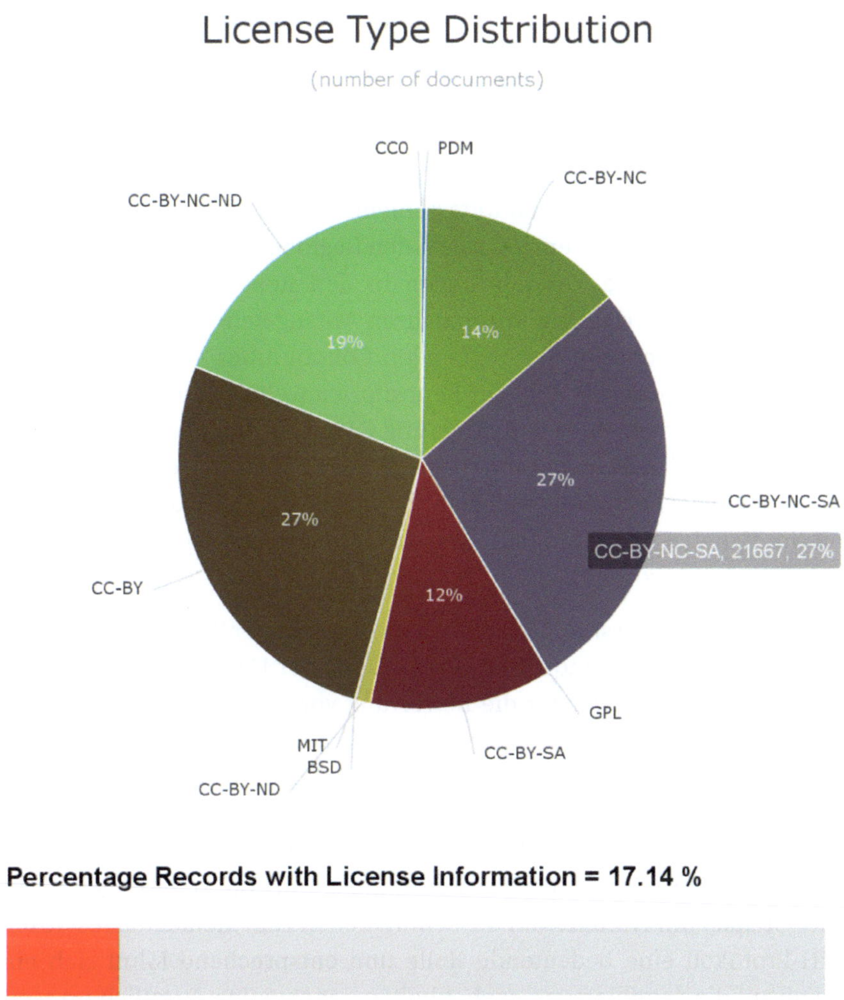

Abb. 12: Verteilung Lizenzbedingungen in österreichischen Repositorien in BASE (Stand 01.10.2021)

5. Fazit

Repositorien haben sich zu einer festen Größe in der globalen Publikations- und Informationsinfrastruktur entwickelt. Über die Jahre hat es immer wieder Entwicklungen und Veränderungen gegeben, auf die sich sowohl die Betreiber:innen als auch die Endnutzer:innen und Datenaggregator:innen einstellen mussten. Oftmals sind diese Entwicklungen regional unterschiedlich ausgefallen und vor allem setzen sie sich global mit zeitlichem Verzug in den Regionen durch. Deutlich lässt sich erkennen, wie bestimmte Veränderungen in den Repositorien-Schwerpunkten (insbesondere Nordamerika und Europa) ihren Anfang nehmen und sich dann mit beträchtlichem Zeitverzug in den regionalen Communities verbreiten. Das führt auch weiterhin dazu, dass die Zahl der Repositorien weltweit zunimmt, auch wenn es Verschiebungstendenzen, z. B. in Richtung Crossref, gibt. Für diese quantitative Zunahme waren und sind insbesondere zunehmend Nachweise und damit erweiterte Materialien aus Forschungsinformationssystemen und Plattformen mit Digitalisaten (in digitalen Sammlungen), Forschungsdaten und Open Educational Resources (OER) verantwortlich.

Aus diesen Tendenzen lässt sich ableiten, dass auch in der Zukunft die Kernmerkmale Sichtbarkeit, Metadatenqualität und Umfang der Nachweise und Publikationen grundlegende Parameter für die Bewertung von Repositorien bleiben. Daher lohnen sich auch aktuell und weiterhin Maßnahmen zur Verbesserung in diesen Bereichen. In diesen Punkten treffen sich die Interessen von Datenanbietern und Datenaggregatoren wie BASE. Für letztere kommt als weiteres Anforderungskriterium die Stabilität der Schnittstelle und die Transparenz der Systemeigenschaften hinzu, was sich insbesondere bei der Kommunikation von Änderungen auswirkt. Nach wie vor spielt im Hinblick auf die Schnittstellen zum Metadatenaustausch das OAI-PMH-Protokoll eine bedeutende Rolle und entsprechend lohnt sich ein genauer Blick auf die detaillierten Gegebenheiten der Nutzung. Letztlich transportieren die Schnittstellen das im System aufgebaute Qualitätsniveau und damit auch die Sichtbarkeit.

Bibliografie

Müller, Uwe; Scholze, Frank; Vierkant, Paul et al. (2019): DINI-Zertifikat für Open-Access-Publikationsdienste. (DINI Schriften 3). Humboldt-Universität zu Berlin.

Pieper, Dirk; Summann, Friedrich (2015): 10 Years of "Bielefeld Academic Search Engine" (BASE). Looking at the Past and Future of the World Wide Repository Landscape from a Service Providers Perspective. OR2015, 10th International Conference on Open Repositories, Indianapolis, Indiana. https://pub.uni-bielefeld.de/download/2766308/2766316/or2015_base_unibi.pdf (abgerufen am 13.10.2021)

Summann, Friedrich; Czerniak, Andreas; Schirrwagen, Jochen; Pieper, Dirk (2020): Data Science Tools for Monitoring the Global Repository Eco-System and its Lines of Evolution. In: Publications 8 (2), p. 35. https://doi.org/10.3390/publications8020035

Tennant, Roy (2004): Digital Libraries. Metadata's Bitter Harvest. In: Library Journal 129 (12), p. 32.

Vanderfeesten, Maurice; Summann, Friedrich; Slabbertje, Martin (Hg.) (2008): DRIVER Guidelines 2.0. Guidelines for Content Providers – Exposing Textual Resources With OAI-PMH. https://pub.uni-bielefeld.de/download/2491610/2491613/DRIVER_Guidelines_v2_Final_2008-11-13.pdf (abgerufen am 05.01.2022)

Friedrich Summann war bis 2022 Leiter der LibTec-Abteilung (Bibliothekstechnologie und Wissensmanagement) der Universitätsbibliothek Bielefeld. Er arbeitet aktiv in zahlreichen Projekten im Kontext digitaler Informationsversorgung (u. a. BASE, ORCID-DE, Digital Humanities, GO:AL).

Lisa Hönegger

Das Teilen und Archivieren von Daten in den Sozialwissenschaften

Handbuch Repositorienmanagement, Hg. v. Blumesberger et al., 2024, S. 549–572
https://doi.org/10.25364/97839033742323

Lisa Hönegger, Universität Wien, Universitätsbibliothek, lisa.hoenegger@univie.ac.at |
ORCID iD: 0000-0001-6530-7343

Zusammenfassung

Die Ansprüche der Open-Science-Bewegung hin zu FAIRen Forschungsdaten stellen Forschende der Sozialwissenschaften und Archive vor eine große Herausforderung: der Umgang mit personenbezogenen Daten und die daraus entstehende Spannung zwischen Datenteilen und Datenschutz. Dieser Beitrag setzt sich mit dem Bedarf an Forschungsdatenmangement (FDM)-Services im sozialwissenschaftlichen Bereich auseinander und thematisiert unterschiedliche Maßnahmen, die das Datenteilen unter Einhaltung rechtlicher und forschungsethischer Anforderungen möglich machen. Anhand von allgemeinen datenschutzrechtlichen Grundlagen, dem internationalen Vergleich von FDM-Praxen und den etablierten Prozessen bei AUSSDA – The Austrian Social Science Data Archive wird dargelegt, wie Datenteilen und Datenschutz vereinbar sind.

Schlagwörter: Sozialwissenschaft; Datenschutz; Open Science; Daten teilen; Datenarchiv; Forschungsdatenmanagement; personenbezogene Daten; sensible Daten; Österreich

Abstract

Sharing and Archiving Data in the Social Sciences

The demands of the open-science movement towards FAIR research data pose a major challenge to researchers in the social sciences and to archives: the handling of personal data and the resulting tension between data sharing and data protection. This contribution addresses the need for research data management (RDM) services in the social sciences and addresses different measures that make data sharing possible while complying with legal and research ethics requirements. Based on general data protection principles, an international comparison of RDM practices, and the established processes at AUSSDA – The Austrian Social Science Data Archive, this contribution shows how data sharing and data protection are compatible.

Keywords: Social science; data protection; open science; data sharing; data archive; research data management; personal data; sensitive data; austria

1. Einleitung

Die Anforderung an Forschende, Forschungsdaten über den gesamten Forschungsprozess adäquat zu managen, steigt kontinuierlich an – Forschungsdatenmanagement (FDM) etabliert sich als Teil des wissenschaftlichen Prozesses und der guten wissenschaftlichen Praxis. Ein für viele Forschende dabei relativ neuer Aspekt ist neben der Publikation der Forschungsergebnisse auch die Veröffentlichung der zugrundeliegenden Forschungsdaten, welcher von immer mehr Fördergebern durch dezidierte Fördervorgaben zu Open bzw. FAIR[1] Data verpflichtend wird. Auch wissenschaftliche Fachzeitschriften können mittels Publikationsrichtlinien ein ähnliches Ziel verfolgen, ebenso wie die eigene Forschungsinstitution beispielsweise durch eine Policy zu Forschungsdatenmanagement. Daten sollen FAIR – also auffindbar, zugänglich, interoperabel und nachnutzbar – gemacht werden, um so für mehr Transparenz in der Wissenschaft zu sorgen und eine Nachnutzung der Daten durch andere Forschende zu ermöglichen. Der österreichische Fonds zur Förderung der wissenschaftlichen Forschung (FWF) inkludiert in seiner Open-Access Policy die Verpflichtung zu „Open Access to Research Data“ und die FAIR Prinzipien.[2] Auch die erst kürzlich verabschiedete Open-Science Policy Austria[3] legt den Fokus darauf, dass Forschungsdaten im Einklang mit den FAIR-Prinzipien verfügbar gemacht werden sollen. Die Deutsche Forschungsgemeinschaft (DFG) hat die Forderung der Veröffentlichung bzw. Zugänglichmachung von Forschungsdaten bereits in den Kodex „Leitlinie zur Sicherung guter wissenschaftlicher Praxis“ aufgenommen und spezifiziert, dass „soweit dies möglich und zumutbar ist, die den Ergebnissen zugrunde liegenden Forschungsdaten, Materialien und Informationen [...] verfügbar zu machen“ sind.[4] Auch auf europäischer Ebene werden offene Wissenschaft und offene bzw. FAIRe Daten gefordert, u. a. von der Europäischen Kommission in „The EU's open science policy“.[5]

Um diesen Ansprüchen gerecht zu werden, sind Forschende auf Repositorien bzw. Archive angewiesen, die die nötigen Infrastrukturen liefern, um Daten nicht nur langfristig und sicher zu verwahren, sondern diese auch zu veröffentlichen. Neben der Unterstützung, um Daten entsprechend den FAIR-Prinzipien aufzubereiten,

---

1 FAIR Principles von GO FAIR: https://www.go-fair.org/fair-principles/

2 Siehe https://www.fwf.ac.at/en/about-us/what-we-do/open-science/open-access-policy/open-access-policy-for-research-data

3 BMBWF, BMDW, BMK: Open Science Policy Austria: https://www.bmbwf.gv.at/Themen/HS-Uni/Hochschulgovernance/Leitthemen/Digitalisierung/Open-Science/Open-Science-Policy-Austria.html

4 Deutsche Forschungsgemeinschaft (2019), S. 9.

5 https://ec.europa.eu/info/research-and-innovation/strategy/strategy-2020-2024/our-digital-future/open-science_en

brauchen Forschende vor allem auch Informationen und Beratung zu den rechtlichen Aspekten der Datenveröffentlichung. Hier treten Fragen in den Vordergrund, ob, in welcher Form oder wie lange die Daten überhaupt veröffentlicht werden dürfen bzw. welchem Personenkreis unter welchen Bedingungen und mit welchen Nachnutzungsrechten die Daten zur Verfügung gestellt werden können. Genau dieser Schritt der Veröffentlichung weckt erwartungsgemäß viele Unsicherheiten bei Forschenden, die sich mit komplexen rechtlichen und auch ethischen Fragestellungen auseinandersetzen müssen. Besonders, wenn es sich bei den Forschungsdaten um personenbezogene Daten handelt, ist zusätzliche Sorgfalt geboten, damit der Datenschutz gewahrt wird.

Einerseits gibt es also verschiedenste, auch rechtlich relevante Anforderungen, die Forschende zum Teilen der Daten verpflichten. Andererseits ist es oft gar nicht so leicht festzustellen, wie oder ob Daten überhaupt geteilt werden dürfen. Die Gründe gegen das Teilen von Daten können vielfältig sein und je nach Datenart und -inhalt variieren, z. B. um Urheberrecht, Nutzungsrechte oder potenzielle Verwertungsinteressen nicht zu verletzen. Diese Aspekte gilt es zwar bei allen Veröffentlichungen zu beachten, in diesem Beitrag liegt der Fokus aber auf dem Umgang mit personenbezogenen Daten und den datenschutzrechtlichen Einwänden bei Veröffentlichungen in den Sozialwissenschaften. Sozialwissenschaftliche Daten sind häufig personenbezogene Daten – wie zum Beispiel Umfragedaten, Interviewdaten, Beobachtungsdaten, aber auch Register- und Verwaltungsdaten[6] – und ihre Verarbeitung ist dann auch datenschutzrechtlichen Gesetzen unterworfen, allen voran der Datenschutzgrundverordnung (DSGVO)[7]. Diese Daten stehen in diesem Beitrag im Fokus und dienen als Beispiel, auch wenn für personenbezogene Daten anderer wissenschaftlicher Disziplinen die gleichen datenschutzrechtlichen Regeln gelten und die hier behandelten Aspekte ebenfalls Gültigkeit haben können.

Die Ambivalenz von Open Data und Datenschutz entsteht nicht nur durch diverse rechtliche oder vertragliche Anforderungen, sondern bei der Veröffentlichung von Forschungsdaten stehen auch forschungsethische Interessen im Spannungsverhältnis miteinander. Forschende sind moralisch verpflichtet, ihre Forschungssubjekte (und damit auch die zugehörigen Daten) zu schützen:

---

6 Für einen Überblick zur Bandbreite von sozialwissenschaftlichen Daten siehe u. a. Perry, A.; Rekker, J. (2018).

7 Verordnung (EU) 2016/679 des Europäischen Parlaments und des Rates vom 27. April 2016 zum Schutz natürlicher Personen bei der Verarbeitung personenbezogener Daten, zum freien Datenverkehr und zur Aufhebung der Richtlinie 95/46/EG (Datenschutz-Grundverordnung) unter https://eur-lex.europa.eu/legal-content/DE/TXT/PDF/?uri=CELEX:32016R0679&from=DE. Siehe auch Leitfaden der österreichischen Datenschutzbehörde zur Verordnung unter https://www.dsb.gv.at/recht-entscheidungen/gesetze-in-oesterreich.html

> Verstöße gegen den Datenschutz widersprechen der Handlungslogik und den Interessen wissenschaftlicher Forschung, da sie unethisch wären, zu einem Vertrauensverlust in der Bevölkerung führen und damit die Forschung von ihrer empirischen Basis abschneiden könnten.[8]

Andererseits ist es ein Anliegen, Zugriff zu vollständigen und umfassenden Forschungsdaten zu erhalten und Daten in demselben Zustand der Wissenschaft zur Verfügung zu stellen. Einige Maßnahmen, die grundsätzlich das Datenteilen und deren Nachnutzung ermöglichen, wie z. B. die Anonymisierung oder Pseudonymisierung[9], lassen sich aber nur schwer mit dem vollständigen Erhalt der vorhandenen Informationen vereinbaren.[10] Die Veröffentlichung von Daten in den Sozialwissenschaften erfordert daher in der Praxis oft auch eine Abwägung der Interessen der Beteiligten und jenen von Open Science bzw. des Erhalts des wissenschaftlichen Wertes von Forschungsdaten.

Mit der Diskussion von relevanten rechtlichen Grundlagen zum Datenschutz, international praktizierten Standards und den etablierten Prozessen bei AUSSDA – The Austrian Social Science Data Archive sollen folgende Fragen behandelt werden: Welche Aspekte gilt es grundsätzlich bei der Verarbeitung von personenbezogenen Daten zu beachten? Wie können Forschende bei der datenschutzkonformen Veröffentlichung von Forschungsdaten unterstützt werden? Wie können Repositorien selbst mit personenbezogenen Daten umgehen? In Kapitel 2 werden die theoretischen, rechtlichen Grundlagen zu personenbezogenen Daten erläutert, die den nachfolgend beschriebenen Prozessen zu Grunde liegen. Kapitel 3 beschäftigt sich mit einer Einordnung sozialwissenschaftlicher Daten in ihrer Sensibilität. Kapitel 4 stellt dar, wie international mit dem Begriff Anonymität umgegangen wird und wie sich diese Auslegungen auf die wissenschaftliche Praxis und auf das Forschungsdatenmanagement auswirken. Kapitel 5 beschreibt auf Basis all dieser Überlegungen die Prozesse und den Umgang mit personenbezogenen Forschungsdaten beispielhaft bei AUSSDA und zeigt, dass sozialwissenschaftliche Daten unter sorgfältiger Einhaltung datenschutzrechtlicher Vorgaben, ethischer Überlegungen und wissenschaftlicher Standards geteilt werden können.

---

8 Rat für Sozial- und Wirtschaftsdaten (RatSWD) (2015), S. 2.
9 Siehe Abschnitt 5.2 für eine Begriffsbestimmung.
10 Lauber-Rönsberg, A. (2021), S. 100.

2. Personenbezogene Forschungsdaten

Die DSGVO schützt personenbezogene Daten, d. h. Informationen, die sich auf eine identifizierbare Person beziehen.[11] Da sozialwissenschaftliche Forschung oftmals auf der Verarbeitung von personenbezogenen Daten basiert, ist der Umgang mit personenbezogenen Daten eine große Herausforderung im Forschungsdatenmanagement in dieser Disziplin. Sofern Daten anonym sind, d.h. dass die Re-Identifizierung von Personen nicht mehr möglich ist oder überhaupt nie möglich war, findet die DSGVO keine Anwendung und die Daten können (aus datenschutzrechtlicher Sicht) ohne Einschränkungen verarbeitet und auch in Repositorien veröffentlicht werden. Pseudonyme Daten hingegen gelten nach wie vor als personenbezogene Daten und unterliegen weiterhin den Anforderungen der DSGVO. Pseudonym sind Daten, die erst nach Hinzuziehen von zusätzlichen Informationen eine Re-Identifizierung zulassen, sofern diese zusätzlichen Informationen separat gespeichert und nicht frei zugänglich sind.[12] Bei sozialwissenschaftlichen Daten ist es oftmals gar nicht so einfach festzustellen, ob Daten anonym oder personenbezogen (pseudonymisiert oder nicht-pseudonymisiert) sind. Dies spielt aber eine große Rolle für die Verarbeitung solcher Daten und ganz besonders für deren Veröffentlichung, da es aus datenschutzrechtlicher Sicht keine Einwände gegen eine Veröffentlichung ohne Zugangsbeschränkungen oder anderen Sicherheitsvorkehrungen von anonymen Daten gibt, bei lediglich pseudonymen oder nicht-pseudonymisierten personenbezogenen Daten hingegen schon.

Personenbezogene Daten ergeben sich entweder aus direkten oder indirekten Identifikatoren. Direkte Identifikatoren, wie z. B. der Name, die genaue Adresse oder die vollständige IP-Adresse sind relativ gut erkennbar und klar als personenbezogene Informationen klassifizierbar. Indirekte Identifikatoren jedoch – und da ergibt sich die Schwierigkeit für sozialwissenschaftliche Daten – ergeben sich aus der Fülle der verfügbaren (spezifischen) Information zu einem Individuum und ermöglichen dadurch eine Re-Identifizierung. Als Beispiel können hier Umfragedaten dienen, die u. a. Informationen zu Alter, Geschlecht, Wohnort und Beruf enthalten. Für sich alleine stehend wären diese Informationen keine personenbezogenen Daten, gemeinsam können sie es aber sein, sofern eine Rückführung auf einzelne Personen damit möglich wird. Eine Re-Identifizierung könnte potenziell möglich sein, wenn z. B. die Informationen „Beruf" und „Arbeitsort" verfügbar sind und so die Rektorin einer örtlichen Grundschule identifiziert wird oder wenn die Variablen „Wohnort" und „Herkunft" verknüpft werden und damit eine Person mit

---

11 Feiler, L.; Forgó, N. (2017), S. 2f.
12 Art. 4 (5) DSGVO

senegalesischer Abstammung in einer Kleinstadt erkannt wird.[13] Ob es sich also um personenbezogene Daten handelt, kann oftmals nur in der Betrachtung der Gesamtheit der Daten festgestellt werden.

Um einen richtigen Umgang mit diesen Daten zu gewährleisten, ist die Unterscheidung in personenbezogene und nicht-personenbezogene Daten also nötig. Im Zweifelsfall sollte davon ausgegangen werden, dass es sich um personenbezogene Daten handelt, die geschützt werden müssen und nur unter bestimmten Bedingungen verfügbar gemacht werden dürfen.[14] Die DSGVO spezifiziert weitere Kriterien, die für diese Entscheidung herangezogen werden können – so

> sollten alle Mittel berücksichtigt werden, die [...] wahrscheinlich genutzt werden, um die natürliche Person direkt oder indirekt zu identifizieren. [...] [Dafür] sollten alle objektiven Faktoren, wie die Kosten der Identifizierung und der dafür erforderliche Zeitaufwand, herangezogen werden, wobei die zum Zeitpunkt der Verarbeitung verfügbare Technologie und technologische Entwicklungen zu berücksichtigen sind.[15]

Das ist im sozialwissenschaftlichen Bereich insofern relevant, als dass eine Re-Identifizierung durch indirekte Identifikatoren häufig nicht gänzlich ausgeschlossen werden kann, ein Teilen dieser Daten aber trotzdem möglich ist, nämlich mittels geeigneter Sicherheitsmaßnahmen unter Berücksichtigung des Risikos, des Aufwandes für eine Re-Identifizierung und des möglichen Schadens von Personen (siehe dafür Kapitel 4 dieses Beitrages).

3. Sensible Forschungsdaten in den Sozialwissenschaften

Die DSGVO reguliert und schützt grundsätzlich alle personenbezogenen Daten, liefert aber gleichzeitig auch einige Ausnahmen und Möglichkeiten zur Datenverarbeitung (insbesondere der Archivierung und Verfügbarmachung) von personenbezogenen Daten für wissenschaftliche Zwecke, sofern geeignete Garantien für die Sicherheit der Daten bestehen.[16] Diese Garantien können mit passenden technischen und organisatorischen Maßnahmen erfüllt werden, die sich am jeweiligen Risiko der Datenverarbeitung für betroffene Personen orientieren. Dabei soll die Eintrittswahrscheinlichkeit, wie auch die Größe des Risikos oder des denkbaren Schadens beachtet werden.[17]

---

13 Beispiele siehe Meyermann, A.; Porzelt, M. (2014), S. 6.
14 Lauber-Rönsberg, A. (2021), Anm. 10, S. 100.
15 Erwägungsgrund 26 DSGVO
16 Art. 89 DSGVO
17 Art. 32 DSGVO und Erwägungsgründe 74-78 DSGVO

Für die Arbeit von Repositorien und die Veröffentlichung oder Zurverfügungstellung von personenbezogenen Forschungsdaten ist das von großer Bedeutung, da mit diesen Ausnahmen und Möglichkeiten einerseits eine rechtliche Grundlage für die Verarbeitung dieser Daten geschaffen wurde, gleichzeitig aber i. S. der DSGVO Maßnahmen gefordert werden, die Daten von Individuen zu schützen. Für eine Analyse der Risiken und der Festlegung geeigneter, darauf aufbauender Schutzmaßnahmen ist darauf zu achten, dass u. a. eine „unbefugte Offenlegung von oder unbefugter Zugang zu personenbezogenen Daten“ keinen „physischen, materiellen oder immateriellen Schaden“ hervorrufen.[18] Forschende und Repositorien müssen also Maßnahmen setzen, die sicherstellen, dass Daten gemäß dem Risiko einer Verletzung des Datenschutzes und dem potenziellen Schaden nach einer Verletzung desselben verarbeitet werden – besonders, wenn der Verarbeitungsschritt die Veröffentlichung dieser Daten ist. Gewisse festgelegte personenbezogene Daten sind darüber hinaus per Gesetz unter dem Begriff *„besondere Kategorien personenbezogener Daten“* besonders schützenswert, weil sie als „besonders sensibel“ eingestuft werden und „erhebliche Risiken für die Grundrechte und Grundfreiheiten“ von Personen darstellen können.[19] Das sind Daten zur politischen Meinung, ethnischen Herkunft, religiösen Überzeugung, Gewerkschaftszugehörigkeit, sowie genetische und biometrische Daten wie auch Gesundheitsdaten und Daten zum Sexualleben.[20]

Sozialwissenschaftliche Forschungsdaten müssen nicht per se personenbezogen sein und damit der DSGVO unterliegen, sind es aber häufig und können zum Teil auch besonders sensible personenbezogene Daten sein. Bei der Aufbereitung und Veröffentlichung dieser Daten ist es daher wichtig, diverse Risiken und potenzielle Schäden zu beachten und die Veröffentlichung, inkl. Schutzmaßnahmen, an diesen Aspekten festzumachen. Dabei können keine pauschalen Einteilungen anhand von wissenschaftlichen Disziplinen oder Methoden vorgenommen werden – eine Einzelbetrachtung und -entscheidung ist immer notwendig.

Das Risiko einer Verletzung des Datenschutzes bei personenbezogenen Forschungsdaten ist vor allem bei großen Datenmengen oder hohem Informationsgehalt besonders hoch. Das kann bei sozialwissenschaftlichen Umfragen durchaus gegeben sein, dem kann aber angemessen mit Aufbereitungs- und Zugangsmaßnahmen von Repositorien begegnet werden. Im Gegensatz dazu stellt z. B. die Verarbeitung von Registerdaten eine größere Herausforderung dar, weshalb dafür wieder strengere Maßnahmen nötig sind, denen z. B. mit der Schaffung eines Austrian-

18 Erwägungsgrund 83 DSGVO
19 Erwägungsgrund 51 DSGVO
20 Art. 9 DSGVO

Micro-Data Centers bei der Statistik Austria nachgekommen werden soll.[21] Registerdaten sind Daten in Verzeichnissen oder Datenbanken mit Informationen über die Bevölkerung, die gesetzlich vorgesehen sind.[22] Dabei steht das Eindämmen des unbefugten Zugriffs durch nicht berechtigte Personengruppen bzw. die Verhinderung der Nutzung für nicht berechtigte Zwecke im Vordergrund.[23]

Ein weiteres Risiko stellen Daten dar, die sich nicht oder nicht gut anonymisieren/pseudonymisieren lassen, wie z. B. genetische oder biometrische Daten, für die die DSGVO auch weitere Einschränkungen oder Bedingungen durch nationale Gesetzgebung zulässt.[24] Das Bundesministerium für Arbeit, Soziales, Gesundheit und Konsumentenschutz (BMASGK) hielt in einer Stellungnahme zum Schutz sensibler Daten fest, dass genetische Daten eine eindeutige Zuordnung zu Individuen ermöglichen und mit dem Vorliegen von Referenzdaten damit eine Re-Identifizierung ermöglicht wird, weshalb eine Anonymisierung solcher Daten praktisch nicht erfolgen kann.[25] Für die Sozialwissenschaften sind diese Kategorien von Daten eher seltener Bestand, wobei auch „Gesichtsbilder", also Fotografien von Personen, als biometrische Daten bezeichnet werden.[26] Diese werden aber nur dann als besonders sensible Daten eingestuft, wenn ihre Verarbeitung sich spezieller Technik bedient und der Identifizierung von Personen dienen soll, was wiederum einen eher seltenen Vorgang für den Bereich der sozialwissenschaftlichen Forschung darstellt. Allerdings gibt es auch im sozialwissenschaftlichen Bereich Forschungsdaten, wo eine Anonymisierung/Pseudonymisierung nicht gut möglich ist bzw. als nicht sinnvoll erachtet wird. Ein Beispiel wären Daten aus dem Bereich der Biographieforschung, da hier durch die Datendichte zu einzelnen Personen eine Anonymisierung nicht ohne eine Verfälschung oder einen erheblichen Verlust an Information erreicht werden kann.[27]

Die Größe des möglichen Schadens für Studienteilnehmer:innen bei Eintritt einer Datenschutzverletzung hat eine Auswirkung darauf, welche Maßnahmen als geeignet im Umgang mit personenbezogenen Daten gelten können. Solche Schäden können beispielsweise eine Diskriminierung, ein finanzieller Verlust, die Rufschädi-

21 Rat FTE (2021)

22 https://www.bmbwf.gv.at/Themen/Forschung/Forschung-in-%C3%96sterreich/Strategische-Ausrichtung-und-beratende-Gremien/Leitthemen/Registerforschung.html

23 Für einen Überblick zur Relevanz von Registerdaten für die sozialwissenschaftliche Forschung siehe Oberhofer, H. et al. (2019), S. 494-504.

24 Art. 9 (4) DSGVO

25 BMASGK (2019), S. 8.

26 Art. 4 (14) DSGVO

27 Siouti, I. (2018), S. 6f.

gung oder andere Aspekte sein, die zu einem wirtschaftlichen oder sozialen Nachteil für die betroffenen Personen führen.[28] Für den Umgang mit diesen Daten ist es dabei durchaus relevant, ob Betroffene „nur“ mit einem finanziellen Nachteil konfrontiert wären, mit einer Diskriminierung (z. B. am Arbeitsplatz auf Grund von unbefugtem Zugriff auf Gesundheitsdaten) oder der Bedrohung bzw. Verfolgung auf Grund der unbefugten Offenlegung der politischen Meinung (z. B. in Regionen mit eingeschränkter Presse- oder Meinungsfreiheit).[29]

Unabhängig vom Dateninhalt gelten Kinder gemäß DSGVO grundsätzlich als besonders schutzwürdig, weshalb dieser Umstand bei einer Veröffentlichung von Forschungsdaten, die personenbezogene Informationen über Kinder enthalten, in der Risiko- und Schadensabwägung berücksichtigt werden muss.[30] Sollten also z. B. sozialwissenschaftliche Umfragen unter Schüler:innen oder internationale Leistungsvergleichsstudien von Schüler:innen Forschungsgegenstand sein, ist bei einer Datenveröffentlichung besondere Sorgfalt angebracht.

Es kann also festgestellt werden, dass Forschungsdaten im Bereich der Sozialwissenschaften in vielen Fällen personenbezogene Daten enthalten, mitunter auch besonders sensible, die einen noch höheren Schutz benötigen. Wie hoch das Risiko einer Datenschutzverletzung und die möglichen Folgeschäden für die Betroffenen sind, muss vor einer Veröffentlichung immer abgewogen und mit geeigneten Maßnahmen begleitet werden. Welche Daten liegen vor, personenbezogene und besonders sensible? Wie wurden diese Daten erhoben – wurden sie vertraulich im Rahmen einer Umfrage generiert, in der Anonymität zugesichert wurde? Wie sollen diese veröffentlicht werden, pseudonymisiert/anonymisiert oder mit direktem Personenbezug? Wie hoch ist das Risiko, dass sich betroffene Personen re-identifizieren lassen oder dass Unbefugte Zugriff erhalten? Wie hoch wäre der damit einhergehende Schaden? Diese und ähnliche Fragen können dazu dienen, die Sensibilität und damit auch das verbundene Risiko einer Veröffentlichung in Repositorien zu eruieren.

28 Erwägungsgründe 75 und 85 DSGVO
29 Für weitere Beispiele zur Einordnung siehe auch Harvard Information Security (2020).
30 Erwägungsgrund 75 DSGVO

4. Der Umgang mit „Anonymität" im europäischen Vergleich – „faktische Anonymität" und „statistical disclosure control"

Die rechtliche Grundlage für den Umgang mit personenbezogenen Daten sind in Deutschland, genau wie in Österreich, die DSGVO und darüber hinaus weitere nationale Gesetze, die sich auf die Öffnungsklauseln der DSGVO stützen. Eine solche Öffnungsklausel gibt es speziell für die Wissenschaft durch Artikel 89 der DSGVO. Über die DSGVO hinaus regelt Deutschland den Datenschutz durch das Bundesdatenschutzgesetz oder die Landesdatenschutzgesetze.[31] Für die wissenschaftliche Verwendung von personenbezogenen Forschungsdaten wurde auch mit dem deutschen Bundesstatistikgesetz von 1987 eine wichtige Grundlage geschaffen, die wesentliche Vorteile für die Wissenschaft und die wissenschaftliche Nutzung und Weitergabe von Daten hatte – die Aufnahme des Begriffes der „faktischen Anonymität", wie von der European Science Foundation definiert. Die faktische Anonymität (oder auch relative Anonymität) steht in dieser Diskussion im Gegensatz zur „absoluten Anonymität", die nur dann besteht, wenn jegliche theoretische Möglichkeit der Re-Identifizierung ausgeschlossen ist. Schon damals wurde festgehalten, dass es keine hundertprozentige Sicherheit gibt, dass ein Datensatz nicht und niemals de-anonymisiert werden kann, selbst wenn noch so viele Maßnahmen zur Vorbeugung getroffen werden. Das Konzept der faktischen Anonymität basiert auf dieser Annahme und spezifiziert, dass Daten auch noch (faktisch) anonym sind, wenn eine Re-Identifizierung nur durch einen unverhältnismäßig großen Aufwand erreicht werden kann.[32] Auch im Bundesdatenschutzgesetz-alt (welches bis zur Einführung der DSGVO Gültigkeit hatte) wurde am Prinzip der faktischen Anonymität festgehalten, in § 3 Abs. 6.[33]

Mit Einführung der DSGVO wurde aber wieder am Konzept der „faktischen Anonymität" gerüttelt, das für die datenbasierte Forschung und auch für eine Veröffentlichung von Daten im Sinne von Open oder FAIR Data äußerst relevant war. Die DSGVO enthält eine Definition, die an das Verständnis der absoluten Anonymität angelehnt wird, wenn sie festhält, dass Daten nur dann anonym sind, wenn sie gar nicht oder nicht mehr auf Personen zurückgeführt werden können.[34] Diese Ansicht beruht rein auf Auslegungen, da die DSGVO selbst keine Unterscheidung zwischen absoluter und faktischer Anonymität trifft. Die DSGVO spezifiziert aber auch, dass

31 Lauber-Rönsberg, A. (2021), Anm. 10, S. 98f.
32 Wirth, H. (1992), S. 7f.
33 Watteler, O.; Ebel, T. (2019), S. 65.
34 Erwägungsgrund 26 DSGVO

Faktoren, wie der für eine Re-Identifizierung nötige Zeitaufwand und die möglichen Mittel, eine Rolle spielen – was wiederum an die Definition der faktischen Anonymität angelehnt ist.[35] Dass diese Unterscheidung für die wissenschaftliche Praxis vor allem im Bereich der Sozialwissenschaften wichtig ist, geht auch aus der Stellungnahme des Rates für Sozial- und Wirtschaftsdaten (RatSWD) zur DSGVO aus 2015 hervor. Darin wird die Definition der Anonymität dahingehend kritisiert, dass diese nicht mehr der faktischen entspräche, wie es für die Praxis notwendig wäre:

> Es ist nicht ausgeschlossen, dass sich in der Rechtspraxis das Konzept der absoluten Anonymisierung durchsetzt. [...] Absolut anonymisierte Daten sind für wissenschaftliche Analysen kaum geeignet, da ihr Informationsgehalt für fast alle Forschungsfragen nicht mehr ausreichend ist [...]. Aus diesem Grunde war die sukzessive Ablösung des Konzepts der absoluten Anonymität durch das Konzept der relativen Anonymität im BStatG, BDSG und Sozialgesetzbuch ein ganz erheblicher Fortschritt für die empirische Forschung in Deutschland, ohne dass hierdurch die datenschutzwürdigen Belange der Bürgerinnen und Bürger beeinträchtigt worden wären.[36]

Dass das Konzept der faktischen (relativen) Anonymität trotz DSGVO noch nicht aus der Praxis verschwunden ist, sieht man auch anhand des Umgangs der deutschen Forschungsdatenzentren der Statistischen Ämter des Bundes und der Länder. Bei faktisch anonymen Daten soll die Möglichkeit der Identifikation von Individuen nahezu ausgeschlossen werden, dabei aber der Informationsgehalt in den Daten erhalten bleiben. Es wird auch festgehalten, dass für eine faktische Anonymität nicht nur der Datensatz an sich betrachtet werden muss, sondern auch weitere Maßnahmen, wie die Zugangsbedingungen zu den Daten, eine Rolle spielen.[37]

Die Diskussion im deutschen Forschungsdatenmanagement (FDM) im sozialwissenschaftlichen Bereich dient in einem ersten Schritt der Sichtbarmachung einer grundlegenden Herausforderung im Verständnis von Anonymität bei Forschungsdaten, wonach es eine absolute Anonymität praktisch nicht gibt. In der FDM-Praxis geht es also folglich nicht darum, eine absolute Anonymität zu erreichen, sondern viel mehr um die Risikominimierung bei der Veröffentlichung von faktisch anonymisierten Forschungsdaten.

Der britische Datenservice UKDS bedient sich zu diesem Zweck dem Konzept „Statistical Disclosure Control (SDC)". „Disclosure" erfolgt, sobald veröffentlichte Daten genutzt werden, um unbekannte (sensible) personenbezogene Informationen über

---

35 Watteler,O.; Ebel, T. (2019), Anm. 33, S. 65f.
36 RatSWD (2015), Anm. 8, S. 4.
37 https://www.forschungsdatenzentrum.de/de/anonymitaet

Individuen herauszufinden und diese gegebenenfalls auch zu veröffentlichen. Das Ziel von SDC ist es, dieses Risiko so weit wie möglich und nötig zu minimieren, während gleichzeitig so viele Informationen wie möglich erhalten bleiben. „Although SDC aims to prevent the re-identification of a data subject, this is a 'risk minimisation' strategy rather than a 'risk elimination' one. Few would wholeheartedly claim to have removed disclosure risk entirely".[38] Abgesehen davon, dass nicht gewährleistet werden kann, dass Datensätze zu einem gewissen Zeitpunkt und in sich geschlossen absolut anonym sind, inkludiert SDC auch Aspekte, die gar nicht in der Kontrolle der Datenbearbeiter:innen liegen und trotzdem eine Auswirkung auf das Re-Identifizierungsrisiko haben können. So spezifiziert auch die DSGVO, dass zukünftige technologische Entwicklungen bei der Anonymisierung bedacht werden sollen,[39] während gleichzeitig immer mehr persönliche Daten von Individuen offen zugänglich werden, die das Risiko wiederum erhöhen können:

> Trying to eliminate the risk of statistical disclosure entirely would ignore changes in how we think about our data and our appetite for disclosing confidential information about ourselves; and we may ultimately fail in SDC as a result. Instead, risk minimisation takes account of outside conditions that we cannot control.[40]

Einen eindeutigen und unumstrittenen Weg im datenschutzkonformen Umgang mit personenbezogenen Forschungsdaten gibt es grundsätzlich nicht, auch nicht durch die Schaffung eines einheitlichen europäischen Rahmens mit der DSGVO. Es scheint aber klar, dass eine absolute Anonymität von sozialwissenschaftlichen Daten nie zu hundert Prozent sichergestellt werden kann,[41] weshalb für den praktischen Umgang mit diesen Daten auch andere Faktoren beachtet werden müssen, darunter vor allem das schon erwähnte potenzielle Risiko einer Re-Identifizierung inklusive des damit einhergehenden möglichen Schadens. Um das Risiko zu minimieren, müssen angemessene Schutzmaßnahmen eingerichtet werden. Im nachfolgenden Kapitel 5 soll aufgezeigt werden, wie AUSSDA als sozialwissenschaftliches Repositorium mit (sensiblen) personenbezogenen Daten umgeht, welche Maßnahmen zum Schutz von Individuen bestehen und empfohlen werden, um das Re-Identifizierungsrisiko zu minimieren, während der wissenschaftliche Wert bestmöglich erhalten bleibt.

---

38 Griffiths, E. et al. (2019), S. 20.
39 Erwägungsgrund 26 DSGVO
40 Griffiths, E. et al. (2019), Anm. 31, S. 20.
41 Siehe auch Stam, A.; Kleiner, B. (2020), S. 4f.

5. Der Umgang mit personenbezogenen Daten beim Austrian Social Science Data Archive (AUSSDA)

Bisher wurden die rechtlichen Grundlagen erörtert, auf Basis derer die Veröffentlichung von personenbezogenen Daten, speziell im Bereich der Sozialwissenschaften, grundsätzlich stattfinden kann, und wie personenbezogene Daten definiert, erkannt und in ihrer Schutzwürdigkeit eingeordnet werden können. Die etablierten Prozesse der Datenveröffentlichung beim österreichischen sozialwissenschaftlichen Archiv AUSSDA basieren auf diesen Grundlagen und Auslegungen – die Umlegung dieser Überlegungen in die Veröffentlichung von Datensätzen mit hoher Heterogenität und Komplexität ist allerdings stets Gegenstand von Diskussion, Anpassung und Weiterentwicklung.

5.1. Die rechtliche Grundlage – Einwilligung oder Ausnahme für wissenschaftliche Zwecke

Laut DSGVO braucht es für jede Verarbeitung von personenbezogenen Daten eine entsprechende Rechtsgrundlage. Gemäß Art. 6 DSGVO kann eine dieser Grundlagen die Einwilligung der betroffenen Person in die Verarbeitung für einen oder mehrere bestimmte Zwecke sein. Bei sensiblen Daten oder auch „besonderen Kategorien personenbezogener Daten" besteht grundsätzlich ein Verarbeitungsverbot, außer eine der genannten Ausnahmen gemäß Artikel 9 DSGVO trifft zu. Eine dieser Ausnahmen ist ebenfalls die (ausdrückliche) Einwilligung. Die Einwilligung ist eine der wichtigsten Grundlagen für eine rechtmäßige Datenverarbeitung in den Sozialwissenschaften für Forschende. Ob bei einer Online-Umfrage oder bei einem Interview, die Teilnehmer:innen werden gebeten, davor in die Erhebung und Verarbeitung ihrer Daten einzuwilligen. Natürlich gibt es auch einige Szenarien, in denen eine Einwilligung nicht eingeholt werden kann, z. B., wenn öffentlich zugängliche Daten genutzt werden, wie bei Forschung im Bereich der sozialen Medien. Für eine rechtmäßige Verarbeitung solcher Daten muss eine andere Rechtsgrundlage gemäß Art. 6 DSGVO gegeben sein.

Wie genau eine Einwilligungserklärung aussehen muss, hängt wiederum vom Forschungsvorhaben ab und lässt sich nicht pauschal beantworten. Dafür gibt es bereits einige Vorlagen von verschiedensten wissenschaftlichen Einrichtungen zur freien Verfügung – die aber wiederum sehr genau an die Gegebenheiten für jede Situation und jedes Projekt angepasst werden müssen. Damit eine Einwilligung grundsätzlich gültig ist, muss sie gemäß DSGVO folgende Aspekte beinhalten: Sie muss freiwillig, mit einer aktiven Handlung, für einen konkreten Zweck, informiert und unmissverständlich gegeben werden und leicht widerrufbar sein. Das kann mündlich, schriftlich oder auch elektronisch erfolgen.[42] Es empfiehlt sich aus Gründen der Nachvollziehbar- und Beweisbarkeit, die Einwilligung zu dokumentieren.[43] Zumindest ist aber auch (nicht unbedeutend für Online-Umfragen) geregelt, dass eine gültige Einwilligung auch mittels Anklicken eines Kästchens erfolgen kann.[44]

Forschende, die planen, personenbezogene Daten für ihr Projekt zu verarbeiten, und diese Informationen nicht aus öffentlichen Quellen beziehen, sondern direkt von ihren Forschungssubjekten, benötigen im Regelfall deren Einwilligung. Zusätzlich ist das auch ethisch der beste Weg, da damit gleichermaßen eine umfassende und verständliche Aufklärung zur geplanten Datenverarbeitung stattfindet und den Teilnehmer:innen wichtige Informationen über ihre Rechte gegeben werden. Die Einwilligungserklärung soll so formuliert sein, dass die Teilnehmer:innen wissen, welche ihrer Daten gesammelt werden und was damit weiter passiert, bis zu einer allfälligen Löschung oder eben Archivierung und Publikation ihrer Daten.[45] Dieser letzte Aspekt ist oftmals noch nicht Bestandteil solcher Einwilligungserklärungen und auch vieler Vorlagen, die frei zugänglich sind, da die Veröffentlichung von Daten selbst ein Prozess ist, der sich erst als Teil der wissenschaftlichen Praxis etabliert. Hier empfiehlt es sich, den Blick auf Formulierungen zu lenken, die einer Archivierung und Publikation klar entgegenstehen, und diese gegebenenfalls zu vermeiden, wie z. B., dass Daten nicht außerhalb des Projektteams weitergegeben werden; dass Daten nur in aggregierter Form veröffentlicht werden; oder, dass Daten nach Projektende gelöscht werden. Das alles ist im Falle einer Archivierung gemäß den FAIR-Prinzipien nicht zutreffend, sofern es nicht einen guten (datenschutzrechtlichen) Grund gibt, dass die Daten nicht mit Personen außerhalb des Projektteams geteilt, dass die Daten nur aggregiert veröffentlicht oder gelöscht werden. Selbst wenn Archive auf Basis anderer Grundlagen das Recht haben, diese Daten zu archivieren, wäre das forschungsethisch bedenklich, da den Teilnehmer:innen etwas Anderes zugesagt wurde.

Für ein Archiv ist das Stützen der Verarbeitungsprozesse auf die Einwilligung als rechtliche Grundlage gewissermaßen schwieriger, da die Daten dort nicht erhoben werden und kein Kontakt zu den Teilnehmer:innen besteht. Es kann auch nicht überprüft werden, ob eine rechtsgültige Einwilligung an die Forschenden bzw. Datenerheber:innen abgegeben wurde. AUSSDA stützt sich für die Archivierung und

42 Erwägungsgrund 32 DSGVO
43 Erwägungsgrund 42 DSGVO
44 Erwägungsgrund 32 DSGVO
45 Siehe auch Verbund Forschungsdaten Bildung (n. d.)

Zurverfügungstellung daher nicht auf die Einwilligung, sondern auf die Ausnahmen, die u. a. für personenbezogene Daten zu im öffentlichen Interesse liegenden Archivzwecken, zu wissenschaftlichen oder historischen Forschungszwecken oder zu statistischen Zwecken mit Art. 89 DSGVO geschaffen wurden.[46] Für Österreich ist das weiter in § 7 des Datenschutzgesetzes geregelt, wonach für die schon genannten wissenschaftlichen Zwecke personenbezogene Daten verarbeitet werden dürfen, die entweder öffentlich zugänglich sind oder pseudonymisierte Daten sind.[47] Das Forschungsorganisationsgesetz ermöglicht die Arbeit von Repositorien darüber hinaus mit der Berechtigung zum Sammeln und Archivieren von Forschungsdaten, um einen optimalen Zugang zu schaffen.[48]

AUSSDA und andere Archive sind also grundsätzlich dazu berechtigt, personenbezogene Forschungsdaten zu verarbeiten und diese unter Einhaltung bestimmter Maßnahmen zur Einhaltung der Rechte und Freiheiten von betroffenen Personen auch zu archivieren und zu veröffentlichen. Eine dieser Maßnahmen, sowohl in der DSGVO als auch im österreichischen Datenschutzgesetz festgehalten, ist die Pseudonymisierung der Daten.[49]

5.2. Anonymisierung/Pseudonymisierung

Anonyme oder anonymisierte Daten sind von der DSGVO ausgenommen und können ohne weitere Auflagen aus datenschutzrechtlicher Sicht verarbeitet werden.[50] Dass sozialwissenschaftliche Daten in den seltensten Fällen anonym sind oder (absolut) anonymisiert werden können (siehe Kapitel 4), stellt das sozialwissenschaftliche Forschungsdatenmanagement vor Herausforderungen. Die Pseudonymisierung hingegen ist ein Konzept, das in der DSGVO spezifiziert ist und als Maßnahme angewandt werden kann, personenbezogene Daten geschützt zu verarbeiten. Daten sind pseudonym, wenn es ohne Hinzuziehen zusätzlicher Informationen nicht mehr möglich ist, Individuen zu identifizieren, solange diese zusätzlichen Informationen gesondert aufbewahrt werden und Unbefugte keinen Zugriff darauf haben.[51] Der Vorgang der Pseudonymisierung entspricht dabei auch dem Grundsatz der Datenminimierung der DGSVO, nachdem Daten dem Zweck angemessen und nur auf

46 Hönegger, L. et al. (2020), S. 3.

47 § 7 des Bundesgesetzes zum Schutz natürlicher Personen bei der Verarbeitung personenbezogener Daten (Datenschutzgesetz – DSG) StF: BGBl. I Nr. 165/1999.

48 § 2f des Bundesgesetzes über allgemeine Angelegenheiten gemäß Art. 89 DSGVO und die Forschungsorganisation (Forschungsorganisationsgesetz – FOG) StF: BGBl. Nr. 341/1981 idF BGBl. Nr. 448/1981. https://www.ris.bka.gv.at/GeltendeFassung.wxe?Abfrage=Bundesnormen&Gesetzesnummer=10009514

49 Hönegger, L. et al. (2020), Anm. 46, S. 4.

50 Erwägungsgrund 26 DSGVO

51 Art. 4 (5) DSGVO

das für diesen Zweck notwendige Maß beschränkt verarbeitet werden dürfen.[52] Daten sollen also nicht grundlos gesammelt und gespeichert werden, sondern nur, wenn es einen legitimen Grund dafür gibt.

AUSSDA geht bei an das Archiv übermittelten Daten davon aus, dass es sich in den meisten Fällen um pseudonymisierte Daten handelt, da nicht ausgeschlossen werden kann, dass zusätzliche, getrennt aufbewahrte Informationen vorhanden sind, die eine Re-Identifizierung ermöglichen können (z. B. bei den Datenerheber:innen). Solange der Personenbezug theoretisch von allen Personen, die zusätzliche Informationen haben (z. B. die Datenerheber:innen) wiederhergestellt werden kann, sind die Daten nicht anonym, sondern pseudonym.[53] Zur Aufbewahrung von Zusatzinformationen (z. B. Identifizierungsschlüssel) gibt es unterschiedliche Praxen und Aufbewahrungsfristen. AUSSDA veröffentlicht derzeit Daten, die zumindest pseudonymisiert sind, d. h. die Zusatzinformationen (die für eine Re-Identifizierung nötig werden) stehen potenziellen Nachnutzer:innen in weiterer Folge nicht zur Verfügung. Damit Daten aber erfolgreich pseudonymisiert werden, dürfen sie ohne solche Zusatzinformationen eine Re-Identifizierung nicht ermöglichen. Dabei folgen wir wieder, wie bisher dargelegt, dem Konzept der „faktischen Anonymisierung", d. h. der Datensatz, der bei AUSSDA veröffentlicht wird, wird auf ein Re-Identifizierungsrisiko geprüft und den Datengeber:innen Empfehlungen hin zur (faktischen) Anonymisierung gegeben. Diese Empfehlungen sind z.B. im quantitativen Bereich das Löschen von einzelnen Variablen (z. B. Name, Geburtsdatum oder E-Mail-Adresse); das Zusammenfassen in Gruppen (z. B. Angabe von Altersgruppen statt Alter); oder im qualitativen Bereich das Ersetzen von Information durch Pseudonyme (u. a. Name, Herkunft, Wohnort).

Datenprüfungen werden bei Dateneingängen von AUSSDA durchgeführt. Diese Prüfungen werden nach gleichen Prinzipien, allerdings abhängig von Datentyp und möglichem Dateninhalt (inklusive Risikoabschätzung), durchgeführt. Die Voraussetzung für eine Datenübernahme und Veröffentlichung durch AUSSDA ist aber immer, dass Datengeber:innen den Datengewinnungsprozess offenlegen, damit das Risiko bewertet werden kann. Die Datentypen, die derzeit bei AUSSDA veröffentlicht werden, gliedern sich in numerische Daten und Textdaten. Für eine praktische Anleitung zu Anonymisierungsschritten bei AUSSDA für numerische Daten (vor allem Umfragedaten) siehe die AUSSDA-Data-Deposit Guideline[54]. Diese kann jedoch, wie der Name bereits verrät, immer nur als Richtlinie gesehen werden – die kon-

52 Art. 5 (1) lit. c DSGVO
53 Watteler, O.; Kinder-Kurlanda, K. E. (2015), S. 517.
54 Butzlaff, I. (2020), S. 10f.

kreten, für eine Anonymisierung notwendigen Schritte hängen immer von weiteren Faktoren ab (wie z. B. Datenmenge und Informationsgehalt) und müssen kontextbezogen betrachtet, angepasst und nach Ermessen umgesetzt werden. Eine vollständige Liste oder ein vollständig beschriebener Vorgang der Anonymisierung kann nicht pauschal für Forschungsdaten festgelegt werden. Eine besondere Herausforderung stellen dabei die stetig neu entstehenden Datenarten und -typen dar, die immer wieder neue Anonymisierungsschritte erfordern.

Die kritische Frage für Forschende, aber auch für Archive ist, ab welchem Zustand Daten als anonymisiert/pseudonymisiert betrachtet werden können. Da die verbreitete Auffassung im Umgang mit sozialwissenschaftlichen Daten ist, dass eine Re-Identifikation niemals hundertprozentig ausgeschlossen werden kann (siehe Kapitel 4), gibt es dafür keine klare Trennlinie. Vielmehr geht es um Risikominimierung und darum, die Balance zwischen Datenschutz und Wissenserhalt für die Forschung zu finden. AUSSDA agiert bei der Datenkontrolle nach denselben Prinzipien und betrachtet Daten dann als anonymisiert/pseudonymisiert, sobald nur mehr mit unverhältnismäßigem Aufwand eine Re-Identifikation durch Dritte stattfinden könnte. Dabei orientiert sich das Archiv an den oben dargelegten, international vergleichbaren Standards im sozialwissenschaftlichen Forschungsdatenmanagement, bewertet Datensätze in ihrem Kontext und setzt technische und organisatorische Maßnahmen in Abwägung von Datenschutz und Risiko.[55] Sollte der denkbare Schaden nach einer (nur mit unverhältnismäßigem Aufwand möglichen) Re-Identifikation dennoch groß sein, nutzt das Archiv weitere Maßnahmen zum Schutz der Daten – die Zugangskontrolle und die Einschränkung der Nachnutzung.

5.3. Zugangskontrollen und Lizenzen

Nach einer Prüfung der Daten und Betrachtung des Hintergrunds der Datenerhebung wird von AUSSDA (oftmals gemeinsam mit Datengeber:innen) eine Einschätzung des Risikos vorgenommen. Da wir davon ausgehen, dass eine Re-Identifizierung niemals komplett ausgeschlossen werden kann, müssen das Risiko im unwahrscheinlichen, aber möglichen Fall einer Datenschutzverletzung beachtet und Maßnahmen zum weiteren Schutz gesetzt werden. Diese Maßnahmen sind bei AUSSDA die Zugangskontrolle und die Einschränkung der Nachnutzung durch die Vergabe von Lizenzen. Damit folgt AUSSDA international etablierten Empfehlun-

55 Watteler, O.; Ebel, T. (2019), Anm. 33, S. 67.

gen im Umgang mit personenbezogenen, sensiblen Daten. "In case you are archiving sensitive data you should always go for a restricted license or closed access".[56]

AUSSDA hat drei verschiedene Zugangsbedingungen etabliert, die die unterschiedlichen Risiken adressieren gemäß der AUSSDA-Access Policy.[57] Darüber hinaus gibt es grundsätzlich zwei verschiedene Arten von Lizenzen, offene Lizenzen (Open Access – OA) und Lizenzen für die wissenschaftliche Nutzung (Scientific Use File – SUF).

Wenn Daten absolut anonym sind bzw. kein Risiko aufweisen, können diese ganz offen zur Verfügung gestellt werden. Diese Daten können im Online-Katalog[58] eingesehen und direkt heruntergeladen werden. Die Daten sind mit einer Open-Access-Lizenz versehen und können daher auch ohne Einschränkungen, aber mit der Verpflichtung zur Quellenangabe (in der Bibliografie) für alle Zwecke und von allen Personen nachgenutzt werden.

Sind die Daten nicht absolut anonym, sondern so bearbeitet, dass sie als „faktisch anonym" zu verstehen wären, werden Daten eingeschränkter zur Verfügung gestellt, sowohl hinsichtlich der Zugangsbedingungen, als auch der Nachnutzungslizenz. AUSSDA vergibt in diesen Fällen eine Scientific-Use-Lizenz, die regelt, dass Daten nur für wissenschaftliche Zwecke verwendet werden dürfen. Diese Einschränkung ist möglich, weil die DSGVO und auch andere relevante Materiengesetze (z. B. das Datenschutzgesetz oder das Forschungsorganisationsgesetz) Ausnahmen für die wissenschaftliche Nutzung von personenbezogenen Daten erlauben. Gleichzeitig wird diese Einschränkung als nötig erachtet, um einer missbräuchlichen Verwendung solcher Daten vorzubeugen. Wie schon zu Beginn erwähnt, ist der datenschutzkonforme Umgang und die Sicherung von Daten nicht nur aus rechtlicher Sicht nötig, sondern wird auch aus forschungsethischer Sicht gefordert. Forschende sind darauf angewiesen, dass Teilnehmer:innen auf den korrekten Umgang mit ihren Daten vertrauen und die weitergegebenen Daten ausreichend geschützt werden. Forschende sind dazu auch in Richtlinien zur guten wissenschaftlichen Praxis verpflichtet.[59]

Sobald Daten nur mehr für wissenschaftliche Zwecke verwendet werden dürfen und dementsprechend mit einer SUF Lizenz lizenziert werden, wird wiederum je

56 OpenAIRE Sensitive data guide. Storing sensitive data: https://www.openaire.eu/sensitive-data-guide
57 Kaczmirek, L.; Hönegger, L. (2019)
58 AUSSDA Dataverse: https://data.aussda.at/
59 Siehe z. B. Rat für Sozial- und Wirtschaftsdaten (RatSWD) (2017), S. 18.

nach Risiko differenziert, wie diese Daten zugänglich gemacht werden. Daten, die ein geringes Risiko nach einer potenziellen Re-Identifikation haben, können nach einem (institutionellen) Login direkt eingesehen und heruntergeladen werden. Die Nachnutzungslizenz (die die Nutzer:innen der Daten rechtlich bindet) spezifiziert dabei, dass Daten nur für wissenschaftliche Zwecke genutzt werden dürfen.[60] Wird das Risiko als größer eingeschätzt, wird eine zusätzliche Zugangshürde eingebaut. Forschende können solche Daten zunächst nicht einsehen und auch nicht herunterladen, sondern müssen mittels eines Formulars den genauen Zweck darlegen, weshalb sie Zugriff auf die Daten benötigen. Dabei wird von AUSSDA geprüft, ob ein Zugriff auf diese Daten für das dargestellte Forschungsvorhaben nötig ist und das Ansuchen legitim ist. Dieser bei AUSSDA restriktivste Zugang schränkt das Missbrauchspotenzial deutlich ein und wird daher als strengste Maßnahme für besonders schutzwürdige Daten gesetzt.

Als sozialwissenschaftliches Repositorium setzen wir uns aktiv für Open Science und FAIRe Daten ein, weshalb wir bei allen technischen und organisatorischen Maßnahmen nach dem Prinzip „so offen wie möglich, so geschlossen wie nötig"[61] agieren. Wenn aus datenschutzrechtlicher Perspektive keine Einschränkungen nötig sind, werden diese nicht umgesetzt. Gibt es aber begründete Bedenken, werden die Daten mit Zugangsbeschränkungen geschützt. Diese Maßnahmen werden stets unter Interessensabwägung aller Beteiligten getroffen und zielen darauf ab, datenbasierte Forschung unter Einhaltung der nötigen Sicherheitsstandards zu ermöglichen. Damit orientiert sich AUSSDA auch an europäischen Forschungsvorgaben zum Datenmanagement.[62]

6. Fazit

Damit Forschende ihre Daten entweder ganz öffentlich oder zumindest für die wissenschaftliche Nutzung zur Verfügung stellen können, braucht es neben den Infrastrukturen wie Archiven bzw. Repositorien vor allem auch eine Beratung und Unterstützung zur Klärung der rechtlichen Fragen und ethischen Bedenken. Der Schutz von personenbezogenen Daten ist unbedingt notwendig, gleichzeitig muss aber auch der wissenschaftliche Wert der Daten erhalten bleiben und zugänglich sein. Die rechtlichen Grundlagen, die das Datenteilen ermöglichen, sind äußerst komplex und ihre Umsetzung in der Praxis oftmals nicht eindeutig geregelt, was Forschende vor enorme Herausforderungen stellt. Die Praxis des Datenteilens, wie

60 Für den vollen Lizenztext siehe https://aussda.at/vertraege-und-lizenzen-bei-aussda/wissenschaftlicher-zweck/
61 European Commission (2021), S. 34.
62 Ebd., Anm. 61, S. 64.

von der Open-Science-Bewegung gefordert[63], ist mit vielen Hürden konfrontiert, wie z. B. mangelnde Ressourcen für die Aufbereitung der Daten oder mangelnde Anreize für das Datenteilen. Ein für Wissenschaftler:innen aber ebenfalls relevanter Faktor, der das Datenteilen verhindert, sind bestehende rechtliche Einschränkungen und Unsicherheiten im Bereich Datenschutzverletzungen.[64] Um die Praxis des Datenteilens bestmöglich zu unterstützen, brauchen Forschende Ansprechpersonen, um solche rechtlichen Unsicherheiten aus dem Weg zu räumen und datenschutzkonform ihre Daten zur Verfügung zu stellen:

> Angesichts der Komplexität der rechtlichen Rahmenbedingungen sind Wissenschaftlerinnen und Wissenschaftler auf eine unterstützende Infrastruktur der Forschungseinrichtung angewiesen, um ein sachgerechtes und rechtskonformes FDM betreiben zu können.[65]

AUSSDA ist als Repositorium, das sozialwissenschaftliche Daten veröffentlicht, bemüht, rechtliche Fragen zur Archivierung und Zurverfügungstellung von personenbezogenen Daten zu klären – durch umfangreiche Recherchen, Rücksprachen mit Datenschutzbeauftragten und Gutachten von unabhängigen Rechtsberater:innen – damit Forschende, die ihre Daten zur Verfügung stellen, um die Risiken und Möglichkeiten Bescheid wissen. In der Praxis geht es vorwiegend darum, diese Risiken, aber gleichzeitig auch die Möglichkeiten zu erkennen, einzuschätzen und danach Maßnahmen zu setzen, die ein Datenteilen mit dem nötigen Schutz ermöglichen. Dabei sucht AUSSDA gemeinsam mit Forschenden nach Lösungen, wie, aber nicht ob Daten geteilt werden können. Im Vordergrund steht, ein Bewusstsein für Datenschutz zu schaffen, das eine offene Wissenschaft nicht einschränkt, sondern nachhaltig ermöglicht.

Bibliografie

Bauer, Bruno; Ferus, Andreas; Gorraiz, Juan; Gründhammer, Veronika; Gumpenberger, Christian; Maly, Nikolaus; Mühlegger, Johannes Michael; Preza, José Luis; Sánchez Solís, Barbara; Schmidt, Nora; Steineder, Christian (2015): Forschende und ihre Daten. Ergebnisse einer österreichweiten Befragung – Report. Version 1.2., S. 51-53. https://doi.org/10.5281/zenodo.32043

BMASGK (2019): Schutz sensibler Daten. Position der Gesundheitssektionen VIII und IX des BMASGK. https://www.sozialministerium.at/dam/jcr:99d679b8-3676-455e-abfc-

63 https://www.bmbwf.gv.at/Themen/HS-Uni/Hochschulgovernance/Leitthemen/Digitalisierung/Open-Science.html
64 Bauer, B. et al. (2015), S. 51-53.
65 Lauber-Rönsberg, A. (2021), Anm. 7, S. 111.

a6ec27c4d64d/S chutz_sensibler_Daten_-_Position_der_Gesundheitssektionen_VIII_und_IX_.pdf (abgerufen am 19.04.2023)

Butzlaff, Iris (2020): Data Deposit Guideline (Public version) v2.0. Information for Data Depositors. Wien: AUSSDA – The Austrian Social Science Data Archive. https://aussda.at/fileadmin/user_upload/p_aussda/Documents/Data-Deposit-Guideline_SUF_v2_0.pdf

Deutsche Forschungsgemeinschaft (2019): Guidelines for Safeguarding Good Research Practice. Code of Conduct. https://doi.org/10.5281/zenodo.3923602

European Commission (2021): Horizon Europe (HORIZON) Programme Guide. Version 1.3, November. https://ec.europa.eu/info/funding-tenders/opportunities/docs/2021-2027/horizon/guidance/programme-guide_horizon_en.pdf (abgerufen am 18.04.2023)

Feiler, Lukas; Forgó, Nikolaus (2017): EU-DSGVO. EU-Datenschutz-Grundverordnung. Kurzkommentar. Wien: Verlag Österreich.

Griffiths, Emily; Greci, Carlotta; Kotrotsios, Yannis; Parker, Simon; Scott, James; Welpton, Richard; Wolters, Arne; Woods, Christine (2019): Handbook on Statistical Disclosure Control for Outputs. https://ukdataservice.ac.uk/app/uploads/thf_datareport_aw_web.pdf (abgerufen am 18.04.2023)

Harvard Information Security (2020): Data Security Levels. Research Data Examples Quick Reference Guide. https://security.harvard.edu/files/it-security/files/rdslexamples.pdf (abgerufen am 18.04.2023)

Hönegger, Lisa; Butzlaff, Iris; Kaczmirek, Lars (2020): Bereitstellung personenbezogener Daten durch AUSSDA. Gesetzliche Grundlage. Wien: AUSSDA – The Austrian Social Science Data Archive. https://aussda.at/fileadmin/user_upload/p_aussda/Documents/Bereitstellung_personenbezogener_Daten.pdf (abgerufen am 18.04.2023)

Kaczmirek, Lars; Hönegger, Lisa (2019): Access Policy. Open Access and Restricted Access Procedures in the AUSSDA Repository. Vienna: AUSSDA – The Austrian Social Science Data Archive. https://aussda.at/fileadmin/user_upload/p_aussda/Documents/AUSSDA_Access_Policy_v2_0.pdf

Lauber-Rönsberg, Anne (2021): Rechtliche Aspekte des Forschungsdatenmanagements. In: Putnings, Markus; Neuroth, Heike; Neumann, Janna (Hg.): Praxishandbuch Forschungsdatenmanagement. Berlin: Walter de Gruyter, S. 89-114. https://doi.org/10.1515/9783110657807-005

Meyermann, Alexia; Porzelt, Maike (2014): Hinweise zur Anonymisierung von qualitativen Daten. In: forschungsdaten bildung informiert 1.

Oberhofer, Harald; Schwarz, Gerhard; Strassnig, Michael (2019): Registerforschung. Verwaltungs- und Statistikdaten für die Wissenschaft. In: Mitteilungen der VÖB 72 (2): Open Science, S. 494–504. https://doi.org/10.31263/voebm.v72i2.3154

Perry, Anja; Recker, Jonas (2018): Sozialwissenschaftliche Forschungsdaten langfristig sichern und zugänglich machen. Herausforderungen und Lösungsansätze. Was sind sozialwissenschaftliche Daten. In: Das offene Bibliotheksjournal 5 (2). https://www.o-bib.de/bib/article/view/2018H2S106-122/6392

Rat FTE (2021): Registerdatenforschung und Implementierung eines Austrian Micro-Data Centers. Fact Sheet. https://repository.fteval.at/id/eprint/667

Rat für Sozial- und Wirtschaftsdaten (RatSWD) (2017): Forschungsethische Grundsätze und Prüfverfahren in den Sozial- und Wirtschaftswissenschaften. https://www.konsortswd.de/wp-content/uploads/RatSWD_Output9_Forschungsethik.pdf (abgerufen am 18.04.2023)

Rat für Sozial- und Wirtschaftsdaten (RatSWD) (2015): Stellungnahme des Rates für Sozial- und Wirtschaftsdaten zu ausgewählten Punkten des aktuellen Entwurfs der EU-Datenschutz-Grundverordnung (DSGVO). 24.02. https://www.konsortswd.de/wp-content/uploads/RatSWD_Stellungnahme_EUDSGVO.pdf (abgerufen am 18.04.2023)

Siouti, Irini (2018): Forschungsethik in der Biografieforschung. Herausforderungen im Forschungsfeld der politischen Partizipation. In: Forum: Qualitative Sozialforschung 19 (3), 28.

Stam, Alexandra; Kleiner, Brian (2020): Data Anonymization. Legal, Ethical, and Strategic Considerations. In: FORS Guide Nr. 11, Version 1.0. Lausanne: Swiss Centre of Expertise in the Social Sciences FORS. https://doi.org/:10.24449/FG-2020-00011

Verbund Forschungsdaten Bildung (n. d.): FAQ „Muss ich eine Einwilligung zur späteren Archivierung und Nachnutzung der Daten einholen?" https://www.forschungsdaten-bildung.de/faq (abgerufen am 18.04.2023)

Verordnung (EU) 2016/679 des Europäischen Parlaments und des Rates vom 27. April 2016 zum Schutz natürlicher Personen bei der Verarbeitung personenbezogener Daten, zum freien Datenverkehr und zur Aufhebung der Richtlinie 95/46/EG (Datenschutz-Grundverordnung). https://eur-lex.europa.eu/legal-content/DE/TXT/PDF/?uri=CELEX:32016R0679&from=DE (abgerufen am 18.04.2023)

Watteler, Oliver; Kinder-Kurlanda, Katharina E. (2015): Anonymisierung und sicherer Umgang mit Forschungsdaten in der empirischen Sozialforschung. In: DuD – Datenschutz und Datensicherheit 8.

Watteler, Oliver; Ebel, Thomas (2019): Datenschutz im Forschungsdatenmanagement. In: Jensen, Uwe; Netscher, Sebastian; Weller, Katrin (Hg.): Forschungsdatenmanagement sozialwissenschaftlicher Umfragedaten. Grundlagen und praktische Lösungen für den Umgang mit quantitativen Forschungsdaten. Opladen, Berlin, Toronto: Verlag Barbara Budrich. https://shop.budrich.de/wp-content/uploads/2019/01/4.-Datenschutz-im-Forschungsdatenmanagement-Oliver-Watteler-und-Thomas-Ebel.pdf (abgerufen am 18.04.2023)

Wirth, Heike (1992): Die faktische Anonymität von Mikrodaten. Ergebnisse und Konsequenzen eines Forschungsprojektes. In: ZUMA Nachrichten 16 (30). https://nbn-resolving.org/urn:nbn:de:0168-ssoar-209679

Lisa Hönegger ist stellvertretende Leitung von AUSSDA, dem österreichischen sozialwissenschaftlichen Datenarchiv, mit Standorten an den Universitäten Wien, Graz, Linz und Innsbruck. Sie arbeitet seit 2018 an der Universitätsbibliothek Wien und beschäftigt sich hauptsächlich mit Forschungsdatenmanagement und Open Science im österreichischen und europäischen Kontext.

Wolfgang Kraus, Anna Nindl

Managen, Öffnen und Teilen qualitativer Forschungsdaten in den Sozialwissenschaften

Herausforderungen für Forschende und Repositorien

Handbuch Repositorienmanagement, Hg. v. Blumesberger et al., 2024, S. 573–595
https://doi.org/10.25364/978390337423229

Wolfgang Kraus, Universität Wien, Ethnographisches Datenarchiv, wolfgang.kraus@univie.ac.at |
ORCID iD: 0009-0009-9299-608X
Anna Nindl, Universität Wien, anna.nindl@univie.ac.at

Zusammenfassung

Forderungen nach Forschungsdatenmanagement und nach möglichst offenen Forschungsdaten werden heute von allen zentralen Institutionen im Forschungsbetrieb erhoben; in den meisten Forschungsbereichen sind sie nahezu zu einer Selbstverständlichkeit geworden. In den qualitativ orientierten Sozialwissenschaften sind diese Forderungen vielfach mit großer Skepsis aufgenommen worden und werden weiterhin kontroversiell diskutiert. Ausgehend von den Strategien, die in einer Initiative zur digitalen Archivierung ethnographischer Daten entwickelt worden sind, vertritt dieser Beitrag die Position, dass das Bewahren und Verfügbarmachen qualitativer Forschungsdaten sinnvoll und notwendig ist, aber aus anderen Gründen und mit anderen Zielsetzungen als jenen, die im Diskurs um offene Forschungsdaten im Mittelpunkt stehen. Für ein verantwortliches und produktives Öffnen qualitativer Forschungsdaten aus den Sozialwissenschaften braucht es ein dialogisches Verständnis qualitativer Forschung, das die Beforschten als Akteur:innen einbezieht, anstatt der dominanten Rhetorik von Effizienz, Replizierbarkeit und Accountability. Auch dann sind noch diverse Herausforderungen zu lösen, nicht nur für die Forschenden, sondern auch für Repositorien, deren Infrastrukturen meist die Voraussetzungen für das Archivieren qualitativer sozialwissenschaftlicher Daten nur teilweise erfüllen.

Schlagwörter: Datenarchivierung; Ethnographie; Ethnographisches Datenarchiv; Forschungsdatenmanagement; Forschungsethik; Kontext; Open Research Data; Qualitative Sozialwissenschaften

Abstract

Managing, Opening and Sharing Qualitative Research Data in the Social Sciences. Challenges for Researchers and Repositories

Demands for open research data have become a mainstream expectation in most scientific fields and are being articulated by the main academic institutional actors. Many researchers in the social sciences working with qualitative approaches are deeply sceptical about such demands. Based on the strategies developed and experiences made in an initiative for archiving ethnographic data, this contribution argues that it makes indeed sense to preserve and share qualitative research data, but for different reasons and with different objectives from those invoked in much of the open research data discourse. In order to do so in a responsible and productive manner, we argue that a dialogic understanding of the qualitative research process is more pertinent than the dominant rhetoric of efficiency, replicability and accountability. Even so, many challenges remain for researchers but also for repositories, whose infrastructures often are not well adapted to the needs of qualitative social science data.

Keywords: Data archiving; ethnography; ethnographic data archive; research data management; research ethics; context; open research data; qualitative social sciences

1. Einleitung

Forderungen nach „Offener Wissenschaft" sind in den letzten Jahren in allen institutionellen Bereichen des Wissenschaftsbetriebs laut geworden. Ausgehend von den Natur- und technischen Wissenschaften, hat dieser Veränderungsprozess schon vor längerer Zeit eingesetzt, aber vor allem seit der Jahrtausendwende zunehmend alle Wissenschaftsfelder erfasst. Im Zusammenhang mit der Open-Science-Bewegung wurde dabei zunächst vor allem der freie Zugang zu Publikationen debattiert. Aber auch der Zugang zu den Daten, auf denen Forschungsergebnisse aufbauen, ist – verbunden mit Schlagwörtern wie Open-Research Data und Forschungsdatenmanagement – zu einer zentralen Forderung geworden,[1] die sich nun in entsprechenden Policies aller wichtigen Institutionen des Wissenschaftsbetriebs sowie in gesetzlichen Vorgaben abbildet.[2]

Derartige Ansprüche gehen oft mit Verheißungen einer nachhaltigen Verbesserung einher. Offene Wissenschaft verspricht eine transparentere, replizierbarere und verantwortlichere – kurz: eine bessere – wissenschaftliche Praxis.

Im Bereich der qualitativ arbeitenden Sozialwissenschaften (aber auch in den Geisteswissenschaften) sind diese Entwicklungen erst später angekommen als in primär quantitativ orientierten Wissenschaftsbereichen. Sie werden mit größerer Skepsis rezipiert und öfter als äußere Einmischungen wahrgenommen, die gängige Praktiken der Forschung erschweren, gefährden oder sogar unmöglich machen

1 Vgl. z. B. Allianz der deutschen Wissenschaftsorganisationen (2010)

2 Für Österreich siehe etwa Policy für Forschungsdatenmanagement an der Universität Wien. Universität Wien, 2021: https://rdm.univie.ac.at/de/fdm-policy-und-faq/; Forschungsdatenmanagement-Policy der Universität Graz. Universität Graz, 2019: https://static.uni-graz.at/fileadmin/strategische-entwicklung/Dateien/FDM-Policy_DE_FINAL_Layout.pdf; Open Access für Forschungsdaten. FWF Der Wissenschaftsfonds: https://www.fwf.ac.at/de/forschungsfoerderung/open-access-policy/open-access-fuer-forschungsdaten

könnten.[3] Zugleich gibt es aber auch in den qualitativen Sozialwissenschaften intrinsische Motivationen für neue Formen des Teilens, Archivierens und Nachnutzens von Forschungsmaterialien. Diese setzen allerdings ein kritisches Hinterfragen der expliziten und impliziten Vorannahmen des Open-Research-Data-Diskurses voraus, an deren Stelle teils sehr andersgeartete Vorannahmen treten. Wie auch immer Forschende zum Open-Research-Data-Paradigma und dessen Forderungen stehen mögen: Spätestens mit der Etablierung der *FAIR Guiding Principles for scientific data management and stewardship*[4] und deren breiter Rezeption durch institutionelle Akteur:innen ist das Thema unumgänglich geworden.

Eine zentrale Voraussetzung für diese Entwicklungen war der etwa zeitgleich stattfindende Prozess der zunehmenden Digitalisierung der Forschungspraxis, der noch immer anhält. Auch dieser hat sich in verschiedenen Wissenschaftsbereichen sehr unterschiedlich abgebildet. In den qualitativen Sozialwissenschaften denkt man dabei vielleicht zuerst an die softwaregestützte Datenanalyse mit Programmen wie MAXQDA, ATLAS.ti und anderen. Aber auch unabhängig davon hat sich Hand in Hand mit der Digitalisierung vieler Lebensbereiche die Praxis qualitativer Datenerhebung grundlegend verändert. Das gilt nicht allein für die Erforschung digitaler Praktiken und Technologien, die seit Längerem ein wichtiges Forschungsfeld bilden, die zugleich aber durch ihre Alltäglichkeit heute in fast alle Felder sozialwissenschaftlicher Forschung hinein reichen.[5] Weniger beachtet, spielen die selbstverständlich gewordenen digitalen Kommunikations- und Datenpraktiken der Forschenden wie auch der Beforschten in der gegenwärtigen Realität sozialwissenschaftlicher Wissensproduktion eine zentrale Rolle. Soziale Medien und das Smartphone als Instrument für Kommunikation und Dokumentation – um nur die banalsten der heute alltäglichen digitalen Praktiken zu nennen – verändern die Rahmenbedingungen und Möglichkeiten für qualitative Forschung ebenso wie die konkreten Materialien, die daraus entstehen.

Im Bereich der qualitativ arbeitenden Sozialwissenschaften bringen diese Entwicklungen für Forschende wie für Repositorien gleichermaßen neue Herausforderungen mit sich. Einigen davon soll in diesem Beitrag nachgegangen werden, und dies aus einer doppelten Positioniertheit: Einmal aus der disziplinären Perspektive der Kultur- und Sozialanthropologie, einem Fach, in dem sich die spezifischen Eigenarten qualitativer sozialwissenschaftlicher Forschungen in besonderer Weise bün-

---

3 Imeri, S. (2019); Hirschauer, S. (2014); Pels, P. (2018).

4 Wilkinson, Mark D. et al. (2016); https://www.force11.org/fairprinciples

5 Einen Schwerpunkt bilden hier Forschungen im und zum Internet; vgl. z. B. Miller, D.; Slater, D. (2000); Miller, D.; Horst, H. A. (2012).

deln; zum anderen ausgehend von den Überlegungen und Erfahrungen des Ethnographischen Datenarchivs (eda), das Wolfgang Kraus gemeinsam mit Igor Eberhard seit 2017 als Kooperation der Universitätsbibliothek Wien und des Instituts für Kultur- und Sozialanthropologie der Universität Wien entwickelt hat.[6]

Die zentralen Zielsetzungen von eda sind zum einen der Aufbau und Betrieb eines digitalen Archivs für ethnographische und qualitative Forschungsdaten, zum anderen die Entwicklung von Best Practice-Modellen für alle Schritte des Datenmanagements und der Datenarchivierung. Die Langzeitarchivierung des Materials erfolgt im PHAIDRA-Repositorium der Universität Wien. Bei der Archivierung ist bisher historisches Material aus abgeschlossenen Forschungen im Vordergrund gestanden; in der Entwicklung konkreter Strategien und Workflows des Forschungsdatenmanagements geht es aber ebenso sehr um Hilfestellungen bei laufenden und zukünftigen Projekten.

Viele der spezifischen Herausforderungen, mit denen wir uns im eda-Zusammenhang auseinandersetzen, betreffen nicht nur Kultur- und Sozialanthropolog:innen, sondern auch qualitativ Forschende aus anderen sozialwissenschaftlichen Disziplinen, wie die einschlägige Literatur[7] sowie viele Gespräche mit Kolleg:innen deutlich zeigen. Die anthropologische Forschung mit ihrer ethnographischen Methodologie soll daher stellvertretend für das weitere Feld qualitativer sozialwissenschaftlicher Forschung stehen. Zugleich gibt es fachliche Besonderheiten, die die hier diskutierten Herausforderungen besonders dringlich machen, wie eine Fachgeschichte im historischen Zusammenhang von europäischer Expansion und Kolonialismus, die besondere ethische Fragen aufwirft und Forschende zu einer globalen und anti-eurozentrischen Perspektive verpflichtet.[8] Auch das Verständnis der Forschung als eines kollaborativen Prozesses gemeinsamer Wissensproduktion von Forschenden und Beforschten ist in der Kultur- und Sozialanthropologie ausgeprägter als in anderen Sozialwissenschaften. Über disziplinäre Grenzen hinaus weithin geteilt wird aber die Vorstellung, dass der Zugang zu den Lebenswelten der Forschungssubjekte ein Vertrauensverhältnis und oftmals Vertraulichkeit, somit also eine besondere Verantwortung der Forschenden impliziert.[9] Dies wiederum macht das Öffnen und Teilen der so gewonnenen Daten problematisch, manchmal auch unmöglich.

---

6 https://eda.univie.ac.at

7 Siehe etwa Bambey, D. et al. (2018); Chauvette, A. et al. (2019); Hirschauer, S. (2014); Mosconi, G. et al. (2019); van Unger, H. (2018); https://soziologie.de/aktuell/news/bereitstellung-und-nachnutzung-von-forschungsdaten-in-der-soziologie

8 Vgl. etwa Pels, P. (2008)

9 Vgl. etwa Hirschauer, S. (2014), S. 308-311

2. Was sind Forschungsdaten?

Die Schwierigkeiten beginnen bereits mit der Frage, ob ethnographische und ähnlich geartete qualitative Forschungszugänge überhaupt *Daten* produzieren. In Teilen der Sozial- und Geisteswissenschaften wird das verneint; manche ziehen es vor, stattdessen von *Materialien* zu sprechen.[10] Dies ist zunächst eine definitorische Frage. Beginnen wir also mit Definitionen. In den bereits zitierten FDM-Policies der Universitäten Wien und Graz fehlen diese oder bleiben sehr unspezifisch, um inklusiv genug für *alle* Arten von forschungrelevanten Materialien zu sein. Oft behilft man sich, im Bewusstsein der Vielgestaltigkeit dieser Materialien, mit beispielhaften Aufzählungen, was alles als Daten dienen kann.[11] Wird dies als Definition gehandelt, dann ergibt sich rasch eine zirkuläre Logik: Daten werden als die Evidenzbasis des wissenschaftlichen Prozesses bestimmt, während Wissenschaft durch ihre Evidenzbasiertheit definiert wird.

Deutlicher werden andere, substanziellere Definitionen. Diese finden sich eher im englischen Sprachraum und berufen sich oft auf eine Definition des United States Office of Management and Budget: “Research data is defined as the *recorded factual material* commonly accepted in the scientific community as necessary to validate research findings [...]” (unsere Hervorhebung).[12] Eine weitere des Öfteren zitierte Definition lautet: “Data that are *descriptive* of the *research object*, or are the object itself” (unsere Hervorhebung).[13]

Das dominierende Verständnis von Forschungsdaten, für das diese Formulierungen beispielhaft stehen, beruht in unserer Sicht auf einem engen positivistischen Modell des Forschungsprozesses, das generell zu kurz greift und das auf weite Teile sozial- und geisteswissenschaftlicher Forschung überhaupt nicht anwendbar ist. Es geht vereinfacht davon aus, dass Forschungsdaten, methodisch kontrolliertes Vorgehen vorausgesetzt, spezifische Aspekte der realen Welt *unabhängig von der Position der Forschenden* zu dokumentieren vermögen – eine Annahme, die auch im Bereich der Naturwissenschaften seit Beginn des 20. Jahrhunderts zunehmend als

---

10 Z. B. Imeri, S. (2018), S. 72. Zur Ablehnung des Datenbegriffes siehe Hirschauer, S. (2014), S. 303-305; Pels, P. (2018), S. 393-395; siehe auch Drucker, J. (2011).

11 Z. B.: https://www.dfg.de/download/pdf/foerderung/antragstellung/forschungsdaten/richtlinien_forschungsdaten.pdf; https://www.ukri.org/wp-content/uploads/2020/10/UKRI-020920-ConcordatonOpenResearchData.pdf (auf diese Formulierung verweist der FWF, vgl. Fußnote 2); https://www.forschungsdaten.info/praxis-kompakt/glossar/#c269821

12 United States Office of Management and Budget: OMB Circular A-110: https://www.whitehouse.gov/sites/whitehouse.gov/files/omb/circulars/A110/2cfr215-0.pdf (2006). Für eine davon abgeleitete Definition, die mehrere britische Institutionen verwenden, siehe Engineering and Physical Sciences Research Council: EPSRC Policy Framework on Research Data. Scope and Benefits: https://epsrc.ukri.org/about/standards/researchdata/scope/

13 https://wiki.bath.ac.uk/display/ERIMterminology/ERIM%20Terminology%20V4

problematisch erkannt worden ist. Aus dieser Annahme folgen zwei weitere: Diese Daten können ohne Rücksicht auf ihren spezifischen Entstehungskontext wiederverwendet werden, und sie eignen sich dafür, Forschungsergebnisse zu reproduzieren/replizieren oder gar zu verifizieren.[14] Das mag in Teilbereichen pragmatisch möglich und sogar sinnvoll sein, baut aber nichtsdestoweniger auf falschen wissenschaftstheoretischen Vorannahmen auf. Vor allem im Bereich der qualitativen Sozial- und Geisteswissenschaften ist das offenkundig.[15]

Genau dies sind aber die zentralen Forderungen des Open-Research-Data-Diskurses; genau daran setzen seine Heilsversprechen an, die, ganz der neoliberalen Rhetorik verpflichtet, mehr Kosteneffizienz, Transparenz und Accountability in der Wissensproduktion in Aussicht stellen.[16] Da hilft es nicht, wenn die Kategorie „Forschungsdaten" so offen und unscharf gehalten wird, wie es die beispielhaften Aufzählungen versuchen.[17] Der Diversität disziplinärer Datenpraktiken kann nicht durch einen unscharfen Datenbegriff Rechnung getragen werden, wenn die Zielsetzungen offener Forschungsdaten einen bestimmten, problematischen Datenbegriff implizieren. Vielmehr braucht das Öffnen qualitativer Forschungsdaten – dort, wo es überhaupt möglich ist – auch Zielsetzungen, die dem Selbstverständnis und der Epistemologie der zugrunde liegenden Forschungen entsprechen. Ist einmal geklärt, zu welchem Zweck und unter welchen Bedingungen Forschungsmaterialien geteilt werden sollen, dann kann man sich wohl auch pragmatisch darauf einigen, dass sie Daten genannt werden können.

14 „Es ist eine Grundlage der modernen Wissenschaft, dass Ergebnisse repliziert, verifiziert, falsifiziert und/oder für andere Zwecke wiederverwendet werden können. Im digitalen Zeitalter bedeutet dies den freien Zugang zu Forschungsdaten im Internet [...]" (FWF Der Wissenschaftsfonds: Open Access für Forschungsdaten: https://www.fwf.ac.at/ueber-uns/aufgaben-und-aktivitaeten/open-science. Es ist überraschend, dass der seit Poppers Kritischem Rationalismus weithin als überholt erachtete Begriff der Verifikation hier weiterhin als nützlich angesehen wird.

15 Für eine Kritik eines naiven Datenverständnisses aus geschichtswissenschaftlicher Perspektive siehe Fickers, A. (2020), S. 160-163. Zur Epistemologie ethnographischer Forschung im Kontrast zum positivistischen Datenverständnis siehe Kraus, W. (2021); Kraus, W.; Eberhard, I. (2022).

16 Z. B. https://www.openaire.eu/what-is-open-research-data; https://www.sshopencloud.eu/news/caring-sharing-workshop-data-mgmt-and-fairness-migration-data

17 Siehe Fußnote 11

3. Charakteristika ethnographisch-qualitativer Forschungsansätze

Die ethnographische Methodologie ist vor allem im fachlichen Zusammenhang der Kultur- und Sozialanthropologie entwickelt worden, wird heute aber in diversen disziplinären Feldern angewendet.[18] Sie ist überwiegend qualitativ orientiert, kann aber durchaus auch quantitative Verfahren einschließen. Sie soll hier, wie oben erwähnt, stellvertretend für qualitative Zugänge in den Sozialwissenschaften insgesamt stehen.

Ethnographie ist ein integrierter Forschungsansatz,[19] der verschiedene methodische Verfahren auf flexible Weise kombiniert und diverse Datenarten auf unterschiedlichen Datenträgern produziert, die nur im wechselseitigen Bezug aufeinander interpretiert ihr volles Potential entfalten. Ethnographische Feldforschung findet in der Regel über längere Zeiträume statt und erfordert intensive soziale Interaktionen mit jenen Personen, die im „Feld" agieren und dieses konstituieren – also jenen sozialen und kulturellen Raum, den Forschende durch ihre Forschungsfragen, Perspektiven und Vorannahmen definieren.[20] Alles, was Einsichten in das Feld liefert, hat potentiellen Datencharakter.

Anstelle homogener Datensets entsteht so ein diverser Datenkorpus, der auf persönlicher Involviertheit im Feld aufbaut und ergänzt wird durch persönliche Erfahrung und Erinnerung (ein Aspekt, den die rezente Herausbildung einer Anthropologie der Sinne und multimodaler Ansätze noch verstärkt hat). Die Ethnograph:in wird mit ihrer persönlichen Identität, ihrer körperlich/sinnlichen Erfahrung und ihrer Kommunikationsfähigkeit zu einem zentralen Werkzeug der Datenerhebung: „Die allmähliche Akkumulation von Felderfahrungen schafft bei der Forscherin ein umfangreiches Kontext- und Hintergrundwissen, eine Kennerschaft, die über Datensammlungen weit hinausreicht und einzelnen Daten erst ihren Sinn zuweist."[21]

Im Hinblick auf Herausforderungen im Zusammenhang von Datenmanagement und -öffnung lassen sich – aufgrund der hier gebotenen Kürze eher plakativ – folgende wichtige Charakteristika festhalten: Ethnographie ist (1) ergebnis- und prozessoffen, (2) integriert, (3) kontextabhängig sowie (4) sozial eingebettet.

(1) Als sowohl ergebnis- wie auch prozessoffener Zugang ist sie weniger planbar als andere sozialwissenschaftliche Verfahren. Das hat Auswirkungen auf heute zuneh-

---

18 Breidenstein, G. et al. (2020)
19 Breidenstein, G. et al. (2020), S. 38.
20 Gupta, A.; Ferguson, J. (1997), S. 1-46; Amit, V. (1999).
21 Breidenstein, G. et al (2020), S. 38.

mend routinisierte methodische Schritte wie Ethikprüfungen und Informierte Einwilligung. In diesem Zusammenhang ist das Konzept des *Processual Consent* wichtig, das davon ausgeht, dass sich Information und Einwilligung der Forschungssubjekte durch den gesamten Forschungsprozess hindurchziehen.[22] Dies sollte konsequenterweise auch die Schritte der Archivierung und möglichen Öffnung der Forschungsdaten einschließen.

(2) Der Begriff „integriert" meint, dass der ethnographische Zugang nicht aus einer Abfolge von klar abgrenzbaren Phasen besteht, wie es in *linearen* Verfahren der Fall ist. In der *rekursiven* Vorgangsweise der Ethnographie überlappen und durchdringen sich die Elemente des Forschungsprozesses, von der Fragestellung über die Konstruktion des Feldes, die Datenerhebung und -auswertung bis hin zur Textproduktion.[23] Sie befruchten sich gegenseitig und sind voneinander abhängig; Schritte, die in der Prozesslogik zeitliche Priorität haben, wie die Festlegung einer Forschungsfrage, sind bis zu einem gewissen Grad unter dem Einfluss der anderen Elemente revidierbar. Daraus folgt, dass auch Datenerhebung und Interpretation nicht voneinander getrennt werden können. Es gibt keine rohen, uninterpretierten ethnographischen Daten; zugleich ist selbstverständlich auch die Interpretation revidierbar. Nicht zuletzt führt die Rekursivität ethnographischen Forschens dazu, dass meist ein Datenüberschuss produziert wird: Im Verlauf der Forschung ist nicht immer absehbar, welche Daten am besten geeignet sind, die sich entwickelnde Forschungsfrage zu bearbeiten. Und auch die genutzten Daten haben aufgrund ihrer Dichte oft einen Mehrwert, der in der laufenden Forschung nicht ausgeschöpft wird.

(3) Kontextabhängigkeit bedeutet, dass ethnographische Daten, wie erwähnt, grundsätzlich im Bezug aufeinander und auf den Gesamtkontext der Forschung zu interpretieren sind.[24] Dies schließt auch die Positionalitäten der Forschenden zentral mit ein. Zugleich beziehen sie sich auf den weiteren Kontext des jeweiligen Feldes: Ethnographische Interpretation und Erklärung beruht im heutigen Verständnis in einem hohen Maß auf der Kontextualisierung der untersuchten Phänomene.[25] Die Kontextgebundenheit ethnographischer Daten, die grundsätzlich von in Zeit und Raum situierten Einzelfällen sprechen, macht eine Anonymisierung unmöglich und auch die Pseudonymisierung vielfach schwierig und kontraproduktiv, da diese unweigerlich mit Kontextverlust einhergeht.

---

22 Z. B. Rosenblatt, P. C. (1995); vgl. RatSWD (2017), S. 23.
23 Breidenstein, G. et al. (2020), S. 51f.
24 Holstein, J.; Gubrium, J. (2007); Eberhard, I. (2020).
25 Dilley, R. M. (2002)

(4) Ethnographische Forschung beruht darauf, dass Forschende in ein soziales Feld eintreten und darin Beziehungen aufnehmen. Es soll nicht „authentisches" und unbeeinflusstes Verhalten dokumentiert werden; vielmehr geht es darum, ins Feld einzugreifen, um mit den Forschungssubjekten zu kommunizieren und zu interagieren. Aus dieser sozialen Einbettung der Forschung resultiert neben der Verpflichtung zur Reflexivität eine relationale Forschungspraxis,[26] in der auch den Beforschten eine aktive Rolle in der Wissensproduktion eingeräumt wird – darum sprechen wir ja von Forschungssubjekten. Daraus folgt eine weiterreichende ethische Verantwortung als bei anderen sozialwissenschaftlichen Forschungsansätzen: Wenn Forschende mit ihrem jeweiligen Feld interagieren, dann hat das soziale Auswirkungen, die mit besonderer Sorgfalt auf mögliche schädliche Folgen hin geprüft werden müssen. Solche potentiellen Auswirkungen hat auch das Teilen von Forschungsdaten.[27]

Wird die relationale Praxis ethnographischer Forschung bis ans Ende gedacht, dann ergibt sich ein Bild dialogischer und kollaborativer Wissensproduktion, das heute von den meisten Anthropolog:innen geteilt wird,[28] keineswegs jedoch in allen Bereichen qualitativer sozialwissenschaftlicher Forschung. Wir vertreten aber die Position, dass ein solches Forschungsverständnis in letzter Konsequenz eine Voraussetzung für ein sinnvolles und ethisch vertretbares Teilen von Daten darstellt. Grundlage dafür ist wiederum ein Selbstverständnis, das den Forschungssubjekten ein Wissen zugesteht, über das die Forschenden nicht verfügen, und das in der nichthierarchischen Begegnung und dem Austausch unterschiedlicher Perspektiven den produktiven Kern der qualitativ-ethnographischen Methodologie sieht.

4. Archivpessimimus

Regelmäßig wiederkehrende Einwände gegen ein leichtfertiges Öffnen ethnographischer Forschungsdaten führen rechtliche, ethische und forschungspragmatische Gründe an: Forschende bauen in lang andauernder Anwesenheit im Feld soziale Beziehungen auf, die auf wechselseitigem Vertrauen beruhen und zu einem verantwortlichen Umgang mit den Daten verpflichten, was im Fall einer Nutzung durch Dritte nicht sichergestellt werden kann. Die Beziehungen zwischen Forschenden und Beforschten zu öffnen, bringt das Risiko unerwünschter praktischer

---

26 Thelen, T. (2015), S. 20.

27 Eberhard, I.; Kraus, W. (2018), S. 45-48.

28 Lassiter, L. E. (2005); EASA's Statement on Data Governance in Ethnographic Projects: https://www.easaonline.org/downloads/support/EASA%20statement%20on%20data%20governance.pdf

Auswirkungen im Feld, aber auch möglicher Formen der Selbstzensur im Hinblick auf die Datenproduktion.[29]

Während solche Bedenken durchaus mit einer grundsätzlichen Zustimmung zu angepassten Formen des Archivierens und Teilens qualitativer Daten einhergehen können, nimmt Hirschauer aus soziologischer Perspektive eine radikalere Haltung zur Forderung nach breiter Archivierung und Öffnung qualitativer sozialwissenschaftlicher Daten ein.[30] Seine Argumente entsprechen zum Teil den bereits erwähnten; er spricht aber schon den grundsätzlichen Zielen der Archivierung und Nachnutzung solcher Daten die Sinnhaftigkeit ab und warnt vor dem „archivarischen Unsinn" einer bloßen Anhäufung von Daten.[31] Dabei räumt er immerhin Ausnahmen ein: Im Bereich der Ethnologie mache es Sinn, Daten als wertvolle Kulturgüter zu betrachten. Ähnliches gelte für die zeithistorische Forschung und ihre Methodologie der Oral History sowie die Biographieforschung.[32]

Dieses Zugeständnis einer begrenzten Sinnhaftigkeit der Datenarchivierung für die Ethnologie (d. h. Kultur- und Sozialanthropologie) stützt sich allerdings auf eine zynische Karikatur ihrer Forschungsziele:

> Die gesamte Ethnologie ist nicht nur in ihren Sammlungen, sondern auch in ihren Ethnografien von einem empirischen Rettungsmotiv durchdrungen. So wie der Klimawandel Inseln überspült, so verschluckt die Globalisierung das kulturhistorische Erbe der Menschheit, *heißt es*. Museale Sammlungen von Artefakten und Videoaufzeichnungen von Kulturtechniken und Sprachen sollen das Schlimmste verhüten.[33]

Nun hat die Haltung einer „Salvage Ethnography", auf die Hirschauer hier verweist, in der Vergangenheit des Faches zweifellos an verschiedenen Punkten eine wichtige Rolle gespielt und auch Anerkennenswertes geleistet.[34] Der gegenwärtige Mainstream des Faches steht Vorannahmen von kultureller Authentizität und destruktivem Wandel allerdings äußerst kritisch gegenüber, und gerade seine Sicht

---

29 Imeri, S. (2019), S. 49.

30 Hirschauer, S. (2014). Für eine weit nuanciertere und konstruktivere Form des Archivpessimismus siehe Meier zu Verl, C.; Meier, C. (2018), S. 80-90.

31 Hirschauer, S. (2014), S. 301f.

32 Hirschauer, S. (2014), S. 301.

33 Hirschauer, S. (2014), S. 301 (unsere Hervorhebung). Quellenangaben, wo es das „heißt", fehlen. Sie aus der rezenten Literatur beizubringen wäre auch schwierig.

34 So etwa vor rund hundert Jahren in der Boas'schen Tradition, die die Anthropologie in den USA nachhaltig geprägt hat.

auf Globalisierung – ein zentrales Thema in der Anthropologie der vergangenen Jahrzehnte – unterscheidet sich diametral von dem, was Hirschauer insinuiert.[35]

Aber zurück zu seinen ernsthaften Argumenten. Soziolog:innen sitzen „inmitten ihrer zeitgenössischen, sprudelnden Datenquellen“; frische Daten können jederzeit mit wenig Aufwand generiert werden; der Aufwand der Datenarchivierung erscheint gegenüber dem potentiellen Nutzen unverhältnismäßig. Qualitative Materialien „leiden [im Gegensatz zu quantitativen Daten] nicht unter Sinnschwäche, sondern unter Sinnfülle“, das heißt, sie müssen für eine Interpretation kontextualisiert werden. Die qualitative Forschung analysiert nicht zuvor gewonnene Daten, sondern „stellt in einer theorieorientierten Analyse den Wert bestimmter Informantenäußerungen *als Datum* erst her.“[36] Eine sinnvolle Verfügbarmachung von Daten kann daher nur in „analytisch geordnete[r] und kommunikativ verstehbare[r] Form“, das heißt in Form von Publikationen erfolgen.[37]

In der Folge führt Hirschauer einige Charakteristika qualitativer und ethnographischer Forschung an, die hier bereits besprochen worden sind – die Kontext-, Erfahrungs- und Interpretationsgebundenheit ihrer Materialien, die sich nicht sinnvoll in jenen Datenbegriff zwängen lässt, der der Forderung nach Datenarchivierung zugrunde liegt. Dem in kleinen Teilbereichen gegebenen Nutzen eines Teilens von Daten stellt er den Aufwand und die Kosten einer breiten Datenarchivierung und ihr massives Potential gegenüber, das zu beschädigen, was er das „Arbeitsbündnis mit den InformantInnen“ nennt. Diese Bilanz ist für ihn klar negativ.[38] Er schließt: „Es ist ein Segen, dass die meisten Daten nach ihrer Gewinnung und analytischen Verarbeitung aus unserem Gedächtnis und unseren Dateien verschwinden. Das macht den Kopf frei für die Erfindung neuer und besserer Forschungsfragen.“[39]

Wenn wir auch die Grundhaltung und die Schlussfolgerungen Hirschauers nicht teilen, so gibt es in seiner Argumentation doch eine Reihe von Übereinstimmungen mit den Überlegungen, die unserer Arbeit im Ethnographischen Datenarchiv zugrunde liegen. Ihnen stehen aber zwei grundsätzliche Unterschiede gegenüber. Der eine betrifft die Historizität der Materialien: Diese ist für Hirschauer nur in wenigen Teilbereichen relevant; im Kernbereich soziologischen qualitativen For-

35 Vgl. etwa Hannerz, U. (1992)
36 Hirschauer, S. (2014), S. 302f. (Hervorhebung original).
37 Hirschauer, S. (2014), S. 302.
38 Hirschauer, S. (2014), S. 304-311.
39 Hirschauer, S. (2014), S. 311.

schens geht es aber um das Hier und Jetzt. Die Möglichkeit, dass etwa aus Interviews ihre zeitliche Einbettung in einer Weise spricht, die der soziologischen Primäranalyse entgeht, zieht er nicht in Betracht.

Der zweite Punkt, nicht ohne Zusammenhang mit dem ersten, betrifft die Rolle, die den „Informant:innen" zugestanden wird. Sie sind nicht Partner:innen mit eigenen Stimmen, die als Teil eines Dialogs gehört werden können, sondern sind zur Gänze der Analyseleistung der Forscher:in untergeordnet. Wie könnte ihnen da ein eigenes aktives Interesse an den entstandenen Daten eingeräumt werden? Genau diese beiden Punkte, in denen wir uns Hirschauers Sicht entgegenstellen, sind aber zentral in unserer Begründung der Legitimität und Sinnhaftigkeit ethnographischer Datenarchivierung.

5. Archivoptimismus

Mit Archivoptimismus meinen wir nicht ein kritikloses Aufspringen auf den aktuellen Trend, sondern eine konstruktiv-kritische Haltung, die in der einschlägigen Literatur weit häufiger vertreten ist als Hirschauers radikale Verweigerung. Sie weist darauf hin, dass die Forderungen nach der Öffnung qualitativer sozialwissenschaftlicher Daten diverse problematische Aspekte beinhalten und ihre praktische Umsetzung – soweit überhaupt möglich und vertretbar – der Eigenart solcher Daten angepasst werden muss. Diese Haltung sieht aber in einer solchen Öffnung eine grundsätzlich sinnvolle Strategie. Die Argumente und Zielsetzungen sind dabei aber typischerweise andere als die des dominanten Diskurses von Kosteneffizienz, Transparenz und Accountability.

Soll man solche Zwischenpositionen fernab von naiver Begeisterung für das neue Paradigma offener Forschung optimistisch nennen? Wir denken ja, weil sie im Archivieren, Verfügbarmachen und Teilen der Daten eine positive Entwicklung sehen und Schritte unternehmen, diese auf sinnvolle Weise voranzutreiben. Stimmen in diesem Sinn sind in der Literatur zahlreich – selbst wenn möglicherweise eine schweigende Mehrheit von qualitativ Forschenden solchen Bestrebungen weiterhin skeptisch gegenüber steht.

Am relevantesten für unseren Argumentationszusammenhang sind dabei jene Beiträge, in denen es um konkrete Versuche geht, Strategien zur Archivierung qualitativer Forschungsmaterialien zu entwickeln und umzusetzen. Das ist nun keinesfalls ein neues Anliegen. Die analogen Vorläufer solcher Initiativen sind jedoch typischerweise an eine klassische Archivlogik und oft an einzelne Institutionen oder

Nachlässe von Forscher:innenpersönlichkeiten gebunden.[40] Aber bei der Digitalisierung und digitalen Öffnung auch persönlicher Forschungsarchive stellen sich bereits ganz ähnliche Herausforderungen wie bei breiter angelegten qualitativen und ethnographischen digitalen Datenarchiven. Ein frühes, nun aber leider vernachlässigtes Beispiel sind die ab 1990 digital aufbereiteten Ethnographic Data Archives des Anthropologen Paul Stirling, die derzeit nur in Teilen zugänglich sind.[41] Noch deutlicher gilt das für institutionellen Archive.[42]

Dominierte in diesen Beispielen die retrospektive Orientierung, so ist in den letzten Jahrzehnten das Archivieren und Teilen von Materialien aus aktuellen oder rezenten Forschungen in den Vordergrund getreten. Exemplarische Initiativen zur analogen und digitalen Archivierung ethnographischer und qualitativer Forschungsdaten sowie deren Potentiale und Nutzungsformen, aber auch die damit verbundenen Herausforderungen werden in diversen Beiträgen besprochen.[43] Diese sind sich generell einig, dass solche Daten ein wertvolles Gut und ihre Erhaltung eine sinnvolle Maßnahme darstellen. Aber wertvoll und sinnvoll im Hinblick auf welche Ziele?

Neben den oft unspezifizierten allgemeinen Vorteilen einer Sekundärnutzung werden diverse weitere Gründe angeführt, darunter die folgenden: Ein Potential, aber auch ein Handlungsbedarf im Zusammenhang mit den aktuellen Veränderungen der Forschungspraxis durch die Digitalisierung (Weber[44], Murillo[45]) sowie das konventionellere Argument verbesserter Möglichkeiten für Vergleich und Restudy (Parezo et al.[46], Corti und Thompson[47]). Ein wichtiger Punkt ist das (zumindest potentielle) historische Interesse des Materials (Corti und Thompson, Zeitlyn[48]), begründet nicht zuletzt aus einer Analogie der Nutzung qualitativen Archivmaterials

---

40 Z. B. Margaret Mead papers and South Pacific Ethnographic Archives, 1838-1996 in der Library of Congress: https://www.loc.gov/item/mm81032441/; National Anthropological Archives. Smithsonian Institution: https://www.si.edu/siasc/naa; vgl. Leopold, R. (2008).

41 The Center for Social Anthropology and Computing: Forty-five years in two Turkish Villages. 1949–1994. University of Kent at Canterbury: http://era.anthropology.ac.uk/Era_Resources/Era/Stirling/index.html

42 Z. B. Royal Anthropological Institute: Archives and Manuscripts: https://therai.org.uk/archives-and-manuscripts. Das digitalisierte Archiv des RAI ist auf kommerzieller Basis über Wiley Digital Archives zugänglich, siehe https://www.wileydigitalarchives.com/royal-anthropological-institute-of-great-britain-and-ireland/

43 Siehe unter anderem Silverman, S.; Parezo, N. (1995); Parezo, N. J. et al. (2003); Corti, L.; Thompson, P. (2007); Lederman, R. (2016); Weber, F. (2017); Knoblauch, H.; Wilke, R. (2018); Murillo, L. F. R. (2018); Zeitlyn, D. (2021).

44 Weber, F. (2017)

45 Murillo, L. F. R. (2018)

46 Parezo, N. J. et al. (2003)

47 Corti, L.; Thompson, P. (2007)

48 Zeitlyn, D. (2021)

mit der Arbeitsweise von Historiker:innen (Lederman[49]). Damit im Zusammenhang wird auch die Bedeutung für die Fachgeschichte (Parezo et al.) sowie im Bereich der Lehre (Corti und Thompson) unterstrichen.

Dazu kommt noch ein zumindest aus der Perspektive des aktuellen anthropologischen Verständnisses ethnographischer Forschung zentrales Argument: Das Potential des Materials für eine Nutzung durch die Beforschten, die von ganz anderen Interessen geleitet sein kann als die akademische, sich mit dieser aber auch überschneiden kann.[50] Diese Konsequenz aus der dialogischen Produktion ethnographischen Wissens formuliert Murillo am deutlichsten: Er sieht – bei aller Sorge um den Schutz vor Missbrauch – in der Öffnung ethnographischer Daten die Chance, von einem "hyperindividualized regime of academic production" und der Konzeption der Ethnograph:in als "possessive author" abzurücken. Dies könne "possibilities for experimentation with collaborative production, circulation, presentation, and openness of ethnographic datasets" eröffnen.[51] Die Herausforderung, diese Ziele mit jenem des Schutzes der Privatsphäre zu vereinbaren, kann für ihn ebenfalls durch eine "collective curation of ethnographic datasets" bewältigt werden, die auf der Kollaboration von Forschenden, Beforschten und Computerexpert:innen beruht.[52]

6. Grundsätze und Lösungsansätze des Ethnographischen Datenarchivs

Die Zielsetzungen, die in diesen Beiträgen sichtbar werden, decken sich weitgehend mit den Motiven, die der Einrichtung und den Grundsätzen des Ethnographischen Datenarchivs (eda) an der Universitätsbibliothek Wien, zugrunde liegen.[53] Dabei sind wir von der Beobachtung ausgegangen, dass (wie bereits erwähnt) in ethnographischen und qualitativen Forschungsansätzen meist ein Datenüberschuss produziert wird, der in der primären Analyse nicht zur Gänze ausgewertet werden kann. Darüber hinaus können die Daten durch ihre Komplexität und Dichte auch aus anderen analytischen Perspektiven betrachtet und nutzbar gemacht werden.

Eine weitere Motivation für Erhaltung und Archivierung ist der historische Grundcharakter dieses Materials. Da es immer kontextuell in Zeit und Raum situiert ist,

49 Lederman, R. (2016)
50 Beispiele dafür nennen Parezo, N. J. et al. (2003), S. 111.
51 Murillo, L. F. R. (2018), S. 577.
52 Murillo, L. F. R. (2018), S. 581.
53 Siehe Fußnote 6

hat es grundsätzlich das Potential, auf ursprünglich nicht intendierte Weise (d. h. ganz ohne ein „Rettungsmotiv", wie es Hirschauer unterstellt)[54] Prozesse von Transformation und Veränderung zu beleuchten. Das dritte zentrale Argument schließlich ist die Möglichkeit, die Daten den Beforschten zugänglich zu machen und kollaborativ für unterschiedliche Zwecke und Nutzungsformen zu erschließen.

Die Archivierung qualitativer und ethnographischer Forschungsdaten stellt sowohl Forschende als auch Repositorien vor ernsthafte Herausforderungen. Im Kontext des Ethnographischen Datenarchivs wurden dafür wenigstens teilweise Überlegungen und Lösungsansätze entwickelt, die hier kurz vorgestellt werden sollen.[55] Dafür greifen wir nochmals die oben genannten vier Charakteristika ethnographischer Forschung auf.

Die ergebnis- und prozessoffene Vorgangsweise bedingt, dass es keine mechanischen Kriterien im Hinblick auf informierte Einwilligung geben kann, deren Aushandlung stets ein kontextueller und permanenter Prozess bleibt. Ebenso kann in vorab erstellten Datenmanagementplänen höchstens provisorisch festgelegt werden, welche Daten entstehen werden und welche davon für eine Archivierung geeignet sind. Es mag im Projektzusammenhang sinnvoll sein, Datenobjekte in einem Repositorium zu sammeln, das besser als andere Datenspeicher die Datensicherung und den Schutz vor unbefugten Zugriffen gewährleisten kann. Aber erst am (vorläufigen) Ende des integrierten Forschungsprozesses sollte entschieden werden, welche Daten für welche Zwecke zugänglich gemacht werden können. Soweit möglich, sollten diese Entscheidungen und die gesamte Datenkuratierung unter Einbeziehung der Forschungssubjekte erfolgen. Das verlangt Flexibilität und Kooperationsbereitschaft nicht nur von den Forschenden, sondern auch von den Repositorien.

Die Kontextabhängigkeit ethnographischer und qualitativer Daten bedeutet, dass im Hinblick auf eine Nachnutzung ihr Forschungs- und Feldkontext so sorgfältig wie möglich dokumentiert werden und der vernetzte Charakter der Datenobjekte sichtbar gemacht muss. Dies bringt für die Forschenden wie auch die Archivierenden einen erheblichen Zusatzaufwand mit sich. Die unabdingbare Bedeutung des Kontextes erschwert die Pseudonymisierung der Daten, da diese immer mit einem Kontextverlust einhergeht; umgekehrt können Aspekte der Daten selbst (vor allem bei multimedialen Daten) sowie Kontextinformationen zur Erkennbarkeit von Personen und Gruppen führen und ihren Schutz gefährden.

---

54 Hirschauer, S. (2014), S. 301.

55 Für eine ausführliche Darstellung der Grundsätze und Archivierungspraxis von eda siehe Kraus, W. (2021).

Überlegungen zur Kontextualisierung spielen im eda-Metadatenschema eine zentrale Rolle und reichen über die eigentlichen Metadaten weit hinaus. Im PHAIDRA-Repositorium, in dem die die Objekte des ethnographischen Datenarchivs archiviert werden, sind Metadaten grundsätzlich immer öffentlich. Das schränkt ihre Tauglichkeit für gewisse Kontextinformationen ein, bei denen ohnehin das Risiko besteht, dass sie die Metadaten überfrachten und von deren primärem Zweck, der Auffindbarkeit der Objekte, ablenken. Daher haben wir eine neue Datenkategorie entwickelt, die wir Kontextdaten nennen. In der Regel in Textform, sind dies beschreibende Kontextinformationen, zu denen, sofern erforderlich, der Zugang eingeschränkt oder ganz gesperrt werden kann. Da die Erstellung von Kontextdaten eine Recherche- und Forschungsleistung erfordert, können sie auch, anders als Metadaten, eine Urheberschaft haben. Eine besondere Form von Kontextdaten sind forschungsbiographische Interviews, wie sie beispielsweise Igor Eberhard mit Elke Mader zu ihren Forschungen in Peru und Ecuador (1979-99) geführt hat.[56]

Eine Konsequenz der Einbettung ethnographischer Forschungen in kollaborative soziale Beziehungen ist das potentielle Interesse der Forschungssubjekte an den Daten sowie ihr Anrecht darauf. Dilger et al. halten dazu fest: "The first duty in ethnographic research is [...] to recognize this joint production and joint ownership of research materials. All forms and norms of managing data depend on it."[57] Das bedeutet, dass die Beforschten oder ihre Nachkommen nach Möglichkeit in alle Schritte des Managements und der Archivierung eingebunden werden sollten, sofern sie das wollen.[58] Immer öfter knüpfen auch die Communities der Beforschten ihre Zustimmung an eine Mitsprache bei der Planung und Durchführung der Forschung und beim Datenmanagement.[59]

Die Interessen der Forschungssubjekte an den Daten können auch gängige Grundsätze des Datenschutzes und Schutzes der Privatsphäre in Frage stellen, wie Zeitlyn nachdrücklich argumentiert.[60] Im ethnographischen Zusammenhang geht es dabei nicht primär um abstrakte individualistisch gedachte Schutzprinzipien, sondern um den konkreten Schutz der Forschungssubjekte unter Rücksicht auf ihre spezifischen Interessen und ihre soziale Einbettung. Daraus können sich zusätzliche Gründe für Zugangsbeschränkungen ergeben (so schlägt Zeitlyn eine langfristige

56 Siehe https://phaidra.univie.ac.at/o:1146526. Zu Kontextdaten sowie zur neuen Kategorie Containerobjekte vgl. Eberhard, I. (2020).
57 Dilger, H. et al. (2019), S. 4.
58 Anders als manche anderen Initiativen ähnlicher Art haben wir in eda noch keine Erfahrungen damit sammeln können, wollen aber in der nahen Zukunft damit beginnen.
59 Vgl. Eberhard, I.; Kraus, W. (2018), S. 47f. Für den größeren Kontext der Forderungen konkreter indigener Gruppen im Hinblick auf Daten, die sie betreffen, siehe Imeri, S.; Rizzolli, M. (2022).
60 Zeitlyn, D. (2021)

Sperre mancher Arten von Daten statt ihrer Pseudonymisierung vor).[61] Bei allen diesen Entscheidungen ist die Mitsprache der Beforschten essentiell, vor allem aber bei Fragen der Datenkuratierung und des Zugangs zu spezifischen Daten: Welche Daten sollen von welchen Kategorien von Personen eingesehen werden können? Für Repositorien erfordert das die Implementierung komplexer Modelle eines gestaffelten Zugangsmanagements mit erheblichem personellem und technischem Aufwand.[62]

7. Conclusio: Von der Forderung zur Förderung

In seiner Konsequenz bedeutet das heutige dialogisch-reflexive Selbstverständnis ethnographischer Forschung, dass das dominante Bild von Datenmanagement und offenen Forschungsdaten mit seinen oft abstrakt gedachten Akteur:innen – neben den Forschenden sind das vor allem *die Scientific Community* und *die Öffentlichkeit* – um weitere, sehr konkrete Akteur:innen erweitert werden muss, nämlich die Forschungssubjekte und ihre spezifischen Communities. Das bringt Komplikationen im Hinblick auf die geforderte Praxis der Öffnung von Forschungsdaten und ihre Ziele mit sich; es bringt aber auch eine andere, intrinsische Motivation für das Teilen von Daten. Daraus resultieren Herausforderungen sowohl für Forschende als auch für Repositorien, die ihre Infrastruktur entsprechend anpassen müssen.

Bei der Archivierung von Forschungsdaten können die meisten dieser Herausforderungen nicht mit institutionellen Regeln, sondern nur in kontinuierlicher enger Kooperation mit den Forschenden bewältigt werden. Dazu kommt noch die wichtige und produktive Kollaboration mit den Beforschten sowie die Rücksichtnahme auf ihre Interessen, die nicht zuletzt aus forschungsethischen Gründen geboten ist.

Es mag disziplinäre Zusammenhänge geben, in denen es für das Erfüllen der Forderung nach offenen Forschungsdaten nicht viel mehr braucht als das Ablegen vorhandener Daten in geeigneten Repositorien. Aber schon 2010 vermerkte die Allianz der deutschen Wissenschaftsorganisationen: „Die Bereitstellung von Forschungsdaten zur weiteren Nutzung ist eine Leistung, die der Wissenschaft als Ganzer zu Gute kommt. Die Allianz ermutigt zur Anerkennung und Förderung dieses zusätzlichen zeitlichen und finanziellen Aufwands."[63] Wie sehr diese Sicht zutreffend und notwendig ist, das wird in kaum einem Bereich so deutlich wie bei qualitativen und

61 Zeitlyn, D. (2021)
62 Sterzer, W.; Imeri, S.; Harbeck, M. (2018)
63 Allianz der deutschen Wissenschaftsorganisationen (2010)

ethnographischen Daten, die erst mit großem Aufwand kuratiert, kontextualisiert und aufbereitet werden müssen.[64]

Eine Bereitstellung und teilweise Öffnung dieser Daten auf breiter Basis verlangt von den Forschenden nicht nur Archivoptimismus, sondern auch die Fähigkeit, zwischen widersprüchlichen Anforderungen und Zielkonflikten zu navigieren, Kompromissbereitschaft im Umgang mit den anderen am Prozess Beteiligten, sowie entsprechende Prioritäten bei der Zuteilung von viel Arbeitszeit (die auch finanziert sein muss). Bei den Repositorien braucht es ebenfalls Flexibilität und Kompromissbereitschaft sowie eine Personalausstattung, die den erforderlichen Ausbau, die aufwändige Betreuung von Forschenden und Daten und das oft noch ungeklärte Zugangsmanagement ermöglicht. Auch institutionell ist das eine Frage von Prioritäten. Im im Zusammenhang mit dem Ethnographischen Datenarchiv werden wir bei der engen und guten Zusammenarbeit mit dem Team des Repositoriums PHAIDRA stets bereitwillig und bestmöglich unterstützt; an Arbeitskapazität fehlt es aber an allen Ecken und Enden. Mit der Forderung nach offenen Forschungsdaten ist es nicht getan: Es bedarf neben der Motivation aller Beteiligten auch einer entsprechenden Förderung aller dafür nötigen Aktivitäten. Gerade in Österreich ist da noch sehr viel zu tun.

Bibliografie

Allianz der deutschen Wissenschaftsorganisationen (2010): Grundsätze zum Umgang mit Forschungsdaten. Helmholtz-Zentrum Potsdam Deutsches GeoForschungsZentrum – GFZ. https://doi.org/10.2312/ALLIANZOA.019

Amit, Vered (Hg.) (1999): Constructing the Field. Ethnographic Fieldwork in the Contemporary World. London: Routledge.

Bambey, Doris; Corti, Louise; Diepenbroek, Michael; Dunkel, Wolfgang; Hanekop, Heidemarie; Hollstein, Betina; Imeri, Sabine; Knoblauch, Hubert; Kretzer, Susanne; Meier zu Verl, Christian; Meyer, Christian; Meyermann, Alexia; Porzelt, Maike; Rittberger, Marc; Strübing, Jörg; von Unger, Hella; Wilke, René (2018): Archivierung und Zugang zu Qualitativen Daten. (RatSWD Working Paper Series 267). Berlin: RatSWD. https://doi.org/10.17620/02671.35

Breidenstein, Georg; Hirschauer, Stefan; Kalthoff, Herbert; Nieswand, Boris (2020): Ethnografie. Die Praxis der Feldforschung. 3. Aufl. München: UVK-Verlag (= utb 3979).

Chauvette, Amelia; Schick-Makaroff, Kara; Molzahn, Anita E. (2019): Open Data in Qualitative Research. In: International Journal of Qualitative Methods 18, pp. 1-6. https://doi.org/10.1177/1609406918823863

64 Vgl. Pels, P. (2018)

Corti, Louise; Thompson, Paul (2007): Secondary Analysis of Archived Data. In: Seale, Clive; Gobo, Giampietro; Gubrium, Jaber F.; Silverman, David (eds.): Qualitative Research Practice. Thousand Oaks: SAGE, pp. 297-313. https://doi.org/10.4135/9781848608191.d26

Dilger, Hansjörg; Pels, Peter; Sleeboom-Faulkner, Margaret (2019): Guidelines for Data Management and Scientific Integrity in Ethnography. In: Ethnography 20 (1), pp. 3-7.

Dilley, R. M. (2002): The Problem of Context in Social and Cultural Anthropology. In: Language & Communication 22, pp. 437-456. https://doi.org/10.1016/S0271-5309(02)00019-8

Drucker, Johanna (2011): Humanities Approaches to Graphical Display. In: Digital Humanities Quarterly 5 (1). http://www.digitalhumanities.org/dhq/vol/5/1/000091/000091.html (abgerufen am 30.12.2021)

Eberhard, Igor (2020): Der Kontext bestimmt alles. Kontextdaten und Containerobjekte als Lösungsmöglichkeiten für den Umgang mit sozialwissenschaftlichen qualitativen Daten. Erfahrungen aus dem Pilotprojekt „Ethnographische Datenarchivierung“ an der Universitätsbibliothek Wien. In: ABI Technik 40 (2), S. 169-176. https://doi.org/10.1515/abitech-2020-2007

Eberhard, Igor; Kraus, Wolfgang (2018): Der Elefant im Raum. Ethnographisches Forschungsdatenmanagement als Herausforderung für Repositorien. In: Mitteilungen der Vereinigung Österreichischer Bibliothekarinnen und Bibliothekare 71 (1), S. 41-52.

Fickers, Andreas (2020): Update für die Hermeneutik. Geschichtswissenschaft auf dem Weg zur digitalen Forensik? In: Zeithistorische Forschungen 17 (1), S. 157-168. https://doi.org/10.14765/zzf.dok-1765

Gupta, Akhil; Ferguson, James (1997): Discipline and Practice. „The Field“ as Site, Method and Location in Anthropology. In: Gupta, Akhil; Ferguson, James (Hg.): Anthropological Locations. Boundaries and Grounds of a Field Science. Berkeley: University of California Press, pp. 1-46.

Hannerz, Ulf (1992): Cultural Complexity. Studies in the Social Organization of Meaning. New York: Columbia University Press.

Hirschauer, Stefan (2014): Sinn im Archiv? Zum Verhältnis von Nutzen, Kosten und Risiken der Datenarchivierung. In: Soziologie 43 (3), S. 300-312. https://publikationen.soziologie.de/index.php/soziologie/article/view/795 (abgerufen am 25.4.2023)

Holstein, James; Gubrium, Jaber (2007): Context. Working It Up, Down, and Across. In: Seale, Clive; Gobo, Giampietro; Gubrium, Jaber F.; Silverman, David (eds.): Qualitative Research Practice. Thousand Oaks: SAGE, pp. 267-281. https://doi.org/10.4135/9781848608191.d24

Imeri, Sabine; Rizzolli, Michaela (2022): CARE Principles for Indigenous Data Governance. Eine Leitlinie für ethische Fragen im Umgang mit Forschungsdaten? In: O-Bib. Das Offene Bibliotheksjournal, 9 (2), S. 1-14. https://doi.org/10.5282/o-bib/5815

Imeri, Sabine (2019): „Open Data“ in den ethnologischen Fächern. Möglichkeiten und Grenzen eines Konzepts. In: Klingner, Jens; Lühr, Merve (Hg.): Forschungsdesign 4.0. Datengenerierung und Wissenstransfer in interdisziplinärer Perspektive. Dresden: Institut für Sächsische Geschichte und Volkskunde, S. 45-59. https://doi.org/10.25366/2019.07

Imeri, Sabine (2018): Archivierung und Verantwortung: Zum Stand der Debatte über den Umgang mit Forschungsdaten in den ethnologischen Fächern. In: Bambey, Doris et al.: Archivierung und Zugang zu Qualitativen Daten. (RatSWD Working Paper Series 267). Berlin: RatSWD. S. 69-79. https://doi.org/10.17620/02671.35

Knoblauch, Hubert; Wilke, René (2018): Forschungsdateninfrastrukturen für audio-visuelle Daten der Qualitativen Sozialforschung – Bedarf und Anforderungen. In: Bambey, Doris et al.: Archivierung und Zugang zu Qualitativen Daten. (RatSWD Working Paper Series 267). Berlin: RatSWD, S. 47-57. https://doi.org/10.17620/02671.35

Kraus, Wolfgang (2021): Setting up a Digital Archive for Ethnographic Data. Challenges, Strategies, Experiences. In: Dreiser, Anja; Samimi, Cyrus (Hg.): Frontiers in African Digital Research. (= University of Bayreuth African Studies Online 10). Bayreuth: Universität Bayreuth. https://doi.org/10.15495/EPub_UBT_00005720

Kraus, Wolfgang; Eberhard, Igor (2022): Managing Data, Managing Contradictions. Archiving and Sharing Ethnographic Data. In: Burkhardt, Marcus et al. (eds.): Interrogating Datafication. Towards a Praxeology of Data. Bielefeld: Transcript, S. 185-206. https://doi.org/10.14361/9783839455616

Lassiter, Luke Eric (2005): The Chicago Guide to Collaborative Ethnography. Chicago: University of Chicago Press.

Lederman, Rena (2016): Archiving Fieldnotes? Placing "Anthropological Records" among Plural Digital Worlds. In: Sanjek, Roger; Tratner, Susan W. (eds.): eFieldnotes. The Makings of Anthropology in the Digital World. Philadelphia: University of Pennsylvania Press, pp. 251-271. https://doi.org/10.9783/9780812292213-015

Leopold, Robert (2008): The Second Life of Ethnographic Fieldnotes. In: Ateliers d'anthropologie 32. https://doi.org/10.4000/ateliers.3132

Meyer zu Verl, Christian (2018): Probleme der Archivierung und sekundären Nutzung ethnografischer Daten. In: Bambey, Doris et al.: Archivierung und Zugang zu Qualitativen Daten. (RatSWD Working Paper Series 267). Berlin: RatSWD, S. 80-90. https://doi.org/10.17620/02671.35

Miller, Daniel; Horst, Heather A. (Hg.) (2012): Digital Anthropology. London: Berg.

Miller, Daniel; Slater, Don (2000): The Internet. An Ethnographic Approach. Oxford: Berg.

Mosconi, Gaia; Li, Qinyu; Randall, Dave; Karasti, Helena; Tolmie, Peter; Barutzky, Jana; Korn, Matthias; Pipek, Volkmar (2019): Three Gaps in Opening Science. In: Computer Supported Cooperative Work 28, pp. 749-789. https://doi.org/10.1007/s10606-019-09354-z

Murillo, Luis Felipe Rosado (2018): What Does "Open Data" Mean for Ethnographic Research? In: American Anthropologist 120 (3), pp. 577-582. https://doi.org/10.1111/aman.13088

Parezo, Nancy J.; Fowler, Don D.; Silverman, Sydel (2003): Preserving the Anthropological Record. A Decade of CoPAR Initiatives. In: Current Anthropology 44 (1), pp. 111-116.

Pels, Peter (2018): Data Management in Anthropology. The Next Phase in Ethics Governance? In: Social Anthropology / Anthropologie Sociale 26 (3), pp. 391-396. https://doi.org/10.1111/1469-8676.12526

Pels, Peter (2008): What Has Anthropology Learned from the Anthropology of Colonialism? In: Social Anthropology / Anthropologie Sociale 16 (3), pp. 280-299. https://doi.org/10.1111/j.1469-8676.2008.00046.x

RatSWD (2017): Forschungsethische Grundsätze und Prüfverfahren in den Sozial- und Wirtschaftswissenschaften. RatSWD Output 9 (5). Berlin: RatSWD. https://doi.org/10.17620/02671.1

Rosenblatt, Paul C. (1995): Ethics of Qualitative Interviewing with Grieving Families. In: Death Studies 19, S. 139-155.

Silverman, Sydel; Parezo, Nancy (ed.) (1995): Preserving the Anthropological Record. 2nd edition. New York: Wenner-Gren Foundation for Anthropological Research. https://copar.umd.edu/preserving-the-anthropological-record-second-edition/ (abgerufen am 30.12.2021)

Sterzer, Wjatscheslaw; Imeri, Sabine; Harbeck, Matthias (2018): Zugriff auf ethnologische Forschungsdaten. Anforderungen und Lösungen (Poster). 107. Deutscher Bibliothekartag in Berlin. Berlin: Berufsverband Information Bibliothek. https://nbn-resolving.org/urn:nbn:de:0290-opus4-157193

Thelen, Tatjana (2015): Wege einer relationalen Anthropologie. Ethnographische Einblicke in Verwandtschaft und Staat. Wien: Institut für Kultur- und Sozialanthropologie, Universität Wien. (Wiener Arbeitspapiere zur Ethnographie 4), S. 20. https://ksa.univie.ac.at/fileadmin/user_upload/i_ksa/PDFs/Vienna_Working_Papers_in_Ethnography/vwpe04.pdf (abgerufen am 30.12.2021)

von Unger, Hella (2018): Forschungsethik, digitale Archivierung und biographische Interviews. In: Lutz, Helma; Schiebel, Martina; Tuider, Elisabeth (Hg.): Handbuch Biographieforschung Online. Wiesbaden: Springer VS, S. 681-693. https://doi.org/10.1007/978-3-658-18171-0

Weber, Florence (2017): Towards a Digital Architecture of Reflexive Ethnographic Data. In: Ethnography 18 (3), pp. 287-294. https://doi.org/10.1177/1466138117724482

Wilkinson, Mark D. et al. (2016): The FAIR Guiding Principles for Scientific Data Management and Stewardship. In: Scientific Data 3, 160018. https://doi.org/10.1038/sdata.2016.18

Zeitlyn, David (2021): For Augustinian Archival Openness and Laggardly Sharing. Trustworthy Archiving and Sharing of Social Science Data from Identifiable Human Subjects. In: Frontiers in Research Metrics and Analytics 6. https://doi.org/10.3389/frma.2021.736568

Wolfgang Kraus, Universitätsprofessor (i.R.) am Institut für Kultur- und Sozialanthropologie der Universität Wien. Zwischen 1983 und 2005 hat er in Zentralmarokko zu Fragen der tribalen Identität und Organisation sowie des oral tradierten historischen Wissens geforscht. Weitere Forschungsschwerpunkte und -interessen sind Kinship, Visuelle Anthropologie, Audiodokumentation, Datenmanagement und Datenarchivierung, ethnographische Forschungsethik sowie Bildungsanthropologie. Er war bis September 2023 wissenschaftlicher Leiter des Ethnographischen Datenarchivs (eda) an der Universitätsbibliothek Wien.

Anna Nindl hat kürzlich ihre Masterarbeit zu politischen Subjektivitäten junger Erwachsener in Split, Kroatien abgeschlossen. Zuvor war sie wissenschaftliche Mitarbeiterin am Institut für Kultur-und Sozialanthropologie und am SSC Sozialwissenschaften der Universität Wien. Zudem wirkte sie an der Datenerhebung für das Projekt VERSUS-Corona am Institut für Sozialforschung der Goethe Universität Frankfurt mit. Ihre Schwerpunkte liegen auf politischer Anthropologie und ethnographischen Methoden.